HER MASTER'S TOOLS?

Society of Biblical Literature

Global Perspectives on Biblical Scholarship

General Acquisitions Editors

Benjamin D. Sommer,
Old Testament/Hebrew Bible

Sharon H. Ringe,
New Testament

Number 9

HER MASTER'S TOOLS?
Feminist and Postcolonial Engagements
of Historical-Critical Discourse

HER MASTER'S TOOLS?

Feminist and Postcolonial Engagements of Historical-Critical Discourse

Edited by

Caroline Vander Stichele and Todd Penner

Society of Biblical Literature
Atlanta

HER MASTER'S TOOLS?
Feminist and Postcolonial Engagements
of Historical-Critical Discourse

Library of Congress Cataloging-in-Publication Data

Her master's tools? : feminist and postcolonial engagements of historical-critical discourse / edited by Caroline Vander Stichele and Todd Penner.
    p. cm. — (Global perspectives on biblical scholarship ; no. 9)
    Includes bibliographical references and indexes.
    ISBN–13: 978-1-58983-119-3 (pbk. : alk. paper)
    ISBN–10: 1-58983-119-3
    1. Bible—Criticism, interpretation, etc. 2. Bible—Feminist criticism. 3. Bible—Hermeneutics. I. Vander Stichele, Caroline. II. Penner, Todd C. III. Series.
    BS511.3 .H47 2005
    220.6'082—dc22   2005011239

13 12 11 10 09 08 07 06 05   5 4 3 2 1

Printed in the United States of America on acid-free, recycled paper conforming to ANSI/NISO Z39.48-1992 (R1997) and ISO 9706:1994 standards for paper permanence.

In memory of all those left behind
between the pages of history . . .

". . . and all those without names
because of their short and ill-environed lives"

—Adrienne Rich, "Culture and Anarchy"

CONTENTS

PREFACE

The Editors

Just over half the essays in this volume originated as presentations in the "Whence and Whither? Methodology and the Future of Biblical Studies" unit, coordinated by the editors, at the International Society of Biblical Literature Meetings in Berlin (July 2002) and Cambridge (July 2003). The general rationale for the two related sessions offered on these occasions was to engage traditional, dominant historical-critical discourse from a variety of feminist perspectives. This particular theme seemed to offer a suitable follow-up to our earlier sessions on Acts, which interacted with newer approaches to that book, while remaining in conversation with more conventional methodologies and approaches (now published as Todd Penner and Caroline Vander Stichele, eds., *Contextualizing Acts: Lukan Narrative and Greco-Roman Discourse* [SBLSymS 20; Atlanta: Society of Biblical Literature, 2003]). With this follow-up project, we envisioned opening up a similar kind of dialogue with respect to the history of scholarship from the perspective of feminist studies. The title chosen for this volume—"Her Master's Tools?"—also reflects this ambition. That the location for the meetings should have been in two of the great bastions of historical-critical scholarship—Berlin in Germany and Cambridge in England— provided further inspiration for the shape of the conversation that took place, which remained structurally consistent as the papers were transposed into this current collection. Our goal was to supply a context for a diverse and lively engagement of the issues of critical relevance to contemporary scholarship on the Bible. In the process, the perspective of the sessions and the volume expanded from feminist to gender-critical and postcolonial engagements of historical-critical discourse. We also sought to broaden the horizon by including voices that challenge hegemonic Western biblical discourse both from its center and its margins, from without and within. However, we are well aware that, given the specific contours of that discussion, there are also limitations in the material and traditions covered—and this fact, as always, is regrettable, even if also symptomatic, given the growing diversity in the field of biblical studies.

Our focus on *engagement* of dominant discourse has remained in full view throughout, but how that is enacted in each contribution varies widely. Reflected in the order of the essays are three fairly broad areas that we sought to highlight: general methodological considerations (Stenström, Scholz, Martínez-Vázquez, Marshall, Geisterfer, Robbins), Hebrew Bible/Old Testament (De Troyer, McKinlay, Masenya, Lee, Fuchs, Boer), and New Testament and early Christian writings (Brock, Marchal, Vander Stichele–Penner, Økland). What is presented in this volume is obviously only a very small sample of the great vitality and divergence that persists in (post)critical discourses on the Bible. As with the previous volume on Acts, our aim has been to establish a springboard for further study and conversation, hoping that others will find within these pages inspiration to push the boundaries of the conversation further, to create new modes of discourse, and perhaps to re-engage and reconfigure neglected features of past scholarship in the process.

In terms of the publication of these essays, we are particularly grateful for the help received in editing from Thomas Randall (University of Amsterdam), Andrea Fryrear (Austin College), and Gillian Grissom (Austin College)—these reliable and astute students played formative roles in seeing this project through to its completion. We are also grateful for the financial support received from our respective academic institutions, which made it possible for us to attend the International Meetings and to organize editorial assistance for this volume. Rex Matthews, the former Society of Biblical Literature Editorial Director, was supportive of this project when we first brought it to his attention in Berlin, and provided invaluable guidance in its decisive, early stage. Bob Buller, his successor, has been a major force in guiding this volume through its final stages, and Sharon Ringe, the SBL consulting editor on the project, was immensely encouraging throughout—it was an honor to work with this seasoned academic. Indeed, Sharon has proved to be a constant reminder of the great debt we ourselves owe not only to the "forefathers" but to our "foremothers" as well. Without their "tools," we would not have a discourse or method with which to converse and engage in the first place. Last but not least, we also want to thank our family, friends, and felines for their continued support and for reminding us that "there is Something More."

ABBREVIATIONS

AB   Anchor Bible
ABD   *Anchor Bible Dictionary.* Edited by D. N. Freedman. 6 vols.
            New York: Doubleday, 1992.
ABRL   Anchor Bible Reference Library
AJT   *Asia Journal of Theology*
ANTC   Abingdon New Testament Commentaries
ASNU   Acta seminarii neotestamentici upsaliensis
ATD   Das Alte Testament Deutsch
BA   *Biblical Archaeologist*
BCTSA   *Bulletin for Contextual Theology in Southern Africa and
            Africa*
BETL   Bibliotheca ephemeridum theologicarum lovaniensium
BibInt   *Biblical Interpretation*
BJS   Brown Judaic Studies
BKAT   Biblischer Kommentar, Altes Testament
BNTC   Black's New Testament Commentaries
BOTSA   *Bulletin for Old Testament Studies in Africa*
BR   *Biblical Research*
BS   The Biblical Seminar
BZAW   Beihefte zur Zeitschrift für die alttestamentliche Wissen-
            schaft
BZNW   Beihefte zur Zeitschrift für die neutestamentliche Wissen-
            schaft
CBQ   *Catholic Biblical Quarterly*
CC   Continental Commentaries
CIS   *Corpus inscriptionum semiticarum*
Colloq   *Colloquium*
ConBNT   Coniectanea biblica: New Testament Series
Cont   *Continuum*
CurTM   *Currents in Theology and Mission*
DBI   *Dictionary of Biblical Interpretation.* Edited by John H.
            Hayes. 2 vols. Nashville: Abingdon, 1999.
EKKNT   Evangelisch-katholischer Kommentar zum Neuen
            Testament
ESEC   Emory Studies in Early Christianity

EUZ	Exegese in unserer Zeit
ExAud	*Ex auditu*
FCB	Feminist Companion to the Bible
FCNTECW	Feminist Companion to the New Testament and Early Christian Writings
HDR	Harvard Dissertations in Religion
HNT	Handbuch zum Neuen Testament
HR	*History of Religions*
HTR	*Harvard Theological Review*
HTS	Harvard Theological Studies
JAAR	*Journal of the American Academy of Religion*
JBL	*Journal of Biblical Literature*
JBQ	*Jewish Bible Quarterly*
JFSR	*Journal of Feminist Studies in Religion*
JR	*Journal of Religion*
JRS	*Journal of Roman Studies*
JRT	*Journal of Religious Thought*
JSNT	*Journal for the Study of the New Testament*
JSNTSup	Journal for the Study of the New Testament Supplement Series
JSOT	*Journal for the Study of the Old Testament*
JSOTSup	Journal for the Study of the Old Testament Supplement Series
JTS	*Journal of Theological Studies*
KEK	Kritisch-exegetischer Kommentar über das Neue Testament
LCL	Loeb Classical Library
NIB	*The New Interpreter's Bible.* Edited by L. E. Keck et al. 12 vols. Nashville: Abingdon, 1994–2002.
NICOT	New International Commentary on the Old Testament
NICNT	New International Commentary on the New Testament
NovT	*Novum Testamentum*
NovTSup	Novum Testamentum Supplements
NTD	Das Neue Testament Deutsch
NTOA	Novum Testamentum et Orbis Antiquus
NTS	*New Testament Studies*
OBT	Overtures to Biblical Theology
OTE	*Old Testament Essays*
PRSt	*Perspectives in Religious Studies*
RelEd	*Religious Education*
RSR	*Recherches de science religieuse*
SBLBSNA	Society of Biblical Literature Biblical Scholarship in North America

SBLDS	Society of Biblical Literature Dissertation Series
SBLRBS	Society of Biblical Literature Resources for Biblical Study
SBLSCS	Society of Biblical Literature Septuagint and Cognate Studies
SBLSP	*Society of Biblical Literature Seminar Papers*
SBLSymS	Society of Biblical Literature Symposium Series
SBLTCS	Society of Biblical Literature Text-Critical Studies
SBLWGRW	Society of Biblical Literature Writings from the Greek and Roman World
SBT	Studies in Biblical Theology
SC	Sources chrétiennes
SCJ	Studies in Christianity and Judaism; Etudes sur le Christianisme et le Judaisme
SemeiaSt	Semeia Studies
SJLA	Studies in Judaism in Late Antiquity
SJT	*Scottish Journal of Theology*
SNTSMS	Society for New Testament Studies Monograph Series
SR	*Studies in Religion*
ST	*Studia theologica*
StBL	Studies in Biblical Literature
STDJ	*Studies on the Text of the Desert of Judah*
STK	*Svensk teologisk kvartalskrift*
STL	Studia theologica Lundensia
STRev	*Sewanee Theological Review*
SVTP	Studia in Veteris Testamenti pseudepigraphica
TDNT	*Theological Dictionary of the New Testament.* Edited by G. Kittel and G. Friedrich. Translated by G. W. Bromiley. 10 vols. Grand Rapids: Eerdmans, 1964–1976
TJ	*Trinity Journal*
TS	*Theological Studies*
TSAJ	Texte und Studien zum antiken Judentum
TynBul	*Tyndale Bulletin*
VT	*Vetus Testamentum*
VTSup	Vetus Testamentum Supplements
WBC	Word Biblical Commentary
WTJ	*Westminister Theological Journal*
WUNT	Wissenschaftliche Untersuchungen zum Neuen Testament
ZNW	*Zeitschrift für die neutestamentliche Wissenschaft und die Kunde der älteren Kirche*

Mastering the Tools or Retooling the Masters? The Legacy of Historical-Critical Discourse[*]

Caroline Vander Stichele and Todd Penner

> *Homo sum, nil historicum a me alienum puto—I am human and consider nothing historical alien to me.*
>
> —Adolf von Harnack[1]

> *What does it mean when the tools of a racist patriarchy are used to examine the fruits of that same patriarchy? It means that only the most narrow perimeters of change are possible and allowable ... For the master's tools will never dismantle the master's house. They may allow us to temporarily beat him at his own game, but they will never enable us to bring about genuine change.*
>
> —Audre Lorde[2]

The opening quotes from Harnack and Lorde set two very different worlds, ideas, and even cultures in juxtaposition to one another. On the one hand, Harnack, one of the premiere scholars of early Christian historical studies, denotes his firm belief in the underlying unity of human experience. For Harnack, one must distinguish between histories and history, the latter being a unified story of development and succession. In this framework of historical research, one suspends personal bias and

---

* We would like to express our thanks to Sian Hawthorne and Jane Clifford of the Centre for Gender and Religions Research in the Department of the Study of Religions at the School for Oriental and African Studies (London), who convened the session "Mapping Gender and Religion: Where We've Been, Where We Are, Where We're Going ... " at the British Association for the Study of Religion annual meeting, Manchester College, Oxford, September 16, 2004. This forum proved immensely helpful for engaging an earlier version of this essay.

1. Adolf von Harnack, *Adolf von Harnack: Liberal Theology at Its Height* (ed. M. Rumscheidt; The Making of Modern Theology 6; London: Collins, 1988), 57.

2. Audre Lorde, "The Master's Tools Will Never Dismantle the Master's House: Comments at 'The Personal and the Political' Panel (Second Sex Conference, October 29, 1979)," in *This Bridge Called My Back: Writings by Radical Women of Color* (ed. C. Moraga and G. Anzaldúa; 2d ed.; New York: Kitchen Table, 1983), 98–99 (emphasis hers).

seeks to "construct an edifice of greatest objectivity,"[3] so that, in the end, one achieves the fullest assessment of the unity that comes from the spirit, which manifests itself in ideas, which, in turn, are embodied in institutions.[4] Harnack accents the unity of human experience, affirming that "nothing historical is alien" to humans—thereby in principle collapsing particularity into universality.

African American feminist and lesbian poet/writer Lorde could probably not be further removed from the white, European, middle-class, heterosexual, male world of Harnack. The worlds that they inhabited and that they sought to change and challenge were fundamentally different. Indeed, the activist Lorde saw Harnack's world and his institutions precisely as those that stood over hers in oppression. In her critique of mainstream feminist theorists, Lorde stated emphatically that "the failure of the academic feminists to recognize difference as a crucial strength is a failure to reach beyond the first patriarchal lesson. Divide and conquer, in our world, must become define and empower."[5] Indeed, *difference* was the critical concept for Lorde's own feminist manifesto—human experience was not unified and universal; it was, rather, discrete and particular. And being a white, heterosexual female analyzing patriarchal patterns of power and persuasion without being attuned to the voices of "poor women, black and third-world women, and lesbians"[6] meant that one was missing a large part of the picture. The "me" to which Harnack refers cannot, in Lorde's view, be the "us" which she denotes—and therein lies a huge and largely unbridgeable gulf in theory, method, and identity. Harnack died four years before Lorde was born, but what separated them was less a matter of time and geography—it was, rather, a significantly different conception of what it meant to be human in relation to history and culture. It was precisely out of this profound discontinuity between their worlds and experiences that Lorde could raise the essential question as to the utility of the "master's tools."

Taking the difference between Harnack and Lorde as our starting point, this present collection of essays seeks to explore the juxtaposition that exists between the world of interpretation offered by traditional historical criticism and that proffered by the various and diverse feminist and postcolonial interpreters who have often found the methods or, at

---

3. Harnack, *Adolf von Harnack*, 47.
4. Ibid., 57, 59. See further G. Wayne Glick, *The Reality of Christianity: A Study of Adolf von Harnack as Historian and Theologian* (Makers of Modern Theology; New York: Harper & Row, 1967), 101–2.
5. Lorde, "Master's Tools," 100.
6. Ibid., 98.

the very least, the results offered by early practitioners lacking, largely because their own later experiences simply did not resonate with those projected in the metaphors, myths, and meanings of their "forefathers." The contributors to this volume thus take up what has turned out to be a prolonged, varied, and often volatile conversation regarding the useful-ness of historical criticism, and they do so from multiple angles, both from within and without. In what follows, we will outline in a general way some of the fundamental issues involved in the transformations from the past to the present in both methods and ideologies, seeking to place the essays contained herein within a broader context.

The Master's Voice?

In his essay "The Essence of the Modern Spirit," Ernst Troeltsch sketches a portrait of modernity, noting that the natural sciences served as a model to be followed by historical and social sciences. Still, he believed that the study of history ultimately escapes the "all-conquering rationalism that is more than willing to overlook the gaps and inconsis-tencies in our knowledge of nature";[7] it rather "inclines us to an antirationalistic contemplation, an aristocratic individualism, a resigned wisdom that everywhere seeks and honors greatness but accepts the unfathomable and unpredictable variety of human life as a dark faith."[8] This positive appreciation of the modern approach to history is also pres-ent elsewhere in Troeltsch's work. In an earlier essay entitled "Historical and Dogmatic Method in Theology," he takes up the defense of the his-torical method for the study of religious history and tradition, contrasting that with the earlier dogmatic approach. Whereas the first, considered modern and termed "history-of-religion method" (*religionsgeschichtliche Methode*), has as its focus universal history, the latter, considered tradi-tional and premodern, focuses on the history of salvation (*Heilsgeschichte*), which is only knowable to the believer. For Troeltsch, the dualistic notion of history presumed by the dogmatic method and consisting of a secular and sacred realm ultimately reflects a dualistic concept of humanity and the divine, which needs to be replaced by a conception of history as the sphere for the "disclosure of the divine reason."[9] In the context of this dis-cussion, Troeltsch proceeds to stress the fundamental importance of the

---

7. Ernst Troeltsch, *Religion in History* (ed. and trans. J. L. Adams and W. F. Bense; Fortress Texts in Modern Theology; Minneapolis: Fortress, 1991), 253.
8. Ibid., 255.
9. Ibid., 27.

principle of analogy for historical criticism, affirming, as Harnack did, the basic unity of human experience:

> [T]he omnipotence of analogy implies the similarity (in principle) of all historical events—which does not, of course, mean identity.... At every point there do indeed emerge unique and autonomous historical forces that, by virtue of our capacity for empathy, we perceive to be related to our common humanity. At the same time, however, these unique forces also stand in a current and context comprehending the totality of events, where we see everything conditioned by everything else so that there is no point within history which is beyond this correlative involvement and mutual influence.[10]

One can perceive quite readily here Troeltsch's attempts to navigate the complexity posed by the admission of particularity amidst (the desire for) universality.[11] As such, his position stands over and against much more positivistic conceptions of the historical-critical task,[12] and Troeltsch in

---

10. Ibid., 14. See further Hans W. Frei, *The Eclipse of Biblical Narrative: A Study of Eighteenth and Nineteenth Century Hermeneutics* (New Haven: Yale University Press, 1974), 195–96.

11. This tension is present in numerous thinkers of the period. For this same phenomenon in Tübingen theology, see John E. Thiel, "The Universal in the Particular: Johann Sebastian Drey on the Hermeneutics of Tradition," in *The Legacy of the Tübingen School: The Relevance of Nineteenth-Century Theology for the Twenty-First Century* (ed. D. J. Dietrich and M. J. Hines; New York: Crossroad Herder, 1997), 56–74. Thiel labels the resultant theological insights almost "postmodern" in their scope and application (69–70), especially given the role of "experience" in this model. It should be noted, however, that the constancy of the universal is never sacrificed in the same way that postmodernism promotes, and this distinction makes for a radical difference.

12. Although Leopold von Ranke is often placed in this category, he in fact shared epistemological views on history and historiography much closer to Troeltsch's (especially with respect to the flow of the particular into the universal; see further Hayden White, *Metahistory: The Historical Imagination in Nineteenth-Century Europe* [Baltimore: John Hopkins University Press, 1973], 165, 174–75). More in line with the historical scholarship Troeltsch is criticizing in this instance are those scholars who come under the critical scrutiny of Martin Kähler in his *The So-Called Historical Jesus and the Historic Biblical Christ* (ed. and trans. C. E. Braaten; Fortress Texts in Modern Theology; Philadelphia: Fortress, 1964), esp. 46–57, who remarks, somewhat caustically, that such positivistic scholars believe that "pious thinking can dissect God as the anatomist can dissect a frog" (48). This type of scholarship can also be designated as "biblical realism," since it considers the reconstructed original text, its original meaning, as well as the history behind the text to be more "real" and therefore also closer to the truth than its alternatives (see further Roland Boer, *Novel Histories: The Fiction of Biblical Criticism* [Playing the Texts 2; Sheffield: Sheffield Academic Press, 1997], 187–89; and Gunter Scholtz, "The Notion of Historicism and 19th Century Theology," in *Biblical Studies and the Shifting of Paradigms, 1850–1914* [ed. H. G. Reventlow and W. Farmer; JSOTSup 192; Sheffield: Sheffield Academic Press, 1995], 159–62). It is an ironic feature of modern biblical criticism that the "memory" of past scholarship in both more liberal and

many respects seeks to mediate between those more purely objectivist approaches and those that fall into complete relativism.[13] He would affirm the objectivity and impartiality of the historical interpreter, as well as the objective content of history, but eschew the "rationalistic tyranny of the universal concept," noting that history shows a "plurality of analogous structures" that "retain their unique value."[14] This emphasis arises from Troeltsch's commitment to the individual as the primary agent of the historical process.[15] Herein we observe the fundamental indebtedness to the modernist enterprise, which provides the foundation for contemporary historical criticism. The Christian (especially Protestant) underpinnings of this commitment to the individual help explain the widespread

---

more traditional communities of scholarship is largely not of the historical positivists, who have almost vanished from the scholarly scene (although one of the first proponents and perhaps the source of this form of historicism, David Friedrich Strauss, is generally remembered [cf. Scholtz, "Notion of Historicism," 161–62]), but rather of the critics of such scholarship (like Kähler and Troeltsch). On the Cartesian basis of this objectivist component in biblical studies, see Klaus Scholder, *The Birth of Modern Critical Theology: Origins and Problems of Biblical Criticism in the Seventeenth Century* (trans. J. Bowden; London: SCM, 1990), 110–42.

13. Troeltsch considered Ernst Renan to be a prime example of this other tendency (Scholtz, "Notion of Historicism," 163). On this facet of Troeltsch's work, see esp. ibid., 150–51, 163–65.

14. Troeltsch, *Religion in History*, 304. In this respect, Troeltsch regards Enlightment historiography as fundamentally flawed: "While the Enlightment (due to the after-effects of supernaturalism) had sought the content of history in a rational truth that remains perpetually and rigidly the same, history has more recently been viewed as the manifestation of manifold basic tendencies of human nature and, in their interconnection, as unfolding the totality of human reason in the course of the generations" (79). Herein Troeltsch also stands opposed to the model developed by Ferdinand Christian Baur, who retained much more of the explicit metaphysical dynamics of German Idealism (cf. Hans Rollmann, "From Baur to Wrede: The Quest for a Historical Method," *SR* 17 [1988]: 446–47).

15. Troeltsch, *Religion in History*, 305; cf. Harnack, *Adolf von Harnack*, 50. The influence of Christian incarnational theology can hardly be missed in this emphasis on the individual, for it is precisely the transposition of this divine principle to humans that Troeltsch and Harnack accomplish: humans manifest the divine in history. In this respect, as in almost all other components of his historical vision, Troeltsch was highly influenced by the German theologian Richard Rothe (1799–1867). Rothe articulated an early (pre-Darwinian) conception of the world historical process as evolutionary in nature, arguing that the Protestant Reformation made the turn toward the secularizing of Christianity, which now embodies its fundamental moral principles in the state. Thus, the "moral process of creation and incarnation" was being continued in the "profane political and social movements of the modern world," making "the whole common life … a cultus in a higher sense" (Claude Welch, *Protestant Thought in the Nineteenth Century: Volume 1, 1799–1870* [New Haven: Yale University Press, 1972], 290–91; see also Sheila Briggs, "The Deceit of the Sublime: An Investigation into the Origins of Ideological Criticism of the Bible in Early Nineteenth-Century German Biblical Studies," *Semeia* 59 [1992]: 11).

adaptability and attraction of this approach to history in Europe (particularly Germany) and then on the North American liberal theological and biblical-historical scene. In the "new" historical humanism, which historians like Troeltsch were advocating, the principle of analogy also takes on greater significance, as it is not just a historical method, but also a humanistic-theological axiom that asserts and affirms the centrality of humans to the historical process. Ultimately, then, in this new post-Hegelian world, history becomes much more intelligible to humans—as *moral* beings—than nature itself, to which "man" is considered superior.[16] In essence, this secularized view of "salvation history" fundamentally sacralizes history itself—God may disappear, but the "project" remains the same and the antidualistic criticism levelled at dogmatic theology is herein "resolved" (or, more precisely, the dualism has been erradicated by collapsing the sacred and the profane). Several fundamental features of Troeltsch's historical approach are thus explicable on this basis: the centrality of humans and culture to the very conception of history and historical process/progress; the emphasis on universal *meaning* in history as an inherent unifying feature despite acknowledged particularity in the unfolding; and the firm belief in a humanistic, objective, scientific method that, although correlative in some respects, would of necessity be different from that used to study nature and thereby more clearly achieve the aims of a *humanistic* historical inquiry.

Given this broader framework, the ideological elements present in this discourse come readily to the fore. It is critical to mention these features, even if briefly, as they have had a profound bearing on the use of the tools propagated by the framework. First of all, the established methods used for historical-critical analysis cannot be separated from their "confessional" framework. In the end, the universalism and individualism that Troeltsch saw as the pinnacle of human religious achievement are, he thought, most profoundly manifested in Christianity and the religion of ancient Israel—these two alone, in his view, had "completely broken the spell of the religion of nature."[17] Troeltsch himself believed

---

16. The primary goal of history is therefore moral education, which implied something akin to "spiritual progress" for scholars like Troeltsch. Troeltsch, *Religion in History*, 25, 27; cf. Harnack, *Adolf von Harnack*, 45–46, 57–59, 66; and Welch, *Protestant Thought*, 290–91.

17. Troeltsch, *Religion in History*, 83 (cf. 81–84). The inherent binary opposition that Troeltsch establishes between "Christianity and Judaism" (as revelatory religions according to the salvation history model) and "nature religions" finds replication in other binary oppositions such as that between the humanistic methods for the study of history and the methods for the study of the natural sciences or between culture and nature (one might add here the inherent opposition that is posited between Protestantism and Catholicism as well). While the relationship between these varied structural oppositions is complex, there seems

that a scholarly investigation of Christianity would demonstrate its superiority: "Indeed, no comprehensive view can any longer fail to see in the
mighty movement of Christianity the culmination of antiquity."[18] This
rise of Christianity is made possible by the disintegration of Judaism,
which is thus reduced to setting the stage for Jesus. Troeltsch is convinced that the historical approach can substantiate his claim that in the
person of Jesus "a religious power manifests itself, which to *anyone* sensitive enough to catch its echo in one's own soul, seems to be the
conclusion of all previous religious movements and the starting point of
a new phase in the history of religion, in which nothing has yet emerged.
Indeed, even for us today it is *unthinkable* that something higher should
emerge, no matter how many new forms and combinations this purely
inward and personal belief in God may yet enter."[19] Apart from this overt
religious emphasis, one also perceives in these statements a distinct focus
on progress and development as a constituent and necessary part of the
historical process.

Alongside this overt Christian bias, one can also find references in
Troeltsch's work to the larger cultural framework of his thinking and the
discourse to which it belongs. In the opening paragraph of his essay on the
essence of the modern spirit, Troeltsch refers to "the complicated life of
the white race today."[20] Although he does not further develop the idea of
race, it literally frames his analysis, which contains further, more specific

---

to be a broad correlative pattern that emerges between the results of Troeltsch's historical
method and the inner logic of the method itself.

18. Ibid., 15.

19. Ibid., 27–28 (italics added). Elsewhere Troeltsch confirms more clearly his confessional bias, insofar as he perceives the modern spirit, and especially its individualism, as a
further development of Protestantism (239; cf. 244, 253, 262). One might go one step further,
in fact, to suggest that there exists a distinctive correlation between the historical task outlined by scholars such as Harnack and Troeltsch and a strongly engrained "Protestant
Principle" of interpretation, articulated most clearly by Johann Philipp Gabler. In his thor-
oughgoing critique of the dogmatic theological method for interpreting Scripture over 200
years ago, Gabler's "reformative" and indeed also "revolutionary" mode of discourse dramatically shaped thinking about historical tradition. Gabler's attempt to separate out the
task of "true biblical theology" from that of "pure biblical theology" was much akin to the
way in which Troeltsch and Harnack (and also Ranke) understood that historical inquiry
ought to be conducted. In the former category, the emphasis was on documentary source
work and reconstruction, while the latter opened up a space for Sachkritik, allowing for the
penetration behind the history to its inner meaning and core (see the translation and discussion of Gabler's seminal address in John Sandys-Wunsch and Laurence Eldredge, "J. P.
Gabler and the Distinction between Biblical and Dogmatic Theology: Translation, Commentary, and Discussion of His Originality," *SJT* 33 [1980]: 133–58). Thus, not only the content of
Troeltsch's project, but indeed also its explicit method, had deep Protestant roots.

20. Troeltsch, *Religion in History*, 237.

indicators of his sociocultural location as well, the most important of which are references to European history and civilization as being based on Greco-Roman culture and Christianity, and his identification of Christianity as "European religion" over and against the religions of the Orient,[21] a distinction that reflects the Orientalist and colonial views of his time.[22] Troeltsch's discourse, moreover, becomes more nationalistic when he mentions the "qualities and forces peculiar to the Germanic nations," which manifest themselves in the sphere of law as well as political and social organization, and are further expressed in "Protestantism, which is experienced essentially along Germanic lines."[23]

Apart from race, references to (social and economic) class can be found in Troeltsch's work as well, insofar as he refers to the educated classes, which form the upper strata of society, who are "influenced by what they read" and differ from the great masses.[24] He also points to the individualism of scientists, which "always tends to a certain pride in belonging to an educated aristocracy."[25] It is clear from the context that Troeltsch situates himself within this group. Last but not least, the gendered nature of Troeltsch's analysis is apparent in his identification of humanity with "the brotherhood of men," which is clear from his statement that one of the far-reaching effects of modern humanitarianism upon the social structure is "the appreciation of the individual personality, *even of women and children*." The fact that "women" are coupled here with "children" denotes a particular kind of masculinist discourse that operates essentially on the exclusion (or at least domestication) of the feminine. Indeed, throughout Troeltsch's work one receives the distinct impression that not only is the subject essentially masculine in content,[26] but the presumed audience is as well.

---

21. Ibid., 28.

22. Shawn Kelley, *Racializing Jesus: Race, Ideology and the Formation of Modern Biblical Scholarship* (Biblical Limits; New York: Routledge, 2002), 64–88, traces the connection of the specific reconstruction of early Christianity in this time period to the orientalizing frame of reference that saw the "Western" conceptual system winning out over the "Eastern."

23. Troeltsch, *Religion in History*, 239. In a note, however, Troeltsch adds that he is not exclusively thinking here of the Germans "but of the entire North-European and American world," thus toning down the nationalistic overtones in his observations, but affirming at the very least the perceived distinction between the predominantly Protestant North and the Catholic South of Europe.

24. Ibid., 262.

25. Ibid., 253.

26. Harnack's analysis equally designates history as the assessment of decidedly male institutions and forms, promoting men as the signifiers of true action and influence: "We study history ultimately in order to know institutions. Whether we are dealing with war, diplomacy, politics or art and science, Church and school, etc., historical research must be

This brief analysis of Troeltsch's work on historiography, stressing the relation of what he states overtly with what still remains implicit, reveals a basic tension of this modernist project: much of the so-called "objectivity" for which historians aimed appears to be a universalization of their own particularity.[27] From an ideology-critical perspective, Michel Foucault aptly captures the interest involved in the historical endeavor to explicate the "logic" of the past when he observes: "we want historians to confirm our belief that the present rests upon profound intentions and immutable necessities. But the true historical sense confirms our existence among countless lost events, without a landmark or a point of reference."[28] The two types of approaches to and desires for history to which Foucault refers in many respects represent a broader narrative of the history of historiography in the post-Enlightenment period. On the one hand, there exists a longing for a history of certainty and objectivity— laying bare, at least to a degree, the rational unfolding of human events, making sense and providing *meaning* to a past (and present) that sustains hope and offers an element of logic for the future. On the other hand, these basic structures of "certainty" mask particular and acute forms of power relationships that postulate white, European, Christian (predominantly Protestant) upper class males as the significant signifiers of the spirit in history. In Foucault's terms, this masking represents a form of "demagoguery" that hides "its singular malice under the cloak of universals."[29] Historical engagement can in fact be much more illuminating of a cultural time period once this basic "malice" is uncovered, or, at the very least, admitted.

From within this ideological perspective pursued here one can look more closely at the broad construction of particular subjects in discrete time periods (past and present), examining how "truth" claims are

---

directed steadily towards learning to know what results development led to. We meet those results in the form of contracts, constitutions, law codes, school curricula and organization, Church organization, liturgies, catechisms, etc." (*Adolf von Harnack*, 54). The "traditional" spheres of female interaction in this time period are not considered to add significantly (if at all) to the "development" that the historian is to ascertain.

27. Terry Eagleton's pointed observation on "disinterest" equally applies to the so-called "objectivist" aims of historical-critical discourse: "What is considered most disinterested, in any society, is the most revealing and transparent model of what interests it is most significantly unconscious of" ("Ideology and Scholarship," in *Historical Studies and Literary Criticism* [ed. J. J. McGann; Madison: The University of Wisconsin Press, 1985], 121).

28. Michel Foucault, "Nietzsche, Genealogy, History," in *The Essential Foucault: Selections from Essential Works of Foucault 1954–1984* (ed. P. Rabinow and N. Rose; New York: The New Press, 2003), 361. However, Foucault's claim to present "the true historical sense" is itself problematic, because it obscures his own interpretation.

29. Ibid., 363.

manufactured within discourses such as Troeltsch's.[30] This emphasis, finally, results in a scrutiny of the "politics of truth" and indeed also the modes of its production (resting squarely in institutions of higher learning and the church).[31] The implication of this observation for our analysis here is that the historical constraints of the modern time period preclude even the ability for the awareness of the ways in which the scientific method pushed for an objectification of the "truth" of the present, which itself was the product of that present. The rule of analogy became, then, a universalization of the political, cultural, and social truths of the nineteenth century. This move provided not just a diachronic extension, it also had synchronic effects in terms of constructing a perception of stability in a particular given historical epoch of the past. Herein lies one of the major thrusts of the modernist project—the universalization of the individual subject, the reentrenchement of authority, and the stabilization of human experience, which secures, finally, the aforementioned power.[32]

From the standpoint of the twenty-first century, of course, it is easy to identify the situatedness of earlier texts, thinkers, and traditions. Indeed, we have so far only delved into the most explicit and obvious cultural, religious, and political elements embedded in these "foreign" rational discourses. As already noted, there existed a strong desire to universalize contextualized and boundaried experience—not least because of the stabilization and security such moves establish. Still, based on his own principle of analogy, Troeltsch as historian and thinker embodied the notion that experience is intricately bound up with the interpretation of history. Implicit in this principle is the idea that different experiences would generate different perceptions of history. This reconfiguration of the interpretative moment did not receive serious consideration by the "forefathers," for it is evident that within their paradigm the fundamental signifier with respect to the past was/is the historian *himself.* Yet what

---

30. Ibid., 306–7.

31. Ibid., 316–17.

32. It is in fact surprising that the anti-authoritarian stance of much early historical-critical discussion should so thoroughly reestablish authoritative and authoritarian epistemologies. Stephen D. Moore offers the astute (and correlative) observation that historical criticism has often been fettered by an ecclesiastical superego that "has always compelled it to genuflect before the icons it had come to destroy" (*Poststructuralism and the New Testament: Derrida and Foucault at the Foot of the Cross* [Minneapolis: Fortress, 1994], 117). In a similar vein, Roland Boer argues that so-called scientific approaches to the Bible "have their triggers in the Enlightenment's repression and removal of theology from its position of intellectual and cultural dominance" (*Knockin' on Heaven's Door: The Bible and Popular Culture* [London: Routledge, 1999], 8).

happens when the historian becomes a *woman* and a differently gendered subject becomes a legitimate focus of historical inquiry?

Challenging and/or Changing the Paradigm?

Foucault once noted that "history is the discourse of power," which accounted, in his view, for why so much "history" was preoccupied with the "history of sovereignty."[33] In many respects not only the history of biblical criticism in the modern era but also the history of modern feminist challenges to traditional historical criticism readily affirm the broader pattern elucidated by Foucault. In examining the development of feminist biblical criticism one is at once aware of the power issues and relations evident not only in the content of study, but also in the "home"/context of that activity. For early social activists like Elizabeth Cady Stanton, for instance, challenging dominant discourse was at heart a political exercise from without. Indeed, her interest in the Bible was largely brought about because of the role it played in the political agenda of her time. Stanton's engagement of the Bible from an early feminist viewpoint, then, represented the firm belief that an alternative history could only be written when the sovereignty in text, interpretation, and institution was challenged head on. As Stanton establishes in her introduction to the *Woman's Bible,* without the feminist awareness necessary to make a difference, the women who use the historical-critical tools simply reinscribe the status quo: "Those who have undertaken the labor are desirous to have some Hebrew and Greek scholars, versed in Biblical criticism, to gild our pages with learning. Several distinguished women have been urged to do so, but they are afraid that their high reputation and scholarly attainments might be compromised by taking part in an enterprise that for a time may prove very unpopular. Hence we may not be able to get help from that class."[34] Thus, the early social and political agenda of Stanton and others represented a movement from outside of the academy and church. As Stanton notes in the above quote, given the risks, women who were *within* these institutions did not readily support the secular feminist agenda. Indeed, merely the presence of women in the institutions was not enough to change them—it was the explicitly feminist agenda that performed that task.

---

33. Michel Foucault, *"Society Must Be Defended": Lectures at the Collège de France 1975–1976* (ed. M. Bertani and A. Fontana; trans. D. Macey; New York: Picador, 2003), 68.

34. Elizabeth Cady Stanton, *The Woman's Bible: A Classic Feminist Perspective* (New York: European Publishing Company, 1895–1898; repr. Mineola, N.Y.: Dover, 2002), 9.

The "sovereign" powers, however, did not easily give way. This statement is true on multiple levels in this early context. On the one hand, since Stanton was operating from outside the established institutions, changes occurred only gradually and over time. On the other hand, the early feminist movement's articulation and execution of its own agenda did not escape the powerful discursive pull of history as the "history of sovereignty." While Stanton and others moved decidedly against dominant male paradigms, seeking to demonstrate the male elite perspective from which this social and cultural bastion produced its "truths" and "facts"—a context that was categorically *not* the world of females—they reproduced dominant discourse in other ways. It is only in this way that we can fully appreciate how the *Woman's Bible,* touted as so "freeing" for its time, nonetheless continued to affirm essentialist racial and social views in the process.[35] Stanton herself belonged to the same Christian, white, educated class as the biblical scholars in question, but was well aware she did not have the theological/historical tools necessary, as Lorde so aptly articulated, to "beat [them] at their own game." Indeed, from early on the engagement of the dominant paradigm ensured that, to some extent at least, early feminist interpreters would not necessarily or easily set their own agenda.

Jorunn Økland has recently observed that "we as feminist interpreters make ourselves dependent on the same foundation that we criticize. But exactly this shows that women—feminists included—do not have a different language and other thought structures to speak in and from than those given us by contemporary discourse. We cannot not inhabit our father's house."[36] Herein exists an inevitable bind, in that the very discourse that challenges rational, scientific Enlightenment paradigms depends, in part, on that framework to make the criticism to begin with.[37] Stanton was at the forefront of the suffragette movement, and she

---

35. Elizabeth A. Castelli, "Heteroglossia, Hermeneutics, and History: A Review Essay of Recent Feminist Studies of Early Christianity," *JFSR* 10 (1994): 78; cf. Elisabeth Schüssler Fiorenza, "Transforming the Legacy of The Woman's Bible," in *A Feminist Introduction* (vol. 1 of *Searching the Scriptures;* ed. E. Schüssler Fiorenza with S. Matthews and A. Brock; 2 vols.; London: SCM, 1993), 1–24. Lorde's comments at the outset of this essay engage this same point. See more recently Amy-Jill Levine's criticism that "feminist postcolonial biblical scholars often re-create the dichotomizing rhetoric of the Bible and many of its interpreters" ("The Disease of Postcolonial New Testament Studies and the Hermeneutics of Healing," *JFSR* 20 [2004]: 91; cf. 94).

36. Jorunn Økland, "Feminist Reception of the New Testament: A Critical Reception," in *The New Testament as Reception* (ed. M. Müller and H. Tronier; JSNTSup 230; CIS 11; Sheffield: Sheffield Academic Press, 2002), 153.

37. The relationship of feminist criticism to the modernist agenda is traced out in an intriguing way by Minoo Moallem, "Transnationalism, Feminism, and Fundamentalism," in

was manifestly a political and social activist. Still, her blazing of the trail of feminist biblical scholarship demonstrates at once the connection of this new enterprise to the (re)claimed experience of women in her time period and, at the same time, reveals how difficult it was for things to change, how women themselves were often complicit in the maintenance of patriarchal structures, and how easy it was to affirm specific features of the dominant discourse while rejecting others. These patterns persisted even once real change in the academy began to take place from the late 1960s and through the 1970s.[38] Rather than presenting this as a problem per se, however, it is helpful to explore more fully this contextualized nature of feminist interpretations.[39]

Although Stanton had much earlier initiated the first "feminist" commentary on the Bible, it was not until the political and social agenda was appropriated by women in the church/synagogue that biblical criticism as traditionally practiced by male scholars came under radical critique by women from *within* ecclesial/religious and academic structures. As a result, the debate shifted in fundamental ways, because feminist scholars were interested, for instance, in reclaiming women *in* the biblical tradition for women in the church/synagogue of their time. Criticism was reserved especially for the conception of history as that which "actually happened" and an articulation of the historical task in objectivist positivist terms.[40] As Carole Fontaine pointedly observes, "What was supposed to have been a universally valid starting point for inquiries of the text some communities hold as 'Scripture' has turned out instead to be a startling example of the particularity of race, class, and gender of the established group of 'authorized' readers, namely, men of educational and ecclesial status whose

---

Women, Gender, Religion: A Reader (ed. E. A. Castelli with R. C. Rodman; New York: Palgrave, 2001), 119–45.

38. On the relationship of burgeoning feminist criticism to some of the essential historical and cultural interactions of this period, see Sue Thornham, *Feminist Theory and Cultural Studies: Stories of Unsettled Relations* (London: Arnold, New York: Oxford University Press, 2000), 44–70.

39. See further the helpful comments by Elizabeth A. Castelli, "Heteroglossia, Hermeneutics, and History," 83–84.

40. Elisabeth Schüssler Fiorenza has been a particularly strong voice in the criticism of this feature of past scholarship. See esp. Schüssler Fiorenza, "Remembering the Past in Creating the Future: Historical-Critical Scholarship and Feminist Biblical Interpretation," in *Feminist Perspectives on Biblical Scholarship* (ed. A. Yarbro Collins; SBLBSNA 10; Chico, Calif.: Scholars Press, 1985), 44–55; idem, "Text and Reality—Reality as Text: The Problem of a Feminist Historical and Social Reconstruction Based on Texts," *ST* 43 (1989): 19; and idem, "What She Has Done Will Be Told…": Reflections on Writing Feminist History," in *Distant Voices Drawing Near: Essays in Honor of Antoinette Clark Wire* (ed. H. E. Hearon; Collegeville, Minn.: Liturgical, 2004), 3–18.

personal or group power interests have been marketed as 'universal' and 'human'. "[41] The problem noted here is not with partiality per se, but in the denial thereof. Indeed, from this perspective the tools themselves are not to be blamed in principle, but rather the ways in which they have been used. Feminist criticism could therefore use them to serve different ends, "for the sake of presenting an alternative interpretation of biblical texts and history to public scholarly discussion and historical assessment,"[42] and to recover the voices and traditions about women—all women—in the sources of the past.[43] In other words, from the beginning, feminist scholars were not abandoning the historical-critical enterprise; they were reconfiguring its goals of recovery based on their alternative experiences as women.[44] In this way, then, feminist scholarship provided a voice of critical inquiry—offering in particular a hermeneutics of suspicion in terms of examining not only the patriarchal texts of the past (and their consequent exclusion of women), but also the history of scholarship that replicated both the structures and results of that patriarchal legacy.[45] Feminist critics are thus explicit about

---

41. Carole R. Fontaine, "Preface," in *A Feminist Companion to Reading the Bible: Approaches, Methods and Strategies* (ed. A. Brenner and C. R. Fontaine; Sheffield: Sheffield Academic Press, 1997), 12.

42. Schüssler Fiorenza, "Remembering the Past," 56.

43. A particularly strong methodological case for the shift to a "history of women" was made by Bernadette J. Brooten, "Early Christian Women and Their Cultural Context: Issues of Method in Historical Reconstruction," in Yarbro Collins, *Feminist Perspectives*, 65–91; see also Bernadette J. Brooten, *Women Leaders in the Ancient Synagogue* (BJS 36; Chico, Calif.: Scholars Press, 1982). Numerous studies on the role of women in and behind biblical texts and ancient cultures were undertaken around this same time. See, e.g., Elisabeth Schüssler Fiorenza, *In Memory of Her: A Feminist Theological Reconstruction of Christian Origins* (New York: Crossroad, 1983); Carol Meyers, *Discovering Eve: Ancient Israelite Women in Context* (New York: Oxford University Press, 1988); Antoinette Clark Wire, *The Corinthian Women Prophets: A Reconstruction through Paul's Rhetoric* (Minneapolis: Fortress, 1990); Ross Shepard Kraemer, *Her Share of the Blessings: Women's Religions Among Pagans, Jews, and Christians in the Greco-Roman World* (New York: Oxford University Press, 1992); Karen Jo Torjesen, *When Women Were Priests: Women's Leadership in the Early Church and the Scandal of Their Subordination in the Rise of Christianity* (San Francisco: HarperSanFrancisco, 1993); and Ross Shepard Kraemer and Mary Rose D'Angelo, eds., *Women and Christian Origins* (New York: Oxford University Press, 1999).

44. For a positive evaluation of historical criticism for feminist interpretation, see Monika Fander, "Historical-Critical Methods," in Schüssler Fiorenza, *Feminist Introduction*, 205–24; and Luise Schottroff, Silvia Schroer, and Marie-Theres Wacker, *Feminist Interpretation: The Bible in Women's Perspective* (trans. M. Rumscheidt and B. Rumscheidt; Minneapolis: Fortress, 1998). It should not escape notice that the most positive endorsements of historical criticism for feminist biblical interpretation have come from scholars situated predominantly in German-speaking European countries (Germany, Austria, Switzerland).

45. See, e.g., Luise Schottroff, *Lydia's Impatient Sisters: A Feminist Social History of Early Christianity* (trans. B. Rumscheidt and M. Rumscheidt; Louisville: Wesminster John Knox, 1995).

their own social location—and the way in which that location affects their historical reconstruction—in a way that earlier male-stream scholars could not possibly be.[46] Awareness of the resultant subjectivities and their impact on the production and performance of discourses thus represents an indispensable element that feminist and other liberationist scholars have brought to the conversation.[47]

Yet, if feminist biblical scholarship existed as a discourse of contestation, it also replicated in a sense the broader discursive structures of historical-critical methodology more generally by its existence as a discourse of opposition and reformulation. Although both feminist critics and earlier scholars like Troeltsch were critical of the purely scientific nature of historical positivism, they had different ends in sight. Yet the stark differences between the two should not obscure that there are also aspects of continuity on the level of the underlying modernist premises. Feminist biblical scholars may want to reconstruct a different past, but in that case the aim still is to reconstruct a past, the starting point for such a reconstruction being women's experiences in the present. Methodologically speaking, the same principle of analogy noted earlier in Troeltsch's work is used here as well. In both cases, historically analogous experiences, when brought to light and voiced, provide a possibility for *present* change and empowerment. Different experiences have, however, altered the sense of analogous experience in the past, as the framework for what constitutes experience and who in fact is allowed to speak has shifted dramatically. The "master's tools" are thus thoroughly deployed against the androcentric paradigm, albeit with a *different* political end in sight. Still, the identity politics of traditional historical-critical practice are reinscribed in the process, as the essential function of *doing* history has remained the same:

> Texts going through historical-critical analysis "tell" the critic about themselves and others in the past and present. In making interpretations, the critic retells those stories. And the process is organized around the horizons of pre-understanding which shape the present of the interpreter ... The security of the modern against the traditional is defended by such measure. The modern here includes an understanding of the

---

46. On this point, see the helpful discussion by T. Dorah Setel, "Feminist Insights and the Question of Method," in Yarbro Collins, *Feminist Perspectives*, 38–39.

47. See, e.g., Silvia Schroer and Sophia Bietenhard, eds., *Feminist Interpretation of the Bible and the Hermeneutics of Liberation* (JSOTSup 374; London: Sheffield Academic Press, 2003), as well as the detailed discussion and application by Kerry M. Craig and Margret A. Kristjansson, "Women Reading as Men/Women Reading as Women: A Structural Analysis for the Historical Project," *Semeia* 51 (1990): 119–36.

interpreter's self within a community of interpretation as the primary locus of authority and value.[48]

In this way, while feminist biblical scholarship provided numerous challenges to the dominant paradigm and discourse, it also manifested a degree of continuity as well. On an ideological level, for instance, the emphasis on the freedom of the subject and the idea that all subjects are equal readily connect with the modernist enterprise underlying traditional historical criticism. The liberationist impulse in feminist critical work affirms that same commitment and, although the universal subject of "western white middle-class Christian male" is challenged (and in some cases obliterated), it tends to be replaced or opposed by another universal subject, as the category "woman," initially used to counter dominant male discourse, often displayed the same universalist and essentialist overtones. A feminism of difference in such instances turned out to be a feminism of uniformity.[49] This fundamental but also recurring problem is noted by Miriam Perkowitz: "What happens as we write about women and gender while simultaneously making visible the Enlightenment constructs that restrict the imagination of women and gender in the first place?"[50] Scholars such as Judith Butler have pointed out the fine line that feminists have always had to walk in this respect:

> The critical task for feminism is not to establish a point of view outside of constructed identities; that conceit is the construction of an epistemological model that would disavow its own cultural location, and, hence, promote itself as a global subject, a position that deploys precisely the imperialistic strategies that feminism ought to criticize. The critical task is, rather, to locate strategies of subversive repetition enabled by those constructions, to affirm the local possibilities of intervention through participating in precisely those practices of repetition that constitute identity and, therefore, present the immanent possibility of contesting them.[51]

This problem is not easily dismissed, for, while they could readily contest androcentric discourse, feminist practitioners often overlooked the subtle and hidden/masked universalization of their own value

---

48. David H. Fisher, "Self in Text, Text in Self," *Semeia* 51 (1990): 144.

49. See Linda Nicholson, "Interpreting Gender," in *Social Postmodernism: Beyond Identity Politics* (ed. L. Nicholson and S. Seidman; Cambridge: Cambridge University Press, 1995), 54.

50. Miriam Peskowitz, "What's in a Name? Exploring the Dimensions of What 'Feminist Studies in Religion' Means," in Castelli and Rodman, *Women, Gender, Religion*, 29.

51. Judith Butler, *Gender Trouble: Feminism and the Subversion of Identity* (New York: Routledge, 1990), 147.

system and discursive structures.[52] Criticism, in this respect, also came from those whose experience was once again decidedly different. As Dolores Williams contends, "It is no wonder that in most feminist literature written by white-American women, the words 'woman' and 'women' signify only the white woman's experience. By failing to insert the word 'white' before 'woman' and 'women,' some feminists imperialistically take over the identity of those rendered invisible."[53] Feminist Jewish scholars, such as Bernadette Brooten and Judith Plaskow, have similarly taken Christian feminist biblical scholars to task in addressing latent issues of anti-Judaism in feminist biblical interpretations.[54]

In light of these observations, we thus suggest that notable elements of continuity exist between feminist biblical scholarship and the dominant discourse, much of which results from the acceptance of certain principal assumptions regarding the historical-critical task. Yet if at one level feminist biblical scholarship has something in common with the historical-critical endeavor (particularly the role of *analogous* human experience), at another level feminist critics became the first to demonstrate in a forceful and sustained manner that within the androcentric paradigm *difference* with respect to the presumed masculinist signifiers had to be brought into the conversation. This dramatic insight and the consequent shift in focus paved the way for other liberationist discourses and reading practices to voice their concerns in the field of biblical studies.

MOVING BEYOND AND MOVING BACK

By the end of the twentieth century, multiple postmodern agendas had challenged and often also replaced the earlier modernist project. These developments were gradual, multitextured, and by no means linear or uniform in nature, but they had a pervasive impact on the discussion of the usefulness of the "master's tools" nonetheless. First of all, the development of a new historicism with its overt politicization of history and historiography implied a different perception of the task of the

---

52. As Gayatri Chakravorty Spivak has pointed out, however, feminism constantly has to mediate the politics of exclusion and inclusion within masculinist frames of reference, which would apply, in her view, to the criticism just raised here ("The Politics of Interpretation," in *In Other Worlds: Essays in Cultural Politics* [London: Methuen, 1987], esp. 129–33).

53. Dolores Williams, "The Color of Feminism: Or Speaking the Black Woman's Tongue," *JRT* (1986): 50.

54. See further Katharina von Kellenbach, *Anti-Judaism in Feminist Religious Writings* (AAR Cultural Criticism Series 1; Atlanta: Scholars Press, 1994); and Luise Schottroff and Marie-Theres Wacker, eds., *Von der Wurzel getragen: Christlich-feministische Exegese in Auseinandersetzung mit Antijudaismus* (BibInt Series 17; Leiden: Brill, 1996).

historian. Second, as a result of the influx of new methods in the field of biblical studies, historical criticism lost its monopoly and became one— even if still dominant—method among others. Third, developments in feminist critical theory led to more sustained reflection on the meaning and impact of gender for the construction of identities. And fourth, the emergence of postcolonial criticism in more recent years further ques- tioned the universalist pretensions of Western hegemonic discourses.

Many of the debates that the new(er) historicism rekindled were already present on the scene much earlier, and are similar to the ones outlined above with respect to feminist biblical scholarship: the recog- nition of the political nature of text and interpreter.[55] Hayden White, for instance, forcefully challenged the pursuit of univocal meaning in his- torical interpretation, and was at the forefront of abandoning determinism as an axiom of historical inquiry. As he affirmed in 1966, "The historian serves no one well by constructing a specious continuity between the present world and that which preceded it. On the contrary, we require a history that will educate us to discontinuity more than ever before; for discontinuity, disruption, and chaos is our lot."[56] It is not difficult to perceive how the tumult of the 1960s (in both Europe and North America) should have evoked such passionate reconfigura- tions of the historian's task. As Catharine Gallagher notes, the New Left agenda had influenced dramatically the theory of literary and historical critics, and brought about a complete break with the notion of "a privi- leged realm of representation" or "privileged referent."[57] The overt political nature and context of both the texts and the historian are explicitly admitted, articulated, and affirmed, as is the awareness of the "excluded" voices submerged behind dominant textual discourses. Typical for this approach are the observations by the noted American

---

55. The work of Hayden White represented a significant stream of interpretation wherein ideology, narrative, and politics were intricately connected to historical study. See the collection of his essays in Hayden White, *Tropics of Discourse: Essays in Cultural Criticism* (Baltimore: Johns Hopkins University Press, 1978); and idem, *The Content of the Form: Narra- tive Discourse and Historical Representation* (Baltimore: Johns Hopkins University Press, 1987). As Frank Lentricchia notes, this political awareness brought with it a reclamation of Marx and Foucault in historical studies ("Foucault's Legacy: A New Historicism?" in *The New His- toricism* [ed. H. A. Veeser; New York: Routledge, 1989], 234–35).

56. Hayden White, "The Burden of History," in *Tropics of Discourse*, 50.

57. Catherine Gallagher, "Marxism and the New Historicism," in Veeser, *New Histori- cism*, 41. In a similar vein, the influence of various poststructuralist critics such as Jacques Derrida and Jacques Lacan also had a dramatic influence on the new developments in his- torical study (Rasiah S. Sugirtharajah, *Postcolonial Criticism and Biblical Interpretation* [Oxford: Oxford University Press, 2002], notes this connection with respect to the development of postcolonial criticism in particular [21–22]).

historian Elizabeth Fox-Genovese: "Ultimately, to insist that texts are products of and participants in history as structured social and gender relations is to reclaim them for society as a whole, reclaim them for the political scrutiny of those whom they have excluded, as much as those whom they have celebrated ... And it is to reclaim them for our intentional political action, and ourselves for political accountability."[58]

As was the case with feminist biblical scholarship earlier, outside political and academic movements also found their way into the guild of biblical studies. The Society of Biblical Literature's journal *Semeia* (1974–2003) proved to be one of the highly influential fruits of this influence, ensuring that a variety of postmodern concerns, theories, discourses, and methods would not easily be repressed by more dominant paradigms in the academy. The seminal collection edited by Norman K. Gottwald and Antoinette Clark Wire in 1976 and expanded substantially in 1993 is another major indicator of the gradual but profound impact of political, social, and cultural readings of the Bible on the field of biblical studies.[59] The fruit of these developments was also reflected in the 1995 publication of *The Postmodern Bible,* which solidified such new(er) discourses as serious contenders in the Western biblical studies guild.[60] In the area of feminist research, the Feminist Companion to the Bible Series played a major role in documenting the growing diversity of approaches in the field.[61] From the very beginning this series aimed to provide visibility for feminist research and to open up space for different voices and viewpoints. The refusal to harmonize or unify these contributions also helped in pushing the agenda of gender-critical engagements of biblical texts further. Also in the 1990s, several feminist commentaries on the whole Bible, including extracanonical texts, were published, commemorating the centennial of the Woman's Bible and presenting an assessment of the state of

---

58. Elizabeth Fox-Genovese, "Literary Criticism and the Politics of the New Historicism," in Veeser, *New Historicism,* 222.

59. Norman K. Gottwald and Antoinette Clark Wire, eds., *The Bible and Liberation: Political and Social Hermeneutics* (Berkeley: Community for Religious Research and Education, 1976); and Norman K. Gottwald and Richard A. Horsley, eds., *The Bible and Liberation: Political and Social Hermeneutics* (Bible and Liberation Series; Maryknoll, N.Y.: Orbis, 1993). The volume went from a collection of 176 pages to over 550, demonstrating in many ways the major shift in acceptance and reception in the ensuing fifteen years.

60. The Bible and Culture Collective, *The Postmodern Bible* (New Haven: Yale University Press, 1995).

61. Athalya Brenner, ed., *A Feminist Companion to the Bible* (10 vols.; Sheffield: Sheffield Academic Press, 1993–1996); and Athalya Brenner (and Carole R. Fontaine for vols. 2, 6, and 8), eds., *A Feminist Companion to the Bible* (2d series; 9 vols.; Sheffield: Sheffield Academic Press, 1997–2001). See also Amy-Jill Levine with Marianne Blickenstaff, eds., *A Feminist Companion to the New Testament and Early Christian Writings* (13 vols.; London: Continuum, 2001–).

the question at the end of the twentieth century.[62] In that same time period, a shift can also be noticed in the direction of gender-critical engagements of biblical texts,[63] which took a dramatic leap forward in the late 1990s and proved formative in shifting the conversation in biblical studies more decidedly toward a focus on gender construction and the destabilization of the traditional male subject, moving beyond the dominant male-female dualism and the heterosexual norm.[64] Michel Foucault's unfinished but still legendary *History of Sexuality* project had an enormous impact in terms of the exploration of difference between the ancient world and the modern with respect to issues of sexuality and gender.[65]

---

62. Carol A. Newsom and Sharon H. Ringe, eds., *The Women's Bible Commentary* (London: SPCK, Louisville: Westminster John Knox, 1992); Elisabeth Schüssler Fiorenza with Ann Brock and Shelly Matthews, eds., *A Feminist Commentary* (vol. 2 of *Searching the Scriptures*; New York: Crossroad, 1994); and Luise Schottroff and Marie-Theres Wacker, eds., *Kompendium Feministische Bibelauslegung* (Gütersloh: Gütersloher Verlagshaus, 1998).

63. See, for instance, Athalya Brenner and Fokkelien van Dijk-Hemmes, *On Gendering Texts: Female and Male Voices in the Hebrew Bible* (BibInt Series 1; Leiden: Brill, 1993); and Athalya Brenner, *The Intercourse of Knowledge: On Gendering Desire and "Sexuality" in the Hebrew Bible* (BibInt Series 26; Leiden: Brill, 1997). On the connections of feminism and gender, and the impact of both on the study of religion, see the very helpful navigation of this complex field by Sian Hawthorne, "Feminism: Feminism, Gender Studies, and Religion," and "Gender and Religion: History of Study," in *Macmillan Encyclopedia of Religion* (2d ed.; New York: Macmillan, 2004).

64. Noteworthy here are contributions focusing on a wide range of gender-related issues, from masculinity to homosexuality to transgender and queer readings. For a diversity of influential studies, see, e.g., Bernadette J. Brooten, *Love between Women: Early Christian Responses to Female Homoeroticism* (The Chicago Series on Sexuality, History, and Society; Chicago: University of Chicago Press, 1996); Martti Nissinen, *Homoeroticism in the Biblical World: A Historical Perspective* (trans. K. Stjerna; Minneapolis: Fortress, 1998); Stephen D. Moore, *God's Gym: Divine Male Bodies of the Bible* (New York: Routledge, 1996); idem, *God's Beauty Parlor: Queer Spaces in and around the Bible* (Contraversions; Stanford: Stanford University Press, 2001); Stephen D. Moore and Janice Capel Andreson, eds., *New Testament Masculinities* (SemeiaSt 45; Atlanta: Society of Biblical Literature, 2003); Dale B. Martin, *The Corinthian Body* (New Haven: Yale University Press, 1995); Virginia Burrus, *"Begotten, Not Made": Conceiving Manhood in Late Antiquity* (Figurae; Stanford: Stanford University Press, 2000); idem, *The Sex Lives of Saints: An Erotics of Ancient Hagiography* (Divinations; Philadelphia: University of Pennsylvania Press, 2004); Daniel Boyarin, *Carnal Israel: Reading Sex in Talmudic Culture* (The New Historicism 25; Berkeley and Los Angeles: University of California Press, 1993); and idem, *Unheroic Conduct: The Rise of Heterosexuality and the Invention of the Jewish Man* (Contraversions 8; Berkeley and Los Angeles: University of California Press, 1997). Earlier work by classical scholars such as John J. Winkler, Froma I. Zeitlin, and David M. Halperin, as well as scholars of Christian history like Peter Brown and John Boswell, provided significant impetus for the developments in biblical studies.

65. Michel Foucault, *History of Sexuality* (trans. R. Hurley; 3 vols.; New York: Pantheon, 1978–1986). On his influence in early Christian studies, see the summary by Averil Cameron, "Redrawing the Map: Early Christian Territory after Foucault," *JRS* 76 (1986): 266–71; and

Assuming the social-historical construction of conceptions of sex and bodies, more recent studies have further developed the notion of contextualized sexual and gendered identities in the ancient world.[66] A similar stress on *difference* can also be found in the largely simultaneously developing field of postcolonial studies, especially in relation to the analysis of cultural and political hegemonic discourses and colonizing/colonial bodies. In this vein, Homi Bhabha has argued that change in the paradigmatic quality of the modern and the Western can only happen if "cultural difference" rather than diversity is affirmed as paramount.[67] Noteworthy in this respect are the affirmation of difference but also the continued examination of *both* oppressive structures *and* the ways in which those are perpetuated in dominant texts, discourses, and modes of interpretation.[68] Scholars from a variety of contexts introduced postcolonial approaches into biblical studies. Fernando F. Segovia was an early proponent of integrating social location in biblical interpretation[69] and has more recently moved toward more overt postcolonial

---

Elizabeth A. Clark, "Foucault, the Fathers, and Sex," *JAAR* 56 (1988): 619–41. The study by Elizabeth A. Castelli, *Imitating Paul: A Discourse of Power* (Literary Currents in Biblical Interpretation; Louisville: Westminster John Knox, 1991), was highly influential more generally for bringing Foucaultian readings more directly into biblical studies. One should also note in this respect the significant effect of new historicism on the development of gender-critical inquiry. Some of these movements have been traced by Stephen D. Moore, "History after Theory? Biblical Studies and the New Historicism," *BibInt* 5 (1997): 289–99. See most recently Elizabeth A. Clark, *History, Theory, Text: Historians and the Linguistic Turn* (Cambridge: Harvard University Press, 2004). A helpful framework for this discussion is provided in the groundbreaking article by Harold C. Washington, "Violence and the Construction of Gender in the Hebrew Bible," *BibInt* 5 (1997): 324–63, where he makes the explicit connection between emphases on ideology-critical analysis and the development of gender(ed) readings.

66. Influential studies appeared at the beginning of the 1990s that helped shape the agenda for the burgeoning developments in biblical studies. See, e.g., Thomas Laqueur, *Making Sex: Body and Gender from the Greeks to Freud* (Cambridge, Mass.: Harvard University Press, 1990); Margaret R. Miles, *Carnal Knowing: Female Nakedness and Religious Meaning in the Christian West* (Boston: Beacon, 1989); and David M. Halperin, John J. Winkler, and Froma I. Zeitlin, eds., *Before Sexuality: The Construction of Erotic Experience in the Ancient World* (Princeton: Princeton University Press, 1990).

67. Homi K. Bhabha, *The Location of Culture* (New York: Routledge, 1994), 32–37.

68. In his comments on Joseph Conrad's *Heart of Darkness*, for instance, Edward Said notes that there is no such thing as a *"direct* experience, or reflection, of the world in the language of the text." He goes on to detail how Conrad's image of Africa was in fact a "politicized, ideologically saturated Africa," which was the product (and itself continued the process of) colonial imperialism (*Culture and Imperialism* [New York: Knopf, 1993], 67).

69. See esp. Fernando F. Segovia and Mary Ann Tolbert, *Social Location and Biblical Interpretation in the United States* (vol. 1 of *Reading from This Place*; Minneapolis: Fortress, 1995); and Fernando F. Segovia, ed., *What Is John? Readers and Readings of the Fourth Gospel*

engagements in and of the field.[70] The noted scholar Rasiah S. Sugirtharajah has also played a significant role in placing postcolonial concerns at
the center of study.[71] As with feminism earlier, in the cases of Segovia and
Sugirtharajah as well, one can observe the decisive and persistent influence of liberationist agendas in the discipline. Moreover, critics such as
Musa Dube[72] and Kwok Pui-lan[73] were equally formative in establishing
postcolonial feminist agendas in non-European contexts.[74]

The development of postcolonial and gender-critical engagements of
traditional historical criticism have thus been significant if varied, and
their impact on approaches to the Bible can be conceptualized in fairly
radical terms.[75] Sugirtharajah, for example, has recently provided a manifesto of sorts with respect to traditional historical criticism, seriously
questioning whether such "neocolonizing" discourses have any further
utility in the world today. He argues that biblical critics rather need to
find a wider public than simply the cloistered and sterile world of the

---

(2 vols.; SBLSymS 3; Atlanta: Scholars Press, 1996–1998). The earlier and highly influential
collection edited by Cain Hope Felder, examining African American engagements of the
history of biblical interpretation, proved to be at the forefront of these developments in
biblical studies (see Cain H. Felder, ed., *Stony the Road We Trod: African American Biblical
Interpretation* [Minneapolis: Fortress, 1991]).

70. See most recently Fernando F. Segovia, ed., *Interpreting Beyond Borders* (Bible and
Postcolonialism 3; Sheffield: Sheffield Academic Press, 2000); and idem, *Decolonizing Biblical
Studies: A View from the Margins* (Maryknoll, N.Y.: Orbis, 2000).

71. See esp. Rasiah S. Sugirtharajah, ed., *Voices from the Margin: Interpreting the Bible in
the Third World* (Maryknoll, N.Y.: Orbis, 1994); idem, ed., *The Postcolonial Bible* (Bible and
Postcolonialism 1; Sheffield: Sheffield Academic Press, 1998); idem, *The Bible and the Third
World: Precolonial, Colonial, and Postcolonial Encounters* (Cambridge: Cambridge University
Press, 2001); idem, *Postcolonial Criticism*; and idem, *Postcolonial Reconfigurations: An Alterna-
tive Way of Reading the Bible and Doing Theology* (London: SCM, 2003).

72. See Musa W. Dube (Shomanah), *Postcolonial Feminist Interpretation of the Bible* (St.
Louis: Chalice, 2000); idem, ed., *Other Ways of Reading: African Women and the Bible* (Global
Perspectives on Biblical Scholarship 2; Atlanta: Society of Biblical Literature, 2001); and
Musa Dube and John L. Staley, eds., *John and Postcolonialism: Travel, Space and Power* (Bible
and Postcolonialism 7; London: Continuum, 2002).

73. Kwok Pui-lan, *Discovering the Bible in the Non-Biblical World* (Bible and Liberation
Series; Maryknoll, N.Y.: Orbis, 1995).

74. For further glimpses into the developments, see the two seminal volumes of *Semeia*
that helped situate this perspective in biblical scholarship: Laura E. Donaldson, ed., *Postcolonialism and Scriptural Reading* (*Semeia* 75; Atlanta: Society of Biblical Literature, 1996); and
Roland Boer, ed., *A Vanishing Mediator? The Presence/Absence of the Bible in Postcolonialism*
(*Semeia* 88; Atlanta: Society of Biblical Literature, 2001).

75. See, e.g., the discussion by Richard A. Horsley, "Subverting Disciplines: The Possi-
bilities and Limitations of Postcolonial Theory for New Testament Study," in *Toward a New
Heaven and a New Earth: Essays in Honor of Elisabeth Schüssler Fiorenza* (ed. F. F. Segovia;
Maryknoll, N.Y.: Orbis, 2003), 93–96.

guild.[76] In some respects, the earlier shift toward social location has also brought about an alteration in the meaning and end of biblical studies, insofar as the focus of newer methods is on discrete historical reception in particular communities by specific peoples.[77] One can readily perceive how it is that such conceptions can be said to eradicate the common analogous experience of humanity articulated in the Harnack citation given at the outset of this essay. "I am human and consider nothing historical alien to me" finds little support in this postmodern framework, since human cultures and individuals are perceived as fragmented in their experience, and the analogous nature of human culture as a nontemporal, universalizing phenomenon is repeatedly challenged.[78] One rather finds discrete communities (past and present) and different experiences, which can only be brought into conversation with great difficulty, and then always at the risk of being subjected to one colonizing project/power or another.

Similarly, the postmodern focus on globalization and particularity has found its way into the biblical studies guild through a diversification of methods. For our purposes here we have highlighted postcolonial and gender-critical interactions, since these methods continue the feminist-liberationist agenda, pushing it further, in most cases, by emphasizing *differences* between various contiguous communities of interpreters, while also promoting *diversity* as a phenomenon embedded in all human experience, thereby placing greater emphasis on examining such multiplicity in biblical texts and traditions.[79] The universalist assumptions that

---

76. Rasiah S. Sugirtharajah, "The End of Biblical Studies?," in Segovia, *Toward a New Heaven,* 133–40.

77. See, e.g., the recent essay by Vincent Wimbush, "In Search of a Usable Past: Reorienting Biblical Studies," in Segovia, *Toward a New Heaven,* 179–98.

78. It goes without saying that not all appropriations of postcolonial and gender-critical perspectives in biblical studies necessarily challenge the fundamental frame of reference of more traditional historical-critical discourses and methods. The emphases on difference are not simply inherent in or intrinsic to the theories or methods themselves, but result to a significant degree from the predilections of and uses by particular interpreters.

79. Although still more traditionally inclined, newer historical studies on everything from the revisionist approach to biblical/Israelite chronology (Philip R. Davies, *In Search of "Ancient Israel"* [JSOTSup 148; Sheffield: JSOT Press, 1992]); to the analysis of the role of imperialism in the production of biblical texts (James W. Watts, ed., *Persia and Torah: The Theory of Imperial Authorization of the Pentateuch* [SBLSymS 17; Atlanta: Society of Biblical Literature, 2001); to the study of diversity in social conflict in early Christian origins (William E. Arnal, *Jesus and the Village Scribes: Galilean Conflicts and the Setting of Q* [Minneapolis: Fortress, 2001]), all demonstrate the influence of the postmodern stress on difference, diversity, and power structures in the study of biblical texts and traditions. Not only do we then perceive the impact of newer methods on reassessments of historical criticism, but we also see the role that such plays in reconstructions of the past itself. See also Philip R. Davies, *Whose Bible Is It Anyway?* (2d ed.; London: Continuum, 2004).

dogged earlier formulations of historical study of the Bible—even if implicitly—are here categorically questioned. Moreover, the liberationist impulses already operative in feminist analyses take on an even larger function in terms of eradicating at an even more fundamental level the basic normative assumptions and values of Western discourse and institutions. Finally, insofar as the combination of gender-critical discussions with postcolonialism provides "a combined offensive against the aggressive myth of both imperial and nationalist masculinity,"[80] this association also offers to push the potential insights of each method further through such collaboration.

Still, the postmodern turn in biblical studies reflects the fundamental Western orientation of these discourses, theories, and methods, providing, in the process,[81] confirmation of the biblical meta-narrative that places humans at the center of the discourse and of history.[82] While negating universal human experience, such counterdiscourses thereby also affirm that it is *human* experience that is at stake and in question.[83] As Roland Boer has recently contended, in terms of its intersection with biblical studies postmodernism is still often "resolutely modernist, if the emphasis on autonomy in modernism is taken into account."[84] Certainly this consideration bears further scrutiny, especially in light of the ways in which

---

80. Leela Gandhi, *Postcolonial Theory: A Critical Introduction* (New York: Columbia University Press, 1998), 98.

81. Western discourses find their home in Western educational institutions, although this is rarely acknowledged or noted in the discussion itself. See further the comments by Roland Boer, "Introduction: Vanishing Mediators?," *Semeia* 88 (2001): 3; and esp. idem, "Western Marxism and the Interpretation of the Hebrew Bible," *JSOT* 78 (1998): 3–21.

82. In broad terms, one might consider this move to represent "the illicit transfer from the ontological to the historical" (Jonathan Z. Smith, *Drudgery Divine: On the Comparisons of Early Christianities and the Religions of Late Antiquity* [Chicago Studies in the History of Judaism; Chicago: University of Chicago Press, 1990], 39). This focus of both historical criticism and its critics on the human and the individual subject demonstrates, at one level, the broad tendency for interpreters to reinscribe biblical-theological value judgments in their inquiry. To some degree, the seeming inevitability of the reinscription confirms our earlier suggestion that there exists a latent (albeit secularized) salvation-historical framework to the philosophical and historical logic of post-Enlightenment thought. The methods and tools of study seem to encourage this reinscription, so even in cases where challenge is adamantly and tenaciously affirmed there exists a basic reaffirmation of the edifice.

83. For a recent challenge to this well-entrenched legacy of the Western tradition, see John Gray, *Straw Dogs: Thoughts on Humans and Other Animals* (London: Granta, 2002).

84. Boer, *Novel Histories*, 193. It is this connection to modernist premises that causes some scholars such as Sugirtharajah to distinguish quite sharply between the aims of postmodernism and those of postcolonialism, arguing rather for the closer connection between postcolonialism and cultural studies (*Asian Biblical Hermeneutics and Postcolonialism: Contesting the Interpretations* [BS 64; Sheffield: Sheffield Academic Press, 1998], 15–16).

postmodern discourses as a whole continue to privilege the individual,[85] and re-entrench authority squarely in the "eye of the beholder." In many respects, in fact, this embracing of the individual at the heart of the postmodern moment in biblical studies heightens the modernist impulse, leaving the individual as the final arbiter of meaning and significance— the lone vantage point in an otherwise fragmented world. Furthermore, the very structures that are dismembered in the newer methods are often re-membered on another level.[86] Indeed, pushing this reflection still further, not only does humanity take central stage in what can perhaps be considered the "final grand narrative,"[87] but privileged classes of individuals do as well. Troeltsch clearly acknowledged the nature and extent of his audience. Very significant features of that earlier audience have now changed—but postcolonial and gender-critical methods are also linked to the educated elite of societies.[88] Although much has shifted in these newer discourses, there is also significant commonality with the dominant

---

85. One might note in this respect that even when *community* life and thought are appealed to or constructed in postmodern discourses, it is a task often undertaken from the vantage point of the *individual* writer and interpreter functioning as a hegemonic voice.

86. For instance, with respect to postcolonial criticism, it is relatively easy to point to matters of application, wherein there are broad re-inscriptions of the very colonial and imperial structures being repudiated. Levine has criticized the use of Judaism in Third World exegesis, for example, noting the way in which colonial historical-critical methods and assumptions are simply taken over by liberationist biblical scholars from other parts of the world ("Disease of Postcolonial New Testament Studies," 91–99). In a similar vein, the preoccupation with gender issues represents a decidedly Western phenomenon as well, as it furthers the modernist focus on the individual even as essentialist perspectives on the subject are increasingly questioned and replaced by a valorization of difference. This particular problem with the reconstitution of power in the very act of its dismemberment has been engagingly assessed (with respect to the frequent use of Foucault) by Jonathan Culler, "The Call to History," in *Framing the Sign: Criticism and Its Institutions* (Norman: University of Oklahoma Press, 1988), esp. 64–68; cf. Briggs, "Deceit of the Sublime," 19–20.

87. One might include here the work of Frantz Fanon, who seeks to establish a new postcolonial non-European humanistic philosophy (see the discussion in Alfred J. López, *Posts and Pasts: A Theory of Postcolonialism* [Explorations in Postcolonial Studies; Albany, N.Y.: State University of New York Press, 2001], 121–42).

88. The rhetoric of postcolonialism could in this view be read as the reflection of a bourgeois mentality. For instance, one could note that postcolonial criticism, in arguing for a fragmentation in terms of experience and the value of individuality as normative, also thereby affirms fundamental Western liberal *democratic* ideals that help fuel the global capitalism it so resolutely resists (see the discussion by Fredric Jameson, where he posits that postmodernism as a discourse represents the "cultural logic" of late capitalism [see esp. "Postmodernism, or the Cultural Logic of Late Capitalism," *New Left Review* 146 [1984]: 53–92; and idem, "Postmodernism and Consumer Society," in *The Cultural Turn: Selected Writings on the Postmodern, 1983–1998* [London: Verso, 1998], 1–20).

discourses of the past. Such associations should thus cause us to reengage the past from the standpoint of the present with increased fervor.

THE TOOLS AND THE HOUSE

In the above discussion our main aim has been to create a broad context for understanding and assessing the relationship of historical criticism to the critical engagement of that discourse that followed first in feminist-critical biblical scholarship and then later in postcolonial and gender-critical assessments of the same. We have argued for a unity of intent in these various and diverse interactions with the "traditions of the fathers," without intending to generalize the various discrete concerns of the diverse post-historical-critical methods under consideration.

Moreover, we have also argued for viewing both continuity and discontinuity between the work of historical criticism and the critics of it who followed. In the approach developed here, we have suggested that one of the underlying elements providing for continuity lay in the particular conception of history and historical investigation proffered by Troeltsch and his contemporaries. Georg Iggers has categorized the historiographical method reflected in the work of Troeltsch as a form of "hermeneutical historiography."[89] Iggers notes that while there was a scientistic objective component to what these historians were after—"definitive accounts of past events were possible"[90]—they were also aware that historical inquiry could not mimic the method of the natural sciences. The basic difference for Troeltsch and others was that the latter "sought causal explanation of recurring phenomena," while the former "dealt with meaningful human phenomena which … [had] to be understood in their unique individuality."[91] As Leopold von Ranke, the oft-touted major figure of this historical school, states, the primary charge of the historian lay beyond mere fact gathering but was rather to be concentrated in a "documentary, penetrating profound study … devoted to the phenomenon itself … to its essence and content."[92] From the stress on documentary sources to the emphasis on development, all of the essential features of historical-critical scholarship of the Bible derive from this broader, predominantly German Protestant approach to the study of human culture and history. It is relatively easy to appreciate, of course, just how deeply committed to the post-Enlightenment modernist agenda such approaches in fact were,

---

89. Georg G. Iggers, *New Directions in European Historiography* (rev. ed.; Middleton, Conn.: Wesleyan University Press, 1984), 19.

90. Ibid., 17.

91. Ibid., 18.

92. Ibid.

with their celebration of the "freedom" of the historical interpreter and the fundamental accent on categorical individuality and uniqueness.[93]

In some sense the tools of this form of historical criticism are embedded in the larger framework out of which it arose. One can readily perceive the degree of continuity in terms of theory and perception, at the very least, between the early "masters" and their later critics. The latter's ascendancy is predicated to a significant extent on the affirmations related to human culture and history advocated by the former. There is thus a direct relationship between so-called modernist and postmodernist concerns in this respect,[94] establishing a broad line of continuity between historical criticism and what followed. That continuity is often lost, repressed, or easily passed over in the rhetoric of self-identification that is necessary for defining a "new" task and theory. Yet, as we have argued above, as radical a critique as feminist scholarship and postcolonial criticisms may have levelled against traditionally dominant discourses, there is also a marked degree of indebtedness to those same entities being so engaged.[95] Indeed, the gap noted at the outset between Harnack and Lorde both hints at the radical *difference* between the two, but also, in a way, the connectedness of their two respective enterprises in terms of seeking to grapple with human nature and culture in its distinctiveness and individuality.

An inherent ambiguity thus persists in the engagements over the past—there is both a contesting of the dominant discourses but also a degree of complicity as a result. The appeal to the ethics and politics of interpretation therefore becomes particularly acute at this juncture. One can use the tools of traditional discourse, doing so uncritically, or one can reject them altogether (although it would remain to be seen if one could

---

93. As David Harvey notes, such forms of modernism "took on multiple perspectivism and relativism as its epistemology for revealing what it still took to be the true nature of a unified, though complex, underlying reality" (*The Condition of Postmodernity: An Enquiry into the Origins of Cultural Change* [Oxford: Blackwell, 1990], 30).

94. Cf. the following comments by Harvey: "there is much more continuity than difference between the broad history of modernism and the movement called postmodernism. It seems more sensible to me to see the latter as a particular kind of crisis within the former, ... while expressing a deep scepticism as to any particular prescriptions as to how the eternal and immutable should be conceived of, represented, or expressed" (ibid., 116).

95. As a cautionary tale, one might note that in its inception historical criticism, whether it was proffered against the church's dogmatic dominance or that reflected in the theories and methods of the evolving natural sciences, was, for its time, a "radical" discourse. It was only gradually over time that it moved from the margins to the center, becoming dominant discourse as a result. Thus, the pattern of contestation followed by solidification and then domination (and also domestication) is attested by the history of biblical criticism itself.

in fact continue to engage the guild of biblical studies in this instance). Finally, one can also engage the dominant discourses and create counter-discourses and communities, reconfiguring and reconstituting traditional tools, methods, and aims in alternative directions and contexts. In the latter case, voices within and without of the guild find each other, and those at the center and the margins can establish (some) common cause. Herein also lies the possibility and prospect for the creation of shifting identities and the development of subversive discourses amidst the employment of alternative ones.

But critical discourses also need to be self-reflective and self-critical, an agenda put front and center by the work of Elisabeth Schüssler Fiorenza in her collection *Rhetoric and Ethic*.[96] It is at this juncture that the *raison d'être* of this present volume exists, for we see precisely this agenda operative in this collection of essays. There is an attempt to incorporate widespread interaction with the traditional historical-critical task, while at the same time engaging that tradition of contesting scholarship. There are meta-levels of interaction herein, with the accent falling emphatically on the continued need for both contest and conversation, dialogue and differentiation, criticism and continuity. We thus see at work in this volume a diversity of approaches and questionings, coupled with divergent reasonings and methodological inquiries. There is no one right way to carry on the task of wrestling with the traditions and the tools of the "masters"—and it is not at all our agenda to suggest a replacement or a "better" path. Insofar as this volume contributes to this necessary and critical discussion in the field, it does so at the point of contestation, as every essay in one way or another employs the discursive logic of opposition, definition, and distinction. Some essays are more clearly indebted to the tools and traditions of historical criticism, others are evidently more inclined to "rage against the machine." In the end it is not only the cumulative effect of these divergent voices that provides a challenge to the reader, but also the gaps and spaces (and at times also fissures) that open up in and between the alternative, subversive, distinctive, reconfigured, and sometimes just simply tweaked and nuanced discourses related to historical engagement of the Bible. We thus consider this combination of methodological and textual studies to provide a springboard for future discussion and debate.

And discussion and debate there will—or, at the very least, should—be, for such interactions will remain essential if we are to move forward, creating new insights and viewpoints for the future. In this process, querying the utility of the "master's tools" will no doubt prove to be one

---

96. Elisabeth Schüssler Fiorenza, *Rhetoric and Ethic: The Politics of Biblical Studies* (Minneapolis: Fortress, 1999).

central component of the larger task. But this move is also just a beginning, as a valid concern arises insofar as the Bible continues to occupy
central stage in Western discourses and institutions. For, while we see in
this volume serious contention over the precise matter of how the tools,
methods, and theories of past historical-critical scholarship can be used
and (re)appropriated in new contexts with different concerns, we also
perceive there to be some fundamental questions as of yet unasked (and
power structures still masked as a result). Primary in this respect may be
the determination of what precisely constitutes the "master's house,"
which the tools presumably built? Is it Western discourse itself, which the
Bible has been formative in shaping? Is it academic and/or political institutions, which continue to "house" the discourses, often reconstituting
them in the process? Is it the mode of production and the ideology
thereby produced, which sustains the late capitalism of our contemporary period? One notes in this respect that the Bible has always played a
critical role in colonial imagination and practice, and as such is often
simultaneously both a source of liberation from but also re-embracing of
the terror and injustice that the tools have helped to construct.

In all of this, of course, one thing is for certain, and that is that the
"master's house" has as its cornerstone the Bible, which provides its sure
foundation. Thus, it remains to be explored further and in other contexts
what it might mean to take Lorde seriously in terms of "dismantling the
master's house."[97] The contributors to this volume make an initial foray
into this larger conversation by engaging the "tools"—but it will remain
the purview of scholars who are critically concerned about our world to
take the task further … and however that dismantling is done—if
indeed it can be done—it is likely to be undertaken at a gradual pace,
brick by brick.

---

97. The conclusion by Miriam Peskowitz is thus provocatively apropos: "[A]n anticolonial refusal means that we release our attachments to the Bible, and in doing so,
question most intently the claims and metaphors and stories that have become part of a collective Western consciousness. It means refusing the Bible's status as a privileged text of the
West, and refusing to be privileged by it" ("Tropes of Travel," *Semeia* 75 [1996]: 192).

HISTORICAL-CRITICAL APPROACHES AND THE EMANCIPATION OF WOMEN: UNFULFILLED PROMISES AND REMAINING POSSIBILITIES*

Hanna Stenström

My contribution to the discussion of the pros and cons of historical-critical approaches to the Bible for feminist biblical scholars and other feminist readers will take as its point of departure a story from an autobiographical work by a Swedish woman, Emilia Fogelklou.[1] The story shows how one form of historical-critical biblical scholarship, the *religions-*

---

* I am indebted to Cecilia Johnselius Theodoru for sharing some of her research with me. Cecilia is a doctoral student in the Department of Literature and History of Ideas at the University of Stockholm, and she is writing a dissertation on Emilia Fogelklou and other Swedish women's interpretations of the Bible in the early twentieth century. Also see her essay "'Så ock på jorden': Emilia Fogelklous gudsrikestanke – en feministisk utopi" (Idéhistoriska uppsatser 37; Stockholm: Stockholms universitet, Avdelningen för idéhistoria, 2000). I am also indebted to Margareta Järlström, "Förmoder: Emilia Fogelklou—teologen" *Kvinnovetenskaplig Tidskrift* 10 (1989): 80–83 (see esp. 81, where the passage quoted and discussed below is treated). It was in this article that I first read about Fogelklou's struggle with the New Testament scholarship of her time. I also want to express my gratitude to Professor Birger Olsson, who read and commented on an earlier version of this essay, providing some valuable comments. The responsibility for the final result and any faults is, of course, my own.

1. Emilia Fogelklou (1878–1972) was an author, theologian, philosopher, and scholar without a permanent position at any university. She was also a mystic and worked as a teacher in children's schools, as well as in different kinds of adult education and later as a freelance author and lecturer. She wrote on such diverse subjects as pedagogy, psychology of religion, sociology, history, and women's issues. She belonged to the women's movement and was also active in peace work. She grew up in the Church of Sweden (Lutheran), but became a Quaker and was one of the founders of the Society of Friends in Sweden. In 1909 she was the first female to receive a Bachelor of Divinity degree in Sweden and in 1941 she was the first woman to receive an honorary doctorate in theology at the University of Uppsala. For more about her life, see Malin Bergman Andrews, *Emilia Fogelklou, människan och gärningen—En biografi* (Skellefteå: Artos, 1999). For biographical information in English, see Emilia Fogelklou, *Reality and Radiance: Selected Autobiographical Works of Emilia Fogelklou* (trans. H. T. Lutz; Richmond, Ind.: Friends United, 1985), esp. 19–66. This translation is the one I will use in this essay.

geschichtliche Schule, came as a form of liberation to Emilia Fogelklou when she was a student of theology in the earliest years of the twentieth century. The story also shows how the conflict between this radical form of historical-critical biblical scholarship and a conservative, apologetic way of doing exegesis was taken into the very body of a woman—as will be shown below, Fogelklou herself got physically ill when she, as a student, encountered such different approaches. I will continue with some questions about what current feminist biblical scholars can learn from such stories, gradually turning toward the issues of the possible uses of historical-critical scholarship in feminist biblical criticism today.[2]

The story I relate is part of *Barhuvad,* published in 1950, one of three autobiographical books by Emilia Fogelklou. In this volume she describes her childhood, youth, course of studies, and the beginning of her career. Fogelklou wrote her autobiographical works in the third person, as a story about a girl called Mi. Not all details in the story necessarily correspond to historical events; not only because memory is seldom exact but also because this book is a consciously constructed narrative and rhetorical piece. However, the central elements in the conflict described in this story correspond to an actual crisis experienced by Emilia Fogelklou in Uppsala at the beginning of the twentieth century.[3]

Recurrent topics in *Barhuvad* are Mi's exposure to biblical scholarship, especially historical-critical approaches, and the nature of her own reading of the Bible.[4] She is, for example, excited by studies in Hebrew language and literature in which philological issues and perspectives from the *religionsgeschichtliche Schule* were central. Reading the prophets in Hebrew, for instance, makes evident for her the poetic character of their texts—the rhyme, the imagery, and the power of the texts. Reading Gen 1 in Hebrew, paying close attention to the connections with Babylonian and Phoenician mythology, opens her eyes to the poetic quality and rhetorical force of the text that is lost in translation and in dogmatic Christian readings where the mythological influences are not acknowledged.[5]

---

2. In what follows, I deliberately write as a biblical scholar, focusing my attention strictly on the encounter between this particular woman and biblical scholarship and on the relevance of this story for feminist critical concerns. I leave aside the more general theological questions implied by the story, such as, for instance, the mariological issues at stake in Fogelklou's work.

3. Cf. Andrews, *Emilia Fogelklou,* 81–83; and Ingrid Meiling Bäckman, *Den resfärdiga: Studier i Emilia Fogelklous självbiografi* (Stockholm/Stehag: Brutus Östlings Bokförlag Symposion, 1997), 166–68.

4. See, e.g., Fogelklou, *Reality and Radiance,* 78; and the Swedish original, *Barhuvad* (Stockholm: Bonniers, 1950), 44, 59.

5. Fogelklou, *Reality and Radiance,* 88; and idem, *Barhuvad,* 83, 94–96.

Mi and the New Testament Seminar—A Story

So far, we have followed Mi's (and her author's) encounter with studies in the Hebrew Bible. Her encounter with New Testament studies, however, is something quite different, since New Testament research in Uppsala at the time was dominated by a conservative exegesis that combined historical work with an apologetic for the traditional Christian dogma, strongly opposing the radicals in the history of religions school. The following events in Mi's story can be dated to 1907. The anonymous professor of New Testament in this story is Adolf Kolmodin (1855–1928), a conservative exegete, who regarded Theodor Zahn and Bernhard Weiss as his teachers and authorities.[6] The identity of the "old professor with sideburns" is not certain, but he may be Waldemar Rudin, professor of biblical exegesis at the Faculty of Theology of Uppsala University from 1877 to 1900.[7]

It was part of Mi's theological course requirement to attend a seminar on the New Testament. It took up the matter of the virgin birth. Mi was the only woman in the group.[8] It became more and more uncomfortable to be present as the old-fashioned orthodox presentation went forward. She experienced a dreadful nausea each time she had to attend. It was her belief at least, that it resulted from the abstruse way of approaching

---

6. Adolf Kolmodin is regarded as one of the last representatives within the field of biblical scholarship of a "dogmatic exegesis," in which teachings of Christian traditions provided the framework for academic exegesis. Here the exposition of the biblical texts supported church dogma. The New Testament Professor who succeeded him, Gillis P:son Wetter (1887–1926, professor 1923–1926), belonged to the *religionsgeschichtliche Schule*. Wetter had studied in Berlin, Marburg and Göttingen, and was influenced by Wilhelm Bousset and Richard Reitzenstein. However, the designation "historical-critical scholarship" represents a very broad spectrum of approaches—even Kolmodin considered himself a "historical critic." It is obvious from his writings that he regarded works by the *religionsgeschichtliche Schule* to be both irresponsible and careless historical work and an attack on the sacred truths of Christianity, thus combining in his own work historical and apologetic aims (see, e.g., Adolf Kolmodin, *Bibliska Tids—och Stridsfrågor* [Stockholm: Evangeliska Fosterlandsstiftelsens förlag, 1906], 103.) Ironically, Kolmodin was at the same time considered too much of a "biblical critic" himself in some conversative Christian circles of his time. See further Birger Olsson, "Förändringar inom svensk bibelforskning under 1900-talet," in *Modern svensk teologi—strömningar och perspektivskiften under 1900-talet* (ed. Håkan Eilert et al.; Stockholm: Verbum, 1999), 67–135 (on Wetter, see 78, 85–87, 88–90; on Kolmodin, see 69–70, 83–84).

7. I owe this suggestion to Birger Olsson.

8. The Swedish original has "församlingen" here. "Församling" is the word used for "religious assembly," "worshipping community," and for "parish." In the translation of the New Testament used in 1950, "församling" is the place where women are supposed to be silent according to 1 Cor 14:34. I think one finds here a deliberate choice on the part of the author to use a word that evokes such associations.

the whole subject, not as an aspect of the history of religion, but rather as a kind of dogmatic man-talk.[9]

An old theology professor with sideburns lived in the same house. One day when Mi was returning home from the unpleasant seminar, she met his kindly wife on the stairs. And when the old lady, with some anxiety in her voice, asked how she was, Mi blurted out her disgust and despair at what she had just come from.

The next day, just as Mi's roommate was holding a little party for her brother and a couple of his fellow law students, the professor came up and knocked on the door. He wanted to see Mi. The party moved quickly to another room, while the professor, a broad smile on his face and two heavy books under his arm, sat himself down on the red and white striped sofa. He had heard from his wife that Mi was having trouble with the question of the virgin birth, and he had come to clear away all the difficulties.[10] He opened up his encyclopedias to several articles on parthenogenesis in animals and humans. He read aloud, sermonized, expounded, greatly satisfied with himself at being able so easily to remove all obstacles.

It became so quiet in the next room, where earlier there had been talking and laughter. Mi was filled with indignation. She was ready to throw the well-meaning old man out. His exposition struck her as strange and repulsive. Finally he left. The company in the next room looked terribly amused. How much they had heard she did not know. The kindly old fellow would doubtless not have objected to letting his brilliance shine over all of them as well.

Mi developed a high fever, and a couple of days later was in the hospital with an advanced case of appendicitis. Whatever the price, she experienced a blessed relief at getting out of the seminar. She couldn't help feeling that it had been the cause of her illness, no matter how unreasonable the coincidence might appear.[11]

At the end, Mi asks herself whether she should terminate her theological studies, but she finally decides to continue. She also realizes that it will not be possible for her to talk to the professor about the seminar.

---

9. The expression used in Swedish original ("manfolksaktigt dogmatiskt") is difficult to translate, but "dogmatic man-talk" captures the sense if not also the feeling.

10. The English "difficulties" is used for the Swedish "stötesten," a word that often translates the Greek *skandalon* (as well as words with similar sense and imagery such as is found in Rom 9:33). This use of vocabulary must thus be a deliberate choice by the author.

11. I have here used the translation available in Fogelklou, *Reality and Radiance*, 87–88. For the Swedish original, see idem, *Barhuvad*, 90–91.

REFLECTIONS ON THE STORY

In this story we encounter three approaches to the traditions related to Jesus' being born of a virgin. The first is Kolmodin's exegesis, which seems to have been a defense of Christian dogmatics rather than a critical analysis of the biblical texts. The second is the "old professor's" apologetic efforts to resolve the problem this dogma caused through proving that *parthenogenesis* is in fact not uncommon in nature. These two approaches, the dogmatic and the apologetic, are contrasted with a consistent historical-critical approach, more specifically the one of the *religionsgeschichtliche Schule*. My primary interest here is in both Mi's relation to these different approaches and her approach viewed on its own terms.[12] I am particularly concerned to address the following two questions: What was liberating in the emerging historical-critical approach? How can this story be read and used from a contemporary feminist perspective? I begin with the second of the two questions.

The story is explicitly about a woman who is alone in a man's world. She is not allowed to formulate her own opinions about the subject discussed and is without options for putting her problems and her solutions on the agenda. Read in this way, the story offers a vivid example of the marginalization of women in general and feminist criticism in particular. It thus represents a chapter in the history of feminist criticism of both the Bible and biblical scholarship. Reading the segment about Mi's nausea and appendicitis, one can even say that Mi—and her author—took the conflict between exegetical approaches into her very body when she fell ill after her encounter with an exegesis of the texts of Jesus' virginal birth that treated the story as historical fact in order to defend the dogma. One may even describe her body as an arena for the conflict between exegetical approaches in a period of transition.

By contrast, the liberating potential of a consistent historical-critical approach, such as the *religionsgeschichtliche Schule's* method of analysis, on Mi's understanding of the biblical virgin birth traditions is made explicit later in *Barhuvad*.[13] This approach made it possible for Mi to problematize the traditions that Jesus was born of a virgin and begotten by the Holy Spirit; at the same time, it also presented some solutions. Mi has learned that traditions of the virgin birth cannot be taken as historical

---

12. Mi's encounter with historical-critical approaches to the Bible is also mentioned in Fogelklou, *Barhuvad*, 44, 59, 83, 92, 94–95.

13. Those passages are missing in Fogelklou, *Reality and Radiance*. See also idem, *Barhuvad*, 96.

fact, as completely unique traditions that prove the truth of Christianity, or as stories about one specific human case of a rather "common phenomenon" among animals. Obviously, she has learned that heroes born of virgins with the help of a divine parent are a recurrent motif in antiquity, and are to be understood in terms of mythological language, not as reports of actual events.[14] For Mi, this means that these traditions force the story of Jesus into a context of "ancient mythical notions of the virgin birth."[15] When Jesus is not conceived and born in the same way as other humans, and when he is thereby transferred to a mythical realm, "the vital connection"[16] between Jesus and human beings is lost.

Furthermore, both Mi and her author have learned, through historical-critical studies, to understand the historical Jesus as a successor to the prophets of the Hebrew Bible. Using a historical-critical approach, Mi's encounter with the prophetic writings in Hebrew made the prophets come alive for her.[17] Understanding Jesus as a successor of these prophets made him real and intelligible in a new way. Since *Barhuvad* is a story, not a piece of academic writing, Fogelklou's argument on these issues is brief and open to different interpretations. For example, it is possible that she recognizes the concern for social justice in the prophetic writings as a constituent element of the message that became contemporary and demanding for the reader, but this is not made explicit. To quote her own words:

> To read part of the pronouncements of the prophets *in Hebrew* made them several degrees more real and immediate. There stood the man—there, the living God—over there, the message. They were contemporary. They had a *here*-and-*now quality, and they were demanding*.... And the figure of Jesus became far more real and understandable when she could place him in the context of the succession of prophets. His message was universal and yet personal. But one destroys the vital connection with human beings by forcing him into ancient mythical notions about the virgin birth.[18]

---

14. This point is not formulated explicitly in the text, but represents my interpretation of both the references to a "history of religions approach" to the virgin birth traditions in the Gospels (Fogelklou, *Barhuvad*, 90) and the emphasis on the presence of a kind of fairy tale motif in those same texts (ibid., 96). See also Fogelklou, *Reality and Radiance*, 87, 89.

15. Fogelklou, *Reality and Radiance*, 89; cf. idem, *Barhuvad*, 96. The word translated as "mythical" in this context is, in the original, derived from a word meaning "fairy tale" or "folk-tale." As I understand it, calling the New Testament stories about Jesus' virginal birth "fairy tales"—which is certainly less correct than labeling them "mythic"—is a deliberate choice for a more disparaging designation.

16. Fogelklou, *Reality and Radiance*, 89; cf. idem, *Barhuvad*, 96.

17. Fogelklou, *Reality and Radiance*, 88–89; cf. idem, *Barhuvad*, 94–96.

18. Fogelklou *Reality and Radiance*, 88–89 (italics original); cf. idem, *Barhuvad*, 96.

For Fogelklou this was no mere academic exercise. Basic to her own life story was a spiritual experience, which she described as a momentary meeting with Reality—with God.[19] Although this is not made very explicit, I find it possible to claim that Fogelklou was convinced that she shared this kind of experience with the prophets and with Jesus.[20] Thus, there is a vital connection, as mentioned above, between a Jesus liberated from mythical notions and Fogelklou herself. In this way, scholarly hypotheses are integrated with personal, spiritual experiences.

The story of Mi and the professors is also a story about a woman struggling for the right to become a subject speaking with some degree of authority on theological issues. Just as in the life of the actual author, two forms of authority actually meet and reinforce one another in her life. The first is an authority based on knowledge given and legitimated by the academic system, the other an authority based on spiritual experience. In fact, both Mi's and her author's theological studies were motivated by the need to have formal knowledge in view of the work that she was convinced that her spiritual experience had called her to do. When both the results of recent research and the spiritual authority of women are denied, and some dogmatic tradition and its male representatives are made the rule and norm, she is denied the right to be a subject who formulates problems and solutions. All she can do is to refuse to digest the dogma, and her body reacts correspondingly with displays of nausea and appendicitis. Thus, the historical-critical approaches are liberating for Mi because they make it possible to criticize and, I would even say, deconstruct interpretive traditions. They also present alternatives such as understanding Jesus as a human being in the prophetic tradition rather than as a savior born of a virgin and conceived by God.

In another passage, from works dealing with the history of early Christianity, Mi learns about different readings of the phrase "Jesus is born of God." These readings provide alternatives to a supernatural, physical interpretation—that he was literally born of God—and rather move in the direction of a nonphysical, symbolic understanding centered on his baptism. These approaches provide her with a number of possible new theological options that she can test with both her reason and her spiritual experience. Out of them, she can form a Christology that supports her in her struggle to be a woman with authority who actively

---

19. For Fogelklou's description of this experience, see Fogelklou, *Reality and Radiance,* 82–83; cf. idem, *Barhuvad,* 53.

20. Fogelklou, *Reality and Radiance,* 84, 86; cf. idem, *Barhuvad,* 55, 66. It is also crucial for Fogelklou that this kind of experience is not related to a specific religious tradition, but is available to all human beings (so, e.g., Fogelklou, *Barhuvad,* 54, 56).

participates in a struggle for a different society. She does not care about
the fact that as such her Christology is "heretical."[21]

In the Swedish original, there is also a passage in the story about Mi's
appendicitis that I consider a decisive part of the rhetoric of the narrative.[22] In the hospital Mi proofreads three of her own writings, which in
actuality are written by Fogelklou herself. One of them is called "Hosea
och Gomer" ("Hosea and Gomer").[23] It takes Hos 1:2 as a point of departure, but is actually a free retelling of the story about Hosea and Gomer.
Fogelklou herself labels this short story "a biblical fantasy." This passage
is decisive in the narrative, since, for the reader acquainted with Fogelklou's "Hosea och Gomer," the mentioning of this story points to an
alternative for both apologetics and "dogmatic man-talk." In "Hosea och
Gomer," a work that is certainly not a piece of analysis but of fiction, the
woman's (Gomer's) own perspective is taken into account, and through
this viewpoint psychological perspectives on human action emerge.

RETELLING THIS STORY TODAY

Having come this far I find it necessary to stop and ask the following question: What is the use of retelling such stories today, for
example, at the International Society of Biblical Literature Meeting in
2002, where an earlier version of this essay was presented? In my mind,
there are at least three trajectories that one can follow from here. The
first is to read this story as an illustrative example from history. Feminist biblical scholars, for instance, can read it as an example of how
historical-critical approaches came into existence promising to be allies to
women active in the women's movement, those who were disillusioned
with traditional dogmatic religion and with the church. In such a feminist
reading, Mi's statement that the stories of the virgin birth of Jesus were
approached "not as an aspect of the history of religion,[24] but rather as a
kind of dogmatic man-talk," becomes crucial. Not only does a history of
religions approach demonstrate that the virgin birth story wraps Jesus in
mythic clothing from which he must be unwrapped and put back in his

---

21. Fogelklou, *Reality and Radiance*, 89; cf. idem, *Barhuvad*, 96.

22. Fogelklou, *Barhuvad*, 96.

23. Emilia Fogelklou, "Hosea och Gomer: En biblisk fantasi," in *Medan gräset gror: En
bok om det växande* (2 vols.; Stockholm: Bonniers, 1911) 1:94–111. According to the information available in that volume, "Hosea och Gomer" was originally published, or at least
written, in 1905.

24. Fogelklou, *Reality and Radiance*, 90; cf. idem, *Barhuvad*, 90. The Swedish formulation
makes it clear that you can read it as a reference to approaches characteristic of the *religionsgeschichtliche Schule*.

place as a successor to the prophets and as one like us, it is also opposed to "dogmatic man-talk" and therefore becomes a resource for female (and male) scholars seeking to break free from this model as well as possibly for women searching for truth and for a living and life-giving spirituality. Furthermore, studies of the early church provide Mi with christological options other than those present in the dogmatic theological tradition. Moreover, "Hosea och Gomer" also implies that studies of the prophets inspire new projects where psychological perspectives and women's perspectives are integrated; although, in the early twentieth century, readings from the vantage point of the biblical women were formulated as "biblical fantasies," not biblical scholarship.

However, as a feminist reader of this story, I am aware that historical-critical approaches did not live up to the potential for liberation that they promised in the beginning. At the time when Emilia Fogelklou wrote her autobiography, Swedish New Testament historical-critical biblical scholarship had forged new alliances with theology and church politics, and had become an ally of the resistance to the ordination of women in the Church of Sweden.[25] We can all add examples to the list. It is obvious that from the perspective of male-stream scholarship, the two professors in Mi's story were among the last representatives of an old order that was to be replaced by representatives of modern historical-critical exegesis. But from a feminist and other marginal perspectives, history was repeated. The story of Mi and the professors could be read as one about all those times and situations when women and other marginalized persons have been subjected to a dominant scholarship and to a theology whose representatives take the right to formulate both problems and answers without giving the "others" the right to think and speak for themselves. Read as such a story, it is as much about historical-critical approaches as about the forms of exegesis against which the founding fathers of historical-critical scholarship revolted. The story therefore reminds us of the fact that in the end we should not discuss methods only but power structures as well. When the power structures are left unchallenged, uncriticized, and

---

25. Regarding this development, see Krister Stendahl, "Dethroning Biblical Imperialism in Theology," in *Reading the Bible in the Global Village: Helsinki* (Atlanta: Society of Biblical Literature, 2000), 61–67 (esp. 62–63); Birger Olsson "Förändringar," 116–19 (esp. 119); Björn Skogar, *Viva vox och den akademiska religionen: Ett bidrag till det tidiga 1900-talets teologihistoria* (Stehag/Stockholm: Symposion Graduale,1993), 214, 287 (esp. 210, n. 64); Birger Gerhardsson, *Fridrichsen, Odeberg, Aulén, Nygren: fyra teologer* (Lund: Novapress, 1994), 75–79, and Annika Borg, "Att lära av misstagen. Några nedslag i svensk 1900-talsexegetik," in *Var kan vi finna en nådig Gud? Om könsmaktsordning i kyrka och teologi* (ed. A.-L. Eriksson; Working Papers in Theology 2; Uppsala: Uppsala University, 2002), 33–48.

unchanged, scholarly methods will continue to serve those in power, and the liberating potential of these methods will remain unrealized.

Finally, to tell the story of Mi and her nausea is part of rewriting the history of biblical interpretation, including the specific kind of interpretation that historical-critical scholarship represents, a rewriting which is now being done by feminists, postcolonialists, and other interpreters analyzing literature and history from the margins. This history is no longer only a history of church fathers and *Doktor Väter*, of professors and schools, and of the martyrs of critical biblical scholarship (e.g., D. F. Strauss)—it is also a history of the victims and survivors of biblical interpretation.

Having followed the first trajectory this far, I realize that much of what I have said is already well known. There is, however, more to say when this story is retold as part of the discussion of feminist biblical scholarship in the early twenty-first century. The second possible trajectory, then, is concerned with the writing of the history of biblical scholarship, but is more specific than the broad sketch above. There are similar kinds of writings to Fogelklou's, such as those by Swedish women active in the women's movement and in the Church of Sweden. The women in question were academics—some of them even theologians, who consciously related their theological reflection and their struggle for women's rights for ordination to biblical scholarship and its findings, although they were not biblical scholars themselves. The writings I talk about can be dated, roughly, from the 1890s to the late 1950s. There are a number of reasons for regarding further research into those works as possibly fruitful for contemporary feminist biblical scholarship, apart from the obvious reason that we would get a more complete historical picture as a result.

One reason is that it could provide more substance to the claim that historical-critical approaches can be an ally of women's liberation, showing more concretely in what kinds of contexts and under what circumstances this has been the case. At the same time, we could perhaps also find more precise answers to the questions concerning why and how historical-critical approaches became adversarial toward women instead, or at the very least an upholder of the status quo. Through such an examination it will also be possible to obtain answers that are contextually relevant, answers that are specifically Swedish, German, Finnish, and so on. Another reason is that such an endeavor could make feminist biblical scholarship more contextual. The reason for talking about Swedish material in an international context is simply that Sweden is not the only European country where feminist theology and research in theological disciplines, such as biblical studies, have been heavily influenced by American scholarship. We have been grafted into a largely American history of feminist interpretation of the Bible. Since a basic feature of feminist research and theological reflection is that it should be contextual, it is important that we do work in our local context using texts such as the one I used here. I regard such an endeavor to be part of a wider project to create a European feminist biblical exegesis with an identity of its own, or, rather, with a number of local identities related to our different national and social contexts.

Furthermore, what I find most interesting in the writings I have addressed thus far is perhaps not so much the interpretations of specific biblical texts they offer but the way in which actual women relate themselves to biblical scholarship. In texts such as the one I read, women write biblical scholarship into the stories of their lives, using it as part of their rhetoric, describing it and its representatives as a force in their lives. Thus, we move from writing the history of an academic discipline to the writing of women's life histories in which biblical scholarship has played a role, and then back again to the discussion of our academic discipline in the past, present, and future. These texts could be approached in two ways: *both* as sources of information and windows to a past *and* as deliberate literary and rhetorical constructions which must be approached with methods appropriate for studying them as such.

Following this second trajectory, I am admittedly sometimes afraid that such a project will either end up as just another illustration of what we already know or in a collection of the work of "Strong Foremothers" typical of those written in the 1970s. To avoid that risk, we must find a suitable theoretical framework. I myself think it must be possible to approach this material within the theoretical framework that I mentioned in my dissertation[26] and developed somewhat further in a recent article.[27] I am inspired here by Sheila Greeve Davaney[28] and Kathryn Tanner,[29] who draw on postmodern theories. At the same time, Davaney positions

---

26. Hanna Stenström, "The Book of Revelation: A Vision of the Ultimate Liberation or the Ultimate Backlash? A Study in 20th Century Interpretations of Rev 14:1–5, with Special Emphasis on Feminist Exegesis" (Ph.D. diss., Uppsala University, 1999), 309–10.

27. Hanna Stenström, "Is a Liberating Feminist Exegesis Possible without Liberation Theology?" *lectio difficilior* 1 (2002), n.p. [cited 20 October 2004]. Online: http://www.lectio.unibe.ch/02_1/stenstroem.htm.

28. Sheila Greeve Davaney, "Continuing the Story, but Departing the Text: A Historicist Interpretation of Feminist Norms in Theology," in *Horizons in Feminist Theology: Identity, Tradition and Norms* (ed. R. S. Chopp and S. Greeve Davaney; Minneapolis: Fortress, 1997), 199–205. I am also dependent on Sheila Greeve Davaney, "Historicist Interpretations of Subjectivity, Tradition and Norms in Feminist Theology," in *STK* 76 (2000): 170–78, esp. 175–76.

29. Kathryn Tanner, "Social Theory Concerning the 'New Social Movements' and the Practice of Feminist Theology," in Chopp and Davaney, *Horizons in Feminist Theology*, 179–97.

her work as an alternative to those postmodern theories that have been criticized for losing the connection to concrete, social, historical phenomena. In this framework it is acknowledged that all values, claims, and identities are historically conditioned and subject to change.[30] Traditions—scholarly, religious, national—are not stable and monolithic, but diverse. They are streams of different, and sometimes contradictory, elements of tradition.[31] We are both "fundamentally situated within and conditioned by our historical locales"[32] and capable of agency and change. As Davaney states, "It is as we creatively interact with our environments, both cultural and natural, that human agency is made possible: it is in and through our embeddedness that human subjectivity emerges, shaped by but also shaping our worlds."[33] Tanner, on the other hand, builds on Marxist and poststructuralist theories of culture, which view "culture as one ... important ... site of political struggle in the West. Political struggle of a cultural sort takes place in the fights over both the meaning and articulation of a society's cultural stakes or symbolic resources."[34]

It is obvious that such a framework, when developed in greater depth than is possible here, is suitable for the study of the writings in question. Writers such as Emilia Fogelklou were certainly shaped by the tradition in which they lived, but they also consciously interacted with their traditions, taking over different elements, including the emerging historical-critical biblical scholarship, and created something new, thereby participating in the struggle over their cultural resources. What they did can perhaps teach us something. Their writings can become part of the stream of tradition in which we live, traditions we can relate to in our cultural struggles and engage in our creation of a feminist biblical scholarship.

This leads me to my third trajectory. Here I ask if we can integrate historical-critical approaches into feminist exegetical projects and realize their liberating potential or if we must necessarily abandon them, just as the two professors in Mi's story have been left behind. My first reaction is to offer a word of caution. As we all know, neither "feminist exegesis" nor "historical-critical approaches" represent uniform entities that one can describe or define exhaustively through a very specific set

---

30. Davaney, "Continuing the Story," 203–8; and idem, "Historicist Interpretations," 172–73.
31. Davaney, "Continuing the Story," 209–10; and idem, "Historicist Interpretations," 173–76.
32. Davaney, "Historicist Interpretations," 173.
33. Ibid.
34. Tanner, "Social Theory," 179.

of characteristics, although all of their different forms share some basic traits. Yet neither can we isolate a central core in order to compare them nor can we free the liberating elements of historical-critical approaches to the Bible from their patriarchal wrappings. As all streams of tradition, they are diverse and unstable, consisting of a number of elements that may exist in tension or even in conflict. And these specific streams can also be seen as elements in various other traditions—theological, confessional, academic, cultural, national, and so forth. We can, therefore, all of us, pile up examples of situations in which historical-critical approaches have been liberating and of contexts in which they have been oppressive or irrelevant. Answers to the questions that are central here are not possible to reach by counting the examples in order to determine which of the piles is the biggest. Rather, our task is to ask when, in which contexts, and under what circumstances historical-critical approaches have been liberating, oppressive, or irrelevant and for whom, in order to reach a number of answers to the question as to whether feminist biblical scholars can use historical-critical approaches. The answers will be strictly contextual but must always be formulated in an ongoing dialogue with feminists in other contexts, either contemporary or historical. For a feminist scholar, a choice to integrate or not to integrate historical-critical approaches is finally dependent on the consequences of doing so for concrete human beings in our specific context, not on preformulated standards for acceptable scholarship, whether they be androcentric or feminist.

What we may do as feminist exegetes, and in fact already do, is to participate in a "[p]olitical struggle of a cultural sort" in that specific part of our culture that is biblical scholarship, criticizing the forms it actually takes, but also struggling to claim elements of that tradition as our own. We claim the right to combine certain elements of diverse traditions of historical-critical scholarship with other elements, for example feminist theory, in order to create new forms of scholarship, which may grow into a stream of tradition as complex, diverse, paradoxical and full of tensions as any other. We neither leave aside the liberating elements of historical-critical approaches nor return to some pristine original state of these methods. Too many presuppositions in the original versions of the historical-critical approach—especially the belief in the possibility of an unbiased, presuppositionless search for truth—are simply no longer tenable. To this observation can be added the methodological and theoretical diversity that exists in contemporary biblical studies and the recognition of the impossibility and undesirability of reaching *the* truth about a historical event or *the* meaning of a text.

It was certainly possible in the early twentieth century for Emilia Fogelklou to read Hosea from Gomer's perspective with psychology as an interpretative tool, and to be liberated from an indigestible dogma such as the virgin birth of Jesus with the aid of historical-critical approaches, but there was no room in biblical scholarship for such ways of interpreting texts even when historical-critical approaches were firmly established. This implies that the problem is not with the methods in and of themselves but with the structures of power. It was necessary for feminist scholars to access places of power—at least of some power—to put Gomer's perspective on the agenda for those who remain within the field of biblical scholarship. This very simple statement about power must be developed and refined through studies of specific cases in which the workings of power become evident, as well as those cases in which feminists exerted power over the methods and used them for their own purposes.

If we question the extent to which historical-critical approaches such as form criticism and redaction criticism are used for feminist ends, the answer seems trivial: some feminists use them, others do not. In my opinion, we should rather ask ourselves how we can use the most basic element of historical criticism: interpreting biblical texts and working with historical issues concerning the contexts of those texts independent of commitments to modern religious communities. Today this focus represents a search for the many possible truths about the past and the many possible meanings of the texts, wherein all truths are allowed expression, however much they evidence a past or textual meaning that is alien, unacceptable, or irrelevant for us today. Here I side with those who do not consider a constructive theological task an inherently necessary part of a project of feminist biblical scholarship.[35] I argue for a form of feminist research in which history is not normative, but may still help us understand our present circumstances more fully or teach us other lessons. This work with historical issues, and its open and ambivalent results, may lead us onwards to a number of different tasks. It may push us to ethical criticism or to deconstruction of texts and convictions, but it may also lead to constructive work in which the diversity of early Christian Christologies relativizes the Christologies of the established churches and makes other and alternative christological options clear. In such a work, we would continuously try to be relevant for human communities other than just the communities of biblical scholars, including

---

35. For a more developed version of my position presented here, see Stenström, "Is a Liberating Feminist Exegesis Possible without Liberation Theology?" With respect to the issue of whether or not the discussion of feminist scholarship on early Christianity is necessarily theological in nature, see Elizabeth A. Castelli, "Heteroglossia, Hermeneutics and History: A Review Essay of Recent Feminist Studies of Early Christianity," *JFSR* 10 (1994): 73–98, esp. 79–92.

but not solely limited to religious communities. Feminist biblical scholarship that refrains from a constructive theological task can still play a role in discussions within religious communities regarding the use of the Bible in theological and ethical discussions. Simply put, such a task performs the critical role of being a nuisance. By this I mean to suggest that feminist scholars do not provide a safe truth about history, one that can be used as normative for contemporary religious communities, not even feminist ones. Rather, even within feminist scholarship there are many possible truths about the role of women in the early church, as the past was complex and it will never be possible to reconstruct it fully or with certainty. One thing seems to be certain, however: biblical texts, the belief systems of the communities in which they were written, and the social structures reflected in the texts were and continue to be androcentric. If we want to formulate a theology and ethics about gender relations, and therefore also sexuality, with the Bible as its basis, and do not accept its androcentrism as well as its heterosexual norm, we will run into difficulties. There are no easy solutions since no texts provide a safe or obvious way out of the mire of the androcentric system. When we reiterate this insight again and again we can hopefully challenge other theologians to rethink and speak clearly about their understanding of the authority of the Bible as well as the relation between the Bible and other norms and sources for theology.

I do not think this is the only engagement feminist biblical scholars should and can undertake. Further, I do not claim that this is relevant or liberating at all times and in all places. I am personally convinced, however, that this task may be necessary in my own context—that is, to insist on how deeply problematic the Bible is for those of us who, like Emilia Fogelklou, do not accept its androcentrism. While this is not the only way to build a better world, it is at least one way to shake the present establishment, and that itself is also a task worthy of feminists.

"Tandoori Reindeer" and the Limitations of Historical Criticism

Susanne Scholz

Powerful political, social, economic, and spiritual-religious developments have been under way since the end of the so-called 'Second World
War' in 1945.[1] Anticolonial movements in the Third World emerged and
succeeded in removing colonial rule. Moreover, the Western social movements of the 1960s and 1970s led to major changes in social and cultural
dynamics. At the same time the human population exploded to more
than six billion. Nuclear and biological-chemical weapons have threatened to destroy our planet several times by now. Corporate capitalism
has grown exponentially. Wars, famine, and political unrest have created
hundreds of thousands of refugees and immigration movements worldwide. Western societies rely on information technology more than ever,
while the gap between rich and poor is widening everywhere, and worldwide 800 million people live in hunger and starvation. At the same time,
institutionalized religious traditions, especially the established Christian
churches, have seen their power and influence decline in the West. Many
Westerners of mainstream Christian, Jewish, and secular backgrounds
are looking elsewhere to satisfy their spiritual needs. Consequently,
Christian fundamentalism and the New Age movement have risen to
become remarkable religious forces in many Western countries in recent
decades. And worldwide religious fundamentalism is on the rise as well.
These and other developments have far-reaching consequences for
humanity and nature on planet earth.

Yet the field of biblical studies seems strangely disconnected from
these changes in our world and hardly takes notice of them. In fact, biblical research, at least Western biblical scholarship, is a field that has
remained mostly unchanged during the past fifty years; little change is

---

1. The term "Second World War" is often criticized for its Eurocentric perspective, see,
e.g., Enrique Dussel, "The Sociohistorical Meaning of Liberation Theology: Reflections About
Its Origin and World Context," in *Religions/Globalizations: Theories and Cases* (ed. D. N. Hopkins, E. Mendieta, and D. Batstone; Durham: Duke University Press, 2001), 33–45, esp. n. 18.

to be expected of it in the near future as well. Despite the crises in our world, both in wealthy countries located mostly in the Northern hemisphere and in impoverished countries located mostly in the Southern hemisphere, established scholars of the Bible are not even expected to relate to social, political, economic, and religious developments in our societies. Courses on biblical literature are usually taught as if not much has changed since they were first designed. How is such detachment possible? I suggest that the dominant methodology in biblical studies—historical criticism—is one of the reasons for this lack of involvement in contemporary affairs. Historical criticism allows interpreters to position biblical literature in a distant past, far removed from today's politics, economics, or religion. Although the exclusion of contemporary questions is not an essential requirement of historical methodology, especially not as understood by many historians during the last decades,[2] biblical scholars often continue using historical criticism in a way that keeps the Bible separate from today's world.

From Subversion to Status Quo

Not all historical critics have used the method in this way; indeed, some, among them feminist interpreters, have examined the Bible's historical context with contemporary questions in mind. For instance, Monika Fander, a feminist critic in New Testament studies, insists on the value of historical criticism for a feminist reading of biblical literature. She writes: "It is not the methods of historical criticism as such that are unsuitable for feminist historical research. The tensions between the historical-critical method and feminist historical study are hermeneutical in character.... Every scholar addresses a text in terms of a particular pre-understanding that is marked, consciously or unconsciously, by the cultural context and questions of the researcher's own time."[3] Similarly, the pioneer of feminist New Testament analysis, Elisabeth Schüssler Fiorenza, sees historical analysis as connected to the hermeneutical interests of the exegete:

---

2. See, e.g., Mary Fulbrook, *Historical Theory* (London: Routledge, 2002); Georg G. Iggers, *Historiography in the Twentieth Century: From Scientific Objectivity to the Postmodern Challenge* (Hanover, N.H: University Press of New England, 1997); and Bruce Mazlish and Ralph Buultjens, *Conceptualizing Global History* (Boulder, Colo.: Westview, 1993). For further reference, see n. 14 below.

3. Monika Fander, "Historical-Critical Methods," in *A Feminist Introduction* (vol. 1 of *Searching the Scriptures*; ed. E. Schüssler Fiorenza with S. Matthews and A. Brock; New York: Crossroads, 1993), 221.

> A critical feminist analysis takes the texts about wo/men out of their
> contextual frameworks and reassembles them like mosaic stones in a
> feminist pattern or design that does not recuperate but counteracts the
> marginalizing or oppressive tendencies of the kyrio-centric text. To
> that end, one has to elaborate models of historical and socio-cultural
> reconstruction that can subvert the biblical text's kyriocentric dynam-
> ics and place the struggles of those whom it marginalizes and silences
> into the center of the historical narrative.... This calls for an increase in
> historical imagination.[4]

This viewpoint is still not the norm, however, and so younger scholars often accept traditional methodology uncritically. The pressure to
promote and protect the dominance of historical criticism is strong even
today[5] because, for the most part, Western biblical scholars do not see
the need to engage systematically theological, political, and international
issues of our day. This detachment often serves conservative theological
and cultural-religious purposes, and so, unsurprisingly, the field of biblical studies is largely dominated by a conservative agenda—religious,
political, and academic.[6]

The fact that historical criticism serves conservative purposes is
indeed a remarkable development. Initially, during the nineteenth and
early twentieth centuries, biblical scholars found in historical criticism a
method that liberated them from the religious and academic status quo.
At that time, historical criticism was a subversive approach. This was particularly true in Germany, the center from which historical criticism
emerged. It began with what we know today as source criticism and
expanded into a full-blown method during the first part of the twentieth
century when historical criticism became the standard in many European
and liberal U.S.-American schools of theology. Yet, in the nineteenth century, scholars who applied historical methodology were welcomed
neither by the church nor the established theological scene of the day. For

---

4. Elisabeth Schüssler Fiorenza, *Wisdom Ways: Introducing Feminist Biblical Interpretation*
(Maryknoll, N.Y.: Orbis, 2001), 146, 148.

5. For a description of the increasing prominence of historical criticism in the West, see
John W. Rogerson, *Old Testament Criticism in the Nineteenth Century: England and Germany*
(Philadelphia: Fortress, 1985); and Hans-Joachim Kraus, *Geschichte der historisch-kritischen
Erforschung des Alten Testaments von der Reformation bis zur Gegenwart* (3d ed.; Neukirchen-
Vluyn: Neukirchener Verlag, 1982).

6. For instance, Elisabeth Schüssler Fiorenza pointed out that "since 1947 no [SBL] presidential address has explicitly reflected on world politics, global crises, human sufferings, or
movements for change;" see her SBL presidential address delivered on December 5, 1987,
entitled "The Ethics of Biblical Interpretation: Decentering Biblical Scholarship," in *Reading
the Bible in the Global Village: Helsinki* (Atlanta: Society of Biblical Literature, 2000), 113.

instance, in the middle of the nineteenth century a highly influential and powerful theology professor in Berlin, Ernst W. Hengstenberg (1802– 1869), made sure that proponents of historical criticism would not gain access to tenured faculty positions.[7] And so the historical critic Johann K. W. Vatke (1806–1882), later recognized as a key figure in the development of historical criticism, did not become a full professor as long as Hengstenberg and like-minded colleagues held influential faculty positions in Berlin. They prevented Vatke's promotion for decades and defended the Christian doctrinal position according to which the starting point for reading the Bible was "the atoning work of Christ."

Among these like-minded colleagues was Old Testament scholar Franz Delitzsch (1813–1890). In 1853, he dismissed historical-critical work. In the first edition of his renowned Genesis commentary he writes:

> If one reads J. Severin Vater's (3d ed., 1802–05) critical, arbitrary, exegetically spiritless commentary on the Pentateuch and Peter v. Bohlen's (1835) apparently learned but sloppy and extremely impudent interpretation of Genesis, one feels the pain about the depth of the decline from scriptural faith.... They all do not appreciate Holy Scripture as a book of divine revelation and are not interested in Christianity as a religion of reconciliation. Therefore, their indifference, which culminates in [August W.] Knobel's commentary and is deeply saddening, deprives Christianity of the inalienable prehistoric basis that is contained in Genesis.[8]

In later editions of his commentary, Delitzsch changed his position on historical criticism and included what he called "preparatory works of [Julius] Wellhausen, [Abraham] Kuenen and preferably [August] Dillmann." Yet he also emphasized that, "the spirit of this [commentary = 5th ed.; 1887] remained the same since 1852 [year of 1st ed.]."[9] From 1828 to 1869, then, the opponents of historical criticism prevailed. Only when the old school retired did historical critics gain ground. After Julius Wellhausen's *Prolegomena to the History of Israel* came out in 1878, ten years after Hengstenberg's reign in Berlin, the situation was reversed and historical criticism instead came to dominate the field of biblical studies.

Many churches also tried their best to prevent what they considered the worst, namely, the application of historical criticism to the Bible. In

---

7. See Rogerson, *Old Testament Criticism*, 85–90.

8. Franz Delitzsch, *Die Genesis* (2d ed.; Leipzig: Dorffling & Franke, 1853), 59–60 (my translation).

9. Franz Delitzsch, *Neuer Commentar über die Genesis* (5th ed.; Leipzig: Dorffling & Franke, 1887), iii.

the United States several Protestant denominations tried to fire historical critics who taught at Christian seminaries. Among them is the famous case of Charles A. Briggs (1841–1913), who taught Hebrew and cognate languages at Union Theological Seminary in New York City, then a Presbyterian institution.[10] In 1892, the Presbyterian Church subjected this scholar to a presbytery trial for heresy. The denomination demanded that Briggs should either refrain from applying historical methodology to the Hebrew Bible or leave his post. Supported by Union's faculty, Briggs did not waiver, continuing his work and keeping his position. The Presbyterian denomination did not accept this situation and cut its ties with the seminary, which has been nondenominational ever since. Many other such stories exist, which illustrate that academic integrity persevered over ecclesiastical intimidation. Scholars risked and sometimes lost their positions when they maintained that the Bible is historical literature like any other document of the past and is to be studied as such.

In the twentieth century, the historical-critical method became part of the standard curriculum in Protestant theological studies, and Catholic and Jewish academic institutions eventually accepted it as the standard for biblical interpretation as well. Since the retirement of Ernst W. Hengstenberg, historical criticism symbolizes the success of the modern scientific worldview, which reveres objectivity and value-neutrality. Historical criticism made the reading of the Bible acceptable in modern academia and validated biblical research as a scientific activity. It is still very effective in discussions with fundamentalist Christians. And so publications on the history of biblical literature abound, even though many critics in this tradition of scholarship ignore the considerable challenges of our age.

---

10. On the trial, see Robert T. Handy, "The Trials of Charles Briggs (1881–1893)," in idem, *A History of Union Theological Seminary in New York* (New York: Columbia University Press, 1987), 69–93. See also Charles A. Briggs, *The Case Against Professor Briggs* (New York: Scribner, 1892–1893); idem, *Authority of Holy Scripture: Inaugural Address and Defense, 1891/1893* (New York: Arno, 1972); and Mark Stephen Massa, *Charles Augustus Briggs and the Crisis of Historical Criticism* (Minneapolis: Fortress, 1990). This kind of dispute continues even today. See, for instance, the court case between New Testament scholar Gerd Lüdemann and the University of Göttingen (Germany). Lüdemann's research on the historical Jesus and the doctrine of Christ's resurrection led the regional Protestant *Landeskirche von Niedersachsen* to withdraw Lüdemann's teaching authority. For detailed information, see http://www.gerdluedemann.de/, as well as Horst Hirschler, "Wir wollen kein Lehrverfahren: Der hannoversche Landesbischof zum Streit um den Göttinger Theologieprofessor Gerd Lüdemann," *Das Sonntagsblatt* (23 February 1995), n.p. [cited 13 October 2004]. Online: http://www.sonntagsblatt.de/1996/8/8–10.htm. Also see Jennie Brokkman, "German Heretic Remains in a Chair," *The Times Higher Education Supplement* 1365 (1 January 1999): 10.

OPPOSITION FROM THE MARGINS

The situation has, however, begun to change. During the past decade, a sustained and strong opposition to historical criticism as an adequate methodology for biblical exegesis has come prominently from scholars marginalized by ethnicity, race, or continental location. Asian American, African American, and Hispanic diasporic scholars in the United States as well as African and Asian exegetes have started to articulate their concerns openly and forcefully in numerous publications. They view historical criticism as a Eurocentric tool that facilitated Western imperialistic practice and distanced the academic field of biblical studies from the issues of our time. Accordingly, Asian American theologian Russell Moy asserts that "the historical-critical method of biblical scholarship is Eurocentric in its methods and ideology due to its historical roots. With the dominance of this method, its practitioners uncritically exalt its cultural worldview over others and view its methods as normative and objective. Its exclusivity prevents an appreciation of non-Western hermeneutical approaches such as oral tradition."[11] Moy locates the formation of historical criticism in Europe, which cannot be denied, and then continues to limit the method's validity to the European cultural-philosophical context—the modern scientific worldview. What is perceived as universal is in fact limited to a particular social location. Moy therefore reminds historical critics of the need to integrate non-Western approaches into their exegetical repertoire.

Other scholars as well contend that historical criticism is a Western endeavor and thus belongs to a particular geographical context. They also emphasize that the method prevents researchers from making much needed connections between biblical literature and the challenges of our time. William H. Meyers, an exegete of African American descent, questions the usefulness of historical criticism because it distances scholarly work from contemporary issues. He observes that "this method tends to lock the interpretative task in the past (e.g., in debates over authorial intent) while evading key contemporary issues like racism or intercultural dialogue... One rarely finds any discussion of an African American interpretation of the Scriptures."[12] This situation has changed only slightly since Meyers made this comment. Even though major studies on African American interpretations of the Bible are now available,[13] many

---

11. Russel G. Moy, "Biculturalism, Race, and the Bible," *RelEd* 88 (1993): 424.

12. William H. Meyers, "The Hermeneutical Dilemma of the African American Biblical Student," in *Stony the Road We Trod* (ed. C. H. Felder; Minneapolis: Fortress, 1991), 41.

13. See, e.g., Vincent L. Wimbush, ed., *African Americans and the Bible* (New York: Continuum, 2001). For the related African context, see also Kurt Holter, *Yahweh in Africa: Essays*

exegetical commentaries continue to stress historical meaning over and against cultural-contextual analysis and therefore separate biblical meaning from contemporary questions.[14]

Scholars from African and Asian countries are among the most vocal critics of historical criticism. Some of them regard the method as a politically, religiously, and economically powerful tool of past and present imperialistic practices of industrialized nations. Although the influence of historical criticism on international politics and economics seems overstated, the connection between intellectual perspective and political practice is important and needs to be taken seriously. After all, Christian missionary movements from Western countries have promoted politically and theologically conservative agendas, which have shaped the beliefs of many Christians in Africa, Asia, and Latin America. In fact, conservative positions in African, Asian, and Latin American Christianities now haunt Western Christians when they try to implement progressive religious policies, as became evident in the election of the first openly gay Episcopalian bishop in the United States.[15] The idea that historical criticism has contributed to the success of imperialistic practices and policies in the past and present is thus a claim not to be dismissed too quickly.

African feminist exegete Musa W. Dube rejects historical criticism outright, arguing that, as an imperialistic instrument of the West, it has at best left political and economic structures of exploitation and oppression in the world unchallenged. She writes that "to divorce biblical interpretation from current international relations, or to discuss it primarily as an ancient text, becomes another western ideological stance that hides its direct impact on the postcolonial world and maintains its imperial domination of Two-Third World countries."[16] Dube suggests that the Bible has profoundly shaped society and thus the

---

on *Africa and the Old Testament* (Bible and Theology in Africa 1; New York: Peter Lang, 2000); and Gerald O. West and Musa W. Dube, eds., *The Bible in Africa: Transaction, Trajectories and Trends* (Leiden: Brill, 2001).

14. More recently the field of historical criticism has developed approaches that account for the relationship between a historian's social location and her or his historical analysis. Besides the works mentioned in n. 2 above, see also Paul Hamilton, *Historicism* (2d ed.; New York: Routledge, 2003); Peter N. Stearns, Peter C. Seixas, and Samuel S. Wineburg, eds., *Knowing, Teaching, and Learning History: National and International Perspectives* (New York: New York University Press, 2000); John Kucich and Dianne F. Sadoff, *Victorian Afterlife: Postmodern Culture Rewrites the Nineteenth Century* (Minnesota: University of Minnesota Press, 2000); and Keith Jenkins, ed., *The Postmodern History Reader* (New York: Routledge, 1997).

15. See, e.g., Marc Lacey, "African Anglican Leaders Outraged Over Gay Bishop in U.S.," *New York Times* (November 4, 2003): A21.

16. Musa W. Dube, *Postcolonial Feminist Interpretation of the Bible* (St. Louis: Chalice, 2000), 20.

Susanne Scholz

Bible's formative role in the postcolonial world requires that scholars engage this body of literature not just as historical material related to the ancient Near East or the early Christian and rabbinic eras. It continues to impact today's world in manifold ways, and therefore the Bible needs to be explicated with care and in detail. For Dube, historical criticism enables Western scholars to ignore the Bible's relationship with political and economic structures of exploitation on the one hand and religious ideology on the other hand. According to Dube, therefore, the historical-critical approach has prevented Western interpreters from opposing colonialism, imperialism, and the systematic socioeconomic impoverishment of countries in Africa and elsewhere. In short, the method has fostered in Western Bible readers an acceptance of the societal status quo.

The situation has affected Western Bible readers, as well as non-Western people who came into contact with Western Christian missionaries and their Bibles. In fact, Sri Lankan exegete Rasiah Sugirtharajah goes as far as to characterize historical criticism as a "legacy of colonial hermeneutics,"[17] which "effectively eclipsed allegorical, symbolic, figurative, and metaphorical ways of appropriating the text" intrinsic to the interpretation of indigenous Hindu sacred texts. "Indigenous reading practices" disappeared when colonized Asian Christian scholars learned to accept historical criticism. For Sugirtharajah, their work illustrates "creative Asian mimicry."[18] Even though these scholars themselves view historical criticism "as an effective weapon of decolonization,"[19] they have been successfully brainwashed, Sugirtharajah contends. He indicts them for employing the tools of the colonizers. For Sugirtharajah, then, historical criticism is not an approach well suited for Asian biblical studies.[20]

Kwok Pui-lan, a Chinese feminist theologian, joins in the opposition against historical criticism, suggesting that historical criticism was created by the "white, male, middle-class academics" to whom this method belongs. People of other social locations need to rely on alternative approaches because "many Asian and indigenous Christians live in cultures

---

17. Rasiah S. Sugirtharajah, *The Bible and the Third World: Precolonial, Colonial and Postcolonial Encounters* (Cambridge: Cambridge University Press, 2001), 71–72.

18. Rasiah S. Sugirtharajah, *Asian Biblical Hermeneutics and Postcolonialism: Contesting the Interpretations* (BS 64; Sheffield: Sheffield Academic Press, 1998), 11.

19. Ibid., 129.

20. For a critical reception of Sugirtharajah's position, see, e.g., Heikki Räisänen, "Biblical Critics in the Global Village," in *Challenges To Biblical Interpretation: Collected Essays 1991–2000* (BibInt Series 59; Leiden: Brill, 2001), 283–309; repr. from *Reading the Bible in the Global Village*, 9–28.

that understand history and historiography in a totally different way. The Eurocentric positivist approach must not be taken as the sole norm for the historical quest. The Bible is too important to be subject to *only* one norm or model of interpretation."[21] This Asian feminist scholar does not want the Bible to be seen as a relic of the past, a document that exists solely to inform readers about ancient worlds. She rather suggests reading biblical literature in conversation with our worlds and experiences, in dialog with multiple religious and cultural practices and beliefs. A strict historical-critical approach disallows such dialogical and imaginative work, which is needed in our religiously pluralistic world. The model of white, middle-class, academic males who, after all, developed historical criticism, is too restrictive for a world in which people of different geographical, racial, ethnic, and religious contexts live together.

Finally, the American Hispanic scholar Fernando Segovia describes clearly and matter-of-factly the problems inherent in historical criticism. It gives scholarly readers the illusion of objective, universally valid, and value neutral analysis, as if they were not reading from their respective social locations. They claim to be doing "exegesis" and not "eisegesis," the latter being regarded as unacceptable. Revered teachers select a small group of future experts as their students who continue the task of the historical project. Segovia characterizes this process as "highly hierarchical and authoritative in character, with strong emphasis on academic pedigree (who studied under whom) and school of thought (proper versus improper approximations to the text)."[22] The approach deliberately and forcefully excludes anybody who does not subscribe to the agenda of historical criticism. Therefore Segovia, too, classifies historical criticism as "colonialist and imperialist":

> It emerged out of a Eurocentric setting, and, as such, it was and remained thoroughly Eurocentric at every level of discourse and inquiry. As a result, the construct unreflectively universalized its bracketed identity, expecting on the surface all readers everywhere to become ideal critics, informed and universal, while in actuality requiring all readers to interpret like Eurocentric critics. In fact, the entire discussion, from beginning to end and top to bottom, was characterized

---

21. Kwok Pui-lan, *Discovering the Bible in the Non-Biblical World* (Bible and Liberation Series; Maryknoll, N.Y.: Orbis, 1995), 86 (emphasis original).

22. Fernando F. Segovia, "'And They Began to Speak in Other Tongues': Competing Modes of Discourse in Contemporary Biblical Criticism," in *Social Location and Biblical Interpretation in the United States* (vol. 1 of *Reading from This Place*; ed. F. F. Segovia and M. A. Tolbert; Minneapolis: Fortress, 1995), 13. See also Mary A. Tolbert's commentary on the situation of graduate work in the field of biblical studies, "Graduate Biblical Studies: Ethos and Discipline," n.p. [cited 20 October 2004]. Online: www.sbl-site.org/Article.aspx?ArticleId=195.

and governed by the fundamental concerns, questions, and horizons of this particular group, uncritically disguised as the fundamental questions, horizons, and concerns of the entire Christian world. To become the ideal critic, therefore, was to enter into a specific and contextualized discussion, a Eurocentric discussion.[23]

In light of this critique, it is not surprising that Segovia proposes, as an alternative, to connect biblical exegesis with cultural studies.[24]

Feminist Compliance with Androcentric Historiography

In contrast to these unambiguous challenges, Western feminist scholars of the Hebrew Bible do not exhibit an equally strong opposition to historical criticism. In fact, many of them appear invested in this method even when they acknowledge its inherent difficulties. For instance, exegete Silvia Schroer of the University of Bern (Switzerland) recognizes "traces of European-imperialistic theory" in historical criticism but wants to remedy past interpretative practice with what she calls "expanded historical research." By this assertion she means that historical critics need to disclose their hermeneutical interests and renegotiate their agenda for historicizing biblical literature. The renegotiated agenda includes addressing the history of interpretation, rewriting the history of women in the Yahweh-religion, reconceptualizing the development of monotheism, and re-emphasizing the legal traditions of the Hebrew Bible.[25] This agenda is impressive but remains firmly rooted in historical criticism. A sustained critique of this method and an integration of contextualized approaches are not considered to be options for the biblical critic.

The severity of the problem is obvious in a short essay by Old Testament exegete Phyllis Bird. Ambivalent about characterizing her work as a feminist reading, she distinguishes between two exegetical steps that have to be kept apart.[26] The first step requires "formulat[ing] the sense of

---

23. Segovia, "They Began To Speak," 29–30.

24. See Fernando F. Segovia, "Cultural Studies and Contemporary Biblical Criticism: Ideological Criticism as Mode of Discourse," in *Social Location and Biblical Interpretation in Global Perspective* (vol. 2 of *Reading from This Place*; ed. F. F. Segovia and M. A. Tolbert; Minneapolis: Fortress, 1995), 1–17.

25. Silvia Schroer, "Bibelauslegung im europäischen Kontext," in *Hermeneutik, sozialgeschichtlich: Kontextualität in den Bibelwissenschaften aus der Sicht (latein)amerikanischer und europäischer Exegetinnen und Exegeten* (ed. E. S. Gerstenberger and U. Schönborn; EUZ 1; Münster: LIT, 1999), 126–30.

26. Phyllis A. Bird, "What Makes a Feminist Reading Feminist? A Qualified Answer," in *Escaping Eden: New Feminist Perspectives on the Bible* (ed. H. C. Washington, S. L. Graham, and P. L. Thimmes; New York: New York University Press, 1998), 124–31.

the text in its ancient social and literary context."[27] An interpreter has to understand a biblical passage as an author's effort to communicate a particular position or message to the ancient audience. This step is "descriptive" and "analytical" and "may not contain any clearly recognizable feminist message," Bird maintains. Only in the second step may a feminist reader identify "signs of feminist orientation in readings of biblical texts..."[28] This step is based on a *"systemic analysis* of gender relations ... a *critique* of relationships, norms and expectations that limit or subordinate women's thought, action and expression."[29] It alone decides whether a feminist interpretation "rings true for women readers"[30] and "makes sense to men as well."[31] Yet historical criticism is key, and so Bird asserts:

> I find no tension between historical criticism and feminist commitment, between attempts to view the past on its own terms and a commitment to change the terms of participation and discourse generated by that past. I see no reason why an attempt to enter sympathetically into the minds or consciousnesses of historical persons and empathize with their feelings, motives and actions should exclude critique and ultimate rejection of those views.... Dismissal of historical criticism simply means that unexamined assumptions are read into the text. Historical criticism makes no claims concerning the normativity, or representativeness, of the ancient texts; in fact, it alerts readers to the dangers of such assumptions by considering the perspective, location and interests of the ancient author (including class, gender, religious party, etc.).[32]

Bird values historical criticism because it provides insight into the authorial context and alerts contemporary readers to potential projections of their assumptions onto ancient Israelite times. Creating exegetical distance, the method allows interpreters to understand the textual-historical meaning first and only then to formulate a response. To feminist Bible scholars like Bird, historical criticism is a tool suited for the feminist interpretative task.

The willingness among Western feminist scholars of the Hebrew Bible to rely on historical criticism is particularly obvious when these scholars examine biblical stories and laws on rape. The problem is that

---

27. Ibid., 126.
28. Ibid., 128.
29. Ibid. 129 (italics original).
30. Ibid.
31. Ibid., 130.
32. Ibid., 128.

historical readings, even when undertaken by feminist readers, seem not to promote feminist views but to support androcentric notions of rape and gender. Yet the conviction that it is possible to describe the intentional meaning of a biblical passage independent of a reader's hermeneutical interest limits the interpretative task. Three examples illustrate the problem. One example relates to the rape of Dinah in Gen 34, another to the rape laws in Deut 22:25–29, and yet another to the rapes of Bilhah and Zilpah in Gen 29:31–30:24. It is a matter of debate whether these texts can be classified as rape texts and how they might be read as androcentric literature.

In the case of Gen 34, interpreters, feminist or not, have long debated whether the story favors Shechem—Dinah's rapist—or Dinah's brothers. Two interpreters, Danna Nolan Fewell and David Gunn, joined the debate several years ago. Fewell and Gunn use mostly literary reading strategies to describe how the narrator tries to have the reader side with the rapist, but then, in an unexpected move, they leave the terrain of literary analysis and fortify their position with a historical assertion. They contend that Shechem deserves our sympathy because he "loves her [Dinah] and takes delight in her."[33] In fact, Shechem's sincerity is apparent in his marriage proposal, which, to these interpreters, was in Dinah's "best interests within the narrow limits of this society."[34] A reference to ancient customs serves to exonerate the rapist. The interpreters claim that the marriage proposal helped Dinah survive in a society that offered no other option for raped women but to marry their rapist. Fewell and Gunn, however, sense the difficulty of their position and acknowledge that "to advocate a woman marrying her rapist might itself seem to be a dangerous and androcentric advocacy," but, in the end, they suggest that "the story world" offers no "other liberating alternatives."[35] A reference to ancient Israelite society thus defends the action of the rapist and, even worse, justifies his marriage proposal. Fewell and Gunn call their reading "feminist," but something went terribly wrong in this interpretation when it is examined from the perspective of feminist theories dealing with rape.[36] From this perspective it is not a "feminist" position to approve of a rapist marrying the

---

33. Danna Nolan Fewell and David M. Gunn, "Tipping the Balance: Sternberg's Reader and the Rape of Dinah," *JBL* 110 (1991): 210.

34. Ibid.

35. Ibid.

36. See also Meir Sternberg's reply to Fewell and Gunn's interpretation in his "Biblical Poetics and Sexual Politics: From Reading to Counterreading," *JBL* 111 (1992): 463–88. For an extended discussion of this and other interpretations, see Susanne Scholz, *Rape Plots: A Feminist Cultural Study of Genesis 34* (StBL 13; New York: Peter Lang, 2000), 116–27.

raped victim-survivor.[37] Promoting androcentric values, this reading not only offers a badly argued historical position, it also illustrates the dangers involved in justifying patriarchal habit with historical argumentation.

The rape laws found in Deut 22:25–29 provide another example, demonstrating the difficulties when feminist interpreters apply historical criticism to rape stories. Old Testament professor Carolyn Pressler, who has written extensively on Deuteronomic law,[38] rejects the possibility that rape laws existed in ancient Israel. She explains that "it is anachronistic to speak about the Deuteronomistic view of sexual laws."[39] Pressler does not want to mix contemporary assumptions with her historical reconstructive work and instead considers a historian's task to be merely to describe "authorial intent." Pressler's writing reveals the conflict that she senses between her description of the historical task and her feminist convictions. On the one hand, she disallows bringing contemporary terminology and concepts to the biblical text. On the other hand, she accepts the need to read with contemporary questions in mind. She writes: "This is not to say that it is inappropriate to bring modern categories to the biblical texts. It is appropriate to ask how Deuteronomy views acts that we consider acts of sexual violence.... It is important to analyze and criticize these and any 'texts of terror'."[40] Yet she also insists that "the offense [described in Deut 22:25–29] is not 'rape' according to the modern definitions of that term."[41] Pressler goes back and forth, but, when it is time for her description of the legal situation, she follows almost exclusively the perspective of the "redactors." She explains that "the Deuteronomic laws regard female sexuality as the possession of the woman's father or husband. The father's claims are akin to property claims; the husband's claims are more extensive. *It follows* that the woman has no claims over her own sexuality; *she therefore cannot be sexually assaulted*."[42]

---

37. Feminists in Peru, for instance, fight vehemently against the legal situation in their country that approves of a rapist marrying the raped woman; see Susanne Scholz, "Was It Really Rape in Genesis 34? Biblical Scholarship As a Reflection of Cultural Assumptions," in Washington, Graham, and Thimmes, *Escaping Eden*, 182–98, esp. 195–97.

38. See, e.g., Carolyn Pressler, *The View of Women Found in Deuteronomic Family Law* (BZAW 216; Berlin: de Gruyter, 1993).

39. Carolyn Pressler, "Sexual Violence and Deuteronomic Law," in *A Feminist Companion to Exodus to Deuteronomy* (ed. A. Brenner; FCB 6; Sheffield: Sheffield Academic Press, 1994), 102–12.

40. Ibid., 112.

41. Ibid., 103.

42. Ibid., 111 (my emphasis).

Historical perspective traps this feminist reader here. The apparently historical description is no longer grounded in feminist analysis but presents an androcentric view of the ancient law as the norm. It is important to note that feminist scholars using historical-critical arguments often seem anxious when they explain the supposedly historical meaning of a rape text. Perhaps they worry about reinforcing androcentric values since, from a contemporary feminist perspective, a woman can, of course, be sexually assaulted even when a father owns her like property. So Pressler is careful at this point. She acknowledges that Deuteronomistic laws "negate women's will, deny women's right to sexual and physical integrity and erase women's personhood." But then she affirms explanations provided by decades-old scholarship about the historical "intention" of the biblical law.[43] Historical argumentation does not serve this feminist analysis well.

Our lack of historical data regarding ancient Israelite life, especially as it relates to rape, sometimes persuades feminist exegetes to ignore certain stories altogether since they are known for containing little historical information. An example is the story about the rapes of the enslaved women Bilhah and Zilpah, found in Gen 29:31–30:24. The story has received little treatment in traditional literature, which usually remembers the story for its genealogical value and summarizes it as a tale about "The Birth and Naming of Jacob's Sons: Genesis 29:31–30:24,"[44] "The Birth of Jacob's Children (29:31–30:43),"[45] or, including the mothers' names, "Jacob's Four Sons by Leah (29:31–35)" and "Jacob's Children by Bilhah (30:1–8)."[46] Yet, besides an emphasis on genealogy, the story is no longer viewed as providing historical information about premonarchic times in ancient Israel, a period that, according to a large segment of current scholarship, cannot reliably be reconstructed on the basis of biblical literature.

This scholarly consensus has also affected feminist work. Feminist exegetes rarely discuss Gen 29:31–30:24, although the passage includes four women who speak and act prominently. Feminist comments are usually limited to a historical reference on surrogate motherhood, as it appears here as well as in Gen 16, the story of Hagar and Sarah. For

---

43. See Pressler, "Sexual Violence," 103 n. 3, where she refers to the source of her arguments: D. R. Mace, *Hebrew Marriage: A Sociological Study* (London: Epworth, 1953).

44. Claus Westermann, *Genesis* (trans. J. J. Scullion; 3 vols.; CC; Minneapolis: Fortress, 1984–1986), 2:469.

45. Nahum M. Sarna, *Genesis* (The JPS Torah Commentary; Philadelphia: Jewish Publication Society, 1989), 206.

46. Victor P. Hamilton, *The Book of Genesis: Chapters 18–50* (NICOT; Grand Rapids: Eerdmans, 1995), 265, 269.

instance, Susan Niditch explains that the custom of having children through another woman is reported in several ancient Near Eastern texts. And so Niditch justifies the exploitative treatment of Bilhah and Zilpah, the enslaved women of Leah and Rachel, when she writes that "surrogate motherhood allowed a barren woman to regularize her status in a world in which children were a woman's status and in which childlessness was regarded as a virtual sign of divine disfavor."[47] The custom of surrogate motherhood is accepted as a legitimate solution for infertile women of the ancient Near East. In fact, historical interrogation hinders feminist readers from considering this text as a story about class privileged women replicating androcentric values, and so many feminist interpreters move on to other texts. Only one interpreter, Renita J. Weems, characterizes the action of Leah and Rachel as "nothing less than reprehensible."[48]

The difficulty for feminist interpreters in identifying the procreative activities in Gen 29:31–30:24 as rape appears clearly in the interpretation of feminist commentator Elyse Goldstein. She writes from a literary-theological and not a historical perspective, but her explanations have the air of universality, as if what was told then makes sense now. She writes: "God rewards Leah with fertility to make up for her troubles with her husband, and the women [Leah and Rachel] are now equalized. One [Rachel] gets a man's love; the other [Leah] gets a child's love. One woman [Rachel] gains status through her husband, the other woman [Leah] status through her children."[49]

In Goldstein's feminist commentary, which focuses almost exclusively on Leah and Rachel, the enslaved women are absent from the discussion. Yet they are forced into sexual intercourse with Jacob, the husband, when the slave-holding wives are desperate for children or husbandly love. Goldstein assumes that the androcentric values surrounding motherhood caused Leah and Rachel to compete with each other. When they accomplished their goals, all is well. The enslaved women, Bilhah and Zilpah, receive no consideration, and the power differential between socially privileged and exploited women remains unexplored. The historical conviction that ancient Israelite society respected women only as

---

47. Susan Niditch, "Genesis," in *The Women's Bible Commentary: Expanded Edition with Apocrypha* (ed. C. A. Newsom and S. H. Ringe; 2d ed.; Louisville: Westminster John Knox, 1998), 20.

48. Renita J. Weems, "Do You See What I See? Diversity in Interpretation," *Church & Society* 82 (1991): 34.

49. Elyse Goldstein, *ReVisions: Seeing Torah through a Feminist Lens* (Woodstock, Vt.: Jewish Lights, 1998), 65. For the idea of God as the equalizer between the women, see also John Calvin, *Genesis* (trans. John King; Carlisle, Pa.: The Banner of Truth Trust, 1992), 140.

mothers prevents Goldstein as well as other interpreters[50] from reading Gen 29:31–30:24 as a critique of women's divergent social positions in a patriarchal order and as a story about the repeated rapes of the enslaved women, Bilhah and Zilpah. Instead, historical clichés about surrogate birthing customs and universalizing assumptions about love between husband and wife/wives prevail in this feminist commentary on Gen 29:31–30:24. A powerful story about the co-option of women into an androcentric structure and class oppression turns into a story about two women becoming mothers.

CULTIVATING ALTERNATIVE WAYS OF READING BIBLICAL LITERATURE

So the problem is how to read the Bible in Western societies in which historical criticism, though initially subversive, has turned into supporting the political, cultural, and religious status quo, as pointed out by postcolonial scholars but overlooked by many Western feminist historical critics. It seems to me that at the dawn of the twenty-first century biblical studies has to be brought up to speed with the Western culture of "Tandoori Reindeer," in which Norwegian-Indians prepare their tandoori with the meat of the land, reindeer, or in which American Jews celebrate Hanukah alongside Christmas. In the Western and secularized societies of Europe and much of North America, people live in a world in which East meets West and North encounters South, diasporic people become increasingly visible, and multireligious and poly-cultural sensibilities represent the hope for a future in which human rights and the planetary ecosystem will flourish.[51] Ours is a culture that lives with much freedom in religious, social, and cultural interaction and experimentation. For many, though not for all, syncretism is no longer a bad word but an everyday occurrence, if not in our town, then on television, in film, or on the Internet.

---

50. For another example, see Esther Fuchs, *Sexual Politics in the Biblical Narrative: Reading the Hebrew Bible as a Woman* (JSOTSup 310; Sheffield: Sheffield Academic Press, 2000), 158. Fuchs limits her analysis to Leah and Rachel and does not consider the dynamics of class as an integral element for understanding the dynamics between socially privileged and marginalized women. She also makes historical arguments supported largely by out-of-date anthropological scholarship; cf. the reference to an anthropological study of 1974 on p. 158 n. 48. See further Susanne Scholz, "Gender, Class, and Androcentric Compliance in the Rapes of Enslaved Women in the Hebrew Bible," *lectio difficilior* 1 (2004), n.p. [cited 20 April 2004]. Online: http://www. lectio.unibe.ch/04_1/Scholz.Enslaved.htm.

51. For the phrase "Tandoori Reindeer," see Craig S. Smith's report on the Muslim Norwegian comedian Shabana Rehman in "Where East Meets West Warily, She Makes Them Laugh," *New York Times* (November 14, 2003): A4.

In light of this multicultural dynamic in our lives, historical criticism seems obsolete. In biblical studies other approaches hold more promise for communicating the ongoing need for the academic study of the Bible than a method developed in confrontation with the experiences of the nineteenth century. In particular, two such methods stand out to me that take into account the questions, concerns, and developments of our time and place. One approach, which defines the study of the Bible in terms of cultural studies, envisions the field as a radically interdisciplinary project that cooperates with such fields as sociology, political science, history, and anthropology. This notion is not entirely new but needs to be pursued more actively and broadly in mainstream biblical research than is currently done. The interdisciplinary character of such work supports research that goes beyond the text-focused approach so dear to many scholars of biblical studies, and takes seriously the contextual and cultural histories and traditions of reading the Bible. Biblical analysis, defined accordingly, illuminates the material conditions of interpretations and helps explore how biblical meanings are constructed in a wide range of reading communities across time and space. This approach looks at the Bible as a document of abundant histories of interpretation in the East, West, South, and North, as a reflection of past and present cultures, political structures, and religions. Bible research turns into a multidisciplinary and multicultural endeavor that examines multiple geographies, histories, and sociologies of reading.

Some of this work is already under way. For instance, the *Global Bible Commentary*,[52] edited by Daniel Patte and others, is based on the insight that contextualized readings represent the future for biblical studies and that different contexts yield different meanings, many largely unknown to Western Bible scholars and readers. The volume is text-focused, but commentators address the assigned biblical books from their own sociopolitical and religious situations. Another example of the kind of work that biblical scholars increasingly need to pursue in a multireligious world comes from Chinese Hebrew Bible scholar Archie Lee. In a society that is mostly nonbiblical and non-Christian, Lee is developing a paradigm for examining the Bible that values cross-cultural and cross-religious exchange. His work on Chinese and biblical creation myths, for instance, explores similarities and differences in the scriptural traditions prevalent in a Chinese Buddhist context.[53]

---

52. Daniel Patte et al., eds., *Global Bible Commentary* (Nashville: Abingdon, 2004).

53. Archie C. C. Lee, "The Chinese Creation Myth of Nu Kua and the Biblical Narrative in Genesis 1–11," *BibInt* 2 (1994): 312–24. Cf. Lee's essay in this volume. For similar works located in other geographical contexts, see, e.g., nn. 11–13, 16–18, and 21–22 above.

The work of Vincent Wimbush, New Testament professor and director of The Institute for Signifying Scriptures at the School of Religion of Claremont Graduate University,[54] also contributes to the study of the Bible as a culminating artifact of many cultures, histories, and peoples. The mission statement of the institute makes an important and—for the field of biblical studies—crucial claim, namely, that "interpretive meaning is less about the codified text, and more about the encoded meanings in cultural behaviors," especially in the context of "historically enslaved and colonized peoples of the world" such as African Americans. To politically, culturally, and religiously dominated Bible readers, "signifying Scriptures" has often meant appropriating texts in performance and "alternative" modes of interpretation rather than to limit the investigation to the text itself or the world behind the text. The exploration of alternative approaches is therefore a central aspect of the institute's work. Yet these and other projects are still on the margins of the academic field and deserve sustained support from scholarly societies, such as the Society of Biblical Literature, or departments of religious and theological studies. All of this work contributes to an understanding of the Bible as a part of our syncretistic way of life.

In a contemporary Western society brimming with multiple languages, cultures, and traditions, a second direction also needs to be developed. Within a societal context of "tandoori reindeer," biblical studies would benefit from a focus on "ordinary" readers. The idea of taking seriously "ordinary" readers in the study of the Bible is most prominently developed so far by South African researchers.[55] They claim that an indigenization of the Bible has been underway among African Christians for some time, but gone unnoticed by researchers in biblical studies. South African scholars decided to remedy this situation and deliberately attend to lay people's readings. In the process, their work has focused on the needs of their political, cultural, and religious context.[56]

Western biblical scholarship is far behind in this movement. One of the problems is, of course, that in Western secularized countries many people do not read the Bible anymore and feel alienated from the religious tradition of their families. Still, many of them consider themselves as being on a spiritual quest and are often part of what is commonly, and perhaps mistakenly, called the "New Age movement." The latter is an attempt by largely secularized people to bring religious-spiritual

---

54. For more information on the Institute, see www.cgu.edu/inst.
55. See, e.g., Gerald O. West, *The Academy of the Poor: Towards a Dialogical Reading of the Bible* (Sheffield: Sheffield Academic Press, 1999).
56. See, e.g., Madipoane Masenya's essay in this volume.

meaning to their lives, a concern they actually share with Christian fundamentalists. In postbiblical Western societies many of these ordinary readers come from the North American and Western European white, middle-class, and reasonably educated strata of society.

If biblical researchers want to reach those ordinary readers, they need to go beyond the exoteric, analytical approach of traditional biblical research and develop an experiential, inner understanding of the Bible so that people understand the Bible's contribution to their religious-spiritual quest. This turn toward an inner reading can enable teachers and professional readers of the Bible to explain to ordinary readers of secularized Western societies that an understanding of the Bible is not only an academic, perhaps historically interesting, subject matter, but also of significance to their lives. In a time in which the Bible plays a central role only to fundamentalist Christians and to Jews and Christians committed to their respective religious institutions, scholars cannot simply assume the importance of the Bible anymore. Rather, the field has to articulate in its work that the study of this sacred text matters even today. In my view, this process of communicating the relevance of biblical studies is twofold. On the one hand, the Bible has to be studied deliberately as an artifact of diverse and manifold worlds, which informs us about past and present cultures. On the other hand, scholars need to introduce ordinary readers of Western secularized societies to the Bible as a sacred text by capturing the attention of an audience that is already committed to easternized approaches to the meaning of life.

The latter approach takes seriously a group of people that has little interest in the Bible but is already committed to spiritual-religious concerns.[57] It also recognizes that Western postbiblical societies sentimentalize, ignore, or are indifferent toward biblical literature and, at best, privatize, individualize, and socially marginalize its role. Sometimes, especially in the United States, Christian fundamentalists organize themselves politically in order to foster change, trying to reinstate the Bible's political centrality, and, although many of them claim spiritual understanding of biblical texts, they remain mostly stuck in literalist viewpoints. Their theologically and politically reactionary struggles

---

57. Marie-Theres Wacker, Professor of the Old Testament and Theological Research on Women at the University of Münster (Germany), was among the first Hebrew Bible scholars of a Western country to articulate this dynamic so prevalent in Western societies. In December 1999, she organized a conference entitled "How To Read the Bible in a Post-Biblical World" at the University of Münster. To my knowledge, the group of scholars did not develop a future agenda for pursuing research on the Bible in a post-biblical society such as Germany.

confront an indifferent majority that favors the Western scientific world-view over biblical primacy. Among this majority are many people who are nevertheless quite interested in issues related to spirituality and religion. They look for religious meaning beyond the institutionalized religious traditions of Christianity and Judaism. Does biblical studies have anything to offer to these "ordinary readers" of the Western secularized world?

Some suggest that an experientially based, inner reading practice might be an answer. For instance, J. Kakichi Kadowaki, professor of philosophy at the University of Sophia, who is a Westerner and a Jesuit, aptly observes the detachment of biblical studies from embodied spiritual practice. He writes: "Most students of theology will agree that their academic biblical studies do little for their spiritual lives."[58] Yet, when he began to practice Zen, he learned to read with the body and learned to appreciate the quest for inner meaning. He considers the Western disembodied approach to the Bible as the reason for feelings of alienation among many Western Christians. As a solution, Kadowaki offers his own story about combining both Zen and the Bible to discover the "inner" meaning of the Bible, a meaning completely detached from a historical or materially focused understanding.

The effort of regaining the "inner" or "esoteric" meaning of the Bible is not new but has a long tradition both in Christianity and Judaism. The mystic traditions of the Kabbalists and the medieval Christians are probably among the most well-known examples. The Catholic tradition has been particularly rich in developing esoteric practices such as the Prayer of the Heart, Christian meditation, or *lectio divina*, all of them interiorized forms of prayers and Bible meditations.[59] Others combine Eastern spiritual practices, such as Yoga, with the study of Western religious texts like the Bible. For instance, Jay G. Williams published a book entitled *Yeshua Buddha: An Interpretation of New Testament Theology as Meaningful Myth.*[60] As the title indicates, Williams offers a reading of the Jesus story based on eastern religious ideas. Each chapter of the book focuses on selected New Testament passages and relates them to eastern teachings. Presented as the "Enlightened One," Jesus emerges as Buddha, not in a historical but an existential and spiritual sense.

---

58. J. Kakichi Kadowaki, *Zen and the Bible* (trans. J. Rieck; Maryknoll, N.Y.: Orbis, 2002), ix.

59. For more on these and related practices in the Catholic tradition, see Thomas P. Ryan, *Prayer of Heart and Body: Meditation and Yoga as Christian Spiritual Practice* (New York: Paulist, 1995).

60. Jay G. Williams, *Yeshua Buddha: An Interpretation of New Testament Theology as Meaningful Myth* (Wheaton, Ill: Theosophical Publishing House, 1978).

Another, much smaller, pamphlet-like publication by Albrecht Frenz relies on individual Bible passages to prove the compatibility of Christianity with the interior practice called Yoga. In *Yoga in Christianity,* the author shows that some of Yoga's basic tenets are also found in the Bible. For instance, the emphasis on developing an attitude of quietude and stillness, so prevalent in the Eastern traditions, appears in Exod 14:14 and Isa 30:15, and is crucial for the notion of the Sabbath. Frenz is defensive at times—as, for instance, when he says: "If the content is clear, then Christian Yoga cannot lead to Hinduism, but is and remains a Christian expression of life."[61] Nonetheless, Frenz recognizes the great overall benefit of the esoteric Eastern practice for the Christian tradition.

Yet another example is Joseph Leeming's *Yoga and the Bible,* first published in 1963.[62] Each of the eighteen chapters begins with a quote from a New Testament passage, mostly from Matthew and John, and uses these texts as clues for describing the nature of spiritual-religious growth. Leeming's study is based on the conviction that the teachings of the Yoga masters are "in essence" similar to the teachings of the New Testament. Since Leeming addresses a Western and Christian-oriented audience, he introduces the spiritual teachings of "past and present Masters" with the words of the "enlightened teacher" of the first century C.E. For instance, the first chapter quotes Matt 7:7–8 ("Ask and it shall be given you...") in order to elaborate on the age-old spiritual quest of humanity. Many of today's seekers do not find their needs satisfied by religious institutions, such as the churches, Leeming presciently observes. Writing in 1963, he points out that those seeking spiritual enlightenment are searching elsewhere, including the Eastern traditions. Yet Leeming also cautions seekers not to give up too quickly on their own religious tradition. They can find in Jesus Christ a teacher who will accompany them on their spiritual journey, once they come to appreciate his wisdom.

These and other works aim at recapturing spiritually meaningful interpretations of the Bible through the embodied experience of Eastern religious traditions. Whether or not the academic field is ready for this direction remains to be seen, but the need is clearly there. In short, both suggestions—researching biblical meaning as reflections of cultural, political, and religious contexts of readers, and teaching the Bible experientially as esoteric literature—represent new ways of reading and studying the Bible at the dawn of the twenty-first century. The former

---

61. Albrecht Frenz, *Yoga in Christianity* (Madras: Christian Literature Society, 1986), 13.

62. Joseph Leeming, *Yoga and the Bible* (Punjab, India: Radha Soami Satsang Beas, 1978). For another publication in a similar vein, see Noëlle Perez-Christiaens, *Le Christ et le Yoga* (Paris: Institut de Yoga B.K.S. Iyengar, 1980).

aligns itself with scholarly efforts particularly under way among subaltern scholars. The latter relates to the context of the postbiblical West, and might or might not be suited to other social locations. Both approaches, the exoteric and the esoteric, offer alternatives to the historical-critical paradigm and may also complement each other.

CONCLUSION: TOWARD A HOLISTIC HERMENEUTIC OF THE BIBLE

Once, not so long ago, in the nineteenth century of Western societies such as Germany and the United States, historical criticism was a radical, even subversive method. Yet not long after that, in the twentieth century at many Western European universities and North American seminaries, the approach turned normative and became a method of the political and religious status quo. Its success was its downfall when it became the litmus test of academic legitimacy. This dynamic is particularly well described and understood by scholars who come from socially, ethnically, racially, and geographically marginalized locations. They tell the story about the failure of historical readings that have come to dominate and oppress their ancestors and contemporaries. For them, historical criticism signifies a method that has helped Westerners to colonize and exploit the world. Accordingly, they reject this method and offer alternatives such as the cultural study of biblical literature.

The clarity of postcolonial scholars is unfortunately not always shared in Western feminist readings of the Bible. A brief discussion about feminist interpretations on rape stories illustrates the problem. Feminist historical treatment of these passages demonstrates the inability to read against androcentric assumptions, often excusing or justifying them. Unlike postcolonial interpreters, many Western feminist historians of the Bible align themselves with the status quo of male-stream scholarship. Historical criticism does not enable them to read against the political, cultural, or religious grain. They find it difficult to read the biblical text from a socially progressive perspective. Consequently, their readings illustrate quite well the hermeneutical and ethical difficulties of the historical method.

The question thus arises how Bible scholars are supposed to study biblical literature in a Western "tandoori reindeer" culture, especially since historical criticism has proved to fail on so many accounts. In this essay I suggest that we need to cultivate alternative ways of reading, which help us to leave behind the historical-critical paradigm, by combining two different approaches to biblical literature that are also found in the world at large: the exoteric and the esoteric ones. The exoteric approach is analytical and examines the Bible's cultural, political, and religious meanings as part of the wide range of histories of biblical interpretation past and present. The esoteric approach develops inner meanings of the Bible and so communicates the value of the biblical text to an audience that has often abandoned its conventional Christian and Jewish traditions. Both approaches promise to connect biblical studies to the political, economic, social, and religious dynamics of our time and place. Leaving behind the narrow confines of historical criticism, this model represents a holistic hermeneutic that will give new validity to the academic study of the Bible in secularized societies of the West.

Indeed, the exoteric and esoteric approaches to the study of the Bible may well become what historical criticism once was in its early stage: new ways of reading. But even historical criticism holds a place in this holistic hermeneutic since historical interpretations provide insights into the assumptions and outlooks of people who read the Bible in the past and present. Both approaches, the exoteric and the esoteric, aim for an integrated view of biblical literature as a book in and of the world as well as a sacred text of Judaism and Christianity. The result of this combination may well be as innovating and inspiring as tandoori reindeer.

BREAKING THE ESTABLISHED SCAFFOLD: IMAGINATION AS A RESOURCE IN THE DEVELOPMENT OF BIBLICAL INTERPRETATION

Hjamil A. Martínez-Vázquez

The bitter present we confront demands that our words, our gestures, and our works consecrate as the true fulfillment of our vocation the aim to express the sorrow, the danger, and the uncertainty—but also the hope and courage—of a humanity that resists disappearance. In the middle of this extreme situation, the mission of an artist cannot degenerate into an inhumane aestheticism but must move toward an ethic of obligation that leads the artist to express the tears of millions of men and women whose lives have been reduced to silence through arms, violence and exclusion.[1]

These are the words of the ninety-year-old Argentinean writer Ernesto Sábato. These words challenge us to step away from our comfort zones and live out our real vocations, whatever they may be. As a historian, I understand this challenge to mean taking the silences within the traditional historical discourses and making them speak. My attempts to complete this task began in the world of imagination. Traditional historiography has constructed an imaginary by establishing a universal knowledge that prohibits imagination by the people who live on the borderlands of society.[2] This imaginary, which I will designate as a colonial entity, does not allow for imagination because it would open the door for an understanding of reality beyond the borders constructed by the universal, as imagination "leads inescapably in artistic direction[s] in which

---

1. Ernesto Sábato, "Valores para la Paz," paper presented at the Inter-American University of Puerto Rico (August 15, 2002) (my translation).
2. I am using the concept of the imaginary to name the overarching set of ideological, philosophical and theoretical paradigms that guide the social, economic, political and academic structures of society. The imaginary should not be seen or interpreted as something that lacks factual reality. The imaginary is responsible for discourses, theories, ideologies and philosophies that dictate the way we live in the world.

truth is told in a way and at an angle that assures it will not be readily co-opted or domesticated by hegemonic interpretative power."[3] This movement represents a subversive action against both the view that only rational things are important and against the imposition of the established colonial imaginary. It thus generates resistance and reconstruction. Through imagination, the existent colonial imaginary can be deconstructed and a decolonial imaginary can be developed in its place.[4] While the colonial one is "a framework, a set of ideological strategies of containment by which everything is explained and organized, ensuring thereby the consensus of the dominated and their consent to their domination,"[5] the decolonial imaginary is a framework filled with ideologies, perspectives, and histories that seek social justice and liberation.[6]

We, scholars and students, have been taught to use facts and their meanings to construct a narrative of the "real." Only the "real" is important, so that everything which cannot be explained through the "real" is deemed to be nonexistent, pure fiction. To go beyond that which is considered "real" is to step out of the boundaries of society into new terrain where the colonial imaginary does not dominate, to those fields

---

3. Walter Brueggemann, *The Prophetic Imagination* (2d ed.; Minneapolis: Fortress, 2001), xiv.

4. The existing imaginary, which I already characterized as colonial, is based on the function of the modern/colonial system. This colonial imaginary is impregnated with racism, capitalism, ethnocentrisms, imperialism, and heterosexism. This system that arbitrarily allows some to dominate over many needs to be decolonized so that a new one can be built, that which I call the decolonial imaginary. It is important to establish that my own conception of a decolonial imaginary differs from that of Emma Pérez, although her work has been influential in the formation of my own understanding. See Emma Pérez, *The Decolonial Imaginary: Writing Chicanas into History* (Bloomington: Indiana University Press, 1999). Pérez describes the decolonial imaginary as "that interstitial space where differential politics and social dilemmas are negotiated" (6). That definition resonates with my understanding of borderlands, which will be explored later in this essay. Yet, while for her the decolonial imaginary is an already existent space, for me it is a work in progress. In the same sense, it is important to explain my use of the terms "postcolonizing," "decolonization," and "decolonial." The first two terms can be used interchangeably since both imply a movement from coloniality to decoloniality. My use of the terms suggests that I visualize this enterprise as an ongoing process, not a finished one. The term "decolonial" implies the already-attained end of colonialism. In this essay, however, "decolonial" will only be used to characterize an imaginary.

5. Rosaura Sánchez, "The History of Chicanas: A Proposal for a Materialist Perspective," in *Between Borders: Essays on Mexicana/Chicana History* (ed. A. R. del Castillo; Encino, Calif.: Floricanto, 1990), 4.

6. While political, social, religious, and economic leaders base their actions in the existing colonial imaginary (manifest destiny, racism, heterosexism, misogyny, and socioeconomic and cultural dominance of the North Atlantic empire and global capitalism), the development of a decolonial imaginary destroys this construction so that people would leave behind oppression, searching instead for social justice.

characterized as ahistorical. Through imagination we can go beyond the established parameters of our disciplines, beyond the established imaginary of U.S. American society and the overarching scheme of global capitalism, in order to transform not only our respective disciplines, but also, and especially, our society. As Walter Brueggemann acknowledges, "clearly, human transformative activity depends upon a transformed imagination. Numbness does not hurt like torture, but in a quite parallel way, numbness robs us of our capability for humanity."[7] This transformative imagination is the ethical obligation that Ernesto Sábato demands of us. It is the vehicle to see beyond the extreme situation and envision change. For example, reading the Bible differently and opening its interpretation to imagination can help in the development of change, since traditional biblical interpretation has been dominated and shaped by the colonial imaginary.

The use of imagination as a counterhegemonic practice helps the scholar to see and hear the silences within traditional historical narratives. These narratives, including those engaged by historical-criticism, while acting under the premise that truth (the "real") and objectivity are readily supplied, have become instruments of the colonial imaginary by muting voices and destroying memory. Moreover, these narratives become colonial discourses as they are embedded within the modernist presupposition that history-telling is the description of "what actually happened." These representations of the past, founded upon the assumption of universality, remove sources of imagination by defining, naming and labeling the past in final and ultimate ways. I believe it is important to step away from this colonial method of representation, which closes spaces of interpretation, negates perspective, and silences voices. It is important to uncover the scaffold behind these narratives constructed by the historical-critical method in order to open the door to imagination, to challenge and deconstruct the established systems of power, and to reconstruct new ways of interpretation. In other words, it is important to create a decolonial imaginary.

Since I am a historian and come to the topic of biblical interpretation from a different perspective than those in the area of biblical studies, I intend to focus on the issue of traditional representations of the past, which the historical-critical method adopts, and to examine how these narrow the opportunities for different readings of texts. A strong connection can be noted between the established representations and the way a person will read a text related to those representations. For example, once

---

7. Brueggemann, *Prophetic Imagination*, xx.

people in power establish a fixed and universal narrative of what happened in a certain period, then all the subsequent readings of texts of that period will be defined based upon that representation. As a result, the reader loses all power to imagine beyond that which is already established, and her or his voice, as well as those of the people in that period whose lives do not participate in the modern constructed narrative, tend to be silenced, which ultimately eliminates the ways in which such voiceless individuals can relate their words to the world.[8]

In the past decades, biblical scholars and laity have developed "new" readings and approaches to the biblical texts, ranging from rhetorical to psychoanalytic analysis, from feminist to ideological criticism, among others. In this sense, then, I am not arguing that alternative voices and perspectives are not already being brought to the forefront of the conversation. Rather, I am suggesting that the constraints (and restraints!) embedded in methods and theories that came out of traditional historiography still impact the way most people read and interpret the Bible. People still believe that the text is part of a particular era and that by understanding that era the text itself acquires meaning.

CONFRONTING TRADITIONAL HISTORIOGRAPHY

In the past century, history as a discipline has gone through many revisions. In the nineteenth century, it gained prominence within various academic settings, but twentieth-century scholars, as well as particular schools of thought and theories, began to question the validity of the discipline. In order to understand these changes and challenges, one needs to acknowledge and examine the work of Leopold von Ranke (1795–1886). Ranke advocated the prominence of history to the extent that it replaced philosophy as the chief discipline in academia. He thought of history as a scientific enterprise whose product was truth. Truth, in this sense, should be understood as a reality, a fact, which cannot be disputed because of its assumed accuracy and precision. Thus, history relates an event "as it actually happened" ("wie es eigentlich gewesen ist").[9]

---

8. Paulo Freire and Donaldo Macedo, *Literacy: Reading the Word and the World* (Westport, Conn.: Bergin & Garvey, 1987).

9. For a better understanding of Ranke's vision, see Leopold von Ranke, *The Theory and the Practice of History* (ed. G. G. Iggers and K. von Moltke; trans. W. A. Iggers and K. von Moltke; Indianapolis: Bobbs-Merrill, 1973); and Georg G. Iggers and James M. Powell, eds., *Leopold von Ranke and the Shaping of the Historical Discipline* (Syracuse: Syracuse University Press, 1990).

According to Ranke's framework, history produced scientific knowledge, verifiable by the facts that were the building blocks to reconstruct the past exactly as it happened. Although he rejected the theories of knowledge of his time (Romanticism, Positivism, and Idealism), Ranke's conception of history is imbued with notions inherent within these theories, such as Positivism's conception of objectivity and the absence of any kind of speculation in the study of a phenomenon. History, according to Ranke, should be seen as the discovery of the past presented in a unilinear way without any kind of human judgment. The historian could not impose her/his own criteria on the study of a specific time. In contrast to Romanticism, Ranke promoted an objectivist epistemology, in which the development of grand narratives led to the truth, and in which, even if facts were studied separately, in the end they had to be located within the larger picture. History became a mirror of reality, a universal reality. This Rankean model ultimately became the authoritative way of understanding history.

By the end of the nineteenth century, many institutionalized historians claimed to be presenting what really happened and were enjoying top rank among their peers. The promotion of history as primarily an academic discipline brought forth the idea that the content of history was knowledge and truth, an idea that Friedrich Nietzsche challenged in his treatise *On the Advantage and Disadvantage of History for Life*. Nietzsche argued that searching for knowledge and truth is "a part of the task of existing and, like every human enterprise, it receives its value from being integrated into the task of which it is a part."[10] In this sense, history is to serve the enterprise of life and should not be seen as the result of the process of searching for knowledge and truth. Nietzsche agreed with the importance of history, but not with Ranke's idea that history should be the central, all-encompassing discipline.

The impetus behind both traditional historiography and, in an ironic twist, also the challenges to it listed above, comes from modernity and the system it created/s. Understood as a period in time, modernity emerged with Columbus's voyage to the Amerindian territories, and developed through the period of the Reformation, the Renaissance, the scientific revolution, and the Enlightenment.[11] Rather than simply viewed

---

10. Friedrich Nietzsche, *On the Advantage and Disadvantage of History for Life* (trans. Peter Preuss; Indianapolis: Hackett, 1980), 1.

11. This definition differs from the common understanding, which situates the development of modernity, as Enrique Dussel argues, "from the Italy of the Renaissance to the Germany of the Reformation and the Enlightenment, to the France of the French Revolution" ("Beyond Eurocentrism: The World-System and the Limits of Modernity," in *The Cultures of*

as an epoch or a period in time, modernity also denotes a discourse, "a highly complex yet coherent narrative containing assumptions about how it is possible to represent the state of nature as supported by a new realist historical consciousness of change over time."[12] In other words, beliefs, characteristics, cultural trends, and rules define modernity. The period of the conquest and colonization of the Amerindian territories gave Europe, represented in this case by Spain, a reason to locate itself at the center of a world-system—a modern/colonial entity. Subsequently, events like the Enlightenment and the scientific revolution helped northern Europe displace Spain as the center of the system.[13] The Reformation was also part of this process of displacement and marginalization since it re-located Catholicism at the periphery of the Christian world. The discourse of modernity, then, locates Europe, which becomes the West, at

---

Globalization [ed. F. Jameson and M. Miyoshi; Durham: Duke University Press, 1998], 4). This understanding leaves Spain and the ideology of conquest and colonialism out of the development of modernity. Dussel argues for the existence of at least two modernities, the first one began with the conquest of the Amerindian nations and the second with the development of Anglo-Germanic Europe in Amsterdam.

12. Alan Munslow, *The Routledge Companion to Historical Studies* (London: Routledge, 2000), 163.

13. The modern/colonial system can be dated to the end of the fifteenth century when Europe found itself confronted with an Other besides Islam. Thus, Spain and Portugal, with their voyages to Africa and the "New World," become the initial location for the construction of the colonial Eurocentric system. These events put Europe in contact with an Other who could provide a sense of comparison. This meant that Europe, as it became the West, could shape its self-identity in the light of this Other, and, for that matter, it could position itself in the center while the newly encountered territories stayed on the periphery. Colonialism, then, is the mechanism used to define and support this relationship of center/periphery. The modern/colonial system is premised on not only this assumed superiority of Europe, but also the subjugation and oppression of the periphery, both physically (political and economic control) and mentally (control of history). The modern/colonial system depends on colonial discourses, which are based on colonial difference. Through these discourses the West writes the history of the colonized by projecting its own history and agenda. Colonial discourses serve the colonizer by creating an imaginary that details the "truth" about the world, a world in which the colonized needs the colonizer because of the constructed superiority of the latter. This imaginary maintains its apparent superiority by giving rationality and scientific knowledge the greater status within society. The idea of the superiority of the rational over the irrational is one of the principles of modernity, and this particular concept fueled the birth and rise of Western imperialism. Since the colonizers have these specialized forms of knowing and understanding and the colonized do not, they are placed in the position of helping the colonized. It is in this regard that the colonized will see the colonizer as their benefactor without necessarily perceiving the system operative behind this relationship. Economic and political exploitation serve this purpose as well, working in the same way since the colonized do not readily observe the exploitation in practice. Colonial discourses create and support "representations" of the Other, and, since these are defined by the colonizer, power over the colonized is secured.

the center of the modern/colonial system and the rest at the periphery. This phenomenon is what Stuart Hall refers to as the concept of "the West and the Rest."[14]

As Enrique Dussel and other scholars have argued, "modernity is, in fact, a European phenomenon."[15] But Dussel goes further by stating that modernity is "constituted in a dialectical relation with non-European alterity that is its ultimate content. Modernity appears when Europe affirms itself as the center of a *World* History that it inaugurates; the periphery that surrounds this center is consequently part of its self-definition."[16] In this sense, then, modernity cannot be explained with respect to a Europe considered as an independent system, but a Europe conceived as center of the system, a "move" that promotes its own superiority and that establishes a connection between Europe and a universal, modern historical consciousness.[17] In this light it is not surprising to observe that the history of European civilization coincides with the very notion of "universal history."[18] As Dale Irvin states,

> Among the more pernicious attributes that have characterized this modern historical consciousness has been the assumption that the historical horizon of modern European civilization coincides with the horizon of universal human history. The concept of universal history is itself a product of modern Europe. It emerged only at the end of the eighteenth century from the intellectual milieu of the European Enlightenment, and had at its center a particular human subject, the modern European.[19]

Immanuel Kant illustrates well this concept of universal history in his treatise, "Idea for a Universal History with Cosmopolitan Intent."[20] For Kant, "The history of mankind could be viewed on the whole as the

---

14. Stuart Hall, "The West and the Rest: Discourse and Power," in *Formations of Modernity* (ed. S. Hall and B. Gieben; Cambridge: Polity, 1992), 275–322.

15. Enrique Dussel, "Eurocentrism and Modernity," in *The Postmodernism Debate in Latin America* (ed. J. Beverley, M. Aronna, and J. Oviedo; Durham: Duke University Press, 1995), 65.

16. Ibid.

17. Dussel, "Beyond Eurocentrism," 3–31.

18. This universal history is based on the bourgeoisie class of Europe, which considered itself to be the prime example of civilization.

19. Dale Irvin, *Christian Histories, Christian Traditioning: Rendering Accounts* (Maryknoll, N.Y.: Orbis, 1998), 23.

20. Immanuel Kant, "Idea for a Universal History with Cosmopolitan Intent," in *Basic Writings of Kant* (ed. A. W. Wood; trans. C. F. Friedrich; New York: Modern Library, 2001), 117–32.

realization of a hidden plan of nature in order to bring about an internally—and for this purpose also externally—perfect constitution; since this is the only state in which nature can develop all predispositions of mankind."[21] The writing of a universal history is thus considered to aid and advance "this intention of nature."[22] European civilization, because of its superiority and its position at the center of the system, then, becomes the overseer of humankind and the bearer of this universal history, from the Greeks to the period of the Enlightenment.

Ranke followed this idea of universal history and developed it into a method. He argued that it was not enough to write the history of several nations and combine them in a collection, but that it was important to look for the interrelationships between them: "This is precisely the task of the study of universal history: to recognize these interrelationships, to indicate the course of large-scale events, which bind all the peoples together and dominate their history."[23] This universal is what every historian should strive for, using "critical research" and "comprehensive understanding."[24] According to this idea, historians should examine closely nations' pasts. More importantly, they should look at connections between these pasts, for in these connections Kant's "perfect constitution" could be found. This universal history is the one through which the particular can be explained,[25] and Europe, the center of the system, becomes the foundation for it, leaving the people outside this center (i.e., on the periphery) without historical consciousness as such. Indeed, although they are not part of that history, these peripheral others should see in the universal history their own past story. Thus, Ranke's conception of universal history and the notion of history as the past itself are the sources of traditional historiography, which gave European civilization its "true" historical consciousness.

As noted earlier, toward the end of the nineteenth century critiques of particular aspects of this traditional way of doing history came to the forefront of the discussions within the discipline. Criticism reached a new height when, in 1940, Walter Benjamin wrote his "Theses on the Philosophy of History," which seeks to bring down the supports of the scaffold that sustain traditional historiography.[26] The first point Benjamin made is

---

21. Ibid., 128–29.
22. Ibid., 131.
23. Leopold von Ranke, *The Secret of World History: Selected Writings on the Art and Science of History* (ed. and trans. R. Wines; New York: Fordham University Press, 1981), 249.
24. Ibid., 250.
25. Ibid.
26. Walter Benjamin, "Theses on the Philosophy of History," in *Illuminations* (ed. H. Arendt; trans. H. Zohn; New York: Schocken, 1985), 253–64.

that it is impossible to retrieve the past "as it really was." History looks for an image, a picture of the past, "which flashes up at the instant when it can be recognized and is never seen again."[27] Historical processes are thus ephemeral entities, not concrete, uniform elements that can be abstracted and concretized. In contrast to traditional modes of analysis, Benjamin called for a historical materialist approach, which avoids connections and complicity with the rulers and the victors, but focuses instead on "the tradition of the oppressed."[28] This understanding breaks with the idea of truth proposed by traditional historiography and opens the door for those communities outside of the center of power to enter the historical discussion. Even more, following a Marxist approach, he states, "Not man or men but the struggling, oppressed class itself is the depository of historical knowledge."[29] Benjamin also turned to a critique of the concept of progress within historiography, because, in his mind, revolutions shatter the continuum established by those in power. In historical materialism, then, the historian does not fall prey to the concept of progress and transition, which supports the whole idea of a perpetual past, but the historian "supplies a unique experience with the past," which aids in understanding her/his position in the present.[30] This critique of progress both serves as the basis for Benjamin's later criticism of universal history, which he viewed as silencing and erasing other events from the past, and explains his attempt to redescribe those "silenced moments" as being as legitimately historical as those introduced in the "universal history." As a result of this approach, the universal appears as particular to Europe. Benjamin also wanted to remove control over history from the center of power by proving that time and history are characterized by disruptions; this move, in turn, makes it possible for the Others (those on the periphery) to possess historical consciousness.[31]

After World War II, especially after the 1960s, histories of marginalized groups, the non-Western alterity, became audible to some degree, and in many ways this recognition called into question the credibility of the prior grand narratives.[32] Multiple histories displaced universal history

---

27. Ibid., 255.

28. Ibid., 257.

29. Ibid., 260.

30. Ibid., 262.

31. Ultimately, Benjamin appeared to be arguing for the presence of disruptions throughout historical time, while also wanting to criticize the traditional way of selecting certain moments to represent the past, thereby silencing others. This kind of argument opened the door for the critique of the so-called "universal history" as actually being another "particular history."

32. My point here is that while histories of subaltern groups were written in the past, it is not until this period that they acquire some importance within institutionalized academic circles.

by challenging the content of the master narratives of the West and its loosely erected scaffolds, thus continuing Walter Benjamin's task. The Others now become agents in their own historical consciousness, and, as Dale Irvin acknowledges, "the otherness of these multiple histories, and especially their otherness to the master narrative(s) of the dominant modern West, or Europe, gives them potentially a critical and liberative capacity."[33] In this challenge to the traditional approach, narrative, as the primary form in which historical writing was in fact cast, quite naturally came to the forefront of discussion among theorists and postmodern historians. The work of Hayden White is seminal in this respect.

Hayden White argued that historiography has been and is a discourse that is formed by the narratives that account for the historian's "findings" and "inventions" about the past. These historical narratives are "verbal fictions, the contents of which are as much invented as found and the forms of which have more in common with their counterparts in literature than they have with those in the sciences."[34] Historians take the events and the structures of the past and put them together through the process of emplotment so that they look like a story, a narrative. In other words, the historian imposes a narrative form on the past and its events. It is in this process of emplotment, which is defined by White as "the way by which a sequence of events fashioned into a story is gradually revealed to be a story of a particular kind," that the invention takes place precisely since the past itself (or in actuality) is not structured in the form of a narrative.[35] White goes on to argue that "this implies that all narrative is not simply a recording of 'what happened' in the transition from one state of affairs to another, but a progressive redescription of sets of events in such a way as to dismantle a structure encoded in one verbal mode in the beginning so as to justify a recoding of it in another mode at the end."[36] Through the process of emplotment, then, the historian imposes meaning on events in the past.[37]

White's argument that historical narratives follow a rhetorical/literary structure has been widely accepted, but not his conclusion that the

---

33. Irvin, *Christian Histories*, 26.

34. Hayden White, *Tropics of Discourse: Essays in Cultural Criticism* (Baltimore: Johns Hopkins University Press, 1978), 82.

35. Hayden White, *Metahistory: The Historical Imagination in Nineteenth-Century Europe* (Baltimore: Johns Hopkins University Press, 1973), 7.

36. White, *Tropics of Discourse*, 98.

37. This process of emplotment described by White is closely related to the Aristotelian concept of mimesis used by Paul Ricoeur. Ricoeur develops this concept in detail in the first volume of his *Time and Narrative* (3 vols.; trans. K. McLaughlin and D. Pellauer; Chicago: University of Chicago Press, 1984–1988).

content of it is as much invented as found. Historians still focus their attention on evidence and "facts" of the past to prove that history goes beyond literature in its argumentation, and that it produces knowledge, which, in most cases, is still considered "scientific" and "universal." White does not question that knowledge comes out of historical inquiry; he simply challenges the kind of knowledge that is produced. He argues:

> I have never denied that knowledge of history, culture, and society was possible; I have only denied that a scientific knowledge, of the sort actually attained in the study of physical nature, was possible. But I have tried to show that, even if we cannot achieve a properly scientific knowledge of human nature, we can achieve another kind of knowledge about it, the kind of knowledge which literature and art in general give us in easily recognizable examples. Only a willful, tyrannical intelligence could believe that the only kind of knowledge we can aspire to is that represented by the physical sciences. My aim has been to show that we do not have to choose between art and science, that indeed we cannot do so in practice, if we hope to continue to speak about culture as against nature—and, moreover, speak about it in ways that are responsible to all the various dimensions of our *human* being.[38]

Here White responds to his critics, especially those who want to perpetuate the modernist approach to history and try to draw scientific and universal knowledge out of the past. Since interpretation mediates the work of the historian and the events of the past, history cannot develop scientific knowledge.[39] The historian is involved in a process of construction in which she/he uses tropes in order to impose a story structure on the events of the past. In this imposition, meaning is given to the events and to the narrative itself. The process of construction of a historical account, in this view, is similar to the process engaged by a writer of literature in order to create a novel, story, or poem.[40]

---

38. White, *Tropics of Discourse*, 23.

39. I agree with White's statement that historians tend to downplay the role that knowledge of literature and art provide by privileging scientific knowledge, the latter being perceived as the only one that provides exactitude and truth. This downplaying proves that historians still participate in the modernist project of favoring science and rationality over other kinds of epistemological ventures. For example, centers of power have controlled for so long now the products of history that the memories and stories of most of the revolutionary history in Latin America have been left out. In novels, poetry and other kind of art, however, people do find a space to address these issues. For instance, the Colombian writer Gabriel García Márquez seeks to confirm this space in his various writings.

40. Although the process of construction of the historical narrative is similar to that of fiction, scholars like Michel-Rolph Trouillot expose the break between history and fiction. Trouillot argues that "historically specific groups of humans must decide if a particular

I do not believe there is a way beyond this use of narrative form in historiography, although White and others have proposed the use of poetry and other literary genres as ways to step away from narrative. The problem, rather, resides in the definition and status given to narrative by the modernist project as that vehicle that propagates universal truth. As White insists, "it is historians themselves who have transformed narrativity from a manner of speaking into a paradigm of the form that reality itself displays to a 'realistic' consciousness. It is they who have made narrativity into a value, the presence of which in a discourse having to do with 'real' events signals at once its objectivity, its seriousness, and its realism."[41]

Yet, in its original state, narrative is just another literary genre and it should not be elevated as a result of its use in history. Historians have to become aware of their unreflected use of narrative as a conveyer of truth in order to challenge it and to advocate for its recognition as a literary genre, nothing more. Narrative represents a manner of speaking and is a vehicle of communication, but not an instrument of truth. Historical narratives should be seen as representations (*mimesis*) or constructions of the past, whereas the voices of the historians, rather than being hidden behind "facts," should always be heard with attentive ears focused on embedded agendas. As a result, historical narratives would become self-critical and self-referential discourses, rather than conveyers of universal truths. They would also become counterdiscourses to the modernist project. Moreover, since they are self-referential and do not claim any universal power, they cannot be co-opted by a colonial agenda or be established as colonial discourses themselves.

It is the use of imagination that allows for the envisioning of new discourses, not only by exposing and confronting the modernist project within traditional historiography, but also by dis-covering the voices and memories that have been concealed.[42] Imagination also provides the

---

narrative belongs to history or to fiction. In other words, the epistemological break between history and fiction is always expressed concretely through the historically situated evaluation of specific narratives" (Michel-Rolph Trouillot, *Silencing the Past: Power and the Production of History* [Boston: Beacon, 1995], 8). Of interest here is the designation of those specific groups of humans. It is essential that the process of verification does not rely on dominant groups who will likely make a decision based on their exercise of power over those un-represented groups; a control that is not limited to a consciousness and identity issue but that readily turns into material dominance, since they would thus still make (and write) the history.

41. White, *Content of the Form*, 24.

42. *Dis-covery* is not the process by which someone finds for the first time a land or an idea. It should be understood as a process in which the subjects realize that covering up has

people doing historical interpretation with a resource for change and transformation because they can see beyond the colonial discourses, beyond the silences, beyond the narratives that have been imposed as "truth." Imagination thus promotes change by dis-covering and un-silencing the voices that erupt and break through the normative and dominant histories. These voices, to use a metaphor from Subcomandante Marcos of the Zapatista National Liberation Army, are like "a little piece of paper among the damp scars of history."[43] Once they begin to articulate themselves they do not only speak about the discourses and its silences but also about the transformation of society. In other words, it is important to read that little piece of paper in order to achieve social transformation. As Marcos writes, "perhaps the little piece of paper speaks of a world where all worlds fit and grow, where the differences of color, culture, size, language, sex, and history don't serve to exclude, persecute, or classify, where the variety may once and for all break the grayness now stifling us."[44] But where can these voices be found? How do/can we encounter them? These questions are answered by going to the borderlands.

BORDERLANDS AS A THEORETICAL PARADIGM AND DISCURSIVE LOCATION

The term *borderlands* has been understood as a physical space, and is usually reserved for the space along the U.S.–Mexico border. But Gloria Anzaldúa has expanded the notion of the term beyond physical reality. In the past decades, Mexican American and Chicana/o scholars have challenged the traditional and dominant discourses in the United States by bringing to the table the perspectives, voices, and histories of the people in the borderlands, particularly the Southwest. Most of them participate

---

been part of their past. In this sense, I am using the term discovery following María Pilar Aquino's conception. See María Pilar Aquino, "The Collective 'Dis-covery' of Our Own Power: Latina American Feminist Theology," in *Hispanic/Latino Theology: Challenge and Promise* (ed. A. M. Isasi-Díaz and F. F. Segovia; Minneapolis: Fortress, 1996), 240–58. Writing from the standpoint of Latin American women, she states, "the five hundred years of European presence in Latin America have served not so much as an occasion for imagining what our history actually was or could have been but rather as an occasion for a continuing dis-covery" (241). She goes on to say, "The great European invasions did not discover but rather covered whole peoples, religions, and cultures and explicitly tried to take away from natives the sources of their own historical memory and their own power" (241). Thus, dis-covery becomes a process of un-covering and re-creating this people's past and memory. It serves the subalterns in their quest for an identity, a self-identity different from that which the people who covered up their memory have imposed upon them.

43. Subcomandante Insurgente Marcos, *Our Word Is Our Weapon: Selected Writings* (ed. J. Ponce de León; New York: Seven Stories, 2000), 276.

44. Ibid.

in what has been called "border studies" and have opened the door for new ways of interpretation.[45] Although the field of border studies has developed, Anzaldúa's conception of "borderlands" is still the leading notion in the field: "physically present wherever two or more cultures edge each other, where people of different races occupy the same territory, where under, lower, middle and upper classes touch, where the space between two individuals shrinks with intimacy."[46] While "border" and "borderlands" suggest a physical space in the U.S.–Mexico territorial contact, for most border studies scholars there are actually multiple borderlands. Borderlands are not a definitive geographical location. Rather, the concept of borderlands has become a metaphor and a theoretical space, acquiring different interpretations as a result.[47]

The borderlands are areas for encounter: spaces where voices are heard, memories are recovered, and where resistance is lived. Through the metaphoric use of the borderlands, Chicana feminists, for instance, have engaged in a theoretical conversation. Gloria Anzaldúa has pointed out that there is a need for theories outside of the dominant academic circles. Anzaldúa finds that, while theory "is a set of knowledges" and "some of these knowledges have been kept from us," people of color (and women of color in particular) need to transform the theorizing space with new methodologies and approaches in order *not* to "allow white men and women solely to occupy it."[48] In this vision, the borderlands become those places where theory is lived out and produced, and imagination is operative. Anzaldúa goes on to assert:

> Necesitamos teorías [We need theories] that will rewrite history using race, class, gender and ethnicity as categories of analysis, theories that

---

45. Renato Rosaldo, *Culture and Truth: The Remaking of Social Analysis* (Boston: Beacon Press, 1989); Héctor Calderón, and José David Saldívar, eds., *Criticism in the Borderlands: Studies in Chicano Literature, Culture, and Ideology* (Durham: Duke University Press, 1991); D. Emily Hicks, *Border Writing: The Multidimensional Text* (Minneapolis: University of Minnesota Press, 1991); Carlos G. Vélez-Ibáñez, *Border Visions: Mexican Cultures of the Southwest United States* (Tucson: University of Arizona Press, 1996); José David Saldívar, *Border Matters: Remapping American Cultural Studies* (Berkeley and Los Angeles: University of California Press, 1997); and Frank Bonilla et al., eds., *Borderless Borders: U.S. Latinos, Latin Americans, and the Paradox of Interdependence* (Philadelphia: Temple University Press, 1998).

46. Gloria Anzaldúa, *Borderlands/La Frontera: The New Mestiza* (San Francisco: Aunt Lute, 1999), 19.

47. See Scott Michaelsen and David E. Johnson, eds., *Border Theory: The Limits of Cultural Politics* (Minneapolis: University of Minnesota Press, 1997).

48. Gloria Anzaldúa, "Haciendo Caras, Una Entrada," in *Making Face, Making Soul/Haciendo Caras: Creative and Critical Perspectives by Feminists of Color* (ed. G. Anzaldúa; San Francisco: Aunt Lute, 1990), xxv.

cross borders, that blur boundaries—new kinds of theories with new theorizing methods. We need theories that will point out ways to maneuver between our particular experiences and the necessity of forming our own categories and theoretical models for the patterns we uncover. We need theories that examine the implications of situations and look at what's behind them.[49]

To develop a theory from the borderlands that breaks down the colonial imaginary and transforms the social conditions it generated is to focus on resistance instead of exclusion, on the inclusion of difference instead of homogenization. It is to understand that actual struggle is necessary in order to dismantle traditional history from a different perspective. It is not about adding names and places to books, but to understand and build theories out of the people's call for justice. These theories analyze existing perspectives and their roots in order to criticize them and formulate their own, while addressing differences and multiplicity of experiences.[50] Borrowing words from Audre Lorde's project, I would also conclude: "It is learning how to stand alone, unpopular and sometimes reviled, and how to make common cause with those … identified as outside the structures, in order to define and seek a world in which we can all flourish. It is learning how to take our differences and make them strengths."[51]

In the borderlands, we can (re)locate ourselves and look for that resistance and strength to which I refer. A view of the borderlands as a physical and metaphorical reality, coupled with the struggle of the people residing in them, has provided the theorizing space that Anzaldúa proposed. Thus, this space produces the imagination that seeks decolonization of discourses and dominant/dominating imaginaries, a process which can be termed the "decolonial imaginary." To put it another way, we need to locate ourselves in the borderlands and live out the practice of imagining in order to become involved in a critical organic intellectual practice.[52] From the perspective of the borderlands, we can see how colonial discourses operate, and how the colonial imaginary tries to define

49. Ibid., xxv–xxvi.

50. See Sonia Saldívar-Hull, *Feminism on the Border: Chicana Gender Politics and Literature* (Berkeley and Los Angeles: University of California Press, 2000), 73.

51. Audre Lorde, "The Master's Tools Will Never Dismantle the Master's House: Comments at 'The Personal and the Political' Panel (Second Sex Conference, October 29, 1979)," in *This Bridge Called My Back: Writings by Radical Women of Color* (ed. C. Moraga and G. Anzaldúa; 2d ed.; New York: Kitchen Table, 1983), 99.

52. For more on the critical organic intellectual practice, see Mark D. Wood, "Religious Studies as Critical Organic Intellectual Practice," *JAAR* 69 (2001): 129–62.

the Other. We need to see the resistance, struggle, and hope of the borderlands as the source of the theoretical models generated in this space. We need to break out of the boundaries of traditional historiography and the colonial imaginary, which perceives the subaltern as objects and not as subjects. Going to the borderlands is to step out of the traditional realm of historiography and locate ourselves in the margins, arguing and exposing that which no one will risk, daring to be dubbed "a-historical."[53] We need to write from the place "imprinted with the legacies of imperialism, colonization, race wars, and gender and class hierarchies."[54]

For example, the history of the Southwest has been dominated by the stories of "pioneers" and "cowboys," on the one hand, and those "savages," "dirty and greasy Mexicans," on the other. These stories have portrayed the "cowboys" and the "pioneers" as subjects and the Mexicans as the Others, as objects of a history impregnated with success and glory at their expense. These stories covered and silenced not only the voices of these Others but also the stories of violence, persecution, and oppression. In the last two decades new studies on the Southwest have emerged that challenge the traditional narratives. It is certainly good that these silenced voices are now being heard. Here I agree with the argument made by Daisy Machado that, "if an entire population group has no historical voice, and if that group seems to have occupied no significant historical space, then it is very easy to relegate that group to the margins of a national and religious epic."[55] Without a doubt these new stories bring people to the forefront of history, but the issue is not merely about their visibility; it is also about transforming systems of thought and the theories of interpretation that codified them as objects in the first place.

To be sure, these new stories and histories are facilitated by the academic discourses of multiculturalism—but the latter should not be confused with what I am articulating here, for multicultural discourses are still sustained by capitalist-transnational powers. These discourses seek appreciation and openness to diversity, but leave unexamined the power relationships responsible for the constant oppression and marginalization of certain peoples. In this sense, the discourses of multiculturalism in the United States make people visible but the colonial imaginary remains un-changed/challenged—it is only from the

---

53. Emma Pérez, *Decolonial Imaginary*, xiii.

54. Ibid., 15.

55. Daisy Machado, "The Writing of Religious History in the United States: A Critical Assessment," in *Hispanic Christianity within Mainline Protestant Traditions: A Bibliography* (ed. P. Barton and D. Maldonado Jr.; Decatur, Ga.: Asociación para la Educación Teológica Hispana, 1998), 83.

borderlands and through imagination that we can dismantle it. In this sense it is not sufficient to talk about diversity and to refer to the history of Mexicans in the Southwestern United States or to open biblical interpretation to these same voices. It is not enough to create programs and courses that open the curriculum to diversity. It is not adequate to add a couple of books to the syllabus. It is not satisfactory to admit into our schools people from "minoritized" communities simply because of legal demands. While the multicultural agenda promotes diversity and plurality, the patterns of oppression, marginalization, and persecution continue.[56]

Left unexamined is the fact that the people who clean our tables and our bathrooms and fix our roofs are mostly people of color and that their working conditions are deplorable. The methodologies and theories, not to say the education and pedagogies in general, that we are developing in the schools in this country do not challenge the present conditions of global capitalism. We, students and scholars, have to move beyond the comfort zones to rename, remap, reclassify, and redefine the world in order to promote liberation and social justice. It is important to locate ourselves in the borderlands in order to build new methodologies and theories based on the experiences of struggle and hope, not based on visibility and "tokenism." We have to step away from the dominant ideologies that promote the "real" based on the "fictional."

In order to attain this location in the borderlands, however, we need first to acknowledge our physical location and our participation within the dominant academic circles. This first step is crucial; if we do not realize our involvement within that sphere of influence, we will participate in and reproduce the same ideology and methodology that silenced and covered people's voices in the first place. In this sense, we must recognize that our voice is not the voice of the subaltern. The subaltern voice is in constant action (often against us), speaking up against colonialism and oppression through social movements, art forms and other media. We are not the voice of the subaltern, since we do not speak for them. Rather, we are responsible for constructing an academic counterhegemonic discourse and culture through which the subaltern may acquire a discursive (academic) presence. We thus arrive at the borderlands when we not only agree to confront the system we are involved in, but also when we listen to the subaltern and engage in its attempts to resist

---

56. See Arturo J. Aldama, "Millennial Anxieties: Borders, Violence, and the Struggle for Chicana and Chicano Subjectivity," in *Decolonial Voices: Chicana and Chicano Cultural Studies in the 21st Century* (ed. A. J. Aldama and N. H. Quiñonez; Bloomington: Indiana University Press, 2002), 11–29.

silence, understanding our responsibility for the growth of a more equitable tomorrow. Instead of looking up to the dominant system and structures for answers, we need to look and search below, where struggle and hope reside. This shift is not the trivial practice of "identification with the poor," but rather the habit of engagement with subalterns in their projects through a different context—the discursive setting.[57]

Building New Modes of Interpretation, Breaking Down Old Ones

I began my argument with a call to imagination and I will finish it with the same call, because imagination can help us see beyond apparent changes in discourses, and realize that colonial practices are still operative, and the liberal discourse of multiculturalism is, today, a prime example of them. The discourses of "savagism" still dominate the understanding of the subaltern as colonizing cultures "attempt to regulate and contain subaltern subjects in static and oppressable modes of production."[58] In the field of biblical interpretation, it is important to acknowledge changes and new approaches, and yet writing and teaching have still not fully dismantled the "aura" of dominance established and sustained by Western epistemologies. In this case, then, "new" voices are heard, but the dominant paradigm remains unchanged. Actually, since the colonial paradigms and scaffolds are still operative, they take over difference and homogenize it. It is precisely in this context that imagination, in the sense I have argued for here, works as a postcolonizing tool.

This essential role of imagination urges the development and use of new methods of biblical interpretation, and I want to offer some suggestions for future work in this field in order to promote a postcolonizing agenda. As Rasiah S. Sugirtharajah clearly states, postcolonial criticism "challenges the context, contours and normal procedures of biblical scholarship." He continues by arguing that postcolonialism "enable[s] us to question the totalizing tendencies of European reading practices and interpret the text on our own terms and read them from our specific locations."[59] I agree with these statements, but I would add that in order to question established reading practices it is important to see beyond the

---

57. It is essential to mention and understand that history is produced outside of academia in the concrete activities of the subaltern. See Trouillot, *Silencing the Past*, 12–13.

58. Arturo J. Aldama, *Disrupting Savagism: Intersecting Chicana/o, Mexican Immigrant, and Native American Struggles for Self-Representation* (Durham: Duke University Press, 2001), 33.

59. Rasiah S. Sugirtharajah, "Biblical Studies after the Empire: From a Colonial to a Postcolonial Mode of Interpretation," in *The Postcolonial Bible*, (ed. R. S. Sugirtharajah; Bible and Postcolonialism 1; Sheffield: Sheffield Academic Press, 1998), 16.

present condition, and this can only be accomplished through transformative imagination as a counterhegemonic subversive practice. It is only then that actual practices as well as present conditions will change, as we challenge the content of colonial narratives, the way in which they are constructed, and the colonial imaginaries they create.

The constant search for new interpretations and new voices, which is clearly important, has also limited the analysis needed of the modes of interpretation and theories provided by the modern/colonial system—both the constructive and deconstructive task must thus work together in tandem. A thorough analysis would seek the deconstruction of theories and methods that have been used to exclude and oppress the subalterns of society by erasing their memory and subverting their imaginative power. Power is the basis for the construction of a colonial imaginary, which leaves the subaltern outside of the discourse. The deconstruction and decolonization of the scaffolds created space for the construction of a decolonial imaginary by providing the subaltern with a voice. If we continue to uncover voices and interpretations, but do not challenge traditional ways and methods of interpretation, we become agents of oppression and the recovered voices are reduced to a footnote (in our texts and our histories).

It is from the borderlands and through the process of imagination that we can construct new theories and methods that will help with the process of interpretation in the context of our own unique places. The way we, as people in the borderlands, do history, theology, sociology, biblical research, or other academic work is still considered particular and political. It is political, and it should continue to be such, because liberation and decolonization are political actions. In order to change the traditional narratives of biblical scholarship it is therefore important to challenge, through the use of a political and subversive agenda for liberation, those institutional practices that reproduce modernist epistemological values and aims. It is equally important to help free traditional views and methods from their presumption of universality, demonstrating, rather, their particularity. Fernando Segovia observes in this respect that "biblical criticism ... become[s] ... but another example of a much more comprehensive process of liberation and decolonization at work in a number of different realms—from political to the academic and, within the academy itself, across the entire disciplinary spectrum."[60] In order to be part of this process, it is important that we maintain a voice filled with life and imagination, and a discursive location in relationship to those

---

60. Fernando F. Segovia, "Biblical Criticism and Postcolonial Studies: Toward a Post-colonial Optic," in Sugirtharajah, *Postcolonial Bible*, 52–53.

who suffer in the borderlands of academic discourse and society in general. In this way, we can step away from modern epistemology and dis-cover a "borderish way of knowing," an epistemology brought out of the experience of oppression and colonization. It is not for the South (subaltern) to become the North (colonial power), but for us to develop open systems of knowledge based on justice.

It is also important to move into the borderlands in order to reconfigure the world through the creation of a decolonial imaginary. It is not a matter of speaking out until one's voice is incorporated into the dominant discourse (or, for that matter, until somehow it becomes a dominant discourse of its own). It is about speaking out and telling stories so we can build bridges in order to destroy the colonial imaginary that treats the subaltern as an object. Of course, this is not a task for one individual but for everyone who wants to confront the existing social order and the power of dominant colonial discourses. Imagination is what brings us together in the borderlands. Imagination is what moves us to re-take history from those in power. Imagination helps us to see that our differences are the essence of our struggle and not assimilation or homogenization. In other words, imagination makes it possible to construct not only counterhegemonic discourses but also the scaffold for a decolonial imaginary.

We cannot, therefore, let scientific approaches to history, biblical interpretation, and life/culture rob us of our stories and our collective memories. We cannot allow dominant discourses to write our histories and define our identities. We cannot let the colonial imaginary make sense of our words and our worlds. Let us speak out and live out (of) our imaginations. The colonial has already built its own imaginary that prohibits any other imagination from taking (up) space, so let us step out of that imaginary and get to the borderlands where there is oppression and death, but where there is also resistance and hope. In the borderlands, we are allowed to imagine a better world, which becomes the source for the reconfiguration of our respective academic fields.

This use of imagination against the colonial system comes from the future in order to build the present. Subcomandante Marcos expresses this conception eloquently in the following lines:

> In our dreams we have seen another world, an honest world, a world decidedly more fair than the one in which we now live. We saw that in this world there was no need for armies; peace, justice and liberty were so common that no one talked about them as far-off concepts, but as things such as bread, birds, air, water, like book and voice. This is how the good things were named in this world. And in this world there was reason and goodwill in the government, and the leaders were clear-thinking people; they ruled by obeying. This world was not a dream

from the past, it was not something that came to us from our ancestors. It came from ahead, from the next step we were going to take. And so we started to move forward to attain this dream, make it come and sit down at our tables, light our homes, grow in our cornfields, fill the hearts of our children, wipe our sweat, heal our history. And it was for all. This is what we want. Nothing more, nothing less.[61]

It is time to use our transformative imagination in all our scholarly endeavours and vocations. Let us move into the borderlands so we can find the hidden voices, the broken memories, and read "the little piece of paper" that becomes "an enormous burden, which frees the person who carries it. It is a work, a mission, a task, something to do, a path to walk, a tree to plant and nurture, a dream to look after."[62]

---

61. Subcomandante Marcos, *Our Word Is Our Weapon*, 18.
62. Ibid., 276.

POSTCOLONIALISM AND THE PRACTICE OF HISTORY

John W. Marshall

Over the last half-century the roles that race, class, and gender bias played in biblical scholarship have been exposed and, in a limited manner which demands further advancement, have received correction. The skeleton lying in the closet of so much study of early Christianity—anti-Judaism and anti-Semitism—has received similar productive attention.[1] In the last fifteen years, a trend in historical-critical and literary-critical practice has drawn another phenomenon to critical attention: colonialism. The movement that focuses on this element of human culture and scrutinizes its attendant effects on the history and practice of scholarship has taken the name *postcolonialism.* As part of the ongoing development of historical-critical investigation, I explore in this essay the role that postcolonial theory and historiography can play in investigations of early Christianity. The postcolonial movement is wide and diverse, so what is offered here is, admittedly, programmatically focused on a subset of postcolonial scholarship that addresses the reconstructive and analytical practices of history, which I will refer to as *historical-critical postcolonialism.*

Before facing the methodological issues that allow traditional historical-critical and contemporary postcolonial methodologies to intermingle, let me articulate two questions that will form micro-case studies for the following methodological discussion, since examples are the arena in which methodology proves its worth. First, within the first-person narrative that the larger martyrdom of Perpetua and Felicitas contains, Vibia Perpetua has absolutely nothing to say about Felicitas, her co-martyr, co-mother, and co-namesake of the larger martyrdom narrative that binds the women

---

1. Samuel Sandmel, *Anti-Semitism in the New Testament?*(Philadelphia: Fortress, 1978); John G. Gager, *The Origins of Anti-Semitism: Attitudes Toward Judaism in Pagan and Christian Antiquity* (Oxford: Oxford University Press, 1983); Peter Richardson and David Granskow, eds., *Anti-Judaism in Early Christianity* (2 vols. Waterloo, Ont.: Wilfrid Laurier University Press, 1986); Peter Schäfer, *Judeophobia: Attitudes toward the Jews in the Ancient World* (Cambridge, Mass.: Harvard University Press, 1997); and Shawn Kelley, *Racializing Jesus: Race, Ideology, and the Formation of Modern Biblical Scholarship* (Biblical Limits; London: Routledge, 2002).

together in historical memory; why would that be? That is to say, under what conditions is it explicable? Question two: in the apocryphal Acts of the Apostles, what wider literary and sociocultural program encompasses the well-known phenomenon of the apostles effectively seducing upper-class women into chaste devotion to the Christian God? These two questions address the more general issue of the intersection of gender and class in these narratives. Let these two questions hang in the air, so to speak, suspended only on the broad hint provided so far that postcolonial theory can influence historical-critical practice and so sharpen and improve on the answers currently available in historical-critical readings of these texts. Before addressing the questions directly, however, it is necessary to gain a sense of the varieties of viable approaches within postcolonial criticism that can be partnered with historical-critical modes of analysis.

METHODOLOGICAL ISSUES

Rasiah Sugirtharajah, Fernando Segovia, and Musa Dube, among others, have pioneered the integration of the wide and established movement of postcolonial studies into the practice of biblical criticism.[2] Much of what I have to say here is clearly indebted to these scholars and could not be proffered without standing on their shoulders. I want, however, to focus attention more narrowly than is usually done in order to understand ways in which historical-critical studies of the development of Christianity can benefit from contemporary postcolonial study, but also make the strategic choice to stand apart from some of the issues that occupy most postcolonial critics.

S. G. F. Brandon, writing in the middle of the twentieth century from the heart of the recently contracted British Empire, sets the scene well. Frantz Fanon had already penned *Black Skin, White Masks* and *The Wretched of the Earth* (though the latter was not yet available in English), and Alfred Memmi had written *The Colonizer and the Colonized*, when, in 1967, Brandon, the former British army chaplain, suggested that antipathy toward the Zealots of 66–70 C.E. came naturally to "those troubled by revolutionaries, whether Russian, Irish, or Indian, who threatened the Western capitalist society or British rule." Brandon went on to note that "the Second World War has, however, apparently wrought a change of

---

2. Rasiah S. Sugirtharajah, *The Bible and the Third World: Precolonial, Colonial and Postcolonial Encounters* (Cambridge: Cambridge University Press, 2001); idem, *Postcolonial Criticism and Biblical Interpretation* (Oxford: Oxford University Press, 2002); Fernando F. Segovia, *Decolonizing Biblical Studies: A View from the Margins* (Maryknoll, N.Y.: Orbis, 2000); and Musa W. Dube, *Postcolonial Feminist Interpretation of the Bible* (St. Louis: Chalice, 2000).

sentiment: the administration and encouragement given to 'resistance' groups in various Nazi-occupied lands seem to have stirred a new and sympathetic interest in the Zealots."[3] Not likely directly indebted to the canonical precursors just noted, Brandon here hints at a principle that would occupy a central place in postcolonial theory. Brandon saw how contemporary structures of domination and hegemony condition scholarly attitudes in the study of specific political and social circumstances of antiquity. When immersed in a society that maintains an empire, in Brandon's case the British Empire, scholars are habituated to suspicion of subaltern resistance movements. When scholars are formed in a context of resistance to empire, in this case Britain's close affiliation with resistance to the short-lived German Empire in continental Europe, they are apt to gain greater understanding of the pervasive pressures that are crucial to the character of subaltern movements and cultures. Brandon's formulation is postcolonial in two senses: chronologically, he has seen the apex of the British Empire pass away in the maelstrom of the Second World War, and methodologically he has entered, if only fleetingly, a postcolonial mental space in the recognition that the mindset of empire has hindered historical-critical investigation. He goes on to name the utter centrality of the Roman *imperium* to the social, religious, and material context for Jesus of Nazareth. It is no revelation that Jesus lived and died on the margins of a great empire, but with the advent of postcolonial studies scholars are in a position to realize the import of this common insight through dialogue with a rich body of theory and comparative material from which we can benefit and to which we can contribute.

How then can Brandon's comment lead into a methodologically reflective integration of postcolonialism and historical criticism? Three insights are important here. First, it is necessary to recognize as a programmatic principle that colonial domination is not a given or natural state for human relations. Second, we must realize that colonization conditions particular circumstances as extensively and decisively as the objects of other analyses do; it operates as pervasively as race, as powerfully as gender, as persistently as class. That is to say that the effects of colonization and imperial domination are woven inextricably into the circumstances and texts that are the objects of our study. Third is the acknowledgment that an untenable naturalizing of colonial domination has deeply conditioned the history of investigation of early Christianity. In order to work out the implications of these foundational insights for the historical-critical study of early Christianity, I propose first to treat

---

3. S. G. F. Brandon, *Jesus and the Zealots: A Study of the Political Factor in Primitive Christianity* (New York: Scribners, 1967), 24.

several issues that are customarily prominent in postcolonial studies but programmatically pushed out of the foreground in the vision of historical-critical postcolonialism that I am striving to articulate here; and, second, to examine briefly two texts that will showcase the relevance of historical-critical postcolonialism for the study of women in early Christianity. Finally, I want to provide a summary sketch of the character and task of a historical-critical postcolonialism as I see it.

Representation and Advocacy

The first issue under consideration is that much of contemporary postcolonial scholarship is engaged in a renegotiation of rights of representation.[4] In the biblical field, Segovia, Sugirtharajah, and Dube all give prominence, and perhaps preeminence, to the task of representing the readings of non-Western, nonacademic, and nonbourgeois interpreters. This endeavor of representation reaches its apex in the generalized task of representing the subaltern.[5] For John Beverley, the central focus of subaltern studies is the power and problem of representation and the task of subaltern studies is the dismantling of subalternity itself.[6] More notoriously, one finds a negative theology of the oppressed (in which a cloud of unknowing ever separates the academic researcher from the subaltern subject) in Gayatri Chakravorty Spivak's declaration that the subaltern cannot speak, or transact speech, without ceasing to be subaltern.[7] As theoretically productive and methodologically salutary such cautions may be, the most common understanding of the question implied by Spivak and asked by Beverley might be formulated thus: Who speaks for the subaltern? For a historical-critical postcolonialism, the difficulty of this already insoluble question is compounded by the complexity of any contemporary claim to "own" the primary texts of,

---

4. Chinua Achebe's *Home and Exile,* for instance, is essentially a tale of a struggle for African narrative sovereignty in the face of centuries of colonial control of the representation of Africa. On this specific theme, see Dorothy Hammond and Alta Jablow, *The Africa That Never Was: Four Centuries of British Writing about Africa* (New York: Twayne, 1970).

5. See Gayatri Chakravorty Spivak, "Can the Subaltern Speak?" in *Colonial Discourse and Postcolonial Theory: A Reader* (ed. P. Williams and L. Chrisman; New York: Harvester Wheatsheaf, 1993), 66–111.

6. John R. Beverley, *Subalternity and Representation: Arguments in Cultural Theory* (Postcontemporary Interventions; Durham: Duke University Press, 1999), 1, 166.

7. Spivak, "Can the Subaltern Speak?" Also see Spivak's comments on this essay in *The Spivak Reader: Selected Works of Gayatri Chakravorty Spivak* (ed. D. Landry and G. M. MacLean; New York: Routledge, 1996), 286–305. Cf. Ania Loomba, *Colonialism/Postcolonialism* (The New Critical Idiom; London: Routledge, 1998), 231–44.

for instance, the second century—no one can speak for the apologists or the Valentinians or the Marcionites from the position of an autochthonous insider; no historically or critically credible claims to do so are forthcoming. The pursuit of legitimate representation in the study of antiquity consists largely of dead-ends and dubious claims of simple continuity. But even if such claims could be credibly made, the study of religion as a discipline does not, in principle, give way to insider interpretive claims as having final legitimacy within its discourse. Solutions that have some credibility in an advocacy-driven postcolonialism—such as, for example, replacing a hermeneutics of authority with one of popular reception[8]—often constitute an abandonment of the historical-critical enterprise itself.

The priority of concern with the redistribution of the right and power to represent also tends to infuse some postcolonialisms with identity politics that, by implication or declaration, circumscribe the legitimate practice of postcolonial criticism. Sugirtharajah understands postcolonial criticism as claiming to represent minority voices.[9] Such a claim coincides with a "definition" of postcolonial criticism that first of all locates the practitioners as former colonized peoples.[10] Though the role of identity in historical-critical endeavors merits constant scrutiny, rights to historical-critical postcolonial criticism do not flow from identities. In the study of religion—where our approach to our subject matter is already programmatically oblique to the questions that our data actively raise—we must be able, when we choose, to free ourselves from the idea that our postcolonialism needs to have direct application outside the academy.

---

8. See Beverley, *Subalternity and Representation,* 183.

9. Sugirtharajah, *Bible and the Third World,* 244.

10. Ibid., 246–47: "I define postcolonial criticism as a textual and praxiological practice initially undertaken by people who were once part of the British, European, and American Empires, but now have some sort of territorial freedom while continuing to live with the burdens from the past and enduring newer forms of economic and cultural neo-colonialism. It was also undertaken by ethnic minorities who live in diaspora, namely British blacks and British Asians in England and racial minorities in the United States and Canada—African Americans, Native Americans, Hispanic Americans, and Asian Americans—who had been victims of old imperialism, who are now current victims of globalization and who have been continually kept away from and represented by the dominant first world elements" (but cf. pp. 269–70).

Scope and Modernity

The second issue that arises relates to the scope of postcolonial analysis, especially in connection to the overwhelming preoccupation with contemporary politics that characterizes some forms of postcolonial inquiry. There may be several reasons why studies of biblical texts and of ancient empires have not been prominent in the growth of postcolonial studies, but the most basic one is the confusion of origins and essence[11] that has plagued the study of religion in so many ways and also interferes with the understanding of the scope of the postcolonial endeavor. While modern and early modern empires undoubtedly provided the context for the literary fiction in which the impulses of postcolonial analysis first arose[12] and to which the initial theoretical apparatus was applied, it should be clear that the narrative of the birth of postcolonial analysis does not set the limit on the theory's application. Of course, particular features of modern imperial domination may not be easily mapped onto every other era. Nevertheless, the analytical task before us is to construct working definitions of the most basic apparatuses—colony, empire, imperialism—and to track their applicability across periods and areas of study. Some such basic definitional attempts are made in several contemporary works on postcolonialism,[13] and it is by no means clear that those sketches of the field effectively stamp "Best after 1492" on the postcolonial analytical framework.

Such an examination of the scope of a postcolonial analytical framework is already taking place in several disciplines. Supported by the continuous contact of Christian and Muslim Empires through the Middle Ages, and by Edward Said's foundational attention to the dynamics of that encounter,[14] medievalists are thinking through the implications of postcolonial analysis for their field.[15] Likewise, in classical studies examination of the dynamics of empire and the relationship of colonizer to colonized has been tempered by a turn to the thinkers and theorists of postcolonialism.[16] Marc Ferro's history of colonization is overwhelmingly focused on the early modern and modern European

---

11. These terms come from Jacques Derrida, *Of Grammatology* (trans. G. C. Spivak; Baltimore: Johns Hopkins University Press, 1974), 74.

12. Sugirtharajah, *Bible and the Third World*, 272.

13. See, e.g., Bill Ashcroft, Gareth Griffiths and Helen Tiffin, eds., *Key Concepts in Post-Colonial Studies* (London: Routledge, 1998).

14. Edward W. Said, *Orientalism* (New York: Pantheon, 1978).

15. See J. J. Cohen, ed., *The Postcolonial Middle Ages* (The New Middle Ages; New York: St. Martin's, 2000).

16. See Clifford Ando, *Imperial Ideology and Provincial Loyalty in the Roman Empire* (Classics and Contemporary Thought 6; Berkeley and Los Angeles: University of California Press, 2000).

empires, but it starts with a guilty admission that a history of colonization could also start with Russian trading colonies in central Asia,
Venetian and Genoan outposts on the Black Sea, the succession of
Islamic Empires, the Crusades and the crusader states, or any of the
ancient empires of Greece and Rome.[17]

In their programmatic introduction to a volume of essays on postcolonialism and medieval studies, Ingham and Warren make the telling
point that by chronologically restricting the applicability of postcolonial
insight to the modern period, postcolonial theorists treat "colonial
'modernity' as a fact of history rather than an ideology of colonialism."[18]
In its reification of modernity, postcolonial studies fails to live up to its
own mandate, and here the study of the origins of Christianity stands to
make a key contribution as a discipline. Jeremy Cohen suggests that
medieval studies can participate in postcolonial analyses by "undermining
contemporary discourses of origin, arguing against the transhistoricity of
normative liberal discourses of unified subjectivity, and cautioning
against myths of purity and wholeness."[19] It should be clear from an
observation like this just how vibrant the potential contribution of the
study of early Christianity to such a body of theory could be.

Universality and Meta-narrative

In the third place I want to refashion Ingham and Warren's insight
concerning the uncritical acceptance of the western meta-narrative of
modernity. The new context I have in mind is the array of Christian meta-
narratives that have often characterized postcolonial interpretations of
early Christianity. The acceptance of the meta-narrative of canonicity
shows up in the selection of documents interpreted—they are overwhelmingly canonical and thus the product of exactly the sort of
hegemonic process that postcolonial critics try to avoid reproducing in
their own work. Segovia may programmatically present a "view from the
margins,"[20] but his work just as resolutely contains its view to the center
(his published work, for instance, focuses on methodology, Hispanic
identity, and Johannine research). The same is the case with Sugirtharajah
and Dube, for, while both speak of broadening the canon, one strives in
vain to watch them do so in the range of ancient documents they actually

---

17. Marc Ferro, *Colonization: A Global History* (London: Routledge, 1997), 1–3.
18. Patricia Clare Ingham and Michelle R. Warren, *Postcolonial Moves: Medieval through Modern* (New York: Palgrave Macmillan, 2003), 2.
19. Cohen, *Postcolonial Middle Ages*, 17 n. 25.
20. Cf. Segovia, *Decolonizing Biblical Studies*, 91.

treat. By reproducing the centrality of canon in the study of ancient texts and traditions such scholarship inevitably allies itself with the kyriarchal processes that facilitated the formation of the canon in the first place.

The canonical meta-narrative also has a twin: the meta-narrative of coherence. Treating the Bible as a unity not only implies a coherence, but usually also maintains a claim that the coherence lies within the set of documents rather than proceeds from readerly activity. This dimension of the Christian meta-narrative shows up in synthetic treatments of the biblical text or the expectation of a unified "biblical voice."[21] The historically necessary task of treating the Bible as it functioned in history—often as a unified entity deployed by or against or within a colonial apparatus—can easily be essentialized into a disposition taken toward the text that reproduces the conditions under which the Bible was deployed in the colonial endeavor.

The third Christian meta-narrative that too often characterizes postcolonial critiques in the study of early Christianity is the overly linear account of development. The most common form of this is a progress from the Hebrew Bible to the New Testament to the Reformation and finally arriving at the modern colonial endeavor.[22] This line of four points skips over huge movements in Judaism and Christianity and actually buttresses the edifice that so many postcolonial critics seek to undermine. While postcolonial critics have rightly criticized the teleology of the history of empire, they have also reified the same movement in the history of Christianity. Such a reification drags in its wake the host of the negative effects in the history of Jewish-Christian relations that the narrative of linear progress has facilitated. Thus, although these three meta-narratives—canonicity, coherence, and progression—are untenable from a historical-critical point of view, they may have strategic value in other parts of the postcolonial project, especially with respect to redressing the politics of legitimate confessional interpretation and application of the authoritative textual resource. Bill Ashcroft has remarked that "history is a method rather than a truth." In light of that statement, then, when we seek to integrate postcolonial insight with historical-critical method, we are thus unabashedly specifying and narrowing postcolonial studies, but with the hope that the transformation of historical-critical studies will intensify its own analytical, explanatory, and descriptive powers.[23]

---

21. Dube, *Postcolonial Feminist Interpretation*, 9, 16, 17.
22. See, e.g., ibid., 13–14.
23. Bill Ashcroft, *Post-colonial Transformation* (London: Routledge, 2001), 86.

Moreover, these meta-narratives of Christianity detailed here are further compromised by their resemblance to Ashcroft's description of "the ideology of imperial history: sequentiality, inevitability, purpose, authority; a teleology that is divinely ordained."[24] It is at this juncture that the historical-critical and postcolonial imperatives coincide. The implication of such a coincidence of imperatives is the homology of religion and empire. At least in the case of religions spanning multiple cultural-linguistic groups and multiple political entities—Christianity is in focus here, but the insight may apply to other "world" religions—the intertwined history of religions and empires suggests that the counter-imperial movement of postcolonial studies stands in tension with the project of advocacy *within* Christianity. Retreat from the embrace of these three meta-narratives—which amount to containment, synthesis, and teleology—is most feasible, then, when the tasks of direct advocacy and quasi-subaltern representation leave the foreground.

CASE SKETCHES: PERPETUA, FELICITAS, AND THECLA

With the intention to be illustrative rather than fully analytical, and to be brief, rather than exhaustive, I return to those two questions posed at the beginning of the essay and examine how the historical-critical postcolonialism I have tried to sketch can address those questions: one—why does Felicitas vanish when Perpetua writes? And two—what context can explain the prominent trope of seduction for the Lord in the apocryphal Acts of the Apostles? The latter question I want to narrow down in asking what draws together the two key features of the seduction motif, namely gender (male apostles attracting women followers) and class (almost invariably the women drawn to the apostolic preaching come from the top echelons of Greco-Roman society).

Martyr Acts: Slavery and Ethnicity

Turning to the martyrdom of Perpetua and Felicitas, let me first reiterate the problem: The dominant scholarly consensus is that the text consists of several portions, one being an original first-person vision-filled account of the imprisonment, which proceeds from the pen of Vibia Perpetua herself. Around this text an initial editor wrapped brief introductory and connecting material. Subsequently, the dream vision of Saturnus was appended and, later still, the account of the martyrdom of the group was added. The latter redaction juxtaposed the two women and at the same

---

24. Ibid.

time occluded much of the agency that is so prominent in Perpetua's own writing.[25] To tease apart the dynamics of slavery in the ancient world,[26] let me turn to Spivak's essay "Three Women's Texts and a Critique of Imperialism,"[27] in which she offers a reading of *Jane Eyre, Wide Sargasso Sea,* and *Frankenstein,* focusing substantially on the role of Bertha Mason as Jane's counterpoint across lines of class and colonial position. Spivak argues that the process of identity formation that occurs in *Jane Eyre* is dependent on the reduction of the colonial other and that the formation of subjectivity itself in Jane Austin's context was conditioned by colonialism and empire.[28] Perpetua, for her part, writes an intensely relational text focusing on her father and brothers, mentioning by name fellow martyr Saturnus and the deacons Pomponius and Tertius. Felicitas, the slave and other woman in the group, who, according to the narrative, gave birth in prison and would share so many of the concerns that Perpetua foregrounds in her discussions of the fate of her own infant son, is not mentioned at all.

The position of the slave in the Roman family was often one of deep intimacy and affection coupled with radical subjugation and inferiority in the same family. Understandings of slaves and slavery spanned a contradictory continuum from Varro's characterization of a slave as "a speaking instrument" to an understanding of the slave as a confidante, so intimate as to form an aspect of the master's self (*Rerum Rusticarum de Agri Cultura* 1.17.1).[29] This density of interaction with slaves might facilitate affective bonds that are brought to the fore in certain circumstances, but such a density also means that the slave cannot easily be attended to as genuinely and independently other. Both ends of the continuum imply a dissolution of the slave's subjectivity from the master's point of view. This characterization is, of course, oriented to the position of the house-

---

25. See Brent D. Shaw, "The Passion of Perpetua," *Past and Present* 139 (1993): 21–22.

26. Especially useful is William Fitzgerald, *Slavery and the Roman Literary Imagination* (Roman Literature and Its Contexts; Cambridge: Cambridge University Press, 2000); Keith R. Bradley, *Slavery and Rebellion in the Roman World, 140 B.C.-70 B.C.* (Bloomington: Indiana University Press, 1989); idem, *Slaves and Masters in the Roman Empire: A Study in Social Control* (Collection Latomus 185; Brussels: Latomus, 1984), and Keith Hopkins, *Conquerors and Slaves* (Sociological Studies in Roman History 1; Cambridge: Cambridge University Press, 1978).

27. Gayatri Chakravorty Spivak, "Three Women's Texts and a Critique of Imperialism," *Critical Inquiry* 12 (1985): 243–61.

28. See criticisms of Spivak's reading in Loomba, *Colonialism/Postcolonialism,* 82–83.

29. Fitzgerald, *Slavery,* 11–14. Fitzgerald brilliantly maps the range, contradiction, and ambiguities of life with slaves, but his sources are necessarily all male writers. This circumstance introduces an additional measure of uncertainty into an effort to read the relationship of Perpetua and Felicitas. Women in the household had a wide range of relationships to slaves and the *paterfamilias,* which could range from cooperation and intimacy to competition and scapegoating and more.

hold slave in terms of a density of interaction, but the continuum from tool to aspect of self would apply to more than the household. This is the condition of ancient slaves, so present in their utility as often to be invisible in their subjectivity. As Perpetua comes into her own and makes the transition from daughter to lady, *filia* to *domina*,[30] Felicitas has disappeared much like Jane Eyre's Bertha Mason.

The most basic circumstances of the martyrdom of Perpetua and Felicitas, inscribed throughout the narrative in characters (jailers, procurators), places (town hall, amphitheatre), and time (Caesar's birthday), highlight the omission of Felicitas that Brent Shaw describes simply as "puzzling."[31] But perhaps Perpetua's action in ignoring Felicitas in her own account of identity formation is no surprise when the dynamics of colonial rule, including the social hierarchy of the settler/colony and its attendant unfree labour, are placed at the center of analysis. The narrative focuses on the status she gains in her relation to male authority figures, her father and brother,[32] and in the display of her "special patronal relationship with her Lord"[33] attested in the civic space. Similar dynamics show up in the transgendering vision in which Perpetua changes into a male fighter and enters into combat with a "certain Egyptian, horrible in appearance," who turns out to be the Devil and the Empire.[34] Attention to the colonial context of the account of Perpetua thus draws together the narrative's treatment of class and gender.

The Apostolic Acts: Portals of Colonization[35]

With the advent of feminist analyses, the apocryphal Acts of the Apostles gained notoriety as texts that foregrounded ways in which some

---

30. Shaw, *Passion of Perpetua*, 6–7.

31. Ibid., 25. Shaw suggests that Felicitas is omitted due to Perpetua's "diary-like concentration on herself," but this position ignores the room her "diary" made for so many significant others in her life and experience apart from Felicitas. Shaw's tenuously offered explanation does not address this oddity.

32. Ibid., 6–7.

33. Ibid., 7.

34. The slurs against Egyptians were proverbial in the empire. Combat with the Egyptian in Perpetua's vision claims her status within the imperial context and simultaneously criticizes that same context. On the one hand, her slur of the Egyptian positions her as a right-thinking settler in a colonial empire. On the other hand, the interpretation of that scene contained within her vision allegorizes the imperial apparatus as the Egyptian that Perpetua will conquer. In both of these instances, the attention to colonial Empire enables us to see how a historical-critical postcolonialism can work to coordinate concerns of gender, ethnicity, and class in the ancient contexts we study.

35. By the phrase "Apostolic Acts," I mean to refer both to the canonical Acts of the Apostles and to the noncanonical "Apocryphal Acts."

forms of Christianity provided space for women's agency within the undoubtedly patriarchal world of antiquity. The title of Virginia Burrus's volume, *Chastity as Autonomy*, aptly captures the spirit of those early feminist investigations.[36] Subsequent feminist analyses, including Burrus's own, have tempered what may have been an overly celebratory picture. Still, I would argue that a postcolonial analysis has an important contribution to make in the analysis of gender in the Apostolic Acts.[37]

For my purposes here, I note that the emblematic romance between colonizing man and colonized woman is a clear trope of the narratives of colonization. In its strongest form, the female partner, or property, of the leading male of the colonized people is won over by the leading male of the colonizers, symbolizing or enacting the transfer of prized property. The hierarchy of gender within which the man is customarily cast symbolizes the hierarchy of colonization itself, and marriage becomes a metaphor for the colonial relationship. Wittingly or not, the emblematic romance also hints at the hybridity engendered in cultural colonial contact. Alexander's generals and their relationships with the princesses of Persia form an ancient historical reminiscence of this motif (cf. Arrian of Nicomedia, *Anabasis*, 7.4.4–5.6). In the literary realm, Aeneas's seduction of Dido puts the motif to work in Virgil's piece of imperial propaganda.[38] The examples of Cortez's mistress Marina[39] and of Pocahontas[40] bring the motif into the modern world.

The relationship of the Apostolic Acts to the motif of emblematic romance in which women are portals of colonization is quite complex and entails several illuminating inversions. In many of these texts, the women are "seduced" to chastity, but the texts take great delight in alluding to the intense sexuality that the seduction scenes conventionally entail. While a quick sketch must stand in for more extensive analyses, the following is noteworthy: Paul draws Thecla from engagement to the powerful Thamyris (*Acts of Paul* 7–19); Peter causes a tumult in Rome by enticing all four concubines from Agrippa, the prefect of Rome, and

---

36. Virginia Burrus, *Chastity as Autonomy: Women in the Stories of the Apocryphal Acts* (Studies in Women and Religion 23; Lewiston, N.Y.: Mellen, 1987).

37. Here I am indebted to Musa Dube's treatment of Rahab. See Dube, *Postcolonial Feminist Interpretation*, 73–83.

38. Ibid., 81–82.

39. René Maunier, *The Sociology of Colonies: An Introduction to the Study of Race Contact* (trans. E. O. Lorimer; International Library of Sociology and Social Reconstruction; London: Routledge & Kegan Paul, 1949), 70.

40. See David Price, *Love and Hate in Jamestown: John Smith, Pocahontas, and the Heart of a New Nation* (New York: Knopf, 2003); and Ann Uhry Abrams, *The Pilgrims and Pocahontas: Rival Myths of American Origin* (Boulder, Colo.: Westview, 1999).

Xanthippe from Albinus, the friend of Caesar (*Acts of Peter* 33 [4], 34 [5]); John convinces Drusiana to abstain from sexual relations with her husband Andronicus, the Praetor (*Acts of John* 63–86); and Thomas hijacks the bridal chamber of the daughter of King Gundaphorus at the moment of consummation and seduces Mygdonia away from Charisius, the friend of King Misdaeus of India (*Acts of Thomas* 11–14, 82–106).

All these texts consistently foreground the sexual tension that proceeds from their inversion of the role or mode of sexual liaison in the apostle's embassy. Mygdonia's representation of the situation to her husband, who, according to a minor character, is "a hard man" who will not long tolerate his wife's zealous continence, emphasizes the role of Jesus as the new man in her life, replacing her husband (*Acts of Thomas* 93–98). Likewise, the daughter of King Gundaphorus makes it clear that she has abandoned her short-term husband for a real man (*Acts of Thomas* 14). This sort of play with the sexual dynamics of the situation effectively associates the Apostolic Acts with the traditional understanding of women as portals of colonial contact rather than distancing them from it.

There is also a political class reversal operative in these texts. Christianity remains a minority religious movement in both the narrative setting of the Acts and almost certainly in the historical circumstance of their composition. Though interpreters have long noticed the role of class and gender in the Apostolic Acts, the motif of seducing upper-class women away from their husbands and marriage beds to chastity for the Lord and faithfulness to his apostles operates not only in the realms of gender and class, but most clearly also as a trope of evangelism modeled narratively on clichés of the means by which one group of people is made subject to another—whether Persians to Macedonians or Gentiles to Christ and his ambassadors. Postcolonialism provides the theoretical apparatus that draws gender and class analyses together in a coherent manner in these settings. Further, postcolonialism helps us appreciate better how ancient understandings of group-over-group dominance (notably imperial domination) were formed in interaction with conceptions of person-over-person dominance (notably gender, sexual relations, and marriage in particular).

CONCLUSION: PROGRAMMATIC CONTRIBUTIONS

These two examples, treated with scandalous brevity, nevertheless point to the way in which postcolonial insights can transform historical-critical investigation. The undoing of mastery (over tools) happens on two axes: first, and preeminently, the axis of colonizer and colonized rises to visibility above the assumptions of normalcy that too often occlude it; second, and in relation to the specific concern of this volume, the focus on colonial context enables an understanding of women in the ancient world that complicates a patriarchal/proto-feminist binary under which one might read the texts. Further, stepping back from the examples for a moment, let me suggest ways in which postcolonial studies can help us theorize movements that already exist in the study of early Christianity and Second Temple Judaism and ways in which we can undertake our work. I am convinced that a historical-critical study of early Christianity and Second Temple Judaism has several elements in it that are acting on a postcolonial insight—like Brandon's—even if they are not in explicit dialogue with postcolonial theory. For example, postcolonialism provides a helpful methodological framework for the endeavors of Richard Horsley in his attention to bandit groups,[41] for Jonathan Z. Smith in his understanding of apocalyptic literature as a response to a loss of native kingship,[42] for Seth Schwartz in his focus on the effects of imperialism in the formation of Judaism in the common era,[43] for Brent Shaw in his attempts to assess violence in the empire without adopting an implicitly Roman view on the data,[44] and for Elisabeth Schüssler Fiorenza in her efforts to relate the phenomenon of patriarchy in the ancient world to other forms of domination.[45] Horsley and Schüssler Fiorenza have already acted on these possibilities and opened up a dialogue with postcolonial theorists and critics. More than most historical disciplines, the study of early Christianity and Second Temple Judaism has expended massive resources on the recovery of subaltern knowledge, movements, texts, and lives. The fact that this is mainly due to the distinctly uncommon transition made by Christianity from subaltern to dominating force has often adversely affected our work, but our successes have still been

41. Richard A. Horsley and John S. Hanson, *Bandits, Prophets, and Messiahs: Popular Movements in the Time of Jesus* (Minneapolis: Fortress, 1985); and Richard A. Horsley, *Jesus and the Spiral of Violence: Popular Jewish Resistance in Roman Palestine* (San Francisco: Harper & Row, 1987).

42. Jonathan Z. Smith, "Wisdom and Apocalyptic," in *Map Is Not Territory: Studies in the History of Religions* (SJLA 23; Leiden: Brill, 1978; repr., Chicago: University of Chicago Press, 1993), 67–87.

43. Seth Schwartz, *Imperialism and Jewish Society: 200 B.C.E. to 640 C.E.* (Jews, Christians, and Muslims from the Ancient to the Modern World; Princeton: Princeton University Press, 2001).

44. Brent D. Shaw, "War and Violence," in *Interpreting Late Antiquity: Essays on the Postclassical World* (ed. G. W. Bowersock, P. R. Lamont Brown, and O. Grabar; Cambridge, Mass.: Harvard University Press, 2001), 130–69.

45. Within Elisabeth Schüssler Fiorenza's substantial oeuvre, see especially *Rhetoric and Ethic: The Politics of Biblical Studies* (Minneapolis: Fortress, 1999); and idem, *Jesus and the Politics of Interpretation* (New York: Continuum, 2000).

impressive. And in dialogue with theorists of postcolonialism, I am convinced we have much (more) to contribute.

Finally, let me outline programmatically a set of principles that have helped me clarify what I mean by a historical-critical postcolonialism and that may facilitate further discussion:

1. In a historical-critical postcolonialism, the concern with ancient empire would not be subordinate to a concern with modern empire.
2. The implied reader of a historical-critical postcolonialism would not be outside the academy, but within it in its changes, its multiculturalism, its transconfessional methodology. This context is not static but is constantly evolving for a host of reasons, including cultural and political.
3. In its treatment and selection of evidence, a historical-critical postcolonialism would stand outside of confessional/canonical boundaries.
4. In its effort to situate the particularity of formative Christianity or late Second Temple Judaism within a larger historical context, a historical-critical postcolonialism would be skeptical of confessional meta-narratives.
5. With consciousness of the social construction and deployment of racial categories, a historical-critical postcolonialism would orient itself to a different map of ethnicities than the one obtained in the modern and contemporary periods. In its history of scholarship, however, a historical-critical postcolonialism must attend to the way in which racialized and colonialized discourses impinge on our discipline's reading of its evidences, the formulation of its guiding questions, and its own self-understanding.[46]
6. A historical-critical postcolonialism would name its readings as local within the academy rather than present them as universal in human society.

The general nature of what I have offered here is not a prescription for what a postcolonial approach to the Bible ought to be. The diversity of postcolonial approaches is well recognized, as is the strength that lies in this diversity. Segovia and Sugirtharajah have been particularly generous in two refusals. Both refuse to universalize postcolonialism as the only valid methodological stance, and both refuse to homogenize postcolonialism. Within the space created by their work, there is ample room

---

46. See Kelley, *Racializing Jesus*.

to think out the character of a historical-critical postcolonialism. Even if the costs of a historical-critical postcolonialism will be the temporary and local occlusion of some types of knowledges, or the limitation of some rationalities that are not able to claim space in an essentially post-Enlightenment discourse, the benefit of a historical-critical stance that produces an account of "other" humans—preserving a substantial measure of their particularity—will make the endeavor worthwhile. The methodological elaboration of historical-critical method seeks to halt the tendency to remake the past in our own image. Historical criticism attempts to circumscribe a forum for intersubjective discussions—which, in the study of religion, is crucially important—and this forum, in turn, creates a discourse that is not bound to a particular confessional context. Such a claim needs to be distinguished sharply from any claim to a universal context of discourse (principle six above is crucial in this respect). More than any discourse on ancient religion, historical-critical work provides materials that can anchor a critique of current practices in the field. It is the methodological rigor with which historical criticism ideally operates that gives it the ability to make its account of otherness convincing and human. The master's house is being dismantled from several sides and the master's tools are constantly being redeployed. Although feminist and postcolonial efforts of dismantling have not always been complimentary,[47] historical-critical work on the ancient world can be a particularly fertile site for methodological cooperation.

---

47. See Leela Gandhi, *Postcolonial Theory: A Critical Introduction* (New York: Columbia University Press, 1998), 81–101.

THE RHETORICAL FULL-TURN IN BIBLICAL INTERPRETATION AND ITS RELEVANCE FOR FEMINIST HERMENEUTICS*

Vernon K. Robbins

In her address at the Rhetoric and Religion Conference held at the University of South Africa, Pretoria (August, 1994), Elisabeth Schüssler Fiorenza asserted that those who have reintroduced rhetoric into biblical interpretation during the last quarter of a century have "become stuck in a rhetorical half-turn."[1] Recently, her essay has been republished in *Rhetoric and Ethic: The Politics of Biblical Studies.*[2] Her assertion is that in the context of the revival of rhetorical criticism "biblical scholarship has not yet made the full epistemological turn to a rhetoric of inquiry insofar as it has barely recognized the contributions which feminist and liberationist scholarship have made to the New Rhetoric."[3]

Schüssler Fiorenza proposes both a rationale and a justification for the rationale in order to explain the situation. The reason rhetorical biblical scholarship has not incorporated feminist and liberationist scholarship,

---

* This essay is a substantially reconfigured version of one that was presented at the 1998 Florence Rhetoric Conference and that appeared in print in 2002 (Vernon K. Robbins, "The Rhetorical Full-Turn in Biblical Interpretation: Reconfiguring Rhetorical-Political Analysis," in *Rhetorical Criticism and the Bible: Essays from the 1998 Florence Conference* [ed. S. E. Porter and D. L. Stamps; JSNTSup 195; London: Sheffield Academic Press, 2002], 48–60). It describes my sense of what a rhetorical full-turn in feminist interpretation might look like. The essay invokes Elisabeth Schüssler Fiorenza as a discussion partner, since she contrasted a rhetorical full-turn with a rhetorical half-turn in an earlier treatment of sociorhetorical interpretation (Elisabeth Schüssler Fiorenza, "Challenging the Rhetorical Half-Turn: Feminist and Rhetorical Biblical Criticism," in *Rhetoric, Scripture and Theology: Essays from the 1994 Pretoria Conference* [ed. S. E. Porter and T. H. Olbricht; JSNTSup 131; Sheffield: Sheffield Academic Press, 1996], 28–53).

1. Schüssler Fiorenza, "Challenging the Rhetorical Half-Turn," 29.

2. Elisabeth Schüssler Fiorenza, *Rhetoric and Ethic: The Politics of Biblical Studies* (Minneapolis: Fortress, 1999), 83–102.

3. Schüssler Fiorenza, "Challenging the Rhetorical Half-Turn," 29–30; and idem, *Rhetoric and Ethic*, 3, 84.

she asserts, is that interpreters remain in "captivity" to "empiricist-positivist science." This captivity takes the form of expending much "energy in applying and reinscribing to Christian Testament texts ancient rhetorical methods, disciplinary technology, terminological stylistics and the scattered prescription of oratorical handbooks in antiquity."[4] Later in the essay she proposes a reason for this captivity: Rhetorical interpreters, she asserts, find themselves unable or unwilling to acknowledge "their feminist and liberationist critical partners" because of "the contested character of the field" of rhetorical studies. She suggests it is "the 'fear' that [they] could be seen as 'unscientific' [that] prevents engagement with such critical political intellectual discourses."[5]

Schüssler Fiorenza continues her Pretoria essay with a critical discussion of sociorhetorical interpretation, since it "is one of the few Christian Testament studies that attempts to take rhetorical and feminist theoretical insights seriously."[6] As she proceeds, her stated goal is "to illustrate how even a socio-rhetorical analysis that is aware of gender studies in the end resorts to a positivist social-scientific approach in order to validate its interpretation in terms of the logic of identity as the best reading and 'reliable scientific' interpretation."[7] When Schüssler Fiorenza wrote this in 1994, she did not have my *Tapestry of Early Christian Discourse*[8] to consult, and I have acknowledged this in my response to her criticisms at the 1998 Florence Rhetoric Conference.[9] She did not, however, revise her response in the 1999 republication of the essay. As a result, her description does not fully apply to the strategies I use in sociorhetorical interpretation and the goals I have for those strategies.

Schüssler Fiorenza's description was based on a perception that socio-rhetorical interpretation "discusses rhetorical, literary, social-scientific, and ideological approaches as separate methodological investigative procedures."[10] It is true that I did not explicitly draw these procedures together in my earlier work. However, the goal of my approach has been,

---

4. Schüssler Fiorenza, "Challenging the Rhetorical Half-Turn," 32; and idem, *Rhetoric and Ethic*, 86.

5. Schüssler Fiorenza, "Challenging the Rhetorical Half-Turn," 47; and idem, *Rhetoric and Ethic*, 97.

6. Schüssler Fiorenza, "Challenging the Rhetorical Half-Turn," 33; and idem, *Rhetoric and Ethic*, 86.

7. Schüssler Fiorenza, "Challenging the Rhetorical Half-Turn," 33; and idem, *Rhetoric and Ethic*, 87.

8. Vernon K. Robbins, *The Tapestry of Early Christian Discourse: Rhetoric, Society and Ideology* (New York: Routledge, 1996).

9. Robbins, "Rhetorical Full-Turn," 51.

10. Schüssler Fiorenza, "Challenging the Rhetorical Half-Turn," 33; and idem, *Rhetoric and Ethic*, 87.

and is, to use an interpretive analytics that brings disciplines together rather than one that drives them apart. Indeed, the overall goal of my interpretive strategy is to undertake a full-formed rhetoric of inquiry in the field of biblical studies. Such an approach is not new, of course, as the basic strategies of an interpretive analytics emerge from the work of Michel Foucault: "An interpretive analytics approaches texts as discourse and 'sees discourse as part of a larger field of power and practice whose relations are articulated in different ways by different paradigms'."[11] According to Dreyfus and Rabinow, an interpretive analytics moves through three steps:

> 1) [T]he interpreter must take up a pragmatic stance on the basis of some socially shared sense of how things are going; 2) the investigator must produce a disciplined diagnosis of what has gone on and is going on in the social body to account for the shared sense of distress or well-being; 3) the investigator owes the reader an account of why the practices he [or she] describes should produce the shared malaise or contentment which gave rise to the investigation.[12]

The sense of distress in the social body of biblical interpretation that I addressed in 1996 was the dividing of exegetical strategies into separate methodological investigative procedures. Thus, Schüssler Fiorenza has not acknowledged the manner in which sociorhetorical interpretation directly confronts the problem of methodological division that she herself also dislikes. One of the results of the division of exegetical strategies was and is the isolation of feminist studies from various arenas of biblical interpretation. One of the goals of my interpretive analytics was and continues to be to articulate how feminist studies and other developing modes of interpretation are internal participants in the movement of biblical studies toward a new paradigm.[13]

THE LOCATION OF SOCIORHETORICAL INTERPRETATION IN TRANSMODERNISM

It may be helpful at the outset to explain, as I understand it, the philosophical location and ideology of sociorhetorical interpretation. The

---

11. Robbins, *Tapestry of Early Christian Discourse,* 12, quoting Hubert L. Dreyfus and Paul Rabinow, *Michel Foucault: Beyond Structuralism and Hermeneutics* (Chicago: University of Chicago Press, 1983), 199.

12. Robbins, *Tapestry of Early Christian Discourse,* 12, quoting Dreyfus and Rabinow, *Michel Foucault,* 200.

13. To this end, writings by twenty-one women appear in the bibliography of Robbins, *Tapestry of Early Christian Discourse,* which was published in 1996.

philosophical ideology of sociorhetorical interpretation is most appropriately identified as relational transmodernism.[14] On the one hand, this ideology is an alternative to particularist modernism. On the other, it represents an alternative to antimodernism and ultramodernism.[15] With the triumph of historicism in biblical interpretation between 1775–1875, particularist modernity began to drive biblical exegesis.[16] Freedom entailed a relocation of authority and historical criticism was its champion. Rejecting Aristotle's concept of form as a designation of essence, philosophers treated form as an external, sensuously perceived, aspect of existence.[17] In this context, biblical interpreters valued particularist and individualist phenomena. Content (*Inhalt*) was separated from other aspects of form, and individualistic interpretation guided the reconstruction of sources.[18] The feminist hermeneutics of Schüssler Fiorenza has continued in the tradition of a relocation of authority nurtured by modernism. Her approach combines historical criticism with a rhetorical hermeneutics of suspicion and thereby functions to relocate the authority of male-stream interpretation. As a result of the merger of modernist and antimodernist strategies in its procedures, it is difficult for this approach to enact a rhetorical full-turn in biblical interpretation.

According to Martin J. Buss, postmodern approaches began to emerge after 1875 and have only gradually found their way into biblical studies. Three major postmodern lines, he asserts, functioned alongside

----

14. Recent publications by Martin J. Buss, my colleague at Emory University, provide helpful resources for locating sociorhetorical interpretation within postmodern analysis. See the Festschrift in his honor by Timothy J. Sandoval and Carleen Mandolfo, eds., *Relating to the Text: Interdisciplinary and Form-Critical Insights on the Bible* (JSOTSup 384; Sheffield: Sheffield Academic Press, 2003).

15. Martin J. Buss, *Biblical Form Criticism in Its Context* (JSOTSup 274; Sheffield: Sheffield Academic Press, 1999), 156–66.

16. Ibid., 121–25.

17. Ibid., 137.

18. Between 1807 and 1817, e.g., W. M. L. de Wette divided the Hebrew psalms into groups based on content and focused on each psalm individualistically as "the living effusion of an emotion-filled heart." He emphasized the lack of poetic similarity among the various psalms: "Every writing requires its own hermeneutic; it can be known and understood only in its own form" (Buss, *Biblical Form Criticism*, 152). Interpreters of the New Testament, focusing on particularist features in the earliest Greek manuscripts of the New Testament, overturned the centuries-old view that the Gospels were written in the chronological order of Matthew, Mark, Luke, and John (their canonical order) to argue that Mark was the earliest narrative Gospel to be written. Stylistic particularities, guided by "special hermeneutics," emphasized analysis and interpretation of individual books, writers, and sources throughout the Old and New Testaments. The highest goal was to move beyond the writing itself to an understanding of the person who produced the writing (ibid., 154–55).

one another during the twentieth century: antimodern, transmodern, and ultramodern. As Buss defines them, the antimodern line "opposes the disorderliness that is inherent in modernity, especially individualism and a strong sense of historical change." The transmodern line believes that major features of modernity are valuable "but problematic when they are emphasized one-sidedly." The ultramodern line attempts to eliminate generality, moving "from moderate nominalism to extreme nominalism" into "scepticism or nihilism, especially when held without a belief in God."[19] In terms of my interests here, the emergence of relationism as a new paradigm in the transmodern line is particularly noteworthy. In Buss's words:

> According to this theory, ... relations, which can recur, are real. At the same time, the theory holds that the particular objects, the items that stand in relations, are also real, even to the extent of having a semi-independent existence, for real relations must have endpoints with some independence, so that they are not simply absorbed into a larger whole. Thus it is said that relations "both combine and separate."[20]

Buss contrasts relationism, on the one hand, to nominalism, which can handle only the extremes: "monadism (radical pluralism) and monism (tight connectivity within a large unit)."[21] On the other hand, essentialism "considers some associations as necessary ('essential') and others as accidental."[22] Relationists replace a theory of causality with a notion of probability, including both conditional probability and correlation. In this context, a new paradigm emerges for form: "Form is held ... to be a *complex of relations* which are shared (at least potentially) with some other existents and can thus be understood, but which together form a whole that evades complete understanding; for, since relations even within a whole require some distancing between the items related, a real whole cannot be completely unified."[23]

For sociorhetorical interpretation, the following conclusion is central:

> Since relationism (like nominalism) makes no distinction between essential and accidental features, a given object can be classified in terms of several different forms, according to one's principle of selectivity, which depends on one's purpose. However, while nominalism holds that a

---

19. Buss, *Biblical Form Criticism*, 156.
20. Ibid., 158.
21. Ibid.
22. Ibid.
23. Ibid., 159 (emphasis original).

form or structure is in the mind of the observer rather than in the object, relationism holds that form emerges interactively as an aspect of a reality revealed to a subject with its questions, thus formed cooperatively by object and observer.[24]

The statement that "form emerges interactively" is especially important for sociorhetorical interpretation since this approach is an "interactive" mode of interpretation, always perceiving "form" to be "an aspect of reality revealed to a subject with its questions, thus formed cooperatively by object and observer." This principle means, in fact, that the best sociorhetorical interpretation results from scholarly collaboration. When a group of specialists work together in a sustained manner to interpret a set of texts they perceive to be "somehow related," the "interactive" product regularly is an exhibition of "forms" that interpreters are enabled, through interactive interpretation, to see and communicate to others.

One of the most important presentations of "transmodern" thought, and one in which the term is specifically used, is Couze Venn's *Occidentalism: Modernity and Subjectivity*.[25] In this essay I make extensive use of this book to present a full rhetorical turn in biblical interpretation. A major goal of Venn's book is "to subvert the conventional opposition between a philosophy of experience and a philosophy of concept" by refiguring historicity and transforming the discussion of subjectivity into intersubjectivity.[26] Focusing on both the materiality and sociality of the world we inherit, inhabit, and transform, Venn emphasizes that we learn to dwell in this world by relying

> on the hospitality of those closest to us and on order in the surrounding world, the regularities of which we can learn through an apprenticeship. Language is central in this process ... , *and thus*, crucially, the relation to the other. This involves both the culturally normed mode of this relation and what Levinas calls the face relation.... So apprenticeship involves a way of learning to be ethical beings, at the same time as one learns to be a particular subject and to act on the world according to particular technologies of transforming and appropriating the world, that is to say, apprenticeship instructs us into the ways of coupling with the objectal and inter-subjective worlds in which we dwell.[27]

---

24. Ibid.
25. Couze Venn, *Occidentalism: Modernity and Subjectivity* (Thousand Oaks, Calif.: SAGE, 2000).
26. Ibid., 33.
27. Ibid., 33–34 (emphasis original).

An implication of this approach is that the most mature human being is not an isolated, autonomous being but one who engages continually in interhuman apprenticeship in the world one inherits, inhabits, and transforms.[28] This apprenticeship "includes learning to deal in culturally specific ways with both the liminal and the material side of beingness, so that we learn to figure and refigure our experiences, and so give meaning to them, in terms of a whole set of rules and stories, beliefs and values inscribed in performative as well as in reflexive practices of becoming instituting particular subjectivities."[29]

This focus on continual interhuman and interobjectal apprenticeship is central to sociorhetorical interpretation. Analysis and interpretation is an ongoing process of learning, because "the world of other bodies and the world of objects constitute the 'dwelling' for subjectivity."[30] Venn uses the notion of choreography to describe our manner of working with others in contexts of hospitality, generosity, pleasure, suffering, mourning, "attachment, mingling the time of the body with the 'time of the soul'."[31] Since "[t]he models for the emplotment of experience already exist in the culture ... they circumscribe the discursive and 'textual' world from which we draw in order to question ourselves regarding the meaning of our experiences, and to rectify our 'selves,' since the subject is always in process."[32] Analysis and interpretation, then, are journeys of intersubjective "being-with and being-towards the other."[33] Sociorhetorical interpretation invites a commentator into an ongoing journey through multiple textures, social systems, cultures, ideologies, and discourses, for the purposes of redrawing, re(con)figuring, and transfiguring intersubjective boundaries of understanding. This transmodern nature of the journey emphasizes its continual movement. It is not a matter of posturing one's analysis and interpretation against modernism in a manner that creates new polarities or binaries, but a matter of working through alternatives that modernism, feminism, postmodernism, poststructuralism, postdeconstruction, and postcolonialism have made accessible to us. Sociorhetorical interpretation as an interpretive analytics introduces choreographies for translocational,

---

28. See Donna Haraway, *Simians, Cyborgs, and Women: The Reinvention of Nature* (London: Free Association, 1991) for her emphasis on the analytical poverty of holding on to the dualities of nature and culture, the human and the machine, given their profound inter-relationships. Cf. Venn, *Occidentalism*, 31, 221.

29. Venn, *Occidentalism*, 35.

30. Ibid., 42.

31. Ibid.; and vol. 3 of Paul Ricoeur, *Time and Narrative* (3 vols.; trans. K. McLaughlin and D. Pellauer; Chicago: University of Chicago Press, 1984–88).

32. Venn, *Occidentalism*, 43.

33. Ibid., 11.

transtextural, transsocial, transcultural, transideological, transsexual, and transtraditional analysis, interpretation, and commentary.

OPPOSITIONAL RHETORIC AS A HALF-TURN

In her Pretoria essay, Schüssler Fiorenza describes the task of rhetorical biblical scholarship in the following manner: "How meaning is constructed depends not only on how one reads the social, cultural, and religious markers inscribed by the text but also on what kind of 'intertexts,' preconstructed 'frames of meaning,' common sense understandings, and 'reading paradigms' one utilizes when interpreting linguistic markers and textualized symbols."[34] I agree fully with this description of our task. In the essay, she refers to her book *Discipleship of Equals* and calls for "a political rhetoric of inquiry in biblical studies" grounded in "the ekklesia as the public assembly of free and equal citizens in the power of the Spirit."[35] Yet, instead of enacting a procedure of "equality" that would have invited a full rhetorical turn in an assessment of the contexts of interpretation for analyzing and interpreting the various versions of the story of the woman who anointed Jesus, for example, Schüssler Fiorenza uses oppositional rhetoric containing inner attributes of domination and separation.[36] Characterizing my work as objectivist, scientistic, empiricist, and male-stream,[37] in contrast to her work as open, free, and based on equality, she took a political half-turn that set her work in opposition to mine in a manner that did not invite further deliberation about the issues involved.

Thus, there is substantive disjunction in Schüssler Fiorenza's Pretoria essay between what she says and what she does. She says many excellent things about the manner in which rhetorical scholarship should proceed, but her discourse enacts an oppositional mode of rhetorical argumentation that would appear to conflict with the openness, freedom, and equality that she establishes as her modus operandi. The issue is what kind of full rhetorical turn we can make as we construct a context of interpretation for a particular text. The scholarly issues at stake become lost when oppositional rhetoric dominates. Schüssler Fiorenza claims a goal

---

34. Schüssler Fiorenza, "Challenging the Rhetorical Half-Turn," 40; and idem, *Rhetoric and Ethic*, 92.

35. Schüssler Fiorenza, "Challenging the Rhetorical Half-Turn," 36; and idem, *Rhetoric and Ethic*, 89.

36. Contrast Kathleen E. Corley, *Private Women, Public Meals: Social Conflict in the Synoptic Tradition* (Peabody, Mass.: Hendrickson, 1993).

37. Schüssler Fiorenza, "Challenging the Rhetorical Half-Turn," 30–31, 35; and idem, *Rhetoric and Ethic*, 84–85, 88.

of enabling "biblical scholars to investigate the discursive arguments, which perform particular kinds of actions in particular historical situations and at particular political sites."[38] I agree with this aim. The question, then, is the particular historical situation and political site that caused Schüssler Fiorenza to use oppositional rhetoric in her essay rather than a rhetoric that would invite discussion and debate among equals.

Schüssler Fiorenza's adoption of oppositional rhetoric as a preferred mode of discourse in a context where she was pleading for a full-turn in rhetorical biblical scholarship presents an opportunity to reflect on the nature of oppositional rhetoric not only in our own personal discourse but also in New Testament discourse more generally. Stephen D. Moore has made the point that as we interpret literature we reenact certain rhetorical practices present in that literature.[39] Feminist scholars have helped us to understand how easy it is to reenact certain male rhetorical practices in the literature we interpret. It is also just as easy for feminist interpreters themselves to reenact oppositional rhetoric in biblical literature. In an address I delivered at the University of Stellenbosch at the Second African Symposium on Rhetoric (July 1996), I briefly described oppositional rhetoric in the New Testament as follows:

> Central to opposition discourse is the reasoning that people to whom God has given a tradition of salvation in the past currently enact a misunderstanding of God's saving action that must be attacked and replaced by an alternative system of belief and behavior … It presupposes an alignment of the speaker with God, against people who claim to understand God who really do not know the will and the ways of God.[40]

Such oppositional rhetoric is present in many places in the New Testament. One immediately thinks of Jesus' controversy with "the Jews" in John 8:43–47, which reaches a point where Jesus asserts that the Jews are "sons of the devil." This is not the time and place to present a sociorhetorical analysis and interpretation of this oppositional discourse. Gail R. O'Day provides many excellent observations about it in her *New Interpreter's Bible* commentary on John. In particular, O'Day speaks directly to one of the major pleas made by Schüssler Fiorenza, namely,

---

38. Schüssler Fiorenza, "Challenging the Rhetorical Half-Turn," 36; and idem, *Rhetoric and Ethic*, 89.

39. Stephen D. Moore, "Deconstructive Criticism: The Gospel of Mark," in *Mark and Method: New Approaches in Biblical Studies* (ed. J. Capel Anderson and S. D. Moore; Minneapolis: Fortress, 1992), 93.

40. Vernon K. Robbins, "The Dialectical Nature of Early Christian Discourse," *Scriptura* 59 (1996): 360.

"to investigate the discursive arguments which perform particular kinds of actions in particular historical situations and at particular political sites."[41] Many New Testament scholars join with O'Day in viewing the Johannine community as a minority group speaking out in protest against a majority culture.[42] She expresses concern about the resultant oppositional rhetoric and explains the difficulty of reconciling it with other discourse in the New Testament.[43] In other words, she does not herself wittingly or unwittingly reenact the oppositional rhetoric in the text. The discourse attributed to Jesus introduces strong polarities to separate Jesus fully from "the Jews." For various reasons, which she explains in her commentary, she does not wish to replay this kind of rhetoric in her commentary but calls attention to other modes of discourse in the New Testament that stand in relation to it. When O'Day makes this move, she takes major steps toward a rhetorical full-turn in interpretation.

SOCIORHETORICAL INTERPRETATION
AS TRANSLOCATIONAL AND TRANSDISCURSIVE

There is a beautiful moment in Schüssler Fiorenza's Pretoria essay when she introduces the metaphor of the African American circle dance or the European folk dance to destabilize a binary frame of reference for figuring the practices of a critical feminist biblical interpretation. Within this description, I suggest, lies an image very close to the one that has guided my development of sociorhetorical interpretation. Schüssler Fiorenza proposes

---

41. Schüssler Fiorenza, "Challenging the Rhetorical Half-Turn," 36; and idem, *Rhetoric and Ethic*, 89.

42. Gail R. O'Day, "John," *NIB* 9:648: "The virulent language of chap. 8 must be read against this backdrop of being cast out of the synagogue, of being excluded from the religious centers that once helped to define one's religious and communal identity. The language of this chapter is the language of the minority group spoken in protest to the majority culture. The Johannine Jewish Christians had no way to back up this language—that is, they had no power to take any actions comparable to their own exclusion from the synagogue. They were outnumbered by the Jewish community and had no political resources at their disposal. Their only 'power' rested in the force of their rhetoric, in their ability to denounce those who had excluded them."

43. Ibid., 9:647: "John 8 presents the reader of the Gospel of John with some of the Gospel's most difficult interpretive issues. The Jesus who emerges from these verses speaks with staggeringly sharp invective to his opponents and holds nothing back in his attack on his theological adversaries. It is very difficult to harmonize this picture of Jesus with the images of him that shape our theological imaginations: Jesus as the one who eats with outcasts and sinners, who cares for the lost sheep, who is the model of how we are to love."

an image of interpretation as forward movement and spiraling repetition, stepping in place, turning over and changing of venue in which discrete methodological approaches become moving steps and artful configurations. Clumsy participants in this dance that figures the complex enterprise of biblical criticism may frequently step on each other's toes and interrupt each other's turns but they can still dance together as long as they acknowledge each other as equals conscious of dancing through a political minefield.[44]

This image of movement and spiraling repetition introduces a very different mode of procedure than one that places oppositional rhetoric at the forefront, and I applaud it. It is an image that evokes well the goal of sociorhetorical analysis and interpretation.

In sociorhetorical terms, the movement and spiraling to which Schüssler Fiorenza refers takes the form of translocational, transtextural, and transdiscursive interpretation. The translocational covers a spectrum of social locations from the intersubjective body to the household, village, city, kingdom, and empire. The transtextural weaves through inner texture, intertexture, social and cultural texture, ideological texture, and sacred texture.[45] The transdiscursive enacts stepping in place, turning, and changing of venue from wisdom discourse to miracle discourse to prophetic discourse to precreation discourse to priestly discourse to apocalyptic discourse.[46]

Yet, despite these common concerns and goals, the oppositional nature of Schüssler Fiorenza's rhetoric becomes a point of division. Indeed, such rhetoric runs the risk of attempting to corral its audience into one location and targeting the audience with one major kind of discourse. Emphasizing only one location, the *ekklesia* as the public, political assembly, and championing only one major mode of discourse, Divine Wisdom, she inadvertently reinscribes only one major location and one major discourse in early Christian literature. New Testament literature itself shows us a better way. It is not all Divine Wisdom discourse, and it is not all located in the *ekklesia* as public, political assembly. Patterns of negotiation in multiple discourses and locations

---

44. Schüssler Fiorenza, "Challenging the Rhetorical Half-Turn," 51; and idem, *Rhetoric and Ethic,* 101.

45. And, if possible, psychological texture should be included as well.

46. Robbins, "Dialectical Nature"; and idem, "Argumentative Textures in Socio-Rhetorical Interpretation," in *Rhetorical Argumentation in Biblical Texts: Essays from the Lund 2000 Conference* (ed. A. Eriksson, T. H. Olbricht, and W. Übelacker; ESEC 8; Harrisburg, Pa.: Trinity Press International, 2002), 27–65.

in the literature interweave diversity, conflict, separation, and concilia-
tion into a thick configuration of history, society, culture, and ideology.

Venn's description, using the work of Emmanuel Levinas, describes
well a person's ethical embodiment among others in the enactment of
sociorhetorical analysis and interpretation: "Generosity and (vigilant)
passivity, readiness to receive what exceeds the I, the welcoming of the
Other, a kind of dispossession of the ego: these are the modalities of the
face relation. It is in that sense that the relation with the Other is an ethical relation."[47] A patience of reception combined with a "readiness to
receive what exceeds the I" guides sociorhetorical analysis and interpretation. The interpreter seeks to engage in heteronomous responsibility
rather than autonomous freedom, in intersubjective exploration rather
than egological imposition. Both the text and the interpreter negotiate the
other with particular goals, that is, modes of desire. Becoming conscious
of these desires requires continual crossing and redrawing of boundaries,[48] movement across textures of texts,[49] and movement through
multiple argumentative modes of discourse.[50]

My hypothesis is that transtextural sociorhetorical analysis and interpretation[51] yields six major *rhetorolects*[52] that interweave in early Christian
discourse: wisdom, miracle, prophetic, precreation, priestly, and apocalyptic.[53] Each rhetorolect embodies conventional religious goals in the
first-century Mediterranean world. In Venn's terminology, this means that
each rhetorolect enacts social, cultural, and ideological desires. The *wisdom*
rhetorolect uses household imagery to bring divine knowledge into intersubjective bodies, namely, all the secrets that lie within an ordered
universe, to enable people to prosper and flourish in the world we inherit,
inhabit, and transform. The *miracle* rhetorolect uses imagery of intersubjective bodies to bring God's powers at work in the created universe inside
an intersubjective body that, for one reason or another, is not fully opera-
tional, positively functional, or constructively interactive. The *prophetic*
rhetorolect uses imagery of a kingdom to transmit the will of God to

---

47. Venn, *Occidentalism*, 211.

48. Robbins, *Tapestry of Early Christian Discourse*, 18–43.

49. Ibid., 44–236; and idem, *Exploring the Texture of Texts: A Guide to Socio-Rhetorical Interpretation* (Valley Forge, Pa.: Trinity Press International, 1996).

50. Robbins, "Dialectical Nature"; and idem, "Argumentative Textures."

51. By this I mean programmatic sociorhetorical analysis and interpretation of inner, inter, social and cultural, ideological, and sacred textures (Robbins, *Tapestry of Early Christian Discourse*; and idem, *Exploring the Texture of Texts*).

52. I define the term thus: "A rhetorolect is a form of language variety or discourse identifiable on the basis of a distinctive configuration of themes, topics, reasonings, and argumentations" (Robbins, "Dialectical Nature," 356).

53. Robbins, "Dialectical Nature"; and idem, "Argumentative Textures."

people and groups who will challenge others—kings, priests, elders, interpreters, lawyers—to bring justice, love, care, and nurture to all people. The *precreation* rhetorolect uses images of the household of an emperor to bring eternal forces of life into intersubjective bodies for a complete realization of well-being. The *priestly* rhetorolect uses imagery of the temple to create beneficial exchange between humans and God. The *apocalyptic* rhetorolect uses imagery of an empire both to enact total annihilation of powers (including earthly leaders and institutions) that disrupt and destroy the comforts of well-being (e.g., food, water, shelter, and supportive community) and to create new beginnings in divine time.

The presence of these major rhetorolects in early Christian discourse means that the interpreter must recognize key modes of desire in early Christian discourse, in traditions of interpretation of this discourse, and in current interpreters of this discourse. Some early Christian texts negotiate these desires with loud, totalizing discourse. Others set totalizing discourses in dynamic dialogue with one another. Still others gather local voices in ways that create lively communities of alternative points of view. Interpreters must negotiate the desires of the text, rather than simply allow the desires to seduce them. Some interpreters, following a hermeneutics of suspicion, try to "negate" the desires of the text. Sociorhetorical interpretation exhibits desires of the text and refigures contemporary narrations of these desires. In this way, interpreters choreograph activities of a heteronomous subject interpreting the heteronomous desires of texts.

Following Venn's terminology further, "every self is a storied self. And every story is mingled with the stories of other selves, so that every one of us is entangled in the stories we tell, and are told about us."[54] Each storied world splices phenomenal time, or temporality as lived, into the cosmological time of history and of the sublime, that is, into the "time of the soul."[55] Each storied world enacts an apprenticeship in the lifeworld. This apprenticeship "concerns learning a particular language game and an (alchemical) practice, that is, it involves at the same time a discursive and a material, transformative and transmutative practice."[56] This means that each early Christian rhetorolect is a storied world that intertwines temporality as lived and the cosmological time of history and the sublime in particular ways.

To put it in other terms that Venn uses, the six early Christian rhetorolects invoke in particular ways "both the inhospitable world into

---

54. Venn, *Occidentalism*, 42.

55. Ibid., 223; and Paul Ricoeur, *Oneself as Another* (Chicago: University of Chicago Press, 1992).

56. Venn, *Occidentalism*, 220.

which being is thrown and the world as the homely shelter for being-in the world."[57] Following Venn still further, time is the horizon of both the cosmological and the phenomenal dimensions of intersubjective being. The major interhuman rhetorolects in early Christianity present time in these alternative ways.[58] Venn's discussion leads to assertions about the interhuman project of becoming responsible for humanity and the world that humanity inhabits. In his words, "the becoming-responsible of humanity is the result of a difficult apprenticeship, requiring explicit critical narratives of being, implicating an ethics of responsibility and solicitude for the other, extending to the natural world in which being exists as 'flesh' of the world. Modernity has been a crucial stage in that apprenticeship."[59] Sociorhetorical interpretation as I apply it represents an exploration and explication of early Christianity as a crucial stage in the difficult apprenticeship of "the becoming-responsible of humanity." Wisdom rhetorolect initiates one into the apprenticeship of learning how to live in basic, everyday interhuman relationships (filial commitment, friendship, community). Miracle rhetorolect invites one into the apprenticeship of bringing the bodies of others to powers of healing, recognizing the illnesses within one's own interbody, and moving toward powers

---

57. Ibid., 223. Wisdom rhetorolect thus grounds itself in the world as "the homely shelter for being-in-the-world" and then struggles with the "mysterious" manner in which righteous people suffer; miracle rhetorolect exists in the world as a place of disruption, illness, and crisis and then explores the amazing ways in which people experience moments of healing, restoration, and peace; prophetic rhetorolect is localized in the world as a place of disobedience and then probes the courageous confrontation of leaders to reform their leadership toward justice and care for the needy; precreation rhetorolect is in the world as a place of darkness which light continually presses against and then searches for the source of light which can be a home away from a place always threatened by darkness; priestly rhetorolect is centered in the world as a place of unholiness and then evokes human sacrifice as a means of beneficial exchange between humans and God; and apocalyptic rhetorolect is grounded in the world as an evil-infested place into which humans are thrown and then journeys beyond the inhabited world in search of a paradisiacal space.

58. In wisdom rhetorolect, time is the moment of insight, the context of learning, of receiving instruction that leads one beyond the world into the mind of God; in miracle rhetorolect, time is the moment of healing, of becoming completely integrated with society as a well being who does not endanger someone else with disease, confront someone else with embarrassing deficiencies, or impede the efficient operations of society; in prophetic rhetorolect, it is the moment of confrontation, of exercising the courage to speak out for the enactment of justice in society; in precreation rhetorolect, time is the appearance and disappearance, presence and absence, of light in a world of darkness; in priestly rhetorolect, time is the moment of sacrifice that removes defilement and wrongs that fracture the well-being of communities who have a responsibility to enact God's love for the created world; in apocalyptic rhetorolect, it is the sequence through which all evil in the world is destroyed and God's goodness and righteousness is fully established.

59. Venn, *Occidentalism*, 235.

that can energize healing of those illnesses. Prophetic rhetorolect moti-
vates the apprenticeship of confrontation of leaders for the sake of others.
Precreation rhetorolect offers one the apprenticeship of special knowledge that leads to the innermost mind of the divine and the innermost
truth about being-in-the-world. Priestly rhetorolect introduces the
apprenticeship of disciplined action and thought designed to purify the
inner resources of one's own inter-body and of one's community of daily
life, thought, and action. Apocalyptic rhetorolect throws one into an
apprenticeship of rewriting the history of the world in terms of the emergence of aggressive evil in the world and its removal from the world.

If our rhetorical analyses reenact only one or two rhetorical modes
within this literature, we are making only a quarter or half-turn within
the rich discursive texture of early Christian discourse. To make the task
complete, one must engage in political rhetoric both by joining voices
and actions with feminist-critical scholars (male and female) and by
employing liberationist modes of analysis within the wide regions of
the global village. We must engage in translocational, transtextural,
transdiscursive, transcultural, and transtraditional interpretations that
includes disenfranchised voices, marginalized voices, recently liberated
voices, and powerfully located voices. In order to make a rhetorical full-
turn as we do this, we must learn how to enact confrontational strategies
in forms and styles of rhetoric that enable free and open discussion and
controversy. We must nurture a transmodern environment where we
keep our colleagues on an equal playing field. Moving forward, spiraling, stepping in place, turning around, and changing venue, we explore
with each other, debate with one another, and disagree with each other
as equals, inviting other voices into the dialogue in a manner that
makes a rhetorical full-turn through sciences, humanities, genders, ethnicities, geographies, races, economies, societies, and cultures, which
thereby become arenas of disputation, dialogue, and commentary.

SOCIORHETORICAL INTERPRETATION
AS TRANSCULTURAL RHETORICAL CRITICISM

In addition to being transtextural and transdiscursive, sociorhetorical
interpretation is transcultural, wherein ethnocentrism is the primary issue
addressed. Against Charles Taylor, Steven Mailloux asserts that judgments
are always ethnocentrically located within the culture making them.[60] But

---

60. Steven Mailloux, "Articulation and Understanding: The Pragmatic Intimacy between
Rhetoric and Hermeneutics," in *Rhetoric and Hermeneutics in Our Time: A Reader* (ed. W. Jost
and M. J. Hyde; New Haven: Yale University Press, 1997), 387–88.

this is not some kind of "wrong thing," according to Mailloux. Rather, "it is our own ethnocentric web of beliefs and desires that gives us interpretive purchase on any object of attention, including the texts or classification systems of another culture. The validity of our interpretation is a function of the rhetorical context in which we argue them: who participates in the conversation, when and where, with what purposes, and so on."[61] As Mailloux develops his argument, he refers to "transcultural judgments" and crossing boundaries thus:

> If transcultural judgments are always cross-cultural translations, then such interpretations are liminal acts opening up a space in which boundaries are transformed yet paradoxically maintained even as they are crossed. Boundaries are crossed in interpretation when one culture becomes the conversational topic or interpretive object of another; boundaries are maintained as the interpretive act in its rhetorical exchanges figures and persuades within the context of the interpreting culture; and boundaries are moved as interpretation changes the shape—trivially or dramatically—of the culture in which the interpretation is produced and received.[62]

This observation moves us into the arena of understanding the other. Relational philosophy understands, in the words of Buss, that the "other" is "neither completely strange nor completely familiar."[63] This takes us one step further to the epistemological issue of transcultural understanding and the practices of transcultural sociorhetorical interpretation. In Mailloux's words, "To understand an act within a foreign culture, the differences must be found in the margins of our own.... [A]s we interact with other communities, traditions, cultures, we can reweave our webs of belief to take account of the other, and we do this more or less successfully from differing points of view within and outside our own groups."[64]

Mailloux's use of the term "transcultural" and his perception of the importance of finding differences "in the margins of our own culture" are thoroughly coherent not only with the thought of Mikhail Bakhtin but

---

61. Ibid., 388.

62. Ibid., 388. Cf. Vernon K. Robbins, "Redrawing the Boundaries with Socio-Rhetorical Criticism," in Robbins, *Tapestry of Early Christian Discourse*, 18–43.

63. Buss, *Biblical Form Criticism*, 159.

64. Mailloux, "Articulation and Understanding," 388–89; cf. Robbins, *Tapestry of Early Christian Discourse*, 170–76; idem, *Exploring the Texture of Texts*, 88–89; and idem, "The Reversed Contextualization of Psalm 22 in the Markan Crucifixion: A Socio-rhetorical Analysis," in *The Four Gospels 1992: Festschrift Frans Neirynck* (ed. F. van Segbroeck et al.; BETL 100; 3 vols.; Leuven: Leuven University Press, 1992), 2:1161–83.

also with the thought and practice of Ellen Berry and a successor of Bakhtin named Mikhail Epstein. After working in the Center for Mind and Thought in Moscow until 1990, Epstein came to the United States and accepted a position in the Department of Russian and Eastern European Languages, Literatures, and Culture at Emory University. Berry began to work with Epstein, and together they produced *Transcultural Experiments*.[65] The work of Berry and Epstein displays yet another aspect of sociorhetorical interpretation as it participates in transcultural rhetorical interpretation.

Moving across boundaries is a challenging task in the context of interpretive/exegetical practice. It calls for a "transcultural context of interpretation." As Wilhelm Wuellner asserts, a rhetorical reading must be "a corporate, cultural experience, and never mainly a private, individualistic one."[66] But it is exceptionally difficult for Western interpreters located either in a humanistic or theological tradition to nurture truly corporate forms of exegesis. Western tradition rewards individualism, not only in the academy but also in the marketplace of religion and the world of modern media. "Dialogue" in Western tradition regularly does not achieve a profound interweaving of webs of understanding, since while one person is talking the other person is thinking about an individual response that will bring attention to the respondent's individual creativity and insightfulness.

Transcultural rhetorical criticism begins with a presumption that any one culture is fundamentally insufficient and incomplete, and thus it needs "radical openness to and dialogue with" other cultures.[67] This includes interpretive cultures, discursive cultures, ethnic cultures, national cultures, alongside many others. Transculturalism avoids "oppositional binaries, especially center and periphery, and emphasizes cultural identity as a dynamic, unstable, and ongoing construction."[68] The goal is "a model of cultural interaction that would not unify cultures but diversify them further through their mutual interaction."[69] This approach invites and welcomes interference, "the spontaneous interaction between various kinds of cultural activity."[70] As Berry and Epstein aptly note, "within a transcultural model, spaces between diverging cultures are

---

65. Ellen E. Berry and Mikhail N. Epstein, *Transcultural Experiments: Russian and American Models of Creative Communication* (New York: St. Martin's, 1999).

66. Wilhelm Wuellner, "Putting Life Back into the Lazarus Story and Its Reading: The Narrative Rhetoric of John 11 as the Narration of Faith," *Semeia* 53 (1991): 115.

67. Berry and Epstein, *Transcultural Experiments*, 3.

68. Ibid., 4.

69. Ibid., 8; cf. Heikki Räisänen, *Marcion, Muhammad and the Mahatma: Exegetical Perspectives on the Encounter of Cultures and Faiths* (London: SCM, 1997), 1–16, 189–203.

70. Berry and Epstein, *Transcultural Experiments*, 9.

filled by the effects of their interferences.... Instead of isolated spots or separate points, interference produces polychromatic patterns" and three-dimensional cultural spaces.[71] Interference "transposes the borders of interacting cultures, mentalities, and disciplines in multiple directions."[72] A major goal, then, is to transform "a divisive politics of identity into a politics of creative interference."[73]

Both Judaism and Christianity have inherent within their formation multiple transcultural dynamics. Much of the genius of the biblical canon lies in its transcultural nature. The story of Israel recounts interaction among multiple cultures in a manner that introduces "canonical transculturalism." The New Testament extends the Israelite story even further into transculturalism. Previously "canonical" modes of discourse are deconstructed and reconstructed into new transcultural modes. Transcultural rhetorical criticism investigates the power of the biblical texts in a manner that invites interpreters to produce transcultural meanings themselves.

One of the practices Berry and Epstein recommend for the production of transcultural interpretation is "collective improvisation." They gather talented people located in different cultures—whether those are the differing cultures of interpretation in the humanities, sciences, arts, and business; or United States, Russia, India, and the Middle East.[74] All the people agree to write on a particular topic for a period of one hour. Then all of them read their essays aloud, and all agree to write commentaries on the texts of the others. This new round of activity then turns into the next round of communication.[75] In an uncanny way, Berry and Epstein's process of culturally diversified people writing on a particular topic has analogies with the process of invention among Christians during the first century. People in significantly different social, cultural, and ideological locations wrote in multiple ways on related topics in order to articulate their understanding of the relation of humans to Jesus and the relation of Jesus to the attributes and actions of God and the Holy Spirit. Gathering authors together in dialogue from as many cultural locations as possible to write commentary on sacred texts from multiple traditions represents a significant step toward transcultural commentary in the twenty-first century. In fact, there are projects like this emerging.[76]

---

71. Ibid.
72. Ibid., 10.
73. Ibid., 12.
74. Ibid., 31.
75. Ibid., 33.
76. See Vernon K. Robbins and Gordon D. Newby, "A Prolegomenon to the Relation of the Qur'an and the Bible," in *Bible and Qur'an: Essays in Scriptural Intertextuality* (ed. J. C. Reeves; SBLSymS 24; Atlanta: Society of Biblical Literature, 2003), 23–42.

Interpreters should now analyze sacred texts, and other literature and media, using transmodern strategies of sociorhetorical interpretation interactively with their own strategies of interpretation and commentary. Engaging in such a diverse range of interactive commentary could begin to move biblical interpretation significantly beyond the circumscribed strategies of modernist commentary into significant transmodern modes of investigation and interpretation. To be sure, it is also an effective way of seeking to overcome the oppositional rhetoric embedded in the text—leading to expansive readings that hope to avert domination through the multiplicity (and sometimes ambiguity) generated in open-ended dialogue.

Conclusions

The primary issues for me in this essay have concerned the nature of feminist hermeneutics. The thesis I have advocated throughout is that feminist hermeneutics can make a rhetorical full-turn in biblical interpretation by moving forthrightly beyond one major political location and one primary discourse. A rhetorical full-turn includes a journey through multiple locations, textures, discourses, societies, cultures, ideologies, and traditions. Feminist interpretation, in my understanding, is amenable to taking this journey too, and more and more the scholarship coming out seems to press forward in making ever greater strides toward exhibiting a rhetorical full-turn. As we diverse interpreters labor together, then, we may, in this community of discovery and dialogue, come to recognize more fully a rhetorical full-turn in biblical studies. Such collaborative recognitions and achievements with respect to a rhetorical full-turn may help us all to fulfill responsibilities of leadership, of assistance, and of transformation in a world that always too easily moves toward violence, abuse, and destruction, rather than reconciliation, healing, and renewal.

Full Turns and Half Turns: Engaging the Dialogue/Dance between Elisabeth Schüssler Fiorenza and Vernon Robbins

Priscilla Geisterfer

In the fall of 1998, while engaged in graduate studies, I was introduced to an ongoing discussion between Elisabeth Schüssler Fiorenza and Vernon K. Robbins. I had by this time aligned myself with both scholars, as I found a great deal of complementarity in their approaches to biblical interpretation, one of the major features of commonality being that the methods of both Schüssler Fiorenza and Robbins have developed as responses to a more traditional historical-critical approach to biblical interpretation. While Schüssler Fiorenza sees the scientistic-positivist ethos of historical criticism as an obstacle to a much-needed paradigm shift "from a scientistic-hermeneutical to a rhetorical-political, from a kyriarchal Eurocentric to a radical egalitarian cosmopolitan model of interpretation,"[1] Robbins's method developed as a response to the competitive nature of historical-critical biblical interpretation. Rather than to participate in the interpretive arena wherein voices compete for a single prescriptive interpretation of biblical texts, Robbins seeks to engage the plethora of biblical methods and the diversity of approaches in a "round-table discussion." In this dialogic forum, biblical interpretation weaves together diverse perspectives into a multifaceted interpretation. Both Robbins and Schüssler Fiorenza approach biblical interpretation from the perspective of rhetoric and share the understanding that language not only carries meaning across time and space, but that it also has the ability to subvert, effect, or maintain values in the world of the hearer/reader. Therefore, although Robbins does not say it as explicitly as Schüssler Fiorenza does, they both insist that interpreters must be as critical of the texts they are creating as they are of the texts they are interpreting.

---

1. Elisabeth Schüssler Fiorenza, *Rhetoric and Ethic: The Politics of Biblical Studies* (Minneapolis: Fortress, 1999), 33.

Although Robbins's and Schüssler Fiorenza's responses to historical-critical biblical interpretation agree concerning these very critical elements, their independent rhetorical approaches differ in quite distinct ways. In her use of rhetoric, Schüssler Fiorenza strategically places herself in direct opposition to the historical-critical approach in order to negate biblically based validation of oppressive structures and to make overt the relationship that exists between interpreter, text, and reader. While Robbins's approach addresses this same relationship between interpreter, text, and reader, his strategy has been more covert, representing a movement from within the tradition.

Moreover, the discussion between them also tends to focus on the way in which they are antithetical to one another. In her article "Challenging the Rhetorical Half-Turn: Feminist and Rhetorical Biblical Criticism," Schüssler Fiorenza had argued that Robbins's use of socio-rhetorical criticism is wrought with empiricist-positivistic scientistic thinking,[2] while Robbins, in his response, "The Rhetorical Full-Turn in Biblical Interpretation: Reconfiguring Rhetorical-Political Analysis," criticizes Schüssler Fiorenza's choice of rhetoric in her assessment of one of his own exegetical works.[3] He describes her rhetoric as oppositional and explains that the use of such rhetoric is not consistent with the methodology she has developed and the message it is supposed to convey.

In this essay, I will enter into this discussion using both Robbins's and Schüssler Fiorenza's methodologies to illuminate the reasons why the use of oppositional rhetoric may occur and to assess the consequences of this rhetorical approach for the message embodied in Schüssler Fiorenza's feminist hermeneutic. In order to do this, I will first outline the rhetorical methodologies of both Robbins and Schüssler Fiorenza. I will then clarify the problem raised by Robbins's critique and enter into it by looking at some of the rhetorical textures in Schüssler Fiorenza's work. The concluding reflection will consider some influences of historical and political time and space upon Schüssler Fiorenza's rhetorical approach. I come to this conversation as a feminist doctoral candidate in biblical theology. Like Schüssler Fiorenza, I hold a marginal position. As a feminist, I am

---

2. Elisabeth Schüssler Fiorenza, "Challenging the Rhetorical Half-Turn: Feminist and Rhetorical Biblical Criticism," in *Rhetoric, Scripture and Theology: Essays from the 1994 Pretoria Conference* (ed. S. E. Porter and T. H. Olbricht; JSNTSup 131; Sheffield: Sheffield Academic Press, 1996), 28–53.

3. Vernon K. Robbins, "The Rhetorical Full-Turn in Biblical Interpretation: Reconfiguring Rhetorical-Political Analysis," in *Rhetorical Criticism and the Bible: Essays from the 1998 Florence Conference* (ed. S. E. Porter and D. L. Stamps; JSNTSup 195; London: Sheffield Academic Press, 2002), 48. Cf. Robbins's essay in this volume.

often asked whether I am a "radical feminist" or a "good feminist." If, through the use of sociorhetorical analysis, I develop a radical interpretation of a text, does this make me a "radical feminist"? If I use Schüssler Fiorenza's rhetorical emancipatory paradigm without using oppositional rhetoric, does this make me a "good feminist"? Since I aim to show the complementarity of feminist biblical hermeneutics and sociorhetorical analysis, seeking to understand both the place and price of oppositional rhetoric, I prefer to call myself a "radically good feminist."

Vernon Robbins's Sociorhetorical Criticism

In his book *The Tapestry of Early Christian Discourse*, Vernon Robbins clearly states that his method of biblical interpretation arose out of the "challenge to integrate the major strategies of the new movements and methods."[4] He includes the perspectives of scientific, literary, rhetorical, and theological methods in a discursive and interactive way as a means to enter into the thickest texture of a text.[5] The term "sociorhetorical" integrates the resources of anthropology and sociology with the communicative aspects of language. In other words, it "integrates the ways people use language with the ways they live in the world."[6] The aim is not to arrive at one agreed-upon interpretation, but rather to nurture a cooperative effort in the acquisition and interpretation of the data.

In his sociorhetorical analysis, Robbins characterizes the text using the metaphor of a densely woven tapestry, whose threads intertwine to create complex patterns and imagery, which come into view only through observing the tapestry from different vantage points. Thus, the changing angle of the interpreter allows her or him to bring into view the different textures of the text. Five such textures are programmatically addressed in sociorhetorical analysis: inner texture, intertexture, social and cultural texture, ideological texture, and sacred texture.

Inner texture stays within the boundaries of the text itself. It looks primarily at the author, narrator, and characters as the reader encounters them in the text. Features considered in inner texture include the following: repetition of words, the use of verb tense, the beginning and ending of a textual unit, the text's rhetorical and argumentative styles,

---

4. Vernon K. Robbins, *The Tapestry of Early Christian Discourse: Rhetoric, Society and Ideology* (New York: Routledge, 1996), 1.

5. Vernon K. Robbins, *Exploring the Texture of Texts: A Guide to Socio-Rhetorical Interpretation* (Valley Forge, Pa.: Trinity Press International, 1996), 2; and idem, *Tapestry of Early Christian Discourse*, 14.

6. Ibid.

as well as its aesthetic qualities.[7] In contrast to the fixed boundaries of inner texture, the boundaries of intertexture are permeable, reaching beyond the text to the world outside of it. In intertexture, other texts play an important and even decisive role in the formulation of new texts. Intertexture regards the text as a series of verbal signs and codes, which incorporate through language the social, cultural, and historical realities outside of the actual text.[8] This texture is also referred to as oral-scribal intertexture.

The social and cultural texture of the text provides an awareness that the characters and narrators are functioning in a represented world, which reflects aspects of the world in which the text was originally written. The reader's perception of the narrator and the characters in the text is mediated through the voice used. Social and cultural texture is used to explore special, common, and final rhetorical topics that Robbins describes as "manifestations of social responses to the world, enactments of social and cultural systems and institutions, and performances of cultural alliances and conflicts" respectively.[9]

The focus of ideological texture shifts attention away from the text, the narrator and characters, and the represented world to both the real reader of the text and the reader for whom the text was intended. The reader of the text becomes the locus of empowerment for the message of the text.[10] Language embedded in texts and interpretations "evokes and nurtures ... alliances and conflicts"[11] within the reader and forms the fabric of ideological texture. This texture concerns the reception and empowerment of the message of the text by the implied and "real" reader(s) (including subsequent reception and interpretive histories). It extends beyond social and cultural texture "into the ways in which people advance their own interests and well-being through action, emotion, and thought."[12] Thus, each text and each interpretation has its own ideological texture. Sacred texture is Robbins's final texture, and it is particular to all texts, including the Bible, which reflect on the relationship

---

7. Robbins, *Tapestry of Early Christian Discourse*, 27–30; and idem, *Exploring the Texture of Texts*, 7–39.

8. Robbins, *Tapestry of Early Christian Discourse*, 30–33; and idem, *Exploring the Texture of Texts*, 40–70.

9. Robbins, *Tapestry of Early Christian Discourse*, 34. See also idem, *Exploring the Texture of Texts*, 71–94.

10. Robbins, *Tapestry of Early Christian Discourse*, 36–40; and idem, *Exploring the Texture of Texts*, 95–119.

11. Robbins, *Exploring the Texture of Texts*, 4.

12. Ibid.

between humanity and the divine. Here the diverse breadth of relationships between the human and divine are systematically explored.[13]

Sociorhetorical criticism recognizes language to be "the inner fabric of society, culture, ideology and religion."[14] Language functions in a multifaceted way to convey meanings, which in turn construct complex relations with other meaning-making mechanisms. Through its multitextured approach, sociorhetorical criticism seeks to uncover, in a programmatic way, these layers of meaning within texts. It does so by respecting and valuing the interaction of and exchange between reader and text, including the respective worlds that each bring into contact with the other. Sociorhetorical criticism is thus an interactive method, one that embraces the challenge of introducing dialogue on a scene of individual interest, embodying inclusion and integration through dialogue as a result.

It is precisely this dialogical approach that I consider to be Robbins's seminal contribution to the study of biblical texts. It allows for the many facets of the text, the interpreter, and the reader to be considered in a respectful and, in Robbins's own words, "responsible" manner.[15] I do become more cautious, however, with respect to his approach to ideological texture. I agree with Robbins that, "every mode of discourse is ideological, but not just ideological."[16] Nevertheless, there has been a tendency in mainstream biblical interpretation to perceive as purely ideological those interpreters, such as feminists (among others), who overtly express their political views at the outset of their interpretation. This tendency could be perpetuated rather easily by a practitioner of sociorhetorical analysis because of the programmatic nature of the interpretive process, which can, in the beginning, appear linear in orientation. Robbins, however, refers to this process as the unraveling of a thickly woven tapestry and not simply as the isolation of the individual threads—it is, rather, the discovery of the "networks of meaning and meaning effects" that exist in the text.[17] The interpreter's ideology is part of this process and should therefore not be equated with the whole of her or his interpretation.

---

13. Ibid., 120–31.
14. Robbins, *Tapestry of Early Christian Discourse*, 1.
15. Ibid., 27.
16. Ibid., 213.
17 Ibid., 20.

Elisabeth Schüssler Fiorenza's Feminist Biblical Criticism

The impetus for Schüssler Fiorenza's development of a feminist biblical criticism is rooted in the overwhelmingly patriarchal or "kyriarchal"
nature of the biblical text and mainstream biblical interpretation, which
perpetuates patriarchal structures of dominance and subservience. "Kyriarchy" is a neologism, which Schüssler Fiorenza has derived from "the
Greek word for the domination of elite propertied men over women and
other men"; patriarchy, by contrast, "is generally understood in feminist
discourses in terms of the western sex/gender system which posits a
man/woman opposition."[18] Hence, the rhetoric of kyriarchal biblical texts
and mainstream historical-critical interpretation reflects structures of
dominance and subservience in their social and cultural situation.

In her work, Schüssler Fiorenza explains that not only does rhetoric
respond to a social and cultural situation, it also reconstructs the world to
which it is responding. Thus, the rhetor has an ethical responsibility to
the world in front of the text as well.[19] In her method, Schüssler Fiorenza
engages kyriarchal modes of biblical interpretation only after using a
feminist practice of interpretation to "interrupt the perspectives and relations between text, reader and context which have been construed by
dominant doctrinal, literary, or historical reading formations."[20] In other
words, once aware of the androcentric presuppositions and patriarchal
underpinnings of texts and their interpretations, feminist criticism enters
into dialogue with other, more traditional strategies and methods of
interpretation.[21] Schüssler Fiorenza seeks, theoretically at least, to integrate and create such a dialogue between the diverse voices of both
feminist criticism and other approaches to biblical criticism. Practically,
however, she holds "scientific" biblical criticism accountable for its inherent and seemingly unconscious ability to exclude and dominate.[22] In this,
her position is not unlike Robbins's approach, which has as one of its
goals to "criticize the dominating interpretive practices that exclude . . .
marginal voices."[23]

In view of this end, Schüssler Fiorenza has distinguished between four
critical hermeneutical moments, which are set forth in her earlier paradigm

---

18. Elisabeth Schüssler Fiorenza, "Struggle Is a Name For Hope: A Critical Feminist
Interpretation for Liberation," *Pacifica* 10 (1997): 225. See also idem, *But She Said: Feminist
Practices of Biblical Interpretation* (Boston: Beacon, 1992), 117.
19. Schüssler Fiorenza, *Rhetoric and Ethic*, 66.
20. Schüssler Fiorenza, *But She Said*, 53.
21. Ibid.
22. Schüssler Fiorenza, "Challenging the Rhetorical Half-Turn," 28–53.
23. Robbins, *Tapestry of Early Christian Discourse*, 11.

for a feminist biblical interpretation for liberation developed in *Bread Not Stone:* ideological suspicion, historical reconstruction, theoretical assessment, and creative imagination. In *Rhetoric and Ethic,* these four hermeneutical moments have been woven into her "rhetorical-emancipatory paradigm," adding an experiential moment to the beginning, an internal analytical moment, and a moment of active transformation at the end. She describes these moments not in terms of a linear progression, but as movements in a circle dance, which are continually repeated throughout the interpretation of biblical texts.[24] In this dance, the feminist biblical critic is best situated as the one who performs the movements and embodies the interpretation. In other words, the feminist critic will seek to come to an interpretation of biblical texts that honors her or him as a whole person. Thus, the critic attempts to tease out the hidden nuances, which may either be affirming or oppressive in nature, opening up the possibility for being nurtured by texts that are liberating for her or him and for all of humanity.[25]

These movements can only be sustained when contextualized in what Schüssler Fiorenza calls "a feminist critical process of 'conscientization'," a process of learning to recognize sociopolitical, economic, cultural, and religious contradictions through an experience of cognitive dissonance in which there is a perceived difference between the givens of the patriarchal framework and one's lived experience.[26] This process of conscientization, along with a systemic analysis, initiates the

---

24. Schüssler Fiorenza, *Rhetoric and Ethic,* 49–53. A hermeneutics of experience and social location forms the starting point of this paradigm, which is rooted in Schüssler Fiorenza's view that in rhetorical analysis the context is every bit as critical as the text itself (19). It is essential, therefore, to identify the socioreligious and intellectual location of both the interpreter and the text. The next move in this interpretive dance is the shift to a hermeneutics of suspicion, which scrutinizes and interrogates biblical interpretive methods and biblical texts in order to tease out androcentrisms, patriarchal oppression, and hierarchical thinking, with the aim of uncovering the voices that have been silenced (50). A hermeneutics of ethical and theological evaluation moves the rhetorical-emancipatory critique toward assessing the rhetorics of texts and traditions, as well as contemporary discourses (51). A hermeneutics of remembrance and reconstruction increases the distance between the interpreter and the world of the text, while at the same time increasing historical knowledge and solidarity through a retelling of the stories of the past and present in order to create written history that complements a hermeneutics of imagination. A hermeneutics of imagination is based on the premise that the ability to imagine is the beginning of freedom, bringing about a new sense of justice and peace in the world (52). Finally, a hermeneutics of transformation and action for change has as its goal the alteration of structures of domination in biblical texts, traditions, and all of life. It must answer first to women who stand at the bottom of the "kyriarchal" pyramid.

25. Schüssler Fiorenza, *But She Said,* 52.

26. Ibid., 53.

transformative dance of feminist biblical interpretation, which seeks to realign the power structures of domination prevalent in patriarchal culture.[27] Thus, while the goal of Robbins's approach is to engender dialogue, the goal of Schüssler Fiorenza's paradigm is to prompt change and transformation through ethically responsible rhetoric. Indeed, Schüssler Fiorenza does place her ideological perspective at the forefront of her paradigm, prescribing as well the need to adopt analytical tools in the process of interpretation.[28] Her vision of a rhetorical-emancipatory approach to biblical interpretation insists on understanding biblical studies as a public discourse that holds interpretations, interpreters, interpretive methods, and texts accountable to a theo-ethics of interpretation wherein discourses of domination are eradicated. Her position provides a vision of conscientization, articulation, and redemption, which moves from the heart of even the greatest oppression (and oppressors) toward emancipation. Schüssler Fiorenza suggests that the most conducive setting for biblical interpretation is, therefore, what she calls the "ekklesia of women."[29]

In her earlier work, Schüssler Fiorenza named the *ekklesia* of women the *ekklesia gynaikon* (women-church), which she described as "the movement of self-identified women and women-identified men in biblical religion."[30] The phrase "women-identified men" is used by Schüssler Fiorenza to indicate the need for men to advocate for "a theology of relinquishment" that recognizes the oppressive structures of patriarchy and actively participates in liberating women and men from their restrictive hold. The term "women-church," rather than being an exclusive concept, is used here by Schüssler Fiorenza as a politically-oppositional term to patriarchy, one that focuses on the *ekklesia* as the public assembly of free citizens—women and men—who gather in order to determine their own

---

27. Ibid., 52.

28. In comparison, then, it seems that Schüssler Fiorenza's approach is primarily ideological in its basic orientation, having perhaps a single aim, while Robbins's approach appears to be comprehensive in nature, viewing the text from a broader interpretive spectrum. While he identifies helpful tools and sets up a programmatic interpretive process for their use, Robbins never prescribes the ideological perspective of the interpreter. It is the perspective of the interpreter that breathes life into the interpretation; thus, in Robbins's framework, the ideological perspective of the interpreter is critical to the dialogue of interpretation. This element represents another point of complementarity between the approaches of both Robbins and Schüssler Fiorenza: they present different facets (or tempos) of the larger interpretive dance. The essential difference is that one focuses more directly on the text and tradition, and the other more squarely on the interpreter.

29. Ibid., 55.

30. Elisabeth Schüssler Fiorenza, *Bread Not Stone: The Challenge of Feminist Biblical Interpretation* (Boston: Beacon, 1984), xiv.

and their children's communal political and spiritual well-being.[31] In her more recent work, Schüssler Fiorenza alters the term *ekklesia gynaikon* so that now *ekklesia* used on its own can denote first and foremost the multiplicity represented in the "Discipleship of Equals" rather than be seen as prioritizing one voice within it.[32]

THE CONTRADICTION OF OPPOSITIONAL
RHETORIC IN FEMINIST INTERPRETATION

It is precisely from Schüssler Fiorenza's *ekklesia* of equals that Robbins's challenge to her use of rhetoric stems. He points out that she claims to stand within this *ekklesia*, while at the same time using oppositional rhetoric in her critique of Robbins's own work.[33] Considering that the fundamental principle of this *ekklesia* is that of equality, Robbins explains that Schüssler Fiorenza's methodological use of oppositional rhetoric is discordant with her message of equality. Robbins adds that oppositional rhetoric closes down discussion due to its "inner attributes of domination and separation [which Schüssler Fiorenza claims, in her feminist biblical criticism and her rhetoric of inquiry, that] she must move beyond."[34] He then articulates the "deep antipathy" that exists "between what [Schüssler Fiorenza] says and what she does." In Robbins's words, "her discourse enacts a dominating, alienating, oppositional mode of rhetorical argumentation."[35]

In her earlier article, "Challenging the Rhetorical Half-Turn," Schüssler Fiorenza had argued that Robbins's sociorhetorical criticism is wrought with empiricist-positivistic scientistic thinking, which is rooted in a "political conservatism [that] has legitimated relations of domination."[36] For Schüssler Fiorenza, this problem is present neither in his own rhetorical expression nor in his analysis of texts, but, rather, in his actual development and use of sociorhetorical analysis and the entire framework that it presupposes. If Robbins, whom Schüssler Fiorenza describes as quite inclusive of feminist scholarship, thus stands accused, then even more so does the rest of the biblical scholarly guild.

---

31. Furthermore, she explains that "women-church" must be understood "as the dialogical community of equals in which critical judgment takes place and public freedom becomes tangible" (Schüssler Fiorenza, *Bread Not Stone*, xiv).

32. Schüssler Fiorenza, *Rhetoric and Ethic*, 11.

33. Robbins, "Rhetorical Full-Turn," 51.

34. Ibid.

35. Ibid.

36. Schüssler Fiorenza, "Challenging the Rhetorical Half-Turn," 35.

As already mentioned earlier, Schüssler Fiorenza explains elsewhere that rhetoric is a major factor in the construction of the world around us. She states that "[r]hetoric seeks to persuade the person to *act right*."[37] The hearer/reader engages in the text's rhetorical motivation, which evokes in her or him a particular response. Schüssler Fiorenza understands a *rhetorical* analysis to necessitate a "communicative praxis" wherein "knowledge" is linked with "action and passion."[38] She asserts that a rhetoric of inquiry "enable[s] biblical scholars to investigate the discursive arguments which perform particular kinds of actions in particular kinds of historical situations and at particular political sites."[39] The success of the rhetorical approach becomes evident in the actions of the hearer/reader.[40] In other words, rhetoric forms and constructs the world around us, the way we speak in that world, and the questions we ask about it. In addition, Schüssler Fiorenza points out that the environment into which a rhetorical approach moves is one of public discussion and communication, as opposed to the "value-detached scientistic posture" of "authoritarian" monologue.[41]

In light of Schüssler Fiorenza's rhetorical stance, which he happens to agree with, Robbins proposes an inquiry into the historical site and political situation that elicited her use of oppositional rhetoric. Rather than proceeding to this inquiry, however, Robbins shifts his discussion to the use of oppositional discourse in New Testament texts. His discussion reveals many instances of oppositional rhetoric in the early Christian writings, as well as in subsequent interpretations of them. His conclusion remains: oppositional rhetoric "closes off issues rather than [moving] them into a context of free exchange among equal partners in dialogue."[42] However, Robbins leaves two issues unresolved: the historical site of Schüssler Fiorenza's use of oppositional rhetoric and its political context.

HISTORICAL SITE AND POLITICAL CONTEXT
OF SCHÜSSLER FIORENZA'S USE OF OPPOSITIONAL RHETORIC

In "Challenging the Rhetorical Half-Turn," Schüssler Fiorenza engages positivist and scientistic scholarship's "radical detachment, [its]

---

37. Elisabeth Schüssler Fiorenza, "Rhetorical Situation and Historical Reconstruction in 1 Corinthians," *NTS* 33 (1987): 387 (emphasis original).

38. Elisabeth Schüssler Fiorenza. "Biblical Interpretation and Critical Commitment," *ST* 43 (1989): 10.

39. Schüssler Fiorenza, "Challenging the Rhetorical Half-Turn," 36.

40. Schüssler Fiorenza, "Rhetorical Situation," 387.

41. Schüssler Fiorenza, "Biblical Interpretation," 9–10.

42. Robbins, "Rhetorical Full-Turn," 51.

emotional, intellectual and political distancing,"[43] which continues to result in the marginalization of liberationist, African American, and feminist theologies. A rhetoric of inquiry reveals that the historical world reconstructed by the interpreter is necessarily configured through the linguistic and conceptual framework of the viewer.[44] In short, no interpretation is completely free of the social and political interests of the interpreter. Schüssler Fiorenza therefore advocates for a rhetorical shift in scientistic biblical scholarship. She insists that biblical scholarship, under the guise of scientistic universalist objectivity, covers up its "masculine embodiment"[45] and therefore results in the legitimation of "relations of domination."[46] Schüssler Fiorenza thus identifies herself "as a 'connected critic' who speaks from a marginal location,"[47] recognizing herself as marginalized within the political site of scientistic biblical scholarship.

In delineating Schüssler Fiorenza's historical situation, it is important to keep in mind that she is both a woman and a feminist. Both aspects add character to her historical situation, as well as to her historical perspective. She enters a long line of women's history marked by subordination to men. Quoting Virginia Woolf, Schüssler Fiorenza refers to this historical situation as her rhetorical context. Her female identity permits only the "outsider's view":

> It is a solemn sight always—a procession like a caravanserai crossing a desert. Great-grandfathers, grandfathers, fathers, uncles—they all went that way wearing their gowns, wearing their wigs, some with ribbons across their breasts, others without. One was a bishop. Another a judge. One was an admiral. Another a general. One was a professor. Another a doctor ... But now for the past twenty years or so, it is no longer a sight merely, a photograph ... at which we can look with merely an esthetic

---

43. Schüssler Fiorenza, "Biblical Interpretation," 7; cf. idem, "Challenging the Rhetorical Half-Turn," 31.

44. Schüssler Fiorenza, "Biblical Interpretation," 7; and idem, "Challenging the Rhetorical Half-Turn," 31.

45. Schüssler Fiorenza, "Biblical Interpretation," 6.

46. Schüssler Fiorenza, "Challenging the Rhetorical Half-Turn," 35; cf. idem, *In Memory of Her: A Feminist Theological Reconstruction of Christian Origins* (2d ed.; New York: Crossroad, 1993), xviii.

47. Elisabeth Schüssler Fiorenza, "The Ethics of Biblical Interpretation: Decentering Biblical Scholarship," *JBL* 107 (1988): 5. See also Ronald Thiemann, "Faith and the Public Intellectual," in *Walk in the Ways of Wisdom: Essays in Honor of Elisabeth Schüssler Fiorenza* (ed. S. Matthews, C. Briggs Kittredge, and M. Johnson-Debaufre; New York: Continuum, 2003), 91–93.

appreciation. For there, trapesing [sic] along at the tail end of the procession, we go ourselves. And that makes a difference.[48]

At first learning only male-stream biblical interpretive methods, Schüssler Fiorenza, through her own experience of cognitive dissonance in the face of biblical texts and interpretive methods, moved from developing a feminist hermeneutics of biblical interpretation to becoming the first woman president of the Society of Biblical Literature.[49] She clarifies, however, that acceptance of women in such positions of authority in the guild does not imply that the interests and perspectives of women are at the forefront in biblical scholarship.[50] As a matter of fact, Schüssler Fiorenza points with undeniable persistence to the pervasive character of scientistic and positivist biblical scholarship in maintaining the marginalization of women.[51] It is the male-embodiment of the scientistic perspective that, when looking at the social and cultural texture of Schüssler Fiorenza's text, represents the dominant culture, and those in the dominant culture possess power and function in impositional ways.[52] Although they do not have the need to use oppositional language, representatives of the dominant culture do use language that is closed and restrictive to those outside of that culture. Although raised in this culture, Schüssler Fiorenza operates from its margins. Hence, in Robbins's categorization of cultures, she would fall under "liminal culture," which exists on "the outer edge of identity."[53] Still, I think her culture can be much better characterized as "countercultural," as it arises out of the dominant culture and rejects its central value: androcentrism.[54] As a result, the political, historical, and cultural situation of Schüssler Fiorenza, as I have sketched it here, is one of struggle against kyriarchal structures, which represent dominant male-stream society as it stands in opposition against anyone or anything defined as other than itself.

---

48. Virginia Woolf, *Three Guineas* (New York: Harcourt, Brace & World, 1966), quoted in Schüssler Fiorenza, "Ethics of Biblical Interpretation," 16.

49. Schüssler Fiorenza, "Ethics of Biblical Interpretation," 6.

50. Ibid.

51. Schüssler Fiorenza, "Challenging the Rhetorical Half-Turn," 28–53. This is also a recurrent theme in her earlier work; see, e.g., idem, "Remembering the Past in Creating the Future: Historical Critical Scholarship and Feminist Biblical Interpretation," in *Feminist Perspectives on Biblical Scholarship* (ed. A. Y. Collins; SBLBSNA 10; Chico, Calif.: Scholars Press, 1985), 43–63.

52. Robbins, *Tapestry of Early Christian Discourse*, 168.

53. Ibid., 170.

54. Ibid., 169.

In the midst of this struggle against a dominant structure, Schüssler Fiorenza recognizes that "[s]truggle is a name for hope." She argues that:

> feminists in religion ... must neither abandon nor defend kyriarchal texts and religions. Rather, we must articulate what it means for wo/men to have religious theological agency, voice and authority to participate in the critical construction and assessment of religious, biblical, and theo-ethical meanings and to assert their authority to do so. In reclaiming the authority of wo/men as religious-theological subjects for interpreting biblical texts, for shaping religious communities and for defining biblical religions ... [b]iblical interpretation becomes the site of struggle, and emancipatory struggles are the site of feminist biblical interpretation.[55]

Inherent to feminist biblical interpretation, then, is the movement toward liberation from oppressive structures. Schüssler Fiorenza recognizes that the need for liberation presupposes an oppressor/oppressed dynamic, basing her understanding of this dynamic on the work of Paulo Freire. In this framework, as Freire argues, it becomes natural and to some extent inevitable for the struggle of an oppressed people "against" their oppressor to involve opposition.[56] He cautions that "in order for the struggle to have meaning, the oppressed must not ... become in turn oppressors of the oppressors but rather the restorers of the [full] humanity of both."[57] Freire perceives the task of the oppressed as liberating their oppressors as well as themselves, pointing out that in the process, however, the shift of the oppressed to oppressor is a natural transition in the struggle for liberation.[58] This transitory reaction is a result of the conditioned state of the very structure of the thoughts of the oppressed. If the oppressed have successfully internalized the dualistic nature of oppressor/oppressed relations, then, as they struggle toward liberation, they seek to move from one side of the dualism to the other. This level of success is not liberation since the limitations of the dualism persist. Deliverance occurs only when the oppressed are able to transform the dualism into that which is its opposite: liberation from dualistic structures altogether. The use of oppositional rhetoric, then, may compromise the desired emancipation rather than bring it to fruition. This does not mean, however, that there is no

---

55. Schüssler Fiorenza, "Struggle Is a Name for Hope," 226.
56. Paulo Freire, *Pedagogy of the Oppressed* (New York: Seabury, 1968), 28.
57. Ibid., 61.
58. Ibid., 29–30. This point is similar to the concept of "mimicry" as developed by postcolonial theorist Homi K. Bhabha (see "Of Mimicry and Man: The Ambivalence of Colonial Discourse," in *The Location of Culture* [New York: Routledge, 1994], 85–92).

place for oppositional rhetoric and oppositional positions. In order to be able to move away emphatically from dualisms both sides of the dualism need to be articulated, and thus sometimes an oppositional stance may be strategic in identifying the less obvious side of the dualism. Thus, oppositional rhetoric can provide a critical step in the unmasking of the power structures by uncovering and naming the implicit dualistic systems that are in fact operative.

Schüssler Fiorenza understands feminist biblical interpretation to be an active participant in the struggle toward the emancipation of religion at the site of biblical interpretation. Her discourse has been referred to as utopian, meaning that her discourse activates "a critical practice of creatively imagining the world otherwise ... in the political present."[59] Such a different world as this, which does not reconstruct oppressive dualisms, necessarily stands in opposition to a world that is constructed of dualisms, thereby creating, ironically, yet another dualism. Although it is not inevitable that oppositional rhetoric be used in a discourse representing an opposing paradigm, it is almost unavoidable in practice when the (in this instance utopian) discourse is bound by time and place to use the same language as the world that it opposes. As Schüssler Fiorenza acknowledges in her rhetorical-emancipatory paradigm, "utopian visions *are always both informed and deformed by our present sociopolitical location.*"[60]

ENGAGING THE DISCUSSION

Taking into account Schüssler Fiorenza's own sociopolitical location, the occurrence of oppositional rhetoric in her discourse appears to be strategic. As discussed earlier, she places herself on the margins from which she struggles with *all* marginalized people for liberation from androcentrism, patriarchy, and kyriarchy. Dominant cultures are ideologically predisposed to impose their own culture on others. The most effective way of accomplishing this goal is through language, which, as both Robbins and Schüssler Fiorenza admit,[61] is an integral thread in the "inner fabric of society, culture, ideology and religion."[62] The effect of dominant culture on fringe societies is pervasive and all-encompassing,

---

59. Elizabeth A. Castelli, "The *Ekklesia* of Women and/as Utopian Space: Locating the Work of Elisabeth Schüssler Fiorenza in Feminist Utopian Thought," in *On the Cutting Edge: Study of Women in Biblical Worlds,* (ed. J. Schaberg, A. Bach, and E. Fuchs; New York: Continuum, 2003), 40.

60. Schüssler Fiorenza, *Rhetoric and Ethic,* 53 (emphasis hers). A similar point is made by Jorunn Økland, "Why Can't the Heavenly Miss Jerusalem Just Shut Up?," in this volume.

61. Schüssler Fiorenza, "Biblical Interpretation," 7.

62. Robbins, *Tapestry of Early Christian Discourse,* 1.

as the dominant culture is the one that controls the shifts in language, society, culture, ideology, and religion. Clearly language serves as a powerful tool in this agenda, and Freire's strategy for the emancipation of the oppressed is derived from precisely this insight. In teaching people who were illiterate to read and write, Freire noticed that they had "come to new awareness of selfhood and beg[a]n to look critically at the social situation in which they found themselves, often tak[ing] the initiative in acting to transform the society that has denied them this opportunity of participation."[63] Yet the danger of replicating or mimicking the discourse of the dominant culture is ever present.

Robbins's critique of Schüssler Fiorenza recognizes this dualism in her discourse as an opposition "between what she says and what she does." By using oppositional rhetoric, Schüssler Fiorenza runs the risk of creating a rhetorical situation of opposition in response to her message. As a result, the feminist vision of equality and integration seems to be compromised. The question then becomes whether the use of oppositional rhetoric in a feminist method of biblical interpretation provides an effective way of moving toward equality and liberation. Schüssler Fiorenza does note that "tensions and slippages in any text that struggles to dislocate established discursive paradigms of interpretation" are unavoidable.[64] Yet, while the dominant culture may well have shaped the language and historical context that gave birth to feminist biblical interpretation, transformation from within can be affected nevertheless—and this is a serious issue that needs further consideration by those practicing liberationist models of interpretation.

Feminist biblical scholars must use their language and stand in their historical and political space and time in order to imagine "a different world of justice and well-being."[65] It is for this reason that conscientization has been placed at the forefront of feminist biblical interpretation. Schüssler Fiorenza insists on the need for consciousness in seeking androcentrisms in texts and their interpretations,[66] and Robbins addresses this need at the level of the historical influences that have shaped the interpreter.[67] Both aspects are vital in a feminist critical hermeneutic. Oppositional rhetoric, although strategic at times, does not serve the aims of a critical feminist hermeneutic for biblical interpretation, as it maintains the dualism and places the focus of feminist scholarship on the

---

63. Freire, *Pedagogy of the Oppressed*, 9.
64. Schüssler Fiorenza, *In Memory of Her*, xvii.
65. Schüssler Fiorenza, *Rhetoric and Ethic*, 52.
66. Schüssler Fiorenza, *But She Said*, 52.
67. Robbins, *Tapestry of Early Christian Discourse*, 27.

struggle against patriarchy rather than on the liberation of all. Other forms of rhetoric can more creatively be engaged to express a contentious point, while at the same time "enabl[ing] free and open discussion and controversy in an environment where we [invite] our colleagues"[68] to join us in the circle dance. Robbins recognizes this metaphor as a guiding principle in the development of his own sociorhetorical method. This dance, as it etches out practices of a critical feminist biblical interpretation, disturbs the balance of binary perspectives. Schüssler Fiorenza describes this phenomenon thus:

> [It is] an image of interpretation as forward movement and spiraling repetition, stepping in place, turning over and changing of venue in which discrete methodological approaches become moving steps and artful configurations. Clumsy participants in this dance that figures the complex enterprise of biblical criticism may frequently step on each other's toes and interrupt each other's turns but they can still dance together as long as they acknowledge each other as equals conscious of dancing through a political minefield.[69]

Robbins and Schüssler Fiorenza are partners in this dance. Yet, while they share the same vision, the battles they fight are different. Robbins circles from within, while Schüssler Fiorenza turns on the margins. Their integrated dance propels historical-critical interpretation by placing embodied interpreters before richly textured texts in order to develop interpretations that respond to real communities. Therefore, the dance between Robbins and Schüssler Fiorenza needs to continue according to its natural rhythm, a full turn here, a half turn there. And consciousness is the beat that drives this dance. The movement into liberation out of oppression necessitates grace and circumspection as the dancer moves through the "political minefield" that has been laid by the structures of oppression and dominance. Indeed, clumsy moments are to be expected, for the participants are new and the dance newer still. Yet as we embrace this dance of cooperation and conscious communication, we may well find ourselves one step closer to liberating not simply ourselves, but others as well.

---

68. Robbins, "Rhetorical Full-Turn," 58.
69. Schüssler Fiorenza, "Challenging the Rhetorical Half-Turn," 51.

"AND THEY DID SO":
FOLLOWING ORDERS GIVEN BY OLD JOSHUA

Kristin De Troyer

Most scholars regard text criticism as a boring enterprise that has no relevance for feminist issues. One incident that happened a few years ago might shed light on this perception. I was invited to a panel session at the annual meeting of the Society of Biblical Literature consisting of women who had recently completed feminist-oriented dissertations. Two women presented their work and two other women were invited to give a response. This panel was then followed by questions from the audience. One woman raised her hand and asked me this critical question: "How could I label myself a feminist," she wanted to know, "and still be occupied with one of the most dated methods of exegesis?" Indeed, many feminists do not see the need for text criticism, as it generally does not address feminist issues or raise feminist questions. The query deserved a thoughtful answer, and I thus did my best to explain the relevance of text criticism to the focus of the panel. My efforts were apparently not sufficient, for the discussion continued after the session and the negative attitude toward my approach remained. Yet the question is a legitimate one, and I am still fully convinced that a relationship between text criticism and the interests of feminist analysis can be established. Even more, I am persuaded that as feminist scholars of the Bible we must engage this relationship more thoroughly and substantively than we have in the past.

In light of this consideration, the goal of my contribution is twofold. First, I will introduce a more recent form of text criticism, one that also has in view literary- (and redaction-) critical issues and questions. Scholars such as Adrian Schenker, Pierre-Maurice Bogaert, and Emanuel Tov, for instance, already practice this newer form of textual criticism.[1] Second, I will show how this form of text criticism contributes to the field

---

1. See, for instance, Adrian Schenker, ed., *The Earliest Text of the Hebrew Bible: The Relationship between the Masoretic Text and the Hebrew Base of the Septuagint Reconsidered* (SBLSCS 52; Atlanta: Society of Biblical Literature, 2003).

of feminist and gender studies, as well as to the broader field of cultural studies. I will use an example from the Old Greek book of Joshua to illustrate my point. I aim to demonstrate that the approach I have been developing in various projects over the past few years has the potential to have a dramatic impact on the analyses and concerns shared by feminist and gender critics. I will show how feminist questions and issues can be raised at the level of both the primary establishment of a (biblical) text and the reconstruction of the different layers within a text.

Modern Methods?

For many scholars, the actual text of the biblical book with which they work is taken for granted. They usually "start" with an "established text," such as the Masoretic Text printed in *Biblia Hebraica Stuttgartensia*, or, for the apocrypha, the Greek text as printed in Rahlfs' edition of the Septuagint. Followers of both modern and traditional approaches share such standardized biblical texts. This situation exists, for instance, in the cases of Benedict Otzen and David Clines—two well-respected biblical scholars, who demonstrate the history of the development of a given biblical text in order to explain how the "established text" came into being.

In my recent review of Benedict Otzen's book on Tobit and Judith,[2] I express my admiration for his analysis of Tobit, an area that is certainly Otzen's greatest strength. In his book, Otzen applies a Proppian analysis to the story of Tobit.[3] Using a synchronic approach for diachronic ends, he thus reconstructs the history of the literary layers of the book. In his analysis, Otzen distinguishes various older forms of the narrative, ranging from a cross-cultural fairy-tale to a Jewish legend. In total, Otzen recognizes four stages in the formation of the book. I was especially interested in the last stage—the stage where the story of Tobit becomes the biblical book, as we now know it. In this last stage of its formation, elements from Jewish history, religious motifs, themes regarding the exile, and elements from other biblical and nonbiblical writings were added to the final form.[4] In 1984, David Clines made a similar reconstruction of the history of the book of Esther.[5] He showed how various strands and

---

2. Benedikt Otzen, *Tobit and Judith* (Guides to Apocrypha and Pseudepigrapha; Sheffield: Sheffield Academic Press, 2002). For my review, see *RSR* 29 (2004): 378.

3. See the influential study by Vladimir J. Propp, *Morphology of the Folktale* (trans. L. Scott; 2d ed.; Publications of the American Folklore Society, Biographical and Special Series 9; Austin: University of Texas Press, 1968).

4. Otzen, *Tobit and Judith*, 16–20.

5. David J. A. Clines, *The Esther Scroll: The Story of the Story* (JSOTSup 30; Sheffield: Sheffield Academic Press, 1984).

elements were added to a shorter book, which finally became the Masoretic Text. Although he used a different method of analysis (literary as opposed to folklorist), Clines's reconstruction followed a pattern similar to the one suggested by Otzen. However, whereas Otzen tried to explain how a nonreligious story became a Jewish religious one, Clines tried to explain the precise opposite: why in an earlier form the book of Esther was a religious text but in the later, final Hebrew text edition God was entirely absent and references to religious discourse were omitted.

The underlying presupposition of both analyses, however, was the same: an author had been adding or omitting elements from a former story, adapting the narrative to a new context or audience. Both the textual history and the literary growth of the books of Esther and Tobit are thus understood as a process of adding and omitting material to an already existing text. While both Clines and Otzen clearly used newer or modern modes of analysis to make their point, these methods, although bearing new names and labels, are, in my opinion, essentially earlier approaches dressed in fresh garb. Clines in fact used redaction and literary criticism, which are classical exegetical methods, while Otzen's Proppian analysis can be seen as a form-critical study combined with redaction critical insights, both of which are also traditional exegetical methods. As I will demonstrate in what follows, these methods all have a similar relationship to text criticism as traditionally practiced.

TRADITIONAL TEXT CRITICISM

In textbooks on method, such as Odil Hannes Steck's introduction to exegetical approaches to the study of the Old Testament/Hebrew Bible,[6] a clear distinction is made between text criticism and literary criticism as two separate stages of analysis. Text criticism first defines and delimits the text, and then literary criticism analyzes the building blocks, textual units, and/or sources within that text. According to Steck, text criticism is mainly concerned with manuscript transmission. He states that "manuscript transmission is, as a rule, not without error" and that therefore "a distinction between unintentional mistakes and intentional changes"[7] must be made. According to Steck, the task of text criticism is "to locate the errors and if possible, to establish the 'original' text of the O[ld] T[estament]."[8] Text criticism thus has no other goal

---

6. Odil Hannes Steck, *Old Testament Exegesis: A Guide to the Methodology* (2d ed.; SBLRBS 39; Atlanta: Society of Biblical Literature, 1996).

7. Ibid., 39.

8. Ibid., 40.

than the establishment of the original text, which in this framework can also be labeled the "final form" of the biblical text. Indeed, very often scholars simply operate on the assumption that the text printed in *Biblia Hebraica Stuttgartensia* is in fact the original or final version of the Hebrew Bible, but that is not necessarily the case. I will return to this matter below. For the moment, however, it bears repeating that in this traditional paradigm, briefly outlined here, text criticism is understood to focus on determining the text itself, while literary criticism is deemed essential for investigating the evolution of the material contained within the text. It unravels the text's different literary units, locates these units in literary layers, explains how one can recognize those different layers, and reconstructs the textual genesis of these layers. Literary criticism thus tries to determine/reconstruct the different parts out of which the so-called "final form" of the biblical text is formed.

According to the traditional division between literary criticism and text criticism, literary criticism can only be undertaken after text criticism has defined the text, which literary critics then analyze further. This strict division between the two methods is still present in most of the handbooks and introductions to the Hebrew Bible/Old Testament and regarded as the paradigm within which the exegete should work. Indeed, most of my colleagues still work within this paradigm. Even those who criticize so-called older methods still operate within a traditional historical-critical paradigm when working with a strict division between text and literary criticism.

RENEWED TEXT CRITICISM

The paradigm just outlined has, however, been challenged. In his double handbook on text criticism—one on the Hebrew Bible[9] and one on the Septuagint[10]—Emanuel Tov addresses the more recent shift in the goal and function of textual criticism. The discoveries in the Judean desert are the main factor in this new development, because, although the majority of the biblical texts found at Qumran confirm the existing established Masoretic Text, a small minority do not. This small minority of texts therefore point to the existence of versions that differ from their Masoretic counterpart. Jeremiah is one of the prime examples here.[11]

---

9. Emanuel Tov, *Textual Criticism of the Hebrew Bible* (2d ed.; Minneapolis: Fortress; Assen: Van Gorcum, 2001).

10. Emanuel Tov, *The Text-Critical Use of the Septuagint in Biblical Research* (2d ed.; Jerusalem Biblical Studies 8; Jerusalem: Simor, 1997).

11. Ibid., 243–45.

While two text-fragments reflect the Masoretic Text of the book of Jeremiah, two others correspond with the Old Greek text of Jeremiah. A variety of other biblical books were found at Qumran as well, which also seem to exist in more than just the masoretic form. These texts now beg the question: Which form is the earlier? Or, stated more neutrally, what is the relation between the different texts of the same biblical book? Some scholars accept that different and independent texts of the same biblical book existed side by side at Qumran. Tov, for instance, considers the various forms of the book of Joshua to be independent texts of the same biblical book.[12] If there are two independent texts of the book of Joshua, then which one is the original biblical text? Or, are they both original biblical texts? And how is one to use the two variants in text criticism and in literary criticism? Others explain the different texts as representing different stages in the development of the Masoretic Text. Eugene Ulrich, for instance, reconstructs the history of the book of Joshua using the Masoretic Text, the Old Greek, Josephus, and the Qumran text of 4QJosh[a], acknowledging a dependence of one text on the other.[13] This perspective still allows one to regard the Masoretic Text as the reference or target text in and for textual criticism, whereas in Tov's hypothesis the selection of a primary target text has become more problematic. Tov and Ulrich's positions, however, have contributed to the change in goal and function of text criticism and its relationship to literary criticism.

Although the discoveries in the Judean desert have indeed been very influential and crucial in shaping a new understanding of the field and method of text criticism, scholars could have come to similar conclusions using other textual evidence long before the scrolls emerged.[14] In other words, we could already have known a lot if we had studied and taken seriously witnesses different from those found at Qumran. Take, for instance, the Old Greek text of Joshua.[15] For over a century, the differences between the Old Greek and the Hebrew Masoretic Text have been recognized and studied within the framework of the old division between text criticism and literary criticism, with the goal of establishing

---

12. Ibid., 245–49.

13. Eugene Ulrich et al., *Qumran Cave 4—IX: Deuteronomy, Joshua, Judges, Kings* (DJD 14; Oxford: Clarendon, 1996), 143–46; and idem, *The Dead Sea Scrolls and the Origins of the Bible* (Studies in the Dead Sea Scrolls and Related Literature; Grand Rapids: Eerdmans; Leiden: Brill, 1999), 27–28.

14. Kristin De Troyer, "Fifty Years of Qumran Research: A Different Approach," *RSR* 28 (2002): 115–22.

15. Another example would be the so-called extracanonical psalms from Qumran, namely, Pss 151–55. We could have learned a lot more about these alternative traditions if we had earlier studied the Syriac text more carefully. Cf. ibid., 121.

the final or the original text. Once this "originality" was established, a literary analysis could start, but very few commentators actually used the differences in their analysis. Little attention was given to establishing the hermeneutical principles at work during the process of literary formation of the Bible—or, more precisely, the biblical texts (in the plural!).

It is, however, precisely the tracing of the editorial changes or the hermeneutical principles from one text to another that can shed light on the literary development of a given text. Thus, when one turns to the analysis of the literary development of the biblical texts, one enters the realm of literary criticism. Hence, the study of witnesses and texts, formerly considered the domain of text criticism proper, becomes part of the study of the redactional development of a text and thus part of literary criticism and redaction criticism. In other words, the witnesses from the Judean Desert alongside the Old Greek, Old Latin, Syriac and other textual witnesses are no longer used now solely to reconstruct or establish the final form of the text, but have become tools with which to reconstruct the history/histories of the biblical text/s.[16] Indeed, one might say that this shift has also called into question the very idea of an "original" or "final form" text—a strikingly postmodern observation from a highly modernist enterprise!

Although these critical shifts may seem rather technical and theoretical, they do affect the realities of feminist and broader cultural studies. I will elaborate on one example from the book of Joshua to shed light on this change in method and its consequences for the field of feminist, gender, and cultural studies. The example focuses on orders given in the book of Joshua.[17]

Orders Need To Be Followed!

I begin my discussion with an analysis of the commands, or the orders, given by God, Joshua, or other important figures in the book of Joshua, both in the Masoretic Text and in the Old Greek text.[18] I selected

---

16. For further elaboration of this topic, see Kristin De Troyer, *Rewriting the Sacred Text: What the Old Greek Texts Tell Us about the Literary Growth of the Bible* (SBLTCS; Atlanta: Society of Biblical Literature, 2003).

17. The material in this section is based on my contribution to the Festschrift for Emanuel Tov. See Kristin De Troyer, "Did Joshua Have a Crystal Ball? The Old Greek and the MT of Joshua 10:15,17 and 23," in *Emanuel: Studies in Hebrew Bible, Septuagint and Dead Sea Scrolls in Honour of Emanuel Tov* (ed. S. M. Paul et al.; VTSup 94; Leiden: Brill, 2003), 571–89. See also idem, *Rewriting the Sacred Text*, 29–58.

18. I am most grateful to Udo Quast from the Septuagint Unternehmen at Göttingen for allowing me to consult his work on the critical edition of Joshua (to be published in *Septuaginta. Vetus testamentum graecum. Auctoritate academiae scientiarum gottingensis editum* [Göttingen:

this topic because I had noticed a marked attempt throughout the narrative to highlight the authority (and hence importance) of leaders of the community. It is not enough to "order," however, the other element that is critical for establishing a character's authority is whether or not his or her orders are obeyed in the ensuing narrative. In the book of Joshua, both God and Joshua appear as important characters, but are their orders also executed? Do people follow their commands or not?

After delineating the commands given by God and Joshua in the narrative of the Hebrew book of Joshua, I will examine whether or not the orders are followed by those who are commanded to do so. The first order appears in Josh 4:5, where Joshua gives the following command: "Pass on before the ark of the LORD your God into the middle of the Jordan, and each of you take up a stone on his shoulder, one for each of the tribes of the Israelites" (NRSV). The command is heeded, as the narrator's report reflects: "And the children of Israel did so, as the Lord commanded Joshua; and they took up twelve stones out of the midst of Jordan ... and carried these stones with them into the camp, and laid them down there" (Josh 4:8). The twelve stones are set up at Gilgal precisely as the Lord commanded Joshua. In 10:22, Joshua gives another command: "open the cave and bring out the kings." The text reports that the command is followed (10:23). Again, as in 4:8, the words "and they did so" appear. Further, the next line includes the phrase "and they brought out the kings," thus repeating part of the command just given. As a result, the command uttered by Joshua is confirmed twice: by the phrase "and they did so" and by the repetition of part of the command in the process of describing the response. Something similar also happens in the next verse. In 10:24, a command is given and the command is literally executed. The narrator repeats the words of the command in the execution line, but the words "and they did so" do not occur. The command of verse 24a—"come and put your feet on their necks"—is simply followed in verse 24b by "and they came and put their feet on their necks." In this case the entire command is repeated.

Apart from the two cases just mentioned, the phrase "and he/they did so" also appears in Josh 5:15. In his vision, "the 'commander of the army of the Lord' said to Joshua, 'Remove the sandals from your feet, for the place where you stand is holy'. And Joshua did so." This verse reminds the reader of the famous passage in Exod 3:5, where Moses is

---

Vandenhoeck & Ruprecht]) and to use the "Kollationshefte" prepared for that volume. The edition of the Old Greek Joshua manuscript from the Schøyen collection will be published in Kristin De Troyer, *Joshua* (ed. R. Pintaudi; Catalogue of the Schøyen Greek Papyri; Oslo-London: The Martin Schøyen Collection, 2004).

similarly ordered to remove his sandals. Here Joshua receives the same command. The narrator, however, does not repeat the words of the command, but simply states "and he did so."[19] By this inclusion he stresses that Joshua obeys God's command. A distinctive pattern can thus be observed in the Hebrew textual tradition of the book of Joshua, where commands by authoritative figures are given. The authority of the character in question receives narrative confirmation in a variety of ways, from direct mention of the fulfillment of the order to the repetition of words from the command in the description of the response. The question now is if this pattern also occurs in the Greek text.

Turning to the Greek text of Joshua, one notices that LXX Josh 4:5 and verse 8 contain both the line of command and the line of execution and that LXX 10:24 also has the command and its execution, although the execution line has a different form of the verb. The Greek of Josh 5:15, however, lacks the words occurring in the Hebrew text of 5:15: "and he did so." Similarly, in Josh 10:22–23 Joshua gives a command to open the cave and to bring out the kings. The statement that the kings are brought out repeats the execution of the command, but, unlike the Hebrew text, the words "and they did so" are not present. It can therefore be noted that, whereas in the Masoretic Text the execution of the command is offered by either the repetition of the command or the short phrase "and he/they did so," the Septuagint only repeats the words of the command in two instances and skips the short phrase "and he/they did so" in two other cases. As a result, there is less stress on the execution of the commands in the Greek text than in the Masoretic. The following overview further demonstrates that the repetition of the line of command in the execution seems more typical of the Hebrew Masoretic Text than the Greek version of the book of Joshua.

		MT	LXX
4:5	command	pass on before...	=[20]
		pick up stones	=
4:8	execution	and they did so	=
		and they picked up stones	=
5:15	command	remove your sandals	=
	execution	and Joshua did so	no parallel
10:22	command	open the cave	=
		bring out the kings	=

---

19. For comparative purposes, it is important to note that nowhere in the book of Exodus do execution lines immediately follow the command lines. God commands, but the reader does not really know whether or not Moses actually took off his sandals!

20. The = sign means that the Greek has the same sentences as the Hebrew does.

10:23	execution	and they did so	no parallel
		and they brought out the kings	=
10:24a	command	come	=
		and put your feet	=
10:24b	execution	while coming	≈[21]
		they put their feet	=

It can be noted that in most of the cases the Masoretic Text repeats the command in the line of the report detailing the execution. Sometimes the report of the execution of the command is rather short: "and they did so." The Old Greek text does not have this short execution line in two cases (5:15, 10:23). There is only one case in the Old Greek of Joshua where the execution line of the order follows precisely the order itself, when God commands the people to pass on before the ark and to pick up the stones (4:5). In verse 8 the report of the execution of this command repeats the order: and they passed on and they picked up the stones. There is thus a noticeable difference between the Hebrew and Greek texts with respect to the following of orders given by an authority figure in the narrative. The Greek text appears to put less stress on the execution than the Hebrew. Yet there is some evidence that further complicates this picture.

For example, there is another line of command in the Hebrew text not discussed so far, where the writer not only repeats more or less literally the command in its execution but also explicitly mentions the chain of authority: God-Moses-Joshua-people. A good example of such a line of command can be found in Josh 11:15: "As the LORD had commanded his servant Moses, so Moses commanded Joshua, and so Joshua did; he left nothing undone of all that the LORD had commanded Moses" (NRSV). Similarly, in 1:17, 8:35, and 14:5 the chain of command is again indicated. In all of these cases, the Greek, like the Hebrew, contains these references to the chain of authority.

The question naturally arises, then: How is one to explain the differences amidst the similarities in the reports of the execution of orders? At least three explanations are possible: (1) the differences represent omissions by the Greek translator; (2) the differences reflect additions by the final redactor of the Masoretic Text; (3) the differences point to different texts of the same book.

According to the first explanation, the Greek translator decided to omit the words "and they did so" and slightly changed the wording of

---

21. The ≈ sign means that the Greek has a form that differs from the Hebrew.

the execution line, deliberately removing several words from the Hebrew text he/she was translating. In this case, it is presumed that the translator worked with a Hebrew parental text that was similar, if not identical, to the Masoretic Text.[22] According to the second explanation, the translator is not considered responsible for the omissions. To the contrary, the translator faithfully followed the Hebrew text, which simply did not have the words "and they did so." In this case, the Old Greek of the book of Joshua reflects a Hebrew *Vorlage* that did not yet have the words "and they did so," thus reflecting an earlier stage than the Masoretic Text of the book of Joshua.[23] Following the third option, the "longer" and "shorter" versions, that is, the texts with or without the words "and they did so" respectively, existed both simultaneously and independently from one another.[24]

The first option is the one presumed by most Hebrew Bible scholarship. With regard to Joshua, most scholars still work with the Hebrew text and dismiss the witness of the Septuagint as a later development, with differences being due to the Greek translator. Do we, however, have any convincing arguments for the second option? There is indeed proof for a "shorter" Hebrew text of Joshua. Here I can point to the Old Greek text itself and to its witnesses. For most scholars who accept the first option, however, that is not enough proof, as they consider their own arguments regarding the translator's activity as stronger. What they overlook, though, is the hermeneutical principle at work in the text. In my opinion, it is easier to explain that one redactor changed the Hebrew story and made all the commands, including especially the execution lines following the commands, consistent than that the Greek writer deliberately deleted them from the Hebrew text. A late, Hebrew redactor made sure that all the commands and the orders given by God or Joshua were followed. Again and again, the words "and they did so" were added or, at the very least, the execution line of the command was made similar to the command itself. In this hypothesis, the Old Greek text reflects a text of the book of Joshua in which it was less necessary to mention that the orders were followed, whereas for the Masoretic Text precisely this point was important. Hence, in the Masoretic Text all orders are reported together with a short phrase "and he/they did so" or with the long execution line reiterating the command line. I am convinced, therefore, that the Old Greek of the book of Joshua reflects a

---

22. See n. 1 above.

23. This is the position I take in my own work; see n. 16 above.

24. Tov can be regarded as representative of this third option. See esp. Emanuel Tov, "The Growth of the Book of Joshua in the Light of the Evidence of the LXX Translation," in *The Greek and the Hebrew Bible: Collected Essays* (VTSup 72; Leiden: Brill, 1999), 385–96.

pre–Masoretic Text in which the orders given by authoritative (and hence important) figures were not followed by an execution line.

So far, I have argued that the Old Greek text offers us a glimpse into an older stage of the Hebrew book of Joshua. More generally, different versions of the same biblical book, such as the Greek and Hebrew texts, need to be studied independently in order to reconstruct a textual literary history of that text and to evaluate the consequences of the possible simultaneous existence of different texts of the same biblical book. Whereas in the earlier method of study, textual criticism represented a different stage from literary analysis, here, in this mode of inquiry, text criticism has now been fused with literary analysis of the biblical book. Indeed, going one step further, one can even state more precisely that, in this instance, the study of the Old Greek text of Joshua has become part of the study of the formation of the Hebrew text of Joshua.

RELEVANCE FOR FEMINIST AND CULTURAL STUDIES

I now return to my original query posed at the outset of this essay: What does text criticism have to do with feminist analysis? My answer to this question would be thus: applying this form of text criticism can help identify themes and motifs added by late(r) redactors in the formation of the Hebrew Bible and such an identification is critical for feminist analysis of the text. Again, I will use Joshua as an example to make my point. In the second century B.C.E., a Hellenistic redactor most likely made changes to the Hebrew text of Joshua. In doing so, he probably wanted to stress the precise execution of commands and, thus, the importance of orders and the authorities who issued them.

In the second century B.C.E., following orders given by key authority figures became of pivotal importance because of the rising conflict between the Seleucid party[25] and traditional Jews. Whether or not this conflict was economic, political, or religious, it had consequences for the cultural and religious life of Jews. There were those who stressed the importance of the law of God. The Torah of Moses needed to be the centerpiece for Jewish life and not the Hellenistic gymnasium or Antiochian citizenship. According to the books of the Maccabees, Mattathias took leadership in the revolt against the Seleucid king (1 Macc 2). In his response to the king's request to follow Seleucidian rule, Mattathias explicitly refers to the religion of his ancestors and especially to the law and ordinances of Judaism (1 Macc 2:21). Leadership, in his opinion, was

---

25. With the term "Seleucid party," I refer to both the Seleucid leadership and that segment of Jews who followed the Seleucid mindset.

not about following the king's commandments, but God's! To show that the commandments of God or the orders of important characters like the leaders of the Maccabean revolt or their great grandfathers, such as Joshua, were obeyed, second-century B.C.E. editors of some of the stories added phrases or sentences in order to indicate that the commandments or orders given in the narrative were in fact followed. Obedience to the law of God or to the commandments given by Jewish leaders thus became a central concern. It is interesting in this light to observe that an example of how a group of Jewish people followed an order given by Mattathias is reported immediately after Mattathias's answer to the king. Mattathias first cries out "let everyone who is zealous for the law and supports the covenant come out with me!" (1 Macc 2:27), and then he and his sons flee to the hills. He instantly has followers: "at that time many who were seeking righteousness and justice went down to the wilderness to live there." Mattathias's outcry had an immediate effect. His order was followed. I believe that the final redactors of some of the biblical texts similarly stressed the importance of orders or characters by making explicit that the orders were indeed followed and they did so by adding a line repeating the command or a phrase indicating that the commands were executed. These biblical additions thus increased the paradigmatic value of the stories in question for the new social situation.

This interpretation of the final layer of the biblical book of Joshua is, of course, hypothetical. The only evidence to prove this hypothesis is the existence of two texts of the same biblical book, namely, the Hebrew Masoretic book of Joshua and the Greek (pre-Masoretic or alternative) version. A comparison between the two texts has led to the formulation of a hermeneutical principle and has allowed me to distill those elements from the text that seem to come from a later period in time and a late moment in the development of the Hebrew text of the Bible.

In my view, this renewed form of text criticism can also prove to be useful for feminist exegesis. First, it can support, in this case, the questioning of the status and authority of the dominant text of the Bible. As more and more alternative texts become known, such as the majority biblical text of Qumran, the text of the Septuagint, the text of the Old Latin, and so forth, the more the single authority of one biblical text can be put to the test. The existence of a plurality of biblical texts may already pose a tremendous challenge to a majority of biblical scholars, as their Archimedean point of reference might have just disappeared. The desire for an absolute textual reference point relates to larger concerns with respect to claims of absolute authority and objectivity in the guild. We cannot deny that the authority of texts and textual traditions (such as the Masoretic) directly correlate, even if implicitly, with power structures of/in the academy. Moreover, the study of this renewed text criticism, in combination with literary (and redaction) critical approaches, can lead to a clearer view of the hermeneutical principles at work in the final stages of the development of the biblical text. These interpretive principles are not value neutral, and therefore need to be submitted to an ideological critique.

Finally, renewed text criticism can also reveal which party had control over the biblical text, a position that brought with it the power to set or change the biblical text. In her contribution on text criticism of the New Testament in this volume, Ann Graham Brock points to very similar issues.[26] She asks questions such as: Who had control? Who could change texts? How were texts manipulated in order to serve someone's goal or opinion? Just as Brock discerns voices of different competing groups within early Christianity, so scholars of (renewed) text criticism of the Hebrew Bible can discern different voices from the period before or concurrent with the final stages of the development of the text. With regard to text criticism of the Hebrew Bible, then, we now have in our hands documents from different groups within late Judaism. The hermeneutical principles that one discovers by comparing these documents—namely, different texts of the same biblical book—can thus buttress critical analysis done by feminists, gender theorists, and cultural studies scholars. Feminist exegesis can therefore play a crucial role in voicing questions regarding the authority of the text in general and the authority of characters mentioned in the biblical texts in particular. The study of text criticism by feminist and gender critics may therefore well represent the beginning of a promising liaison![27]

---

26. Ann Graham Brock, "Scribal Blunder or Textual Plunder? Codex Bezae, Textual-Rhetorical Analysis, and the Diminished Role of Women," in this volume. Especially useful is Brock's analysis of the diminishment of the role of women in the book of Acts as reflected in Codex Bezae.

27. Kristin De Troyer, "Septuagint and Gender Studies: The Very Beginning of a Promising Liaison," in *A Feminist Companion to Reading the Bible: Approaches, Methods and Strategies* (ed. A. Brenner and C. R. Fontaine; Sheffield: Sheffield Academic Press, 1997), 366–86.

SARAH AND HAGAR:
WHAT HAVE I TO DO WITH THEM?

Judith E. McKinlay

Now Sarai was barren; she had no child (Gen 11:30). It is in this way that
the Bible introduces Sarah,[1] with a barrenness that hangs over and settles
upon those whose lives intersect with hers in the early chapters of Genesis, coming to rest most particularly on Abraham and Hagar. Poignantly
interwoven in the Abraham cycle is Hagar's story, appearing in two
episodes (Gen 16 and 21), a cycle that is layered with that thick clustering
of motifs so significant for Israel's story: wilderness, divine annunciation,
divine notice of affliction, even the naming of God (however enigmatic).
Abraham may be the "father" of ancient Israel, but in the foreground of
his narrative stand Sarah and Hagar, two biblical women, met in an
ancient text, who continue to haunt our memories and imaginations. But
is it possible for me to find connections with them, and should this be the
aim of my reading? Is the question of my title—"what have I to do with
them?"—even an appropriate one?

These questions lead to that most basic issue for biblical readers:
which hermeneutical key do I use? The "I" is a crucial element in this
question, for it is "I," the reader that I am, who is attempting to meet the
Sarah and Hagar of the text; it is not only a matter of who is Sarah, and
who is Hagar, it is also a matter of who am I, the reader. So if I am
coming to this tale as a feminist reader, I need to consider how this will
influence how I hear these texts. While feminist readings have become,
and continue to become, more nuanced with an increased awareness of
difference and of the multiple interests that impact on the lives of
women, biblical as well as contemporary, Teresa de Lauretis's description
of the feminist task written in the 1980s still sets important perameters:
"to seek out contradictions, heterogeneity, ruptures in the fabric of representation so thinly stretched—if powerful—to contain excess, division,

---

1. The ancestor pair is designated "Sarai" and "Abram" until Gen 17, but for the sake of
simplicity I shall use the later names "Sarah" and "Abraham" throughout.

difference, resistance; to open up critical spaces in the seamless narrative space constructed by ... dominant discourses."[2]

The feminist task is one that takes seriously the ethics of interpretation, keenly aware of how our biblical understandings, gained through whichever critical approach we choose to employ, impact upon our present.[3] Of course, the texts are already complex enough in themselves: Abraham's narrative is complicated by Sarah's barrenness; Sarah's narrative is complicated by her gifting of Hagar, the fertile Egyptian slave woman; Hagar's narrative is complicated by the birth of Ishmael, a complication that spills out into two wilderness flights, which finally leave Hagar as an occupier of the wilderness, the biblical Other space. Complications and complexities abound.

First Close Reading

So how am I to read these narratives? Do I begin by asking the questions of the whence of such an ancient surrogacy move, or the whence of Abraham's, Sarah's and Hagar's journeyings in the ancient Near East, which were frequently the beginning points of previous historical-critical approaches? At what time were they moving through the lands of the ancient Near East? Yet such "behind the text" matters take me only so far, providing background information that is hypothetical at best. Nor do they involve me as the reader in my engagement with these women and their seemingly shared man. Employing a literary tradition criticism, I note the motifs so significant in Israel's story, of wilderness wandering, divine annunciation, and the divine notice of affliction, and find myself watching an itinerary reversed as Hagar comes up from Egypt to serve the one who, in Gen 12, went down to Egypt and seemingly served the Pharaoh. But if the writer in that case left a careful ambiguity surrounding Sarah's serving, this time there is no question: it is Sarah herself, the barren one, who plans a sexual serving for Hagar. I am already being drawn into this story, wanting to tackle the ethical issues and confront these women.

But past training nudges me to take critical note of the literary context, so, following Sarah and Hagar in a canonically ordered reading, I watch the sharp cut of the covenant slicing these chapters into sections, just as it slices Ishmael's flesh in Gen 17, until finally the message of the promised heir reaches Sarah. And Sarah laughs. Reading in sequence,

---

2. Teresa de Lauretis, *Alice Doesn't: Feminism, Semiotics, Cinema* (Bloomington: Indiana University Press, 1984), 29.

3. See the work of Elizabeth Schüssler Fiorenza, J. Cheryl Exum, and others.

with the Sodom and Gomorrah/Lot episodes followed by the second sister/wife tale, the motifs of sin, punishment, intercession and reprieve, breaches of the hospitality code, incest, invitations to rape, and divine protection from violation tumble into view in quick succession. What a world this is for Isaac—this promised child of laughter—to enter, as the motifs of birth and cutting come together when "the laughing one" is cut into covenant relationship at eight days old (Gen 21:4). Sarah makes the connection with God; it is God who has made "laughter" come, who has made the unbelievable happen—a child in their old age. But again we observe the ambiguity: do her words *everyone who hears will laugh* imply laughter *with* or laughter *at* (Gen 21:6)?[4] And what is Ishmael doing three verses later? Is he masquerading as an Isaac or simply laughing? I am now hesitating, recognizing a disturbing elusiveness in this text, and aware that laughter in this narrative has become heavy with the weight of divine promise, too weighty in the eyes of Sarah, whose talk is now of separation and division; the son of the slave woman is not to share inheritance with the child of the miraculous laughter (21:10).

I realize that I am already engaging in a close reading of the text, following the rhetorical-critical steps of Phyllis Trible.[5] Adding the narratological questions—who speaks and who sees and acts—reveals a Sarah who names neither mother nor son;[6] objectified and unwanted they are to be cast out (21:10). Nor does Sarah mention the fathering; she has the one son, Abraham has the two. It is the narrator who relates that the fate Sarah demands for t/his son causes Abraham deep distress (21:11). One might ask where God is to be found in this, but the theological underpinning is sound: it is God who recognizes Abraham's distress and acknowledges his double sonship. There is to be a double line of descendents, separated by the naming of Isaac's offspring for Abraham.

---

4. R. Christopher Heard notes that "in its only other biblical occurrence (Ezek 23:32), *sehoq* clearly takes the sense 'object of ridicule'. If Sarah has this sense in mind in v. 6a, she may be anticipating that her bearing of a child will turn her into a laughingstock ... If so, the simple sight of Ishmael laughing may be enough to arouse her anger ... She may project her own feelings of embarrassment onto Ishmael, and imagine that he is laughing *at her*" (*Dynamics of Diselection: Ambiguity in Genesis 12–36 and Ethnic Boundaries in Post-Exilic Judah* [SemeiaSt 39; Atlanta: Society of Biblical Literature, 2001], 85). Mark G. Brett translates the verse as "Laughter has Elohim made for me; whoever hears will laugh at me" (*Genesis: Procreation and the Politics of Identity* [Old Testament Readings; New York: Routledge, 2000], 60).

5. Phyllis Trible employed this approach for her reading of Hagar in *Texts of Terror: Literary-Feminist Readings of Biblical Narratives* (OBT 13; Philadelphia: Fortress, 1984), 8–35.

6. Neither Abraham nor Sarah refers to Hagar by name; she is named only by God and the narrator. The three questions are associated with the work of Mieke Bal (see *Lethal Love: Feminist Literary Readings of Biblical Love Stories* [Bloomington: Indiana University Press, 1987], 21).

There is immediate consolation for Abraham, but immediate distress for Hagar, now returned to the wilderness—for the second time. But was it for a second time? Redaction criticism has long raised the question: could this second wilderness experience be a textual replay of Gen 16 but with variations?[7] While there are parallels, for in both there is life-giving water and promise of a nation from Hagar's son, there are also significant differences; whereas her earlier flight was on her own initiative, in the second Hagar is sent out by the very father of the child promised in the first, with the skinful of water given by Abraham soon running dry and death looming for the boy. This second narrative ends with a wilderness life for Ishmael, with God, and with two Egyptian women, a closure, which, in its final textual reading, serves to round off the brief Hagar cycle.[8]

Engaging with the Gaps

Yet such readings have only laid the groundwork for my initial questions: Who are these women and what have I to do with them? If, as a feminist reader, I apply the lens of ideological criticism, further questions arise: For whose benefit is Sarah's surrogacy ploy? Is it for herself, as I am told in 16:2, or is it for Israel, as the larger canonical narrative would insist? Or is it for Abraham, as the previous chapter might lead us to believe? Certainly it involves a silent/silenced Abraham, who acquiesces in this bodily, sexual entry, but then allows the mother of his child to be driven out—twice. If I were to explore t/his repeated acquiescence in Hagar's dismissal further with the aid of psychoanalytical criticism, I might read it as a fear of the "other" woman that he cannot shake off and which dogs him compulsively.[9] In turning the focus upon Hagar, however, what is very clear to me, as it is told in Gen 16:1–6, is that she has no voice in Sarah's planning; she offers merely a "look" after the deed. Yet it is a look that changes the tenor of the tale, turning Sarah's talk (v. 5) to

---

7. So T. D. Alexander, "Are the Wife/Sister Incidents of Genesis Literary Compositional Variants?" *VT* 42 (1992): 145–53. See Sean E. McEvenue for an example of redaction-critical attribution of different source material behind each account ("A Comparison of Narrative Styles in the Hagar Stories," *Semeia* 3 [1975]: 64–80).

8. Note Danna Nolan Fewell's point, that the ending of this story might answer the questions asked in the time of Ezra and Nehemiah—"Where will these women and children go? How will they live?"—with the "opiate" response: "Don't worry. God will take care of them" ("Changing the Subject: Retelling the Story of Hagar the Egyptian," in *Genesis* [FCB 2.1; ed. A. Brenner; Sheffield: Sheffield Academic Press, 1998], 194).

9. See J. Cheryl Exum's application of this approach to the sister/wife tales of Genesis in *Fragmented Women: Feminist (Sub)versions of Biblical Narratives* (JSOTSup 163; Sheffield: Sheffield Academic Press, 1993), 148–69.

one of suffered wrong and hurt.[10] Power shuttles between husband and wife to end with Sarah, who deals with the situation harshly, to Hagar's detriment. Power is an issue in this text, and all those engaged with it suffer hurt.

But if both chapters reveal a story of emotion, hurt, and suffering, little of this is expressed in the text; most lies hidden beneath the textual surface. While the historical-critical method encouraged scholars to pay careful attention to the surface levels of the text and the historical contexts behind them, it paid little attention to the gaps and omissions within the texts themselves. Yet they are there, left by the storyteller for the reader to tease out. So if I, as the reader confronting the text, am seeking a credible and identifiable Sarah and Hagar, I need to read those gaps along with the surface narrative. While the ancient storytellers no doubt recognized that their listeners would make this move subconsciously, I am interested in bringing these subconscious fillings to the surface. The question now is: How does one do this? In a recent article, the scholar Pamela Reis has imagined Abraham saying to Sarah (in 16:6), "Whatever you do to her is fine with me, for I have no feelings for her whatsoever," in an attempt to reassure Sarah "that she is still the sole wife, that she, alone is loved."[11] But I wish to move outside the scholarly guild and look to the writers whose skill rests in creative imaginings, such as Jenny Diski who, in her novel *Only Human*, supposes that:

> Sarai discovered that playing God at his own game gave her all God's disadvantages. She could manipulate the world, but she could not participate in it. The world swelled with the life that she had willed into being, and mocked her for being unable to indulge in her achievement with any of her senses but that of sight ... Sarai could do no more about her behaviour to Hagar than Hagar could do about her innately youthful triumph over her mistress. They were both prisoners of human conflict, of wishes perversely come true.[12]

If so, what was the emotional impact of that behavior? For Hagar? For Sarah? How am I to imagine still further into the gaps of this tale of

---

10. As Heard notes, "the almost exact correspondence between Sarai's words in 16:5 and the narrator's words in 16:4 invites readers to see the situation described in 16:4 through Sarai's eyes ... (one might wonder whether this) represents a projection of Sarai's own lowered self-esteem onto Hagar" (*Dynamics of Diselection*, 66). The textual ambiguity of the genitive (subjective or objective), which Heard highlights in v. 5, may well indicate the careful and deliberate subtlety of the writer. For "indeed the ambiguity is poignant: perceiving herself as a victim of wrongdoing, Sarai in turn inflicts wrongdoing on Hagar" (67).

11. Pamela Tamarkin Reis, "Hagar Requited," *JSOT* 87 (2000): 87.

12. Jenny Diski, *Only Human: A Comedy* (London: Virago, 2000), 180–81.

sexual using and human conflict? Mikhail Bakhtin and others have opened up the possibility of dialogic conversations between texts quite removed from each other, introducing an "intertextuality" that as "a reading strategy works by deliberately bringing disparate texts together, to see how one looks through the lens of another."[13] Bakhtin's understanding of all "utterances" being linked "in a very complexly organized chain of other utterances," where each speaker ends "to make room for the other's active responsive understanding,"[14] and of discourse living "on the boundary between its own context and another, alien, context,"[15] encourages me to expand this chain and draw upon writers whose interest is in exploring the depths and heights of sexual knowings. Luce Irigaray's work, *Elemental Passions,* with its offer of "some fragments from a woman's voyage as she goes in search of her identity in love,"[16] allows such a dialogical reading. Heard within the silences of the Genesis script, her work may provide a way of exploring the emotional subtext of this Sarah/Hagar narrative. In this attempt to reveal the hidden, to allow an "I" to emerge in the silenced voices, I am quite deliberately disrupting the surface unity of the text by introducing a female voice in dialogic response to the male code of the Genesis writer.[17] So I imagine these words of Irigaray as those of Hagar addressing Abraham:

> And I was speaking, but you did not hear. I was speaking from further than your furthest bounds. Beyond the place you were penetrating ... From a captive and forgotten childhood lying beneath any of your potential gestures of mastery or appropriation.... And it was not that I

---

13. David Jobling, Tina Pippin, and Ronald Schleifer, "Part III. The Conscience of the Bible: Introduction," in *The Postmodern Bible Reader* (ed. D. Jobling, T. Pippin, and R. Schleifer; Oxford: Blackwell, 2001), 254.

14. Mikhail M. Bakhtin, *Speech Genres and Other Late Essays* (ed. C. Emerson and M. Holquist; trans. V. W. McGee; Austin: University of Texas Press, 1986), 69, 71. Cf. Vernon K. Robbins's essay in this volume.

15. Mikhail M. Bakhtin, *The Dialogic Imagination: Four Essays by M. M. Bakhtin* (ed. M. Holquist; trans. C. Emerson and M. Holquist; Austin: University of Texas Press, 1981), 284.

16. Luce Irigaray, *Elemental Passions* (trans. J. Collie and J. Still; London: Athlone, 1992), 4.

17. It is to be noted, as Karen Hohne and Helen Wussow point out, that Bakhtin himself stressed that "language is never unitary" so that "for a patriarchal language to exist, it must speak in conflict with the languages of the others it tries to marginalize and silence" ("Introduction," in *A Dialogue of Voices: Feminist Literary Theory and Bakhtin* [ed. K. Hohne and H. Wussow; Minneapolis: University of Minnesota Press, 1994], xi). While gender and feminism were not of concern to Bakhtin, Suzanne Rosenthal Shumway notes that "feminism and Bakhtinian theory share a concern for the oppressed and marginalized others created by the hegemony of dominant, authoritarian, and 'internally persuasive' languages" ("The Chronotope of the Asylum: *Jane Eyre,* Feminism, and Bakhtinian Theory," in Hohne and Wussow, *Dialogue of Voices,* 153). Cf. Jorunn Øklund's essay in this volume.

was withholding myself from you, but that you did not know where to find me. You searched and searched for me, in you. Wanting me still to be virgin material for the building of your world to come. But how could it ever be reached if, in that quest, once again you wanted yourself as you already are? ... Nothing from outside the place where you already are reaches you.[18]

Yet if, in turn, I place a Genesis template over Irigaray's text, the talk of sexual passion almost inevitably becomes entwined with the political; what may be metaphorical in Irigaray can be heard with sobering recognition of the more literal in Genesis:

You only encourage proximity when it is framed by property ... Always you assign a place to me ... You frame. Encircle. Bury. Entomb? ... The frame you bear with you, in front of you, is always empty. It marks, takes, marks as it takes: its fill ... You mark out boundaries, draw lines, surround, enclose. Excising, cutting out. What is your fear? That you might lose your property.[19]

The following words may be the very ones that lock Sarah within her destiny: "You close me up in house and family. Final, fixed walls."[20] Perhaps addressed not so much to Abraham as to the world in which she lives, the world from which Hagar both flees and is driven out. But the story is also the story of the limitations of Hagar's flight; she, the outsider, the "other," is destined to remain within Israel's narrative:

What you intend for me is the place which is appropriate for the need you have of me. What you reveal to me is the place where you have positioned me, so that I remain available for your needs. Even if you should evict me, I have to stay there so that you can continue to be settled in your universe. And this world takes place neither simply inside you or outside you. It passes from inside to outside, from outside to inside your being. In which should be based the very possibility of dwelling ... Already inside and outside, I am continuously divided between the two spheres of your space, and you never meet me as a whole. You never meet me ... where am I? Nowhere. Disappeared forever in your presence.[21]

These words that describe the universal as well as the particular physical and emotional turmoil of bodily encounter are here read with an

---

18. Irigaray, *Elemental Passions*, 9–10.
19. Ibid., 24–25.
20. Ibid., 25.
21. Ibid., 47–48.

added layer of meaning in the desperation of a sexual act enjoined for the sake of an heir to the covenant community that would be Israel. As Irigaray so poignantly observes, "I gave you something to play for, let you have some play ... The privilege of an omnipotent God ... I had not begun to exist save in my pretension to be a needed womb and mother for you.... You filled me with your emptiness. You filled me up with your lacks.... You were the one who became a gaping hole, I became full."[22]

Irigaray was not intending her words to be read through any lens but the emotional and sexual relationship between a woman and a man, yet it is clear that what she has written can be heard speaking on many levels. Heard as the voice of difference, the words speak again for Hagar, the biblical "Other," destined for the wilderness, the borderland: "The whole is not the same for me as it is for you.... Can never be completed, always in-finite. When you talk about Infinity, it seems to me that you are speaking of a closed totality.... The absolute of self-identity—in which you were, will be, could be."[23] The political undertones heard in this parallel reading have a further interest for me, because the interests that I bring to my reading of this text include those of a woman of the dominant culture, living in the postcolonial context of Aotearoa, New Zealand. The addition to the agenda of biblical studies of not only feminist and ideological criticisms, but also of more recent postcolonial and cultural criticisms, is an acknowledgement in itself that context makes a difference. The assumption of the historical-critical method was that knowledge was "*perspectiveless. If it represents a particular point of view, this point of view is accessible to anybody, insofar as they are suitably trained.*"[24] But if the quest for such a universal objectivity is abandoned, then I as the reader am able to recognize and accept that my situated placement, my context for reading, does indeed make a difference. And it does so whether I am conscious of the fact or not. As Stephen Fowl and Gregory Jones comment in their discussion of Scripture and Christian ethics, "the very shape of the question concerning which interpretive strategy to adopt in any situation will be determined by the political nature of the

---

22. Ibid., 61.

23. Ibid., 89.

24. Elizabeth Grosz, *Space, Time and Perversion: The Politics of Bodies* (New York: Routledge, 1995), 28. While James Barr, in his defense of "historical criticism," argues that much depends on what exactly is meant by this term, many of us have recognized the charge of eisegesis as against exegesis as having much to do with introducing any element of subjectivity (see James Barr, "Remembrances of 'Historical Criticism'," *in God Who Creates: Essays in Honor of W. Sibley Towner* [ed. W. P. Brown and S. D. McBride Jr.; Grand Rapids: Eerdmans, 2000], 59–72).

context in which interpretation takes place," adding that "[h]ermeneutics is inevitably, though not restrictively, a 'political' discipline."[25]

OPENING UP A DIALOGUE

For me, the details of wilderness and ethnic tensions make immediate connection with the contemporary and political postcolonial dialogues in my own country (New Zealand), which in turn resonate with the writings of postcolonial critics, in which there is considerable discussion about borderlands, margins, and spaces of tension. As Rasiah Sugirtharajah defines it, postcolonialism is "a critical enterprise aimed at unmasking the link between idea and power." As "a reading posture ... a mental attitude rather than a method," it is acutely attuned to signs of dominance that render others powerless or subordinated.[26] Relegating such Others to the margin has, of course, long been a ploy of those concerned to mark difference and identity, a practice employed both by Ezra and Nehemiah and the later colonial world.[27] But postcolonial criticism has brought these issues both into sharper focus and into dialogue with the lived experience of readers from colonial or postcolonial contexts. Read in the context of Aotearoa, New Zealand, the fear of "mixing"

---

25. Stephen E. Fowl and L. Gregory Jones, *Reading in Communion: Scripture and Ethics in Christian Life* (Grand Rapids: Eerdmans, 1991), 16.

26. Rasiah S. Sugirtharajah, "A Postcolonial Exploration of Collusion and Construction in Biblical Interpretation," in *The Postcolonial Bible* (ed. R. S. Sugirtharajah; The Bible and Postcolonialism 1; Sheffield: Sheffield Academic Press, 1998), 93 (the longer comment by Sugirtharajah is also worth citing in this context: "It is a critical enterprise aimed at unmasking the link between idea and power, which lies behind Western theories and learning. It is a discursive resistance to imperialism, imperial ideologies, imperial attitudes, and their continued incarnations in such wide-ranging fields as politics, economics, history, and theological and biblical studies"). Cf. Fernando F. Segovia, "Biblical Criticism and Postcolonial Studies: Towards a Postcolonial Optic," in Sugirtharajah, *Postcolonial Bible*, 56: "Postcolonial studies is a model that takes the reality of empire, of imperialism and colonialism, as an omnipresent, inescapable and overwhelming reality in the world: the world of antiquity, the world of the Near East or of the Mediterranean Basin; the world of modernity, the world of Western hegemony and expansionism and the world of today, of postmodernity, the world of postcolonialism on the part of the Two-Thirds World and of neocolonialism on the part of the West."

27. It is not easy to categorize or interpret the appearance of marginalization even in the biblical account. Thomas B. Dozeman, for example, has suggested two quite different roles for its part in the Genesis drama, one following Victor Turner's rites of passage readings, where it functions as the place of the hero's initiation and transformation, and the other as "the drift or borderland between civilization and chaos ... where entire nations can live at risk with God" ("The Wilderness and Salvation History in the Hagar Story," *JBL* 117 [1998]: 32–33).

so evident in this Genesis text is immediately familiar, being present from the earliest days of so-called European "settlement." For me, then, a feminist postcolonial exploration of these ancient texts will have a twofold aim: to understand the dynamics of power, particularly gendered political power, within the text, and to watch for any possibility of collusion of the text with present politics. With respect to the latter concern, if the biblical text comes from an ancient past, so too is the world of the reader an inheritor of its own past. In Aotearoa, New Zealand, for instance, there are issues of ethnic power imbalance whose origins lie in the settler and colonial worlds of the nineteenth century that are not yet fully resolved.

This double-angled awareness of the impact of past traditions leads me once again to apply that Bakhtinian intertextual reading strategy of "deliberately bringing disparate texts together, to see how one looks through the lens of another." This approach is, of course, a reader-driven exploration, for it is my own interests that lead to my choosing a text to set in dialogic conversation with Gen 16 and 21, and to act as the new sounding board. In this case it is a text from the nineteenth-century missionary world of Aotearoa, New Zealand, that will provide the postcolonial lens, for it also records an ethnic power imbalance. By this very choice, then, it is I, the reader, who may be determining to some extent "the new things that emerge when we read together texts that do not belong together."[28] The hope is that the dialogue will both allow a deeper understanding of the dynamics of the texts themselves and provide a connection with the context of my own world.

The "disparate" text to be heard in this dialogic conversation comes from the nineteenth-century diaries and writings of Elizabeth and William Colenso, a Church Missionary Society (CMS) couple joined in what was, in effect, a missionary marriage of convenience encouraged by Bishop Selwyn.[29] But, as in Genesis, there was another woman in this household. Ripeka, a young Maori woman, had been gifted to William by her parents as a domestic worker in the house. In 1848, five years after his marriage to Elizabeth, William had a child by Ripeka. Unlike Sarah, however, Elizabeth had had no hand in this encounter, and indeed was unaware for some time of what was happening. Echoes of Genesis begin

---

28. Jobling, Pippin, and Schleifer, "Conscience of the Bible," 255.

29. Colenso noted in his autobiography that when they married "we two had no love for each other," although he believed "that mutual affection would surely follow ... all that I wanted was a suitable partner, particularly in mission work " (quoted by Frances Porter and Charlotte Macdonald, eds., *'My Hand Will Write What My Heart Dictates': The Unsettled Lives of Women in Nineteenth-Century New Zealand as Revealed to Sisters, Family and Friends* (Auckland: Auckland University Press, 1996), 296.

to be heard, rather, after the birth of the child whom Ripeka bore to William. Not surprisingly, the ramifications were significant for all involved: Ripeka was married (off) to another of the house servants, Hamuera,[30] as Elizabeth did her best to turn Ripeka's feelings away from William, who subsequently wrote in his autobiography that "there followed a terrible time for us all."[31] Elizabeth's letter to William some time later provides an echo of that much discussed "look" directed at Sarah by Hagar: "I recollect that Rebecca (aka Ripeka) had said something to the same effect ['that I was not fit to be any man's wife'] to the girls in the house which they told me of, and that she had it from you."[32]

Like Abraham, William loved his son, but, in marked contrast, refused to allow him to leave with his mother in her comings and goings over the next two years. There are, of course, some notable differences with the Genesis story, for in this case it was Ripeka who made the decision to leave, and William who acted to keep his son in his own household. Elizabeth also left. Initially she wrote to William that "I look upon him [i.e. the child Wi(remu)] now as my own—given into my charge to bring up for God, and as long as life lasts I shall never forsake him. I trust I have been able to forgive all who have done me wrong from my heart."[33] Once Elizabeth reached Auckland, however, and met the refusal of her own missionary father even to have Wi in his house, matters changed, as the following letter indicates: "I solemnly assure you it was nothing but the fear of you that induced me to retain the child. You forced upon me in utter disregard of my natural feelings.... *I was your slave and dare not refuse*, and therefore I prayed continually and most *earnestly* for grace to be kind towards him."[34]

But while William Colenso loved his son and wished him brought up alongside the other children (born to him and Elizabeth), the colonial missionary world had other views. The archdeacon George Kissling wrote to his colleague of "the most afflictive and disgraceful shock which our Mission has sustained" and Elizabeth herself records a Mr. Grace, a

---

30. The date is debated. It may have been the same year (1848), although William recorded it as 1850 in his autobiography.

31. Quoted by Austin G. Bagnall and G. C. Petersen, *William Colenso, Printer, Missionary, Botanist, Explorer, Politician: His Life and Journeys* (Wellington, New Zealand: Reed, 1948), 306.

32. William Colenso, "Letters from his wife, Elizabeth 88–103–1/22," (Alexander Turnbull Library, 1843–1899; Wairoa, 24 September 1853). I am indebted to Cathy Ross for this reference, which was sent to me in personal correspondence and taken from her Ph.D. dissertation, "More Than Wives? A Study of Four Church Missionary Society Wives in Nineteenth-Century New Zealand" (University of Auckland, New Zealand, 2004).

33. Porter and Macdonald, *"My Hand Will Write,"* 298.

34. Ibid., 301–2 (emphasis added).

CMS missionary from Taupo, advising her against taking Wi to Auckland on the grounds that "[i]t would be such an injury to the *Cause* for Wi to be publicly seen."[35] Once in Auckland, Elizabeth seems to have wanted to deny the European paternity of this child altogether, writing several times to William suggesting both that "Wi grows more and more like Hamuera" and that "everyone who knew Hamuera says he is his child. He grows more and more like him." William regarded this suggestion as "strange, bitter and spiteful."[36] The end result was that Wi was "decisively dumped as being a blot on the missionary escutcheon."[37] Frances Porter and Charlotte Macdonald have suggested that Elizabeth's about-face in regard to Wiremu is yet another instance of the "sense of duty to 'the Cause',"[38] and, indeed, Elizabeth writes to William in those terms in the letter quoted above dated May 1854, accusing him of "the irreparable injury you have done to the Cause." The "injury" could be either the "adultery," its result, or both.

William's devotion to Wiremu seems to have been unambiguous, most marked perhaps by his defiance of Bishop Selwyn's order that Wi be returned to his mother, although Cathy Ross suggests another possible interpretation of this event: "although William was happy enough to 'cohabit' with a Maori woman, he did not want his child brought up by Maori."[39] Her term "cohabit" hints, at the very least, at the flow of boundaries, the overflow, the refusal of containment. The connections between the loved, but ultimately excluded, Ishmael and Wiremu are challenging. As the results of a sexual act—a desire, differently motivated but each with alarming consequences—the exclusions of both stand as embodied "moments of panic," that historical moment that Homi Bhabha describes as resulting from "a contingent, borderline experience (that) opens up *in-between* colonizer and colonized," [40] threatening the prescribed sense of decency and order. If Sarah and Hagar have appeared set in binary opposition over and against each other, so too have Elizabeth and Ripeka. Yet gender and postcolonial analysis come together in highlighting the limitations of binary categories when reading the lives of women of dominant

---

35. Ibid., 297–98. In the same letter, Elizabeth writes, "Do not make yourself uneasy about Wi. I shall not alter my conduct towards him, let people say what they will." It is, of course, difficult to separate the issues of the extramarital sexual "affair" and that of the mixed-race child.

36. Ibid., 300.

37. Ibid., 299.

38. Ibid., 300.

39. Cathy Ross, draft chapter for "More than Wives?" 19.

40. Homi K. Bhabha, *The Location of Culture* (New York: Routledge, 1994), 206–7, uses this term in his discussion of "the margin of hybridity."

cultures; so often they are inside and outside, at the center and on the periphery at the same time. Both Sarah and Elizabeth were wives of the culture later assumed as dominant, and viewed through its lens this was, in all probability, the cause both of their problems and their actions. Sarah's barrenness was not acceptable in the world of chosen covenant partners required to replicate themselves over generations; Elizabeth's guardianship of her husband's mixed child Wiremu was not acceptable in the white European missionary world of her time.[41] No wonder Sarah reacted as she did to Hagar's pregnancy, and Elizabeth was so ambivalent about Wiremu. But both Ripeka and Hagar disappear from view, finally so peripheral that they are lost from sight; little is known of Ripeka's later life, Colenso seeing her again only once, ten years later. Hagar is already moving out of focus at the end of chapter twenty-one; the reader's gaze is now firmly fixed upon Ishmael, with Hagar, his mother, mentioned only as negotiating his wife.[42] Setting Hagar and Ishmael alongside Ripeka and Wiremu, and Sarah and Abraham in relation to William and Elizabeth, albeit with all their differences, and applying both a gender and a postcolonial lens, has been a sobering exercise, making me aware of the complexities as well as the miseries in these lives that are dominated by a power imbalance and ethnic tension, as alive in nineteenth-century New Zealand as it was in sixth-century Yehud.

Revisiting History through a New Historicist Lens

If, as is currently being proposed, the Genesis material was gathered together in Yehud, in the Persian era, there is yet another dimension to this text; the Sarah-Hagar narrative would also need to be read keeping in mind those foreign wives driven out by their husbands in obedience to the requirements of the powers of their day (Ezra 9–10; Neh 13). In which case, the text may, in fact, be acting as a code, as Christopher Heard argues:

---

41. Note the view expressed only a few years earlier: "It may be deemed a cold and mercenary calculation; but we must say, that instead of attempting an amalgamation of the two races, Europeans and Zealanders, as is recommended by some persons, the wiser course would be, to let the native race gradually retire before the settlers, and ultimately become extinct" (Robert J. C. Young, *Colonial Desire: Hybridity in Theory, Culture and Race* [New York: Routledge, 1995], 9, quoting Anon., "The New System of Colonization—Australia and New Zealand," *The Phrenological Journal and Magazine of Modern Science* 11 [1838]: 258).

42. I am indebted to Professor Exum for drawing my attention to this parallel between Hagar and Ripeka. In December 1885, William writes in a letter to his son, now called Willie, that 1861 was the first time he had seen Rebecca since she had left the household in 1852, and that it was also the last time he ever saw her. Noted by Bagnall and Petersen, *William Colenso*, 429.

> Ishmael functions basically as object lesson for the "proper" Yehudian
> response to intermarriage ... Abraham's dismissal of Hagar and Ish-
> mael stands as both a paradigm for action and a reassurance for the men
> called upon to undertake similar drastic actions. God demands that the
> voice of Sarah (or that of Nehemiah) be obeyed. No matter what one's
> attachment to one's half-Egyptian son, no matter whether he was cir-
> cumcised at eight days (or thirteen years), God insists that the children
> of intermarriages, and their mothers, be dismissed from Abraham's
> household and from Yehud.[43]

As an Egyptian, Hagar would have had a particular significance in a
world where the Egypto-Greek threat to Persian control of its lands was
high on the list of concerns.[44] She would have been a useful tool for such
a political writer, emphasizing that no foreign wives and mixed-raced
children were acceptable, and that those of Egyptian origin in particular
were to be driven out. Such historical questioning is no longer about
Nuzi parallels and datings for the wandering of Israel's ancestors; the
focus has now shifted to having an eye firmly fixed upon the scribe or
scribes responsible for the form of the narrative as it appears on the scroll,
who, far from being historicists concerned with preserving past traditions
for their own sake, were "directly engaged with the issues of their *own*
day."[45] The tools of historical criticism, traditionally understood, have
been exchanged for those of the New Historicism, where the emphasis is
on the reciprocal relationship of text and context, noting how traditions of
the past are used to serve the interests of the present.[46] As a result, the
whence of the origins of the ancestor tradition has slipped out of view.
Situated now in Persian Yehud, Sarah and Hagar are both shaped by and
shapers of the world of the scroll-writer(s).[47]

But the questions do not stop there. Is the biblical text in effect acting
as an agent in this Ezra-Nehemiah world, or is it criticizing such an anti-
Egyptian stand? The God who is "seen" or "seeing" in Gen 16 seems

---

43. Heard, *Dynamics of Diselection*, 176.

44. See Brett, *Genesis*, drawing on the work of Kenneth Hoglund, *Achaemenid Imperial Administration in Syria-Palestine and the Missions of Ezra and Nehemiah* (SBLDS 125; Atlanta: Scholars Press, 1992).

45. Brett, *Genesis*, 137.

46. In Stephen Greenblatt's words, "representations are not only products but produc-
ers, capable of decisively altering the very forces that brought them into being" (*Marvellous Possessions: The Wonder of the New World* [Oxford: Clarendon, 1991], 6).

47. See Claire Colebrook, *New Literary Histories: New Historicism and Contemporary Criti-
cism* (Manchester: Manchester University Press, 1997), 28: "New historicism ... moves towards the idea of the text as practice: the critic focuses on the material effects and circumstances produced by the text and in which the text is produced."

double-faced; turning to Hagar this God offers a divine annunciation and a compassionate hearing for her affliction, but, turning toward Sarah, this deity sends the servant back to her harsh and bitter mistress.[48] So in the second retelling God expresses consolation for Abraham with divine promise of a nation of descendents, while seemingly allowing (endorsing?) the pitiless expulsion of Hagar with Ishmael. Readers can watch the Egyptian Hagar sent—not once, but twice—into the wilderness. We get the message: no Egyptian wives! Yet, as Mark Brett suggests, "the name of her son indicates divine concern with all such suffering,"[49] so the message heard is that one may drive out such m/Others but one may not drive them out beyond the concern of Israel's God, for the angel of God speaks to Hagar in the wilderness, even if the speaking comes at a distance, from heaven. Repeated in the wilderness is the promise that God will make a great nation of Ishmael.[50] We are reading here the countermessage: "divine blessing flows extravagantly over the covenant's borders to include Ishmaelites, Ammonites and Moabites."[51] Ishmael, moreover, is not going to kowtow to anyone; he emerges as a fiercely independent character and, not insignificantly, with an Egyptian wife. In effect, it seems, in Brett's reading, that in their skilful of a double-voiced text, these ancient scribes were virtually employing that decolonizing strategy, which, in postcolonial terms, effectively "undermines the operation of colonial power by inscribing and disclosing the trace of the other so that it reveals itself as double-voiced."[52] One suspects that the missionaries in Auckland missed this biblical message!

In this decolonizing strategy, the role of the wilderness space is a crucial element. Traditional literary criticism has long recognized the thematic significance of the wilderness, which provides parallels for the God/Moses and God/Israel stories,[53] thereby allowing one to read the Genesis

---

48. In the text the order is reversed, and Brett may well be right in reading this as stating the status quo of the dominant ideology first, before providing the undermining promise to Hagar (*Genesis*, 59).

49. Brett, *Genesis*, 61, marking this with the "if" of Hagar being taken as "exemplary" of the dispossessed.

50. Cf. Brett's comments: "it is striking that the promise of a 'great nation' was precisely the first of the series of promises, given to Abram, that climaxed in the language of covenant. In passing on this promise to Hagar and Ishmael, Elohim devolves it to descendents of Abraham who were ostensibly separated from the privileged covenant lineage in 17.19–22" (ibid., 71).

51. Ibid., 84. It is to be noted that Brett describes his work as combining "older styles of historical scholarship with a pastiche of narratology, reader-orientated criticism, anthropology, the so-called New Historicism and postcolonial studies" (2).

52. Young, *Colonial Desire*, 23.

53. See David Daube, *The Exodus Pattern in the Bible* (London: Faber & Faber, 1963), 23–38; and, more recently, Trible, *Texts of Terror*; Claus Westermann, *Genesis* (trans. J. J. Scullion;

chapters as one episode or phase in the larger "rhythm of a divinely appointed destiny in Israelite history."[54] What is arresting for a feminist reader, of course, is that it is Hagar who sets this rhythm in motion, being canonically the first person approached by God in the wilderness.[55] The fact that she is Egyptian becomes all the more significant when read with Exodus in mind: what is God doing, coming to the rescue of an Egyptian?[56] A world where an Egyptian Hagar experiences a theophany and divine annunciation in the wilderness is surely dissonant with the supposedly Israelite-focused world of Abraham and Sarah. There is, of course, the inherent irony that the wilderness should have any role at all, being, in terms of the surface plot, a place of the dispatched and excluded, similar to the nonspace of the ghetto or the closet. This is markedly not the space of Sarah and Abraham, but it is also not Egypt. Where Thomas Dozeman describes the wilderness as a "borderland between civilization and chaos," postcolonial writers might take this further, seeing it, in the words of bell hooks, as that "site of creativity and power, that inclusive space where we recover ourselves, where we move in solidarity to erase the category colonizer/colonized" and which "offers one the possibility of radical perspective from which to see and create, to imagine alternatives, new worlds."[57] And so Gen 21 ends with Hagar, the Egyptian subaltern,[58] and her son Ishmael as the narrative representatives of that destabilizing space with its message of divine blessing that

---

3 vols.; CC; Minneapolis: Fortress, 1984–1986), 2:344; Dozeman, "The Wilderness and Salvation History"; Brett, *Genesis*; and Reis, "Hagar Requited."

54. Robert Alter, *The Art of Biblical Narrative* (New York: Basic Books, 1981), 60.

55. Dozeman notes "the absence of the wilderness in all other stories in Genesis" apart from three peripheral references. He asks whether "Hagar's repeated journey there is intended to embed her story in a larger history in which parallels are created between the lives of Hagar and Moses, and also between the Ishmaelites and Israelites" ("The Wilderness and Salvation History," 24). As he suggests, the wilderness of Paran is both the dwelling place of Ishmael and the entry point for the Israelites after they leave Sinai in Num 10. His form-critical thesis is that the Hagar story was reinterpreted by Priestly writers who shifted the point of comparison away from Hagar and Moses "to the similar wilderness experiences of Ishmaelites and Israelites" and "structured the additions within their preferred framework of promise and fulfillment" (34–35). In this, the later genealogy of Ishmael (Gen 25:12–18) plays a significant role.

56. Dozeman quotes Tsevat's statement that "Sarai does to a child of Egypt . . . what the Egyptians would later do to Sarai's children" ("The Wilderness and Salvation History", 29).

57. bell hooks, *Yearning: Race, Gender, and Cultural Politics* (Boston: South End, 1990), 152, 149–50. The wilderness often functions as the mestiza borderlands in the frequently quoted writings of Gloria Anzaldúa. Cf. Hjamil Martínez-Vásquez's essay in this volume.

58. On the term "subaltern," see Gayatri Chakravorty Spivak, "Can the Subaltern Speak?" in *Colonial Discourse and Postcolonial Theory: A Reader* (ed. P. Williams and L. Chrisman; New York: Harvester Wheatsheaf, 1993), 66–111.

borders cannot prevent. Sarah, while remaining in the dominant narrative, has already been returned to textual silence.

CONCLUSION

It now remains to be seen exactly where this essay has taken me in my quest for understanding Sarah and Hagar. Setting the Genesis account alongside a colonialist narrative has served as a reminder for those of us living in colonial/postcolonial contexts that this text cannot be dismissed as simply being an ancient story. A postmodern understanding would, in any case, deny that texts could be relegated to the category of "ancient" if this implies a closed meaning. The New Historicist emphases highlight the continuing performance of texts, the way in which they "both produce and reveal mechanisms of power" in each new context of performance.[59] To recognize this speaking of texts over the span of time is to recognize that our own historical texts are also not locked in a past; that our own present is equally built on the inequalities of an "Othering" history, which must be acknowledged before the transformative readings of the wilderness can be celebrated.[60]

A feminist postcolonial lens also links this discussion with the sexual intertwining of the three Genesis players explored in the earlier parallel reading with Irigaray, for it recognizes the ways in which the sexuality of the human body has been used, and continues to be used, as the foregrounding site of political and ideological issues. If it is true that "[b]ody and body politic, body and social body, body and city, body and citizen-body, are intimately linked productions,"[61] it is all the more true of colonial discourse, where, to quote Homi Bhabha,

[T]he construction of the colonial subject in discourse, and the exercise of colonial power through discourse, demands an articulation of forms of difference—racial and sexual. Such an articulation becomes crucial if it is held that the body is always simultaneously (if conflictually) inscribed in

---

59. Colebrook, *New Literary Histories*, 27–28.

60. It should be noted that missionary attitudes in Aotearoa, New Zealand, varied and were as complex as any other human endeavor. While I was first working on this essay, the bones of Bishop Pompellier, New Zealand's first Roman Catholic bishop, were being brought back for reburial with "his" people, and his respect for the Maori was being remembered and celebrated by Maori at each stopping place.

61. Barbara Hooper, in an unpublished manuscript quoted by Edward W. Soja, "Thirdspace: Expanding the Scope of the Geographical Imagination," in *Human Geography Today* (ed. D. Massey, J. A. Sarre and P. Sarre; Cambridge: Polity, 1999), 273.

both the economy of pleasure and desire and the economy of discourse, domination and power.[62]

My thesis is that both Hagar and Ripeka are notably inscribed in both. Following Brett, however, what is striking about the biblical account is the way in which the telling became a double-voiced production, allowing a colonialist reading of excluded space in a conceived world of binaries, and at the same time destabilizing that reading with its underside of inclusive possibility. The multivoiced readings with parallel texts took the exploration of double-voice in quite other directions. Were such explorations permissible? I would argue they were, insofar as "[a] story is *not* just a story. Once the forces have been aroused and set into motion, they can't simply be stopped at someone's request. Once told, the story is bound to circulate; humanized, it may have a temporary end, but its effects linger on and its end is never truly an end."[63]

I would suggest that interpretive explorations likewise never come to an end. Historical-critical methodology, together with its more radical turn to the New Historicism, will continue as one voice among the many, but accompanied by new and sometimes highly experimental, if tentatively presented, ways to bring the text into meaningful dialogue with the world of the reader, as I have attempted in this essay. The quest for understanding the dynamics of texts may lead to drawing upon resources far removed from those of the more traditional approaches. Conversations about texts will spiral out and spill over into new contexts. A feminist reading works with this expectation, for it is inherently a committed reading, which refuses to leave texts in a closed world of the past. They are not to be locked up and examined only under the rubric of "what the text meant," but read with an eye opened to the present and the future, with a concern for their political and ethical influence. Most particularly, "feminism does not 'forget' or 'bracket' or 'erase' the situation and concerns of the reader in her or his attempts to capture the meaning of a text," but offers a reading, which, with others, takes an ethical responsibility in its interpretative task, considering *"value in relation to its future (its consequences) rather than in its past (its cause)."*[64] The feminist hope is that the whither of biblical interpretation continues to ask the ethical question: Whom does this

---

62. Bhabha, *Location of Culture*, 67.

63. Trinh T. Minh-ha, *Woman, Native, Other: Writing Postcoloniality and Feminism* (Bloomington: Indiana University Press, 1989), 133.

64. David Jobling, Tina Pippin, and Ronald Schleifer, "Part I. Rereading the Bible: Introduction," in Jobling, Pippin, and Schleifer, *Postmodern Bible Reader*, 44.

reading serve?[65] Sarah and Hagar will not be contained in a biblical time-warp, but will continue to offer their story for readers to take with them into the complications of their own lives. What we do with that offer is the challenge. For on the question of "what have I to do with Sarah and Hagar?" hangs the other: what have Sarah and Hagar to do with me, and us—here, today? I think the scribes of Genesis would be saying "Amen."

---

65. I am in agreement here with Drucilla Cornell, "What is Ethical Feminism?" in *Feminist Contentions* (ed. S. Benhabib et al.; New York: Routledge, 1995), 78: "I use the word 'ethical' to indicate the aspiration to a nonviolent relationship to the Other and to otherness in the widest possible sense. This assumes responsibility to struggle against the appropriation of the Other into any system of meaning that would deny her difference and singularity."

THEIR HERMENEUTICS WAS STRANGE! OURS IS A NECESSITY! REREADING VASHTI AS AFRICAN-SOUTH AFRICAN WOMEN

Madipoane Masenya (ngwana' Mphahlele)

Can I afford to take refuge in the study of the biblical past?
While harsh economic realities and social problems
*   look me in the eyes?*
Can I afford the luxury
*   of sophisticated, controversial exegetical methods?*
While rape, malnutrition, women and child abuse
*   are the order of the day in my environs?*
I dare not!
Make my context a hermeneutical key,
Let the Bible become the women's (people's) Bible![1]

Despite the fact that South Africa's government is secular and its citizens religiously diverse, the Christian Bible continues to play a formative role in the lives of many of South Africa's church-going people, the majority of which are primarily women. The ongoing impact of the Bible on African-South African[2] Christians is rooted in history, especially missionary history. Although the latter was not always helpful, particularly with respect to the affirmation of the identity of African peoples in this country, the Bible's positive influence will continue to be felt by many South African Christians. Such a situation necessitates, as I will argue here, the need for women-friendly methods of biblical interpretation. The

---

1. Madipoane Masenya (ngwana' Mphahlele), *Making the Context of African-South African Women a Hermeneutical Focus in Theological Education* (A National Initiative for the Contextualisation of Theological Education Publication 21; Johannesburg, South Africa: NICTE, 2000), 21.

2. Hereafter, I will use the apparently repetitive phrase "African-South African" rather than "Black South African" to refer to the women who belong to the indigenous peoples of South Africa: The Xhosas, Sothos, Swathis, Ndebeles, etc. This specification is prompted by the observation that there is no universal women's experience. In my view, the different experiences of South African women from various racial groups will impact the ways in which these women read and interpret the Bible.

latter will hopefully liberate these women from the strange biblical hermeneutics in which they have been steeped through the years.

Though African women form the vast majority of church-going and Bible-reading communities in the South African context, historically and currently, men have interpreted the Bible for them from a male perspective. What these women received was indeed a strange way of interpreting the Bible. Such foreign perspectives cannot enable Christian African women to rediscover and redefine who they really are in God's divine scheme. There is, therefore, a need for African women of South Africa to reread the Bible through the lens of their own female experience. The argument presented here is more specifically an attempt to reread the Bible from a *bosadi* (womanhood) perspective.

By way of introduction, I will provide a short autobiography in order to highlight the particular interpretative context that has produced African-South African women Bible readers. This autobiography will include a description of what I have called a *bosadi* approach to the reading of biblical texts. Such an approach is strongly committed to making the Bible a more accessible, empowering spiritual resource for African women in South Africa. Next, I will present two readings of the story of Vashti in Esther 1, a historical-critical as well as a *bosadi* reading.

A JOURNEY AND STRUGGLE

I grew up during the early sixties in the repressive sociopolitical context of South Africa at that time. I was living in a rural area, which has been and still is the primary lot of the African peoples in this country. It is worth noting here that Africans have always been at the bottom of the segregation ladder. The urban areas, particularly the city's quiet, decent suburbs, were reserved for whites only, while Indians and colored people resided in the settlements located on the city's outskirts. This situation was typical for the *apartheid* setting.

It is no wonder that due to the conservative nature of the rural context in which I lived, coupled with the oppressive conditions under which African-South Africans lived in apartheid South Africa, I did not immediately come to appreciate fully the crisis caused by segregation. My inability to realize the severity of the racial crisis was, in my view, caused by the fact that I was not able to interact with white folks on a regular basis. Such an interaction could have enabled me to develop a better understanding of the evil nature of the apartheid policy, a policy that advocated the separate development of peoples of different races, deliberately making one race the norm for all others.

Vivid, painful memories of separately designated areas for blacks and whites underscore the harmful effects of apartheid on African people. One did not have to be exceptionally observant to perceive the pattern existing at the time; the physical appearance of an area quickly revealed those for whom it was reserved. Blacks and whites could, for example, visit the same medical doctor but they would have very different waiting rooms. The dilapidated one would be reserved for blacks, while a well-kept, clean room was reserved for the white folks. A beautiful, breath-taking park would feature a board with the words "White Only" printed upon it. Such a situation could only breed a generation of resident aliens, a group of people who are exiled in what is supposed to be their own home. How could one not feel foreign in such a context? How could one's sense of self-worth and self-esteem remain unaffected?

In the domestic setting, especially in rural areas, this sense of foreignness and strangeness became even more pronounced depending on one's gender. As this world was, and still largely is, patriarchal, female folk have found themselves on the margins of African society. It is not an exaggeration to suggest that the lives of African-South African females are typified by foreignness from birth to death: foreign to the then-normative white race, foreign to the normative male sex, foreign to one's own culture with its tendency to marginalize women, foreign to one's own family in communities that idolize marriage, foreign to the in-laws, and so on.[3]

This feeling of utter foreignness was aggravated by the fact that even the low-quality education reserved for blacks then, the so-called Bantu education, was not helpful in addressing black contextual issues, let alone issues directly pertaining to the lives of African women in South Africa. Even the Christian churches, including theological institutions such as the historically black and Afrikaner[4] ones, were not helpful. Given the status quo of the time, it is no wonder that the theologies and biblical hermeneutics in which all of us were trained were geared toward affirming those who were in power, that is, white males. Though this subgroup lived and continues to live on the African continent, most of their theological and biblical hermeneutical endeavors have remained untouched by the reality of the African contexts.[5] It is no wonder, then, that even today theology and studies of the Bible remain foreign to African peoples

---

3. Madipoane Masenya (ngwana' Mphahlele), "'... But You Shall Let Every Girl Live': Reading Exodus 1:2–2:10 the Bosadi (Womanhood) Way," *OTE* 15 (2002): 99.

4. The word "Afrikaner" refers to a white Afrikaans-speaking person. Afrikaans is a language derived from Dutch. Afrikaners were the originators of the apartheid regime and thus the historical oppressors of black peoples during the apartheid era.

5. Madipoane Masenya (ngwana' Mphahlele), "Is White South African Old Testament Scholarship African?" *BOTSA* 12 (2002): 3–8.

in South Africa. Moreover, these limited endeavors still leave African women on the receiving end of theological discussions, because the male-focused academic contexts in which theological discussions take place often continue to exclude women.

As noted earlier, the churches also refused to affirm the full human-ity of women. As a matter of fact, it may be argued that the current South African secular state with its affirmation of the rights of women has become more prophetic on this matter than the South African church! It is in this context that black liberation theologians emerged, dissatisfied with the incapacity and/or unwillingness of Western theologies to challenge the oppressive status quo. Advocating such radical theologies at the time could have easily landed these people in prison, but these theologians addressed the real needs of the African people. Yet these theologies were not so helpful in addressing issues pertaining to African women in South Africa. Perhaps it is no wonder, then, that, in my case, it was only in the early 1990s that I became aware of the harsh realities of patriarchy not only in the academy, but also in the churches.

Once I was introduced to feminist and womanist theologies and bib-lical interpretation, I was never to be the same again. At that point I began a painful journey, as I started fighting for the liberation of African-South African women through writing, speaking, and living. I have fought in the academy, which remains both basically white and conse-quently foreign to the African context,[6] and also largely male and therefore less concerned with women's issues. I have also fought in the church, which, though black, remains male in terms of its leadership and decision-making practices. It is a church that has continued to marginal-ize and push aside the female folk through foreign—particularly colonial, apartheid and male—biblical interpretations. I have fought in a largely African context whose male folk, although acknowledging the rights of people of all races enshrined by the South African constitution, in practice still believe that the full humanity of women can only be affirmed in the public sphere of work and not in the realm of church or home. My strug-gle to affirm the full humanity of African women in this country is motivated by my own desire to discover my self-identity as a human being created in the image of God. It is motivated by the desire to call myself by my own name and in my own voice.

It is this desire that has motivated me to move beyond familiar Western terms such as "feminism" and "womanism" in order to develop what I have since called the *bosadi* approach to the reading of biblical

---

6. See further ibid; and idem, "A Response to Himbaza and Holter," *BOTSA* 13 (2002): 9–12.

texts. In what follows, I offer a brief description of the basic nature of this methodology.

THE *BOSADI* APPROACH

My doctoral dissertation, entitled "Proverbs 31:10–31 in a South African Context: A Bosadi (Womanhood) Approach,"[7] focused not only on the sociohistorical context of the text of Prov 31 but, even more importantly, on the contexts/social locations of African-South African women readers of biblical texts. Such a study not only enhanced my knowledge of the ideological nature of the Bible, but it also deepened my appreciation for the critical role that readers in different social locations play in producing texts, thus undermining the myth of the "objective" and/or "scientific" biblical scholarship in which we had been so deeply and thoroughly steeped. Such a study has been helpful to me not only as I interact with socially engaged academics, but also as I engage with grassroots communities.

In terms of basic definition, the Northern Sotho word *bosadi* (womanhood) is an abstract noun derived from the word *mosadi*. The latter has the following meanings: "woman," "married woman," "wife."[8] The word *mosadi* comes from the root *-sadi*, which denotes "womanhood." The word *bosadi* may similarly be translated as "womanhood" or "private parts of a woman." The word *mosadi* (woman) is also used in other African-South African languages, such as the Nguni (*umfazi*), Venda, (*musadzi*), Xitsonga (*wansati*), and Setswana (*mosadi*), a fact revealing the basic commonalities of language and experience among the various indigenous peoples of South Africa.[9]

Reclaiming the use of the Northern Sotho word *bosadi* not only makes sense to African-South African women at the grassroots level, women with whom I interact constantly and thus naturally, it also succeeds in enabling these women to read the Bible in a way that affirms them, because the *bosadi* approach acknowledges the uniqueness of the context of African-South African women. Theirs is a context characterized by

---

7. Madipoane Masenya (ngwana' Mphahlele), "Proverbs 31:10–31 in a South African Context: A Bosadi (Womanhood) Approach" (Ph.D. diss., University of South Africa, 1996); and idem, *How Worthy Is the Woman of Worth? Rereading Proverbs 31:10–31 in African-South Africa* (New York: Peter Lang, 2004).

8. Cf. Dirk Ziervogel and Pothinus C. Mokgokong, *Comprehensive Northern Sotho Dictionary* (Pretoria: van Schaik, 1975), 1154.

9. Cf. Madipoane Masenya (ngwana' Mphahlele), "Rereading the Bible the *Bosadi* (Womanhood) Way," *BCTSA* 4 (1997): 15–16. See also idem, *How Worthy is the Woman of Worth*, 122–27.

sexism, postapartheid racism, and classism among other factors. This context shapes the way they interact with the Bible. In its analysis of the context of the reader, the *bosadi* approach highlights the significance of the element of faith in the life of an African woman in her encounter with the Bible. It also acknowledges the common points between the world-views of Africans and those of the Israelites. Like many other women's liberation approaches, the *bosadi* approach foregrounds the liberating elements of the Bible and challenges and resists the oppressive ones. The approach is not only critical of the biblical text; it also criticizes African cultures, thus reflecting a degree of self-criticism and analysis. Although the *mosadi* reader acknowledges the significance of the contexts that produced the biblical texts, the context of the modern female reader takes priority over the former. Such an approach enables and empowers the reader to approach the Bible, first and foremost, informed by her own social location thereby escaping the temptation to read the text with strange (white/male) eyes. This contextual gendered reading of the Bible draws its inspiration from the author's commitment to foreground African women's contexts in biblical hermeneutics. While a variety of terms could possibly be used, *bosadi* symbolizes in its essence an engagement of the Bible as read by African women in South Africa through their own eyes.

With the preceding observations in mind, let us now turn to two different readings of the story of Vashti in the Hebrew Bible in order to illustrate further the methodology I am advocating here. The first reading I present is the traditional (historical-critical) reading of the character of Vashti. It is the kind of reading that typically has dominated the scene of biblical interpretation. This approach, particularly if it is used as an end in itself and not in order to allow the Bible to interact with the context of African women, may be designated as "strange" in our contexts. It also becomes problematic if it is regarded as the only legitimate approach to the Bible for all Bible-reading communities. The second reading of the Vashti character represents the *bosadi* approach to the text. Together, the two methods placed side by side, evidence the wide gap that exists in the South African context between the methods of the colonial and apartheid past and the anticipation of new methods for the present and future.

TRADITIONS OF A FOREIGN MASTER

In my training as a biblical scholar, the historical-critical approach to the study of the biblical texts proved to be a dominant methodological force and voice in my education. Indeed, it can even be considered the only acceptable methodology for "serious" engagement of issues related to the text. The advocates of this methodology stressed the need to trace the historical background of biblical books, examining issues related to a particular book's genre, authorship, original audience, possible date of composition, content (e.g., whether the book was true history or not; major themes), history of textual transmission, and redaction history. Coupled with such an approach to the biblical text, students of the Bible were encouraged or even forced to study the original languages in which the Bible was written. The traditional reading of the book of Esther below will highlight some of these emphases.[10]

The main focus of the book of Esther is the celebration of the Feast of Purim, found toward the end of the book.[11] In the month of Nisan, in the twelfth year of Ahasuerus, the king of Persia, *pur* (i.e., the lot) was cast and it fell on the thirteenth day of the month (Esth 3:7; 9:26). This was to be the day on which the destruction of the Jews would take place. As a result of the reversal of fortunes (a wisdom motif running through the book of Esther), however, the Jews were the ones who destroyed their enemies on the proposed day instead. Esther and Mordecai decided that this thirteenth day of the twelfth month would be a day of celebration and gift giving to the poor. This was to be the day on which they would remember the salvation God had provided for them in a foreign land.

The book of Esther depicts the conditions of a people in exile. It purports to record the historical events that took place when the Jews were under the rule of the Persian Empire. The history of the Persians' dealings with the Jews reveals that the Persian masters were relatively tolerant toward the exiles. According to this book, it was even possible for Esther to become queen, even though, being Jewish, she was a foreigner; in the case of her relative Mordecai, he could also find himself in a high position in the empire, being appointed second-in-command by King Ahasuerus.

The book of Esther certainly has the pretense of being historical, as evidenced by the description of the situation at the royal court in Esth 1, which matches the historical context quite well. Indeed, a historically verifiable person, the Persian king known as Xerxes I, is referred to as Ahasuerus in the Hebrew text. The advanced arrangement of communication portrayed in the text also matches the Persian system in place during the historical period depicted in the book. Despite these glimpses into the possible historical world of the production of the text, some scholars consider the story to be fictional. It is argued that the book does

---

10. See further Carey A. Moore, *Esther: Introduction, Translation and Notes* (AB 7B; New York: Doubleday, 1971), 12–14; and James A. Loader, *Das Hohelied, Klagelieder, Das Buch Esther* (ATD; Gottingen: Vandenhoeck & Ruprecht, 1992), 228–29.

11. The word "Purim" comes from the Hebrew word *pur* for the English "lots/casting of lots" (cf. Esth 9:24–28).

not portray true historical events, since it contains many implausibilities and improbabilities, elements that bear witness to its unhistorical character. It is implausible, for instance, that a leader could organize a feast for so many days in his kingdom. It is also unclear why the king would order the destruction of his own people. Additionally, the name "Esther" is not recorded anywhere in Persian history as the name of one of the Persian royal family. As a matter of fact, the Persians never allowed foreigners to be queens in their own royal courts. According to archaeological discoveries and records, there was never a queen by the name Vashti in Persian history either. Such inconsistencies, among many others, have prompted biblical scholars to hesitate in regarding the book as a reflection of actual historical events. Even its admission into the canon was a matter of contention among Jewish scribes, primarily because the name of God does not appear anywhere in the Hebrew manuscripts of this book. Modern scholars therefore choose to read Esther as a narrative rather than a history. Some would specifically designate it as a historical novella,[12] while others regard it as a political novella.[13]

Wherever scholars settle on the historical and literary character of the book, one thing is apparent: in any interpretation little space is given to the character of Vashti. The traditional pattern in the interpretation of Esth 1 is to regard as its main purpose the contextualization of the story of Jewish survival in the events at the Persian court. These events are passed over quickly, particularly those surrounding the character of Vashti, in order to give way to the main focus of the story: the veiled hand of God that ensures Jewish survival in the midst of threat in a foreign country, an event which culminated in the celebration of the feast of Purim. A quick glance at the commentaries reveals that Vashti's character is often neglected, or dealt with in only a few paragraphs. Vashti's act of refusing to appear before the king when summoned by him, an act that outraged the king and quickly led to her deposal as queen, is usually regarded simply as a narrative technique intended to introduce the more important queen of the story, Esther. Vashti's appearance thus only serves as a foil for the narration of the events related to the Jewish people—she herself is incidental and marginal.

This tendency to pass over the character of Vashti reveals the readers' and commentators' natural tendency to collude with the author of the

---

12. See Gerrie F. Snyman, "From Text to Sermon: Reading and Creating Religious Texts," in *Congregational Ministry* (Pretoria: UNISA, 2003), 116–23.

13. See Sarojini Nadar, "Power, Ideology and Interpretations: Womanist and Literary Perspectives on Esther as Resources for Gender-Social Transformation" (Ph.D. diss., University of Natal, 2003), 55–60.

text—to read "with the text" rather than against its powerful and persuasive grain. In this context, particular ethnic groups, male leaders, and socioeconomic classes predominate at the expense of others in the story. It reflects the way our academies, seminaries, and churches have always trained us to read the Bible. Women are trained and encouraged to read the Bible from a male perspective. Black people are equipped with the skills to read the Bible with a white person's agenda. Poor people are socialized to collude with elitist texts and interpretations.[14] This is a strange situation indeed, one that can easily entrench systemic forces of racism, classism, patriarchy, ethnocentrism, and so forth, not only in the biblical text, but also in the homes, churches, and societies of the readers. Such a hermeneutic cannot help marginalized readers to rediscover their self-identity and affirm their self-worth. I would go as far as to suggest that a male-oriented reading and analysis of the text of Esther cannot affirm the full humanity of women. Such readings can only re-entrench the existing problematic structures of the status quo. I will return to an example of what may be regarded as a male-oriented reading of the Vashti character at the end of this section.

Those who are patriarchally-oriented will view Vashti's story with distaste. How can a wife refuse to appear before her *baal*, master—a man of status at that? Indeed, she deserved the punishment that was supposed to remind not only her, but also all the people in the Persian kingdom, that "every man should be master in his own house" (1:22). In my view, such a declaration from a king who has failed to be master in his own house is ironic. Still, according to traditional interpretation, a woman like Vashti cannot be a model for the modern women readers of this story. The ideal and biblical model for a Christian woman, from a patriarchal perspective, is that of a wife who submits herself unquestioningly to her husband. This allegedly "feminine" virtue is stated explicitly in Eph 5:21–33 and can even be quoted by men who have hardly read the Bible. Such statements reveal not the Word of God, but male power dynamics. It is no wonder that such readings have encouraged our churches through the ages to read the Vashti character unsympathetically and, in fact, to read Esther sympathetically, as one who "obeys." The following example can serve as a case in point.

I had the opportunity to listen to two women, who happened coincidentally to be pastors' wives, interpret the Vashti character in their attempt to encourage Christian women in their *bosadi* (womanhood) journeys. The pattern was the same: the two main female characters in this

---

14. In this regard, see the caution demonstrated by Itumeleng J. Mosala, *Biblical Hermeneutics and Black Theology in South Africa* (Grand Rapids: Eerdmans, 1989).

book were brought together, made to compete with each other, not for their own welfare as persons in their own right, but in terms of whether or not they were good wives to their husbands, that is, in terms of their husbands' welfare. Vashti was cited as an example of a bad woman, a disobedient wife who, by not honoring her husband, thereby failed also to honor God. It seems that the underlying assumption was that a Christian woman should respect her husband at all costs; I say "at all costs" because neither of them criticized the drunken state of the king when he summoned his wife to appear before him. Neither questioned the integrity of such a king in relation to his spouse. I was left with the impression that what husbands command is always right; the wife's role is to respond in silence and submission.

In contrast to Vashti, Esther was cited as a model woman, one whose example Christian women should aspire to emulate. She was portrayed as a humble woman who showed respect for her husband. One of the pastor's wives argued that husbands are women's "lords," and, as such, they deserve to be honored as women's God-given gifts. Therefore, for example, wives are to ensure that they always take responsibility for the preparation of the meal of their "lord." It is disturbing to see how these women naturally collude with the narrator's portrayal of Esther. They could not question what they referred to as her obedience. But was Esther obedient when she manipulated her speech before the king in order to save, not the Persian king's people, but her own Jewish people? Was she obedient (at least according to the Persian laws) when she dared to appear before the king without being summoned? Such an act could have cost even Esther, the Persian queen, her life. But Esther went ahead and did it, neither out of her commitment to honor and obey her husband nor out of a commitment to her husband's people. Esther ventured to take such a risky step as a result of her commitment to save her own people. The contrast with the reading of Vashti's behavior is indeed striking.

In my view, such androcentric readings of biblical texts as those offered by these pastors' wives will not only estrange females from their experiences as women, but they will also hinder them from hearing the Word and will of their divine Mother in the text. My conviction concerning God's will for women's lives is that since they were originally born to belong to the human feminine species, they should never aspire to be anything but just that. They must therefore refuse to be copies of men, lest they fail to fulfill the purpose for which their Heavenly Parent has created them.

An important question I want to ask as I conclude this section is this: what perceptions might such masculinist readings enforce on female readers, particularly on the coming generation of women? These readers will primarily observe that women are not allowed to act independently.

They must make sure that they submit to the demands of their husbands at all costs, and, in that way, they will be revealing their commitment to Jesus Christ. But can such notions encourage Christian women to exercise their God-given potential, not only in the churches, but also in their homes and the broader society? Can these interpretations encourage women to take up the tasks of the different ministries to which they are called? Can women be encouraged to interrogate the biblical text to be able to discern the life-giving Word of God from the death-dealing word of males? It does not seem so.

Vashti from a *Bosadi* Perspective

In my past scholarship, I have attempted to read the Vashti character in a way that I thought would make sense to African women in South Africa, hoping to liberate this character from the strange interpretations she has received through the years and to replace the former with a woman-friendly interpretation.[15] Before I begin, however, I wish to point out the procedure that I normally follow when I reread a particular Bible text from a *bosadi* perspective. As the *bosadi* approach is committed to African-South African women's contexts or a gendered-contextual reading, even before I start researching on a particular biblical text I deliberately choose to read and write from my specific social location: as an African woman in South Africa. Though many, if not all, commentaries I read on particular biblical texts have been produced by whites, whether male or female, I endeavor to read them with African *bosadi* (womanhood) eyes, an exercise which is often difficult, given the centrality of the Western perspective in my training. But for me, the context of the African *mosadi* reader is more significant than that which produced the biblical text. In rereading the Bible story, then, I will be looking for ideologies in the text that are unfriendly to my context: patriarchy, misogyny, the narrator's possibly negative attitude toward particular races, classes, ethnic groups, foreigners, and so on. The aim of this approach is to see how these elements may be interpreted in relation to the marginalized peoples in the communities of African-South Africa, particularly women.

---

15. For a more extensive treatment, see Masenya (ngwana' Mphahlele), *Making the Context,* 20–30; idem, "A Small Herb Increases Itself (Impact) by a Strong Odor: Reimagining Vashti in an African-South African Context," *OTE* 16 (2003): 332–42. The following material is based on a paper that I presented for the Feminist Hermeneutics of the Bible Section at the 2002 SBL/AAR Annual Meeting in Toronto on the subject.

When the above approach is applied to the Vashti character the following questions arise: What is the narrator's attitude toward Vashti, the woman? What factors have led to such a position? Which strategies is this character made to use to survive in a foreign patriarchal context? Can she be a model for women of Africa in South Africa today? How is her ethnicity related to that of the narrator? Is she made to suffer narrative violence precisely because she is not of the same ethnic group as the narrator? How was her ethnicity interpreted by past white male South African biblical interpreters? What impact did such perceptions have, and continue to have, on the identity of African peoples in the country? What is Vashti's class? Did her socioeconomic position (as portrayed by the male narrator), in one way or another, help her in her struggle toward survival? If that were the case, how was she helped? If it helped and, particularly, if she were an upper-class woman, in what way can her class serve as an inspiration to many African-South African women who remain at the bottom of society's socioeconomic ladder and may never be like her in their lifetime? On the whole, how may this character empower African women to be what they were meant to be by God? How may she contribute to the enhancement of their spirituality?[16]

From the above analysis, one can see that my approach is geared toward a Bible reading that will make sense to women whose lives are typified by multiple forms of oppressions: gender inequalities, post-apartheid racism/neo-racism, African patriarchy, and socioeconomic discrimination, to name but four challenges. What troubles me is that the South African church is less concerned about such matters. On the whole, it continues to remain silent in the midst of the violent acts committed against women. As a matter of fact, in many instances the church is part of the problem. It is high time that the church reviews the hermeneutics it has taught its members in the past in order to see how the affirmation of such interpretive lenses affects the ability of members to achieve fullness in their human identity. Does it encourage them to experience the abundant life that God has meant and is still meaning for them? If not, something has to be done. We prefer, therefore, to read the Vashti character in Esth 1 the *bosadi* way.

---

16. The last two questions, particularly in my church context, would be viewed as more basic than all the others, as teachings, sermons and so forth focus more on the need for an individual's personal relationship with God than on all these other, more "earthly," concerns. This is an unfortunate dichotomy, which is strange to the African holistic way of thinking. According to the African worldview, life is not compartmentalized into spheres such as the social, economic, religious, and so forth. All these form a whole and the latter is religious. When one aspect becomes disturbed, the whole is affected.

As noted earlier, the book of Esther reveals the situation of Jewish exiles in a foreign country, a context that was characterized by oppression and assimilation. In a parallel way, Vashti was in exile in her own home, a situation that reminds us of African-South Africans in the apartheid era. We lived under suppression and repression in our own country. If we apply this situation to Esth 1, it may be argued that the narrator in this text treats Vashti like a stranger to the Persian community. She is not treated as an independent character, but always delineated in relation to her husband. The mention of her own banquet in the context of her husband's larger feast, for example, probably indicates that the feast was not of her own initiative. She is presented as an uncooperative woman who flatly refuses to "honor" her husband's appreciation of her beauty by refusing to appear before him when summoned to do so. As a matter of fact, Vashti never really appears as an independent character at all, except when she breaks the code of conduct by refusing to appear before the king, an act that culminates in her removal from the scene. Like an exile in a foreign country, Vashti cannot be allowed to possess her own will. She can only survive through being assimilated by patriarchy. Vashti is a stranger in what is supposed to be her own territory.

Vashti's situation is very similar to what is still occurring in post-apartheid African-South Africa. In this context, there is an apparent understanding that the equality clause of the South African constitution pertaining to the equality between women and men applies in the workplace only. In many family and church contexts, African women are still treated as exiles. It is in these settings that one's gender determines the extent of one's assimilation. As in South Africa, what actually makes Vashti an exile in her own country is her gender. Indeed, her gender speaks louder than her ethnicity and her class.

Vashti as Example

The negative portrayal of the Vashti character by the narrator tempts one to speculate that she receives such harsh treatment because she is a woman in a world that did not legitimate women's power. Vashti is an example of one who, although socioeconomically strong and ethnically legitimate and powerful, continues to be haunted by her problematic gender. The latter will also determine the violation she will receive not only from the male narrator who presents her story, but also from fellow Persian characters, who, although socioeconomically not as powerful as she is, belong to the gender that legitimates the power they can exercise over her. When compared with the male characters around her in Esth 1, Vashti's gender speaks louder than her class, but when compared to other female characters, who are mentioned and not named or who are not mentioned at all, her class advantages her over other women in her own context. This situation reminds us that women of all ages, including women in the postapartheid South Africa, have never experienced patriarchy in the same way.

A look at Vashti's character tempts one to classify her as a bold person. She seems to know what she wants, and she will do what it takes to achieve what she wants irrespective of what the repercussions might be. Ironically, her fight is rewarded because she actually gets what she wanted: not to appear before the king. Though the narrator presents her as a fighter who does not care about upsetting the ruler of the empire as well as the patriarchal status quo, I hesitate to classify Vashti as a liberated woman or a feminist.[17] That would, in my view, be reading too much of what is happening in our twenty-first-century contexts back into this fourth-century B.C.E. world.

The challenge that we face as female readers of female characters such as Vashti as they appear in the Hebrew Bible canon is that scant information concerning them is provided. For example, in the present episode the narrator does not provide us any reasons for why Vashti dared to do what she did. Any reasons we may put forward for Vashti's refusal to appear before the king remain mere speculation. In my view, the omission of such important information, given the consequences that this character is made to suffer because of this act, is another proof that the character of Vashti in this book, particularly here in the beginning of the story, is unimportant to the narrator. She is merely used as a foil for the "proper" queen, the Jewish one, to appear on the scene. When Esther enters the picture, by contrast, her reasons for refusing to appear before the king are related by the narrator (Esth 4:11), further entrenching the character of Vashti as a vanishing point in the text.

The omission of the reasons for Vashti's refusal gives readers a glimpse of just how patriarchally-oriented the biblical narrators can be. They do not hesitate to violate the female characters in their narratives. In the present example, the narrator, in order to introduce the story of Esther, vilifies another woman from a different ethnic group, reducing Vashti to a narrative foil. Vashti, the Persian woman, is portrayed negatively as a woman who shames her husband and is made to suffer the consequences of her independent decision. Vashti's boldness, which results in her vulnerable situation as a woman in exile in her own home, is worth holding up as exemplary behavior. Still, considering Vashti's

---

17. Michael V. Fox, *Character and Ideology in the Book of Esther* (Columbia: University of South Carolina, 1991); and Jeffrey M. Cohen, "Vashti: An Unsung Heroine," *JBQ* 24 (1996): 103–6.

socioeconomic position, it is probably not an exaggeration to speculate that her class bolstered her boldness to refuse to appear before the king. It should be kept in mind, therefore, that women from poor contexts are not always in a position to say "no" to patriarchy, given their powerlessness. In this sense, while Vashti's boldness is exemplary, it cannot be as helpful to women in poverty.

Can the character of Vashti as presented in Esth 1 also serve as a model of hope for women of Africa living in South Africa? To use the image of a proverb ("a small herb increases itself by a strong odor"[18]), is the odor she releases in her context strong enough to dismantle the forces that deny fullness of life to women in our day? The answer to this question will naturally differ from one context to another. Women need to be strategic as to which odors to release, when to release them, and to what extent to release them. In this story, Vashti has, in my view, succeeded in showing the people, and particularly the men of her time (and ours), that women also have a will and can exercise that will whenever they want to, irrespective of what the consequences may be. Vashti, symbolizing a small herb, has succeeded in releasing an appropriate odor, one that for a moment challenged even that main upholder of the patriarchal status quo—the king.

In a Bible-reading context where theological education remains the luxury of a few people who have the relevant resources to engage in it, a context in which theology as a discipline receives little subsidy from the government, promoting historical-critical methodology as the only appropriate option for biblical interpretation may prove detrimental to powerless but committed (female) Bible readers. Though these readers embrace the Bible as an important spiritual resource, many cannot afford such an expense in order to access the Bible. The situation becomes even more exacerbated if such tools do not enable the Bible to address the needs of the readers. As a matter of fact, although the historical-critical methodology claimed objectivity, in reality it took care of the needs of its historical proponents. Women (let alone African women) and their contexts were never part of the original agenda of this methodology.[19]

On the other hand, a methodology that takes seriously the social location of African women Bible readers like the *bosadi* approach might prove to be more rewarding. The *bosadi* reading of the Vashti character presented here has hopefully brought this to light. As scholars employ such

---

18. In Northern Sotho, it is stated thus: *Serokolwana se sennyane se ikoketsa ka go nkga*. The sense of the proverb is that one who is deemed small or insignificant has ways of impacting those who are bigger/stronger.

19. Masenya (ngwana' Mphahlele), "Response to Himbaza and Holter," 3–8.

women-friendly approaches to the Bible, African women will benefit from reading texts no longer with *strange eyes,* but with their *own* eyes, employing their *own* biblical hermeneutics.

MOTHERS BEWAILING: READING LAMENTATIONS

Archie Chi Chung Lee

The conventional historical-critical approach generally adopted in academic circles is inadequate for understanding the complicated reality of cries of lament as they are articulated and textualized in the book of Lamentations. The reason for this is that historical criticism largely deals with recovering the historical scenario behind the text, focusing on the tragic fate of the holy city Jerusalem and what its chosen people did to bring calamity upon themselves. This preoccupation with the theological themes and concepts of sin, punishment, forgiveness, and hope of redemption has been so rigidly formulated that the significance of lament in human life is undermined as a result. The agonizing experience of YHWH turned enemy of the people, the latter personified in the female character of Jerusalem, is also not given its due. What I am attempting, therefore, is to reread the book of Lamentations in the light of the contemporary experience of bewailing mothers at the Tiananmen Square Massacre of 1989. Cross-textual reading, which acknowledges the encounters of different texts in the reading of the Bible, is proposed here as an alternative mode of interpretation that seeks to enhance these two textual formulations of the deep human quest for meaning in the midst of great grief and pain. It is my hope that the confluence of these two texts will enable the understanding of human responses to suffering through the "crossings" made in the process of "cross-textual reading."

READING THE BIBLE CROSS-TEXTUALLY

The cross-textual method assumes that readers, who are shaped by their own cultural and social texts, have always interpreted the Bible in an interactive process that accommodates the multiplicity of texts. I use the term "social text" here to refer to the religio-cultural as well as the socio-political milieu that makes up the background of the reader.[1] I designate

---

1. There is an Asian background to the development of this approach found in the missionary movement and Asian theology analyzed from a postcolonial perspective. See Archie

as "Text-A" a social text such as the Tiananmen Square Massacre of 1989, which represents the identity and underscores the agony and aspiration of Asian peoples. Text-A includes both the literary and orally transmitted articulation and construction of human reality as it is lived and experienced. It can take the form of stories, legends, myths, or folktales in either narrative or lyric compositions.[2] However, these nonbiblical Asian texts should not be read merely as a context into which the Bible, taken mostly as *the text,* is to be contextualized in order to be properly understood. Rather, these texts are to be perceived and treated, both theoretically and practically, as "texts" that interact with other texts in the process of reading and interpretation. They embody "the word" that can come into dialogue with the biblical word and contribute to the interpretation of the Bible, appropriately rendered in the Asian setting as "Text-B."

The dynamics of "the crossing" that takes place in the encounter of Text-A and Text-B engenders both meaning and understanding. There should be multiple crossings between the two texts, one shedding light on the other and being challenged and reformulated by it in the dynamic reading process. Although the Bible as the canon of the believing community has presumably a higher authority for many Christian scholars and interpreters, it cannot be categorically allowed to override and preempt Text-A in the cross-textual approach. Whenever the absolute claim and authority of the Bible are asserted, Text-A is once again relegated to the secondary status of medium used merely for effective communication purposes. This is illustrated by the situation in Asia, where, in order for the target audience to understand the Bible, the missionaries have worked hard to learn the local language and then translated the Bible into the vernacular with the principal goal of communicating the word to the target audience. The language peculiarities and cultural modes embedded in Text-A are adopted only in so far as they can be used in the service of preaching the word of Text-B. They are quite often emptied of their original religiosity and historicity, being domesticated until they are suitable as a tool for communicating the word of Text-B, but then only at a superficial level.

For Asians, the historical-critical method not only does not alleviate the absolute claim of the Bible in its encounter with the reader and other

---

Lee, "Biblical Interpretation in Asian Perspective," *AJT* 7 (1993): 38–48; Kwok Pui-lan, *Discovering the Bible in the Non-Biblical World* (Bible and Liberation Series; Maryknoll, N.Y.: Orbis, 1995); and Angela Wai-Ching Wong, *The Poor Woman: A Critical Analysis of Asian Theology and Contemporary Chinese Fiction by Women* (New York: Peter Lang, 2002).

2. Asian Christian theologians and biblical scholars have been interested in doing Asian theology using Asian resources. See John England and Archie Lee, eds., *Doing Theology with Asian Resources: Ten Years in the Formation of Living Theology in Asia* (Auckland, New Zealand: Pace, 1993).

texts, but it further assumes the so-called "objectivity" established by that method and thereby promotes the tyranny of scientism. This approach leaves no room for the role of the reader and the input of other texts that are part and parcel of the make-up of the reader in the Asian setting. A radical position must therefore be taken to raise the status of Text-A on an equal footing with Text-B, in order to enable fruitful crossings for the two texts and thereby to arrive at a mutually enriching encounter. This admission of Text-A into the dynamics of reading also calls into question the notion of a well-defined, absolute revelation in Text-B, understood in the traditional Judeo-Christian sense.

In what follows, I will first offer a few brief comments on the historical-critical approach to Lamentations and then demonstrate how the cross-textual method works, reading Lamentations in relation to a social text such as the "Tiananmen Mothers Campaign."

The Historical-Critical Approach to Lamentations

In historical-critical scholarship the broken yet hopeful man of Lam 3 is favored as the "high point"[3] and theological core of the book. Thus, scholars often move quickly from the condemned mournful "Widow Zion" of Lam 1–2 to Lam 3 in order to avoid Zion's emotionalism and tragic fate and to seek reason and redemption in the text.[4] Tod Linafelt sees in this common reading strategy the tendency to value lament "only in so far as it leads to something that is less strident and mournful, and more conciliatory and hopeful."[5] In conventional scholarship on the book of Lamentations, the identity of the speaker in Lam 3 ("I am the man … ") has thus received much scholarly attention. Historical-critical scholars have been preoccupied with the historical background, including the traditions incorporated within and transformed by the constructed historical reality.[6] Under the assumption of Jeremiah's authorship, the portrayal of this prophet as a paradigm of suffering has predominated.[7] There is also

---

3. Delbert R. Hillers, *Lamentations: A New Translation with Introduction and Commentary* (AB 7A; Garden City, N.Y.: Doubleday, 1992), 122.

4. Tod Linafelt, *Surviving Lamentations: Catastrophe, Lament, and Protest in the Afterlife of a Biblical Book* (Chicago: Univeristy of Chicago Press, 2000), 2.

5. Ibid., 11.

6. Norman Gottwald, *Studies in the Book of Lamentations* (SBT 14; London: SCM, 1954).

7. Magne Sæbø has provided a good summary of different approaches to the issues in "Who Is 'The Man' in Lamentations 3? A Fresh Approach to the Interpretation of the Book of Lamentations," in *Understanding Poets and Prophets: Essays in Honour of George Wishart Anderson* (ed. A. G. Auld; JSOTSup 152; Sheffield: Sheffield Academic Press, 1993), 294–306.

a tendency to universalize the figure into a typical "pious one" in general or a nonhistorical "everyman."[8]

Sæbø asserts that the traditio-historical context of the interpretation of Lam 3 is to be located in the special Jerusalem tradition of Zion and David.[9] He points to the sequence of chapters 1–5 for the theological position on the fall of Zion, which is portrayed as a mourning widow in the first two chapters as well as in the last two. Sæbø affirms the central position and significance of chapter 3 in his "royal-messianic" interpretation. When Zion failed and fell, as described in Lam 2 and 4, the hope of the future of the people rested on the enigmatic "man" of chapter 3, who is identified as the last monarch of the Davidic House in Jerusalem, King Zedekiah.[10]

This line of investigation claims to be historical and critical, but in actuality it is mostly ideological, framed in terms of the theological interest of the interpreter. Historical-critical interpreters are preoccupied with the theological thrust of the motifs of doom and hope read in light of the different traditions of Zion in the preexilic period. Most of them condone the gender bias directed against the disgraceful woman embodied in the Zionic figure of the mourning widow. She is to be punished and violently treated by the righteous God who has chosen the royal figure of the "man"—the Davidic King—to whom alone salvation is to be given.

The scholarly agenda that favors the central position of Lam 3 and ascribes a theological center to it only reveals the Christian community's uneasiness in dealing with catastrophic tragedies. The emotional expectation from the community in such crisis situations is to overcome and get rid of the calamity if it is too overwhelming. The drive from pain to deliverance is so compelling that the face of the mourning widow becomes insignificant, intentionally disfigured, and necessarily blank. The faceless, suffering woman is hurriedly replaced by the male royal-messianic figure, who embodies the source of comfort and redemption. The voice of the female persona in Lam 1–2 thus becomes insignificant. Her suffering and grief only serve to pave the way for a transition from justifiable punishment to the expectation of redemption in Lam 3. Scholars usually apply the theological assumptions of God's rightful punishment and the superiority of God's mercy as a conventional framework for

---

8. Hillers, *Lamentations*, 122.

9. Here Sæbø picks up the proposal of Bertil Albrektson that Lamentations has its background in the preexilic Deuteronomic tradition of Israel and further develops it to underscore the Jerusalem tradition in Lamentations. See Bertil Albrektson, *Studies in the Text and Theology of the Book of Lamentations* (STL 21; Lund: Gleerup, 1963).

10. Sæbø, "Who Is 'The Man' in Lamentations 3?" 304.

interpretation. The strict causal link between sin and punishment and the expectation of a call for conversion are commonly affirmed.[11]

THE BEREAVED MOTHER IN LAMENTATIONS
AND THE MOTHERS OF TIANANMEN

I will now read the book of Lamentations in parallel with a Chinese social text of the mourning mothers who lost their beloved children as a result of the military crackdown in Tiananmen Square. To date, 115 bereaved mothers have joined together in a coalition called "Tiananmen Mothers Campaign"[12] to have their voices heard and to demand the justice due to them and their dead children. Their unrelieved and unresolved grief has aggregated into bitter pains. Public mourning and remembrance of their dead ones have been denied them on the past fourteen anniversaries of the June 4 Tiananmen Square Massacre. Moreover, the rightful student movement of 1989 is still condemned as counterrevolutionary turmoil, whereas the murdering soldiers who willingly or unwillingly opened fire at the students were honored as people's heroes.[13] This absurdity of life in the Chinese context must be seen in light of the political tyranny of China. Vera Schwarcz, a Jewish scholar of Chinese contemporary history and of the student movement of May 4, 1919, happened to be in Beijing during the 1989 student demonstration. She followed the development closely and has written a succinct summary related to the repression of memory articulated above:

> China today is in danger of losing its past. Like a snail robbed of its shell, it has nothing to pull back into, little to carry forward with certainty. No homecoming to memory is allowed: The mass movement of 1989 did not happen. The government claims it was nothing but "counterrevolutionary turmoil" instigated by a handful of "hooligans." The authorities

---

11. Jože Krašovec, "The Source of Hope in the Book of Lamentations," in *Reward, Punishment, and Forgiveness: The Thinking and Beliefs of Ancient Israel in the Light of Greek and Modern Views* (ed. J. Krašovec; VTSup 78; Leiden: Brill, 1999), 679–88. Westermann sees the confession of sin (1:5, 8–9, 14, 18, 20–21; 2:14; 3:42; 4:6, 13–15; 5:7, 16) and the approval of God's judgment (1:14, 18; 2:17; 3:42; 4:11–16; 5:19) as the two dominant themes in Lamentations (Claus Westermann, *Handbook to the Old Testament* [London: SPCK, 1975], 251). The affirmation of the compassion of God, which will lead the people out of devastation and bitter lament, forms the conclusion to his interpretation.

12. See the resource online at: http://iso.hrichina.org/iso/ (cited 14 April 2004).

13. Vera Schwarcz, "Memory and Commemoration: The Chinese Search for a Livable Past," in *Popular Protest and Political Culture in Modern China* (ed. J. N. Wasserstrom and E. J. Perry; 2d ed.; Boulder, Colo.: Westview, 1994), 170–71. See also idem, "In the Shadows of the Red Sun: A New Generation of Chinese Writers," *Asian Review* 3 (1989): 4–16.

have honored the soldiers who died during the repression of June calling them "revolutionary martyrs," but the students and ordinary citizens killed in Beijing, Chengdu, and other cities may not be mourned publicly. On the first anniversary of the June Fourth Massacre, in fact, even to wear white (the traditional Chinese color of mourning) or black (its Western equivalent) was forbidden. Remembrance of the dead—which has long been the anchor of personal, familial, and to a certain extent national identity in China—is crushed under the weight of officially mandated amnesia.[14]

The brave bewailing "Tiananmen Mothers" under the leadership of Ding Zilin, who lost her seventeen-year-old son and has subsequently been hailed as "the advocate for the dead," have defied the official policy and, in so doing, have refused to submit to the state's power. These mothers' persistent demands represent a strong force of resistance against the state that oppresses and silences them for the sake of national stability and social harmony. The Tiananmen Mothers put forth the following five-point demand to the Chinese government: (1) the right to mourn, publicly and peacefully, the loss of their loved ones; (2) the right to accept humanitarian aid from organizations and individuals inside and outside of China; (3) an end to the persecution of the June 4 victims, including those injured in the massacre, as well as the families of the dead; (4) the release of all detainees who participated in the democratic movement of 1989; and (5) a full investigation and public accountability for the June 4 Massacre that would end impunity for the perpetrators of this crime.[15] In the past ten years since she came out to organize the mothers, Ding has experienced many threats, persecutions, and intimidations from the authorities. She is prepared to sacrifice herself, however, in order to "document death"[16] and to advocate for the right of the dead and their living relatives. The voices of the mothers will never be fully suppressed until they are vindicated.

In reading Lamentations with the social text of the Tiananmen Mothers, the voice of the personified Mother Zion clearly stands out and captures our attention. Her cry and that of the bereaved mothers of Jerusalem forms the hermeneutical key to our interpretation. The female voice in the lament is persistently heard in both Text-A and Text-B, and it

---

14. Schwarcz, "Memory and Commemoration," 170.

15. See Tiananmen Mothers Campaign on the "Human Rights in China," n.p. [cited 14 April 2004]. Online: http://www.hrichina.org.

16. Ding Zilin, "Documenting Death: Reflections after Ten Years," n.p. [cited 20 October 2004]. Online: http://iso.hrichina.org/public/contents/article?revision%5fid=2122&item%5fid=2121.

should continuously turn our attentive ears to the reality of the suffering that her children in Asia and other places experience. The lament does not seek to explain but instead represents the prevailing struggle to counteract national power and massive violence that threatens life. The Mothers of Tiananmen and the bereaved mother of Lamentations embody the resistance to unjustly exercised oppressive force. In the voices of the mother we can hear the cries of her dead children refusing to be pushed aside and neglected. A poem entitled "Weep No More Cicadas," which was dedicated to those who died at Tiananmen Square, underlines the enduring cry of the dead to be heard by the nation.

> Before twilight
> Our sons and daughters
> Were drenched in the blood
> They lay on the square motionless
> Their eyes still open
> Mothers, do not wait for them anymore
> Out of their scattered limbs
> Their crushed skulls
> An immutable race is born
> Weep no more, cicadas
> Though the hills stridulate endlessly
> Forsythias are still blooming
> Red peony sky hangs over the eastern gate
> The oracle has spoken
> China, can't you hear
> History is shouting
> Your chest is aflame
> Your mournful children are awakening.[17]

In Lam 1:1, Zion, here personified as a woman, does not seem to be given dignity and respect. She is only portrayed as "the female other," framed within the context of the national crisis of Israel brought about when the capital city Jerusalem fell captive to the Babylonians. This devastated woman has lost her husband and children. She sits alone, condemned of all the sins committed by the predominantly male leadership:

---

17. "Poems by Mira Foung," n.p. [cited 11 April 2004]. Online: http://www.vedanet. com/Mpoems.htm. For other collections of Tiananmen poetry (in Chinese), see Bai Hua et al., *A Starless Night in June: An Anthology of Poems* (Hong Kong: Breakthrough, 1990); Guangzhong Yu, ed., *My Heart at Tiananmen: A Collection of Poems for the Memorial of June 4th* (Taipei: Zheng Zhong, 1989); and Xuanren Wu and Qing Yang, eds., *Lament Songs and Flaming Blood: Anthology of Original Poems from the Democracy Movement, 1989* (Hong Kong: Shi Fang and Zhongguo Deng Huo Xing Dong, 1999).

> How lonely sits the city
> That once was full of people!
> How like a widow she has become,
> She that was great among the nations! (Lam 1:1)

Both the first sentence about the city and the second in which the state of the widow is described end with an adverbial phrase using the same Hebrew word *rb* ("*full* of people" and "*great* among the nations;" Lam 1:1). Through the contrast between the glorious past and the lowly present, the ruined situation of the city and the shameful state of the widow are underscored as strikingly parallel miserable conditions. The fate of a desolate city is closely linked with a condemned widow in Lamentations. Her "husband" has no part to play in this tragedy. The suggestion seems to be that her friends and lovers have rightly left her, turning to be her enemies instead (1:2). She has no one to comfort her (1:9, 17, 21). She confesses later that her lover has deceived her (1:19).

The first statement providing an explanation for the desperate situation is the motive clause in Lam 1:5: "Because the Lord has made her suffer for the multitude of her transgressions." The use of *rb* in "the *multitude* of sins" echoes her former state of being "full" of people and "great" among the nations in 1:1. Disfigured and deserted, her shame is further spelled out in her nakedness (1:8) and her uncleanness (1:9). The play on words between "filthy thing" and "mockery" is not to be missed (1:8, 17).[18] It is the natural cycle of menstruation that is being caricatured as unclean and abhorrent (cf. Lev 18:19; Ezek 22:10). Her physical condition is portrayed as both her punishment and cause for ridicule. Here the author of Lamentations tries to make her appear ugly and degenerate. She is simply viewed as being justly condemned and rightfully exploited. The phrase "the Lord made her suffer" (1:5) acknowledges that all humiliations and pains come to Mother Zion in the day of God's fierce anger (1:12), and God is justified for bringing about the devastating violence to the woman.

It is no wonder that the woman's voice should appear in the first person at this point of intense unresolved bereavement: "O Lord! Look at my affliction" (Lam 1:9c). She raises her voice again to plead to the Lord in v. 11: "Look, O Lord, and see how worthless I have become." The appeal is then extended to all passers-by. She protests against the incomparable pain she should endure: "Look and see if there is any pain like my pain" (1:12). At the end of the first poem the widow admits that her groans are many (*rb*) and her heart is faint (1:22).

---

18. On the meaning and possible rendering of the root of the word *nwd*, see Hillers, *Lamentations*, 53–54.

Lamentations 2 further affirms that the Lord has humiliated "Daughter Zion" (2:1, 4, 10) and "Daughter Judah" (2:2, 5).[19] In this chapter the Lord is the subject of all the destructive actions taken against Zion and Judah in the first ten verses, which are framed by the humiliation of Daughter Zion (2:1, 10). The questions addressing "Daughter Jerusalem" (2:13, 15) and "Virgin Daughter Zion" (v. 13) do not give any evidence of the identity of the speaker whose voice is in the first person singular. "Daughter Zion" speaks in the first person to pour out her lamentation at the death of her people, with special mention of the innocent infants and babies (2:11), who naturally cry out to their mothers (2:12). The same is also the case in the following fragment of another June 4 memorial poem entitled "Mama! I'm Hungry," written by poet Guangzhong Yu and found in his collection *My Heart at Tiananmen:*

> Mama, I'm hungry
> But I cannot eat
> Such a taste of bitterness
> Choking all day at my throat
> How can I swallow it down?
> Mama, I'm tired
> But I cannot sleep
> Such a heavy feeling
> Pressing all night upon my chest
> How can I sleep tight?
> Mama, I'm dead
> But I cannot die in peace
> Such a tragic country
> Forever scalded my soul
> How can I let go?
> Mama, I'm gone
> At next year's Grave Sweeping Season
> Remember to summon my soul
> In the days of democracy
> Beneath the Tiananmen Square.[20]

---

19. The holy city as divine daughter is a symbol of God's chosen people in relation to God. The expression "Daughter Zion" occurs twenty-six times in the Old Testament, eight of which are found in Lamentations (1:6; 2:1, 4, 8, 10, 13, 18; 4:22). For a comparative study of the notion of the holy city as divine daughter in Hebrew and Greek usage, see Elaine R. Follis, "The Holy City as Daughter," in *Directions in Biblical Hebrew Poetry* (ed. E. R. Follis; JSOTSup 40; Sheffield: Sheffield Academic Press, 1987), 173–84.

20. Guangzhong Yu, *My Heart at Tiananmen*, 20. Unless otherwise stated, translations of poems from Tiananmen are my own.

The agony of the students on hunger-strike at Tiananmen is communicated to their mothers. Although desperate, they are courageous in the face of death. Expressed in the poem is a quest for a day when democracy is realized, and the dead soul wants to be summoned to witness it. In Lam 2:18, which represents a turning point in the chapter, "Daughter Zion" is invited to cry out for the lives of her hungry children who died in their prime (2:19). The ironic questions in 2:20 start with the same demand for attention that one finds in the former chapter (1:9, 11, 20): "Look, O Lord, and consider!" But the intention of the questions is not easy to comprehend.

> Should women eat their offspring,
>   the children they have borne?
> Should priest and prophet be killed
>   in the sanctuary of the Lord? (Lam 2:20)

Obviously, the rhetorical questions assume a negative answer: it should not be so. The lines constitute the woman's daring accusation of God.[21] The death of children is the most desperate and grievous moment encountered by a mother, even before such a horrific event becomes a national concern for the loss of the future to a people. Here we must raise the issue of the nationalistic project that merely co-opts motherhood in metaphorical terms for a national agenda in both the Chinese and biblical texts. Literary representations of "woman" as a sign for the "nation," exhibiting the desired quality of self-sacrifice, benevolence, devotion, and care, appear in national discourse and politics. Based on Kumari Jayawardena's theory,[22] Angela Wai-Ching Wong develops a feminist cultural critique of this construct, which in her view not only serves the national agenda but also erases woman's sexuality and subordinates her to the new patriarchy in Asia. From a postcolonial perspective, Wong explicates that such a project of feminization of colonial territory contributes to the further victimization of women.[23] Here femininity is nationalized and motherhood politicized, just as one also finds in the student demonstrations at Tiananmen Square, in which

---

21. Kathleen M. O'Connor, "Lamentations," in *The Women's Bible Commentary: Expanded Edition with Apocrypha* (ed. C. A. Newsom and S. H. Ringe; Louisville: Westminster John Knox, 1998), 190.

22. See esp. Kumari Jayawardena, *Feminism and Nationalism in the Third World* (London: Zed Books and Kali for Women, 1986); as well as Kumari Jayawardena and Malathi de Alwis, eds., *Embodied Violence: Communalising Women's Sexuality in South Asia* (London: Zed Books and Kali for Women, 1998).

23. Wai-Ching, *Poor Woman*, 34–43.

Mother China was similarly nationalized and politicized, as the following poem suggests:

> Why do you shed tears?
> Because Mother is critically ill.
> Why are you so happy?
> Because people of the whole nation are helping.
> Mother is saved; your esteemed body is safe.
> Mother is in good health; she loves her children.
> I want our Mother
> Because she gives love to us,
> Brings warmth to humankind.
> I love my Mother
> Because Mother raised us into adulthood,
> Brought us to the path of brightness.
> Bless our Mother Country:
> Good health, live long for millions of years.
> Long live Mother Country! Long live democracy and freedom![24]

Such discursive uses of female identity are problematic regardless of who uses them, and they make us painfully aware of the fragility of goodness when placed in the service of political aims and aspirations.

Since the massacre, however, awareness of such discursive practices has become all the more critical, as Mother China has been captured and co-opted by the present political leadership, which has turned into the enemy of the people. The cry of the starving students on hunger-strikes is not being met by any compassionate response from the leaders. Instead, the violent military crackdown brought about murders and massive injuries. Bai Hua's poem, "The Rediscovery of China," exhibits the ironic characteristics of seeing lament and hope in the younger generation of Chinese students who are on a hunger-strike:

> Comes May, the world turns its sight toward the East in shock.
> Innocent and plain faces of childhood
> In hunger and thirst, they lack the strength to get up,
> Cower in the square where seventy years ago their grandfathers
> Hurried and shouted across.
> Occasionally, in the rainstorm, the flowers struggle to raise their heads,
> Swollen mouths speak voicelessly:
> Do you know us? We are China.
> You are China? The very ancient China?

---

24. "I Want Mother" is taken from a poster at Tiananmen Square on May 25, 1989. The poem is published in the collection *Lament Songs and Flaming Blood,* 104.

Today she is so youthful, beautiful, and charming!
Transpiring unshaken strength out of poverty and weakness.
All of a sudden, all the world's beds become concrete,
All the world's dining tables are stripped bare.
All the world's children have learnt one simple Chinese sentence:
"Mother, I am hungry." [25]

We cannot expunge the intensified bitter lament of mothers bereft of their children from the accusation of the Mothers of Tiananmen, who cry out against the murderers of their children. A poem presenting a dialogue between a student on a hunger-strike and his/her mother exhibits aspiration for hope in the young heart and a deep feeling of agony on the part of the mother:

Oh mother, if you hear
My hungry intestine weeps
Same as hearing the full stomachs of the living
If you see me
Fall, spit blood
Same as seeing a human being's explicit dignity standing tall.
* * *
My heart, as if stabbed and broken into pieces, my child,
Severe pain is the only feeling of being alive.
Ask whose heart is so cold and hard
Whose soul is so ugly?
Having sucked full with flaming blood
Seems to be still giggling in the sea of blood!? [26]

Read cross-textually with writings from the Mothers of Tiananmen, Lam 2 portrays the same bereavement of Mother Zion in a narrative movement progressing "from a description *of* Jerusalem (2:1–12) to an address to Jerusalem (2:13–19); and finally to a speech *by* Jerusalem herself (2:20–22)."[27] The eyewitness calls Jerusalem to cry to YHWH passionately and ceaselessly on behalf of the lost children.

Pour out your heart like water
Before the face of Adonai
Lift up your hands to him
On account of your children

---

25. Bai Hua et al., *Starless Night in June*, 17.
26. Ibid., 89.
27. Barbara Bakke Kaiser, "Poet as 'Female Impersonator': The Image of Daughter Zion as Speaker in Biblical Poems of Suffering," *JR* 67 (1987): 176–77.

Who expire from famine
At the head of every street. (Lam 2:19)

It is at the high point of emotional upheaval and grief that the voice of the female persona comes in to cast an ironic invective at YHWH, the *murderer* of her children.

See, O YHWH, and pay heed. . . .
You have slain in the Day of your wrath;
You have butchered mercilessly! . . .
You have summoned as on a feast day
All my terrors round about. (Lam 2:20–22)

Mother Zion implores YHWH to look and see the ironic situation of the death of her children in famine and God's merciless butchering of them on a feast day, where YHWH, the *murderer*, actually invites Zion's enemies to the banquet. Mother Zion openly accuses YHWH of being her enemy in killing her well-cared-for children.

On the Day of the wrath of YHWH
There was no escape or survivor.
As for those whom I formed and raised—
My Enemy has finished them off! (Lam 2:22)

The complaint that God does not seem to see the people's plight and cries of despair—"look and see" (Lam 1:9, 11, 20; 2:20)—is reiterated in the traditional appeal to the Lord to remember:

Remember, O Lord, what has befallen us;
Look and see our disgrace. (Lam 5:1)

The concerns for the women and the mothers are especially underlined in chapter 5: "Our mothers are like widows" (Lam 5:3), and "Women are raped in Zion" (5:11). It is not the generation of the exile, but their descendents who assume and complain that "our ancestors sinned; they are no more, and we bear their iniquities" (5:7). Hunger, famine, hard labor, and the aftermath of war dominate the present reality of life (5:2–6, 8–16). Mount Zion still lays in desolation (5:18). This generation of survivors therefore appeals to the Lord and acknowledges that God's reign endures throughout the generations.

Lamentations appropriately ends with the communal prayer in chapter 5, which does *not* evidently provide hope and promise redemption. Lament lingers on, but the prayer anticipates openness in the midst of ambiguity and uncertainty. The cry in 5:20 sounds like a haunting call that does not yield to any justification in terms of sin (Lam 1:18, 20; 3:42;

4:13; 5:7, 16) and the consequent punishment (1:5, 8–9, 12–15, 17, 21; 2:1, 17, 20–21; 3:1; 4:11) manifested in the brutality of the aggressive enemies. The enduring, unbearable situation of "no consolation" (1:2, 9, 16–17; 2:13, 21) persists. There is no mention of any grounds for God's willingness to restore the people and renew their day (5:21):

> Why have you forgotten us utterly,
>   Forsaken us for so long?
> Take us back, O Lord, to yourself,
>   and we will come back.
> Renew our days as of old.
> Unless truly you have rejected us
>   Raging bitterly against us. (Lam 5:20–22)

The distress is still a present reality, in the midst of which the community cries out in anguish. Lamentations 3 in no way presents a past experience from which deliverance has been brought about.[28]

Nearly fifteen bitter years have come and gone and the cry of the Mothers of Tiananmen has still not been heard. No response has come to the demand for the justice due to the dead and the living. Their rightful claims have to be reiterated time and again. Yet the lack of an answer has given me a sense of the understanding of the communal lament and prayer of Lam 5 and the open-endedness and incompleteness of the book itself. At the end of Lamentations there is no indication of the "strong man" (of the so-called theological center in Lam 3) who comes to initiate restoration, but rather the communal act of prayer in the midst of the harsh reality opens to a future in God. Based on the understanding of the particles in the beginning of 5:22 as indicating a class of conditionals—a protasis without an apodosis (cf. Gen 38:17; Num 5:20; Exod 32:32)—Linafelt constructs the ending of the book of Lamentations as "a willful *nonending*," an incompleteness that anticipates an open future. The nonresponsiveness of YHWH gives way to an ambivalent state of being within the community of lamenters who refuse to move "beyond lament to praise."[29]

AN INCONCLUSIVE POSTSCRIPT

Through cross-textual hermeneutics, we face up to the plurality of texts, which has consequences for our reading of the Bible. This

---

28. Iain W. Provan, "Past, Present and Future in Lamentations III 52–66: The Case for a Precative Perfect Re-examined," *VT* 41 (1991): 164–75.

29. Tod Linafelt, "The Refusal of a Conclusion in the Book of Lamentations," *JBL* 120 (2001): 343.

approach highlights the interactive reading process in the understanding of the biblical text (Text-B) wherein the reader is conscious of the impact of "the other text" (Text-A), whether this text is cultural or political, literary or social in its configuration and function. These other texts are part of the textuality that makes up our life context, shapes our political existence, models our social vision, and enriches our religiosity. They may inform us of our presuppositions, challenge our presumptions, clarify our ambiguity, recast our worldview, and/or reformulate our persuasions. But, first and foremost, they must be taken seriously and given a space in which to operate. Though they are referred to here as "the other text" in the context of the Bible, they are in fact the "indigenous text" vis-à-vis the Bible, the latter of which is only an "acquired text," a newcomer to the already very rich textual and commentarial traditions in the Asian context.

There are no precisely articulated hermeneutical principles to follow in the cross-textual approach. The success of it and the fruitful result it may generate depend on the space allocated to these nonbiblical texts and on the creative imagination the reader is prepared to bring to the reading process. The worlds of the two texts, biblical and nonbiblical, will exercise their individual constraints in terms of the textures that constitute the foundation of texts.[30] As such, there should not be any fear of uncontrolled subjectivity and wild imagination as the parameters of the texts in question delimit a particular scope for interpretation.

This approach may also unveil the limitations and presuppositions of the historical-critical method. In reading Lamentations, it is clear that the historical preoccupation with the issues of the unity and theological structure of Lamentations is totally inadequate for understanding the lamenting cry of the suffering mother. It has not helped to penetrate into the realms of human pain and suffering, social injustice, human violation, and the cries for vindication. The tradition of lament is more about the articulation of grief than about seeking a rational explanation for catastrophic calamities. In the crossings between Text-A and Text-B, then, the voice of the disgraced widow, the representation of human struggles for justice, and the fight against oppressive powers and principalities can be heard more loudly and clearly in the residual cries of the mothers, even though they are thousands of miles and generations apart.

---

30. For further development of these concepts, see Vernon K. Robbins, *Exploring the Texture of Texts: A Guide to Socio-Rhetorical Interpretation* (Valley Forge, Pa: Trinity Press International, 1996); and idem, *The Tapestry of Early Christian Discourse: Rhetoric, Society and Ideology* (New York: Routledge, 1996).

The recovery of the nature of lament gives back to those in distress a voice to articulate the *yuan* in Chinese and *han* in Korean cultures, which is a religious and theological notion expressing a deep feeling of resentment and grievance arising from the experience of being unjustly treated. The persistent cries of the Mothers of Tiananmen and Mother Zion are especially empowering to the bereaved mothers who are always in our midst awaiting vindication.

The massive sufferings of men, women, and children in Asia will fashion Text-A and reconfigure the way in which Lamentations can be read fruitfully in a cross-textual manner. Preman Niles's comments on the task of Korean theology are helpful in this respect: "Like Rachel of Old (Jer. 31:15; Mt. 2:18), mothers, wives and sisters in Asia are lamenting and weeping, not so much for themselves as for their loved ones, and refusing to be comforted with cheap and facile offers of peace because their own are no more. To respond to and surface the cries of the victim both as a dismantling cry and as a lament for vindication is one of the major tasks of *Minjung* theology."[31]

What I have attempted so far in this essay is to use Text-A to reinterpret the role of woman/female in human suffering and the reality of lament cries in Text-B (= Lamentations). The suffering Mothers of Tiananmen are taken as the text through which we come to understand the suffering mother/ widow/daughter of Jerusalem. Thus, the cross-textual approach has the potential for elucidating aspects of gender and feminism that historical criticism has not seen, because the latter only reads in a linear manner; that is, "with the text." One who has experienced suffering through the eyes of these mothers will read Lamentations in a way that moves beyond the limited scope of the historical-critical method. While Text-B in turn does confirm the horror of suffering more generally, overall the accent is placed on the role of Text-A in shaping the reading of Text-B. Cross-textual hermeneutics has been both a theological method for Asian theology and a reading strategy in Asian biblical studies, but the conscious efforts of bringing Text-A to light in order to illuminate the biblical text may also be imperative for biblical studies in other parts of the world.[32]

---

31. D. Preman Niles, "Editorial," *Commission for Theological Concerns Bulletin* 5 (December 1984–April 1985): 2–3. *Minjung* theology is a typical Korean theological construction that takes seriously the experience and location of Korean *minjung* (people).

32. Nancy C. Lee provides an excellent example of how to take a social text and apply it to the study of Lamentations. See her *The Singers of Lamentations: Cities under Siege, From Ur to Jerusalem to Sarajevo* (BibInt Series 60; Leiden: Brill, 2002).

THE HISTORY OF WOMEN IN ANCIENT ISRAEL: THEORY, METHOD, AND THE BOOK OF RUTH

Esther Fuchs

Missing in feminist historical criticism of the Hebrew Bible is an awareness of the methodological and theoretical questioning of funda-mental premises, concepts, and inquiries in the study of history as such.[1] Whether or not history provides a justification of social and cultural norms today, and to what extent history is little more than a story told by a particular individual and endorsed by an interpretive community, are fundamental questions in historiography in general, and in the history of the ancient world in particular. A similar self-questioning regarding the researcher's location and position is carried on in other social scientific areas of study, from anthropology, to sociology, to archaeology. More-over, basic concepts that the social sciences traditionally have taken for granted such as agriculture, kinship, the family, monogamy, and capital-ism have come under considerable scrutiny. The awareness that certain ethnographic phenomena, often referred to as cross-cultural structures, reflect a present state of affairs that should not automatically be projected onto the past has seeped into the theoretical debates of social "science." Basic terms and concepts in the study of history, such as "culture,"

---

1. E.g., What kind of book is the Hebrew Bible? Is it a cultural product of an ancient society in which men dominated, or is it an ideological product of a group of men who set out to establish a male-dominated or patriarchal order in an egalitarian setting? Do stories about women "reflect" historical realities of female subjection, or do they create a fictional world inspired by the male desire for female subjection? As feminists, how should we read the Bible? Should we point to the gaps and fissures, the exclusions and suppressions of women, or should we join the postmodern celebration of the Bible's polysemy and irre-ducible heterogeneity? Should we focus on the alleged world "behind" the text, using the text as a clue to and symptom of a broader historical reality? What is the status of the puta-tive world some of us claim to have discovered "behind" the text? Is the world of biblical women a reconstruction, a discovery, or is it a projection of the researcher's imagination and desire? To the extent that no researcher is free of bias, to the extent that all scholars have a position that is bound up with a particular cultural background, professional train-ing, and religious belief, how can anyone claim to be able to add to our knowledge about Israelite women in ancient Israel?

"experience," and "agency," have become topics of debate in feminist philosophy as well.[2] The possibility of establishing "facts" outside of the framework of a given interpretation and the possibility of studying such "facts" objectively—the so-called "scientific" claims of the social sciences—have both been widely problematized in feminist and post-modern scholarship. The status of scientific knowledge has thus become a matter of major debate. The usefulness of empiricism and positivism has been questioned. The politics of European Enlightenment scholar-ship, which established some of the categories and classifications that contemporary biblical historians continue to use today, have been ques-tioned and debated as well. Knowledge is bound up with the interests of the researcher, and we cannot divorce ourselves from contemporary con-cerns, claiming to attain an unmediated or neutral perspective on the past, as historical-critical approaches to the Bible have so frequently implied. Furthermore, past texts can hardly be read as innocent of bias, as disinterested or unrelated to cultural and creedal contexts. No one can legitimately claim that a book like the Bible, as heavy on axiology and eti-ology as it is, is best mined for clues about the way things actually were rather than how they ought to have been. These concerns and questions are critical for feminist interpretation of the Hebrew Bible.

In what follows here I will provide a brief overview of recent histo-ries of women in ancient Israel, and focus in particular on Carol Meyers's work, which has been especially influential. My critique questions the sci-entific and objective certainty that often colors such histories. What I hope to achieve is an awareness of women's ancient history as *interpretation* of data, as a contingent and tentative reading, as a hermeneutics rather than a collection of ascertainable facts. In the following analysis I will suggest that historians of Israel's past cannot avoid subjectivity and positionality, their own political location and their own interpretive grids, much as modern historians and literary critics cannot avoid theirs.[3] I will suggest that what historians of biblical women do is interpret texts—much as literary critics do—and therefore that what they offer is as much a

<hr />

2. See, e.g., Judith Butler and Joan W. Scott, eds., *Feminists Theorize the Political* (New York: Routledge, 1992); Linda Nicholson, ed., *Feminism/Postmodernism* (New York: Rout-ledge, 1990); Seyla Benhabib et al., *Feminist Contentions: A Philosophical Exchange* (New York: Routledge, 1995); Linda Alcoff and Elizabeth Potter, eds., *Feminist Epistemologies* (New York: Routledge, 1993); and Micaela di Leonardo, ed., *Gender at the Crossroads of Knowledge: Feminist Anthropology in the Postmodern Era* (Berkeley and Los Angeles: University of Cali-fornia Press, 1991).

3. Elizabeth A. Flynn and Patrocinio P. Schweickart, eds., *Gender and Reading: Essays on Readers, Texts, and Contexts* (Baltimore: Johns Hopkins University Press, 1986); and Jane P. Tompkins, ed., *Reader-Response Criticism: From Formalism to Post-Structuralism* (Baltimore: Johns Hopkins University Press, 1980).

construction as a reconstruction of a stable, knowable and representable reality. In the process, I will also draw out some of the submerged debates and contentions that have not been made explicit in the scholarly discourse on the lives of ancient Israelite women.

RECONSTRUCTING WOMEN'S LIVES IN ANCIENT ISRAEL

Margaret Conkey has argued that archaeology and human origins research in general tend to project notions regarding the centrality of fertility and female sexuality, as well as notions of sexual dimorphism, onto data traditionally gathered and interpreted by men. She notes that "the findings of archeology all too easily set certain definitional parameters for the categories and institutions that have been unquestioned anthropological givens. If archeology 'shows' for example, the antiquity of the nuclear family, heterosexual bonding, and the home-base (read domestic unit), these all too easily become legitimate analytical units, as natural, unquestioned elements of human social life."[4] By failing to question the presuppositions of archaeological and historical objects of knowledge, we defend the taken-for-granted status of these objects, thus reproducing a dominant paradigm and the fundamental values on which it rests. Some biblical historians have argued that "patriarchalism" is a "presentist" and therefore inappropriate category of analysis that ought not to be applied to the study of the Hebrew Bible. At the same time, however, as we shall see, they do make use of other categories of analysis that take certain models of social life in modern society as given. In this essay, then, I will query why patriarchalism is less appropriate for use as an analytic frame in biblical studies than say the family unit or the state, or class and other presentist terms.[5]

The study of "women" as a group or category requires that the historian uses gender, or the social meaning attributed to sexual difference, as a primary category of analysis. As Joan Scott states, "[t]he term 'gender' suggests that relations between the sexes are a primary aspect of social organization ... and that differences between the sexes constitute and are

---

4. Margaret Conkey, "Original Narratives: The Political Economy of Gender in Archeology," in di Leonardo, *Gender at the Crossroads of Knowledge,* 126.

5. Indeed, the recent interest in women in ancient Israel and the Hebrew Bible is itself conditioned by a modern or contemporary impulse. Yet, whether or not there is agreement about the shape of the object of knowledge, the inquiry, regardless of the specific terms and concepts it uses, is fueled by the questioning of the hegemony of patriarchalism in the modern world. The recent scholarship on women in antiquity is as such necessarily presentist to some degree.

constituted by hierarchical social structures."[6] Historians whose focus of study has been women often work to reconstruct what some feminists have dubbed "her-story." The point in this case is to give value to an experience that has been ignored or devalued. These historians attempt to fit a new subject—women—into widely used historical categories, and, for the most part, they try to interpret their subjects in terms recognizable to social and political historians.[7] Another approach within the "her-story" framework offers a different periodization, causation, and a new narrative, different from the normative androcentric one. Often this approach frames experience within a female sphere of familial and friendship connections and support systems. Scott argues that for feminist history to achieve its radical potential it cannot confine itself to recounting the great deeds of women. Rather, feminist history must expose the often silent and hidden operations of gender that are nonetheless the defining forces in the organization of most societies.

When it comes to feminist historians of ancient Israel, the problem of reconstructing the lives of women is compounded by the paucity of written sources outside the Bible and the uncertain data offered by archaeology. Succinctly stated, one never knows what is fact and what is fiction, what is a story and what is history. To what extent are biblical historians safe in using distinct stories as "proof" that women's lives or experiences indeed resembled in any way their reconstructions? If the biblical meta-narrative is polemical or prescriptive, as I argue in my book *Sexual Politics in the Biblical Narrative,* then the biblical historian virtually falls into the trap, or at the very least the enchanting web, of the biblical narrator by positing as fact or reality what the narrator wished to construct as such.[8] That the "historical" narratives of the Bible are no more reflective of a certain reality than so-called "nonhistorical" episodes or stories about individuals is suggested by the polemical nature and narrative structure of much of this "history."[9] Indeed, Mieke Bal argues that the only historical coherence that could possibly be found in the book of Judges, for instance, was the scholarly meta-narrative imposed on the text by modern scholars.[10] Yet the distinction

---

6. Joan W. Scott, *Gender and the Politics of History* (New York: Columbia University Press, 1988), 25.

7. Ibid., 19.

8. Esther Fuchs, *Sexual Politics in the Biblical Narrative: Reading the Hebrew Bible as a Woman* (Sheffield: Sheffield Academic Press, 2000), 11–33.

9. Marc Zvi Brettler, *The Creation of History in Ancient Israel* (New York: Routledge, 1995), 1–19.

10. Mieke Bal, *Death and Dissymmetry: The Politics of Coherence in the Book of Judges* (Chicago: University of Chicago Press, 1988), 9–39.

between the scholarly meta-narrative and biblical "history" is often blurred. According to Regina Schwartz, this blurring is dangerous because "the equation of the ideologies of biblical narratives with a positivist historian's understanding of 'real events' turns what could be founding fictions of Western culture that demand critique into 'facts' that seem formidably unassailable."[11] Schwartz demonstrates that contemporary biblical historiographies are rooted in German higher criticism of the nineteenth century, which in turn was implicated in a quest for nationalist roots, identity, and coherence.[12] The understanding of history in the Bible as a moral story and the modern understanding of history as a succession of events that have actually taken place represent radically different conceptions.

Furthermore, returning to a point raised earlier, the radically varying accounts rendered by modern historians suggests that the story of historical criticism is an interpretation rather than a reconstruction. If the object of research were knowable, and if the methods used truly scientific, the picture of the past would have emerged as the same, much as in the natural sciences, where lab tests are expected to lead to identical results. Yet the status of women in ancient Israel emerges as wildly divergent in various historical reconstructions. These differences suggest that much of the resultant reconstruction depends as much on the historian herself, on her theory and methodology, as on the alleged "reality" she has supposedly uncovered. Ideology is just as constitutive a part of social institutions as it is of textual production. To give up the question of ideology as inscribed in the text, to claim innocence and to use the biblical text or archaeological evidence as transparent, unproblematic sources of information is, to say the least, to assume that in antiquity people wrote texts in order to document events and social conditions, which locks us back into a "presentist" mindset. To assume that certain inscriptions are transparent reflections of historical reality is also rather problematic. In addition to questions of philology and correct translation, there are questions of dating, authorship, origination, context, ideological function, and purpose. Despite a fairly confident belief in the validity of historical research and archaeological methods, the various emergent reconstructions of women's lives in ancient Israel diverge substantially.

---

11. Regina M. Schwartz, "Adultery in the House of David: The Meta-Narrative of Biblical Scholarship and the Narratives of the Bible," in *Women in the Hebrew Bible* (ed. A. Bach; New York: Routledge, 1999), 336.

12. Ibid, 335–50.

Phyllis Bird, for example, suggests that women's cultic status in ancient Israel was rather marginal and subordinate to other concerns. Bird argues that women's participation in Israelite cults was "not essential and that it played a less central or less important role in women's lives than in men's."[13] Bird goes on to describe the situation as follows:

> Males occupy the positions of greatest authority, sanctity, and honor and perform tasks requiring technical skill and training. They preside over the presentation of sacrifices and offerings, have charge of the sacred lots, interpret the sacred law and instruct the congregation, pronounce blessing and curse, declare absolution and pardon, and guard the purity of the sanctuary and the worshipers; that is, they perform the priestly service in both sacrificial and oracular functions. Priestly office in Israel, as in the rest of the ancient Near East, was reserved to males. Contrary to popular opinion, Israelite Yahwism was not distinguished from the surrounding religions by its rejection of women in priestly office, but conformed to common practice.[14]

Carol Meyers, by contrast, suggests that women's cultic status was considerably better:

> Circumstantial as this kind of information about household cult and female involvement may be, it surely suggests a place for women in household religion. Furthermore, if any vestiges of goddess worship existed, women would probably have been directly involved with religious activity in domestic and perhaps also public shrines. But even without that possibility, and even excluding the specifically female focus on motherhood that the votary objects may have represented, household worship of any kind could hardly have taken place without female participation, whether normative or heterodox.[15]

Meyers explains the exclusion of women from the priesthood as being the result of pragmatic measures taken in the face of Canaanite cultic practices and thus related to demographic needs. According to Meyers, "[a] coterie of female professionals, diverted from pressing family needs, would not have been in the best interest of the community as a whole."[16] Her reconstruction of a woman's domestic religion in premonarchic Israel is

---

13. Phyllis Bird, *Missing Persons and Mistaken Identities: Women and Gender in Ancient Israel* (Minneapolis: Fortress, 1997), 89.

14. Ibid., 93–4.

15. Carol Meyers, *Discovering Eve: Ancient Israelite Women in Context* (New York: Oxford University Press, 1988), 163.

16. Ibid.

expanded both chronologically and geographically by Susan Ackerman, who finds evidence for the centrality and leadership of women in a cult dedicated to the Queen of Heaven even in the Jerusalem temple:

> [S]urprisingly, this women's cult did not prosper only in those spheres such as the home and the family where we might expect to find women's religion.... And if the worship of the Queen of Heaven was a part of the religion of the monarchy, the Queen's cult may also have been at home in what was essentially the monarch's private chapel, the temple.... But the biblical data about the Queen of Heaven do suggest that the women of late seventh and early sixth century Judah and Jerusalem exercised religious power. They worshiped a goddess whose cult they found particularly appealing and went so far as to introduce the cult of that goddess into the temple compound itself.[17]

Ackerman's thesis flies in the face of Tikva Frymer-Kensky's historical reconstruction of goddess worship in ancient Israel. According to Frymer-Kensky, the authority of the goddess began to wane toward the end of the second millennium in the ancient Near East in general.[18] Frymer-Kensky rejects the possibility that the numerous plaque figurines found in ancient Israel represent a female deity and insists that all vestiges of goddess worship had disappeared from ancient Israel by the beginning of the first millennium. Frymer-Kensky argues that Yahwistic monotheism replaced and displaced the goddess in all her manifestations. Ackerman's reconstruction is also debated by Carol Fontaine, who questions the simplistic correlation between the existence of powerful goddess worship and the high social status attributed to women in ancient societies. She points out that such a correlation may have existed only for women in elite groups. While for Ackerman the Bible represents a questionable source of historical data, for Fontaine archaeological data represent an equally problematic source for accessing historical reality. She notes that "archeological reconstructions of culture are no more free from the biases and preconceptions of their excavators than literary readings of ancient texts are free from the values imposed on them by their modern critics."[19]

Though both Frymer-Kensky and Ackerman note that historical reconstruction is a problematic task, fraught with the usual dangers of

---

17. Susan Ackerman, " 'And the Women Knead Dough': The Worship of the Queen of Heaven in Sixth Century Judah," in Bach, *Women in the Hebrew Bible*, 27.

18. Tikva Frymer-Kensky, *In the Wake of the Goddess: Women, Culture and the Biblical Transformation of Pagan Myth* (New York: Free Press, 1992), 1–6, 70–80.

19. Carole R. Fontaine, "A Heifer from Thy Stable: On Goddesses and the Status of Women in the Ancient Near East," in Bach, *Women in the Hebrew Bible*, 159.

modernist and subjectivist projections, they nevertheless proceed to reconstruct various roles and institutions for women in ancient Israel. Yet both Frymer-Kensky and Ackerman work with a historicist premise without elucidating when they are positing a literary typology and when they are extrapolating a historical existence for the female characters they discuss. In the preface to her book, Frymer-Kensky states, "[t]here is no such thing as the totally objective recovery of history, for something informs our choice of questions to ask and our selection of data that seems significant to us."[20] Yet the bulk of her book does indeed seek to establish historical facts about the centrality of the goddess in the ancient Near East in general and in ancient Israel in particular. Similarly, Ackerman distances herself from the historicist claims she attributes to other historians: "to put the matter more bluntly, I will not suppose that any of the stories I will consider actually happened, nor will I suppose the women actors of these stories actually lived. In fact, in the case of certain of Judges' women, the book's female military heroes, for example, I will not even assume that the 'type' of character the Judges' woman represents ever existed within Israelite society."[21] Nevertheless, the bulk of Ackerman's book (notably chs. 2–5) does make historicist claims even when appearing to deal with literary typologies. Both Ackerman and Frymer-Kensky eschew a developmental chronology, or even an etiology, in their historical reconstructions. Yet, in their (incompatible) reconstructions of ancient Israel, the former argues for the centrality of goddess worship in the first millennium and the latter denies it.

Frymer-Kensky, Ackerman, and Bird offer a fairly static picture of ancient women's lives. For all three, the basic time-line of the first millennium shows few changes or transformations in what Julia Kristeva has defined as "women's time."[22] By contrast, in *Discovering Eve*, Carol Meyers posits that women in the premonarchic period enjoyed a greater measure of autonomy and power than the later centralized hierarchies of the nation-state, the temple, and the palace afforded them. According to Meyers, women in the agrarian villages in the highlands of ancient Israel were crucial to the economic life of the tribal society that preceded the urban society of the monarchy. She suggests that because women were

---

20. Frymer-Kensky, *In the Wake of the Goddess*, ix.

21. Susan Ackerman, *Warrior, Dancer, Seductress, Queen: Women in Judges and Biblical Israel* (ABRL; New York: Doubleday, 1998), 14.

22. Julia Kristeva, "Women's Time," in *Feminist Theory: A Critique of Ideology* (ed. N. O. Keohane, M. Z. Rosaldo, and B. C. Gelpi; Chicago: University of Chicago Press, 1982), 31–55. Kristeva uses the term "women's time" to refer to women's history, specifically to the circulation into culture and various textualizations of the concept.

crucial to the economic survival of the family (or *bet av*, which literally means "the house of the father"), they enjoyed social parity and cultural prestige. Yet she does not explain of what exactly this prestige and high status consisted. Meyer's references to women's "power" are rather nebulous, especially since she does not explain over whom or in relation to what this power was allegedly exercised. Was women's power in ancient Israel exercised in relation to their parents, husbands, fathers, brothers, fathers-in-law, brothers-in-law, co-wives, sons, sons-in-law? What processes did this alleged power affect, and what circumstances enabled this power to come into visible expression? By way of explanation, Meyers posits the binary model of male authority and female power. She notes that "authority is basically a hierarchical arrangement that may be expressed in formal legal or juridical traditions. Power has no such cultural sanctions but nonetheless can play a decisive role in social interactions."[23] But just what are the interactions and circumstances in which this power is exercised? The only example Meyers offers is the case of the daughters of Zelophehad, who manage to receive a temporary inheritance in lieu of their nonexistent brothers until their marriage to male relatives enables the legal transference of this inheritance to their husbands (Num 27: 1–11).

This biblical episode substantiates for Meyers her thesis regarding the equal weight of women's power versus male authority in ancient . Israel. The rest of her evidence is based on work done on a peasant village in southern France. The use of cross-cultural data is of course permitted in some ethnographic research, but the use of this methodology in relation to a society that no longer exists and is thus unobservable is, to say the least, problematic. Nevertheless, Meyers goes on to argue that her evidence is sufficient enough to challenge the notion that early Israelite society was ever patriarchal. Here Meyers introduces what she believes is a crucial distinction, a differentiation between a patrilineal society and a patriarchal one: "there is no doubt about the existence of a system of lineage reckoned through male ancestry and regulating the transmission of property through the male line in ancient Israel."[24] However, she never addresses how or why this system rules out the possibility that men dominated in such a society.

---

23. Meyers, *Discovering Eve*, 41.

24. Ibid., 39. Naomi Steinberg expands Meyers' thesis in her book, *Kinship and Marriage in Genesis: A Household Economics Perspective* (Minneapolis: Fortress, 1993). Steinberg contends that Israelite marriage patterns establish patrilineal descent rather than patriarchal alliance, but she does not explore the significance of this distinction.

Again and again Meyers refers to women's active roles, implying that active work is somehow antithetical to an exploitive system of domination. She repeatedly underscores the reproductive and productive contributions to the household economy, but, given the absence of material compensation for such efforts, and given the admitted lack of symbolic privilege, the question remains how women were credited or recognized for their contributions. If women were charged with greater reproductive duties as Meyers argues, and if, nevertheless, patrilineage remained the existing system of descent, what did women receive in return for their intensified reproductive labor?[25] If, as Meyers further suggests, women were required to intensify their productive efforts as well, and if men nevertheless were the ones who received access to social (i.e., public) power, as well as symbolic authority, what did it benefit the women?

Yet "patriarchy" is precisely the term that Meyers refuses to accept or define.[26] Rejecting the vagueness, misuse, and abuse of the term in some biblical feminist works, and complaining about its alleged rigidity, she goes on to question the usefulness of the category in general. But is it not up to the historian to define the particular kind of patriarchy he or she is studying and to explain its "variations across time?"[27] The flexibility of this paradigm, like all paradigms, lies in the hands of the researcher, not in its abstract formulation. According to Meyers, "analysis of patriarchy originates in earlier feminist movements, particularly those tending to Marxism; and patriarchy as a dimension of human experience to be confronted, understood, and challenged belongs to a recent expansion of feminist consciousness."[28] Yet is not Meyers's own interest in the history of ancient women just as much a result of this expanded feminist consciousness? Why, then, is her inquiry into the experiences of women in ancient Israel more legitimate as a social scientific or historical endeavor than is the use of "patriarchy" as a concept or analytic category? Meyers implies that the Marxist-feminist understanding of patriarchy is biased by a modern

---

25. Scott (*Gender and the Politics of History*, 86) suggests that male domination in patriarchal societies is the effect of men's desire to transcend their alienation from the means of the reproduction of the species. The principle of generational continuity restores the primacy of paternity and obscures the real labor and the social reality of women's work at childbirth.

26. Cf. Tikva Frymer-Kensky's comments: "The question of the usefulness of the term 'patriarchy' is not confined to ancient Israelite society alone. The social system reflected in the Bible did not originate in Israel, nor is it substantially different in the Bible than elsewhere in the ancient Near East" (*In the Wake of the Goddess*, 120).

27. Meyers, *Discovering Eve*, 29.

28. Ibid., 27.

capitalistic frame of reference, but does not she herself use Marxist terms and concepts in her analysis of ancient Israel? Feminist theorists have in fact taken Marxist formulations to task for defining the concept of production too narrowly, without giving adequate attention to the unique productive activities of women.[29] Indeed, in my opinion, Meyers's use of orthodox Marxist terms occludes her insight into the specific exploitation of women as reproductive agents and sexual objects in ancient Israel.[30] After all, if women are active productively and reproductively and are not given access to public and symbolic social systems, or to political leadership positions, in other words, if no credit is offered to them, then the conclusion that they are being used—exploited—by a patriarchal system is inescapable. Meyers thus discusses women's engagements without attending to the credit or compensation—economic or symbolic—offered them in return for their activities.

Meyers rejects as historically inappropriate the notion of gender asymmetry, the assumption of universals, the dualistic modeling of gender differentiation, and the valuation of one gender over another.[31] A misused "universal," in her judgment, is the notion of a primitive matriarchy, yet, at the same time, she uses the model of the heterosexual couple as a universal paradigm for what she defines as gender complementarity. Methodologically, she extrapolates evidence for gender equality and complementarity in ancient Israel from an agrarian Sicilian village "still relatively untouched by industrialization in the early 1960s."[32] Though she rejects the public/private dichotomy as a dualistic model of gender differentiation, she uses the equally problematic dualistic model of male authority and female power. Finally, she presents the interests of men as the interests of the community, without ever questioning the representation of women as members within it.

But the most significant problem in *Discovering Eve* is the lack of connection made between cultic and political centralization in, and urbanization and bureaucratization of, ancient Israel as constituted by the monarchy *and* the demotion that these allegedly brought about in the social and religious status of women. Is there an inevitable connection between processes of institutionalization and the exclusion of women

---

29. Seyla Benhabib and Drucilla Cornell, "Introduction," in *Feminism as Critique: On the Politics of Gender in Late-Capitalist Societies* (ed. S. Benhabib and D. Cornell; Feminist Perspectives; Minneapolis: University of Minnesota Press, 1987), 1–15.

30. Catharine McKinnon, "Feminism, Marxism, Method, and the State: An Agenda for Theory," in Keohane, Rosaldo, and Gelpi , *Feminist Theory,* 1–30.

31. Meyers, *Discovering Eve,* 29.

32. Ibid., 31.

from power? Though Meyers concedes that a search for the origins of gender hierarchy is imperative,[33] her representation of ancient Israel offers little illumination of these origins. What she proffers instead is a description of a putative past that preceded the beginning of the subordination of women. Toward the end of her book, Meyers postulates that the Bible is the product of "male public structures, of male-dominated civil and religious bureaucracies."[34] But just how did these male dominated institutions emerge from the pristine egalitarian society described in most of the chapters of Meyers's book? Are centralized structures, urban institutions, and bureaucratic establishments patriarchal by definition?

Meyers argues that the Bible is the product of a priestly, scribal elite, which, in her reconstruction, was "an all-male, hereditary group ... based in the precincts of the royal palace in Jerusalem."[35] If this is the case, how are we to assess the materials that deal with women, notably with women's private lives? If, as Meyers argues, "the social distance between the shapers of sacred tradition and females is reflected in the androcentric orientation of the Hebrew Bible,"[36] how are we to understand references to real or symbolic women or to female institutions, or the use of fragments of women's traditions? Are we to take these references, as a simple reflection of women's lives and experiences?

One can readily observe the various issues I am raising here. There is a perceivable disjunction between what scholars of the study of ancient Israelite women say they can do and what they actually enact in practice. On some levels there is an evident lack of reflection on historical texts as products of discursive practices, including the difficulties that arise for our interest of reconstruction as a result. On other levels it is clear that some interpreters have prescribed modes of analysis and models for making sense of the data that are rather unreflective with respect to the use of the past in general. Although just a sampling of the panoply of current viewpoints on the matter is offered above, it is enough to demonstrate that feminist scholarship on ancient biblical/Israelite women has far to go methodologically in terms of moving the discussion and agenda forward. To illustrate my point further, I now turn to an analysis of a specific debate related to one particular biblical woman—Ruth.

---

33. Ibid., 8.
34. Ibid., 176.
35. Ibid., 11–12.
36. Ibid., 12.

RECOVERING RUTH

Astonishingly, in her first article on Ruth, Meyers suggested that we take the story of Ruth not just as an authentic story about female experience, but as an authentic expression of a woman's voice as well. According to her, the book of Ruth, or what she understands as its "gynocentricity," interrupts the usual literary "androcentricity" of the Bible.[37] Meyers does not explain, however, how this book slipped into the androcentric anthology of biblical works. Did the editors not notice its "gynocentricity" or the narrative visibility, even centrality, of female figures? The point I would like to make here is that the male composers, authors, scribes, and editors of the Bible, though tending to see the world in male-centered terms, were not opposed to women's visibility and centrality as such. It is neither the historical existence nor the literary presence of women that presented a problem for them. Rather, as I tried to explain in my earlier work, the problem was political power, social hierarchy, and discursive hegemony.[38]

That one or several female characters are afforded a central role in a given biblical story does not preclude or preempt the hypothesis of patriarchalism. We must be careful to distinguish between androcentrism (the male-centered, male-valued perspective of the Bible) and patriarchalism (the cluster of ideologies and discourses aimed at justifying the social domination of men). Though Meyers accepts the premise that the Bible as a whole is androcentric, she rejects my analysis of the story of Ruth, presenting it as a minority view on the tale.[39] Yet I would argue that, if we both agree that the Bible as a whole is androcentric, there is nothing odd or peculiar about my attempt to understand why an apparently gynocentric book like Ruth was included in the biblical canon. Meyers speculates that the book may have been composed or written by a woman, and that the least we can say is that the book represents a "gender perspective" or a female source. But, again, one must

---

37. Carol Meyers, "Returning Home: Ruth 1.8 and the Gendering of the Book of Ruth," in *A Feminist Companion to Ruth* (ed. A. Brenner; FCB 3; Sheffield: Sheffield Academic Press, 1993), 86.

38. Esther Fuchs, "Status and Role of Female Heroines in the Biblical Narrative," *Mankind Quarterly* 23 (1982), 149–60; repr. in Bach, *Women in the Hebrew Bible*, 77–84. Much of my thesis is based on Michel Foucault's conception of power. For the benefit and limits of using Foucauldian theories of power within the framework of feminist criticism, see Irene Diamond and Lee Quinby, *Feminism and Foucault: Reflections on Resistance* (Boston: Northeastern University Press, 1988).

39. Meyers, "Returning Home," 90.

return to the question I raised earlier: why did this particular story find a place in the androcentric and patriarchal canon?

In my earlier article on Ruth, I argued that the patriarchal narrator went out of his way to praise Ruth because her actions helped solidify the patriarchal order. After all, Ruth made it possible for her father-in-law's and her deceased husband's patrimonic and patrilineal genealogy to be re-established. There is therefore every reason for the narrator to present Ruth in a positive light. A positive characterization of a woman does not contradict the interests of patriarchy. On the contrary, it is in the best inter-ests of patriarchal authors to valorize and idealize women who work to insure its continuity. That women present themselves in heterosexual terms (as is done in the Song of Songs), that women encourage men to rule (as is the case in Proverbs), that women go out of their way to protect the interests of men by giving birth to male heirs—these are all elements that are in compliance with patriarchal ideology. There was thus no reason for the biblical editor to preclude or preempt such texts from the biblical corpus. The positive representation of women in their capacity as sexual objects/agents or as son-oriented mothers may perhaps be problematic in the context of misogynous literature, which usually seeks to denigrate all things female, including the sexual and maternal components of feminin-ity. But misogyny should not be confused with patriarchalism, though both certainly do share some strategies in common. Misogyny is driven by the desire to create gender separatism, so any accommodation of women in their sexual or reproductive capacities is intolerable. Such is not, however, the purpose of patriarchalism, which seeks to accommo-date, include, and/or co-opt women by way of subjugation in order to appropriate the products of women's productive and reproductive labor, as well as to insure and control their sexual accessibility.

My understanding of patriarchal ideology does not confine its prac-tice and reproduction to men alone. In most successful patriarchies women's collaboration is essential for the successful functioning of patri-archal authority. Ideology, as a discourse that constructs the subject, seeks to hide its political investments. The oppression of women in a patriarchal system does not mean the elimination of all autonomy or independence, but rather of certain kinds of social actions and symbolic expressions that may subvert patriarchal authority. Ideology "interpel-lates" or hails individuals as subjects.[40] In other words, women acting in

---

40. I am here adapting some of Louis Althusser's discussion of ideology in *Lenin and Philosophy, and Other Essays* (trans. B. Brewster; New York: Monthly Review, 1971). See Fredric Jameson, *The Political Unconscious: Narrative as a Socially Symbolic Act* (Ithaca: Cornell University Press, 1981), for a discussion of the ideological construction of the literary text.

ancient Israel could not possibly act outside of patriarchal ideology; their so-called "voices" must thus be read as multilayered or at least doubled expressions. Biblical representations of women must also be read as composites, reflecting the ideology of the writers as well as what some scholars refer to (rather facilely) as "female experience." In this sense, ideology is both an illusion (an imaginary representation of individuals' relationships with and attitudes to their conditions of existence) and an allusion (a reference to a reality outside of the representation itself). Ideology exists in human actions, practices, rituals, and institutions as well as texts. Ideology is not separable from the subject; it "has no outside but at the same time it is nothing but outside."[41] In my understanding, patriarchal ideology is constitutive of the female subject in biblical history, unless it is exposed and questioned. Thus, to read the biblical text as direct expression of a female archaic experience as Meyers does is to ignore the mediation of a patriarchal imaginary, ideology, and discourse.

Indeed, women's collaboration would not be possible without the occasional praise and accommodation of specific roles, especially if those contribute to the perpetuation of the patriarchal system as a whole. The fact that a woman authored or narrated a particular text, therefore, does not mean that it is nonpatriarchal. Texts that have allegedly been authored or authorized by women should be subjected to a hermeneutics of suspicion as much as texts authored or authorized by men. In addition, to argue that every woman's text necessarily reflects an authentic female experience presupposes that female "experience" is a universal category, natural and self-understood. However, as Joan Scott states: "[E]xperience is at once always already an interpretation and is in need of interpretation. What counts as experience is neither self-evident nor straightforward; it is always contested, always therefore political."[42] The task of the historian is to historicize female experience, to break its essentialist premises and forewarn those who would jump to hasty generalizations and conclusions.

In her interpretation of the book of Ruth, however, Carol Meyers makes the following assertion: "[W]e accept the notion that gender is a culturally determined variable that affects literary production and that female experience, even if submerged in predominantly male literature, cannot be obliterated from a literary fabric precisely because women's

---

Also see Michele Barrett's definitions of ideology in *Women's Oppression Today: The Marxist/Feminist Encounter* (London: Verso, 1988).

41. Althusser, *Lenin and Philosophy*, 175.

42. Joan W. Scott, "Experience," in *Feminists Theorize the Political* (ed. J. Butler and J. W. Scott; New York: Routledge, 1992), 37.

lives are part of the total social cloth."[43] This assertion merely begs the question: just how and why did certain female authorized texts come to be included in male edited/mediated literature—was it done by accident, by mistake? Meyers does not offer a historical explanation for the prominence of Ruth in the Bible. Instead, she focuses on a specific collocation, *bet em* in Ruth 1:8, which signals for her a unique genre of female literature. From there Carol Meyers proceeds to collect additional verses referring to "Mother's Household" (her translation of *bet em*) in Genesis, Song of Songs, and Proverbs and argues that, despite the specific and different historical contexts of each collocation, they all point to a gendered text as well as to an actual historical institution in ancient Israel. The few verses referring to *bet em* are then raised to an equal status with the numerous, indeed overwhelming, number of references to *bet av* ("Father's Household"). From here it is merely a short step to concluding that both institutions were equal in social prestige and importance. By conflating the biblical text with the history of ancient Israel, Meyers concludes not only that women's literature plays a vital role in the Hebrew Bible, but that "Israelite women apparently had a role equal to if not greater than their husbands in arranging the marriages of their children, although this is not always easy to discern under the androcentric layering of the texts."[44] It seems just as possible, however, that mothers' participation in arranging marriages for their daughters, as Naomi does for Ruth, is not at all a feature that the Biblical authors wished to conceal. After all, marriage, notably the marriage that is orchestrated by Naomi in the book of Ruth, does not threaten the patriarchal order. On the contrary, it reproduces and perpetuates it. Now, it could very well be that there was an institution such as a "Mother's Household" in ancient Israel, but for the historian the question should be whether it was replaced by the later *bet av*. Does the predominant use of *bet av* in the biblical text indicate a process of literary suppression?

These questions remain open in Carol Meyers's second article on the book of Ruth, in which she focuses on women's informal associations. Using data based on fieldwork in rural Greece in the 1960s and work done on peasant societies in the 1970s, Meyers argues that women in ancient Israel wielded power and made contributions to the social and economic life of the community in ways that have not been previously acknowledged by scholars. Because she does not define "power" or "authority" as relational concepts, it is never clear over whom women's associations exerted their alleged power. Meyers's reliance

---

43. Meyers, "Returning Home," 90.
44. Ibid., 112.

on cross-cultural approaches leads her to make a sweeping generaliza-
tion regarding all "premodern societies," which she then applies to
ancient Israel without using any specific data from the ancient Near
East.[45] Because "premodern" is a vast and vague category, ranging over
thousands of years, historically speaking her case lacks specificity: "Our
Western eyes often blind us to the possibility that women's productive
labor carried out in household units in premodern societies can be valued
as highly as men's leadership tasks in community-wide structures."[46] In
the absence of written records regarding the allegedly high value placed
on women's domestic labor, this assertion must surely remain a wishful
speculation. This observation, of course, does not mean that women did
not contribute to the economy of their community; after all, a public leadership role is its own compensation in both material and symbolic terms.
My point is rather that, while Meyers does make a strong case for the
recognition of women's hard work and substantive contributions to
Israel's economic life, she fails to prove that this work gained women a
status equal to that of men. To the extent that informal value codes
existed in ancient Israel (a point Meyers does not actually substantiate),
they may have in fact contributed to the ideological illusion of justice and
equality, which is obviously a mechanism essential to the perpetuation of
economic and social exploitation.

Meyers's point about the important social function of women's informal kinship connections through mutual assistance, and their role in
solidifying marital ties, is equally well argued. Although she admits that
there is virtually no evidence for her thesis, she nevertheless suggests that
"women are the ones who effect cooperation between settlements inhabited by affinals."[47] But how does this cooperation prove that the brides
that were exchanged between families were not themselves the very
objects for which the bridegroom's family compensated the bride's
family? Meyers's idea that the exchanged brides indeed "increased the
likelihood that families connected in this way would offer economic or
other assistance"[48] does not engage in any way my analysis of the bride's
economic and social objectification.[49] Similarly, Meyers's point about
women's alleged network and extended kinship associations in their

---

45. Carol Meyers, "'Women of the Neighborhood' (Ruth 4.17): Informal Female Networks in Ancient Israel," in *Ruth and Esther: A Feminist Companion to the Bible* (ed. A. Brenner;
FCB 2.3; Sheffield: Sheffield Academic Press, 1999), 113.

46. Ibid., 115.

47. Ibid., 118.

48. Ibid.

49. Fuchs, *Sexual Politics*, 45–52.

husbands' communities does not intersect with the question of their political subordination to patriarchal authority. As Meyers herself concedes, patrilocal marriages reduced the wife to a rather "precarious position as the newcomer in an established household."[50] If the function of such associations was adaptive, to help ease the transition of the wife into her husband's milieu, they indeed must have performed a crucial role in enabling and stabilizing the patrilocal structure of marriage.[51]

But this adaptive role of the alleged neighborhood association of women does not enter into Meyers's discussion. What she emphasizes is the contribution these networks made to the "community's well-being."[52] Meyers insists that the women's groups performed "essential functions without which the economic survival and social stability of small premodern communities such as existed in ancient Israel would not have been possible."[53] While I do not necessarily disagree with this statement, I would argue that women's contributions ought to be analyzed within a framework that encompasses both public and private, male and female, spheres of power. To focus on the highly elusive concept of female power without relating it to the political investments of the patrilocal order idealizes and mystifies social hegemony of men in ancient Israel. As mentioned earlier, the point of a patriarchal story is not to denigrate women as such; it is, rather, to extol and affirm women who collaborate with patriarchal ideology. To the extent that they spare no effort to reestablish the patrilineal, patrilocal, and patronomial structures of the family unit, Ruth and Naomi are heroines of the patriarchal story, whether we agree that their represented relationship is reciprocal or not.[54]

This observation does not mean that there may not have been a story that originated with women, perhaps even composed by women, about two females who shared a friendship or who managed to survive against the odds, even without men. A story about two women who survive outside of a patrilocal marriage—indeed, two women who form a bond and create an economically viable existence for themselves outside of the heterosexual matrimonial framework altogether—may have been subversive, but the existing structure of the book of Ruth, which begins with female bonding as a precarious phenomenon that is eventually and

---

50. Meyers, "Women of the Neighborhood," 120.

51. Whether we accept Mieke Bal's thesis regarding the transition from patrilocal to virilocal marriage as reflected in the book of Judges, the fact remains that the marital unit was headed by a man. See Bal, *Death and Dissymmetry*, 168–96.

52. Meyers, "Women of the Neighborhood," 124.

53. Ibid., 126.

54. Fuchs, *Sexual Politics*, 77–84.

"successfully" replaced by heterosexual bonding leading to the reestablishment of the male order, is hardly that sort of story. In its present form the book of Ruth cannot be construed as a "woman's story," except in the most superficial sense of thematic orientation. As it stands, the story of Ruth affirms a patriarchal discourse that naturalizes and legitimizes gendered hierarchies. Scholars who seek to reclaim the book of Ruth[55] ought to be wary of the temptations of a hermeneutics of desire, one that projects a presentist fantasy onto a distant past. Historians who seek to reconstruct a history in which women are allegedly equal in status to men ought to resist this temptation even more strenuously, if only because of their claim to represent scientific and objectivist truth. Several historical critics have indeed come up with highly suggestive readings of female characters, but more often than not even the most imaginative among them lay claim to a knowable reality "behind" the text, as it were. Historical criticism has indeed an important contribution to make, in my mind, but this contribution is in the realm of interpretation, rather than reconstruction.

Conclusion

In *Sexual Politics in the Biblical Narrative*, I analyze patriarchal ideology as a narrative strategy at work in the Hebrew Bible. In this essay I prefer to see patriarchalism as a discourse that shapes social and cultic practices and institutions, as an interconnected system of institutional, discursive, and ideological mechanisms. In this sense, this essay further elaborates the thesis that ancient women colluded in their own oppression and that stories about them need not be read as expressions of female experience. The current tendency in feminist biblical historical criticism to refer to women's texts, women's voices, and women's institutions as automatic reflections of female autonomy, authenticity, and authority accepts the concept of female "experience" uncritically as universal and self-understood. My argument against constructing a social scientific, objectivist narrative regarding the status of women in ancient Israel rejects both the assumption of male supremacy and the counterassumption of gender equality. Instead, I would recommend we replace the factual discourse of historical reconstruction with one attuned to the politics of the text and the context of the historian/reader. Judith Butler articulates this need for political self-consciousness thus:

---

55. Judith A. Kates and Gail Twersky Reimer, *Reading Ruth: Contemporary Women Reclaim a Sacred Story* (New York: Ballantine, 1994).

Power pervades the very conceptual apparatus that seeks to negotiate its terms, including the subject position of the critic; and further, ... this implication of the terms of criticism in the field of power is *not* the advent of a nihilistic relativism incapable of furnishing norms, but rather, the very precondition of a politically engaged critique. To establish a set of norms that are beyond power or force is itself a powerful and forceful conceptual practice that sublimates, disguises, and extends its own power play through recourse to tropes of normative universality.[56]

I would thus recommend that we reconsider biblical historical criticism as an interpretive approach, as a hermeneutical theory. As such, all the feminist historians discussed here offer us powerful and highly suggestive readings of the Hebrew Bible and its context. But in my opinion this approach does not go far enough. As an interpretive rather than scientific method, biblical historical criticism will be under no obligation to generate a single, unified reconstruction of ancient origins. As a hermeneutical theory historical criticism will complement rather than exclude literary approaches to the text. Finally, then, the focus on gender or the hierarchical construction of sexual difference can collapse the disciplinary boundaries and destabilize the methods that now divide feminists into incompatible methodological camps. Moreover, in the course of resisting patriarchal politics in the text and in our own approaches, we may have to refine our definition of patriarchy, and to look for diverse definitions and articulations of its discursive, institutional, and ideological manifestations. Because as feminists we ourselves are captives of a phallocentric economy, we may have to exercise a strategy of hermeneutic displacement, one that questions existing normative approaches, while at the same time refusing to generate any alternative authoritative coherence. As Elizabeth Meese aptly observes: "Feminists are those who are in the process of exorcizing the patriarchal consciousness that all of us have internalized because of our place in society."[57] Meese goes on to recommend that we allow for a plurivocal feminist critique that refuses to identify a center, a reading that is self-displacing and sometimes even self-contradictory. This refusal of authority in all forms may well permit several feminist theories to cohere as progressions toward an inclusive horizon of multivocal interpretations. By way of contribution to this larger interpretive project, my

---

56. Judith Butler, "Contingent Foundations: Feminism and the Question of 'Postmodernism,'" in Benhabib et al., *Feminist Contentions*, 39.

57. Elizabeth Meese, *Crossing the Double-Cross: The Practice of Feminist Criticism* (Chapel Hill: University of North Carolina Press, 1986), 147.

critique of feminist biblical historical criticism in this essay seeks to question an emerging orthodoxy that is nevertheless riddled with contradictions, one that has not yet come to terms with the indeterminacy of historical inquiry.

No Road: On the Absence of
Feminist Criticism of Ezra-Nehemiah

Roland Boer

The tendency in feminist biblical criticism has been to focus on texts that include women in the narrative, especially books such as Ruth, Esther, Genesis, Judges, Ezekiel and Hosea. These texts, and others like them, have been the sites of intense literary and postmodern interpretations as well. Meanwhile, other texts have been by-passed as intransigent and arid, resisting feminist criticism since hardly any women appear at all. Among these texts are those of Chronicles and Ezra-Nehemiah, where historical criticism carries on its task virtually untroubled by questions from feminism.

One of the problems is that the well-known methods employed by most feminist critics have operated, and continue to operate, with an agenda based on the recovery of female characters and voices in the biblical materials, or with reconstructions that seek to restore women to the historiography of ancient Israel or early Christianity, relying on both archaeology and the rereading of texts in this light.[1] Even the sustained criticism of the representations of women, for instance in the prophetic literature of Ezekiel and Hosea, seeks to detoxify such representations in a hermeneutics of recovery. Furthermore, in contrast to the concern with presence, that is, with the overt presence of women in the texts and in the history, the problem of absence has rarely been broached. Many feminist critics settle for the point that this lack of female presence is what one would expect in an overwhelmingly patriarchal text in which a host of patriarchies run over each other in an effective removal and silencing of women.

Ezra-Nehemiah is doubly interesting from the perspective of the question of absence: first, feminist critics have by and large avoided it and, as a result, have failed to engage the issue that women rarely, if

---

1. See esp. the work of Carol Meyers and Elisabeth Schüssler Fiorenza, as well as Esther Fuchs's essay in this volume.

ever, appear in the text. Or, we could reverse the relation: the very fact that this double-text contains explicit narratives of the expulsion of women (Ezra 9–10 and Neh 13:23–31) may be read not merely in terms of exogamy and endogamy, but also as a narrative of the expulsion of women themselves (and thereby feminist critics) from the text. Second, after languishing for many years in the doldrums of the postexilic period, where it was felt that the historical record was especially opaque, Ezra-Nehemiah has emerged as a key text in the debates over Second Temple Judaism. In a return to the Teutonic skepticism of nineteenth-century biblical criticism, a return that seeks to shrug off the more recent theoretical developments within biblical studies, some, such as Philip Davies and Thomas Thompson, have argued that the bulk of the biblical material must be dated to the Persian period, if not at times the Hellenistic. And even newer methods such as postcolonial criticism take such a late dating as the starting point for understanding the politics of textual interrelationships. Thus, for instance, Mark Brett argues that Genesis subtly criticizes the exclusionary agenda of Ezra-Nehemiah.[2]

There are, then, two concerns in my discussion of Ezra-Nehemiah, the one historical in the context of current debates and the other feminist, concerned with the chronic absence of feminist criticism of this curious Doppelgänger of a text. In order to deal with the questions of historical criticism[3] and feminism, I begin with a reading of one of the few feminist studies of Ezra-Nehemiah, Tamara Ezkenazi's "Out From the Shadows: Biblical Women in the Post-Exilic Era."[4] Eskenazi's article raises some problems on which I will subsequently dwell, namely, the inescapable tendency toward micro-readings and the isolation of women from the matrix of the text itself.

The premise of Eskenazi's agenda of recovery is that the absence of women in Ezra-Nehemiah is only apparent: "*At first glance* they seem absent."[5] Who is to blame for this presence of ostensible absence?

---

2. Mark Brett, *Genesis: Procreation and the Politics of Identity* (Old Testament Readings; New York: Routledge, 2000). See also Judith McKinlay's essay in this volume.

3. By historical criticism, that peculiar hybrid of biblical studies, I mean the overarching dual desire to construct a history of the literature of the Hebrew Bible and a history of the context in which that literature arose, i.e. the history of Israel itself. All of the various methods—source, form, redaction, socioscientific, archaeological and so on—are held together by this deep desire for the history of the literature and Israel, a mimetic desire for origins.

4. Tamara C. Eskenazi, "Out from the Shadows: Biblical Women in the Post-Exilic Era," in *A Feminist Companion to Samuel-Kings* (ed. A. Brenner; FCB 5; Sheffield: Sheffield Academic Press, 1994), 252–71.

5. Ibid., 252.

According to Eskenazi, "they—translators and commentators, not the biblical text—efface women's presence."[6] Moreover, if we follow the combination of archaeology and the re-reading of biblical texts, a different picture emerges, layered beneath the one that lies on the surface. In itself there is nothing new in such an approach, for biblical historiography has traditionally followed this path, bouncing biblical texts off archaeology and throwing in a good dose of imagination to make the connections. Different about Eskenazi's approach, along with so much other feminist biblical criticism, is that if one approaches such a task with feminist questions in mind, then both archaeology and the biblical text will generate different answers to those feminist questions. Her citations of various critics show this only too well, from Samuel Terrien's lament for the good old egalitarian days of equal worship to L. W. Batten's laughable creation of aporia over the phrase "he and his daughters" in Neh 3:12 (are they really daughters or in fact "hamlets"?).

Rather than debate each point of her argument, I will undertake two lines of response to Eskenazi. First, I will ask why Eskenazi limits herself, like so much feminist biblical criticism, to micro-readings, the fragments and shards of the text, only to make the breathtaking leap to general conclusions of a returning egalitarianism in the postexilic era? Second, I will raise the issue of what happens if we read the narratives of the exclusion of women not in light of purity[7] or xenophobia but as part of a much wider pattern of dissent and disaffection to which the text of Ezra-Nehemiah is a response?

ON THE LIMITS OF MICRO-READINGS

The bulk of Eskenazi's argument rests on citing a series of references to women in the Elephantine documents and then drawing parallels to Ezra-Nehemiah (e.g., moving from Mibtahiah in the Elephantine texts to Noadiah the prophetess of Neh 6:14). To begin, a few necessary details regarding the Elephantine community are important to set forth. This community, a combination of Jewish mercenaries and merchants (a fascinating amalgamation in itself), lasted for the whole of the fifth century B.C.E., spilling backward into the sixth by some twenty-five years and possibly forward into the fourth as well. With all the documents—contracts, family archives, letters, and ostraca—available for most of the twentieth

---

6. Ibid., 265.

7. See, e.g., Mary Douglas, "Responding to Ezra: The Priests and the Foreign Wives," *BibInt* 10 (2002): 1–23.

century, Eskenazi has much to pore over in light of her specific agenda of reading for the lives of women.[8]

What she finds in the documents and contracts of Mibtahiah, Tapmut, and Yehoishma is that these women held certain rights of property and inheritance that influenced marriage and divorce proceedings. Much like prenuptial agreements today, Mibtahiah is able to ensure the continuity of the property that her *father* had bequeathed to her. By the time of her third marriage to an Egyptian architect, after a Jewish husband who disappears and another Egyptian architect whom she divorces, Mibtahiah has significant holdings. Her third and final marriage contract ensures that all her property remains hers. Tapmut, an Egyptian slave who marries a Jew by the name of Anani ben Azariah, holds property rights should her partner die, and either party may initiate divorce, even though she is a slave. Like the daughter of Tapmut and Anani, in Yehoishma's contracts divorce proceedings may also be instituted by either partner. As for Yehoishma herself, after the manumission of both her and her mother, her marriage contract indicates that a good deal of wealth remains her own. For Eskenazi, there thus existed an unheard-of level of legal equality between men and women in marriage—the documents from Elephantine "show women in the Jewish community who are able to rise from slavery to a position of influence in the temple, to divorce their husbands, hold property, buy and sell."[9]

But what is the connection to Ezra-Nehemiah? Eskenazi sidesteps the uniqueness of the Elephantine community and the Egyptian situation by suggesting, arguing, and assuming that the practices in both Elephantine and the Persian province of Yehud are indebted to a common Mesopotamian background. In her mind, this would have been due not only to frequent communication and interaction but also to the dominance and provenance of Jews in Yehud from the metropolitan centers of the Persian Empire, namely, Mesopotamia itself, specifically Babylon.

Thus, given a good postal service and a similar Semitic provenance for the legislators in both communities, the relative separation of Ezra-

---

8. Reading Eskenazi's essay reminds me of an extraordinary library that I encountered when I was studying for my Bachelor of Divinity degree at Sydney University. The Gillespie Library was once very well funded by St. Andrew's College, and it held an extraordinary collection that petered out by the 1980s. As the ceilings sagged above me, I still relish the feeling of opening a journal from 1898 and finding that I had to tear the still-uncut pages. Another memorable experience was the discovery of Budde's collection of Coptic texts from the early twentieth century when I was doing my Honors thesis. I am sure that the various bits and pieces of that library would have contained the texts by A. E. Cowley, Emil G. H. Kraeling, George Rolles Driver, and Bezalel Porten that Eskenazi cites.

9. Eskenazi, "Out from the Shadows," 259.

Nehemiah and Elephantine dissipates. A variety of texts from Ezra-Nehemiah itself make their appearance in the Elephantine context: the overwhelming use of אבות, which should be rendered "families" or "ancestral houses"; Ezra 9–10 and the issue of foreign wives; and the hidden women in Ezra 2:55 (*hassoperet*), Ezra 2:61 and Neh 7:63 (wife of Barzillai), Ezra 2:65 and Neh 7:67 (male and female singers), Ezra 8:10 (Shelomith, whom Eskenazi takes as female), Neh 3:12 (the daughters of Shallum), Neh 6:14 (Noadiah the prophetess), and Neh 8:2–4 (the women present at the public reading of the Torah).

Some of these identifications are more tentative than others, especially "the female scribe" and her descendants in Ezra 2:55 and the female designation of Shelomith in Ezra 8:10, but I do want to question a couple of points before moving on to consider the consequences of Eskenazi's rereading. First, regarding Barzillai, the text reads: "and the sons of Barzillai (who had taken a wife from the daughters of Barzillai the Gileadite, and was called by their name)" (Ezra 2:61). Eskenazi takes this reference as "a clan clearly named after the matriarch's family ... an important example of a deviation from the more common pattern where the woman is incorporated into her husband's family by taking his name."[10] But is the "matriarch's family" really in view? Barzillai is, after all, the *father* of the daughters, and so those daughters bear their father's name, as also do the Judahite man and his sons. Eskenazi here follows the conventional anthropological distinction between matriliny and patriliny (often read as matriarchal and patriarchal), a distinction that effaces the patriarchal nature of both marriage practices. As Mieke Bal had already shown before Eskenazi published her essay,[11] a better distinction would be between virilocal (the wife goes into the man's family) and patrilocal (the husband goes into the wife's father's house). Far from the first (virilocal in Bal's terminology, patrilinial in common anthropological usage) being the "more common pattern"—here Eskenazi retrojects from the dominant Western practice of marriage—many of the biblical narratives show a tension between virilocal and patrilocal practices, with both being essentially patrilineal in nature. Thus, rather than matriarchal, the Barzillai reference is better read as being patrilocal.

My second specific disagreement lies with her reading of the banishment of foreign wives in Ezra 9–10. Her points are well made that issues of ethnic purity also have economic and social dimensions and that the presence of "foreign" partners is only a problem when women and men

---

10. Ibid., 265–66.
11. Mieke Bal, *Death and Dissymmetry: The Politics of Coherence in the Book of Judges* (Chicago: University of Chicago Press, 1988).

can both inherit and thereby potentially take property outside of the community upon divorce or the death of a partner or parents. (Although do not the children of her and her divorced husband still inherit and thereby keep the property inside Israel? How do children play out in these divorce contracts? In a patrilineal system, would they not belong to the father? Should he leave the community, would the property go with him?) However, to argue from here that "an opposition to foreign women, so easy to criticize from a distance, is at the same time an affirmation of women who belong to the group"[12] is extraordinary. Neither xenophobia nor misogyny are issues any longer; rather, the act of dispensing with some women in favor of your own becomes a positive move. In an essay written soon after this one, Eskenazi reveals a certain uneasiness with her earlier position. Teaming up with the sociologist Eleanor Judd and using comparative material from the formation of the modern state of Israel, she argues that the "foreign" wives are in fact women who were initially regarded as Jews and ceased to be so with the strict reforms of Ezra. No longer foreign in the sense she took it in the initial essay, the distinction becomes an intra-Jewish one.[13] Eskenazi here softens her position by moving the issue from a pure exclusion of foreigners to the more gray area of defining an insider out of the Jewish tradition.

Equally extraordinary is the suggestion that texts like Neh 10:30 are reciprocal in terms of women and men—"We will not give our daughters to the peoples of the land or take their daughters for our sons." The very act of exchanging women, giving and taking, is hardly reciprocal. The first question to ask is, "By whom" are these actions undertaken? Who opposes foreign women—whether external or internal "foreigners"? Who affirms one's own women? Who takes and gives daughters in marriage? I am afraid that I cannot see how this is an advance of any sort; not only do Ezra and the men divide the women into insiders and outsiders, Judahites and foreigners, for the sake of property rights, but the very act of preserving a community by expelling some is nothing other than xenophobic. In fact, are not xenophobia and misogyny legitimated in precisely these fashions—in terms of property and marriage—so as to be palatable?

The questions I have raised concerning some of the details of Eskenazi's argument obviously undermine the possibility that we take all of her conclusions as viable. And yet I want to do precisely that, even if it is purely for a hypothetical purpose. What if it were true? What are the

---

12. Ibid., 263.
13. Tamara C. Eskenazi and Eleanore P. Judd, "Marriage to a Stranger in Ezra 9–10," in *Temple Community in the Persian Period* (Second Temple Studies 2; ed. T. C. Eskenazi and K. H. Richards; JSOTSup 175; Sheffield: Sheffield Academic Press, 1994), 266–85.

consequences if all her points were granted? Eskenazi is, at the very least, clear on this point: "[O]ne conclusion is nevertheless inevitable: whatever their precise role, the Jewish women in the post-exilic era have not been effaced from history."[14] Further, we can therefore postulate "a certain practical egalitarianism between women and men in light of shared economic responsibilities"[15] that is characteristic not only of premonarchic Israel but also of the postexilic era. And the main feature of such a society is the family as the significant socioeconomic unit and the pioneer of frontier/rural life, combined with the flux of internal boundaries.

On one level this conclusion seems too close to a conservative, bucolic dream of the past—the family, a return to basics, a removal from the evil influence of the city. But such a response dismisses Eskenazi's conclusions too easily. So, let me take a different tack and begin to respond to the question of consequences by noting the extraordinary shift from the analysis of minute points in the bulk of the essay to the sweeping claims of these conclusions. Most of Eskenazi's analysis, like much of feminist biblical criticism, focuses on the personal and domestic. Such a micro-politics is of course necessary, as Henri Lefebvre's notion of the critique of everyday life has shown,[16] but it leaves the public domains of economics and politics to men. Thus, Eskenazi's essay, as with so many others on various texts in the Hebrew Bible gathered, for instance, in the *Feminist Companion to the Bible*, is concerned with marriage contracts and divorce, genealogical lists, and the family itself.

However, to attribute such a concern with personal and domestic questions to the unconscious agendas of feminist criticism alone neglects the profound influence of archaeology on biblical studies. In the same way that one extracts the fragments and detritus of long-gone peoples from the ground and analyzes each piece in painstaking detail, so also the biblical text becomes a literary *Tel*, a mound of paper from which one draws fragments in an effort to reconstruct that which is largely missing. In this respect feminist criticism is profoundly traditional, pairing textual and artifactual analyses in a pattern that is so familiar it is hardly questioned.

But there is a further reason for the concern with the miniscule focus, one that comes from those in literary criticism outside of biblical studies. On a number of occasions I have discussed matters in biblical studies with critics from English, German, and French literary and cultural studies

---

14. Eskenazi, "Out from the Shadows," 270.

15. Ibid., 260–61.

16. Henri Lefebvre, *The Critique of Everyday Life* (London: Verso, 1991). Also see my discussion in Roland Boer, *Marxist Criticism of the Bible* (New York: Continuum, 2003), 87–109.

contexts (partly because I believe biblical studies needs to reconceive itself as a component of literary and cultural criticism) and a constant refrain is that biblical critics seem to be able to make much out of little, to select the smallest of textual samples and write voluminously about them. This practice is due to the limited amount of material available in the Bible for analysis, a situation that changes little even if we add the various bits and pieces of extracanonical literature and the other ancient Near Eastern texts. But it also has a lot to do with the appropriation by religious bodies of these disparate temporal and spatial texts, declaring them sacred and making small selections of the sacred texts the center-piece of worship in both church and synagogue. Each word and each letter then becomes overloaded with meaning, and one may spend a life-time or two chasing down that elusive significance.

The proclivities of archaeology and feminist method, combined with the scarcity of texts and their sacred status, all tend, therefore, to produce readings of writings like Ezra-Nehemiah in which miniscule pieces come up for intense scrutiny. What I would like to do, then, is locate the micro-concerns of Eskenazi's work within a macro-framework. In this respect, I follow the example of Gale Yee, whose finely balanced attention to the details of family life and gender politics is always undertaken within the context of political economics.[17] But this is because Yee is both a Marxist and feminist biblical scholar. Another way of putting this concern is in terms of the contrast between inductive and deductive readings; the pres-sure from all quarters for inductive readings, for the drawing out of general conclusions from bits and pieces of texts—what in New Testa-ment studies would be called pericopes—comes up against a relative dearth of what David Jobling has called "deductive" readings. I would prefer the term "totalizing" to designate the latter, one that seeks to read the whole first—a whole stretch of text that often runs beyond the bound-aries of the "book"—before making conclusions about the individual pieces.[18] But what this approach also means is that one throws the net well beyond the text in order to deal with political economics, culture, and society in the broad sense of epochs rather than with the specific his-torical events so commonly pursued by biblical critics. And it seems to

---

17. Gale Yee, "Ideological Criticism: Judges 17–21 and the Dismembered Body," in *Judges and Method: New Approaches in Biblical Studies* (ed. G. Yee; Minneapolis: Fortress, 1995), 146–70.

18. David Jobling, "The Salvation of Israel in 'The Book of the Divided Kingdoms,' or 'Was There Any Fall of the Northern Kingdom?'" in *Redirected Travel: Alternative Journeys and Places in Biblical Studies* (ed. R. Boer and E. W. Conrad; JSOTSup 382; New York: T&T Clark, 2003), 50–61.

me that the best use of archaeology in biblical studies is for the pursuit of the whole picture rather than the miniscule focus.

What happens when we locate Eskenazi's work within a macro-framework, filling in those vast areas that she has left untouched, is that one finds that she is dependent on a certain line of Marxist biblical scholarship. She explicitly acknowledges Carol Meyers's highly influential *Discovering Eve*,[19] but the line runs back to Norman Gottwald's *Tribes of Yahweh*,[20] and ultimately to the legacy of Johann Jakob Bachofen, Lewis Henry Morgan, and Friedrich Engels.

Although she has tempered her position, postulating "heterarchy," a point somewhere between patriarchal hierarchy and some version of egalitarianism,[21] Meyers's argument in *Discovering Eve* relies on a de-Marxified (and depoliticized) version of Norman Gottwald's highly influential argument for a "communitarian" mode of production as the basis of the first identifiable Israelite society in the hill country of Judah.[22] More egalitarian and cooperative than that from which it emerged—the Canaanite city-states operating with a "tributary" mode of production— early Israel surfaces by overthrowing the dominant mode of production.

---

19. Carol Meyers, *Discovering Eve: Ancient Israelite Women in Context* (New York: Oxford University Press, 1988).

20. Norman K. Gottwald, *The Tribes of Yahweh: A Sociology of Liberated Israel 1250–1050* (2d ed.; Sheffield: Sheffield Academic Press, 1999).

21. Carol Meyers, "Tribes and Tribulations: Retheorizing Earliest 'Israel,'" in *Tracking the Tribes of Yahweh: On the Trail of a Classic* (ed. R. Boer; JSOTSup 351; London: Sheffield Academic Press, 2002).

22. Given the dearth of basic Marxist theory in biblical studies, a comment on mode of production is probably necessary. For Marx and Engels (see for instance Karl Marx and Friedrich Engels, *The German Ideology* [Moscow: Progress, 1976]), the key is that human beings both produce and are produced; they are produced by the conditions under which they live but they also produce those conditions themselves, including the biological form of life known as "human being." Producing the means of subsistence through the organization of physical resources affects their social, cultural, and biological life, but it also remakes the material life of human beings, altering the conditions under which human beings in fact live. That is, the being and nature of human beings themselves is produced by their production of subsistence in relation to nature. Thus, for Marx and Engels, "mode of production" is the way human beings produce the possibility of their own existence in relation to both nature and the existing mode(s) of production. They identified two dimensions of mode of production: the forces or means of production, which designate human interaction with nature in terms of raw materials, technical knowledge, and the uses of labor; and the relations of production, which refer to the patterns of human interaction, the organization of human resources, and the allocation or division of labor. But mode of production also has a more general sense in Marxist theory, which is no less than the whole reality of a particular historical epoch, including within its orbit culture and economics, ideology and class, politics and philosophy, religion and population, nature and law, and so on. Often the term "mode of production" slides between these two senses—the specific and the all-encompassing.

The monarchy subsequently saw a return to the "tributary" mode under pressure of the dominance of this form in the surrounding areas. For Gottwald, the "communitarian" model is the key, ebbing and flowing from the moment of emergent "Israel" to the early Christian and Jewish practices of communal cooperation rather than domination. Thus, the message of Jesus and the reconstruction of Judaism by the Pharisees after the two revolts (67–74 C.E. and 132–135 C.E.), in this view, attempt to recover and hold onto "communitarian" ideals whose origins lie with the first "Israel." In the Gottwaldian construction, this tradition of production is the subversive ideal of the Bible, that which holds out, more or less successfully, against the "tributary" and then later the "slave-based" modes of production.[23]

Provided with her own particular twist, this meta-narrative underlies Eskenazi's argument, except that it takes Meyers's depoliticized version of it and argues for a return to some form of egalitarianism in the post-exilic era.[24] In fact, with her emphasis on the family and its dynamics, she draws closer to those who have taken Gottwald's argument further toward a "household" or "familial" mode of production in preference to a communitarian one. Thus, David Jobling argues that prior to the monarchy we have such a household mode of production, drawing the term from Marshall Sahlins, a position that is somewhat more egalitarian in terms of its conception of sexual difference in relation to modes of production than what presumably followed under the monarchy.[25] In a similar but more comprehensive fashion, Gale Yee seeks to bring together questions of class, economics, and gender in terms of three modes of production, namely, familial, tributary, and slave.[26] In this respect, she relies heavily on Gottwald, shifting the communitarian mode of production to a familial one and reading Gen 2–3 in terms of the transition from the former to the latter.[27] Like Gottwald, she prefers to avoid the terminology associated with the Asiatic mode of production, yet her three modes of production can be read as transformations of the tribal, Asiatic, and Ancient means of production in traditional Marxist theory.[28]

---

23. See also Norman Gottwald, "Sociology of Ancient Israel," in *ABD* 6:79–89.

24. This argument seems to dissipate in the later essay by Eskenazi and Judd, "Marriage to a Stranger in Ezra 9–10."

25. David Jobling, *1 Samuel* (Berit Olam; Collegeville, Minn.: Liturgical, 1998).

26. Gale Yee, "Ideological Criticism"; and idem, "Gender, Class and the Social Scientific Study of Genesis 2–3," *Semeia* 87 (1999): 177–92.

27. Yee, "Gender."

28. Ronald Simkins ("Patronage and the Political Economy of Ancient Israel," *Semeia* 87 [1999]: 123–44) with debts to Sahlins, Meyers, and Gottwald, also assumes that the domestic, household, or communitarian mode of production precedes the shift to what he calls a patron-client, or clientalistic, mode of production in monarchic Israel. This domestic form

Without immersing myself in the problems with such terminology and in the related conceptions,[29] I observe that such a development in biblical studies has a history within Marxist theory. Unfortunately, the most cited text in these discussions is Karl Wittfogel's *Oriental Despotism*.[30] Using Wittfogel, David Jobling argues that the "transition from a more egalitarian to a tributary mode is typically accompanied by shifts from female-based to male-based patterns of kinship and social organization, from a low-level agriculture dominated by women to an intensive agriculture organized by men, and from the extended family to the nuclear family."[31] I write "unfortunately," since Wittfogel's is an idiosyncratic text, both reactionary (it is directed against the Soviet Union) and technologist (changes in mode of production have to do with uses of water and irrigation) in orientation. But what lies behind it is the fantastical theories of Bachofen and Morgan, with their arguments seeking to sustain the position for a prior matriarchy before patriarchy took over. Jobling's is a gentler version, but it still assumes such a background.

What is sorely needed in biblical studies is a detailed investigation, not merely of the notion of mode of production itself, but especially of Marxist debates over the mode of production in the ancient world.[32] Such an inquiry becomes even more urgent in light of the way articles like those by Eskenazi unwittingly rely on the unreflected appropriations of Marxism in biblical studies.

In response to both Eskenazi and this tradition (which continues largely unreflected upon) in biblical studies, let me return to Gottwald in order to offer a dose of demystification. In his recent book, *The Politics of Ancient Israel*, Gottwald argues that the political make-up of ancient Israel was in no way remarkable or distinct from the other polities that surrounded it in the ancient Near East.[33] He uses a strategy of critical imagination that attempts to move beyond the positivism of both the current minimalist positions that will say nothing apart from the archaeological record and those that reflect trust, for religious reasons, in the basic content of the Hebrew Bible. Noting the current absence of comprehensive comparative studies, he argues that Israel was no different in terms of its

---

represents the primary mode by which surplus was acquired, used, and distributed, and by which social relations operated.

29. For further discussion, see Boer, *Marxist Criticism*, 229–46.

30. Karl Wittfogel, *Oriental Despotism* (New Haven: Yale University Press, 1963).

31. Jobling, *1 Samuel*, 146.

32. For starters, see Stephen P. Dunn, *The Fall and Rise of the Asiatic Mode of Production* (London: Routledge & Kegan Paul, 1981).

33. Norman K. Gottwald, *The Politics of Ancient Israel* (Library of Ancient Israel; Louisville: Westminster John Knox, 2001).

economic, social, and cultural formation from the smaller states of the ancient Near East, such as Moab, Ammon, Syria, Philistia, and Phoenicia. As to the reason why Israel was able to develop and preserve its religious writings in a way that these other states did not, he suggests that the peculiarities of its political history, especially the loss of independence, created a unique situation in which the religious and scribal elite had the opportunity to record and preserve certain literary materials.

The aspect of his wider argument that interests me is the fact that Israel was like any other state in the ancient Near East in terms of its politics and culture. To argue, as Eskenazi does, for a unique Israelite or more broadly Semitic tradition in which women were in some way more equal, flies in the face of the broader context in which Israel existed as a state. Even the highly influential imperial centers of Egypt and Mesopotamia are more like each other than distinct, and so any postulated difference between these two centers—a basis of Eskenazi's argument—collapses.

While Eskenazi suggests that the religious traditions of the postexilic era open up the possibility for different practices in regard to women, she speaks ultimately of social practices that were subject to the political vagaries of Israel's historical context. She argues, in fact, that the marriage practices of Elephantine and postexilic Yehud were dependent on Mesopotamian practices. But we need to ask what the broader socioeconomic context of the texts of Ezra-Nehemiah might have been. Briefly, the basic means of production involved the various techniques associated with widespread hand-tooled agriculture and domesticated animals. Any new developments in technology were directed toward agriculture—improved quality of implement metal, irrigation, and so on. The relations of production involved a multitude of small landholders who paid tribute to various layers of a significant bureaucracy, at a local, "national," and imperial level. At the top of the bureaucracy is the imperial center—Babylon, Egypt, Asshur, and so forth—where the tribute is lavished upon a standing army (used to ensure the regular payment of tribute and to increase the empire), buildings of imperial government and religion, and the relatively large number of officials required to keep the system running. Politically, the concentration and reorganization of power necessary for the formation of a state followed remarkably similar patterns: the gradual differentiation of wealth and power and their concentration in certain individuals, usually called chieftains, and then the elevation of such chieftains into kings of various types as the state became more complex and established. Based on constant conflict and efforts to overcome one's neighbors, the states of the ancient Near East did not, for instance, operate by means of oligarchies or citizen assemblies (as in Greece) or a senate (as in Rome). And this pattern also applied to the smaller states such as Moab, Ammon, Phoenicia, or Judah, which merely struggled to replicate the patterns of the larger imperial states. Culturally and ideologically, religion (or the sacred) was the central language for expressing political, philosophical, juridical, and political control (except that it is a little anachronistic to put it this way). The construction of space in the Asiatic mode of production depended upon the layering of tribute payments enforced upon the peasants: there were very few centers of bureaucracy (i.e., the ancient "city") toward which all tribute was directed, followed by the subservience of even these spaces to a larger center, of which the smaller centers seem like various points on the spokes of a wheel.[34] Spatial practice was then focused upon the flow toward and away from the centers, and this movement was inextricably tied up with the religious centralization in the places of power and their status as the destinations of tribute.

Domestic space was then ordered in terms of the need to maintain such a system, while the family unit was a much larger entity focused on ensuring that enough was produced both to survive and to pay tribute. This familial situation necessitated having as many children as possible with the presence of multiple generations, all co-existing in basic four-roomed dwellings (including cohabitation with animals), resulting in a life-span that did not get one much past the early thirties. In this context, the possibilities for women are extremely limited. The only option seems to have been the tension between what I described earlier as virilocal and patrilocal systems: upon marriage, either she went to her husband's home and became subject to his father, or he came to her home and was subjected to hers. Even the possibility of female inheritance that Eskenazi is keen to find falls within this broader pattern.

A MOTLEY CREW OF DISSENTERS

How, then, might a feminist analysis of Ezra-Nehemiah proceed based on the insights delineated above? Not only do I want to follow a totalizing reading of the text itself, but I also want to bring in certain Marxist categories, as I have already done to some extent. By insisting

---

34. Jonathan Dyck's discussion of a Persian federalist system with local authorities at the periphery, embodied most clearly in Ezra-Nehemiah, and the suggested opposition of Chronicles in applying the federalist position to Israel itself, is consonant with the broad category of the Asiatic mode of production in Marxist theory as I have outlined it here (see Jonathan Dyck, *The Theocratic Ideology of the Chronicler* [BibInt Series 33; Leiden: Brill, 1998]). Problems arise when Dyck sees the opposition itself as in some way unique; rather, the two positions merely operate in a continuum within a larger framework.

that gender should not be understood in isolation from questions of class and economics, the agenda of a Marxist-feminist perspective is to show that the women who do appear are part of a larger pattern within the text. Further, the very possibility of the text itself—the fact that it exists at all—relies upon the narratives of exclusion that saturate Ezra-Nehemiah. Thus, the socioeconomic issues relate directly to scribal production and, indeed, to textuality itself.

With respect to this broader issue, one could focus on any number of viable places of entry into the discussion, such as the sheer monotony of the lists (whether related to the numbers of returnees or the temple vessels), the perpetual concern with money for rebuilding the walls and the temple, the preoccupation with the organization of temple duties, the presence of the interminably long periods of standing and listening to the Torah (that seem to provide us with another dimension of the lists themselves), or even the perpetual interplay of letters (some of which appear whole, as part of the patterns of writing, hearing, and interpretation that permeate the text). However, of interest to me from a Marxist-feminist perspective are the narratives of conflict and tension. My assumption here is that texts rarely if ever overtly reflect their socioeconomic context, but that there does exist a complex and dialectical relationship between texts like Ezra-Nehemiah and their context(s). The question that therefore arises is this: What is repressed in order to make this text work?

In many respects, Ezra-Nehemiah is a classic hegemonic text, to take up Antonio Gramsci's term. By this designation Gramsci means to signal not so much a dominant ideological position, as the term's common usage seems to assume, but a chronically unstable and perpetually threatened position. A particular hegemony, a combination of both force and consent, needs to reassert itself against opposition and other forms of undermining and threat, in order to maintain some semblance of control. Moreover, for Gramsci, hegemony also provided the means for bringing about a revolutionary transformation in terms of a new arrangement of force and consent.[35]

Ezra-Nehemiah overflows with oppositions of all kinds. The most obvious one is the opposition to the rebuilding of the city walls and the temple. In the book of Ezra it takes the form of an approach by the "adversaries of Judah and Benjamin" (4:1) to help rebuild the temple, only to meet with refusal by Zerubbabel, Jeshua, and the "rest of the heads of the fathers' houses in Israel" (4:3). All very legal and correct, the contest between these two groups lasts through the reigns of various

---

35. For more on Gramsci's approach, see my discussion in Boer, *Marxist Criticism*, 42–64.

Persian kings, focusing on letters and decrees that in one instance stop the temple building (4:6–24) and then allow it to resume until completion (5:3–6:15). In the book of Nehemiah the opposition from Sanballat and Tobiah is more direct, sneering, and military in nature. Here the issue is not so much the rebuilding of the temple but of the walls of the city, which then requires armed guards for the builders (Neh 3:33–4:17/Ezra 4:1–23; 6:1–19). Often read as signaling opposition from the people of the land left behind during the exile (the lack of identity of these dissenters in Ezra until 5:3 hints in this direction), in Ezra-Nehemiah it seems to be primarily the governors of the province "Beyond the River" (עבר נהרה) who oppose the project. Against methods legal, literate, and military, as well as against subterfuge, insult, and drawn-out harassment, the walls and temple creep their way toward completion.

If there is a hint of class conflict between the people left on the land and the intellectual, political, and economic elites who return from exile in the narratives of opposition to the rebuilding, then it comes to the fore in Neh 5 over the question of exploitation and debt. Here, in the face of famine, the nobles and officials turn out to be guilty of charging interest on grain and food. Responding to a sequence of three outcries from the people (Neh 5:1–5), all dealing with the loss of fields, vineyards, houses, sons, and daughters through debt, Nehemiah confronts the nobles and officials and tells them to return these, including also the one-hundredth (i.e., 1 percent) interest of money, grain, oil, and wine. They agree, and Nehemiah curses any who would likewise exploit the people. He then follows with a statement that, as governor, he neither exacted the governor's allowance, which was a heavy burden on the people, nor did he acquire land. Before we get too carried away with Nehemiah's benevolence, however, it should be noted that he insists that only the interest and security for defaulted debts (both property and people) be returned, not that the debts themselves should be forgiven. The tributary system itself remains intact, with a few immediate excesses curbed. All that Nehemiah's measures do is to ensure that the immediate threat of wholesale social breakdown does not take place and that the walls continue to be built. His intervention with the nobles and officials is hardly revolutionary, opting, as he does, for a trickle-down system of social justice; as long as the nobles do the right thing, then the economic and social system will keep going. In the end, the voices of the people protesting the actions of the nobles are met with only band-aid measures.

From here we find a whole series of oppositions: Eliashib the priest makes room for Tobiah the Ammonite in the temple during Nehemiah's absence (Neh 13:4–8); the people refuse to tithe and consequently the priests and Levites abandon their temple posts (Neh 13:10–14); merchants from Judah and Tyre arrive in Jerusalem to sell a whole range of wares on the Sabbath (Neh 13:15–18). In the case of the latter, blocked from entering by Nehemiah himself, who shuts the gates, the merchants merely set up shop outside the gates until he tells them to move on (Neh 13:19–23). And we should not forget the false prophets, of whom the prophetess Noadiah is the only one named (Neh 6:14).

Do we have here a widespread pattern of dissent and civil disobedience? The connections made with past practices of the Israelites would suggest so, at least as far as the text is concerned (cf. Neh 1:6–9; 9; 13:18). It is precisely in this context of opposition and dissent across the social spectrum that the stories of foreign wives in Ezra 9–10 and Neh 13:23–27 should be understood. Let me reverse the usual focus on Ezra and pick up the more curious story in Neh 13, which is the last in the series of dissenting practices in that chapter, including the refusal of tithes for the priests and Sabbath trading. Most interesting here is Nehemiah's response. Hearing the languages of Ashdod, Ammon, and Moab spoken by the children of mixed marriages, Nehemiah "writes": "I contended with them and cursed them and beat some of them and pulled out their hair" (Neh 13:25). This response is curiously violent, conjuring up images of a mad governor rushing about, screaming and punching and pulling hair, except that there is a more brutal undertone that suggests some rough law "enforcement." So also with the son of Eliashib the high priest, who seems to have married a daughter of the loathed Sanballat the Horonite (although she is not in fact mentioned), whom Nehemiah chases out of town (Neh 13:28). And who is the "them" with whom he contends? Whose hair does he pull? As the verse unfolds, it would seem to be the Jewish men, who are forced to take an oath and admonished not to be like Solomon by doing "all this great evil" or acting "treacherously" against God by marrying foreign women (Neh 13:25–27). But the proceeding verses after 13:24 make the identity of "them" less clear. Is it the sons, half of whom speak the language of Ashdod? Or is it perhaps the women of Ashdod, Ammon, and Moab themselves (Neh 13:23)?

The image of widespread dissent with respect to the laws of Ezra and Nehemiah appears not merely in the image of intermingled Jews, Ashdodians, Ammonites, and Moabites, but also in the extensive list of culprits in Ezra 10:18–44 and the time it takes—three months from the first of the tenth month to the first of the first month—to deal with the "problem" of the foreign wives (Ezra 10:16–17). Now we find Canaanites, Hittites, Perizzites, Jebusites, Ammonites, Moabites, Egyptians, and Amorites, forming a direct echo of the peoples of the land in the narratives of the Pentateuch and Joshua (Ezra 9:1). I do not want to go into the details of Ezra's response, his hair-pulling and sitting "appalled" (Ezra 9:3), or, for that matter, his prayer of confession, but what is noteworthy is both the proclamation that all exiles should gather in assembly on pain of dispossession of property and banishment from the community, and the response of the people to this declaration. They gather, of course, but then we read: "And all the people sat in the open square before the house of God, trembling on account of the matter and because of the heavy rain" (Ezra 10:9). The rain will become a narrative device, when it offers a reason for requesting that the officials deal with the problem of the foreign wives. But the rain is an exceedingly curious note, a dash of narrative realism that dissipates the repentance of the people themselves. They tremble, but is that because they are truly sorry, or more because they are drenched, cold, and somewhat miserable, annoyed at Ezra's antics?

The foreign wives and their children, banished like the traders or the son-in-law of Sanballat, become part of a pattern that includes the refusal to pay the tithes for the priests, Levites, and singers, the offer to help with the temple and then the opposition to the rebuilding of the walls, and the protests against the exploitation that is enacted by that ever-present yet unclear group of "nobles" who stand with the governor and the scribe. In terms of this comprehensive pattern, one final note should be made: bearing a massive amount of gold, silver, and temple vessels, Ezra and his entourage from Babylon become somewhat concerned over ambush. And so Ezra, having assured Artaxerxes that he required no armed guard since God would be with him, demands a fast and prayer, and also gives all the loot to twelve of the leading priests (strange that he does not carry some himself) (Ezra 8: 12–30). The narrative of the journey ends with the following note: "the hand of our God was upon us, and he delivered us from the hand of the enemy and from ambushes by the way" (Ezra 8: 31). Of course the enemy remains nameless, and the fear of ambush could be explained by the amount of gold and silver in their possession, but, in light of the widespread dissent, one can also imagine an ambush or two not by your garden-variety robber, but by a motley collection of debt-slaves, antiwall protesters, tithe avoiders, false prophets, and foreign women.

If I have overstated the last point slightly, it merely emphasizes the fact that the text of Ezra-Nehemiah seethes with dissent and opposition. My point is that the exclusive focus on the question of foreign women neglects this wider matrix. Women are indeed absent from Ezra-Nehemiah, except in narratives of their disappearance, but only because they are part of a whole range of excluded and rejected groups. However, let me recast all of this in terms of a question that has rarely been dealt with, if at all, in biblical studies, and that is the nature of the political subject. Part of my interest comes from recent debates on the Left, such as those of Slavoj Žižek, Alain Badiou, Antonio Negri, and Michael Hardt. But it is also germane to a text like

Ezra-Nehmeiah in which the burning question is precisely who might be counted as an Israelite—not just Judah and Benjamin, but "Israel" (Ezra 2:2b) and "all Israel" (Ezra 2:70; cf. 2:2 and 3:1). Who, as far as this narrative is concerned, is a political subject?

To begin with, we find what can only be classified as the literary presence of ruling classes, identified with an aggregate of terms, such as "nobles" (החרים), "mighty ones" (אדירים; Neh 10:30/29), "officials" (הסגנים),[36] or "leaders" (השרים; see Neh 4:10/16). Separated from everyone else and named in Neh 10:2–28/1–27, the rulers are followed by the "rest (שאר) of the people, the priests, the Levites, the gatekeepers, the singers, the temple servants, and *all who have separated themselves* from the peoples of the lands to hold fast to the law of God, their wives, their sons, their daughters, all who have knowledge and understanding, join with their brethren, their mighty ones" (Neh 10:29–30/28–29; italics mine). These individuals are unnamed, being political subjects only insofar as they are denoted in conjunction with their rulers; these are the others who come in as a remainder (שאר). And yet they are a rung above the "peoples of the lands" (עמי הארצות).

However, just when it looks as though we have three levels in the text—rulers, sundry hangers-on, and the riff-raff beyond any recognizable status—the second and third levels start to collapse into each other. The singers begin the slide, for, after the litany of men and their sons in the long census-like genealogy in Ezra 2 and Neh 7, we find the following:

> The whole assembly (כל־הקהל) together was forty-two thousand three hundred and sixty, *besides* their menservants and maidservants, of whom there were seven thousand three hundred and thirty-seven; and they had two hundred male and female singers. Their horses were seven hundred and thirty-six, their mules were two hundred and forty-five, their camels were four hundred and thirty-five, and their asses were six thousand seven hundred and twenty.[37]

Here slaves, singers, horses, mules, camels, and asses do not count. Nor, in light of the passages I discussed earlier, are the following included: late arrivals at assemblies, sabbath traders, people who were not in exile and are now opposed to rebuilding Jerusalem, debt-slaves (for they are slaves too), tithe avoiders, false prophets, and, of course, the "foreign"

---

36. This term, cognate with Babylonian *šaknu* and Assyrian *saknu,* appears only in Ezra-Nehemiah (Ezra 9:2; Neh 2:16; 4:8, 13; 5:7, 17; 7:5; 12:40; 13:11), Isa 41:25, Jer 51:23, 28, 57, and Ezek 23:6, 12, 23. In the prophetic texts the reference is directly to Babylonian and Assyrian officials, which indicates a similar usage in Ezra-Nehemiah.

37. Ezra 2:64–67; cf. Neh 7:66–69 (italics mine).

women and their children. All of them are the repressed over and out of which the text of Ezra-Nehemiah comes together.

HALPERIN'S DEMURRER

I have given what may seem like inordinate attention to Tamara Eskenazi's article on Ezra-Nehemiah. But this is because, from what I can ascertain, this piece is the *only* feminist article on Ezra-Nehemiah, appearing rather forlornly at the close of the first *Feminist Companion to the Bible* volume on Samuel-Kings. With insufficient material for a separate volume on Ezra-Nehemiah, even in combination with Chronicles, a fringe attachment with Samuel-Kings must apparently do. Even Eskenazi's later work either favors sociological comparisons with modern Israel over and against any explicit feminist approach[38] or simply abandons her feminist agenda as an artifact of the past. Indeed, her article on Nehemiah is anything but feminist.[39] "Out from the shadows," but all too briefly, it seems, for the exclusion of women from the text of Ezra-Nehemiah continues to determine the absence of feminist criticism of this text.

A decade later, however, the more interesting question may be why this work of recovery was so important in the later 1980s and early 1990s. There is an inextricable link, it seems to me, between the ideas and the context of most of this work, namely, the confessional location within synagogue and church, or at least an obligation to such a constituency. Another way of putting this is that the determining feature of such feminist biblical criticism is that it is ultimately theological in some sense. In fact, it seems to me that the first sentence of Eskenazi's later article betrays this underlying agenda all too clearly: "The people's prayer in Neh 9:6–37 has been recognized rightly as the theological centerpiece of Ezra-Nehemiah."[40] Eskenazi's method of recovery and reconstruction, as with so much feminist biblical criticism, is driven by a theological concern to retrieve a text considered sacred. As long as the biblical text remains a model for contemporary theological reflection and worship, and is granted some form of sacred status, then considerable effort will be

---

38. See Eskenazi and Judd, "Marriage to a Stranger." Even though this article deals with women in Ezra-Nehemiah and is written by two women, it cannot be called a feminist argument.

39. Tamara C. Eskenazi, "Nehemiah 9–10: Structure and Significance," *Journal of Hebrew Scriptures* 3 (2000–2001), n.p. [cited 13 October 2004]. Online: http://www.arts.ualberta.ca/JHS/Articles/article_21.htm .

40. Ibid., 1.1.

expended on retrieving certain elements of the text that can then be claimed as authoritative and/or paradigmatic. So Eskenazi can write: "Recognized, these women can help us reconstruct the world of our mothers with greater precision and enhance our understanding of the roots of our cultural and religious traditions."[41]

In the end, the real distortion is not from the translators and commentators but from the theological and political underpinnings of their work. In response, let me close with the demurrer of David Halperin, a classicist and scholar of Foucault. In a panel discussion concerning the ancient world, Halperin was asked whether he would have liked to live in ancient Greece, the subject of so much of his work. Given the exclusion of women, children, slaves, and foreigners from citizenship in the Greek city-state—in other words, the status of the majority of the population was simply that of being nonpersons—his answer was "no, it would have been terrible." The same applies to the world constructed by Ezra-Nehemiah. Thus, we can try to escape this rather inevitable conclusion by sublimating our sociocultural/political and theological/religious agendas and identities, but all we end up constructing in the end is a fictional world of the past that represents our utopian hopes for tomorrow. This result may be comforting, but it is hardly historical or critical for being that—and, other than in name, it most certainly is not feminist either.

---

41. Eskenazi, "Out from the Shadows," 271.

SCRIBAL BLUNDER OR TEXTUAL PLUNDER?
CODEX BEZAE, TEXTUAL-RHETORICAL ANALYSIS,
AND THE DIMINISHED ROLE OF WOMEN

Ann Graham Brock

To an ever-increasing extent scholars are reevaluating textual criticism for its potential in helping them discover the marginalized voices of the past, as this foundational methodology has immense potential to provide insights into how editors or redactors altered ancient texts, thereby reflecting certain points of view or biases of their time. Competency with the tools of textual criticism is thus essential to the scholar who wishes to discern power relationships, especially when determining who had control of the ancient texts and therefore had the ability to make certain kinds of changes in those texts, as well as how these individuals may have gone about creatively transmitting and manipulating texts.[1]

In decades past, many scholars considered textual criticism to be the most "objective" of all the disciplines of New Testament criticism. It is easy to see how this view could develop: either a textual variant existed or it did not, and, when it did, certain formulae or criteria helped the scholar determine the likely priority of one variant over another. When the scholarly pendulum swung the other way, and the notion of "objectivity" rightly became a questionable premise, textual criticism as a discipline experienced some marginalization and even came to be called the "neglected firstborn" of New Testament scholarship.[2] As of late,

---

1. On this precise theme, see Kim Haines-Eitzen, *Guardians of Letters: Literacy, Power, and the Transmitters of Early Christian Literature* (New York: Oxford University Press, 2000). The following thoughts and research are motivated by the discussion subsequent to a paper I presented entitled "Appeasement, Authority, and the Role of Women in the D-Text of Acts," which was delivered in the session "Acts as a Window into Church History" at the International Meeting of the Society of Biblical Literature in Cambridge, 2003, and published under the same title in *The Book of Acts as Church History—Apostelgeschichte als Kirchengeschichte* (ed. T. Nicklas and M. Tilly; BZNW 120; Berlin: de Gruyter, 2003), 205–24.

2. Bart D. Ehrman, "The Neglect of the Firstborn in New Testament Studies" (presidential lecture presented at the meeting of the Southeastern Region of the Society of Biblical

however, the discipline is experiencing a resurgence of attention as the complexity of the process of textual transmission in antiquity is becoming ever more apparent, which brings with it a recognition of the value of a socioculturally attuned textual criticism for discerning the voices of different, competing groups within early Christianity.[3] In *The Orthodox Corruption of Scripture,* for example, Bart Ehrman has made a compelling case for how proto-orthodox scribes changed early Christian texts to express, more clearly in their view, fundamental "truths" of the faith.[4] He articulates the ways in which scribes, influenced by the polemics of their day, altered the texts upon which they worked to bring them more in line with nascent-orthodox concerns and to make them less vulnerable to heretical interpretations.[5]

In much the same way that textual criticism has proved so effective in tracing changes due to theological concerns (related, for example, to attempts to undermine adoptionist, separationist, and docetic Christologies), so too can it help to highlight alterations with respect to gender issues. Furthermore, this tool becomes even more effective when used in conjunction with rhetorical analysis to categorize the types of textual changes in terms of their persuasive aims and their operative ideological underpinnings. This combination of methodologies becomes especially useful in helping to overcome one of the thorniest issues in textual criticism—that of discerning innocuous scribal blunder from deliberate reframing of source material. Clusters of certain kinds of changes make it possible to identify patterns and possibly discern ideological or theological biases behind the changes, rather than just blithely dismissing similar textual variants as the result of mere scribal carelessness. In this current context I focus specifically upon gender issues within the book of Acts, examining specific patterns of textual alterations. To set the stage I will first briefly employ redactional analysis to indicate gender issues already at work within its predecessor volume, the Gospel of Luke. Then I will explore how Acts not only follows closely in the footsteps of "the former volume" in the way it diminishes the role of women, but, by combining textual and rhetorical criticism, I will show how one of the

---

Literature, Macon, Ga., 14 March 1997), n.p. [cited 14 April 2004]. Online: http://rosetta.reltech.org/TC/extras/ehrman-pres.html.

3. See Eldon J. Epp, "Issues in New Testament Textual Criticism: Moving from the Nineteenth to the Twenty-First Century," in *Rethinking New Testament Textual Criticism* (ed. D. A. Black; Grand Rapids: Baker Academic, 2002), 17–76.

4. Bart D. Ehrman, *The Orthodox Corruption of Scripture: The Effect of Early Christological Controversies on the Text of the New Testament* (New York: Oxford University Press, 1993).

5. For a good summary of the issues at stake, see Eldon J. Epp, "The Multivalence of the Term 'Original Text' in New Testament Textual Criticism," *HTR* 92 (1999): 245–81.

more important manuscript witnesses of Acts (Codex Bezae) reduces women's roles even further.

Textual Variants in Luke

With respect to gender issues, it is extremely interesting to compare how the author of Luke reworks source material from Mark to adapt it to his particular perspective. Through this comparison scholars such as Elisabeth Schüssler Fiorenza have been able to point out how Luke downplays the ecclesial leadership activity of women.[6] Although Luke's diminishment of women's leadership is quite apparent to many scholars, it is difficult to convince others because there is no question that Luke provides the highest number of passages concerning women.[7] For instance, only Luke includes a considerable amount of narrative concerning Jesus' mother, Mary, as well as Elizabeth and the faithful example of Anna. Furthermore, Luke provides his readers with such unique stories as the woman with the coin (15:8–10), the woman with the leaven (13:20–21), the bent woman (13:10–17), the healing of the daughter of Jairus (8:41–42, 49–56), and the woman whose son is healed (7:12–16). The crux of the issue, however, is not the quantity of narratives but the status of the women within them. Despite Luke's significantly greater amount of material focused upon female figures, these stories tend to detract from their portrayal as active leaders. In fact, the vast majority of the depictions are those of quiet, contemplative, and faithful role models.

A comparison with other canonical Gospels with respect to the treatment of Mary Magdalene and the other women at the cross clarifies the ways in which Luke's portrayal diminishes or removes the leadership role of women in the text. For instance, only Luke minimizes the role of the women at the cross by introducing into the scene "other acquaintances," to whom Luke gives greater emphasis by mentioning them first.[8]

---

6. Elisabeth Schüssler Fiorenza, *In Memory of Her: A Feminist Theological Reconstruction of Christian Origins* (New York: Crossroad, 1983), 52.

7. For scholars who perceive Luke's treatment of women more positively, see Leonard Swidler, *Biblical Affirmations of Women* (Philadelphia: Westminster, 1979), 280–81; Ben Witherington III, "On the Road with Mary Magdalene, Joanna, Susanna, and Other Disciples—Luke 8:1–3," *ZNW* 70 (1979): 243–48; Susanne Heine, *Women and Early Christianity: Are the Feminist Scholars Right?* (trans. J. Bowden; London: SCM, 1987), who adds a "corrective" to the feminist angle; and E. Jane Via, "Women in the Gospel of Luke," in *Women in the World's Religions: Past and Present* (ed. U. King; New York: Paragon, 1987), 38–55, who supports Swidler's hypothesis that the author of Luke could have been a woman (50).

8. For more on the ways in which Luke portrays women's roles in a comparatively diminished way, see Ann Graham Brock, *Mary Magdalene, the First Apostle: The Struggle for Authority* (HTS 51; Cambridge: Harvard University Press, 2003), 19–40, esp. 32–38.

Furthermore, while the parallel passages in the other three Gospels each elucidate the identities of the women at the cross, only in the Lukan account do the women at the cross remain nameless. In fact, Luke refers to this group of women four times in the passion narrative, but names them only once at a later point, which is coterminous with the male disciples' harsh reaction to their witness, when they evaluate the women's news as λῆρος (24:11; "futile nonsense"; "idle talk").[9] Most importantly, the Gospel of Luke makes no reference to a resurrection appearance of Jesus to Mary Magdalene or the other women, and it is the only Gospel in the canon that lacks the address from either an angel or Jesus that commissions them to go tell the others.

The pivotal point here is that Luke's presentation of the resurrection narratives portrays the women's tradition in a way that no longer reflects any primacy in their witness and provides no mandate for them to preach or spread the good news. This kind of diminishing of women's witness continues also in the Acts of the Apostles in much the same way.

Textual Variants in Acts

Women's leadership roles are as scarce in the Acts of the Apostles as they are in Luke, and as leaders they are significantly less prominent than in Paul's epistles.[10] Unfortunately, when we look at the book of Acts for the portrayal of gender politics, we do not have access to synoptic parallels for comparison as we have with Luke, but we do have two major textual clusters, represented by Codex B (an Alexandrian text type) and Codex D (also called Bezae; considered by many to be a Western text type or text cluster). When we compare these two codices with respect to gender and politics, and especially with respect to women in leadership roles, the kinds of issues already evident in Luke continue to appear also in the Acts of the Apostles.

Textual criticism helps to highlight some of the subtle differences between these two codices concerning leadership issues. Codex D (Bezae) is approximately 10 percent longer than Codex B,[11] and yet in all of the additional material it offers no additional portrayal of women's

---

9. John's Gospel, on the other hand, does name these women and portrays them in even closer proximity to the cross (within speaking distance) than other versions of the account (John 19:25–27).

10. E.g., in this respect it is useful to compare the preponderance of women's names in Rom 16 and the reference to female leadership in 1 Corinthians in conjunction with the paucity of named female leaders/characters in Acts.

11. Bruce M. Metzger, *The Text of the New Testament: Its Transmission, Corruption, and Restoration* (New York: Oxford University Press, 1968), 51.

leadership roles in its depiction of the emerging church. In fact, just the opposite becomes apparent—a comparison of the two codices shows that D's variations ultimately diminish the roles of women even further than is the case in B. Certain scholars, including John Ropes, Philippe Menoud, Eldon Epp, Elisabeth Schüssler Fiorenza, and Ben Witherington, have discerned and elaborated upon aspects of this tendency.[12] Schüssler Fiorenza, for instance, summarizes the intensification of the diminishment as follows: "Whereas Luke plays down the ecclesial leadership activity of women but underlines the support of prominent women for the Christian mission, Codex D eliminates them totally."[13] Witherington likewise points out what he calls "antifeminist" tendencies in Western texts.[14]

In a recent contribution to text-critical assessment of Acts, however, Michael Holmes challenges this scholarly conjecture of what he calls an "alleged" antifeminist bias in the Western texts, stating that "the claim, though often repeated, has not, to my knowledge, been examined in a thorough or comprehensive fashion."[15] In his detailed examination, he rightly argues, in my view, that many scholars have taken variants or tendencies that appear in Codex Bezae and over-generalized them to describe Western texts as a whole, overlooking that Bezae is only one representative of this text type and possesses idiosyncrasies of its own. In the course of the essay, Holmes proceeds to take each textual variant and offer alternative explanations for alterations in the text, often preferring the explanation of a scribal blunder over intentionality as the possible reason for the changes. However, had he also employed rhetorical criticism to a greater extent, along with the textual criticism he so aptly performs, more of the nuances within the text of Codex Bezae would have become evident and therefore also suspect. The text of Bezae, regardless of the other Western texts, displays enough variants in and of

---

12. See, e.g., James Hardy Ropes, *The Text of Acts* (vol. 3 of *The Beginnings of Christianity*; ed. F. J. Foakes Jackson and K. Lake; London: Macmillan, 1926), 178; Philippe H. Menoud, "The Western Text and the Theology of Acts," *Bulletin of the Studiorum Novi Testamenti Societas* 2 (1951): 30–31 and n. 42; Eldon Jay Epp, *The Theological Tendency of Codex Bezae Cantabrigiensis in Acts* (SNTSMS 3; Cambridge: Cambridge University Press, 1966), 75 n. 3, 167–68 n. 7; Schüssler Fiorenza, *In Memory of Her*, 52; and Ben Witherington III, "The Anti-Feminist Tendencies of the 'Western' Text in Acts," *JBL* 103 (1984): 82–84.

13. Cf. Schüssler Fiorenza, *In Memory of Her*, 52; Jane Schaberg, "Luke," in *The Women's Bible Commentary* (ed. C. A. Newsom and S. H. Ringe; Louisville: Westminster John Knox, 1992), 279.

14. Witherington, "Anti-Feminist Tendencies," 82.

15. Michael W. Holmes, "Women and the 'Western' Text of Acts," in Nicklas and Tilly, *Book of Acts as Church History*, 184.

itself to reveal a pattern of alterations that clearly appears to lessen the female leadership presence in the text. The following is a presentation of some of the salient variants and the ways in which textual criticism used in conjunction with rhetorical analysis brings gender issues to the fore.

"Women" (B) or "Women and Children" (D)

One of the first relevant textual variants concerns Acts 1:14, in which Codex B describes the people surrounding Jesus as apostles, Jesus' brethren, and women. Only the D-text (Bezae) follows the reference to the women with the words: καὶ τέκνοις ("and children"), the effect of which depicts women as no longer an independent group who, along with the men, were "devoting themselves to prayer." With this additional reference to children, the variant in D lends itself more easily to the characterization of this group as the "women and children" of the apostles.[16] Their juxtaposition with children thus alters their presentation as peers and thrusts these women into the category of simply being the wives of the apostles.[17]

"Daughters" (B) or "Some Daughters" (D)

Another textual variant occurs at Acts 2:17: "I will pour out my Spirit upon all flesh, and your sons and your daughters shall prophesy." The article (αἱ) before "daughters" is not present in D as it is in B. Thus, this variant in D makes it appear that only "some of the daughters will prophecy, as opposed to all their sons."[18] Holmes argues against this instance representing a deliberate change, stating that "the omission of the article [in D] is more probably a scribal slip due to homoioteleuton."[19]

---

16. Schüssler Fiorenza, *In Memory of Her*, 52.

17. Witherington, "Anti-Feminist Tendencies," 82, referring also to Walter Thiele, "Eine Bemerkung zu Act 1.14," *ZNW* 53 (1962): 110–11. For more on the emphasis on "family," see Mary Rose D'Angelo, "The ANEP Question in Luke-Acts: Imperial Masculinity and the Deployment of Women in the Early Second Century," in *A Feminist Companion to Luke* (ed. A.-J. Levine and M. Blickenstaff; FCNTECW 3; New York: Continuum, 2003), 44–69; and idem, "'Knowing How to Preside over His Own Household': Imperial Masculinity and Christian Asceticism in the Pastorals, Hermas, and Luke-Acts," in *New Testament Masculinities* (ed. S. D. Moore and J. Capel Anderson; SemeiaSt 45; Atlanta: Society of Biblical Literature, 2003), 265–95.

18. Holmes, "Women and the 'Western' Text," 189. Here he quotes Richard Pervo, "Social and Religious Aspects of the 'Western' Text," in *The Living Text: Essays in Honor of Ernest W. Saunders* (ed. D. E. Groh and R. Jewett; Lanham, Md.: University Press of America, 1984), 229–41, arguing against Pervo's interpretation that the change is a deliberate one.

19. Holmes, "Women and the 'Western' Text," 189.

Such a phenomenon is not that uncommon. Yet if one already perceives a tendency to downplay the role of women and/or to reconfigure it in terms of a domesticating function, then one has to question seriously the alleged accidental character of the missing article.

"Leading Women" (B) or "Wives of Leading Men" (D)

Another noteworthy variant occurs in Acts 17:4, where Codex B has a phrase that could be translated as "leading women": γυναικῶν τε τῶν πρώτων, and which Codex D reads as follows: καὶ γυναῖκες τῶν πρώτων (translating unambiguously as "and wives of the leading men"). Metzger favors the priority of the reading of B because "it was thought much more likely that copyists would replace the less usual connective by the more common καί."[20] Holmes acknowledges that, while the text of B leaves room for some ambiguity and could indicate either "the leading women" or "the wives of the leading men," the text of D completely removes the ambiguity: "the women persuaded are clearly *wives* of leading citizens of the town, not leading citizens in their own right."[21]

"Prominent Greek Women" (B) or "Prominent Men and Women" (D)

In Acts 17:12, Codex B refers to prominent believers and mentions the women first: "a number of prominent Greek women and many Greek men."[22] Interestingly, the opposite order appears in Codex D, which names the men first and reads instead: "And many of the Greeks and prominent men and women."[23] Although this variant appears once again to diminish the prominence of women in the text, Holmes raises the possibility that it could be "merely another example of Bezae smoothing out the grammar to produce better Greek."[24] He points to Metzger's evaluation that the Greek constructions in D are sometimes better than B;[25] however, even if that were the case, it is important to note that this

---

20. Bruce M. Metzger, *A Textual Commentary on the Greek New Testament* (London: United Bible Societies, 1971), 453. The counter-argument would be that it is not Codex D that diminishes the role of women by relegating them to the category of being merely "wives," but that perhaps Codex B is more ascetically-oriented and therefore responsible for the lack of reference to "children."

21. Holmes, "Women and the 'Western' Text," 191.

22. Τῶν Ἑλληνίδων γυναικῶν τῶν εὐσχημόνων και ἀνδρῶν οὐκ ὀλίγοι.

23. Τῶν Ἑλλήνων καί τῶν εὐσχημόνων ἄνδρες καί γυναῖκες ἱκανοὶ ἐπίστευσαν.

24. Holmes, "Women and the 'Western' Text," 192.

25. Ibid. Cf. Metzger, *Textual Commentary*, 454.

improvement to a "preferable grammar" in the Greek also included placing the men ahead of the women.

"Damaris"(B) or [Nothing] (D)

Another textual variant relevant to the status of women occurs in Acts 17:34. Here Codex B makes a specific reference to a woman named Damaris who is listed along with men as a convert. Although she is only one of two people specifically named, she is missing altogether in the same list in Codex D, where these four words are absent: καὶ γυνὴ ὀνόματι Δάμαρις ("and the woman named Damaris").[26] Whereas the absence of the woman's name appears suspicious to some, Holmes contends that in this case the probability is higher that one line has merely fallen out of the text.[27]

"Priscilla and Aquila" (B) or "Aquila and Priscilla" (D)

Finally, one of the most compelling indications of an intentionally diminished role for women in D occurs with the reversing of the order of the names of the missionary couple Priscilla and Aquila in Acts 18. More often than not, when the text refers to them, it refers to Priscilla first. In two out of three references to the pair (18:2, 18, 26), Codex B names the two thus: Πρίσκιλλα καὶ Ἀκύλας, with Priscilla's name coming first. Interpreters have generally understood the order of these names to signify a certain prominence in Priscilla's status in the early Christian community. For no explicable reason, however, in 18:26 Codex D differs from all the other major manuscript witnesses in that it presents these two names in reverse order, reading instead: Ἀκύλας καὶ Πρίσκιλλα ("Aquila and Priscilla").[28]

In this case, arguing mere scribal slip is tenuous indeed, since immediately preceding Aquila's name Codex Bezae presents another variant: a singular verb instead of a plural one, which apparently is intended to

---

26. Scholars such as William M. Ramsay (*The Church in the Roman Empire before A.D. 170* [London: Putnam & Sons, 1893], 161–62) have interpreted the absence of this reference in D as evidence of a diminished portrayal of the role of women in this textual tradition. Cf. Witherington, "Anti-Feminist Tendencies," 82–83, who argues the following: "As in 17:4 and 12, there may also be a tendency to elevate the status of men at 17:34, [the scribe] not being satisfied simply to lessen the prominence of women."

27. Holmes, "Women and the 'Western' Text," 193.

28. Interestingly, in Acts 18:2, D* indicates that Paul came to Aquila alone, with the unique textual variant αὐτῷ (to him), lacking the pronoun αὐτοῖς (to them) found in all the other texts.

correspond in number only with Aquila.[29] Nevertheless, Holmes still offers the possibility that the reversal of names was an "unconscious slip," arguing that "whether this reading was the result of a deliberate alteration or an unconscious slip (due to the cultural habit of mentioning the husband first) can scarcely be determined with any meaningful degree of probability."[30] He concedes, however, that "the change of order, from 'Priscilla and Aquila' to the reverse, certainly does entail some diminution of a noteworthy Lucan emphasis on Priscilla, but it is uncertain whether it can be claimed as evidence of a specific 'Western' theological agenda."[31]

Scholars could, of course, legitimately argue against an intentional desire to diminish the role of women in D by pointing out that this text reverses the order of the names only once, here in 18:26; for if such a desire really existed why not then reverse the order of the names every time Priscilla and Aquila appear? This query highlights exactly why it is so crucial to do rhetorical analysis in conjunction with textual criticism. In the other two instances, the order of the names bears no particularly controversial nature. In 18:2, Paul simply joins this team, Aquila and Priscilla, in Corinth, while in 18:18 the text says Paul set sail for Syria, along with Priscilla and Aquila. The next section, however, portrays this couple's interaction with Apollos, declaring that "Priscilla and Aquila [in that order] heard him, and took him, and taught him the way of God more accurately" (Acts 18:26). The reversal of their names here in D serves as a red flag precisely because of the context of this passage. In this passage these two leaders in the movement are responsible for instructing Apollos. With this alternate order, Codex D's text thus gives greater emphasis to Aquila as the instructor of Apollos, as opposed to Codex B, which gives the first rank to Priscilla. Metzger explains the change thus: "Apparently the Western reviser (D it^{gig} syr cop^{sa} arm *al*) desired to reduce the prominence of Priscilla, for he either mentions Aquila first (as here) or inserts the name of Aquila without including Priscilla (as in vv. 3, 18, and 21)."[32]

---

29. The version of 18:26 in Codex Bezae presents another significant and possibly related variant: in place of the plural ἀκούσαντες (referring to both Priscilla and Aquila), Bezae reads instead the male singular form of the word "to hear": ἀκούσαντος. Such a change, when taking into account the new order of the names in Bezae, makes it appear that only Aquila heard Apollos speaking, which, as a result, minimizes Priscilla's role even further. For an alternative opinion, see Holmes ("Women and the 'Western' Text," 199 n. 60), who argues that "this appears to be a copying mistake by the scribe of Bezae, rather than a significant variant."

30. Holmes, "Women and the 'Western' Text," 199.

31. Ibid.

32. Metzger, *Textual Commentary*, 466–67.

The change of the verb in Codex D, referring to Aquila alone, further reduces the likelihood of a mere scribal slip in 18:26.[33]

This reversal of names is only one of several examples that clearly show the need to undertake rhetorical analysis in conjunction with textual criticism. Just as it helps to explain why a bias may be present even if the names of the two missionaries are not reversed every time they appear, so too does rhetorical analysis assist in helping to explain why other alterations do or do not occur in Western texts. For instance, Holmes contends that those scholars who perceive an antifemale tendency in Western texts have failed properly to account for the instances in which these texts continue to maintain positive statements concerning women and have not produced textual alterations at these points. Thus, as part of his argument against an "antifeminist" Western tendency, Holmes employs the example of Tabitha (Acts 9:36) and points out how positively the text describes her as "full of good works and giving alms."[34] Although we do not actually have the D codex at this point in the narrative, we do have other extant witnesses of the Western texts that he uses to argue against an antifemale tendency within the text-type as a whole. He explains:

> It would be most interesting to know how D transmitted the passage in Acts 9:36 about a "disciple" (μαθητρια) by the name of Tabitha, who is praised in glowing terms (αυτη ην πληρης εργων αγαθων και ελεημοσυνων ων εποιει). Unfortunately, Dd is lacunose for this portion of Acts. Among the surviving evidence there is, apparently, no trace of any "Western" alterations: the positive comments about Tabitha appear to have been left untouched.[35]

This kind of argument underscores precisely the point I am making here—rhetorical criticism makes it possible to counter the argument that the textual variants cannot reveal antifemale tendencies because this text preserves rather than alters specific positive comments. The use of rhetorical criticism here explains why it is perfectly logical that the title μαθήτρια ("disciple")—the only instance of the female form of this word appearing in the New Testament—nevertheless remains unchanged in the extant Western text-types. Having the status of "disciple" and being described as "always doing good and giving alms" threatens no one, thus it naturally stands unaltered. Therefore, what is needed is a critical reevaluation of

---

33. Cf. n. 29 above.
34. Holmes, "Women and the 'Western' Text," 189.
35. Ibid.

exactly what kinds of "positive" comments appear to have been left untouched. The presentation of Tabitha as being full of "kindness" and manifesting the virtue of "almsgiving" is exactly the kind of role model the author of Luke-Acts highlights and advocates for women.[36]

CONCLUSION

The examples provided above are some of the most significant variants concerning female figures in Acts. A close comparison of Codices B and D provides a revealing case study of how variants in ancient manuscripts reflect ideological and sociocultural issues within early Christian communities. Indeed, as evident from this study, there is virtue in preserving multiple versions of texts—and analyzing them precisely in their multiplicity—because taken together they can cast light upon the sociocultural contexts in which they were written and the issues early Christians were facing. As Eldon Epp points out, variants have influence and retain that power even today. For this reason, textual criticism needs to pay careful attention to the history of early Christianity.[37] Study of the history of theological (and cultural) debates in conjunction with the recognition of even subtle textual variants directly related to those debates carries tremendous potential for revealing alterations in the portrayal of power relations within a text.

The textual variants above indicate that in many ways Codex D picks up what is already a tendency in Luke-Acts concerning the weakening of the portrayal of the role of women and takes it even further. The motives behind textual alterations are easily open to debate, but specialists in the field, rather than easily dismissing textual variants such as these, need to examine them with even more seriousness. This is especially so in the case of Codex Bezae, where in many cases a healthy dose of skepticism needs to accompany the term "innocuous scribal blunder."

I hope to have shown ways in which textual criticism can offer a variety of reasons for certain textual alterations, some of which may be unintentional and some of which may only appear to be so. Clearly, what one infers from these textual alterations depends upon one's perspective and the tools one uses. To this end, rhetorical criticism used in conjunction with textual analysis can be immensely helpful. This kind of analysis requires much more than merely evaluating individual variations; it also involves assessing the cumulative force of textual differences, such as those highlighted here in the codices of Acts, and then accounting for the

---

36. See further D'Angelo, "ANEP Question in Luke-Acts."
37. Epp, "Issues in New Testament Textual Criticism," 75.

overall configuration that emerges. Significantly, the variants discussed here do not follow a haphazard pattern that would decrease women's status at one point but then also increase their status at another. Instead, it is the cumulative weight of all these changes, occurring in the same direction of influence, that underscores the point that gender issues are evidently at stake.

Textual criticism, therefore, is not an arcane subdiscipline unworthy of time and attention, but rather has immense potential for supplying scholars with insights into the points of contention within the early church that alterations within the ancient texts helped to diminish or eradicate. With tools and insights such as these, we gain even greater potential for recovering ancient marginalized voices, including other representations of diverse roles for women in early Christianity. One of the important contributions of feminist scholars like Elisabeth Schüssler Fiorenza, for instance, has been to stimulate scholars to think differently about ideology and its role in texts and interpreters—to approach texts with a hermeneutics of suspicion. Textual traditions are not ideologically neutral, and neither are the scholars who examine those traditions. Long promoted as an objective science, textual criticism reveals its vulnerabilities in the way the critic's selections for or against an argument expose ideological and cultural leanings. With the same text in front of two textual critics, Michael Holmes and I saw the material through completely different cultural and ideological lenses. Thus, even in the so-called "hard science" discipline of text criticism, there is no neutrality—not in texts, not in their traditions, not in their transmission, and certainly not in their reception and reconstruction.

Military Images in Philippians 1–2: A Feminist Analysis of the Rhetorics of Scholarship, Philippians, and Current Contexts

Joseph A. Marchal

Feminist interpreters of biblical literature have long advocated a critical reconsideration of historical approaches to interpretation.[1] Such work has shown how our methods ought not to go unexamined; rather, they should be analyzed in terms of their own rhetoricity. This study endeavors to provide just such a reconsideration of a specific group of interpretations of Philippians, in order to examine the rhetorics of scholarship, the letter itself, and the utility of both for inspiring reflection on our own contemporary contexts. In this study I aim to show how certain assumptions about the audience have allowed or encouraged some scholars to ignore the potentially troubling rhetorics (violent, divisive, hierarchical) implemented in the letter. In the process, I seek to demonstrate that sustained engagement of the rhetoricity of the letter and the process of interpretation itself is not only necessary for carrying out the critical interpretive project, whether focused upon the historical horizon or not, but that it carries with it a potentially liberating component as well.

---

*This paper was first presented (in a slightly different form) at the "Rhetoric, Violence, and Evil" conference, sponsored by the Centre for Rhetorics and Hermeneutics at the University of the Redlands (January, 2004). Many thanks go to James D. Hester and J. David Hester Amador for arranging the meeting, as well as to the dialogue participants on this topic, especially those who formally responded to this paper before, during, and after the conference: Leslie Hayes, Avaren Ipsen, Yong-Sung Ahn, and Paul Fullmer. Credit goes to them for insights that strengthened or clarified the ideas contained herein, while responsibility for any missteps or muddled thinking remains with the author.

1. See, for example, some of the earliest resources for feminist interpretation, such as Elisabeth Schüssler Fiorenza, *In Memory of Her: A Feminist Theological Reconstruction of Christian Origins* (New York: Crossroad, 1983); Mary Ann Tolbert, ed., *The Bible and Feminist Hermeneutics* (*Semeia* 28; Chico, Calif.: Scholars Press, 1983); Letty Russell, ed., *Feminist Interpretation of the Bible* (Philadelphia: Westminster, 1985); and Adela Yarbro Collins, ed., *Feminist Perspectives on Biblical Scholarship* (SBLBSNA 10; Chico, Calif.: Scholars Press, 1985).

Since a turn to rhetoric can be seen, by some estimates, as an alternative to violence, the occurrence of violent images (and possibly even threats of enacted violence) presents unique problems for rhetoricians, especially those interested in biblical studies.[2] Beginning with Phil 1 and 2 as a test case, I will examine the role of military images in both the letter and in scholarship on the letter. Seeking a way to engage potential violence in these rhetorical features, I hope to step beyond mere identification of these rhetorics, integrating this identification into a series of feminist responses, including suspicious caution, analysis of domination, ethical evaluation, resistance, and the establishment of creative goals/hopes for change.[3] Such a project has clear resonances with the work of rhetorical scholars like Lucie Olbrechts-Tyteca, Chaïm Perelman, and Elisabeth Schüssler Fiorenza, and could prove to be relevant to current contexts of military declarations and strategies.

---

2. Lucie Olbrechts-Tyteca and Chaïm Perelman wrote that "[r]ecourse to argumentation assumes the establishment of a community of minds, which, while it lasts, excludes the use of violence" (*The New Rhetoric: A Treatise on Argumentation* [trans. J. Wilkinson and P. Weaver; Notre Dame, Ind.: University of Notre Dame Press, 1969], 55). For further discussion of violence and argumentation, see pp. 54–59. Typically, Perelman is credited with the work to the exclusion of Olbrechts-Tyteca. Though all indications support their full partnership in the conception, research, and writing of *The New Rhetoric*, Olbrechts-Tyteca's name and role are literally being written out of the history of rhetoric. It is for this reason that the two authors are listed here in reverse order to the "normal" pattern, as this is also the alphabetical order of their last names. For more on Olbrechts-Tyteca's background, contribution to this tome, and later work, see Barbara Warnick, "Lucie Olbrechts-Tyteca's Contribution to *The New Rhetoric*," in *Listening to Their Voices: The Rhetorical Activities of Historical Women* (ed. M. Meijer Wertheimer; Columbia: University of South Carolina Press, 1997), 69–85. For more on the prominent role assigned to Perelman in North American and European scholarship, see James L. Golden and Joseph L. Pilotta, eds., *Practical Reasoning in Human Affairs: Studies in Honor of Chaïm Perelman* (Synthese Library 183; Boston: Reidel, 1986); and Ray D. Dearin, ed., *The New Rhetoric of Chaïm Perelman: Statement and Response* (Lanham, Md.: University Press of America, 1989).

3. These responses are suggested by the work of Schüssler Fiorenza (among others). For the most recent elaboration of these steps for feminist biblical interpretation, see Elisabeth Schüssler Fiorenza, *Wisdom Ways: Introducing Feminist Biblical Interpretation* (Maryknoll, N.Y.: Orbis, 2001), 165–90; and idem, *Rhetoric and Ethic: The Politics of Biblical Studies* (Minneapolis: Fortress, 1999), 48–55. It should also be noted that this essay's feminist interpretation of Philippians does not emerge in a vacuum but has developed in many important ways in conversation with (and occasional contradistinction to) the work of Cynthia Briggs Kittredge (esp. *Community and Authority: The Rhetoric of Obedience in the Pauline Tradition* [Harrisburg, Pa.: Trinity Press International, 1998]).

Overview of Military Imagery in Philippians

The examination of military images in Philippians has been a provocative development for recent studies of the letter, as well as particularly topical, since such analysis calls attention to Philippi's significant history as a colony and area of veteran settlement.[4] Edgar Krentz's initial study on military language in Phil 1:27–30 surveyed the importance of this terminology as a *topos* in many areas of Greco-Roman society: politics, biographical writing, and philosophy (in particular, ethics).[5] Both Krentz and his student Timothy Geoffrion have read the letter with an ethical backdrop in view, wherein the faithful soldier provides the example for a life of virtue.[6] These initial forays into military imagery in the letter have provoked further consideration by Craig de Vos, Raymond Reimer, and John Schuster.[7] Beyond pointing out the rather obvious uses of military terms in the letter, such as *praitōriō* (1:13) and *systratiōtēs* (2:25),[8] these

---

4. For more on the Roman colonial background of Philippi, see Paul Collart, *Ville de Macédoine: depuis ses origines jusqu'à la fin de l'époque romaine* (Paris: Boccard, 1937); Lilian Portefaix, *Sisters Rejoice: Paul's Letter to the Philippians and Luke-Acts as Received by First-Century Philippian Women* (ConBNT 20; Stockholm: Almqvist & Wiksell, 1988), 59–60; Lukas Bormann, *Philippi: Stadt und Christengemeinde zur Zeit des Paulus* (NovTSup 78; Leiden: Brill, 1995); Peter Pilhofer, *Philippi I: Die erste christliche Gemeinde Europas* (WUNT 87; Tübingen: Mohr Siebeck, 1995); Craig S. de Vos, *Church and Community Conflicts: The Relationships of the Thessalonian, Corinthian, and Philippian Churches with Their Wider Civic Communities* (SBLDS 168; Atlanta: Scholars Press, 1999), 233–50, 275–87; and Peter Oakes, *Philippians: From People to Letter* (SNTSMS 110; Cambridge: Cambridge University Press, 2001), 1–54.

5. Edgar M. Krentz, "Military Language and Metaphors in Philippians," in *Origins and Method: Towards a New Understanding of Judaism and Christianity. Essays in Honour of John. C. Hurd* (ed. B. H. McLean; JSNTSup 86; Sheffield: Sheffield Academic Press, 1993), 105–9. Though primarily focused upon "celestial citizenship," Lilian Portefaix's study (which predates Krentz's) on the reception of Philippians by first-century women offers several initial observations regarding the potential military connotations in the letter. See especially Portefaix, *Sisters Rejoice*, 140–41.

6. Krentz, "Military Language," 109; and Timothy C. Geoffrion, *The Rhetorical Purpose and the Political and Military Character of Philippians* (Lewiston, N.Y.: Mellen, 1993), 38. Geoffrion calls this the *topos* of *militia spiritualis* (*Rhetorical Purpose*, 38–42). See also David McInnes Gracie, "Introduction," in Adolf von Harnack, *Militia Christi: The Christian Religion and the Military in the First Three Centuries* (trans. D. M. Gracie; Philadelphia: Fortress, 1981), 19–20.

7. De Vos, *Church and Community Conflicts*, 277–87; Raymond Hubert Reimer, "'Our Citizenship Is in Heaven': Philippians 1:27–30 and 3:20–21 as Part of the Apostle Paul's Political Theology" (Ph.D. diss., Princeton Theological Seminary, 1997); and John Paul Schuster, "Rhetorical Situation and Historical Reconstruction in Philippians" (Ph.D. diss., The Southern Baptist Theological Seminary, 1997).

8. Harnack, *Militia Christi*, 36; Portefaix, *Sisters Rejoice*, 140; Krentz, "Military Language," 109–10; Schuster, "Rhetorical Situation," 45; and Reimer, "Our Citizenship," 191–92, 201–2.

scholars also argue that the military imagery plays a more direct role in the purpose of the letter: to exhort the Philippians to stand firm.[9]

Following Duane Watson's division of the letter's rhetorical structure, Krentz, Geoffrion, and Reimer focus on 1:27–30 as the section that establishes the purpose of the argument.[10] Paying close attention to the wording and argument of this section, they note that a number of the terms are found in speeches of encouragement given by commanders to their troops when they seem discouraged or intimidated. For example, the verb *politeuesthe*, especially when paired with *euangeliou* in 1:27, recalls admonitions detailing the proper way to live out one's obligations toward the imperial cult.[11] The second reference to "good news" in the verse (*tē pistei tou euangeliou*) could then be viewed as designating a soldier's pledge of allegiance to the general and the emperor.[12] Even the adverb *axiōs* (1:27) can be used to denote excellence in combat.[13]

The military imagery, however, extends beyond the initial clause of this verse. The theme of absence and presence is important for military situations, since a commander's presence in battle is often depicted as a necessary positive example for the troops (1:27, cf. 1:7–8, 19–26; 2:12, 24, 28).[14] The third clause (*stēkete en heni pneumati, mia psychē synathlountes*)

---

9. Krentz, "Military Language," 113, 115; Geoffrion, *Rhetorical Purpose*, 23; and de Vos, *Church and Community Conflicts*, 278–79.

10. Krentz, "Military Language," 113; Geoffrion, *Rhetorical Purpose*, 25, 35–82; and Reimer, "Our Citizenship," 136. In particular, these scholars are following Duane F. Watson in identifying 1:27–30 as the letter's *narratio* ("A Rhetorical Analysis of Philippians and Its Implications for the Unity Question," *NovT* 30 [1988]: 60, 65–67).

11. Krentz, "Military Language," 115–16; Geoffrion, *Rhetorical Purpose*, 45–47; and Reimer, "Our Citizenship," 144–46. See also Raymond R. Brewer, "The Meaning of *politeuesthe* in Phil. 1:27," *JBL* 73 (1954): 76–83. Schuster argues for the importance of the use of *politeuesthe* as a term indicating an alliance in a treaty between Rome and Maroneia ("Rhetorical Situation," 53, 64, 70–72, 177–78). While Krentz and Geoffrion attempt to establish that military terms were generally "in the air" for ethical topics, Schuster's comparative thesis is often premised upon the letter *directly* alluding to such sources as Appian's and Dio Cassius's accounts of the battle of Philippi (see Schuster, "Rhetorical Situation," 114). While such a thesis is problematic and difficult to demonstrate, Schuster's study does further illustrate the wide semantic field for military language and is therefore useful for the purposes of this overview.

12. Harnack, *Militia Christi*, 28–29; Geoffrion, *Rhetorical Purpose*, 62–65; and Reimer, "Our Citizenship," 149–50. In the imperial context, *euangelion* frequently referred to the good news of an important military victory or the rise of a new emperor (who often bears the title *sōtēr*; cf. 1:28; 3:20). See Krentz, "Military Language," 117–18; idem, "De Caesare et Christo," *CurTM* 28 (2001): 343–44; Geoffrion, *Rhetorical Purpose*, 49–50; Reimer, "Our Citizenship," 175–77; and de Vos, *Church and Community Conflicts*, 274.

13. Geoffrion, *Rhetorical Purpose*, 44–45; Reimer, "Our Citizenship," 143–44; and de Vos, *Church and Community Conflicts*, 278.

14. Krentz, "Military Language," 119.

summons the image of soldiers standing in line side by side in proper formation.[15] Furthermore, *stēkete* is an antonym for fleeing (*pheugein*) and thus denotes steadfastness, as well as being an important element in describing how to live worthily as citizens of the empire (*politeuesthe*), especially in times of war.[16] The unity and togetherness that comes to expression in the clause (*en heni pneumati, mia psychē synathlountes*) also indicates the desired mental attitude for the army, since group action is understood to be the hallmark of a successful campaign.[17] The rest of this section only seems to reinforce the battlefield imagery, as the audience is exhorted not to be intimidated (*mē ptyromenoi*, 1:28) with a term typically reserved for frightened and disorderly horses in the midst of a battle.[18] The antithetical language of destruction (*apōleias*) and salvation (or safety, *sōtērias*) in the next clause emphasizes the potential outcomes of any military conflict.[19] One of the soldier's expectations going into battle would certainly have been the possibility of suffering injury (*paschein*; 1:29) from another combatant.[20] Finally, the use of the term for opponents (*antikeimenōn*; 1:28) among this dense cluster of military terms seems to confirm that *agōna* (1:30) should be read primarily as a military, rather than an athletic, term.[21]

Those arguing for the importance of military images in Philippians need to show that such language plays a major role in the organization of the whole, not just one of its parts. It is essentially this endeavor that Geoffrion's monograph takes up, expanding upon Krentz's initial article

---

15. Portefaix, *Sisters Rejoice*, 140; Krentz, "Military Language," 120; Geoffrion, *Rhetorical Purpose*, 60–61; Reimer, "Our Citizenship," 147–49; Schuster, "Rhetorical Situation," 79–81; and de Vos, *Church and Community Conflicts*, 277–78.

16. Krentz, "Military Langauge," 121; Geoffrion, *Rhetorical Purpose*, 24, 36, 55; Reimer, "Our Citizenship," 146; and de Vos, *Church and Community Conflicts*, 278. Gerald F. Hawthorne notes that *stēkete*, as well as *synathloun, agōn*, and *paschein*, could be either military or athletic terms (*Philippians* [WBC 43; Waco, Tex.: Word, 1983], 54).

17. Krentz, "Military Language," 122–23; Geoffrion, *Rhetorical Purpose*, 59; Reimer, "Our Citizenship," 148; and de Vos, *Church and Community Conflicts*, 277–78. The image of "contending together" might be especially potent for veterans to recall as a group (cf. Geoffrion, *Rhetorical Purpose*, 53). Three of the key terms here (*stēkete, synathlountes*, and *politeuesthe*) are also repeated in 3:17–4:3 (Schuster, "Rhetorical Situation," 25).

18. Geoffrion, *Rhetorical Purpose*, 66; Reimer, "Our Citizenship," 150–51; Schuster, "Rhetorical Situation," 83; and de Vos, *Church and Community Conflicts*, 278.

19. Reimer, "Our Citizenship," 155–56.

20. Krentz, "Military Language," 126; Geoffrion, *Rhetorical Purpose*, 71–77; and Reimer, "Our Citizenship," 156–58.

21. Martin Dibelius, *An die Thessalonicher I–II; An die Philipper* (2d ed.; HNT 11; Tübingen: Mohr Siebeck, 1925), 71; Portefaix, *Sisters Rejoice*, 140; Krentz, "Military Language," 126; Geoffrion, *Rhetorical Purpose*, 69–70; Reimer, "Our Citizenship," 152, 159–60; and Schuster, "Rhetorical Situation," 84. Appian used *agōn* to describe the battle at Philippi (Appian, *Civil Wars* 4.117; see also 4.106, 115, 119, 133–34; Schuster, "Rhetorical Situation," 88–89).

by analyzing the other sections in relation to the dominant purpose of the letter—the encouragement of steadfastness—but argued through the prism of military terminology. Such steadfastness is demonstrated by the military images of both staying in line (three forms of *menō* in 1:24–25) and advancing or making progress (*prokopē* in 1:12, 25).[22] The community's shared identity is articulated in terms of remaining steadfast together, as the *koinōnia* language (1:5, 7; 3:10; 4:14, 15) and the frequent appeals to joy are meant to reflect.[23] The exhortations to joy denote the expectation that a good soldier would do his duty joyfully, just as Paul does, even while suffering (1:18; 2:17–18).[24]

Moreover, the role of examples is vital both in military situations and in the organization of the letter to the Philippians. Since the army requires submission and obedience, the Christ hymn could function as a model of such humble submission (2:7–8).[25] Paul seems to be playing the role of both a model and an authority figure (like a military commander), since he calls for the audience to join him in the same conflict (his, 1:30), with obedience (2:12) and without grumbling (2:14) even in his absence (1:27; 2:12).[26] Clearly, Timothy and Epaphroditus (the *systratiōtēn*, "co-soldier" in 2:25) are also presented as models of steadfast devotion.[27] The description of Timothy as *isopsychon* (in 2:20) to Paul might reflect the role of "a confidant" serving especially in military situations.[28] The presentation of

---

22. Geoffrion, *Rhetorical Purpose*, 59; Reimer, "Our Citizenship," 190; and Schuster, "Rhetorical Situation," 58, 62.

23. Geoffrion, *Rhetorical Purpose*, 82–84, 105–17. Schuster sees *koinōnia* as a term of alliance in Josephus and Appian ("Rhetorical Situation," 50–53, 177). *Chara* (joy) and related words appear 21 times in the letter (1:2, 3, 4, 7, 18[2x], 25; 2:2, 17[2x], 18[2x], 28, 29; 3:1; 4:1, 4[2x], 6, 10, 23).

24. Geoffrion, *Rhetorical Purpose*, 41, 118–20. According to Geoffrion, the language of joy and steadfastness belong to the *topos* of *militia spiritualis*.

25. Geoffrion, *Rhetorical Purpose*, 41, 134–40; Reimer, "Our Citizenship," 197–99; and de Vos, *Church and Community Conflicts*, 280–81.

26. Geoffrion, *Rhetorical Purpose*, 85, 100–104, 129–33. In a similar vein, the letter uses many imperatives and refers to Paul's *stephanos* (4:1) (see Geoffrion, *Rhetorical Purpose*, 101, 206–7; Reimer, "Our Citizenship," 206–7; A. H. Snyman, "Persuasion in Philippians 4:1–20," in *Rhetoric and the New Testament: Essays from the 1992 Heidelberg Conference* [ed. S. E. Porter and T. H. Olbricht; JSNTSup 90; Sheffield: Sheffield Academic Press, 1993], 333–34; and Krentz, "De Caesare," 344). Philippians 1 and 2 seem to reflect an argument grounded in the model of Paul throughout, yet as a strategy it will come most explicitly to the fore later in 3:17 (*symmimētai* and *typos*) and 4:9.

27. Geoffrion, *Rhetorical Purpose*, 140–46; Reimer, "Our Citizenship," 201–2; and de Vos, *Church and Community Conflicts*, 278.

28. Reimer, "Our Citizenship," 201. See also Panayotis Christou, "ISOPSYCHOS, Phil 2:20," *JBL* 70 (1951): 293–96; and Davorin Peterlin, *Paul's Letter in the Light of Disunity in the Church* (NovTSup 79; Leiden: Brill, 1995), 163.

their positive models only heightens the contrast between the negative models (1:15–17; 2:14–15) and the positive one of Paul. If one finds this polarization between enemies and allies to be reminiscent of the sides lined up in formation in 1:27–30, then the imagery seems to point the reader even more forcefully in this particular direction.[29]

As a result of the prominence of military imagery in 1:27–30 and its argumentative compatibility with and consistency throughout the rest of the letter, scholars arguing for the relevance of this set of images maintain that the letter is meant as an encouragement for steadfastness.[30] Most of the time, these scholars cite the heritage of military colonists in Philippi as one that would give added credence to the importance and persuasiveness of such images, since they would be familiar as well as favorably received.[31] In this regard, Paul plays an important and "peculiar" role as one with authority in these exhortations,[32] as he presumes that calls for steadfastness and obedience will be followed. Thus, scholars interested in the military imagery in Philippians hold that the audience was receptive to the means, the message, and the sender of the letter.

Feminist Assessment: Reconsidering the Scholarship on Military Imagery in Philippians

Having surveyed the arguments of those scholars who have found military images in Philippians to be a prominent and constituent element of its structure, it is now critical to shift, in this next part, to an analysis based on cautious suspicion.[33] Acknowledging that biblical texts have been used to support oppressive practices throughout the centuries, it is critical to examine closely the positive view of the soldier as an ethical ideal promoted by Philippians-scholarship. Such suspicion is further

---

29. Geoffrion, *Rhetorical Purpose*, 152–58. This contrast between model and antimodel is also particularly evident in the following units: 3:2–3, 18–21; 4:2–3, 8–9.

30. Krentz, "Military Language," 115, 127; and Geoffrion, *Rhetorical Purpose*, 115.

31. Krentz, "Military Language," 127; idem, "De Caesare," 344; and Geoffrion, *Rhetorical Purpose*, 25. Geoffrion maintains that the audience would have consisted of "citizens or residents of a Roman colony," both of whom (he presumes) would receive a letter with such images quite well (*Rhetorical Purpose*, 23).

32. In light of the general tenor of the letter, however, some scholars have argued that, while Paul has authority, it is also limited. Geoffrion, for instance, repeatedly emphasizes this "limited authority figure" conception of Paul (*Rhetorical Purpose*, 85, 100–104). He follows Wayne A. Meeks who sees Paul here being "suggestive rather than prescriptive" (*The First Urban Christians: The Social World of the Apostle Paul* [New Haven: Yale University Press, 1983], 139).

33. On the hermeneutics of suspicion, see Schüssler Fiorenza, *Wisdom Ways*, 175–77; and idem, *Rhetoric and Ethic*, 50–51.

fueled by the lack of reflection on how military images and models function in an order of domination, both in the past of Greco-Roman
antiquity and in the present of Western modernity/postmodernity.[34] The
scholars of military images surveyed above do not make use of any feminist or liberation-oriented approaches in their interpretations and they
rarely (if ever) even refer to these critical interpretive perspectives. As a
result, it should not be surprising that these evaluations of Philippians
fail to undertake a systematic analysis of domination, even though such
an analysis might be especially relevant in the case of military images in a
letter within an imperial setting.[35]

In this essay, I proceed in a different manner by implementing *kyriarchy* as a descriptive analytic concept in my analysis of military imagery
in the context of both modern scholarly interpretation and of the letter
itself. The term kyriarchy is here preferred over patriarchy since it
emphasizes a more comprehensive view of how oppression functions.[36]
Rather than a simplified, dualistic analysis of power in gendered terms,
kyriarchy highlights how multiple and mutually influential structures of
domination and subordination function together, evident not only in
sexism, but also in racism, classism, ethnocentrism, heterosexism, colonialism, nationalism, and militarism. Indeed, this focus on kyriarchy
naturally places special emphasis on colonialism. Though the importance
of the colonial status of the city of Philippi is often noted in these studies,[37]
it has not lead so far to many postcolonial interpretations of the letter,
either by scholars interested in military images or by anyone else in the
field.[38] Since the military is one of the most obvious wings of a colonizing

---

34. On the analytic or hermeneutics of domination, see Schüssler Fiorenza, *Wisdom Ways*, 172–75; and idem, *Rhetoric and Ethic*, 50.

35. The notable exception in Philippians-scholarship would be the work of Cynthia Briggs Kittredge. See her *Community and Authority*. In a secondary fashion, since the work does not focus on Philippians as a whole, see also Elizabeth A. Castelli, *Imitating Paul: A Discourse of Power* (Literary Currents in Biblical Interpretation; Louisville: Westminster John Knox, 1991).

36. The term "kyriarchy," based on the Greek word for "lord," has been coined by Schüssler Fiorenza to treat exactly this phenomenon. For an introductory definition to this neologism, see Schüssler Fiorenza, *Wisdom Ways*, 1, 118–19, 211; and idem, *Rhetoric and Ethic*, ix. See also Schüssler Fiorenza, *Bread Not Stone: The Challenge of Feminist Biblical Interpretation* (rev. ed.; Boston: Beacon, 1995), 211 n. 6; and idem, *But She Said: Feminist Practices of Biblical Interpretation* (Boston: Beacon, 1992), 8, 117.

37. See, e.g., Krentz, "Military Language," 111–12, 127; and Geoffrion, *Rhetorical Purpose*, 23.

38. For some initial insights that move interpretation toward "aspects of a postcolo-
nial reading" for Philippians, see Efrain Agosto, "Paul vs. Empire: A Postcolonial and Latino Reading of Philippians," *Perspectivas: Occasional Papers* 6 (2002): 37–56. Agosto's comments focus upon Paul's imprisonment and the collection for the poor, with some very different results from this study's engagement with military imagery. See also the response to Agosto by Hjamil A. Martínez-Vázquez, "Postcolonial Criticism in Biblical Interpretation:

regime, postcolonial concerns would seem to be most certainly meritorious of consideration once one identifies the prevalence of military imagery in the letter. By noting the sociopolitical context of the letter's writing and reception (e.g., the presence of veterans at Philippi, its status as a Roman colony), scholars focused upon military imagery have reminded interpreters of this oft-neglected factor in the interpretation of Pauline letters.[39] Their work demonstrates the need for further political-ethical engagements with these contexts for the interpretation of Philippians. Though not itself a full postcolonial analysis, the following observations take up this task of engagement in conversation with feminist, postcolonial, and feminist postcolonial interpretive practices.

To begin with, while it may be a rather obvious observation, military images are first and foremost associated with violence. Despite this fairly apparent connection that was as true in the Greco-Roman period as it is today, it is one rarely (if ever) noted by scholars who propose the relevance of military imagery for the letter to the Philippians. Indeed, one of the virtues of scholarly explanation in this vein has been its emphasis on the vivid visualization of the images in the letter. Both Krentz and Geoffrion, for example, write of the battle lines being drawn, as the opponents swing to face each other. The letter points out the opposition to these Pauline "soldiers," labeling them as the enemy (3:18; cf. 1:15–17, 28; 2:15, 21). There is even some brief discussion of suffering (1:29; 2:17, 27–28). Yet, remarkably, there is very little acknowledgment by scholars that these machinations involve, or serve as preludes to, actual violence. The hearkening toward military images stops short, and the considerations are, as a result, quite literally bloodless.[40]

A Response to Efrain Agosto," *Perspectivas: Occasional Papers* 6 (2002): 57–63. For brief introductions to postcolonial analysis in biblical interpretation (especially as it is partnered with feminist analyses), see Musa W. Dube, *Postcolonial Feminist Interpretation of the Bible* (St. Louis: Chalice, 2000); and Kwok Pui-lan, *Discovering the Bible in the Non-Biblical World* (Maryknoll, N.Y.: Orbis, 1995). See also Fernando F. Segovia, *Decolonizing Biblical Studies: A View from the Margins* (Maryknoll, N.Y.: Orbis, 2000); and Rasiah S. Sugirtharajah, *Postcolonial Criticism and Biblical Interpretation* (Oxford: Oxford University Press, 2002).

39. For recent efforts to correct this lack in Pauline studies, see, e.g., the studies collected in Richard A. Horsley, ed., *Paul and Empire: Religion and Power in Roman Imperial Society* (Harrisburg, Pa.: Trinity Press International, 1997); and idem, ed., *Paul and Politics: Ekklesia, Israel, Imperium, Interpretation* (Harrisburg, Pa.: Trinity Press International, 2000).

40. The analogy here to the terms of discussion for modern warfare (especially as it has been described as of late by and for U.S. armed forces) is irresistible. Similarly, conversations stop short of speaking of blood and death, offering, rather, obfuscations and circumlocutory descriptions, such as "surgical strikes," "precision targets," "smart bombs," and "collateral damage."

Ironically, it has been precisely this issue of bloodshed that has been at the heart of previous debates among scholars of early Christianity, focusing on whether participation in this movement could have been compatible with Roman military service. While some have explained the incompatibility of military participation for early believers by reason of the potential for idolatry, others maintain that it is specifically the violence and bloodshed that would have been especially prohibitive for them.[41] If there is any doubt as to whether images of the military or the ideal soldier are strongly affiliated with acts of violence, one can simply survey materials describing the training and enlisted activities of a Roman soldier (*miles*).[42] The essential traits of a soldier in the Roman army included being in strong physical condition and having the facility with weapons so as to inflict harm and cause (mostly mortal) damage to other human beings.[43] If one could not meet this qualification for committing acts of violence, one could not effectively be a soldier, enacting both the violent and threatening roles. Thus, when language recalls the formations and encouragement of soldiers engaged in a battle (as the letter of Philippians seems to do), it implies and anticipates an impending violent, bloody, and (for some) mortal resolution.

Because of the limited reach of the studies examining military images, the considerations of the audience have also been, in the end, partial and brief, especially with regard to possible attitudes about or reactions to military images. This lack in analysis is all the more striking since, as these scholars *have* acknowledged, these images could be connected to Philippi's multiple colonizations.[44] Herein, perhaps, one can begin to explain why most scholarship on the military images in the letter has not questioned the valence of such images for an audience of

---

41. Jean-Michel Hornus, *It Is Not Lawful for Me to Fight* (Scottsdale, Pa.: Herald, 1980); C. John Cadoux, *The Early Christian Attitude to War* (London: Headley, 1918); and Gracie, "Introduction," 14.

42. Roy W. Davies, *Service in the Roman Army* (ed. D. Breeze and V. A. Maxfield; New York: Columbia University Press, 1989), 3–15, 26, 41–43. See also Antonio Santosuosso, *Storming the Heavens: Soldiers, Emperors, and Civilians in the Roman Empire* (Boulder, Colo.: Westview, 2001), 16–22, 89–116.

43. Indeed, the medical service in the field was mainly set up in anticipation of casualties in the Roman army. See Graham Webster, *The Roman Imperial Army of the First and Second Centuries A. D.* (London: Adam & Charles Black, 1969), 250–53.

44. By the mid-first century C.E., Philippi was under the authority of the Roman Empire and designated a *colonia iuris Italicum*. For more on this kind of colony, see de Vos, *Church and Community Conflicts*, 112–15, 246–47; Barbara Levick, ed., *The Government of the Roman Empire: A Sourcebook* (London: Croom Helm, 1988), 73–74, 316; and A. N. Sherwin-White, *The Roman Citizenship* (2d ed.; Oxford: Clarendon, 1973), 316–19. For an overview of the Thasian, Macedonian and Roman colonizations of Philippi, see the resources in n. 4 above.

subjected people: scholars assume a *uniformly* positive reception for these images in the letter of Philippians because of the settlement of veterans at Philippi during the civil wars. This assumption, however, overlooks several factors in terms of the community at Philippi and its relation to the structures of domination in the Roman Empire.

First, it seems unlikely that veterans (or their descendants) were members in any significant way of the relatively small audience Paul was addressing in the Philippian community. In general, the appeal of this movement was not to elite members of society, but to an ethnically and socially diverse mix of subsistence-level (or lower) populations. More recent scholarship that has attempted to reconstruct the "church" community at Philippi confirms that this tendency would have been operative at Philippi as well. De Vos, for instance, writes that it was "unlikely that there were any in the church who were descendants of the original colonists. Certainly nothing remotely hints at his [Clement; Phil 4:3] being a member of the ruling elite."[45]

Similarly, Peter Oakes estimates that if there were any descendants of veterans in the community, they would have been farmers who had fallen on bad times economically, having lost their land.[46] Indeed, Oakes could have been writing about scholars interested in military images in his following assessment: "It is characteristic of much of scholarship that Karl Bornhäuser can look at a letter, two out of three of whose named addressees are Greek women, and take as his exegetical foundation the idea that the recipients are Roman, male, ex-soldiers."[47] Oakes's comment lays bare the scholarly tendency to take one factor (Philippi as a Roman colony) and read it in a rather limited fashion into all situations for the letter, ignoring especially the role of women. This tendency, which Oakes so explicitly names, also shows how traditional biblical and classical scholarship has been inclined to identify first with elite men, who produced and preserved most of our sources for the ancient world. This history of scholarship, then, also demonstrates the need for a feminist analytic of domination as an accompaniment to any accounting of the impact of the veteran settlement in and colonial status of Philippi.

Second, even if veterans were present or somehow affected the reception of such images at Philippi, there are no assurances that this reception

---

45. De Vos, *Church and Community Conflicts*, 255. See also Oakes, *Philippians*, 57–61.

46. Oakes, *Philippians*, 60–61. Oakes also notes that "there was probably a negligible proportion of veterans among the hearers of the letter," since, for the city of Philippi, "the proportion of veterans in the population was extremely small" (*Philippians*, 53).

47. Oakes, *Philippians*, 63–64. He is referring here to Karl Bornhäuser, *Jesus imperator mundi (Phil 3, 17–21 u. 2, 5–12)* (Gütersloh: Bertelsmann, 1938).

would have been uniformly positive (as presumed by scholars of military images in the letter). Veteran loyalty to the emperor was less than assured in the century leading up to the composition of this letter, especially because of the frequent shifts at the top of the sociopolitical and military hierarchies during and after Rome's string of civil wars.[48] It was these wars that brought veteran settlers (primarily from Antony's losing side) to Philippi in 31 B.C.E.[49] Occasions for veteran dissatisfaction at settlement were not rare,[50] a phenomenon advanced perhaps by conscription,[51] frequent delays in land allocation,[52] or by failure to deliver upon promises of reward expected for service.[53]

Turning to the specific situation of Philippi, veterans were more likely to be unhappy if settled there, since its location (far from Italy) was not likely considered ideal.[54] Furthermore, many could have been settled at Philippi as a result of being "on the wrong side at the wrong time," and, for this reason, would have had no lingering affection for the reigning administration that placed them there. These events present problems to scholars who wish to portray veterans (and their descendents) at Philippi as a monolithic entity, sharing the same positive outlook on their time in the Roman military and the resulting colonization and settlement.

Third, even if one were to assume that military imagery would have some inherent appeal to the veterans of Roman campaigns, it does not explain why scholars have presumed that military language as a rhetorical practice would have had a similar appeal across the diverse group that

---

48. For shifts in veteran loyalty during the civil wars, see Lawrence Keppie, *The Making of the Roman Army: From Republic to Empire* (London: Batsford, 1984), 104, 115, 121–28; and Santuosso, *Storming the Heavens*, 39–52.

49. Keppie, *Making of the Roman Army*, 128–29; idem, *Colonisation and Veteran Settlement in Italy: 47–14 B.C.* (London: British School at Rome, 1983), 76; and G. W. Bowersock, *Augustus and the Greek World* (Oxford: Clarendon, 1965), 65.

50. Keppie, *Colonisation and Veteran Settlement*, 36; and idem, *Making of the Roman Army*, 110, 135. On the importance of settling these "near-mutinous soldiers," see Peter Garnsey and Richard Saller, *The Early Principate: Augustus to Trajan* (Oxford: Clarendon, 1982), 8. The late republic, in general, shared the problem that "a large and increasing proportion of discharged veterans had little or no property to support them when they returned to their homes." See Geoffrey E. M. de Ste. Croix, *The Class Struggle in the Ancient Greek World: From the Archaic Age to the Arab Conquests* (Ithaca: Cornell University Press, 1981), 357.

51. Keppie, *Colonisation and Veteran Settlement*, 37–40; A. H. M. Jones, *The Later Roman Empire, 284–602: A Social Economic and Administrative Survey* (Oxford: Oxford University Press, 1964), 618; and P. A. Brunt, *Italian Manpower, 225 B.C.-A.D. 14* (Oxford: Oxford Unversity Press, 1971), 391.

52. Keppie, *Colonisation and Veteran Settlement*, 70, 87.

53. Ibid., 41; and idem, *Making of the Roman Army*, 144.

54. Keppie, *Colonisation and Veteran Settlement*, 32, 59–76. For Antony's own preference for Gaul rather than Macedonia as a power base, see Keppie, *Making of the Roman Army*, 114.

made up the Philippian community. Such scholarship has not adequately explained why, aside from former veterans, those groups (including women, a range of native peoples, and various subgroups among the majority lower class) would be inclined to look upon such terminology or events favorably.[55] For the most part, the people of the Greco-Roman world would have experienced the military (in general) as a component of dominating rule, most recently in the form of Roman imperial government, with its accompanying requirements of subordination and obedience.[56] In terms of the colonization of Philippi by the Romans, residents were more likely to resent the military because of the wholesale confiscation of land and the overall exploitative conditions of their settlement.[57] To the extent that colonization increased the mistreatment of the indigenous populations, an undue amount of that exploitation most likely fell upon women. If there were any members of Philippian society who would have gained socially or economically from Roman rule, women were the least likely to have enjoyed such benefits.

Since scholars interested in military images have not fully acknowledged the violence of these images, they also have overlooked the significantly gendered aspects of military violence.[58] Feminist scholars and allies have asked this rather pointed question: "what could be more

---

55. This oversight represents a particular weakness of Schuster's thesis, as his study presumes that the military families will recall specific speeches and accounts of the military history in the language of Philippians ("Rhetorical Situation," 141). For an audience-oriented approach to the letter that considers the way women would have received it, see Portefaix, *Sisters Rejoice.* For the prominent role of women in Philippi's cultic activities (all but ignored in many of these studies), see Valerie A. Abrahamsen, "Women at Philippi: The Pagan and Christian Evidence," *JFSR* 3 (1987): 17–30; idem, "Christianity and the Rock Reliefs at Philippi," *BA* 51 (1988): 46–56; and idem, *Women and Worship at Philippi: Diana/Artemis and Other Cults in the Early Christian Era* (Portland, Maine: Astarte Shell, 1995).

56. On the importance of the imperial control of the military in the process of increasing the exploitation of the majority, especially as Rome's principate arose from the republic, see de Ste. Croix, *Class Struggle,* 374–92.

57. Keppie, *Colonisation and Veteran Settlement,* 61, 87, 101. Veteran settlement would only exacerbate any lingering enmity in general between civilians and soldiers. See Santosuosso, *Storming the Heavens,* 51. As E. Badian comments, "No administration in history has ever devoted itself so whole-heartedly to fleecing its subjects for the private benefit of its ruling class as Rome ... [in] the last age of the Republic" (*Roman Imperialism in the Late Republic* [2d ed.; Oxford: Oxford University Press, 1968], 87). Again, this misunderstanding of a subject people's potential attitude to a military force's intrusion and occupation is chillingly analogous to current American misunderstandings of how Iraqis would react to their "war of liberation."

58. For the examination of gender, violence and/or war in the context of biblical interpretation, see the collection of articles in Claudia V. Camp and Carol R. Fontaine, eds., *Women, War, and Metaphor: Language and Society in the Study of the Hebrew Bible* (Semeia 61; Atlanta: Scholars Press, 1993). See also Alice Bach, "Rereading the Body Politic: Women and

acutely gendered than war, an activity historically described as performed by men only, in a space containing nothing but men?"[59] Scholars have not explained how a letter exhorting one to be a "good soldier" would have appeal for women in the Philippian community,[60] a group that would not have shared this experience in the Roman military (indeed, scholarship on these images rarely even takes up the subject of women in this community). Perhaps even more critically, these women could have experienced military figures as perpetrators of violence directed against them. Rape has so frequently accompanied war through the centuries that it stands as "part of a soldier's proof of masculinity and success, a tangible reward for services rendered."[61] These connections to military imagery, then, could rather thus create major obstacles for the letter's ability to communicate to women.[62] This observation is not

---

Violence in Judges 21," *BibInt* 6 (1998): 1–19; Yani Yoo, "*Han*-Laden Women: Korean 'Comfort Women' and Women in Judges 19–21," *Semeia* 78 (1997): 37–46; Susan Niditch, *War in the Hebrew Bible: A Study in the Ethics of Violence* (New York: Oxford University Press, 1993); Phyllis Trible, *Texts of Terror: Literary-Feminist Readings of Biblical Narratives* (OBT 13; Philadelphia: Fortress, 1984); and Harold C. Washington, "Violence and the Construction of Gender in the Hebrew Bible: A New Historicist Approach," *BibInt* 5 (1997): 324–63.

59. Washington, "Violence and the Construction of Gender," 329–30. Washington notes that this question is posed in the terms given by Miriam Cooke, "WO-man, Retelling the War Myth" in *Gendering War-Talk* (ed. M. Cooke and A. Woollacott; Princeton: Princeton University Press, 1993), 177.

60. Observation of this lack in interpretation of Philippians should not, however, be taken as making the exact opposite case. This study is not attempting to argue that there is a necessary relationship between women (either ancient Philippian females or those of other times and places) and resistance to military images. The record on such a relationship is, at best, ambiguous. Rather, here I am trying to problematize scholarly assumptions about the reception of and purpose for this letter, while complicating our picture of the ancient community at Philippi. For more on the multiple and ambiguous roles of women and men in both peace-making and militarism, see Mary Condren, "To Bear Children for the Fatherland: Mothers and Militarism," in *The Power of Naming: A Concilium Reader in Feminist Liberation Theology* (ed. E. Schüssler Fiorenza; Maryknoll, N.Y.: Orbis, 1996), 115–23.

61. Susan Brownmiller, *Against Our Will: Men, Women, and Rape* (New York: Bantam, 1976), 33. On the pervasiveness of violence against women as part of warfare across the centuries, see esp. pp. 23–118. As Bach comments, "rape in war is a familiar act with a familiar excuse" ("Rereading the Body Politic," 10). For an example of some of the challenges entailed in reconstructing the contours of violence against women in antiquity, particularly from archaeological remains, see Tal Ilan, *Integrating Women into Second Temple History* (TSAJ 76; Tübingen: Mohr Siebeck, 1999; repr., Peabody, Mass.: Hendrickson, 2001), 208–11.

62. As Washington comments, "even vicarious identifications with texts like these is problematic for a female-identified reader, who soon finds herself aligned with the object of violence. The male is by definition the subject of warfare's violence and the female its victim" ("Violence and the Construction of Gender," 345–46). Washington's comment is based upon Teresa de Lauretis's assertion that "the subject of violence is always, by definition, masculine" ("The Violence of Rhetoric: Considerations on Representation and Gender," in *The Violence of*

insignificant for the audience, because, as Oakes's quote above makes clear, women were central to the community at Philippi. Euodia and Syntyche (4:2–3) are specifically addressed in the letter, and there are strong indications that they played a leading role in the community.[63]

Hence, scholarly investigations into the range and impact of military imagery could benefit from some methodological expansions as well as some further consideration of the Roman military and its impact. This scholarly trajectory has commendably noted the relevance of Philippi's status as a colony within the Roman Empire to the interpretation of the letter. However, these scholars have yet to investigate the role of "empire" as the location for the rhetorical production and reception of these images, a task for which feminist, postcolonial, and other liberation-oriented critics of biblical literature could be of immediate and fruitful aid.[64] This "aid" is all the more essential given the clear implications of violence (against the "enemy" and against women) and mortal threat involved with these images. This fact most likely would not have been lost on an ancient audience living at the site of battles of historical significance for the Roman Empire (such as Philippi). Thus, one who calls up the images of soldiers, enemies, and combat lines, while contrasting destruction with safety (or salvation), is interacting with and reconfiguring an entire thought-world that also involves bloody suffering, death, and assaults against women. Describing scenes like this is, rhetorically speaking, not too far afield from Paul actually threatening his audience. By evoking this imagery, Paul participates in a rhetorical act that echoes, rather than overturns, this violent and oppressive structure. And a reticence or

---

Representation: Literature and the History of Violence [ed. N. Armstrong and L. Tennenhouse; London: Routledge, 1989], 250).

63. On the basis of the description of Euodia and Syntyche as "co-workers" and "those who struggled with me in the gospel" in 4:3, many scholars argue for their prominence and possible leadership roles in the community. For further considerations of their roles, see Kittredge, *Community and Authority,* 90–94, 96, 98–110; Mary Rose D'Angelo, "Women Partners in the New Testament," *JFSR* 6 (1990): 65–86; and Portefaix, *Sisters Rejoice,* 135–54.

64. It should be noted that this study does not aim to produce another monolithic depiction of the audience to replace the previous conception of uniformity. In fact, as this overview has attempted to show, we could expect a range of factors to affect how various members of the Philippian community would have received such arguments in different ways. Categories of people in the community such as veterans, women, or colonized subjects should not be read as uncomplicated subgroups easily boxed in terms of single factors. Women and men in the community would have had a variety of positions within the interlocking relations of kyriarchy, and responses and attitudes to such argumentation would reflect this variety. Here a postcolonial exploration of potential responses (accommodation/collaboration, resistance, nativism, nationalism, hybridity, etc.) to a colonial context like Philippi could be fruitful. See, e.g., Musa W. Dube (Shomonah), "Postcolonial Biblical Interpretations," *DBI* 2:299–303.

unwillingness to engage this element of the Pauline rhetorical strategy is to risk extending the violence inherent in the rhetorics even further.

FEMINIST ANALYSIS: RECONSIDERING
MILITARY IMAGERY IN PHILIPPIANS 1–2

Having reexamined the scholarly assumptions about the use and effect of military imagery in Philippians, I now turn to an analysis of how such assumptions have allowed or encouraged approaches to the letter that leave hierarchical rhetorics unrecognized. The critical point of departure in this investigation is to examine how the use of these military images is tied up with the letter's overarching techniques of argumentation.[65] Throughout Phil 1 and 2 Paul works to establish as models for the audience both himself and those compatible with his ideas for communal identity (Timothy, Epaphroditus, and a particular version of Christ).[66] According to this letter, Paul thinks/feels (*phronein*) the right way about the community (1:7–11), brings about progress (1:12–14), sacrifices himself for them (1:21–26; 2:16–18), and is engaged in the conflict that they should be sharing (1:29–30). This argument that seeks to establish Paul as a model for the audience is then utilized in the first half of the letter in a two-fold manner. First, it supports his calls for them to live a particular way in conformity to Paul's ideas, an argument that is accompanied by a dense cluster of military images in 1:12–30. Second, it clarifies the exhortation to obedience that follows the Christ hymn in 2:6–11 as an argument to obey Paul (2:12–13), their model and their "commander."[67] The military imagery in the letter thus forms part of Paul's strategy to construct a reality where the Philippians will take Paul as their authority and obey him.[68]

---

65. The phrase "techniques of argumentation" refers to the terminology and functional descriptions Olbrechts-Tyteca and Perelman have established in *New Rhetoric*, 185–459.

66. On argument from a model as a relation establishing the structure of reality, see Olbrechts-Tyteca and Perelman, *New Rhetoric*, 362–68. In many ways the argument from a model overlaps with or is premised upon the relation between a person and her/his acts. On the relationship between person and act in argumentation, see pp. 293–305.

67. As noted above with respect to scholars interested in military images, arguments established by a model are common for military contexts and vital for rallying troops to follow orders. It is here that this study parts ways with the analysis of the hymn offered by Kittredge (*Community and Authority*, 99–100, 110). Though the hymn might have offered a pattern of reversal as a hope to those oppressed in various ways by the kyriarchal culture, its imagery and vocabulary are still embedded in this kyriarchal matrix of slave-master (2:7) and subject-ruler (2:9–11). For a similar view, see Sheila Briggs, "Can an Enslaved God Liberate? Hermeneutical Reflections on Philippians 2:6–11," *Semeia* 47 (1989): 137–53.

68. For a convincing and important elucidation of obedience in Philippians, see Kittredge, *Community and Authority*, 1–110. Inherent to the hermeneutics of suspicion, as

The depiction of sides lined up against each other as if in combat formations, aptly articulated by scholars of military images, fits well with the letter's oppositional and dualistic style. Paul often evokes a group of antimodels (1:15–17, 28; 2:15, 21) to serve as opponents or foils for the models presented on "his side" of the matter.[69] This deployment of antimodels is often accompanied by examples of Paul's dissociative rhetoric; these antimodels cause divisions (1:15–17) and bring destruction upon themselves (1:28).[70] That Paul also often backs up these arguments through an appeal to divine authority (1:8, 28; 2:13) only underscores the "all or nothing" tenor of the letter.[71] As mentioned above, when accompanied by allusions to potential destruction with divine approval ("and this from God"; 1:28), these exhortations to obedience and adherence to a particular course of action veer quite close to threats.

By presuming a positive reception of Paul's arguments and not engaging with any feminist or liberation-oriented considerations, scholars interested in the Philippian military imagery have not been able to recognize how one set of hierarchical or authoritative arguments (military rhetorics) overlaps with another set of arguments (modeling, obedience, and dualistic rhetorics) to work for a common purpose. Through the elucidation of kyriarchal structures and arguments, feminist interpretive work emphasizes that military images can and do collaborate in an interlocking fashion as part of an overarching system of subordination and control. Their implementation is not an isolated phenomenon but is

---

described by Schüssler Fiorenza, is the idea that kyriocentric texts *construct* a particular view of reality rather than simply reflect it, in order to produce (or continue producing) kyriarchal power arrangements (*Rhetoric and Ethic*, 50–51).

69. On the use of antimodels and their relation to models, see Olbrechts-Tyteca and Perelman, *New Rhetoric*, 366–68.

70. Dissociations as arguments function to alter the very structure of how two elements were once associated. The classic example for Olbrechts-Tyteca and Perelman would be the dissociation between appearance and reality, expressed in the form term I/term II (appearance/reality), where now term II is preferred over term I. For more on dissociations and the appearance/reality pairing, see *New Rhetoric*, 411–36. In these cases within Philippians, Paul is arguing in terms of division/unity and destruction/safety dissociations, among others. For how division/unity might be characteristic of traditional dissociative pairs, see 420–21.

71. On the argument from authority as an argument based on the structure of reality, see Olbrechts-Tyteca and Perelman, *New Rhetoric*, 305–10. Indeed, "the extreme case is the divine authority which overcomes all the obstacles that reason might raise" (308). One of the virtues of argumentation as described by Olbrechts-Tyteca and Perelman is the emphasis they place on its interactivity; that is, a rhetorical act works best when it integrates different kinds of argumentative techniques from more than one category so that they build upon or complement each other. It is in this "interaction of arguments" that the rhetoric becomes convincing and can produce variant effects based upon differences in interaction. For more on the interaction of arguments, see 460–508.

linked with a system of power that the audience would have palpably experienced. Nor is this implementation isolated in the letter, since it works in tandem with the various modeling and authority arguments.[72] By implementing these images in his rhetoric, Paul makes clear that, though he might be seeking to replace the military, he expects similar kinds of obedience from the community and assumes a similar kind of authority for himself (and those most like him). Thus, whether one is considering these images together or on their own, it is vital for an interpretation that intends to promote a liberating reading to recognize, name, and analyze how military images function to oppress the vast majority of people.[73]

As it has hopefully become clear, if these kinds of argumentative techniques (model, divine authority, dissociation) were associated with the military imagery presented in the letter, this could only prove to be more of a liability rather than a virtue for the development of Paul's argument as a "limited authority figure."[74] One has to wonder how effective

---

72. This kind of rhetorical overlap fits with the perspectives of all three scholars highlighted in this essay (Schüssler Fiorenza, Olbrechts-Tyteca, and Perelman). The collaboration of two different kinds of authoritative rhetorics within the letter very much resembles Olbrechts-Tyteca and Perelman's "interaction of arguments" (elaborated in n. 71 above), while demonstrating how various oppressive power structures are found intersecting in a pyramidal arrangement of rule, that is, to use Schüssler Fiorenza's neologous heuristic concept, kyriarchally.

73. For examples of biblical interpretation concerned with the role of violence (and especially violence against women) in interpretive contexts, recent and historical, see Bach, "Rereading the Body Politic," 1–2, 4–5, 16–18; Yoo, "*Han*-Laden Women," 37–39, 41–45; Washington, "Violence and Construction of Gender," 324–26, 329–30, 332–42, 348, 355–56; Camp and Fontaine, *Women, War, and Metaphor*, vii, ix–xii; Susan Niditch, "War, Women, and Defilement in Numbers 31," *Semeia* 61 (1993): 39, 42–43, 49; and Susan Brooks Thistlethwaite, "'You May Enjoy the Spoil of Your Enemies': Rape as a Biblical Metaphor for War," *Semeia* 61 (1993): 59–61, 71–73. These scholars address issues ranging from (though not limited to) Korean "comfort women," Puritan efforts against Native Americans, German militarism, the rape camps of Bosnia-Herzegovina, the conflict in Rwanda, and American actions in Viet Nam, the Philippines, and the Middle East. It would not be difficult to add relevant contemporary situations, from war situations in Burundi and Liberia to the treatment of women at military training facilities (e.g., at the U.S. Air Force Academy). On the hermeneutics of ethical and theological evaluation, see Schüssler Fiorenza, *Rhetoric and Ethic*, 51; and idem, *Wisdom Ways*, 177–79.

74. Geoffrion, *Rhetorical Purpose*, 85, 100–104. For a similarly defensive view of Paul's modeling, see Frederick W. Weidmann, "An (Un)Accomplished Model: Paul and the Rhetorical Strategy of Philippians 3:3–17," in *Putting Body and Soul Together: Essays in Honor of Robin Scroggs* (ed. V. Wiles et al.; Valley Forge, Pa.: Trinity Press International, 1997), 245–57; and Andrew D. Clarke, "'Be Imitators of Me': Paul's Model of Leadership," *TynBul* 49 (1998): 329–60. In part, Weidmann's article is written in response to Robert T. Fortna, "Philippians: Paul's Most Egocentric Letter," in *The Conversation Continues: Studies in Paul and John in Honor of J. Louis Martyn* (ed. R. T. Fortna and B. R. Gaventa; Nashville: Abingdon, 1990), 220–34.

calls to obedience through military steadfastness would have been, given the variegated context of Philippi and the role of women in the community. Yet, for the most part, it is precisely this rhetorical success that has been presumed (rather than argued for or explained) by scholars interested in military imagery in Philippians. Olbrechts-Tyteca and Perelman have described the creation of a rhetorical act as prominently involving an "adaptation to the audience," since argumentation requires that a rhetor finds a way to appeal to the audience's reasonableness.[75] This orientation toward the audience requires that the rhetor actually cares about and in some way esteems or values the other person's (or people's) opinions and reactions. Since audiences are normally composite (as was the community at Philippi), the rhetor will have to use a multiplicity of arguments in order to be convincing.[76] While it seems that Paul has used a number of different arguments in Phil 1 and 2, it also appears that he might not have valued the perspectives of at least some members of the potential audience, instead seeking authority for himself and obedience from them.

While it may not be surprising that Paul the rhetor does not stand up to the standards and ethics promoted by modern rhetorical scholars, it does not help to rule out (as scholars interested in military images have appeared to do) the possibility that audiences (now or in the mid-first century) could be prone to resisting Paul's arguments. Given the factors sketched above, it is not hard to imagine resistance by some to a message couched in terms of military and other hierarchical arguments.[77] The violence implied, the potential bitterness of veterans, and the consequences of colonial exploitation for the majority of the populace (including most women and all of the lower classes) could be factors, again, for rejection by audiences both ancient and modern. By advocating for an authoritative arrangement similar to (rather than running counter to) military imagery of his time, Paul seeks to establish for himself a secure place in a hierarchical arrangement[78] that could have invoked a range of negative

---

75. As Olbrechts-Tyteca and Perelman note, "There is only one rule in this matter: adaptation of the speech to the audience, whatever its nature" (*New Rhetoric*, 25). On "adaptation to the audience," see pp. 14–26.

76. Ibid., 21–26.

77. Resistance seems to play a role within both the hermeneutics of suspicion and the hermeneutics of ethical/theological evaluation. Feminist interpretation seeks to dislodge and challenge rhetorical practices that help to produce the marginality of those oppressed by kyriocentric texts and in kyriarchal societies. See, e.g., Schüssler Fiorenza *Rhetoric and Ethic*, 51; and idem, *Wisdom Ways*, 175–77.

78. Even when Paul seems to be arguing for a displacement of certain hierarchical structures, it is typically the case that he replaces one hierarchical structure for another, one that benefits himself and reinstalls kyriarchal relations of domination evident in both

reactions (from ambivalence to outright rejection) from his audience at Philippi. Indeed, it seems he might have anticipated or even already experienced such a reaction, as is suggested by instructions like "do all things without grumbling or questioning/arguing" (2:14).[79]

By approaching the letter as an *attempt* to construct such a particular authoritative relationship, rather than a reflection of an apparently already-accepted authoritative position for Paul, we can also note how much effort Paul seems to be expending on arguing for the Philippian community's obedience and his own paradigmatic status. Realizing that this letter and its sender could have been marked as "not yet authoritative" only increases the possibility that the combination of military and other hierarchical rhetorics as a way to recommend Paul and other models like him could have met with limited success. Thus, contrary to the assumption and occasional argument of scholars, one must at least consider the strong possibility that some members of the community that received the letter resisted Paul's rhetoric. The recurring arguments seeking to establish Paul as a model, so that the community will think/feel or act the same way as he does (1:7, 30; 2:2–5, 17–18), suggest that the focused exhortation to Euodia and Syntyche to "think/feel the same thing" (*to auto phronein*; 4:2) should be read as an attempt to get them to "think/feel the same thing" *as Paul*.[80] Noting the effort with which Paul produces a

---

structures. For feminist responses to assertions that Paul's message is anti-imperial, see Cynthia Briggs Kittredge, "Corinthian Women Prophets and Paul's Argumentation in 1 Corinthians," in Horsley, *Paul and Politics*, 103–9; and Antoinette Clark Wire, "Response: The Politics of the Assembly in Corinth," in Horsley, *Paul and Politics*, 124–29. See also Vander-Stichele and Penner's contribution in this volume.

79. In fact, this could be viewed as an instance of where Paul *does* seek to adapt to his audience in response to or anticipation of less-than-positive reactions. Ironically enough, it is also a moment where he is arguing for the audience not to participate in certain rhetorical activities ("questioning," "considering," "debate," or "argument," all of which are ways one could translate the Greek noun *dialogismōn* in 2:14).

80. Most scholarship on Philippians has acquiesced to Paul's division of authority in this manner, thus assuming that the call in 4:2 to "think the same thing" portrays a conflict between Euodia and Syntyche, rather than a difference between Paul and the two women. Among the most recent examples, see Markus Bockmuehl, *The Epistle to the Philippians* (BNTC 11; Peabody, Mass.: Hendrickson, 1998), 238–42; Gordon D. Fee, *Philippians* (IVP New Testament Commentary Series 11; Downers Grove, Ill.: InterVarsity, 1999), 167–71; Paul A. Holloway, *Consolation in Philippians: Philosophical Sources and Rhetorical Strategy* (SNTSMS 112; Cambridge: Cambridge University Press, 2001), 146–47, 164; Oakes, *Philippians*, 114, 123–24; Carolyn Osiek, *Philippians, Philemon* (ANTC; Nashville: Abingdon, 2000), 110–13; and Peterlin, *Paul's Letter in the Light of Disunity*, 101–32. As on previous occasions, Kittredge's argument that Euodia and Syntyche are not in a conflict with each other but with Paul is unique and convincing. See Kittredge, *Community and Authority*, 105–8. Perhaps it is not coincidental that de Vos, who is interested in military images in the letter but does not

range of exclusively male models (Timothy, Epaphroditus, and a specific version of Christ) in support of his own model authority, while potentially serving as a contrast to the leadership or example of Euodia and Syntyche, also further highlights the possibility of resistance by some in the community.

Although it is not necessary to demonstrate this possibility of rejection in order to proceed to the final reflections of this essay, it does lend further credence to the following imaginative turn in service of creative hope for change.[81] Operating with suspicious caution and a desire to evaluate critically the arguments in the biblical tradition in terms of a feminist scale of values, I have here highlighted some of the kyriarchal implications of the letter to the Philippians. To the extent that the letter's military and modeling rhetorics partake of a kyriarchal mindset and reinforce such interrelated oppressive power arrangements, it is vital for a feminist interpretive project not only to address this oppressive function, but also to seek a shift in our basic approaches. This shift involves responding creatively and developing aids for change, rather than simply relegitimizing the text as a static authority.

While the final step in this instance is in some ways speculative, it is nonetheless crucial as an attempt to bring about just such a shift as described above. When we read the arguments establishing Paul (and those like him) as models for the community, we can do so *with* "grumbling and questioning." Assuming that the letter is just one part of an ongoing rhetorical exchange aids us in our desire to *dialogizesthai* ("question," "consider," or "argue"; 2:14) with the letter of Philippians and Paul. We ought to question whether we should imitate anyone claiming to be our leader who "plays" the role of a military figure (whether as a "commander" or a fighter pilot).[82] We should consider and reconsider whether it is best to present arguments in terms of a dualistic rhetoric (safety vs. destruction, us vs. them; "you are either with us or with the terrorists"). We ought to argue over whether there can ever be only one model for our

---

letter but does not address their gendered aspect, is particularly derogatory toward these "notorious" women, arguing that Paul "names them because their behavior is reprehensible and he shames them as an example to others" (*Church and Community Conflicts*, 255–56).

81. On the hermeneutics of creative imagination and the hermeneutics of transformation, see Schüssler Fiorenza, *Rhetoric and Ethic*, 52–54; and idem, *Wisdom Ways*, 179–83, 186–89.

82. The use of military images here is not dissimilar from the ancient rhetorical practice of *prosopopoeia* (writing speech-in character; e.g., composing a speech as one would *imagine* a famous general might). For the interpretation of Paul as playing the role of, or imitating, a "general" or "commander," see Krentz, "Military Language," 114–15, 127; and Geoffrion, *Rhetorical Purpose*, 28, 54, 85, 100–102.

way of life, one perspective for the resolution of issues within our communities (providing us with unity [as in 1:27–28; 2:1–4] or a new unilateralism). We must wonder if "progress" (1:12, 25) can ever be delivered, rhetorically or materially, on military terms.[83]

Turning the calls to imitation on their head, we can imitate those signs of struggle in the letter (regardless of whether the resistance preceded Paul's arguments or the arguments anticipated such a resistant response). Rather than unquestioningly assenting to Paul as authority figure and final arbiter, we can emulate the grumblers and dissenters, those people less convinced about Paul's role in their community, quite possibly including women like Euodia and Syntyche. This orientation toward Philippians demonstrates that *identifying* the military or modeling rhetorics of the letter does not necessarily mean we must, or even can, *identify with* Paul as model or military figure (as many Pauline scholars have previously done).[84] Traditional historical-critical methods might be able to take us through the first task, but the charge of more fully comprehending the rhetorics of Philippians and its interpretation necessarily involves those approaches that seek to engage these rhetorics through various turns of assessment, analysis, and response. Just as the conversation likely continued beyond this letter in mid-first-century Philippi, so our conversations about our models, our methods of liberation, and the authority of our received traditions must continue today.

---

83. Developing rhetorical methods and modes of analysis in terms of just such contextual issues is not a new phenomenon. Feminist (and most liberation-oriented) approaches have developed in response to critical reflections upon one's experience and social location (see Schüssler Fiorenza, *Rhetoric and Ethic*, 49–50; and idem, *Wisdom Ways*, 169–75). To a great extent, the New Rhetoric, as Olbrechts-Tyteca and Perelman (and others) have developed it, was a response to the crisis in Europe after the Second "World War" as to why rationalism and empiricism had not helped to foster greater understanding between human beings. Two multicontinent wars, the Holocaust, and a range of ethically troubling instances of injustice and violence caused them (and other rhetoricians) to seek the grounds of understanding beyond the realm of formal logic. For more on the background and relevance of their work, see Golden and Pilotta, *Practical Reasoning*; Dearin, *New Rhetoric*; Thomas H. Conley, *Rhetoric in the European Tradition* (Chicago: University of Chicago Press, 1990), 285–310; Patricia Bizzell and Bruce Herzberg, eds., *The Rhetorical Tradition: Readings from Classical Times to the Present* (Boston: Bedford Books of St. Martin's, 1990), 899–923, 1066–103; and Sonja K. Foss, Karen A. Foss, and Robert Trapp, *Contemporary Perspectives on Rhetoric* (3d ed.; Prospect Heights, Ill.: Waveland, 2002), 81–115. For a feminist response to the events of September 2001 and the war in Afghanistan, see Mary E. Hunt, "War: A Feminist Religious View," *JFSR* 18 (2002): 51–52; and Betsy Reed, ed., *Nothing Sacred: Women Respond to Religious Fundamentalism and Terror* (New York: Thunder's Mouth, 2002).

84. Schüssler Fiorenza succinctly examines this issue of (mostly male-stream) scholarly identification with Paul in "Paul and the Politics of Interpretation," in Horsley, *Paul and Politics*, 40–57.

PAUL AND THE RHETORIC OF GENDER

Caroline Vander Stichele and Todd Penner

In his recent study of the women at Corinth, Bruce Winter grounds the Pauline admonition against women being unveiled (1 Cor 11:2–16) in a full contextual analysis of the rise of "new women" in the Pauline communities. In particular, he argues that Paul was reacting against the moral laxity of these "new women," who flaunted Roman legal conventions and marriage mores. Paul's push to have the women veiled in worship represents his desire to have his community "appear" morally upright in the light of Roman social values, norms, and laws.[1] As a result, Paul's seemingly harsh treatment of these women becomes perfectly comprehensible, if not also morally applauded.

Winter's reading is to be situated within a long line (and range) of "explanations" regarding Paul's prohibition on women participating unveiled in community worship, with the focus typically on the "public" nature of the Christian ritualistic context.[2] His approach also coheres well with the commitment of historical criticism to explain the context and language of a particular text so as to render it sensible and comprehensible to modern readers. Whether one assesses more clearly the anthropology underlying Paul's arguments,[3] delineates more accurately

---

1. Bruce W. Winter, *Roman Wives, Roman Widows: The Appearance of New Women and the Pauline Communities* (Grand Rapids: Eerdmans, 2003).

2. For an overview, see Caroline Vander Stichele, "Authenticiteit en integriteit van 1 Kor 11,2–16: Een bijdrage tot de discussie omtrent Paulus' visie op de vrouw" (Ph.D. diss.; Katholieke Universiteit Leuven, 1992), 339–47. See also Margaret Y. MacDonald, *Early Christian Women and Pagan Opinion: The Power of the Hysterical Woman* (Cambridge: Cambridge University Press, 1996), 145; and Judith M. Gundry-Volf, "Gender and Creation in 1 Corinthians 11:2–16: A Study in Paul's Theological Method," in *Evangelium, Schriftauslegung, Kirche: Festschrift für Peter Stuhlmacher zum 65 Geburtstag* (ed. J Ådna, S. J. Hafemann, and O. Hofius; Göttingen: Vandenhoeck & Ruprecht, 1997), 153.

3. See, e.g., Dale B. Martin, *The Corinthian Body* (New Haven: Yale University Press, 1995), 229–49, who situates the Pauline argument within ancient conceptions of pollution, especially potent during boundary-crossing activities such as prophecy. Troy W. Martin, "Paul's Argument from Nature for the Veil in 1 Corinthians 11:13–15: A Testicle Instead of a Head Covering," *JBL* 123 (2004): 75–84, offers the most recent example of this kind of

the fuller context of veiling in the ancient world,[4] or underscores in more detail the social meaning of hair itself for Paul and his readers,[5] in all of these instances the focus rests squarely on how to make sense of Paul's arguments from a decidedly *historical* perspective.

---

approach. While scholars have explored the symbolic (and in some cases scientific) associations between female hair and genitalia in ancient Greco-Roman literature (see Martin, *Corinthian Body*, 235–39), one must be cautious about overextending these observations. It is likely that the symbolic control of women's sexuality (denoted by veiling in this instance) should be separated from an assumption of knowledge of technical linguistic associations. The former is clearly functioning in 1 Cor 11, the latter much less obviously so. Troy Martin (Paul's Argument from Nature"), for instance, argues that the περιβόλαιον for women in 1 Cor 11:15b refers to "female genitalia," a move wherein Martin pushes semantic boundaries to conclude that women's "hair" forms (in a literal linguistic way) their counterpart to male testicles. In Martin's construction, therefore, morally decent women would naturally "veil" their hair/genitalia. While this might be true on a cultural symbolic level, the attempt to make the literal connection is more tenuous. Martin's association in this instance turns on his linguistic speculation that μύρον (perfume) in Aristophanes' *Ecclesiazusae* (523–24) is a "play" on its "other" meaning, "semen" (80; cf. his reading of Aristophanes' *Lysistrata* 937–47, which provides the critical link in his argument, but which seems more likely to refer to the "scent of a woman" than of a man).

4. See, e.g., Richard Oster, "Use, Misuse and Neglect of Archeological Evidence in Some Modern Works on 1 Corinthians [1 Cor 7,1–5; 8,10; 11,2–16; 12,14–26]," *ZNW* 83 (1992): 52–73, esp. 67–69. In a shift away from the usual emphasis on women, Oster argues that archaeological evidence "patently demonstrates that the practice of men covering their heads in the context of prayer and prophecy was a common pattern of Roman piety and widespread during the late Republic and early Empire. Since Corinth was itself a Roman colony, there should be little doubt that this aspect of Roman religious practice deserves greater attention by commentators than it has received" (69). Most authors presume that Paul has some kind of headcovering in mind. The traditional view is that reference is made here to a veil: "Man disgraces his head by wearing a veil, woman disgraces hers by not wearing one" (Charles K. Barrett, *A Commentary on the First Epistle to the Corinthians* [BNTC; London: Blackwell, 1968], 251). Others think Paul refers to a particular hairstyle in this passage and see him opposing long hair for men and arguing that women should keep their hair orderly rather than loose; so, e.g., Abel Isaksson, *Marriage and Ministry in the New Temple: A Study with Special Reference to Mt 19.13–12 (sic) and 1 Cor 11.3–16* (ASNU 24; Lund: Gleerup, 1965); J. B. Hurley, "Did Paul Require Veils or the Silence of Women? A Consideration of I Cor 11:2–16 and I Cor 14:33b–36," *WTJ* 35 (1973): 190–220; Jerome Murphy-O'Connor, "Sex and Logic in 1 Cor 11:2–16," *CBQ* 42 (1980): 489; Wolfgang Schrage, *Der erste Brief an die Korinther (1 Korinther 6,12–11,16)* (EKKNT 7.2; Düsseldorf: Benziger; Neukirchen-Vluyn: Neukirchener Verlag, 1995), 492–94; and Gundry-Volf, "Gender and Creation," 151. More recently, Marlis Gielen has argued that Paul primarily opposes short hair for women ("Beten und Prophezeien mit unverhülltem Kopf? Die Kontroverse zwischen Paulus und der korinthischen Gemeinde um die Wahrung der Geschlechtsrollensymbolik," *ZNW* 90 [1999]: 231–37).

5. Winter, *Roman Wives*, 77–96; and Mary Rose D'Angelo, "Veils, Virgins, and the Tongues of Men and Angels," in *Women, Gender, Religion: A Reader* (ed. E. A. Castelli with R. C. Rodman; New York: Palgrave, 2001), esp. 395–99.

Feminist scholars seeking to reconstruct the role of the women prophets find themselves in similar terrain, but with a different loyalty, so to speak, as they are committed to the women whose voices were "silenced" by the androcentric statements perceived to reside in the text and in subsequent male-stream interpretations that continue to neglect these women even today.[6] The history behind the text is every bit as important in these instances as it is in more traditionally aligned studies, demonstrating that feminist scholarship has been concerned to employ the methods of historical criticism, albeit with a view to revealing and assessing the ideologies that have guided the construction of both text and interpretation, acknowledging that no interpretation is free of bias or interest.

Our contribution to this discussion seeks to deepen and expand a feminist hermeneutics of suspicion by broadening the perspective to a gender-critical analysis. This shift to a gender-critical perspective is decidedly located within the Western history of interpretation—and we are keenly aware of the universalizing and essentializing tendencies of that tradition. Nevertheless, we see this effort as part of a deconstruction and de-colonization of the field from within. To take location seriously means to engage it; thus, challenging dominant discourse admittedly becomes a political issue for interpreters, since modern interpretations often mask their own gendered, political, cultural, and religious agendas, in part because the implied religious authority of the text has frequently forced a hermeneutic of suppression on the guild as a whole.

While the approach developed here is also committed to a historical contextualizing of the text, we understand that the meaning of a text is larger than and not limited to what any *one* reading focused on the text's sociohistorical/cultural and literary (i.e., within the surviving Pauline lit-

---

6. See, e.g., Elisabeth Schüssler Fiorenza, *In Memory of Her: A Feminist Theological Reconstruction of Christian Origins* (New York: Crossroad, 1985), 226–33; Antoinette Clark Wire, *The Corinthian Women Prophets: A Reconstruction through Paul's Rhetoric* (Minneapolis: Fortress, 1990), esp. 116–34; and Elizabeth A. Castelli, "Paul on Women and Gender," in *Women and Christian Origins* (ed. R. Shepard Kraemer and M. R. D'Angelo; New York: Oxford University Press, 1999), 221–35. In her gender-critical comments on the same passage, Deborah F. Sawyer (*God, Gender and the Bible* [Biblical Limits; New York: Routledge, 2002], 134–35) shifts the focus from the usual emphasis on the inequality between men and women in the text to the "disempowerment" of both "in relation to the deity." Also see the assessment of some important feminist readings of this passage by Jorunn Økland, "Feminist Reception of the New Testament: A Critical Reception," in *The New Testament as Reception* (ed. M. Müller and H. Tronier; JSNTSup 230; CIS 11; Sheffield: Sheffield Academic Press, 2002), 137–48; as well as the brief discussion of the basic debate between "pro" and "anti" Pauline interpreters in Tal Ilan, *Jewish Women in Greco-Roman Palestine: An Inquiry into Image and Status* (TSAJ 44; Tübingen: Mohr Siebeck, 1995; repr., Peabody, Mass.: Hendrickson, 1996), 9–10 n. 31.

erary canon) contexts can in principle yield for the modern reader. We are especially interested in broadening meaning by moving away from a reconstruction of the historical situation in question or Paul's theological agenda to the engagement of fundamental issues of identity that are central to ancient rhetorical theories of proper comportment. We aim to push to the fore the argumentative logic and function of the Pauline text, paying special attention to Paul's argument *as argumentation*. It is in this nexus of Pauline persuasion that one also comes into closest contact with the patterns of power that pervade all texts, ancient and modern. Our early Christian texts are, as we will argue, truly incarnational, taking on the form of all modes of ancient discourse, manifesting all the power plays (and the masking of the same), all the value-laden agenda, the vying for dominance at the expense of others, including also the gendering of language and concepts to meet these various ends. In short, the move from assessing the content to analyzing the *function* of the Pauline admonition against veiling and his use of the ontological argument from nature (bolstered by a similar appeal to Scripture) demonstrates a different kind of meaning-making than a more traditional conceptual analysis of themes/images, words, or the elucidation of sociocultural parallels in and of themselves achieves. The analysis that follows thus focuses much more squarely on the history *in front* of the text, as well as the rhetorical and ideological underpinnings of Pauline argumentation as a whole.

We will first begin with an analysis of the argumentative texture of the text, exploring both the progression of the argument and the specific appeal to "ontology" with its attendant rhetorical effect. Other instances where Paul makes the same ontological move by grounding sex differentiation in nature (Rom 1:26–27 and 2:27) will also be discussed in order to illuminate the larger argumentative gains that this Pauline discourse achieves. This analysis is then followed by an assessment of the role of similar ontological arguments in Epictetus and Plutarch. As we shall see, Paul's language and argument take on quite a different shade when they are placed within the male gendered "rhetorical culture" of the ancient world.[7]

---

7. In contrast to scholars such as Jennifer Larson ("Paul's Masculinity," *JBL* 123 [2004]: 85–97), who has recently argued that Paul rejected "certain traditional standards of masculinity" (94) and countered "the tendency to equate masculinity ... with outward demonstrations of dominance and power" (95; cf. Brigitte Kahl, "No Longer Male: Masculinity Struggles Behind Galatians 3:28," *JSNT* 79 [2000]: 37–49), the argument developed here is that Paul does in fact employ the masculine/gendered *topoi* of his culture. Paul's rhetorical use of gendered themes and images in the Corinthian discourse is more clearly affirmed by J. Albert Harrill ("Invective against Paul [2 Cor 10:10], the Physiognomics of the Ancient Slave Body, and the Greco-Roman Rhetoric of Manhood," in *Antiquity and Humanity: Essays on Ancient Religion*

THE CRUX OF (THE) MATTER

The precise nature of the practices in the Corinthian community—such as determining whether or not the issue at stake was one of hairstyle or hair covering—has often formed a central concern in historical-critical interpretations of this passage. In our estimation, however, it is more critical to ask how these elements—hair and covering/veiling—further Paul's larger argumentative aims, and, even more so, what they reveal about the guiding framework that is reflected in Paul's statements.[8] This redefinition of the question implies a double shift in focus. On the one hand, attention moves away from a (largely hypothetical) reconstruction of the situation in the Corinthian community to Paul's argumentation. On the other, it also redirects the attention from the traditional image of Paul as pastor, who offers sublime guidance to his struggling communities, to a founder seeking to shape, maintain, and, if necessary, enforce a strongly boundaried Christian identity.[9] This shift becomes more evident as one analyzes Paul's argument in detail.

---

and Philosophy Presented to Hans Dieter Betz on His 70th Birthday [ed. A. Yarbro Collins and M. M. Mitchell; Tübingen: Mohr Siebeck, 2001], 189–213), who, nevertheless, asserts (similar to Larson) that Paul rejected the use of physiognomy in characterization and that his use of gendered tropes had the aim of achieving a rhetorical *inversion* of masculine discourse (211–12), a position which seems to sanction Paul's moves given the seemingly "positive" ends advanced. While, in a more decidedly theological vein, Gundry-Volf admits that "culture plays a significant role in Paul's thinking on gender in this text" and that Paul's theology of gender is "informed by that context" ("Gender and Creation," 169), in her actual assessment this affirmation does not seem to shape in any serious way her reconstructions of Paul's perception of gender (for the most recent version of this argument, see Linda L. Belleville, "Κεφαλή and the Thorny Issue of Headcovering in 1 Corinthians 11:2–16," in *Paul and the Corinthians: Studies on a Community in Conflict. Essays in Honour of Margaret Thrall* [ed. T. J. Burke and J. K. Elliott; NovTSup 109; Leiden: Brill, 2003], 215–31, who strongly affirms that Paul's argument is *theological* rather than *sociological* in nature [226; cf. 215, 229] and that the general language throughout this section emphasizes "gender parity and mutuality" [216; cf. 223]). Ben Witherington (*Women in the Earliest Churches* [SNTSMS 59; Cambridge: Cambridge University Press, 1988], 78–90) achieves a similar "balance" in his correlation of the various Pauline elements related to "new creation" and "old," thereby clearing Paul of charges of "male chauvenism" (90).

8. Cf. Ross Shepard Kraemer, *Her Share of the Blessings: Women's Religions among Pagans, Jews, and Christians in the Greco-Roman World* (New York: Oxford University Press, 1992), 147: "whether this passages pertains to head coverings or hairstyles is probably irrelevant: control and release are really what is at issue."

9. For two recent essays that are particularly helpful in demonstrating this emphasis, especially with respect to Paul's argumentation in 1 Corinthians, see Trevor J. Burke, "Paul's Role as 'Father' to His Corinthian 'Children' in Socio-Historical Context (I Corinthians 4:14–21)," in Burke and Elliott, *Paul and the Corinthians*, 95–113; and Charles A. Wanamaker, "A Rhetoric of Power: Ideology and 1 Corinthians 1–4," in Burke and Elliott, *Paul and the Corinthians*, 115–37.

The critical lynchpin of Paul's argument in 1 Cor 11 is found in v. 5b, where two different situations—to be uncovered and to be shaved—are identified with each other (ἒν γάρ ἐστιν καὶ τὸ αὐτό) in order to transfer the scandalous character of the one to the (disputed) other. The logic behind this reasoning can be reconstructed as follows: to cut or shave is a shame (v. 6b); an uncovered head is one and the same as being shaved (v. 5b); therefore: to be uncovered is a shame (v. 5a). Paul presumes that (or at least proceeds as if) his audience will subscribe to the major premise: for a woman to cut or shave is shameful. He then uses the analogy between hair and headcovering to persuade his readers that to be uncovered is equally shameful. This analogy is most effective, of course, if his readers indeed accept both premises, namely, that cutting or shaving is a shame and that an uncovered head equals shaving, which is the more drastic practice of the two since it implies that all hair is removed.[10] While he immediately goes on to bolster this "conclusion" with further argumentation, the fact that Paul can assume this framework as operative implies, at the very least, that his readers are thought to share these cultural values and assumptions. Paul is thus advancing on the basis of what he believes to be common topics to the goal of his deliberative argumentative formulation.[11]

Before moving to the elaboration of Paul's essential premise, it is worth turning first to the end of the textual unit, where he returns to the practical issue at stake. In v. 13 he addresses his audience directly with an appeal to their own sound judgement: "judge for yourselves: is it proper for a woman to pray to God uncovered?" This appeal to what is "proper" is very much in line with Aristotle's principle of suitability (τὸ πρέπον), which denotes particular actions and attributes that "naturally" apply to

---

10. As Gielen points out, Paul aims at "die Gleichsetzung einer (Männern vorbehaltenen) Kurzharfrisur von Frauen mit der entehrenden Totalentfernung der Haare (Glatze) durch eine Kahlrasur" ("Beten," 232 n. 37). Max Küchler provides examples from contemporary literature that show that being shaved was considered both a mutilation and indecent (*Schweigen, Schmuck und Schleier: Drei neutestamentliche Vorschriften zur Verdrängung der Frauen auf dem Hintergrund einer frauenfeindlichen Exegese des Alten Testaments im antiken Judentum* [NTOA 1; Göttingen: Vandenhoeck & Ruprecht, 1986], 79–82).

11. The use of *konoi topoi* is in line with standard ancient rhetorical procedure, as expressed, e.g., in Hermogenes' *Progymnasmata*: the *topos* is an "amplification of something that is agreed, as though demonstrations had already occurred; for we are no longer inquiring, (for example), whether this person is a temple robber or a war hero but we amplify the fact as proved" (11–12; cf. Theon, *Progymnasmata* 106; Cicero, *De oratore* 3.27.106; Quintilian 2.4.22; translation of Hermogenes is taken from George A. Kennedy, trans. and ed., *Progymnasmata: Greek Texts of Prose Composition and Rhetoric* [SBLWGRW 10; Atlanta: Society of Biblical Literature, 2003]). See further Todd Penner, *In Praise of Christian Origins: Stephen and the Hellenists in Lukan Apologetic Historiography* (ESEC 10; New York: T&T Clark International, 2004), 196–208.

specific individuals depending on their social/cultural standing.[12] We thus observe Paul engaged in an explicit form of cultural discursive practice. In this particular case he seems more specifically focused on establishing the boundaries of gender identity and activity within the Corinthian community's ritualistic context.[13]

The next verses further support this particular focus. In vv. 14–15, Paul introduces a new argument, which to modern ears hardly sounds convincing: "Does not nature itself teach you that if a man wears long hair, it is degrading to him, but if a woman has long hair, it is her glory? For hair is given her for a wrapper." Suggesting that a clear distinction is required in the appearance of men and women, he repeats now in vv. 14–15 for long hair what he already established in vv. 4–5 with respect to covering the head: that which is degrading (ἀτιμία) for a man is a woman's glory (δόξα).[14] It is remarkable that only here, at the very end of his argument, a word for hair (κόμη; cf. κομάω) and a term denoting a specific type of headcovering (περιβόλαιον) occur, for in the previous verses Paul referred to the act of covering or uncovering the head without specifying how it was to be done.[15]

---

12. Aristotle states that "he that entertains suitably and as reason directs is magnificent, for the fitting is the suitable.... But it must be fitting in each particular, that is, suitability to the agent and to the recipient and to the occasion—for example, what is fitting at the wedding of a servant is not what is fitting at that of a favorite; and it is fitting for the agent himself, if it is of an amount or quality suitable to him" (*Eudemian Ethics* 3.6.4; unless otherwise noted, translations from ancient writers are taken from the Loeb Classical Library).

13. Jorunn Økland, "Women in Their Place: Paul and the Corinthian Discourses of Gender and Sanctuary Space" (Ph.D. diss.; University of Oslo, 2000; now published as JSNTSup 269; New York: T&T Clark International, 2004), 273–95, establishes a strong case for viewing 1 Cor 11:2–16 as applying to ritualistic hierarchy rather than reflecting anything specific about the Pauline view on the relationship between men and women in general. However, several tensions do arise when this passage is situated in the broader Pauline context. For instance, there is clearly some slippage between ritualistic and nonritualistic contexts—as the two evidently intersect with one another in a variety of ways (not least in that it is usually understood that these are *house* churches in which worship is being conducted).

14. Similar statements can be found in Plutarch and Pseudo-Phocylides: Plutarch, *Moralia*, 267B: τοῖς μὲν τὸ κείρεσθαι, ταῖς δὲ τὸ κομᾶν σύνηθές ἐστιν ("it is usual for men to have their hair cut and for women to let it grow"; trans. ours); and Pseudo-Phocylides, Sentences 212: ἄρσεσιν οὐκ ἐπέοικε κομᾶν ("long hair is not fit for men"; trans. ours). See further Pieter W. van der Horst, *The Sentences of Pseudo-Phocylides with Introduction and Commentary* (SVTP 4; Leiden: Brill, 1978), 249.

15. Some scholars have argued that ἐξουσία in 11:10 refers to a type of head covering. See most recently George J. Brooke, "Between Qumran and Corinth: Embroidered Allusions to Women's Authority," in *The Dead Sea Scrolls as Background to Postbiblical Judaism and Early Christianity: Papers from an International Conference at St. Andrews in 2001* (ed. J. R. Davila; STDJ 46; Leiden: Brill, 2003), 157–76, who compares this Pauline reference with 4Q270, suggesting

If in vv. 4–6 as well as in vv. 13–15 the analogy with hair is used to settle the issue about covering the head, the argumentation shows that Paul considers hair to be a highly gendered matter: Men and women are supposed to wear their hair differently. Indeed, being uncovered is as shameful for a woman as cutting or shaving her hair—long hair is her glory. Yet, as we will demonstrate below, there is a lot more at stake for Paul in this argument than simply a matter of how women and men should wear their hair or posture themselves in prayer, because such issues are in many respects part of Paul's larger concern to establish and promote a particular ethos of Christian identity in 1 Corinthians, which, as we argue, is a gendered/boundaried phenomenon for Paul. For the moment, however, it is significant to note that the covering of the head is Paul's immediate argumentative aim in this passage—an argument from shame is used in service of promoting proper male and female comportment in worship.[16]

PAUL'S ONTOLOGICAL MOVE

The arguments in favor of the practice that Paul endorses receive an ontological foundation (11:7–12) based on Gen 1 and 2. Here he argues that the difference between man and woman finds its origin, quite literally, in creation and thus in God.[17] To support his case in favor of women covering their heads, Paul goes on to use a second ontological argument in v. 14, where he introduces his reference to long hair with an appeal to "nature" (φύσις): "does not nature itself teach you.... ?" A similar use of nature personified as "teacher" does not occur elsewhere in Paul's letters, but two other references to φύσις are informative because they also relate to the issue of gender: Rom 1:26–27 and Rom 2:27.

In Rom 1:26–27 Paul argues thus: "For this reason God gave [Gentiles] up to degrading passions (πάθη ἀτιμίας). Their women exchanged natural intercourse for unnatural (τὴν φυσικὴν χρῆσιν εἰς τὴν παρὰ φύσιν), and in the same way also the men, giving up natural intercourse (τὴν

---

that Paul here has in mind an "embroidered" cloth similar to the referent of the Hebrew *rwqmh* (172–75).

16. For a more detailed assessment of the gendered nature of this passage and its relationship to community comportment, as well as to Paul's own projected identity, see Todd Penner and Caroline Vander Stichele, "Unveiling Paul: Gendering Ēthos in 1 Corinthians 11:2–16," in *Rhetoric, Ethic, and Moral Persuasion in Biblical Discourse* (ed. T. H. Olbricht and A. Eriksson; New York: T&T Clark International, 2005).

17. Økland regards Paul's use of the Genesis creation account to be selective and (given the context) rather unique ("Women in Their Place," 280–85), while Belleville seems to consider it perfectly appropriate for this argument ("Κεφαλή and the Thorny Issue," 223–25).

φυσικὴν χρῆσιν) with women, were consumed with passion for one another." As in 1 Cor 11:14, in this instance Paul labels as "dishonorable" (ἀτιμία) the blurring of that which is deemed to be "natural": long hair on men in 1 Corinthians and sexual relations that are considered inappropriate in Romans. Bernadette Brooten notes that such terminology also occurs in Philo of Alexandria, who condemns same-sex love as "contrary to nature" (παρὰ φύσιν).[18] That Paul explicitly uses the expression παρὰ φύσιν with respect to female homoeroticism may therefore not be accidental. As Brooten observes: "The most common motif in the condemnation of female homoeroticism in the Roman world is that the woman has become masculine, which in cultural terms means that she has tried to go beyond the passive role accorded to her by nature and rise to the social level of a man."[19] Although in both cases of same-sex love the

---

18. Our focus at this juncture is on Paul's argument with respect to his appeal to nature. It should be noted, however, that while interpreters frequently take παρὰ φύσιν in Rom 1:26 to refer to the act of same-sex sexual interaction, a variety of scholars have recently argued that the use of "unnatural" in this context rather refers to immoderate or excessive desire— i.e., controlled by the passions (see esp. Dale B. Martin, "Heterosexism and the Interpretation of Romans 1:1–32," *BibInt* 3 [1995]: 332–55; and David E. Fredrickson, "Natural and Unnatural Use in Romans 1:24–27: Paul and the Philosophic Critique of Eros," in *Homosexuality, Science, and the "Plain Sense" of Scripture* [ed. D. L. Balch; Grand Rapids: Eerdmans, 2000], esp. 199–207). Given this shift, it is evident that modern assumptions about what is "natural" and "unnatural" do not necessarily cohere with ancient perceptions (cf. Rebecca Fleming, *Medicine and the Making of Roman Women: Gender, Nature, and Authority from Celsus to Galen* [New York: Oxford University Press, 2000], 16–17, who affirms that in essence the appeal to "nature" means an appeal to "constancy" or "giveness," but the specific content of that appeal is highly relative, even in a given historical epoch).

19. Bernadette Brooten, "Paul and the Law: How Complete was the Departure?" *Princeton Seminary Bulletin*, Suppl. 1 (1990): 84; and idem, *Love between Women: Early Christian Responses to Female Homoeroticism* (Chicago: University of Chicago Press, 1996), 235–37. The portrayal of Sappho in Ovid is instructive in this respect, as he gives her an overt male identity, perhaps as a means to rehabilitate her from the negative associations with overt female homoeroticism (cf. Pamela Gorden, "The Lover's Voice in *Heroides* 15: Or, Why Is Sappho a Man?" in *Roman Sexualities*, [ed. J. P. Hallett and M. B. Skinner; Princeton: Princeton University Press, 1997], esp. 280–86). Stephen Moore provides a lengthy list of ancient writers who regarded sexual relations between women as "unnatural" (*God's Beauty Parlor and Other Queer Spaces in and around the Bible* [Contraversions; Stanford: Stanford University Press, 2001], 143–44). Again, however, it should be stressed that "unnatural" in this context may refer to inordinate sexual desire (cf. n. 18 above). Given that one standard ancient *topos* with respect to women (from the perspective of the elite male literary gaze) was their uncontrollable sexual urge and their perceived submission to physicality, it was quite "natural" for these writers to depict female homoeroticism in negative terms and as a deviation from the masculine norm (cf. Ellen Greene, *The Erotics of Domination: Male Desire and the Mistress in Latin Love Poetry* [Baltimore: John Hopkins University Press, 1998], 59; and esp. Sandra R. Joshel, "Female Desire and the Discourse of Empire: Tacitus's Messalina," in Hallett and Skinner, *Roman Sexualities*, esp. 230–35; as well as Judith P. Hallett, "Female Homoeroticism

boundaries between male and female behavior are crossed, female conduct may have been (more) unacceptable because it was more threatening for the culturally established male norm.[20] Similarly, Moore remarks that "in principle, the thought of a woman gaining status was more worrying for elite males than the thought of a man losing status."[21]

A further element of significance in this passage for our assesment of 1 Cor 11:2–16 is the fundamental concern they share: their respective contexts relate to the appropriate worship of God. The rejection of the worship of the "Creator" (Rom 1:25) persists as a thread throughout Paul's slanderous (today libelous) assessment of Gentile behavior. The relationship between homoeroticism and idolatry may therefore not be accidental in this case.[22] In both instances of this theme in 1 Corinthians and Romans, the underlying idea is that a divinely instituted hierarchy was not respected. In the case of the perceived idolatry articulated in Romans, the issue is that the creature rather than the Creator is worshipped, while, in the case of the alleged "sexual perversion," the hierarchy between men and women is thought to be overturned. In this analogy the presumed superiority of God and that of the male correspond to each other.[23] Essentially the same hierarchy between God and

---

and the Denial of Roman Reality in Latin Literature," in Hallett and Skinner, *Roman Sexualities*, 255–73, who notes the Roman association [and dismissal as a result] of this practice with foreign, particularly Greek, influence). On the matter of passivity versus activity and the societal-gendered role of women in Rom 1, see esp. Roy Bowen Ward, "Why Unnatural? The Tradition behind Romans 1:26–27," *HTR* 90 (1997): 263–84; Diana Swancutt, "Sexy Stoics and the Rereading of Romans 1.18–2.16," in *A Feminist Companion to Paul* (ed. A.-J. Levine, with M. Blickenstaff; FCNTECW 6; New York: Continuum, 2004), 53–59; and idem, "'The Disease of Effemination': The Charge of Effeminacy and the Verdict of God (Romans 1:18–2:16)," in *New Testament Masculinities* (ed. S. D. Moore and J. Capel Anderson; SemeiaSt 45; Atlanta: Society of Biblical Literature, 2003), 197–205.

20. Since the "norm" was the establishment of male identity as the "impenetrable penetrator," both penetrating women, as well as passive men, provided a clear threat to this cultural indicator of masculinity. See esp. Jonathan Walters, "Invading the Roman Body: Manliness and Impenetrability in Roman Thought," in Hallett and Skinner, *Roman Sexualities*, 29–43; and Holt N. Parker, "The Teratogenic Grid," in Hallett and Skinner, *Roman Sexualities*, 47–65.

21. Moore, *God's Beauty Parlor*, 150.

22. Cf. Jennifer Wright Knust, "Paul and the Politics of Virtue and Vice," in *Paul and the Roman Imperial Order* (ed. R. A. Horsley; Harrisburg, Pa.: Trinity Press International, 2004), esp. 158, 162–64, 169–72; Swancutt, "Sexy Stoics," 60–63; and idem, "The Disease of Effemination," 205–7.

23. Catherine Edwards has made a similar argument in terms of the relationship of the social order to the authority of the emperor ("Unspeakable Professions: Public Performance and Prostitution in Ancient Rome," in Hallett and Skinner, *Roman Sexualities*, 89–90). For the view that establishment of authority is the critical element in Paul's rhetoric in 1 Corinthians, see Burke, "Paul's Role as 'Father'," 108–10. Wanamaker makes an even stronger

man, with the inclusion of Christ, reoccurs more explicitly in 1 Cor 11:3, where the body metaphor "head" is used to establish a hierarchical order between God-Christ-man-woman.[24] It can thus be noted that a similar connection to nature and creation exists in Rom 1 and 1 Cor 11, and that in both cases the appeal is made to bolster a particular gendered order and relationship in the context of proper worship.[25]

Romans 2:27 represents the second instance in which a Pauline appeal to nature is made. Here the issue under discussion is the difference between Gentiles and Jews. The matter of gender is present too insofar as Paul refers to the presence of the foreskin as the natural condition compared with circumcision. He states: "Then those who are physically uncircumcised (lit. uncircumcision by nature: ἡ ἐκ φύσεως ἀκροβυστία) but keep the law will condemn you who have the written code and circumcision but break the law." Although gender is not the explicit focus in this instance, Paul does describe a certain condition of the male body as "natural." The reference to nature in conjunction with physical characteristics related to gender represents the link between this text and 1 Cor 11:14. But the relevance of this passage for our discussion goes further than that, as Paul goes on to explain the difference between circumcision and uncircumcision with another binary opposition: between "physical circumcision" (v. 28: ἐν σαρκὶ περιτομή) and "circumcision of the heart" (v. 29: περιτομὴ καρδίας). This latter notion is further qualified as "spiritual not literal."

In his book *A Radical Jew*, Daniel Boyarin has stressed the importance of this distinction between spiritual and literal meanings for understanding Paul's hermeneutics of the body. For Paul, the body represents the literal over against the spiritual, the particular over against the universal. Since the universal subject in Paul's letters is a Christian

---

connection in this respect, as he argues that, as "founder," Paul is also "creator" of the Corinthian community, thus drawing convincing if implicit parallels between God as Creator and Paul as the same ("Rhetoric of Power," 124).

24. Scholars have construed the meaning of "head" (κεφαλή) variously. The most prominent metaphorical meanings advanced are as follows: 1) "chief" or "ruler"; 2) "source" (so Heinrich Schlier, "κεφαλή," *TDNT* 3:673–81; Stephen Bedale, "The Meaning of *kephalē* in the Pauline Epistles," *JTS* 5 [1954]: 211–15; and Belleville, "Κεφαλή and the Thorny Issue," 227–30); 3) "preeminence" (thus Richard S. Cervin, "Does *kephalē* Mean 'Source' or 'Authority Over' in Greek Literature? A Rebuttal," *TJ* NS 10 [1989]: 85–112; and Gundry-Volf, "Gender and Creation," 158–59). It seems difficult, however, to avoid a hierarchical connotation altogether (cf. Økland, "Women in Their Place," 294–95). For a more in-depth discussion, see Vander Stichele, *Authenticiteit en integriteit*, 281–336.

25. A further noteworthy point of agreement is the use of Gen 1:26–27, which is cited explicitly in 1 Cor 11 and seems to be alluded to implicitly in Rom 1 (cf. Swancutt, "Sexy Stoics," 61 n. 97).

male, Jews and women embody particularity, or, as Boyarin states: "The quintessentially 'different' people for Paul were Jews and women."[26] In spiritualizing circumcision in Romans, Paul has, in a way, reasoned it out of existence. As a result, it also loses its *raison d'être* and as such it has become irrelevant "in Christ," or, as Paul states in Gal 6:15: "neither circumcision nor uncircumcision is anything, but a new creation is everything." If, however, marks of ethnicity are thus erased in Christ, so also is gender (in a sense). "Femaleness" may lose its meaning when women are incorporated into the spiritual body of Christ, but gender does not therefore cease to exist "in the flesh," nor, for that matter, does ethics as a form of body politics.[27]

It is precisely this distinction that makes it possible for Paul to affirm both universality in the spiritual realm and difference when it comes to ethics. Both tendencies are present in 1 Cor 11 as well. Women can indeed pray and prophesy just as men do, but such "egalitarianism" (if that indeed is an appropriate term for what is manifested therein) has its limits. Freedom in the spirit does not imply freedom from the body. It does not erase difference on the level of the physical, especially not with respect to the female body. Paul's arguments thus reveal his essential interest to keep the boundaries between male and female in place.[28] As Mary Douglas states, "bodily control is an expression of social control,"[29] and such control is by far the interest of upper-class males in the ancient world.[30] In this light, we should note that even when women become incorporated within the "spiritual body," this does not yet imply that this body is perceived as a nongendered zone. In fact, the "spiritual body" in Paul is defined in predominantly masculine terms.[31] The "natural" world thus infuses the spiritual as well, and

---

26. Daniel Boyarin, *A Radical Jew: Paul and the Politics of Identity* (Berkeley and Los Angeles: University of California Press, 1994), 17.

27. See further Daniel Boyarin, "Paul and the Genealogy of Gender," in Levine, *Feminist Companion to Paul*, 17–23.

28. Cf. Økland, "Women in Their Place," 290–95, who sees the presence of the "veil" as possessing a "boundary"-defining function for Paul.

29. Mary Douglas, *Natural Symbols: Explorations in Cosmology* (New York: Pantheon, 1982), 79; quoted in Gail Paterson Corrington, "The 'Headless Woman': Paul and the Language of the Body in 1 Cor 11:2–16," *PRSt* 18 (1991): 224.

30. Cf. David G. Horrell, "The Development of Theological Ideology in Pauline Christianity," in *Modeling Early Christianity: Social-Scientific Studies of the New Testament in Its Context* (ed. P. Esler; New York: Routledge, 1995), 235–36, who has argued, with respect to the Pauline corpus, that one can perceive a clear development in the social legitimation of the interests of the male "heads of households."

31. Moore, *God's Beauty Parlor*, 170–71.

consequently one can only speak of a relative eradication of gender identity in this realm.[32]

If in Rom 1 and 1 Cor 11 Paul uses "nature" as the sure ground for how things ought to proceed in worshipping the Creator, in Rom 2 he turns the tables on his use of what is "natural." As we may presume, a circumcised male himself, Paul not only does *not* want to normativize the "natural" state of the male member, but, even more so, he also seeks to spiritualize "deformity" of the same.[33] This fluctuation could well be viewed as a deliberate negotiation on Paul's part, and evidences the flexibility that such ontological arguments have in Paul's thinking, but with the result, we have argued, that masculine identity is affirmed over against the female "other" in whatever (argumentative) focus Paul has in the moment.[34] Thus, whether the natural order is affirmed or relativized, masculinity as the defining norm stands firm. This position, finally, leaves one with a different framework for understanding 1 Cor 11, especially in

---

32. This case is particularly true with respect to women, since there existed a strong tradition in ancient Christianity that women in fact achieved their spiritual status by "becoming male." Elizabeth Castelli, for instance, observes that in the case of Perpetua her "spiritual progress is marked by the social movement away from conventional female roles and by the physical movement from a female to a male body; these processes of transformation signify her increasingly holy status" ("'I Will Make Mary Male': Pieties of the Body and Gender Transformation of Christian Women in Late Antiquity," in *Body Guards: The Cultural Politics of Gender Ambiguity* [ed. J. Epstein and K. Straub; New York: Routledge, 1991], 35). For a similar phenomenon with respect to Aseneth (and in reference to her lack of need for veiling as a result), see Ross Shepard Kraemer, *When Aseneth Met Joseph: A Late Antique Tale of the Biblical Patriarch and His Egyptian Wife, Reconsidered* (New York: Oxford University Press, 1998), 196–98. See also Marvin Meyer, "Making Mary Male: The Categories 'Male' and 'Female' in the Gospel of Thomas," in *Secret Gospel: Essays on Thomas and the Secret Gospel of Mark* (New York: Continuum, 2003), 76–95, esp. pp. 84–92, where the Philonic and broader Greco-Roman background of this movement of female to male identity is explored (cf. Boyarin, "Paul and the Genealogy," 24–29; 36–39; and Wayne A. Meeks, "The Image of the Androgyne: Some Uses of a Symbol in Earliest Christianity," *HR* 13 [1974]: 165–208).

33. We have not traced out the larger implications of this Pauline rhetoric for his discursive construction of the relationship between Jew and Gentile, but suffice it to say that the "old" boundaries are not simply eradicated in Paul's thought (for an excellent discussion of this point, see most recently Denise Kimber Buell and Caroline Johnson Hodge, "The Politics of Interpretation: The Rhetoric of Race and Ethnicity in Paul," *JBL* 123 [2004]: 235–51).

34. A similar situation can be observed in Paul's use of κόσμος and κτίσις in Romans and 1 Corinthians. As Edward Adams has noted, in the former Paul has a rather positive assessment of the world and creation ("God's good and well-ordered creation, destined to be redeemed"), whereas in the latter it is much more negative ("alienated from God and doomed to perish"). Adams, however, fails to accent the rhetorical use of these terms, and focuses instead on the differing "theological frameworks" and "situational contexts" of the respective concepts (*Constructing the World: A Study in Paul's Cosmological Language* [Edinburgh: T&T Clark, 2000], 242–43).

terms of the overarching cultural framework that guides Paul's argument and the precise nature of the persuasive aim of this text.

THE NATURE OF HAIR IN GRECO-ROMAN MORAL PHILOSOPHERS

Paul's position on hair in 1 Cor 11 resonates with broader cultural patterns of the Greco-Roman world, but a hard and fast rule on covering the female head in public is difficult to establish—and may in fact not exist in the first place,[35] especially since "hair" is a discursive subject that takes on different shape and meaning depending on the argument it is used to promote. Much of this debate depends on how one assesses the predominantly male sources, how one evaluates literary versus archaeological remains, and which geographic and cultural regions one examines for the evidence.[36] For instance, in the elite Roman literary context, female hair is frequently eroticized. Indeed, a woman's beauty is often wrapped up with the outward appearance of her hair (cf. Ovid, *Amores* 1.14; *Ars amatoria* 3.136; Apuleius, *Metamorphoses* 2.8–9). Ovid suggests that, while some aspects of female "grooming" ought to take place behind closed doors, the actual grooming of the hair should be done before male lovers (*Ars amatoria* 3.235). Here the brushing of the hair is something of a performance, which generates and invigorates desire. Of course, the reverse is also true: "Let her who has poor hair set a guard at her door, or always be tired in the temple of the Good Goddess. My arrival was suddenly announced to a woman once; in confusion she put her hair on all awry. Let my foes endure a cause of shame so fearful! Upon Parthian women let that dishonour fall! Ugly is a bull without horns; ugly is a field without grass, a plant without leaves, or a head without hair" (3.240). In this context, the appearance of feminine beauty is intricately bound up with the presentation of a woman's hair; a true reflection of her "glory."[37] By

---

35. Cf. Robert M. Grant, *Paul in the Roman World: The Conflict at Corinth* (Louisville: Westminster John Knox, 2001), 38.

36. A Roman colony like Corinth could have any number of diverse cultural backgrounds represented. On the cultural complexity and multivalence of a thoroughly Hellenized Roman city such as Corinth, see Luca Graverini, "Corinth, Rome, and Africa: A Cultural Background for the Tale of the Ass," in *Space in the Ancient Novel* (ed. M. Paschalis and S. A. Frangoulidis; Ancient Narrative Supplementum 1; Groningen: Barkhuis, 2002), 60–65; but cf. Bruce W. Winter, "The Achaean Federal Imperial Cult II: The Corinthian Church," *TynBul* 46 (1995): 169–78; and idem, *Roman Wives*, who argues that a Roman legal context must be read as the primary cultural and legal lens for interpreters.

37. But this image could just as readily, in another context, be used to represent the danger women pose to men, as in the hair of Medusa; cf. Tina Pippin, "Wisdom's Deviant Ways," in *On the Cutting Edge: The Study of Women in Biblical Worlds; Essays in Honor of Elisabeth*

contrast, men are to "take no pleasure in curling [their] hair with the iron, or in scraping [their] legs with biting pumicestone" (1.505). Ovid even states that "an uncared-for beauty is becoming to men." On the other hand, there is some basic degree of grooming required, for Ovid believes that men should not let their "stubborn locks be spoilt by bad cutting; let hair and beard be dressed by a practised hand" (1.515). Thus, men's hair is also a reflection of their gendered role, and the display of their hair ought to reflect something fitting and proper to them as well.[38]

Given this broader framework, deviations from a perceived norm are particularly significant. In Acts 18:18, for instance, Paul cuts his hair (presumably in a way that is different from the norm) to solemnize a vow.[39] This feature is further reflected in mourning rituals. Women, such as the old mother and her foreign attendants in Euripides' *The Suppliants* (95), shave their head when grieving for their male dead (cf. *Phoenissae* 1485). In the *Iliad*, Hector's mother both throws off her veil and tears her hair (22.405), while his wife throws off her veil (22.470). In a different vein, Thecla's desire for transformation into Christian/male identity in the *Acts of Paul and Thecla* is denoted by her wish to cut her hair short (25) and by the eventual altering of her "female" cloak into a "male" garment (40).[40] However, even while Paul's cutting of his hair (noted above) in some sense signals his masculine comportment in the text from a particular cultural angle, when Hercules loses his hair it has, to the contrary, a disempowering and effeminizing effect.[41] In short, while it may be difficult to

---

Schüssler Fiorenza (ed. J. Schaberg, A. Bach, and E. Fuchs; New York: Continuum, 2003), 146–47. Intriguing in this context is also Euripides' contrasting of Clytemnestra (with long, beautiful hair) and Electra (with short, cropped hair); see further Richard Hawley, "The Dynamics of Beauty in Classical Greece," in *Changing Bodies, Changing Meanings: Studies on the Human Body in Antiquity* (ed. D. Montserrat; New York: Routledge, 1998), 48–49.

38. See the substantive assessment of the use of hair in ancient literature by Molly Myerowitz Levine, "The Gendered Grammar of Ancient Mediterranean Hair," in *Off with Her Head: The Denial of Women's Identity in Myth, Religion, and Culture* (ed. W. Eilberg-Schwartz and W. Doniger; Berkeley and Los Angeles: University of California Press, 1995), 76–130.

39. See the discussion by Rick Strelan, *Strange Acts: Studies in the Cultural World of the Acts of the Apostles* (BZNW 126; Berlin: de Gruyter, 2004), 222–30. The deviation from the normal pattern may designate this action as a sacred duty. Physical transformations/departures were often seen as signs of "cardinal moments"; cf. Angus Bowie, "*Exuvias Effigiemque*: Dido, Aeneas and the Body as Sign," in Montserrat, *Changing Bodies*, 60–61.

40. See further Willi Braun, "Physiotherapy of Femininity in the *Acts of Thecla*," in *Text and Artifact in the Religions of Mediterranean Antiquity: Essays in Honour of Peter Richardson* (ed. S. G. Wilson and M. Desjardins; SCJ 9; Waterloo, Ont: Wilfrid Laurier University Press, 2000), 209–30.

41. Cf. Nicole Loraux, "Herakles: The Super Male and the Feminine," in *Before Sexuality: The Construction of Erotic Experience in the Ancient World* (ed. D. M. Halperin, J. J. Winkler, and F. I. Zeitlin; Princeton: Princeton University Press, 1990), 24.

establish a firm representation of specific "rules" for men and women, in the course of promoting a particular argument hair is frequently used in a gendered manner for the purposes of differentiation of one sort or another (and context is determinative in this respect). In the end, function seems to hold primacy over specific content as such.[42]

At this juncture it is helpful to explore this point further by examining some specific parallels in other ancient writers that bear closely on Paul's argumentation in 1 Cor 11. The most interesting is a series of comments in Epictetus's *Discourses,* which correspond closely with the way in which Paul refers to nature in relationship to hair in 1 Cor 11. The first relates to the discussion of providence:

> Come, let us leave the chief works of nature (τὰ ἔργα τῆς φύσεως), and consider merely what she does in passing. Can anything be more useless than the hairs on a chin? Well, what then? Has not nature used even these in the most suitable (πρεπόντως) way possible? Has she not by these means distinguished between the male and the female? ... Wherefore, we ought to preserve the signs which God has given; we ought not to throw them away; we ought not, so far as in us lies, to confuse the sexes which have been distinguished in this fashion. (1.16.9–12, 14)

Several striking parallels can be noted between this passage and the Pauline texts under discussion. First, as in 1 Cor 11:14, nature is also personified. "She" distinguishes between male and female, and hairs on the chin are her "sign" (σύμβολον) of sexual difference. This differentiation is not just presented as a fact but also as an indicator of specific human behavior. Second, as is the case with Paul in Rom 1, Epictetus is concerned with the proper recognition of God: "by Zeus and the gods, one single gift of nature would suffice to make a man who is reverent and grateful perceive the providence of God" (1.16.7). He then goes on to suggest that anyone not recognizing God's providence, even in the smaller workings of nature, is truly "stupid" and "shameless" (1.16.8). The reference to

---

42. Other divergent examples include the portrayal of young Roman boys—for religious and sexual purposes—as having the "hair of women" (John Pollini, "Slave-Boys for Sexual and Religious Services: Images of Pleasure and Devotion," in *Flavian Rome: Culture, Image, Text* [ed. A. J. Boyle and W. J. Dominik; Leiden: Brill, 2003], 149–66), as well as the essential perceived difference between long hair on a "lover" and long hair on a "bandit" (Keith Hopwood, "'All That May Become a Man': The Bandit in the Ancient Novel," in *When Men Were Men: Masculinity, Power, and Identity in Classical Antiquity* [ed. L. Foxhall and J. Salmon; New York: Routledge, 1998], 201–2; cf. Belleville, "Κεφαλή and the Thorny Issue," 217, esp. n. 10, who, citing Dio Chrysostom 35.11–12, notes that long hair on men became culturally acceptable in general only later in the second century and earlier was deemed more narrowly appropriate depending on the circumstance/context).

"shamelessness" (ἀναισχυντία) in this context represents another element of correspondence with 1 Cor 11:4–6 (cf. Rom 1:27), where Paul uses similar terminology to deprecate the practices he opposes.

Further, Epictetus concludes this discourse with reference to singing hymns to this "great" God (1.16.16), which, for him, is also a sign of human rationality: "sing the greatest and divinest hymn, [for the reason that] God has given us the faculty to comprehend these things and to follow the path of reason" (1.16.18). The opposite idea is present in Rom 1, where, according to Paul, God in fact gives the Gentiles over to a debased mind manifested in "vile" behaviors (1:28). Overall, then, in this first parallel the suggested order in nature is itself presented as a "witness" to an "ordered" (gendered?) deity, and honoring this hierarchy of nature in principle reflects the recognition (and worship) of this Creator. Those "irrational" entities who do not acknowledge the ordered universe are more than just "stupid"—they are also "shameless." This feature is one of the critical lynchpins present in Rom 1 and Epictetus (but probably also implied in 1 Cor 11): the first step beyond the "natural" order of the world initiates chaos and moral depravity.

That human interference should not blur the difference between the sexes becomes even clearer in this second passage from Epictetus, where he is concerned with the presence or absence of hair on the body:

> Woman is born smooth and dainty by nature, and if she is very hairy, she is a prodigy, and is exhibited at Rome among the prodigies. But for a man not to be hairy is the same thing, and if by nature he has no hair he is a prodigy, but if he cuts it out and plucks it out of himself, what shall we make of him? ... Man, what reason have you to complain against your nature? ... Make a clean sweep of the whole matter; eradicate your—what shall I call it?—the cause of your hairiness; make yourself a woman all over, so as not to deceive us, half-man and half-woman.... Shall we make a man like you a citizen of Corinth, and perchance a warden of the city, or a superintendent of ephebi, or general, or superintendent of the games? Well, and when you have married are you going to pluck out your hairs? For whom and to what end? And when you have begotten boys, are you going to introduce them into the body of citizens as plucked creatures too? A fine citizen and senator and orator! (3.1.27–35)

In this passage Epictetus objects to the removal of hair that is present by nature and that is, according to him, a characteristic of sexual difference. By removing hair men obscure the difference between the sexes. He goes even further to suggest that such an action reveals the desire to be a woman. This reference is illuminating because it delves into several interrelated aspects of gender in the ancient world. Here Epictetus challenges a male who clearly appears and presents himself ("cuts" and "plucks" out his hair) as effeminate.[43] The contrast between male and female body types demonstrates both the firm boundaries that Epictetus favors and, in particular, his perception that "nature" witnesses to the "type" each sex should embody. The appeal to nature underscores this emphasis on what the true male will look and act like. It is not surprising, then, that Epictetus is quick to draw associations between the effeminate male and his role in civic life, the primary manifestation of male identity in the ancient world. In an intriguing reference to Corinth, Epictetus questions the suitability of such a "plucked" male for political service. Leadership and pedagogical positions require the demonstration of manly qualities, of which hair is here perceived to be a visible sign.[44] In other words, the (plucked) "male" of this passage ultimately will reproduce citizens in his own image, which, from Epictetus's standpoint, would damage the reputation of the *polis*. Hair, or lack thereof, is not only presented as an outward symbol of the inner character (i.e., manliness) of the adult male but is also taken, as a consequence, to be a sign of his potential contribution to or impotence within the body politic.

---

43. In a similar way, Martial describes Cotilus as a "pretty fellow" (*bellus homo*), who "curls his hair and arranges it carefully, always smells of balsam or cinnamon, hums tunes from the Nile ... moves his plucked arms with changing measures, lounges all day among ladies' chairs and is ever a murmuring ... knows who's in love with whom, scurries from dinner party to dinner party" (3.63; see further Anthony Corbeill, "Dining Deviants in Roman Political Invective," in Hallett and Skinner, *Roman Sexualities*, 111–12, 118–23). See also Lucian, who, in his biting satire *Alexander the False Prophet*, lambastes Alexander for living off old doting women who seek attention (6), noting that, while Alexander may appear in the guise of a "real man" (i.e., hairy; 3), in reality—underneath it all—he is bald (59; cf. his *Professor of Public Speaking* 10, where the hairy Platonic philosopher is contrasted with those who have coiffed their own hair [11–15]). In these various instances hair forms a critical component of masculine identity and demonstrates who is suitable for the public forum and who is not. For further discussion of the evidence for hairstyles of men and women, see Cynthia L. Thompson, "Hairstyles, Head-Covering, and St. Paul: Portraits from Roman Corinth," *BA* 51 (1988): 99–115; David W. J. Gill, "The Importance of Roman Portraiture for Head-Coverings in 1 Corinthians 11:2–16," *TynBul* 41 (1990): 245–60; and Belleville, "Κεφαλή and the Thorny Issue," 215–20. On the rabbinic/Jewish evidence (and its problems), see Ilan, *Jewish Women*, 129–32.

44. The cultural reasoning that supports this connection rests, on one level at least, in Aristotelian science, wherein hairiness was understood to be grounded in the very essence of male identity: the production of sperm (which Epictetus seems to acknowledge in the above citation, since he suggests eradicating the "source" [= male genitals] of hairiness). Women were thought to have sperm as well, so this accounted for the presence of their hair, although they neither had as much nor was it agitated so as to spread throughout their bodies. In this framework, the greater hairiness of males was seen as a sign of their superiority over females (Lesley Ann Dean-Jones, *Women's Bodies in Classical Greek Science* [Oxford: Clarendon, 1994], 83–85).

Although Epictetus does not refer in these passages to hair growing on the head as Paul does, their argumentation has much in common. Nature indicates what type of human behavior is appropriate. Both appeal to nature when speaking about hair and both consider hair to be an important feature of sexual difference. According to Epictetus, the presence of hair on man and its absence on woman is "natural," while, for Paul, long hair is natural on a woman, but not on a man. The similarity is precisely that the situations of men and women are presented as each others' opposite. But there is one further element that becomes particularly evident: in the same way that proper ("natural") comportment of the body in the first example from Epictetus suggests something about one's relationship to God, in the second case suitable comportment says something about the body politic, particularly the role that the individual in question plays in the civic life of the city. A similar concern for gender distinction and identity in relation to both the divine and human order is also present in Rom 1 and 1 Cor 11. Not surprisingly, then, for both Paul and Epictetus the *vir bonus* is the truest reflection of the divine.

The appeal of Paul and Epictetus to nature should be understood against the background of popular Greek ideas (not excluding the elaboration of these notions in philosophical frameworks such as Stoicism),[45] which are also reflected in Hellenistic Jewish writers such as Josephus and Philo. In this Hellenistic framework, φύσις appears as the antipode of νόμος, the latter of which comes about by convention. Hair readily serves as an important example in this respect, since it can be viewed as both nature (a part of the body) and as convention (the styling and preening of the hair).[46] Yet the difference between "nature" and "convention" in this

---

45. The stoic character of Paul's reference to nature in 1 Cor 11:14 has been assessed differently. See, e.g., Johannes Weiss, *Der erste Korintherbrief* (9th ed.; KEK 5; Göttingen: Vandenhoeck & Ruprecht, 1910), 276: "Diese Argumentationsweise, schon bei Plato vorgebildet ... ist echt stoisch." Hans Conzelmann is more skeptical, noting that nature is not an object of systematic reflection for Paul, but only serves here as an additional argument (*Der erste Brief an die Korinther* [12th ed.; KEK 5; Göttingen: Vandenhoeck & Ruprecht, 1981], 224). Gordon D. Fee argues that "Paul makes no theological significance of the idea as one finds it in Stoicism. For him this is not an appeal to Nature, or to 'natural law', or to 'natural endowment'; nor is Nature to be understood as pedagogic (actually 'teaching' these 'laws')" (*The First Epistle to the Corinthians* [NICNT; Grand Rapids: Eerdmans, 1987], 526–27). While in Stoic thought a close connection exists between "nature" and "god" (cf. Troels Engberg-Pedersen, *The Stoic Theory of Oikeiosis: Moral Development and Social Interaction in Early Stoic Philosophy* [Aarhus, Denmark: Aarhus University Press, 1990], 59–60), Paul considers nature to be God's creation (cf. Friedrich Lang, *Die Briefe an die Korinther* [16th ed.; NTD 7; Göttingen: Vandenhoeck & Ruprecht, 1986], 143; and Max Pohlenz, "Paulus und die Stoa," *ZNW* 42 [1949]: 77).

46. Levine, "Gendered Grammar," 88–89.

framework is less clear than may at first be evident. As classicist John Winkler points out, the contrast of φύσις and νόμος "is itself a cultural item, a habit of thought once discovered, promoted, and eventually adopted as convention."[47] We are thus dealing with a highly flexible category, which is all the more convenient for achieving the ends of persuasion.[48] Most determinative in this respect is the argumentative use made of the distinction between φύσις and νόμος.[49] In fact, as Winkler contends elsewhere, we cannot even equate "against nature" with "abnormal" or something that was in fact immoral.[50] For instance, when women acted nobly, they were, in the ancient view, acting contrary to their "own" natures—that is, they were performing like/as men.[51]

This last point finds emphasis in an example of a similar discussion of hair in Plutarch. In his *Roman Questions,* Plutarch queries the following:

> Why do sons cover their head when they escort their parents to the grave, while daughters go with uncovered heads and hair unbound? Is it because fathers should be honoured as gods by their male offspring,

---

47. John J. Winkler, "Laying Down the Law: The Oversight of Men's Sexual Behavior in Classical Athens," in Halperin, Winkler, and Zeitlin, *Before Sexuality,* 172. Not surprisingly in this light, Troels Engberg-Pedersen refers to Paul's "naïve use of 'nature' in support of traditional and social normative perceptions" with reference to Rom 1:24–27 (*Paul and the Stoics* [Edinburgh: T&T Clark, 2000], 209).

48. Depending on the specific argumentative goal or prescription of behavior, the nature of what was considered "natural" could shift drastically. For example, those moral philosophers who eschewed homoerotic sexual relationships used appeals to nature as a "proof" for their arguments (Craig A. Williams, *Roman Sexuality: Ideologies of Masculinity in Classical Antiquity* [New York: Oxford University Press, 1999], 234–44) in much the same way that Martial could employ "nature" as a "proof" for penetration of both males and females by the fully masculine male (cf. 11.22.9–10; Williams, *Roman Sexuality,* 242).

49. In Hellenistic Judaism, this particular distinction becomes more complex, as νόμος is not simply (humanly contrived) "convention" but "law" from God. In 4 Maccabees, for example, νόμος is praised and personified in much the same way as Nature is in Epictetus. Eleazar is in fact extolled as one who is "in harmony with the law" (7:7) (see Stephen D. Moore and Janice Capel Anderson, "Taking it Like a Man: Masculinity in 4 Maccabees," *JBL* 117 [1998]: 252–53).

50. John J. Winkler, *The Constraints of Desire: The Anthropology of Sex and Gender in Ancient Greece* (London: Routledge, 1999), 20–21.

51. E.g., Strabo dismisses the stories of the Amazonian women as an improbable "myth" precisely on this basis (11.5.3). Of course, since "male" is the norm, acting "against nature" can in some contexts be beneficial for those who are inferior, culturally or otherwise (some of these sentiments are based on the Aristotelian one-sex model, in which women were imperfect males measured against the "complete man"; see Guilia Sissa, "The Sexual Philosophies of Plato and Aristotle," in *A History of Women in the West; I. From Goddesses to Christian Saints* [ed. P. S. Pantel; trans. A. Goldhammer; Cambridge: Harvard University Press, 1992], 65–67; and Martin, *Corinthian Body,* 230; cf. n. 32 above).

but mourned as dead by their daughters, that custom (ὁ νόμος) has assigned to each sex its proper part and has produced a fitting result from both? Or is it that the unusual is proper in mourning, and it is more usual for women to go forth in public with their heads covered and men with their heads uncovered? So in Greece, whenever any misfortune comes, the women cut off their hair and the men let it grow, for it is usual (σύνηθές ἐστιν) for men to have their hair cut and for women to let it grow. (267 A-B)

It is remarkable that both Plutarch and Paul refer to length of hair when discussing the covering of the head. They also use similar terminology to do so.[52] They further agree that long hair and a headcovering are appropriate for women, but not for men. On other points, however, they diverge. Plutarch refers to the (apparently legitimate) reversal of this practice in a specific situation, namely, at the funeral of one's parents. Plutarch, moreover, does not refer to nature in this respect, but only to custom (νόμος) and what is usual (σύνηθες), while Paul refers to nature with respect to hair, but to "custom" (συνήθεια) with reference to the wearing of a headcovering (11:16).[53] On the one hand, it is noteworthy that the basic assumptions about hair and headcovering in Plutarch are consonant with what one finds in 1 Cor 11—there is an accepted and expected pattern. On the other hand, the fact that Plutarch allows for exceptions suggests something noteworthy about the function of the distinction in this particular passage. Plutarch tries to explain the deviant behavior of women and men in a specific situation, but does not see this as a problem per se, while, in the previous examples of Paul and Epictetus, appeal to nature affirms the difference between men and women with respect to hair, and both writers react negatively against the blurring of that distinction. They both confirm the ontological character of sex/gender distinctions for the sake of making explicit arguments about proper recognition of the divine and the suitable comportment of the individual in the body politic. Thus, these texts are clearly prescriptive in aim, while the

---

52. According to Cynthia Thompson, the similarity in language "may suggest that this discussion was somewhat conventional.... The true importance of Plutarch's passage is the underlying conviction that in hairstyle and head-covering women and men must be different. Paul, too, is anxious to maintain distinctions" ("Hairstyles, Headcoverings," 105).

53. Some scholars have suggested that συνήθεια rather relates to φιλόνεικος in v. 16a. In that case Paul would be claiming that "we" do not have such a custom of being contentious. So, e.g., Philipp Bachmann, *Der erste Brief des Paulus an die Korinther* (2d ed; KNT 7; Leipzig: Deichert, 1910), 362; and Huub van de Sandt, "1 Kor 11,2–16 als rhetorische eenheid," *Bijdragen* 49 (1988): 420. In light of the use of συνήθεια earlier in the letter, however, where it refers to the practice of idolatry (8:7), it seems more likely that Paul suggests in this instance the existence of another custom in the Corinthian community, that of uncovering the head.

passage from Plutarch, by contrast, has a descriptive function. In short, as the precise purpose of the argument shifts, so does the assessment of what is proper with respect to the physical comportment of the individual.

Thus, in line with the broader argument being developed in this essay, we suggest that the kind of gendered differentiation that relates to discussions on hair and coverings is in principle a highly contextual matter, depending much more on argumentative aim than sociocultural and historical particularities. As the parallels above demonstrate, the bottom line in this appeal to the constancy or giveness of nature is the establishment of a hierachical domain of acting and speaking, which ultimately serves to highlight the dominant values (and social position) of the authority figure in question.[54]

Paul's "Hairy" Rhetoric

Read against the backdrop of its sociocultural discursive environment and through the interpretative lens of a gender-critical analysis, the argumentation in 1 Cor 11 appears as firmly established male gendered discourse. In our estimation, the advantages of this reading are threefold. First, within the broader frame of reference established, this shift in perspective can be considered an important step in moving beyond the idea(l) of a univocal historical/philological sense of the text and in promoting, in turn, a broadening of the range of (Western) interpretive possibilities. Second, drawing on both historical-critical and feminist analysis, such a gender-critical engagement of the text opens up a more expansive forum for dialogue by focusing on the interrelationship of the discursive identities of male and female "players" created in and through Pauline argumentation. Finally, this reading furthers awareness of the embedded politics and cultural identities in this text, as well as in all interpretations (ours included).

As the argumentative force of Paul's ontological claim and his particular rhetorical strategy show, grounding gender distinctions in nature represents a powerful means to establish superiority and/or relegate others to inferiority in the competitive world of ancient (and modern) identity formations. The fate of the letter's recipients may be unknown, but, as its reception history attests, Paul's later success was established by such forms of persuasion—demonstrating not only the cultural resonance of the arguments themselves, but also the readiness of ancient readers (alongside their modern counterparts) to accept the thoroughly gendered

---

54. See further Penner and Vander Stichele, "Unveiling Paul."

rhetorical and political function of Paul's discourse. Pauline argumentation thus engenders a specifically Christian hermeneutic that embraces a sharp distinction between respective male and female comportment.[55] The focus in this case is decidedly on issues related to the gender of Paul's recipients, but frequently unnoticed is Paul's own "hairiness"—his own gendered identity on display in and through the text. Order established in his community, then, reflects not only on the cosmic authority of God, it reveals even more so Paul's own imperial identity and his corresponding cultural masculine "normalcy."

Thus, while modern scholarship is quite willing to see as operative the "power politics of the body politic in Roman Corinth,"[56] it often appears oblivious to Paul's own participation in the same. The result of such "reading with the text" is to encourage a historical universalizing and final affirmation of the text's ideology and the further marginalization of both men and women as mere textual objects. While one might not want to go as far as to suggest that this modern move is initiated solely by Paul's performance, one cannot discount the power of a hermeneutics of desire. The structural parallel between Paul's own "grounding" of his argument and similar moves made by many so-called "modern interpreters" should at the very least give one pause. Such "reading with the text" provides, finally, an "ontology" of its own—a historicizing argument "according to nature." Most problematic, perhaps, is that in this

---

55. This point is aptly demonstrated by the reception history of the Pauline corpus, wherein, more specifically, a battle is waged between so-called "hierarchical" and "egalitarian" texts and interpretations. Particular biblical texts and interpretations are prioritized over others relative to specific religious and (church-)political agendas and convictions. In this respect, the recent major study of the Pauline cultural context (J. Paul Sampley, ed., *Paul in the Greco-Roman World* [Harrisburg. Pa.: Trinity Press International, 2003]) has surprisingly marginalized discussion of 1 Cor 11 in a number of essays that would have seemed to benefit from its inclusion. For instance, while some scholars such as David L. Balch ("Paul, Families, and Households," 277) reference this text in passing as a counter-balance to Paul's acceptance of women as leaders of house churches and their ability to utter charismatic speech, O. Larry Yarbrough's essay on marriage in Paul ("Paul, Marriage, and Divorce," 426 n. 37) relegates reference to this text to a footnote, which he justifies by the "problems" associated with this and similar texts. Yet, as suggested earlier in this essay, Paul's configuration of the ritualistic context reveals broader gendered patterns that support a wider view of male and female identity in the community as a whole (cf. n. 13 above). Further, removing the text in question from the study of Pauline social practice and thought, as those scholars who view it as a post-Pauline interpolation are inclined to do (see most recently Cornelia Cyss Crocker, *Reading 1 Corinthians in the Twenty-First Century* [New York: T&T Clark International, 2004], 157–60), hardly resolves the issue that from very early on 1 Cor 11:2–16 was understood to be integral to the evolving Pauline image.

56. Bruce W. Winter, *After Paul Left Corinth: The Influence of Secular Ethics and Social Change* (Grand Rapids: Eerdmans, 2001), 141.

modern mimicry—if we can call it that—the sense of ambiguity expressed with respect to the "women" in Paul's text is now transferred to another level altogether, one which relates quite strongly to our own cultural-moral discourses in the West. The gendered structures of Paul's texts therefore prove to be far from harmless elements of a by-gone era. Indeed, they are invoked again and again in each reading of the text, as is, for that matter, Paul's "hairy" rhetoric.

WHY CAN'T THE HEAVENLY
MISS JERUSALEM JUST SHUT UP?*

Jorunn Økland

Within the last decade feminist biblical scholarship has relocated its point of departure. Feminist scholars no longer have to begin by pointing out that our sources are androcentric and that androcentric scholarship represents a limited perspective. Instead, many feminist scholars now take issues in gender theory as points of departure and explore what gender theory might contribute to an appreciation of the biblical texts. This shift is not just a result of biblical gender studies becoming more established and, hence, now being in a position to set its own agenda. It also relates to "the linguistic turn" of the humanities, which puts the spotlight back on the complicated process of reading texts and literature, and exposes the "abysmal linguistic oblivion" ("abgründige Sprachvergessenheit")[1] that, according to Hans-Georg Gadamer, had shaped the European philosophical imagination since Kant. Nevertheless, in this linguistic turn language as a historical, material, located phenomenon ironically got lost again, not least through the subsumption of "philology" under "theory" as expressed most clearly by Paul de Man,[2] whose understanding of literary theory as philology and philology as "an examination of the structure of language prior to the meaning it produces"[3] owes more to structuralist method than to traditional, historical-critical philology with its sensitivity toward the fact that texts are written in particular languages under

---

* I am grateful to John Marshall for posing the devastating question as to why the bride is speaking if she is *only* the receptacle, as she was so situated in an earlier phase of this work (see Jorunn Øklund, "Sex, Gender and Ancient Greek: A Study in Theoretical Misfit," *ST* 57 [2003]: 133).

1. Hans-Georg Gadamer, *Hermeneutik II: Wahrheit und Methode* (vol. 2 of *Gesammelte Werke*; Tübingen: Mohr Siebeck, 1986), 361.

2. See, e.g., Paul de Man, "The Return to Philology," in *The Resistance to Theory* (Minneapolis: University of Minnesota Press, 1986), 21–26. I am here building on the analysis of Helge Jordheim, *Lesningens Vitenskap: Utkast til en ny filologi* (Oslo: Universitetsforlaget, 2001), 94–101.

3. De Man, *Resistance to Theory*, 24.

particular historical and material constraints that affect *both* the linguistic
structures *and* their meaning-content. Thus, even the most universalizing
theory is linguistically embedded, although this is not always admitted or
recognized. Theories or theologies formulated in one language make
themselves dependent on the possibilities of that language. When applied
to different linguistic systems they may tease out what is unexpressed or
suppressed, but it is equally plausible that they render important possibilities in that other language invisible. For feminism this is a problem
because feminism began as a Western movement for equality, but unless
feminist theories are applied with critical care toward geographical, linguistic, and historical difference they could serve as just another tool in the
continuing Western colonization of "hearts and minds" around the globe.
Thus, the turn to a more explicitly feminist-theoretical agenda potentially
has its problems—even if as a feminist I mainly welcome such a turn.

This essay is to some extent inspired by Toril Moi, who sometimes
includes reflections on linguistic differences between American English,
French, and Norwegian in her study of literature, although she does not
explore these differences systematically.[4] It is also inspired by Theodor
Adorno, who used foreign words frequently in his writings as an "explosive force."[5] In Sinkwan Cheng's words, "this 'explosive' power comes
precisely from the way the *Fremdwort* functions as an outlaw in the land
of linguistic purity and organicity—as an outlaw which nonetheless
promises to be the founder of a new law in the world 'to come'."[6]

GENDER THEORY, PHILOLOGY, AND LINGUISTIC DIFFERENCE

A coherent and smooth text in only one language might eliminate the
"distraction" that foreign languages and universes of meaning represent
in order to facilitate a firm focus on the content, in this case the theory.
But it would also render invisible the difference of the linguistic and cultural universes that the ancient biblical texts represent, that the modern
theories I use to interpret them represent, and that my own Norwegian
background represents—and thus it would undermine its own content.
Therefore, the variety of languages upon which biblical scholars are

---

4. One exercise in the translingual versatility of feminist concepts and theories might be
to compare the first chapter of her book *What Is a Woman?* with its Norwegian version from
the year before: Toril Mol, *'What Is a Woman?' and Other Essays* (New York: Oxford University
Press, 1999); idem, *Hva er en kvinne? Kjønn og kropp i feministisk teori* (Oslo: Gyldendal, 1998).

5. Theodor W. Adorno, "On the Use of Foreign Words," in *Notes to Literature* (ed. R.
Tiedemann; trans. S. W. Nicholson; 2 vols.; New York: Columbia University Press, 1991), 2:286.

6. Sinkwan Cheng, *"Fremdwörter* as 'The Jews of Language' and Adorno's Politics of
Exile," in *Adorno, Culture and Feminism* (ed. M. O'Neill; London: Sage, 1999), 77.

dependent will be exposed rather than concealed through transcriptions and translations that mimic[7] the essay's main language (even if I—as the Bride [see below]—will for the most part adhere to this strategy). With foreign letters, alphabets, and words constantly interrupting and leaving fissures and channels into other universes of language and meaning, the result is a fractured text that exposes difference, alienation, and mimicry, both in its form and content.[8] But in Adorno's words, foreign or alien[9] words "have their legitimacy as an expression of alienation itself."[10]

Traditional biblical scholarship has often been acutely aware of linguistic difference, although often hopelessly uncritical in its application of philological knowledge. That is why at this point a coupling of critical feminist theory with more conventional, philological biblical criticism could bring out the best in both, which is what I will try here. For this purpose I find Luce Irigaray particularly apt, because much of her theory is developed through close readings of historical texts. She has repeatedly pointed out how passage through the master discourse and rigorous interpretation of its phallogocratism down to the level of syntax and grammar is indispensable *before* a different syntax, grammar, and metaphor can be developed.[11] In her main work, *Speculum de l'autre femme*,[12] Irigaray has interrogated the stranglehold of ancient male discourse on history and pointed out its fissures, from where one could sometimes, perhaps, hear the other (mainly understood as "woman") speaking.[13]

Finally, before moving on to Revelation, I will point out some particularities of the languages hitherto noted compared to the main language of

---

7. The notion of mimicry, and how one can thereby speak sensibly within one discourse/language and simultaneously say something entirely "different," will be developed below in relation to Luce Irigaray and to the incident in Revelation wherein the woman/ bride utters male discourse.

8. Thereby, hopefully, attention is also drawn to how colonialism and alienation affect the very language of our texts, not only (merely) their content.

9. Cheng discusses the problem of translating into English the title of Adorno's other article on the topic, "Wörter aus der Fremde." She prefers the title "Alien Words" to "Words from Abroad," which is the name under which this piece is published in English (Cheng, "Fremdwörter," 77, 95).

10. Adorno, "On the Use of Foreign Words," 289.

11. See, e.g., Luce Irigaray, *Ce Sexe qui n'en est pas un* (Paris: Minuit, 1977), 157.

12. Luce Irigaray, *Speculum de l'autre femme* (Paris: Minuit, 1974). My reference to works in languages other than English will necessarily be inconsistent in this essay. In the case of Irigaray, where I refer to *her* writing or where the French is important in itself, I use the French text. Where I use Irigaray to construct meaning in the English text, I will rely on the English translations by Gillian Gill and Catherine Porter/Carolyn Burke.

13. I leave aside for now the closely related but much larger hermeneutical problem of how to understand ancient Greek and Hebrew texts at all within modern cultural and linguistic contexts, since this is constantly dealt with within traditional biblical scholarship.

this essay, English. This step is taken in order to show how language and meaning cannot be separated, and why therefore I find it a problem that much Anglophone feminist theory is not always aware of the difference that linguistic difference makes. In an Anglophone feminist-theoretical context, the distinction between sex and gender has been very productive. "Sex" in this context may denote biology, materiality, or even essential mental characteristics[14] that some believe to be innate to men and women. "Gender" is the socioculturally constructed system of roles and identities that sorts people into two groups, men and women, and attributes to them a role that influences their self-understanding, mentality, and possibilities from birth.

French and Scandinavian languages do not have the English distinction between sex and gender. On this basis, Toril Moi, from the same small language community as myself, points out that English-language critics, *including* the post-structuralists, have misread the French feminists, above all Simone de Beauvoir, through the lens of the sex/gender distinction: "English-language post-structuralists have largely failed to see how the more inclusive approach to subjectivity and the body could be found in de Beauvoir and other feminists writing in languages that do not operate with such a distinction."[15] Similarly, when, in the English translation, Irigaray's *sexué* is translated "sexualized" (see below), the latter term in English carries very different connotations than "gendered," which, in my view, would have covered the French term better (although not perfectly). On the other hand, the linguistic system into which Scandinavian feminists read the English sex-gender distinction only has one term for the various types of differences between men and women: "kjønn/kön," which, as Moi points out, does not thereby mean that they are unable to distinguish between physiology, social roles, and metaphors *when necessary*. For the moment, this observation only means that my use of the term "gender" will mimic English, while denoting the semantic fields of Norwegian "kjønn" or French "sexe," which allow one to approach Revelation's bodies in their interpreted state without getting caught in the endless Anglophone feminist-theoretical debates on what is more important, sex or gender. This approach means that "gender"

---

14. That these concepts are at least as elusive as "sex" itself only fuels current debates. I will not go into the discussion of all the different entities to which "biological body" can refer. See further Elsa Almås and Espen Esther Pirelli Benestad, *Kjønn i bevegelse* (Oslo: Universitetsforlaget, 2001), 19–31; and Anne Fausto-Sterling, *Sexing the Body: Gender Politics and the Construction of Sexuality* (New York: Basic Books, 2000). I will also not discuss the complicated relationship between modern "biology" and ancient Greek φύσις, an equally elusive term.

15. Moi, '*What Is a Woman,*' 5.

must be read as something more comprehensive than gender as opposed to sex. "Gender" in this "foreign" sense has a material side, but its materiality cannot always be pinned down and defined. Luckily, such terminological recirculation is a possibility in the highly versatile and complex English language, which recently has been hailed as Esperanto's true heir and fulfilment.[16]

Another particularity of Scandinavian languages compared to English is that there are linguistic alternatives to the silent, unstable inclusion of women under a masculine/generic term. In the hegemonic languages of feminist theory today, English and French, women can sometimes be included in the masculine term "man" or *homme,* which then takes on generic meaning, but other times they are excluded. For current French thinkers this possibility of using *homme* in both a masculine and a generic sense represents the core of phallogocentrism.[17] "Woman" is sometimes presupposed within the generic term, other times not. Her inclusion does not make a visible or "hearable" difference to the term[18] and she is rarely mentioned explicitly. For "man" or *homme,* woman is the difference without which the term could not make claims to universality. Woman becomes the necessary support of the universality of "man," operating within the latter term as a constant shadow that cannot be dialectically absorbed—neither obliterated nor fully assumed. This ambiguity was particularly convenient in post-revolutionary France when it came to teasing out what *Droits de l'homme* ("Rights of Man") should mean in practice. The linguistic ambiguity made it easier not to grant women equal rights with men even if they were sometimes subsumed under the *homme*-terminology, thereby loading that designation with universal meaning.[19]

Germanic (including Dutch and Scandinavian) languages have preserved the ancient Greek distinction between the generic ἄνθρωπος and the masculine ἀνήρ. That is, they have a separate word for "human being" as

---

16. Mark Abley, *Spoken Here: Travels among Threatened Languages* (London: Heinemann, 2003), 93–94.

17. I am particularly relying on Irigaray (*Speculum de l'autre,* esp. 58–61) for the idea that the world is understood according to λόγος, an order defined by the masculine.

18. This is not only a problem of anthropological terminology, but of much Western philosophical discourse more generally: Derrida's invention, the term *différance,* which when pronounced in French sounds like the correctly spelled *difference,* illustrates this ambiguous (graphic) difference that does not make a (audible) difference. See Jacques Derrida, "Différance," in *Margins of Philosophy* (trans. A. Bass; Chicago: University of Chicago Press, 1982), 3–27.

19. See Joan W. Scott, *Only Paradoxes to Offer: French Feminists and the Rights of Man* (Cambridge: Harvard University Press, 1996).

individuals and as a whole that both English and French lack. I am not thereby suggesting that phallogocentrism is a French and English phenomenon only or that the generic signifier in Greek and Germanic languages is not frequently used in an exclusively masculine sense too. But this difference accounts for some of the distinct directions gender study takes in the various language communities. In what follows, I pursue the issue of linguistic difference, but now focusing more specifically on the issue of gender and language, engaging whether "woman" can be spoken in any phallogocentric language at all or whether the "organicity" of the phallogocentric text conceals the difference of woman altogether.

MALE AND FEMALE VIRGINS

Drawing on the gender-critical and philological awareness developed in the previous section, I will now apply these insights to the reading of a specific biblical text. In particular, I will explore some of the virginal characters in Revelation's blissful "elsewhere,"[20] where we find odd relationships between lovers, between humans and sheep, and between men and women in general. The book as a whole is dressed in the language of war and conquest, imperial rulership and worship, purity and danger.[21] I will show how the characters in question and their mutual relations represent the blissful "elsewhere" as a specific gendered place.

Feminist biblical scholars have studied Revelation from various perspectives, but a common question seems to arise again and again: can Revelation be saved or reclaimed as sacred Scripture for Christian women? As Hanna Stenström has demonstrated with particular clarity in her thesis, both men and women have looked to Revelation as a writing

---

20. One could call this place neither "heaven" nor "new earth" because the texts simply imply that it moves around (i.e., it is mobile). Under the influence of Theo Angelopoulos's *To Μετέωρο Βήμα του Πελαργού* (*The Suspended Step of the Stork;* Greece: Greek Film Centre, 1991) and also Luce Irigaray (e.g., in "Le Miroir, de l'autre côté," in *Ce Sexe,* 16), I have chosen the term "elsewhere" (αλλού; "ailleurs"/"autre côté"), a term that encompasses all of these possibilities.

21. For language of war and conquest, see in particular Catherine Keller, *Apocalypse Now and Then: A Feminist Guide to the End of the World* (Boston: Beacon, 1996); and Stephen D. Moore, "Revolting Revelations," in *The Personal Voice in Biblical Interpretation* (ed. I. R. Kitzberger; London: Routledge, 1999), 183–200. For imperial ideology and worship, see, e.g., David Aune, "The Influence of Roman Imperial Court Ceremonial on the Apocalypse of John," *BR* 18 (1983): 5–26. Purity issues are touched upon by most feminist readers; see in particular Adela Yarbro Collins, "Feminine Symbolism in the Book of Revelation," *BibInt* 1 (1993): 20–33; and Hanna Stenström, "The Book of Revelation: A Vision of the Ultimate Liberation or the Ultimate Backlash? A Study in 20th Century Interpretations of Rev 14:1–5, with Special Emphasis on Feminist Exegesis" (Ph.D. diss., Uppsala University, 1999).

of Christian hope—which is why feminist biblical scholars cannot just write it off as a misogynist text, but must try to come up with gender-sensitive interpretations of it instead.[22] They have also shown a special interest in the various females of Revelation. Among scholars who draw on feminist and other gender theory in their interpretations of Revelation, the level at which they activate such theory and the outcome of it varies considerably. Elisabeth Schüssler Fiorenza and Adela Yarbro Collins have remained largely within the historical-critical paradigm in their work on Revelation, albeit with gender-awareness.[23] Stephen Moore relates closely—and broadly—to literary and gender theories and constantly draws attention to language as I also attempt to do here, although he does so in a way that one probably has to be a native speaker of English in order fully to appreciate the results.[24]

Catherine Keller, Tina Pippin, and Hanna Stenström are more interested in the social functions and consequences Revelation has or might have for women, and they also engage more systemically with feminist theory.[25] Stenström points out that, in the rhetoric of Revelation, "women" can be used as a "rhetorical means to designate evil when the topic is the struggle between Good and Evil and the necessity to take sides in the struggle."[26] Pippin's comment concerning the bride, the Lamb, and the 144,000 is obviously fundamental to the argument here: the "scene is disturbing because the imagery is that of mass intercourse."[27] These readings focus a greater part on the *influence* of the gender structures of the text on real, embodied women, as analyzed with the help of feminist theory. As a result, they also take cultural location more fully into account.[28]

---

22. See, e.g., Stenström, "Book of Revelation," 32, 240.

23. Among their numerous publications on Revelation, the following are the most important for this essay: Adela Yarbro Collins, *The Combat Myth in the Book of Revelation* (HDR 9; Missoula, Mont.: Scholars Press, 1976); idem, "Feminine Symbolism;" and Elisabeth Schüssler Fiorenza, *Revelation: Vision of a Just World* (Proclamation Commentaries; Minneapolis: Fortress, 1991).

24. Stephen D. Moore, *God's Gym: Divine Male Bodies of the Bible* (New York: Routledge, 1996).

25. Stenström, "Book of Revelation"; Keller, *Apocalypse*; Tina Pippin, *Death and Desire: The Rhetoric of Gender in the Apocalypse of John* (Louisville: Westminster John Knox, 1992); and idem, *Apocalyptic Bodies: The Biblical End of the World in Text and Image* (New York: Routledge, 1999).

26. Stenström, "Book of Revelation," 316.

27. Pippin, *Death and Desire*, 80.

28. In particular, Pippin's *Apocalyptic Bodies* challenges me to think through my own relationship to Revelation. In my upbringing within the context of the Lutheran state church of Norway, Revelation was a book "not to be read"—it was too liminal, too imaginative. Revelation challenged the relatively happy, tempered, grace-full marriage between social democracy and Lutheranism. Revelation is hopelessly socially undemocratic, and it distorts

In relation to these various ways of activating feminist theory, I will combine the tools of traditional philology and feminist theory in order to focus narrowly on how the characters in the scenes of the "elsewhere" contribute to the "kjønning"/gendering of this place. I will then question if the difference of "elsewhere" can be expressed at all within the language of "here." I resist mainstream discourse and its penchant for asking what is figurative and literal speech—a question that I find often sidetracks important discussions of the structures of meaning in the book of Revelation. The gender of the various heavenly characters and the text's concern for the purity of these *male* and *female* bodies will thus be approached with a presupposition borrowed from Swedish sociologist Yvonne Hirdman, namely, that the characters represented in the various spaces contribute to or reflect a gendered discourse of the place in question.[29] According to Hirdman, the "gender system" operates according to two dynamics, segregation and hierarchy. Hirdman underscores their unique structuring abilities: they *make* sense. She shows how character, action, and place are intimately linked to each other and stand in a legitimizing, reinforcing, dialectical relationship with each other.[30]

In Revelation, the most important places are the old world and the new world (coming down from heaven). We learn a lot about these places through the characters that inhabit them. The characters in/from heaven, on which I focus here, are presented at more or less regular intervals throughout the book, such as in chs. 4–5, 7, 14, and 20:11–22:5. The main characters are God and the Lamb. God (θεός), who mostly sits on the throne in heaven (e.g., 4:2–3; 7:11; 11:16; 16:11; 22:1), is described in hypermasculine metaphors and grammar, as demonstrated by Stephen Moore, who finds that Revelation's heaven parallels the modern gym where the male body-builder (God), "the supreme embodiment of hegemonic hypermasculinity," is "mirrored" by the multitudes lining the interior walls of the heavenly city/gym.[31]

---

the rational structures of Lutheran dogmatics—especially in relation to grace and the life hereafter. Like the wedding at Cana incident in John 2, where Jesus turned water into wine, my cultural religious background had a particular way of viewing such incidents:"Me vett de é der, men me liga de ikkje"—"we know it's there, but we don't like it." So maybe it was an act of teenage rebellion to start reading Revelation....

29. The argument behind this assertion can be found in Jorunn Øklund, *Women in Their Place: Paul and the Corinthian Discourse of Gender and Sanctuary Space* (JSNTSup 269; New York: Continuum, 2004).

30. Yvonne Hirdman, "Genussystemet–reflexioner kring kvinnors sociala underordning," *Kvinnovetenskapelig tidsskrift* 3 (1988): 52.

31. Moore, *God's Gym*, 139.

The Lamb (ἀρνίου), a somewhat gender-ambiguous character (cf. Rev. 5:6–8; 14:1–4; 19:7), is generic and grammatically neuter. If we read Revelation "with the grain" within a heterosexual framework, however, we observe that, since the Lamb is eventually married to the bride, the holy Jerusalem, it must be male. This is not the only possible reading, but it is perhaps most adequate if one reads with the gender ideologies of Revelation's historical setting in mind. Indeed, as Steve Moyise demonstrates, this Lamb is rather unstable;[32] it performs as a masculine lion (λέον).

THE 144,000 Παρθένοι

In Rev 14:1–3 we are told that a group of no less than 144,000 stand on Mount Zion together with the Lamb, which they follow wherever it goes. They sing a new song before the throne, which no one can learn except the 144,000. They are described as "virgins" (παρθένοι; 14:4) and also as "blameless" (ἄμωμοι; 14:5) and as "firstfruits" (ἀπαρχή; 14:4), the latter designations borrowed from the sphere of ritual slaughter. Revelation 14:4 includes them among the heavenly bodies: "It is these who have not defiled themselves with women, for they are virgins; these follow the Lamb wherever he goes. They have been redeemed from humankind as first fruits for God and the Lamb" (NRSV).

The same group is also encountered earlier in Rev 7:4–8. There they still seem to be on earth, where they are about to be sealed on their foreheads by an angel with the seal of the living God (7:2). The resonance with the Passover story (Exod 12) is not to be missed, although in the latter 600,000 men are mentioned alongside of "little ones," which is followed by a comment that a mixed group of people went up with the men (Exod 12:37–38). In a similar way as in the Passover story, the seal should prevent the 144,000 from being harmed when God's angels go forth to punish (Rev 7:3). The gender-status of the 144,000 is more ambiguous than the 600,000 men from Exodus since women and children are not mentioned separately, but there may be other reasons for that, as we shall see. In any case, they are described in masculine grammatical terms, and they are taken from each of the tribes of the *sons of Israel* that are named in the list (Rev 7:5–8)—twelve thousand from each tribe. Israel and his sons were male, and usually only men were counted in lists of this kind.

---

32. Steve Moyise, "Does the Lion Lie down with the Lamb?" in *Studies in the Book of Revelation* (ed. S. Moyise; Edinburgh: T&T Clark, 2001), 181–94.

By Rev 14 the 144,000 are redeemed from the old earth. It is uncertain up to this point in the narrative whether they are male or female, as the lack of female designations in Rev 7 may be a result of normal phallogocentric speech where the female is invisibly subsumed under the grammatically male proper names, tribes, and categories. However, the sealing seems to be the differentiating act that makes maleness definitive. The ambiguity of the possibly phallogocentric speech in Rev 7 is removed by the clear reference to the group's avoidance of defilement by women. To borrow the words of Stenström, "the sense of exclusive maleness is rather due to the fact that the group is put in contrast to 'women'.... The real name of the believer is a name in masculine."[33]

In Rev 14:1 we are also given more information about the seal that they received in Rev 7: the seal bears the names of the Lamb and the Father. The 144,000 have not been "inscribed" by women and other defiling agents; they have kept themselves pure by refraining from sexual relations with women. So what the 144,000 have in common are both the presence and absence of inscriptions on their body—foreheads and foreskins are sealed with the seal of the Father but not of women.

Because both their number and the reference to the seal on their foreheads are repeated, I believe, along with the majority of scholars, that Rev 7 and 14 refer to the same group. From a narrative point of view, characterization of two distinctive entities by means of the same referents would be less than elegant. Yet, if the 144,000 are male, the use of the term παρθένος also becomes odd, for παρθένος is usually translated "virgin" and thus, for modern Anglophones, could look like a descriptive term for a female bodily state represented by an intact *hymen*. Further, for modern readers it has become increasingly theologically problematic that Revelation seems to presuppose that there are no women inhabitants in its "elsewhere," most often described as "heaven" or "the New Jerusalem."[34]

---

33. Stenström, "Book of Revelation," 72.

34. In early Christianity this absence of women is unlikely to have caused many problems, as it was believed that virtuous, Christ-believing women were resurrected as men (e.g., Tertullian, *De cultu feminarum* 1,2). It is a recurring theme in Kari Børresen's scholarship that Augustine is the first early Christian author to argue that women are resurrected as women. When Augustine asserts that "the Lord said that there would be no marriage in the resurrection, not that there would be no women" (Latin: *nuptias ergo dominus futuras negavit esse in resurrectione, non feminas;* for edition, see Marie Turcan, ed., *Tertullian: De cultu feminarum / La toilette des femmes* [SC 173; Paris: Cerf, 1971]), he thus disputes with Tertullian, Jerome, and the encratites who all believed women would be resurrected as males, or angelic males (Kari Børresen, "'Patristic 'Feminism': The Case of Augustine," in *From Patristics to Matristics: Selected Articles on Christian Gender Models by Kari E. Børresen* [ed. Ø. Norderval and K. L. Ore; Rome: Herder, 2002], 42).

The modern scholarly silence concerning the gender of the heavenly inhabitants in Rev 7:2–8 and 14:1–5 could be seen as just an ordinary consequence of androcentrism: as long as the interpreters were male, and men inhabited Revelation's "elsewhere," scholars did not really perceive any problems. Before gender had become a burning issue, Ronald Preston and Anthony Hanson could innocently and matter-of-factly state that, "if taken literally it means that only male celibates can be saved!"[35] But in the face of the growing feminist criticism of the Bible, this reading became increasingly problematic as it would imply the *denouement* of the irredeemably sexist plot of this book, which is, after all, part of the Bible, whose authority and reliability was already under attack from so many other angles. Instead, a rather apologetic inclusivism has taken over in traditional, gender-blind scholarship. More recently, scholars have pointed out the theological problem of the exclusion of women; this is especially the case with Tina Pippin, who sees it as symptomatic for the Apocalypse as a whole.[36] More or less implicitly, the demand for male virginity is viewed as a symptom of the misogynist ideology of the text: women are understood as defiling agents, so men who want to be redeemed must not even have touched one.[37] Before returning to alternative solutions, I will, as promised, question what philology might contribute to the issue at hand.

Historical-critical exegesis is highly sensitive toward the problems of translating the term παρθένος. It is commonly known that Matthew, in his fatal (because of the effective history of its interpretation) designation of Jesus' mother as παρθένος (Matt 1:23), was just quoting the Septuagint translation of the Hebrew עַלְמָה (Isa 7:14), meaning "young girl." The Septuagint translator had not chosen the closest Greek equivalents, κόρη or νεᾶνις,[38] but this other term, παρθένος, which more often than the Hebrew original referred to the state of the *hymen*. He was blissfully unaware of the effects and consequences his insensitive translation would have, through Matthew's endorsement as Gospel author, for later dogma and gender models.

From the outset, however, παρθένος was not an unambiguous description of a bodily state either. As Delling pointed out, the ancient

---

35. Ronald Preston and Anthony T. Hanson, *The Revelation of Saint John the Divine* (London: SCM, 1949), 100.

36. Pippin, *Death and Desire*, 70, 86.

37. Ibid., 70, 81; cf. Stenström, "Book of Revelation," 285, 314.

38. For the latter possibility, see Kristin de Troyer, "Septuagint and Gender Studies: The Very Beginning of a Promising Liaison," in *A Feminist Companion to Reading the Bible: Approaches, Methods and Strategies* (ed. A. Brenner and C. R. Fontaine; Sheffield: Sheffield Academic Press, 1997), 337.

Greek use of the term was in no way limited to girls with an unbroken *hymen* even if this state may represent one out of the many elements upon which the use of the term is contingent.[39] For Delling, it is obvious that the term denotes a mature young woman, noting that the bodily state is one option alongside many others, but he also admits that it is difficult to "assign a specific meaning to each occurrence" of the word, given that the various nuances of the term intermingle.[40] In the religious context of the Bible, there are frequent references to a "virgin" who bears a divine child. But, again, Delling pleads for attention to semantic nuance: "one has to ask in *each* case what specific ideas are bound up with the statement."[41] Delling goes on to point out that there is no emphasis on virginity in the Hebrew use of עַלְמָה and that its translation as παρθένος is odd; indeed, even the Septuagint use of παρθένος covers everything from chastity, youth, and young girls, to virginity in a more narrow sense (it can even be used for a raped girl, as it is in Gen 34:3).[42] In true philological fashion, then, he emphasizes that the "well-known" figure of The Virgin is an abstraction of religious history.[43]

I cite Delling in detail here because, as with many of the articles in *TWNT/TDNT* (the chosen representative of philological, historical-critical approaches for my argument here), his article destabilizes what modern readers perceive as the "meaning" of the term in question. His critical *Begriffsgeschichte* thus approaches the deconstructive method. He demonstrates the variety of meanings for παρθένος in ancient Greek, showing how arbitrary the later preoccupation with the *hymen* of the "mother of god" is. Still, having done away with any fixed meaning of the term, he "short-circuits" when he comes to the use of the word in Revelation: here it is suddenly used only figuratively (*nur bildlich*), like πόρνη.[44] Having just deconstructed any "literal" meaning of the term by listing all its possible meanings, why does Delling have this sudden change of mind? The "only figurative" explanation is too often the scholarly safety valve,

---

39. Gerhard Delling, "παρθένος," *TDNT* 5:826–37. Cf. LSJ, s.v. παρθένος/εία. From the examples they mention, the term also seems more closely linked to female gender than to sexual status.

40. Delling, "Παρθένος," 825: "die verschiedenen Klangfarben mischen sich zum Teil in den Aussagen, so daß nicht jedes Vorkommen auf eine bestimmte festlegbar ist."

41. Ibid., 827: "Indessen ist in jedem Falle zu prüfen, welche besonderen Auffassungen sich mit der Aussage verbinden" (emphasis added).

42. Ibid., 831.

43. Ibid., 830: "die 'bekannte' Gestalt der Jungfrau ist eine religionsgeschichtliche Abstraktion."

44. Ibid., 835.

blown when scholars are uncomfortable with Revelation's statements and want to avoid the problems with its meanings.

If none of the aforementioned elements are indispensable and thus none can determine the use of the term παρθένος, its usage for men does not have to be classified as "figurative." Therefore, its use in Revelation is probably contingent on other elements than the physiological feature that became so crucial in the production of dogma in a later period when asceticism had become an ideal. In other words, Revelation's usage of παρθένος for men is only metaphorical to the extent that all language is metaphorical. This perception is reflected in modern English translations such as *Good News for Modern Man*, which translates παρθένος as, "they are unmarried" or "chaste." Yet, however philologically and modern-contextually adequate these translations may be, they are not representative of the importance attached to a physiological, "literal" understanding when women are designated as such elsewhere in the New Testament. If παρθένος in the verses concerning Mary in Matt 1:23 and Luke 1:27 had been translated in similarly flexible ways, exegetes would definitely have had less to discuss, and the church would have produced fewer "heretics."

Even if παρθένος is mostly used for females, Revelation is not the only Christian writing to use this term for men. In the phrase περὶ δὲ τῶν παρθένων (concerning the virgins) in 1 Cor 7:25, the genitive plural is adequate both for masculine and feminine grammatical gender, and because of 7:26 it is reasonable to believe that it refers to both male and female virgins: "I think it is good for a human being (ἀνθρώπῳ) to be/remain like that," namely, a virgin. It is even possible that the author of Revelation is alluding to this saying, because this valorization of life-long virginity is rather foreign to the Jewish discourses on which Revelation otherwise seems to draw. Even the relatively conceptually close Temple Scroll from Qumran states the following about entrance into the New Jerusalem: "a man who lies with his wife and has an ejaculation, *for three days* shall not enter the whole city of the temple in which I shall cause my name to dwell," [45] which is very different from Paul's advice about lifelong abstinence.

---

45. Trans. from Florentino García Martínez, *The Dead Sea Scrolls Translated: The Qumran Texts in English* (trans. W. G. E. Watson; 2d ed.; Grand Rapids: Eerdmans, 1996). 11Q19 (*Temple Scroll*ᵃ), 45, 11–12: ואיש כיא ישכב עם אשתו שכבת זרע לוא יבוא אל כול עיר המקדש אשר אשכין שמי בה שלושת ימים. In the later rabbinic texts it seems rather to be agreed that not to have a wife is "to diminish the image of God"; still, the balancing of marriage and family duties with Torah study is represented as difficult. See Daniel Boyarin, *Carnal Israel: Reading Sex in Talmudic Culture* (Berkeley and Los Angeles: University of California Press, 1993), 134–66.

Having established that the problems with the male παρθένοι are theological rather than linguistic-philological in nature, I return to the discussion of alternative reading strategies. In order to avoid understanding the 144,000 as male, an alternative strategy is to read male names, male categories—like the notion of the firstfruits, which in terms of animal sacrifice meant male victims—and the masculine grammar of the Greek as generic and conventional, a reading strategy also applied to other parts of the New Testament. Among feminists, this approach has been taken by Schüssler Fiorenza, who emphasizes that grammatical gender is not the same as sex, and that using masculine pronouns does not imply that something is imagined as male. Therefore women can read Revelation as gender-inclusive.[46] This interpretation is possible on the basis of two distinctions, between literal and symbolic/metaphorical, and between sex and gender. Schüssler Fiorenza is aware of the gendered dualisms and the androcentrism of Revelation, including the context in which it was produced, but gendered dualisms, in her view, should not be taken in "a literalist sense."[47] Within the rhetoric of Revelation, "sexual language is used metaphorically"; in this case, that is to say that the 144,000 have not participated in the idolatry of the imperial cult.[48]

Since Schüssler Fiorenza has followed her "hermeneutics of suspicion" and unmasked the naturalized truths of centuries of kyriocentric dominance in other contexts, I find her approach to the gendered language of Revelation rather surprising. Not only does she *not* see it as decisive for Revelation's message, but she also suggests that the relation between grammatical gender and sex is arbitrary. I agree that in languages such as German, Norwegian, and Greek, where all nouns are gendered masculine, feminine, or neuter, the reasons why something is grammatically gendered one way or the other do not always conform to modern standards of rational thinking about sex and gender. That cities, countries, and many natural phenomena (e.g., tornadoes) are gendered feminine rather than neutral is not rational according to such measures, but it is explicable because, in a premodern worldview where everything in the cosmos was conceived of as having gender qualities, being hospitable, reproductive, and accommodating were feminine qualities that both women and cities and the soil embodied; moreover, hosting uncontrollable natural forces was something women had in common with natural phenomena. Thus, grammatical gender is not a given. Rather,

---

46. Schüssler Fiorenza, *Revelation,* 14, 130–31.
47. Ibid., 13–14, 88.
48. Extensive arguments against this approach have been presented by Pippin and Stenström, so I will only pursue my philological issue here.

there is often a cultural-historical explanation behind it. The fact that there is not always such an explanation does not mean that it is illegitimate to question the gender designation. In fact, I find such questioning a passageway into ancient webs of gender discourse that are otherwise invisible to the modern feminist gaze, which tends to look for men and women and nothing else. I do, however, strongly agree with Schüssler Fiorenza that masculine grammatical forms can also include women. But for me this does not make Revelation a potentially women-inclusive writing, it only demonstrates the problem of phallogocentric discourse: it *can* include women but no one knows exactly when it does because women are not worthy of representation separately from the males. On other occasions, Revelation expresses gender so explicitly that I end up concluding with Pippin that Revelation resists a generic reading of its anthropology altogether.

Another alternative interpretive strategy would be to read Rev 14:1–5 outside of a heterosexist framework, and take seriously that παρθένος elsewhere more often than not denotes females. In that case, these παρθένοι are women who have not defiled themselves by having sex with other women. If so, it is sexual contact between women, not women *per se*, that is seen as impurity. But such a reading of the 144,000 παρθένοι would presuppose a gynocentric imaginary and a rather unrestrained way of talking about women who are erotically attracted to other women but still able to control themselves. This would be highly unusual in an ancient literary context[49] and would, in my view, not fit with the masculine grammatical forms and the androcentric approach found elsewhere in the book.

Miss Jerusalem

One could argue that Jerusalem, the bride, must be female (e.g., Rev 19:7; 21:9). But she is also a city.[50] The question is thus whether she is a "heavenly character" in line with God, the Lamb, and the 144,000. If so,

---

49. Bernadette Brooten has "combed" ancient texts for references to female homoeroticism in her *Love between Women: Early Christian Responses to Female Homoeroticism* (The Chicago Series on Sexuality, History, and Society; Chicago: University of Chicago Press, 1996), esp. 62–64. The references are hard to find, veiled in obscure language, and adopt an extremely hostile stance toward the phenomenon.

50. The text leads the reader to identify the bride with the holy city, the New Jerusalem (21:2). The New Jerusalem is obviously contrasted with (the Old) Jerusalem, but whether the Zion of 14:1 is identical to the New Jerusalem (with the exception that she is not yet descended to the new earth) is less clear. However, because of their similar characterization as the place for the redeemed, I choose to treat them as identical. It has been suggested that the bride in Rev 21 is rather to be identified with the woman of Rev 12; but see Yarbro Collins, *Combat Myth*, 132.

what does she contribute to the gendering of the "elsewhere" that I am exploring here?

Like Athena, born from the forehead of her omnipotent father Zeus after he had swallowed her mother, so the Miss Jerusalem is similarly born from her father, the Omnipotent (21:22), after he has rid himself of "the great whore," Babylon. In the ancient world, cities were often gendered female through grammar and/or the connection with a city goddess. [51] As in much androcentric discourse concerning women, the femininity of cities could be perceived as either promiscuous or virginal, although in a Greco-Roman context the femininity of cities seems mostly to be a way of expressing its maternal role as home and nurturer. In Revelation, Babylon is the whore and the New Jerusalem is the pure bride (21:2, 9). Thus, holiness is associated with virginity and wholeness and dissociated from fragmentation and brokenness. The formerly holy earthly Jerusalem has to disappear, for she has fulfilled her duty and is defiled through evil invasion/penetration.[52]

Is Miss Jerusalem a character inhabiting the "elsewhere" like the others? Or is her presence of a different kind? If we look at Rev 14, we notice that she is not missing because the 144,000 literally stand on her. She is a brilliant example of Luce Irigaray's "woman who has not yet taken (a) place," which is the *chora*:[53] "Woman is still the place, the whole of the place in which she cannot take possession of herself as such. She is experienced as all-powerful precisely insofar as her indifferentiation makes her radically powerless. She is never here and now because it is she who sets up that eternal elsewhere from which the 'subject' continues to draw his reserves."[54] The preliminary answer must therefore be that she seems to be place, home, and accommodation rather than an inhabitant herself with the possibility to act, move, and make (right) choices, as the

---

51. This motif is also mentioned in Yarbro Collins, "Feminine Symbolism," 26–27.

52. Moving from imagery to possible text-external realities, the Roman invasion of the city could be seen as a kind of rape.

53. Explained briefly, the philosophical use of the term goes back to Plato's *Timaeus* (50D–52D), which understands Space/Place ($\chi\omega\rho\alpha$) as present at the birth of the cosmos alongside Being and Becoming, representing a triad or the three Kinds. *Chora* ($\chi\omega\rho\alpha$) is the space that all bodies occupy and is the substance of which they are made: it is the ever-existing, all-receptive place/space, the amorphous and formless imprint-bearer that nevertheless prevents the imitations from being identical to their origin. Concerning the recent revitalisation of this ancient Greek term, see Jorunn Øklund, "Men Are from Mars and Women Are from Venus: On the Relationship between Religion, Gender and Space," in *Gender, Religion, and Diversity: Cross-Cultural Approaches* (ed. T. Beattie and U. King; London: Continuum, 2004), 152–61.

54. Luce Irigaray, *Speculum of the Other Woman* (trans. G. C. Gill; Ithaca, N.Y.: Cornell University Press, 1985), 227.

other heavenly characters can. The virgin bride is possessed by God and the Lamb and becomes inhabited by them; they do not even need their own temple to dwell in because they are constantly in her, and her space is accommodating them well enough. Also, those whose names have been recorded in the Lamb's Book of Life are allowed to enter her (21:27). The New Jerusalem may be female, but she does not inhabit herself.

This instability in the characterization of Jerusalem as both city and human virgin bride is more comprehensible. In her article "Bodies-Cities," feminist theorist Elizabeth Grosz explores the constitutive and mutually defining relations between corporeality and the metropolis. She points out that "the body is psychically, socially, sexually, and discursively or representationally produced, and ... in turn, bodies reinscribe and project themselves onto their sociocultural environment so that this environment both produces and reflects the form and interests of the body."[55] Humans do not *make* cities (contrary to humanist and Marxist views) any more than cities "produce the bodies of their inhabitants as particular and distinctive types of bodies."[56] There is thus a fluidity between the concepts of the city and the human body. Miss Jerusalem is a city described in a language that explores the multivalent, metaphorical potential of a human female body. However, after twenty-one chapters, all of which contain attempts to get rid of the dangerous and unreliably vulnerable females, in 22:17 the only female left, the city Jerusalem, starts to speak! Her vital function as χώρα means she cannot be allowed to be extinct like the others. With the Spirit, she says ἔρχου ("come").[57]

In Revelation, as in many other ancient writings, speech belongs to males alone. Women give birth, suffer, are acted upon, but they do not speak. It is as if this one word of the bride is a message to her readers that she has survived the treatment given to her in the previous chapters. But if males own the discourse, does this speech (re)constitute the bride as a man too? Does the one word spoken by the bride actually construct her as a speaking character in the book as a whole, thus undermining the representation of her as the χώρα in the Zion/Jerusalem passages?

---

55. Elizabeth Grosz, "Bodies-Cities," in *Sexuality and Space* (ed. B. Colomina; Princeton Papers on Architecture; Princeton: Princeton Architectural Press, 1992), 242.

56. Ibid., 250.

57. This reading presupposes that the end is an inherent part of the text of Revelation, not just a postscript more or less detached from the rest of the text, so that "the bride" in Rev 22:17 refers to the same bride as in Rev 21:2, 9, "Miss Jerusalem." If this is *not* the case, and the book's ending is either a later addition or an unrelated postscript by the same author, then John's heaven is an all-male place sustaining itself on a female, unspeaking χώρα.

Irigaray reflects on the fact that "women" (which cannot be identified), in order to speak intelligently, have to speak as *sexué* males or as *asexué*.[58] As part of male discourse, the bride's ἔρχου would indeed be *parler-homme*, one of the few lines that such discourse "needs" its female character to utter in order for this discourse to appear to itself as nonrapist. Within such structures of meaning, this single word expresses the bride's acceptance of the role male discourse grants to her—as submissive, sexually available, ready for the nuptial chamber of the Lamb and his 144,000 brothers. A woman's *parler-homme* still does not make her male in the same way as them.

But this word ἔρχου (a present imperative, second-person singular verb), in itself a complete finite sentence, the shortest possible one, is not able to mimic any other hierarchy than that between the commanding, speaking subject and the "thou," the second person singular pronoun that is supposed to follow the imperative. Spoken in Greek, its grammatical gender is open, and the fact that it is spoken together with the gender-neutral Spirit does not clarify it any further. In the text, the neutral Spirit and the female bride command, and the male hearer (ὁ ἀκούων) is commanded to repeat after them. But who is to come? Might it not be the Lamb, but an Other?

At this point the text takes a strange step. One would expect that "come" is what the bride says to Jesus *alias* the Lamb, who identifies himself in the previous verse. But in the context of 22:17, the imperative is repeated a third time, only this time in the third person, and the one commanded to follow the bride's imperative is specified as "the one thirsting" (ὁ διψῶν), still in grammatically masculine terms. This theme of thirst, fluid, and saturation indeed opens up other ranges of meaning that cannot be fully explored here. Important for the moment, however, is that ὁ διψῶν is much more ambiguous than the "come Lord Jesus" of v. 20, an ambiguity that allows for the coming of many, not only of the Lord Jesus.

In order to display how the "eschatology" of Irigaray and that of John the Seer could be seen as touching each other at this point, I will use Irigaray's notion of *parler-femme*, literally, "speaking woman." The expression is, as often with Irigaray, highly ambiguous, thereby carrying a range of meanings. Its translation into English, "speaking (as) woman," is somewhat narrower, even if the "as" is put in parentheses. However, if woman has not yet taken place, how can one already speak as woman? Are speaking and writing[59] *causes* or *effects* of a different "sexe"? In the

---

58. Irigaray, *Ce sexe*, 133; 145–46; see discussion of these terms above. For woman as a nonidentifiable entity, see Irigaray, *Speculum de l'autre*, 285.

59. In her discussion of writing, Irigaray gives speech primacy over writing (in contrast to Derrida). A different writing may be an "effect" of *parler-femme*.

case of the ideology of the sexual difference of the "here and now" (labeled phallogocentrism, phallocratism, etc.), Irigaray sees writing that does not question its relation to this ideology as both producer and product (thus both *cause* and *effect*) in the current economy of meaning.[60] Similarly, concerning a different "sexe," she would not limit herself to only one of these options: The creative Word can bring a different "sexe" into being, but it can also be the effect of such a creation.

Thus, in Irigaray's notion of *parler-femme*, there is a tension between "already" and "not yet." Both Irigaray and John the Seer speak of the elsewhere *to come*, and both put this speech into the words and discourses available here and now. John the Seer claims already to speak from "elsewhere" back into this world, but his words and discourse sound depressingly familiar—depressingly "here." Irigaray on the other hand states explicitly that speaking from the other side is not yet possible, and one is tempted to suggest that she aptly diagnoses the problems with John's reversed "elsewhere": "We do not escape so easily from reversal.... There is no simple manageable way to leap to the outside of phallogocentrism, nor any possible way to situate oneself there, that would result from the simple fact of being a woman."[61] However, exactly for this reason she sees it as important to traverse the male imaginary and the dominant phallogocentric discourse in order "to provide a place for the 'other' as feminine."[62]

In order to start *parler-femme*, then, it is necessary to go back into the nuptial chamber and "destroy, but ... with nuptial tools. The tool is not a feminine attribute. But woman may re-utilize its marks on her, in her."[63] If we now take a look at Miss Jerusalem again, in many ways she reminds us of Irigaray's *femme* (wife or woman) of the philosopher.[64] By the end of Revelation, she is the bride in the nuptial chamber: What was required of her in order to arrive at speech was to take part in the wedding (night)[65] with the great multitude, gods and men, and fulfil the role of matter, χώρα, and city for them. And, as does Irigaray, we can assume that this enterprise was not an easy one. When she arrives at speech, she mimics the line given to her by the male discourse in the nuptial chamber. This is fine, however, for still, according to Irigaray, *mimicry* is the one path to

---

60. Irigaray, *Ce sexe,* 129.

61. Luce Irigaray, *This Sex Which Is Not One* (trans. C. Porter and C. Burke; Ithaca, N.Y.: Cornell University Press, 1993), 162.

62. Irigaray, *Ce Sexe,* 133.

63. Ibid., 150.

64. Ibid., 147–48.

65. The nuptial connotations of *faire la noce avec les philosophes* is lost in the English translation; cf. Irigaray, *Ce Sexe,* 147.

which the female condition is assigned. However, she continues: "But this (i.e. mimetic) role itself is complex, for it supposedly lends itself to everything, if not to everyone. That one can copy anything at all, anyone at all, can receive all impressions, *without appropriating them to oneself.* . . . If she can play that role so well, if it does not kill her, quite, it is because she keeps something in reserve . . . she still subsists, otherwise and elsewhere than there where she mimes so well what is asked of her."[66]

Through *mimétisme* the bride can simultaneously deal with male discourse in order to uncover its mechanisms, and at the same time re-utilize the marks these mechanisms leave on her in order to create space for the other woman to come. *Parler-femme* thus remains a possibility through its specific relation to the *otherwise* and *elsewhere*, in a different discourse without any closure of *archè* and *télos*, beginning and end[67]—or, to put it in Revelation's words, ἄλφα and ὦ (22:13; transliterated: *alpha* and *omega*). Whereas Revelation's author seeks to define the *télos*[68] of time, of men, and of God's transactions with himself through the media of the Lamb and the bride, the bride herself has no *télos* within this book, in the sense of a closure and end. Her gates are never closed (21:25), and, as she is just a place, she can have no end in herself. But her openness and infinity somehow make her more eternal than the men who come (and go), and for whom she functions as a receptacle. Hence, seen from a modern perspective, she is not confined to the book of Revelation, she is not confined inside the *alpha* and *omega* of the hardcover of the Bible either; indeed, she has not yet taken place.

As Pippin points out in her reading of Heaven from the perspective of the Bottomless Pit, "the tree and waters of life in the New Jerusalem are repetitions of their Eden versions in Genesis."[69] Similarly, the bride's *parler-femme*, speaking "come," can only be likened to the first page of the Bible where the God, who is helplessly confined within its hardcover and within the logic of its discourse, proclaims, "Let there be light!" (Gen 1:3). I am impressed with the astonishing effects of his creative proclamation—still it sounds like the cry of a claustrophobic who has just entered a narrow, dark room. The bidding of the bride—"come"—may be wholly in accordance with the discourse of the narrow, dark

---

66. Modified English quote from Irigaray, *This Sex*, 151–52.

67. Irigaray, *Ce Sexe*, 149.

68. Τέλος not only denotes end as such, but the purposeful, ultimate aim/fulfillment. See LSJ, s.v. "τέλος."

69. Tina Pippin, "Peering into the Abyss: A Postmodern Reading of the Biblical Bottomless Pit," in *The New Literary Criticism and the New Testament* (ed. E. S. Malbon and E. V. McKnight; JSNTSup 109; Sheffield: Sheffield Academic Press, 1994), 259.

nuptial chamber it is spoken within, and yet it is wholly other too, as the creative word bringing the phantasmic becoming-woman into life, here, there or "elsewhere."

CONCLUSION

I have tried to use feminist theory in combination with philology in order to investigate how male and female virgins in the book of Revelation contribute to its construction of the "elsewhere," but the broader concern has been to investigate how difference (sexual, linguistic or other) can speak through a dominant language (which one could argue, in a most universalizing way, is always nonidentical to itself anyway). I have argued for two main ways in which this is accomplished: through mimicry and taking on an "alien" posture, but, because my overall goal is awareness, I am hesitant to conclude that one is better than or can manage without the other.[70]

As should be clear by now, in my view Revelation's "elsewhere" is a gendered place in that a group of males live on and off the female ground. Revelation has been much explored in terms of intertextuality in recent years with resultant conflicting notions both of intertextuality and of which texts could be linked to Revelation in an intertextually sensible way.[71] One of the intertextual echoes that I hear in Revelation's "elsewhere" is the resonance with Hesiod's account of the paradisiacal existence of ἄνθρωποι ("human beings," definitely used in a male sense since they are contrasted with women) before the arrival of the γένος ("species") of women. Absence of women does not mean that there was no feminine entity surrounding them and accommodating them, for, until the arrival of the devastating Pandora, they lived happily on and off γαῖα ("the earth") and what *she* constantly had to offer them. None of this makes the masculinity of Revelation's 144,000 any more stable. Knowing that femininity is usually lurking somewhere just under the surface of the term παρθένος, the use of this term on men is a bit queer. I wrote about

---

70. Biblical scholars are in a good position to reflect upon such issues, as they study texts in different languages; they do not speak only one language—many use English in het-eroglossic ways that mimic other languages. Such practices have their problems (of fragmented and inconsistent textual surfaces and misunderstandings) but it also creates pos-sibilities.

71. See, e.g., David Aune, "Intertextuality and the Genre of the Apocalypse," in *Society of Biblical Literature 1991 Seminar Papers* (SBLSP 30; Atlanta: Scholars Press, 1991): 142–60; Alison M. Jack, *Texts Reading Texts, Sacred and Secular: Two Postmodern Perspectives* (JSNTSup 179; Sheffield: Sheffield Academic Press, 1999); and Steve Moyise, *The Old Testament in the Book of Revelation* (JSNTSup 115; Sheffield: Sheffield Academic Press, 1995).

Jerusalem as being possessed (by God and the Lamb), but these 144,000 are not their own either. They were purchased and sealed, just like slaves. They are described as firstfruits and as blameless, like appropriate but powerless victims bought for animal sacrifice in the heavenly Temple. In this way, then, their masculinity does not imply any kind of control over the discourse.

Further, the bride, Miss Jerusalem, goes into the nuptial chamber. Whether she speaks this word only because it is expected of her within male discourse or whether she mimics and simultaneously speaks as the woman of a different "sexe," we cannot know. But the attentive listener to the sound coming from the other side may hear ... the bride, Jerusalem, the "phantasmic 'becoming-woman'" not (yet) leaping outside of the Seer's discourse, but situating herself at its borders, on the Bible's very last page, and moving continuously from the inside to the outside,[72] through the canonical Bible's cover and beyond, where she can come and become.

---

72. Paraphrasing Irigaray, *This Sex*, 122, 141.

EPILOGUE: BABIES AND BATHWATER ON THE ROAD

Athalya Brenner

As I was reading this enlightening collection of articles with great interest and a sense of adventure, I used the editors' introduction as my guide. To quote from the beginning:

> [T]his present collection of essays seeks to explore the juxtaposition that exists between the world of interpretation offered by traditional historical criticism and that proffered by the various and diverse feminist and post-colonial interpreters who have often found the methods or, at the very least, the results offered by early practitioners lacking, largely because their own later experiences simply did not resonate with those projected in the metaphors, myths, and meanings of their "forefathers."[1]

Part of their conclusion is that the highly diverse essays in this rich volume—each in its own particular way—eventually illustrate the uneasy if continued partnership between traditional modes of historical criticism and "between so-called modernist and postmodernist concerns in this respect, establishing a broad line of continuity between historical criticism and what followed."[2]

So wherein lies the difference? According to the editors,

> [C]ritical discourses also need to be self-reflective and self-critical.... It is at this juncture that the *raison d'être* of this present volume exists, for we see precisely this agenda operative in this collection of essays. There is an attempt to incorporate widespread interaction with the traditional historical-critical task, while at the same time engaging that tradition of contesting scholarship. There are meta-levels of interaction herein, with the accent falling emphatically on the continued need for both contest and conversation, dialogue and differentiation, criticism and continuity.[3]

---

1. Caroline Vander Stichele and Todd Penner, "Mastering the Tools or Retooling the Masters? The Legacy of Historical-Critical Discourse," in this volume (2–3).

2. Ibid., 27.

3. Ibid., 28.

Ultimately, then, they suggest that "one thing is for certain, and that is that the 'master's house' has as its cornerstone the Bible, which provides its sure foundation."[4]

Babies and Bathwater

I feel I should (and in fact can) agree with the general thrust of these quotations. The editors have assessed the nature of the essays generously and fairly, highlighting the journey: on the way from reassessment and critique to beyond consent; from the feminist to the so-called postfeminist and beyond; from the premodern to the modern to the postmodern and beyond; from the confessional to the nonconfessional cultural (let me not use "secular," which is an overloaded word); from claimed universalism emanating from particularly centered situations (European, Western, Christian) to the paradoxically and potentially globalized discourse facilitated by recognizing contextual geographies and landscapes of varyingly legitimate identities. It is here that this volume is to be situated—*on the road*. And this is a road perhaps not well trodden or traveled at this time, but which promises to handle more traffic, for the benefit of travelers all over. And on this road, to mix metaphors, babies and bathwater had to be somewhat (once again, according to particular tastes and contextual situatedness!) modified, but—thankfully—neither the one nor the other has been completely discarded. Although, mind you, babies and bathwater on the move somehow changed identities, transmuted into each other, a case of alchemy no doubt.

For feminist criticisms to envelop historical criticism is, undoubtedly, a development. And this is a development for which one can be thankful, because, as amply demonstrated in this volume (see, e.g., De Troyer and Brock and, absolutely differently, Boer), the "master's tools"—contra Lourde—may and can be used to dismantle the master's house, if one so wishes. In passing, let me acknowledge that the mere engagement of female scholars in historio-critical criticism (so rare until recently), resolutely dismantling some of the latter's more cherished conclusions to boot, fills me with (de-?)colonizing glee. Because a decentering of methodology, its reexamination and reapplication, is part and parcel of being "post" and seems to me preferable, if and when possible, to the more simplistic option of deletion (or disregarding or "being thrown out"—to keep with the babies and bathwater imagery?). A re-molding through a judicious utilization coupled with departure (Stenström,

---

4. Ibid., 29.

(Stenström, Scholz) is such sweet victory. It does facilitate the Other and the Elsewhere (McKinley, Masenya); when the gaze shifts, previously dark realms can come to light (Martinez-Vázquez), texts can be read anew (Fuchs, Lee, Marchal, Vander Stichele and Penner, Økland, Boer again) and new programs can be sought (Marshall, Robbins, Geisterfer).

COMING CLEAN

So essays such as the ones collected here are by and large prudent. They build on previous methods even if and when they reject past premises or conclusions. Most of them hit a fair balance between past and present concerns, one's own contextuality and otherness-contextuality, individual and collective (however that distinction may be defined), scholarly and personal, scholarly and emotional, and I could go on. And you, the book's readers, could go on in a similar vein as well. (I assume most of you will be appreciative rather than resistant or suspicious readers.) Furthermore, and this, in my mind, connects to the situated-as-facilitating-globalization seeming paradox, I can detect unmasked anger in the two essays by Masenya and Fuchs, perhaps another and relatively better masked one in Boer's. This is certainly different from second, perhaps also third, wave feminist criticism. I note this feature not because I think feminist anger is unwarranted. It is. It still is. But because uncontrolled anger may blind a practitioner from using the master's tools for the ironical purpose of undermining that same master, namely, taking over a methodology for achieving different results.

And to go one step further—to come cleaner (one might say), having praised this collection in no uncertain terms—the time has now come for me to express some, well, not exactly reservations, but certainly uncertainties. To begin with, regarding methodologies, I would like to raise the following question: Having integrated, nay, assimilated, traditional modes of historio-critical investigation, with satisfactory twists, to our (post)modern hearts' content, how do we go further along the trajectory of (self-interested) feminist, postcolonial, race, gender, cultural, liberation modes of Bible criticisms? A prevailing suggestion arising from this volume is that the aim should be renewal, while incorporating the old into the new. Another is the employment of a hermeneutics of suspicion, or resistance, to counteract (or provide an antidote for) habitual or thoughtless readerly collusion. Yet another suggestion is for readers to uphold notions of difference (gender, class, ethnicity, and so on) as hermeneutical keys. This is undeniably good advice. And yet, in the framework of the present volume, is this goal in fact achieved?

In this respect, within a self-avowed framework of extension and inclusion—geographical and contextual and confessional/nonconfessional, to name but a few variables—I find a glaring omission in this book: it is, when all is said and done, a Western Euro-American enterprise! You may object and say, "Look here, you know that Euro-American centrism is unavoidable for biblical studies at this time, but an effort has been made to include non-English European cultures as well as third and fourth and fifth-worlds' contributions; and surely the preoccupation with postcolonialism and demarginalization is a hallmark of this volume?" I grant this protest, but for one factor: the volume remains a decidedly [post]Christian collection. It contains many creeds, but, ultimately, with a [post]Christian agenda, even if this agenda is extended beyond traditional constraints and is, and fortunately so, relevant for a wide variety of particularistic concerns. This volume has a contribution by one, single, Jewish author (Fuchs); two, if you count me as well. Significantly, both of us work in the Euro-American world, although we were born Israelis and maintain Israeli identity. Israel boasts a heavy volume of research in the last decades in Bible and so-called early Jewish history and religious studies, some of it highly innovative, quite a bit of it translated into the Euro-American (yet again) linguistic media. Israeli biblical scholars of the twentieth century, such as Moses Hirsch Segal, Umberto (Moshe David) Cassuto, Ye'hezkel Kaufmann, Meir Weiss and their followers, rejected the sociohistorical approach almost completely, offering alternatives that were narrowly Jewish-ideological at times, to be sure, but their methods of decentering and reading were fruitful and, at times, pioneering. These are also "fore-fathers" of biblical criticism—and important ones. And yet, when it comes to engaging the history of the discipline, the focus tends to be on the purely Western-centered institutions and scholars, with these "others" marginalized. Please correct me if I am wrong: Does this huge body of ongoing Israeli Bible research feature in this book in a meaningful manner? For that matter, does research done by *Jewish* scholars feature largely in this book? Fuchs discusses Carol Meyers's work, and Boer discusses Tamara Eskenazi's; A.-J. Levine is mentioned in a note, in the editors' introduction. Have I forgotten anybody? Ah yes. Boyarin, Brooten, Peskowitz, Plaskow, Kraemer, Sternberg, Schwartz, Frymer-Kensky, Myerowitz, Ilan, Sarna, Derrida, are mentioned in passing, they are indeed. You can comb the notes to find others if you will. However, and this is my impression, the combined weight of [post]modern Jewish scholarship on the Bible and related areas, confessional and nonconfessional, is less noticeable here than I would have thought fair.

Ah, I can almost hear your objections again. There is nothing wrong with this. Not every volume has to include every viewpoint. The editors have informed us of availability—most articles originated in Society of Biblical Literature International Meeting presentations, so availability is a definite factor. In any case, this volume does much by reaching outwards, beyond the Euro-American realm. It is not fair to judge absent components; rather concentrate on what there is. And, finally, on the personal level, Brenner must have her own vested, situated interest and ideology that predisposes her to notice this relative lack of Jewish/Israeli scholarly representation.

To the last imagined charge I readily admit. As for the others, I would find them less convincing. In this volume, contributors deal with canonized sources and canonized interpretations from the Judeo-Christian worlds, of then and now. Geography and context are constructed as a backdrop not only for a multiplicity of methodologies, but also for the deployment of scholarly voices. Voices from North Europe, Australia, Africa and South-East Asia are coupled with American voices in the critique of older biblical studies methods (predominantly German). I hope, indeed I believe, that a political agenda informs all articles, even if the methods or aims differ. The "Judeo" element of the "Judeo-Christian" scholarly worlds from which the interpreters operate is thus made vague, less important—in contradistinction to the "Judeo-Christian" properties of the canonized texts that are explored. This omission, or deletion (for me), can only be excused if returned to later, perhaps elsewhere, and if it is borne in mind. In a Western, [post]Christian volume as the one we have before us (and how can it be otherwise, let me admit), privileging geographically more distant voices over those of the cultural Other within, looking for "borderlands" (Martinez-Vázquez) while overlooking the "borderlands" contained by the inside (or not), is equal to ignoring any other difference. In other words, perhaps a return to religious difference and its implications might be as fruitful for neo-feminist criticisms (should we use this cipher now instead of "Xth wave," and so on?) as inquiries into any other contextual difference.

ON THE ROAD

This volume's editors call us to contest accepted guild practices, with judiciousness and self-reflection. To conclude in that vein, I would like to problematize the assertion that concludes their introduction: "[t]he 'master's house' has as its cornerstone the Bible, which provides its sure foundation."[5]

This task of contestation, of destabilizing, of jagging, of introducing deliberate unevenness, is certainly carried out by the volume's contributors

---

5. Ibid., 29.

in a variety of ways. Insiders and outsiders may find that their positions have shifted: emic has become etic and vice versa—at least for some circles; at least for a while, before the wheel of academic fashion turns a full turn again (Robbins) into another interpretive and imperative rhetoric. The master's house has been invaded by the mistress and her voices and their productive echoes. The mistress has secured at least some space for "herself" and "her" concerns, as those are extended to societal and ethical affairs at large. But does "the Bible" still serve as the metaphorical house's "foundation" and, moreover, how "sure" is that foundation? And which bible, or bibles, and for whom? Once again, such questions have been broached in this volume (by Brock and De Troyer, for instance, and Marshall), but they require more systematic and substantive engagement.

So, while on the road, many questions remain. Questions of gain and loss, and prices to be paid, and so on. "Whence and Whither: Methodology and the Future of Biblical Studies" was the title Penner and Vander Stichele gave to the sessions they organized at the ISBL conferences out of which most of the essays in this volume arose. This is indeed a most pertinent question. So let me conclude by asking some more.

Quo vadis, feminist biblical scholarship? *Quo vadis*, postcolonial scholarship? What is beckoning? Where do you want to go? Is the Master's House still the house you long to possess, only that you would like to become its legitimate(d) masters and mistresses instead of marginal(ized) lodgers? Would you like to move it (houses can be moved now from one location to another)? What is meant by decentering? Will an act of exchanging places within the accepted power paradigms be the object of desire? Are new structures of dominance, a shift in majority/minority balances, being implemented? Are you, we, aspiring to conquistador positions in the names of the proverbial "oppressed"? Should we not simply demolish the house instead of merely deconstructing it and its inhabitants, in order to build a completely new one instead? And if so, who will get right of occupation in the new house, and on what terms? Indeed, whose Bible is it anyway? The contenders are many and the audiences are dwindling, as we are becoming more and more radicalized. Whose scholarship will matter, say, twenty-five years hence?

These are burning questions that must occupy us on the road ahead.

BIBLIOGRAPHY

Abley, Mark. *Spoken Here: Travels among Threatened Languages.* London: Heinemann, 2003.

Abrahamsen, Valerie. "Christianity and the Rock Reliefs at Philippi." *BA* 51 (1988): 46–56.

———. *Women and Worship at Philippi: Diana/Artemis and Other Cults in the Early Christian Era.* Portland, Maine: Astarte Shell, 1995.

———. "Women at Philippi: The Pagan and Christian Evidence." *JFSR* 3 (1987): 17–30.

Abrams, Ann Uhry. *The Pilgrims and Pocahontas: Rival Myths of American Origin.* Boulder, Colo.: Westview, 1999.

Ackerman, Susan. "'And the Women Knead Dough': The Worship of the Queen of Heaven in Sixth Century Judea." Pages 21–32 in *Women in the Hebrew Bible.* Edited by A. Bach. New York: Routledge, 1999.

———. *Warrior, Dancer, Seductress, Queen: Women in Judges and Biblical Israel.* ABRL. New York: Doubleday, 1998.

Adams, Edward. *Constructing the World: A Study in Paul's Cosmological Language.* Edinburgh: T&T Clark, 2000.

Adorno, Theodor W. "On the Use of Foreign Words." Pages 288–91 in *Notes to Literature.* Edited by R. Tiedemann. Translated by S. W. Nicholson. 2 vols. New York: Columbia University Press, 1991.

Agosto, Efrain. "Paul vs. Empire: A Postcolonial and Latino Reading of Philippians." *Perspectivas: Occasional Papers* 6 (2002): 37–56.

Albrektson, Bertil. *Studies in the Text and Theology of the Book of Lamentations.* STL 21. Lund: Gleerup, 1963.

Alcoff, Linda, and Elizabeth Potter, eds. *Feminist Epistemologies.* New York: Routledge, 1993.

Aldama, Arturo J. *Disrupting Savagism: Intersecting Chicana/o, Mexican Immigrant, and Native American Struggles for Self-Representation.* Durham: Duke University Press, 2001.

———. "Millennial Anxieties: Borders, Violence, and the Struggle for Chicana and Chicano Subjectivity." Pages 11–29 in *Decolonial Voices: Chicana and Chicano Cultural Studies in the 21st Century.* Edited by A. J. Aldama and N. H. Quiñonez. Bloomington: Indiana University Press, 2002.

Alexander, Thomas D. "Are the Wife/Sister Incidents of Genesis Literary Compositional Variants?" *VT* 42 (1992): 145–53.

Almås, Elsa, and Espen Esther Pirelli Benestad. *Kjønn i bevegelse.* Oslo: Universitetsforlaget, 2001.

Alter, Robert. *The Art of Biblical Narrative.* New York: Basic Books, 1981.

Althusser, Louis. *Lenin and Philosophy, and Other Essays.* Translated by B. Brewster. New York: Monthly Review, 1971.

Ando, Clifford. *Imperial Ideology and Provincial Loyalty in the Roman Empire.* Classics and Contemporary Thought 6. Berkeley and Los Angeles: University of California Press, 2000.

Andrews, Malin Bergman. *Emilia Fogelklou, människan och gärningen—En biografi.* Skellefteå: Artos, 1999.

Angelopoulos, Theo. *The Suspended Step of the Stork.* Greece: Greek Film Centre, 1991.

Anonymous. "The New System of Colonization—Australia and New Zealand." *The Phrenological Journal and Magazine of Modern Science* 11 (1838): 247–60.

Anzaldúa, Gloria. *Borderlands/La Frontera: The New Mestiza.* San Francisco: Aunt Lute, 1999.

———. "Haciendo Caras, Una Entrada." Pages xv–xxviii in *Making Face, Making Soul/Haciendo Caras: Creative and Critical Perspectives by Feminists of Color.* Edited by G. Anzaldúa. San Francisco: Aunt Lute, 1990.

Aquino, María Pilar. "The Collective 'Dis-covery' of Our Own Power: Latina American Feminist Theology." Pages 240–58 in *Hispanic/Latino Theology: Challenge and Promise.* Edited by A. M. Isasi-Díaz and F. F. Segovia. Minneapolis: Fortress, 1996.

Arnal, William E. *Jesus and the Village Scribes: Galilean Conflicts and the Setting of Q.* Minneapolis: Fortress, 2001.

Ashcroft, Bill. *Post-colonial Transformation.* London: Routledge, 2001.

Ashcroft, Bill, Gareth Griffiths, and Helen Tiffin, eds. *Key Concepts in Post-Colonial Studies.* London: Routledge, 1998.

Aune, David. "The Influence of Roman Imperial Court Ceremonial on the Apocalypse of John." *BR* 18 (1983): 5–26.

———. "Intertextuality and the Genre of the Apocalypse." Pages 142–60 in *SBL Seminar Papers, 1991.* SBLSP 30. Atlanta: Scholars Press, 1991.

Babbitt, Frank C., et al., trans. *Plutarch: Moralia.* 16 vols. LCL. Cambridge, Mass.: Harvard University Press, 1927–1976.

Bach, Alice. "Rereading the Body Politic: Women and Violence in Judges 21." *BibInt* 6 (1998): 1–19.

Bachmann, Philipp. *Der erste Brief des Paulus an die Korinther.* 2d ed. Leipzig: Deichert, 1910.

Badian, Ernst. *Roman Imperialism in the Late Republic.* 2d ed. Oxford: Oxford University Press, 1968.

Bagnall, Austin G., and G. C. Petersen. *William Colenso, Printer, Missionary, Botanist, Explorer, Politician: His Life and Journeys.* Wellington, New Zealand: Reed, 1948.

Bakhtin, Mikhail M. *The Dialogic Imagination: Four Essays by M. M. Bakhtin.* Edited by M. Holquist. Translated by C. Emerson and M. Holquist. Austin: University of Texas Press, 1981.

———. *Speech Genres and Other Late Essays.* Edited by C. Emerson and M. Holquist. Translated by V. W. McGee. Austin: University of Texas Press, 1986.

Bal, Mieke. *Death and Dissymmetry: The Politics of Coherence in the Book of Judges.* Chicago: University of Chicago Press, 1988.

──────. *Lethal Love: Feminist Literary Readings of Biblical Love Stories.* Bloomington: Indiana University Press, 1987.

Balch, David L. "Paul, Families, and Households." Pages 258–92 in *Paul in the Greco-Roman World.* Edited by J. P. Sampley. Harrisburg, Pa.: Trinity Press International, 2003.

Barr, James. "Remembrances of 'Historical Criticism'." Pages 59–72 in *God Who Creates: Essays in Honor of W. Sibley Towner.* Edited by W. P. Brown and S. D. McBride, Jr. Grand Rapids: Eerdmans, 2000.

Barrett, Charles Kingsley. *A Commentary on the First Epistle to the Corinthians.* BNTC. London: Blackwell, 1968.

Barrett, Michelle. *Women's Oppression Today: The Marxist/Feminist Encounter.* London: Verso, 1988.

Bedale, Stephen. "The Meaning of *kephalē* in the Pauline Epistles." *JTS* 5 (1954): 211–15.

Belleville, Linda L. "Κεφαλή and the Thorny Issue of Headcovering in 1 Corinthians 11:2–16." Pages 215–31 in *Paul and the Corinthians: Studies on a Community in Conflict. Essays in Honour of Margaret Thrall.* Edited by T. J. Burke and J. K. Elliott. NovTSup 109. Leiden: Brill, 2003.

Benhabib, Seyla, and Drucilla Cornell. "Introduction." Pages 1–15 in *Feminism as Critique: On the Politics of Gender in Late-Capitalist Societies.* Edited by Seyla Benhabib and Drucilla Cornell. Minneapolis: University of Minnesota Press, 1987.

Benhabib, Seyla, et al., eds. *Feminist Contentions: A Philosophical Exchange.* New York: Routledge, 1995.

Benjamin, Walter. "Theses on the Philosophy of History." Pages 253–64 in *Illuminations.* Edited by H. Arendt. Translated by H. Zohn. New York: Schocken, 1985.

Berry, Ellen E., and Mikhail N. Epstein. *Transcultural Experiments: Russian and American Models of Creative Communication.* New York: St. Martin's, 1999.

Beverley, John. *Subalternity and Representation: Arguments in Cultural Theory.* Postcontemporary Interventions. Durham: Duke University Press, 1999.

Bhabha, Homi K. *The Location of Culture.* New York: Routledge, 1994.

The Bible and Culture Collective. *The Postmodern Bible.* New Haven: Yale University Press, 1995.

Bird, Phyllis A. *Missing Persons and Mistaken Identities: Women and Gender in Ancient Israel.* Minneapolis: Fortress, 1997.

──────. "What Makes a Feminist Reading Feminist? A Qualified Answer." Pages 124–31 in *Escaping Eden: New Feminist Perspectives on the Bible.* Edited by H. C. Washington, S. L. Graham, and P. L. Thimmes. New York: New York University Press, 1998.

Bizzell, Patricia, and Bruce Herzberg, eds. *The Rhetorical Tradition: Readings from Classical Times to the Present.* Boston: Bedford Books of St. Martin's, 1990.

Bockmuehl, Markus. *The Epistle to the Philippians.* BNTC 11. Peabody, Mass.: Hendrickson, 1998.

Boer, Roland. "Introduction: Vanishing Mediators?" *Semeia* 88 (2001): 1–12.

──────. *Knockin' on Heaven's Door: The Bible and Popular Culture.* London: Routledge, 1999.

342 Bibliography

——. *Marxist Criticism of the Bible.* New York: Continuum, 2003.

——. *Novel Histories: The Fiction of Biblical Criticism.* Playing the Texts 2. Sheffield: Sheffield Academic Press, 1997.

——. "Western Marxism and the Interpretation of the Hebrew Bible." *JSOT* 78 (1998): 3–21.

——. ed. *A Vanishing Mediator? The Presence/Absence of the Bible in Postcolonialism. Semeia* 88. Atlanta: Society of Biblical Literature, 2001.

Bonilla, Frank, Edwin Meléndez, Rebecca Morales, and María de los Angeles Torres, eds. *Borderless Borders: U.S. Latinos, Latin Americans, and the Paradox of Interdependence.* Philadelphia: Temple University Press, 1998.

Borg, Annika. "Att lära av misstagen. Några nedslag i svensk 1900–talsexegetik." Pages 33–48 in *Varkan vi finna en nådig Gud? Omkönsmaktsordningi kyrka och teologi.* Edited by A.-L. Eriksson. Working Papers in Theology 2. Uppsala: Uppsala University, 2002.

Bormann, Lukas. *Philippi: Stadt und Christengemeinde zur Zeit des Paulus.* NovTSup 78. Leiden: Brill, 1995.

Bornhäuser, Karl. *Jesus imperator mundi (Phil 3, 17–21 u. 2, 5–12).* Gütersloh: Bertelsmann, 1938.

Børresen, Kari. "'Patristic 'Feminism:' The Case of Augustine." Pages 33–47 in *From Patristics to Matristics: Selected Articles on Christian Gender Models by Kari E. Børresen.* Edited by Ø. Norderval and K. L. Ore. Rome: Herder, 2002.

Bowersock, G. W. *Augustus and the Greek World.* Oxford: Clarendon, 1965.

Bowie, Angus. "*Exuvias Effigiemque:* Dido, Aeneas and the Body as Sign." Pages 57–79 in *Changing Bodies, Changing Meanings: Studies on the Human Body in Antiquity.* Edited by D. Montserrat. New York: Routledge, 1998.

Boyarin, Daniel. *Carnal Israel: Reading Sex in Talmudic Culture.* The New Historicism 25. Berkeley and Los Angeles: University of California Press, 1993.

——. "Paul and the Genealogy of Gender." Pages 13–41 in *A Feminist Companion to Paul.* Edited by A.-J. Levine with M. Blickenstaff. FCNTECW 6. New York: Continuum, 2004.

——. *A Radical Jew: Paul and the Politics of Identity.* Berkeley and Los Angeles: University of California Press, 1994.

——. *Unheroic Conduct: The Rise of Heterosexuality and the Invention of the Jewish Man.* Contraversions 8. Berkeley and Los Angeles: University of California Press, 1997.

Bradley, Keith R. *Slavery and Rebellion in the Roman World, 140 B.C.-70 B.C.* Bloomington: Indiana University Press, 1989.

——. *Slaves and Masters in the Roman Empire: A Study in Social Control.* Collection Latomus 185. Brussels: Latomus, 1984.

Brandon, S. G. F. *Jesus and the Zealots: A Study of the Political Factor in Primitive Christianity.* New York: Scribners, 1967.

Braun, Willi. "Physiotherapy of Femininity in the Acts of Thecla." Pages 209–30 in *Text and Artifact in the Religions of Mediterranean Antiquity: Essays in Honour of Peter Richardson.* Edited by S. G. Wilson and M. Desjardins. SCJ 9. Waterloo, Ont.: Wilfrid Laurier University Press, 2000.

Brenner, Athalya, ed. *A Feminist Companion to the Bible.* 10 vols. Sheffield: Sheffield Academic Press, 1993–1996.

———. *The Intercourse of Knowledge: On Gendering Desire and "Sexuality" in the Hebrew Bible.* BibInt Series 26. Leiden: Brill, 1997.

Brenner, Athalya, and Fokkelien van Dijk-Hemmes. *On Gendering Texts: Female and Male Voices in the Hebrew Bible.* BibInt Series 1. Leiden: Brill, 1993.

Brenner, Athalya, and Carole R. Fontaine, eds. *A Feminist Companion to the Bible.* 2d Series. 9 vols. Sheffield: Sheffield Academic Press, 1997–2001.

Brett, Mark G. *Genesis: Procreation and the Politics of Identity.* Old Testament Readings. New York: Routledge, 2000.

Brettler, Marc Zvi. *The Creation of History in Ancient Israel.* New York: Routledge, 1995.

Brewer, Raymond R. "The Meaning of *politeuesthe* in Phil. 1:27." *JBL* 73 (1954): 76–83.

Briggs, Charles A. *Authority of Holy Scripture: Inaugural Address and Defense, 1891/1893.* New York: Arno, 1972.

———. *The Case Against Professor Briggs.* New York: Scribner, 1892–1893.

Briggs, Sheila. "Can an Enslaved God Liberate? Hermeneutical Reflections on Philippians 2:6–11." *Semeia* 47 (1989): 137–53.

———. "The Deceit of the Sublime: An Investigation into the Origins of Ideological Criticism of the Bible in Early Nineteenth-Century German Biblical Studies." *Semeia* 59 (1992): 1–23.

Brock, Ann Graham. *Mary Magdalene, the First Apostle: The Struggle for Authority.* HTS 51. Cambridge, Mass.: Harvard University Press, 2003.

———. "Appeasement, Authority, and the Role of Women in the D-Text of Acts." Pages 205–24 in *The Book of Acts as Church History, Apostelgeschichte als Kirchengeschichte.* Edited by T. Nicklas and M. Tilly. BZNW 120. Berlin: de Gruyter, 2003.

Brokkman, Jennie. "German Heretic Remains in a Chair." *The Times Higher Education Supplement* 1365 (1 January 1999): 10.

Brooke, George J. "Between Qumran and Corinth: Embroidered Allusions to Women's Authority." Pages 157–76 in *The Dead Sea Scrolls as Background to Postbiblical Judaism and Early Christianity; Papers from an International Conference at St. Andrews in 2001.* Edited by J. R. Davila. STDJ 46. Leiden: Brill, 2003.

Brooten, Bernadette J. "Early Christian Women and Their Cultural Context: Issues of Method in Historical Reconstruction." Pages 65–91 in *Feminist Perspectives on Biblical Scholarship.* Edited by A. Y. Collins. SBLBSNA 10. Chico, Calif.: Scholars Press, 1985.

———. *Love between Women: Early Christian Responses to Female Homoeroticism.* The Chicago Series on Sexuality, History, and Society. Chicago: University of Chicago Press, 1996.

———. "Paul and the Law: How Complete was the Departure?" *Princeton Seminary Bulletin.* Suppl. 1 (1990): 71–89.

———. *Women Leaders in the Ancient Synagogue.* BJS 36. Chico, Calif.: Scholars Press, 1982.

Brownmiller, Susan. *Against Our Will: Men, Women, and Rape.* New York: Bantam, 1976.

Brueggemann, Walter. *The Prophetic Imagination.* 2d ed. Minneapolis: Fortress, 2001.

Brunt, P. A. *Italian Manpower, 225 B.C.-A.D. 14.* Oxford: Oxford University Press, 1971.

Buell, Denise Kimber, and Caroline Johnson Hodge. "The Politics of Interpretation: The Rhetoric of Race and Ethnicity in Paul." *JBL* 123 (2004): 235–51.

Burke, Trevor J. "Paul's Role as 'Father' to His Corinthian 'Children' in Socio-historical Context (I Corinthians 4:14–21)." Pages 95–113 in *Paul and the Corinthians: Studies on a Community in Conflict. Essays in Honour of Margaret Thrall.* Edited by T. J. Burke and J. K. Elliott. NovTSup 109. Leiden: Brill, 2003.

Burrus, Virginia. *"Begotten, Not Made": Conceiving Manhood in Late Antiquity.* Figurae. Stanford: Stanford University Press, 2000.

———. *Chastity as Autonomy: Women in the Stories of the Apocryphal Acts.* Studies in Women and Religion 23. Lewiston, N.Y.: Mellen, 1987.

———. *The Sex Lives of Saints: An Erotics of Ancient Hagiography.* Divinations. Philadelphia: University of Pennsylvania Press, 2004.

Buss, Martin J. *Biblical Form Criticism in Its Context.* JSOTSup 274. Sheffield: Sheffield Academic Press, 1999.

Butler, Judith. "Contingent Foundations: Feminism and the Question of 'Postmodernism.'" Pages 17–34 in *Feminist Contentions: A Philosophical Exchange.* Edited by S. Benhabib et al. New York: Routledge, 1995.

———. *Gender Trouble: Feminism and the Subversion of Identity.* New York: Routledge, 1990.

Butler, Judith, and Joan W. Scott, eds. *Feminists Theorize the Political.* New York: Routledge, 1992.

Cadoux, C. John. *The Early Christian Attitude to War.* London: Headley, 1918.

Calderón, Héctor, and José David Saldívar, eds. *Criticism in the Borderlands: Studies in Chicano Literature, Culture, and Ideology.* Durham: Duke University Press, 1991.

Calvin, John. *Genesis.* Translated by J. King. Carlisle, Pa.: The Banner of Truth Trust, 1992.

Cameron, Averil. "Redrawing the Map: Early Christian Territory after Foucault." *JRS* 76 (1986): 266–71.

Camp, Claudia V., and Carol R. Fontaine, eds. *Women, War, and Metaphor: Language and Society in the Study of the Hebrew Bible.* Semeia 61. Atlanta: Scholars Press, 1993.

Castelli, Elizabeth A. "The *Ekklesia* of Women and/as Utopian Space: Locating the Work of Elisabeth Schüssler Fiorenza in Feminist Utopian Thought." Pages 36–52 in *On the Cutting Edge: Study of Women in Biblical Worlds.* Edited by J. Schaberg, A. Bach, and E. Fuchs. New York: Continuum, 2003.

———. "Heteroglossia, Hermeneutics and History: A Review Essay of Recent Feminist Studies of Early Christianity." *JFSR* 10 (1994): 73–98.

———. "'I Will Make Mary Male': Pieties of the Body and Gender Transformation of Christian Women in Late Antiquity." Pages 29–49 in *Body Guards: The Cultural Politics of Gender Ambiguity.* Edited by J. Epstein and K. Straub. Routledge: New York: 1991.

———. *Imitating Paul: A Discourse of Power.* Literary Currents in Biblical Interpretation. Louisville: Westminster John Knox, 1991.

———. "Paul on Women and Gender." Pages 221–35 in *Women and Christian Origins*. Edited by R. Shepard Kraemer and M. R. D'Angelo. New York: Oxford University Press, 1999.

Cervin, Richard S. "Does *kephale* Mean 'Source' or 'Authority Over' in Greek Literature? A Rebuttal." *TJ* NS 10 (1989): 85–112.

Cheng, Sinkwan. "*Fremdwörter* as 'The Jews of Language' and Adorno's Politics of Exile." Pages 75–103 in *Adorno, Culture, and Feminism*. Edited by M. O'Neill. London: Sage, 1999.

Christou, Panayotis. "*ISOPSYCHOS*, Phil 2:20." *JBL* 70 (1951): 293–96.

Clark, Elizabeth A. "Foucault, the Fathers, and Sex." *JAAR* 56 (1988): 619–41.

———. *History, Theory, Text: Historians and the Linguistic Turn*. Cambridge: Harvard University Press, 2004.

Clarke, Andrew D. "'Be Imitators of Me': Paul's Model of Leadership." *TynBul* 49 (1998): 329–60.

Clines, David J. A. *The Esther Scroll: The Story of the Story*. JSOTSup 30. Sheffield: Sheffield Academic Press, 1984.

Cohen, Jeffrey J., ed. *The Postcolonial Middle Ages*. The New Middle Ages. New York: St. Martin's, 2000.

Cohen, Jeffrey M. "Vashti: An Unsung Heroine." *JBQ* 24 (1996): 103–6.

Colebrook, Claire. *New Literary Histories: New Historicism and Contemporary Criticism*. Manchester: Manchester University Press, 1997.

Collart, Paul. *Ville de Macédoine: depuis ses origines jusqu'à la fin de l'époque romaine*. Paris: Boccard, 1937.

Collins, Adela Yarbro. *The Combat Myth in the Book of Revelation*. HDR 9. Missoula, Mont.: Scholars Press, 1976.

———. "Feminine Symbolism in the Book of Revelation." *BibInt* 1 (1993): 20–33.

———, ed. *Feminist Perspectives on Biblical Scholarship*. SBLBSNA 10. Chico, Calif.: Scholars Press, 1985.

Condren, Mary. "To Bear Children for the Fatherland: Mothers and Militarism." Pages 115–23 in *The Power of Naming: A Concilium Reader in Feminist Liberation Theology*. Edited by Elisabeth Schüssler Fiorenza. Maryknoll, N.Y.: Orbis, 1996.

Conkey, Margaret. "Original Narratives: The Political Economy of Gender in Archeology." Pages 102–39 in *Gender at the Crossroads of Knowledge: Feminist Anthropology in the Postmodern Era*. Edited by M. di Leonardo. Berkeley and Los Angeles: University of California Press, 1991.

Conley, Thomas H. *Rhetoric in the European Tradition*. Chicago: University of Chicago Press, 1990.

Conzelmann, Hans. *Der erste Brief an die Korinther*. 12th ed. KEK 5. Göttingen: Vandenhoeck & Ruprecht, 1981.

Cooke, Miriam. "WO-man, Retelling the War Myth." Pages 177–204 in *Gendering War-Talk*. Edited by M. Cooke and A. Woollacott. Princeton: Princeton University Press, 1993.

Corbeill, Anthony. "Dining Deviants in Roman Political Invective." Pages 111–23 in *Roman Sexualities*. Edited by J. P. Hallett and M. B. Skinner. Princeton: Princeton University Press, 1997.

Corley, Kathleen E. *Private Women, Public Meals: Social Conflict in the Synoptic Tradition*. Peabody, Mass.: Hendrickson, 1993.

Cornell, Drucilla. "What is Ethical Feminism?" Pages 75–106 in *Feminist Contentions*. Edited by S. Benhabib et al. New York: Routledge, 1995.

Corrington, Gail Paterson. "The 'Headless Woman': Paul and the Language of the Body in 1 Cor 11:2–16." *PRSt* 18 (1991): 223–31.

Craig, Kerry M. and Margret A. Kristjansson. "Women Reading as Men/Women Reading as Women: A Structural Analysis for the Historical Project." *Semeia* 51 (1990): 119–36.

Crocker, Cornelia Cyss. *Reading 1 Corinthians in the Twenty-First Century*. New York: T&T Clark, 2004.

Culler, Jonathan. "The Call to History." Pages 57–68 in *Framing the Sign: Criticism and Its Institutions*. Norman: University of Oklahoma Press, 1988.

D'Angelo, Mary Rose. "The ANEP Question in Luke-Acts: Imperial Masculinity and the Deployment of Women in the Early Second Century." Pages 44–69 in *A Feminist Companion to Luke*. Edited by A.-J. Levine and M. Blickenstaff. FCNTECW 3. New York: Continuum, 2003.

———. "'Knowing How to Preside Over His Own Household': Imperial Masculinity and Christian Asceticism in the Pastorals, Hermas, and Luke-Acts." Pages 265–95 in *New Testament Masculinities*. Edited by S. D. Moore and J. Capel Anderson. SemeiaSt 45. Atlanta: Society of Biblical Literature, 2003.

———. "Veils, Virgins, and the Tongues of Men and Angels." Pages 389–419 in *Women, Gender, Religion: A Reader*. Edited by E. A. Castelli with R. C. Rodman. New York: Palgrave, 2001.

———. "Women Partners in the New Testament." *JFSR* 6 (1990): 65–86.

Daube, David. *The Exodus Pattern in the Bible*. London: Faber & Faber, 1963.

Davaney, Sheila Greeve. "Continuing the Story, but Departing the Text: A Historicist Interpretation of Feminist Norms in Theology." Pages 198–214 in *Horizons in Feminist Theology: Identity, Tradition and Norms*. Edited by R. S. Chopp and S. Greeve Davaney. Minneapolis: Fortress, 1997.

———. "Historicist Interpretations of Subjectivity, Tradition and Norms in Feminist Theology." *STK* 76 (2000): 170–78.

Davies, Philip R. *In Search of "Ancient Israel."* JSOTSup 148. Sheffield: JSOT Press, 1992.

———. *Whose Bible Is It Anyway?* 2d ed. London: Continuum, 2004.

Davies, Roy W. *Service in the Roman Army*. Edited by D. Breeze and V. A. Maxfield. New York: Columbia University Press, 1989.

De Troyer, Kristin. "Did Joshua Have a Crystal Ball? The Old Greek and the MT of Joshua 10:15, 17 and 23." Pages 571–89 in *Emmanuel: Studies in Hebrew Bible, Septuagint and Dead Sea Scrolls in Honour of Emanuel Tov*. Edited by S. M. Paul et al. VTSup 94. Leiden: Brill, 2003.

———. "Fifty Years of Qumran Research: A Different Approach." *RSR* 28 (2002): 115–22.

———. *Joshua*. Edited by R. Pintaudi. Catalogue of the Schøyen Greek Papyri. Oslo-London: The Martin Schøyen Collection, 2004.

———. *Rewriting the Sacred Text: What the Old Greek Texts Tell Us about the Literary Growth of the Bible*. SBLTCS. Atlanta: Society of Biblical Literature, 2003.

———. "Septuagint and Gender Studies: The Very Beginning of a Promising Liaison." Pages 366–86 in *A Feminist Companion to Reading the Bible: Approaches,*

Methods and Strategies. Edited by A. Brenner and C. R. Fontaine. Sheffield: Sheffield Academic Press, 1997.

De Vos, Craig S. *Church and Community Conflicts: The Relationships of the Thessalonian, Corinthian, and Philippian Churches with Their Wider Civic Communities.* SBLDS 168. Atlanta: Scholars Press, 1999.

Dean-Jones, Lesley Ann. *Women's Bodies in Classical Greek Science.* Oxford: Clarendon, 1994.

Dearin, Ray D., ed. *The New Rhetoric of Chaïm Perelman: Statement and Response.* Lanham, Md.: University Press of America, 1989.

Delitzsch, Frans. *Die Genesis.* 2d ed. Leipzig: Dorffling & Franke, 1853.

———. *Neuer Commentar über die Genesis.* 5th ed. Leipzig: Dorffling & Franke, 1887.

Delling, Gerhard. "παρθένος." *TDNT* 5:826–37.

Derrida, Jacques. *Margins of Philosophy.* Translated by A. Bass. Chicago: University of Chicago Press, 1982.

———. *Of Grammatology.* Translated by G. C. Spivak. Baltimore: Johns Hopkins University Press, 1974.

Diamond, Irene, and Lee Quinby, eds. *Feminism and Foucault: Reflections on Resistance.* Boston: Northeastern University Press, 1988.

Dibelius, Martin. *An die Thessalonicher I–II; An die Philipper.* 2d ed. HNT 11. Tübingen: Mohr Siebeck, 1925.

Diski, Jenny. *Only Human: A Comedy.* London: Virago, 2000.

Donaldson, Laura E., ed. *Postcolonialism and Scriptural Reading. Semeia* 75. Atlanta: Society of Biblical Literature, 1996.

Douglas, Mary. *Natural Symbols: Explorations in Cosmology.* New York: Pantheon, 1982.

———. "Responding to Ezra: The Priests and the Foreign Wives." *BibInt* 10 (2002): 1–23.

Dozeman, Thomas B. "The Wilderness and Salvation History in the Hagar Story." *JBL* 117 (1998): 23–43.

Dreyfus, Hubert L., and Paul Rabinow. *Michel Foucault: Beyond Structuralism and Hermeneutics.* Chicago: University of Chicago Press, 1983.

Dube (Shomanah), Musa W., ed. *Other Ways of Reading: African Women and the Bible.* Global Perspectives on Biblical Scholarship 2. Atlanta: Society of Biblical Literature, 2001.

———."Postcolonial Biblical Interpretations." *DBI* 2:299–303.

———. *Postcolonial Feminist Interpretation of the Bible.* St. Louis: Chalice, 2000.

Dube, Musa W., and John L. Staley, eds. *John and Postcolonialism: Travel, Space and Power.* Bible and Postcolonialism 7. London: Continuum, 2002.

Dunn, Stephen P. *The Fall and Rise of the Asiatic Mode of Production.* London: Routledge & Kegan Paul, 1981.

Dussel, Enrique. "Beyond Eurocentrism: The World-System and the Limits of Modernity." Pages 3–31 in *The Cultures of Globalization.* Edited by Fredric Jameson and Masao Miyoshi. Durham: Duke University Press, 1998.

———. "Eurocentrism and Modernity." Pages 65–76 in *The Postmodernism Debate in Latin America.* Edited by J. Beverley, M. Aronna, and J. Oviedo. Durham: Duke University Press, 1995.

———. "The Sociohistorical Meaning of Liberation Theology: Reflections about Its Origin and World Context." Pages 33–45 in *Religions/Globalizations:*

Theories and Cases. Edited by D. N. Hopkins, E. Mendieta, and D. Batstone. Durham: Duke University Press, 2001.

Dyck, Jonathan. *The Theocratic Ideology of the Chronicler.* BibInt Series 33. Leiden: Brill, 1998.

Eagleton, Terry. "Ideology and Scholarship." Pages 114–25 in *Historical Studies and Literary Criticism.* Edited by J. J. McGann. Madison: The University of Wisconsin Press, 1985.

Edwards, Catherine. "Unspeakable Professions: Public Performance and Prostitution in Ancient Rome." Pages 66–95 in *Roman Sexualities.* Edited by J. P. Hallett and M. B. Skinner. Princeton: Princeton University Press, 1997.

Ehrman, Bart D. "The Neglect of the Firstborn in New Testament Studies." Paper presented at meeting of the Southeast Region of the Society of Biblical Literature. Macon, Ga., March 14, 1997. No pages. Cited 14 October 2004. Online: http://rosetta.reltech.org/TC/extras/ehrman-pres.html.

———. *The Orthodox Corruption of Scripture: The Effect of Early Christological Controversies on the Text of the New Testament.* New York: Oxford University Press, 1993.

Engberg-Pedersen, Troels. *Paul and the Stoics.* Edinburgh: T&T Clark, 2000.

———. *The Stoic Theory of Oikeiosis: Moral Development and Social Interaction in Early Stoic Philosophy.* Aarhus, Denmark: Aarhus University Press, 1990.

England, John, and Archie C. C. Lee, eds. *Doing Theology with Asian Resources: Ten Years in the Formation of Living Theology in Asia.* Auckland, New Zealand: Pace, 1993.

Epp, Eldon J. "Issues in New Testament Textual Criticism: Moving from the Nineteenth to the Twenty-First Century." Pages 17–76 in *Rethinking New Testament Textual Criticism.* Edited by D. A. Black. Grand Rapids: Baker, 2002.

———. "The Multivalence of the Term 'Original Text' in New Testament Textual Criticism." *HTR* 92 (1999): 245–81.

———. *The Theological Tendency of Codex Bezae Cantabrigiensis in Acts.* SNTSMS 3. Cambridge: Cambridge University Press, 1966.

Eskenazi, Tamara C. "Nehemiah 9: Structure and Significance." *Journal of Hebrew Scriptures* 3 (2000–2001). No pages. Cited 13 October 2004. Online: http://www.arts.ualberta.ca/JHS/Articles/article_21.htm.

———. "Out from the Shadows: Biblical Women in the Post-Exilic Era." Pages 252–71 in *A Feminist Companion to Samuel-Kings.* Edited by A. Brenner. FCB 5. Sheffield: Sheffield Academic Press, 1994.

Eskenazi, Tamara C., and Eleanore P. Judd. "Marriage to a Stranger in Ezra 9–10." Pages 266–85 in *Temple Community in the Persian Period.* Second Temple Studies 2. Edited by T. C. Eskenazi and K. H. Richards. JSOTSup 175. Sheffield: Sheffield Academic Press, 1994.

Exum, J. Cheryl. *Fragmented Women: Feminist (Sub)versions of Biblical Narratives.* JSOTSup 163. Sheffield: Sheffield Academic Press, 1993.

Fander, Monika. "Historical-Critical Methods." Pages 205–24 in *A Feminist Introduction.* Vol. 1 of *Searching the Scriptures.* Edited by E. Schüssler Fiorenza with S. Matthews and A. Brock. New York: Crossroads, 1993.

Fausto-Sterling, Anne. *Sexing the Body: Gender Politics and the Construction of Sexuality.* New York: Basic Books, 2000.

Fee, Gordon D. *The First Epistle to the Corinthians.* NICNT. Grand Rapids: Eerdmans, 1987.

———. *Philippians.* IVP New Testament Commentary Series 11. Downers Grove, Ill.: Intervarsity, 1999.

Felder, Cain H., ed. *Stony the Road We Trod: African American Biblical Interpretation.* Minneapolis: Fortress, 1991.

Ferro, Marc. *Colonization: A Global History.* London: Routledge, 1997.

Fewell, Danna Nolan. "Changing the Subject: Retelling the Story of Hagar the Egyptian." Pages 182–94 in *Genesis.* FCB 2.1. Edited by A. Brenner. Sheffield: Sheffield Academic Press, 1998.

Fisher, David H. "Self in Text, Text in Self." *Semeia* 51 (1990): 137–54.

Fitzgerald, William. *Slavery and the Roman Literary Imagination.* Roman Literature and Its Contexts. Cambridge: Cambridge University Press, 2000.

Fleming, Rebecca. *Medicine and the Making of Roman Women: Gender, Nature, and Authority from Celsus to Galen.* New York: Oxford University Press, 2000.

Flynn, Elizabeth A. and Patrocinio P. Schweickart, eds. *Gender and Reading: Essays on Readers, Texts, and Contexts.* Baltimore: Johns Hopkins University Press, 1986.

Fogelklou, Emilia. *Barhuvad.* Stockholm: Bonniers, 1950.

———. "Hosea och Gomer. En biblisk fantasi." Pages 94–111 in vol. 1 of *Medan gräset gror: En bok om det växande.* 2 vols. Stockholm: Bonniers, 1911.

———. *Reality and Radiance: Selected Autobiographical Works of Emilia Fogelklou.* Translated by H. T. Lutz. Richmond, Ind.: Friends United, 1985.

Follis, Elaine R. "The Holy City as Daughter." Pages 173–84 in *Directions in Biblical Hebrew Poetry.* Edited by E. R. Follis. JSOTSup 40. Sheffield: Sheffield Academic Press, 1987.

Fontaine, Carole R. "A Heifer From Thy Stable: On Goddesses and the Status of Women in the Ancient Near East." Pages 159–78 in *Women in the Hebrew Bible.* Edited by A. Bach. New York: Routledge, 1999.

———. "Preface." Pages 11–14 in *A Feminist Companion to Reading the Bible: Approaches, Methods and Strategies.* Edited by A. Brenner and C. R. Fontaine. Sheffield: Sheffield Academic Press, 1997.

Fortna, Robert T. "Philippians: Paul's Most Egocentric Letter." Pages 220–34 in *The Conversation Continues: Studies in Paul and John in Honor of J. Louis Martyn.* Edited by R. T. Fortna and B. R. Gaventa. Nashville: Abingdon, 1990.

Foss, Sonja K., Karen A. Foss, and Robert Trapp. *Contemporary Perspectives on Rhetoric.* 3d ed. Prospect Heights, Ill.: Waveland, 2002.

Foucault, Michel. *History of Sexuality.* Translated by R. Hurley. 3 vols. New York: Pantheon, 1978–1986.

———. "Nietzsche, Genealogy, History." Pages 351–69 in *The Essential Foucault: Selections from Essential Works of Foucault 1954–1984.* Edited by P. Rabinow and N. Rose. New York: The New Press, 2003.

———. *"Society Must Be Defended": Lectures at the Collège de France 1975–1976.* Edited by M. Bertani and A. Fontana. Translated by D. Macey. New York: Picador, 2003.

Fowl, Stephen E., and L. Gregory Jones. *Reading in Communion: Scripture and Ethics in Christian Life.* Grand Rapids: Eerdmans, 1991.

Fox, Michael V. *Character and Ideology in the Book of Esther.* Columbia: University of South Carolina, 1991.

Fox-Genovese, Elizabeth. "Literary Criticism and the Politics of the New Historicism." Pages 213–24 in *The New Historicism.* Edited by H. A. Veeser. New York: Routledge, 1989.

Frederickson, David E. "Natural and Unnatural Use in Romans 1:24–27." Pages 199–207 in *Homosexuality, Science, and the "Plain Sense" of Scripture.* Edited by D. L. Balch. Grand Rapids: Eerdmans, 2000.

Frei, Hans W. *The Eclipse of Biblical Narrative: A Study of Eighteenth and Nineteenth Century Hermeneutics.* New Haven: Yale University Press, 1974.

Freire, Paulo. *Pedagogy of the Oppressed.* New York: Seabury, 1968.

Freire, Paulo, and Donaldo Macedo. *Literacy: Reading the Word and the World.* Westport, Conn.: Bergin & Garvey, 1987.

Frenz, Albrecht. *Yoga in Christianity.* Madras: Christian Literature Society, 1986.

Frymer-Kensky, Tikva. *In the Wake of the Goddess: Women, Culture and the Biblical Transformation of Pagan Myth.* New York: Free Press, 1992.

Fuchs, Esther. *Sexual Politics in the Biblical Narrative: Reading the Hebrew Bible as a Woman.* JSOTSup 310. Sheffield: Sheffield Academic Press, 2000.

———. "Status and the Role of Female Heroines in the Biblical Narrative." Pages 77–84 in *Women in the Hebrew Bible.* Edited by A. Bach. New York: Routledge, 1999.

Fulbrook, Mary. *Historical Theory.* London: Routledge, 2002.

Gadamer, Hans-Georg. *Hermeneutik II: Wahrheit und Methode.* Vol. 2 of *Gesammelte Werke.* Tübingen: Mohr Siebeck, 1986.

Gager, John G. *The Origins of Anti-Semitism: Attitudes Toward Judaism in Pagan and Christian Antiquity.* Oxford: Oxford University Press, 1983.

Gallagher, Catherine. "Marxism and the New Historicism." Pages 37–48 in *The New Historicism.* Edited by H. A. Veeser. New York: Routledge, 1989.

Gandhi, Leela. *Postcolonial Theory: A Critical Introduction.* New York: Columbia University Press, 1998.

García Martínez, Florentino. *The Dead Sea Scrolls Translated: The Qumran Texts in English.* Translated by W. G. E. Watson. 2d ed. Grand Rapids: Eerdmans, 1996.

García Martínez, Florentino, and Eibert J. C. Tigchelaar, eds. *The Dead Sea Scrolls Study Edition.* 2 vols. Leiden: Brill, 1997–1998.

Garnsey, Peter, and Richard Saller. *The Early Principate: Augustus to Trajan.* Oxford: Clarendon, 1982.

Geoffrion, Timothy C. *The Rhetorical Purpose and the Political and Military Character of Philippians.* Lewiston, N.Y.: Mellen, 1993.

Gerhardsson, Birger. *Fridrichsen, Odeberg, Aulén, Nygren: fyra teologer.* Lund: Novapress, 1994.

Gielen, Marlis. "Beten und Prophezeien mit unverhülltem Kopf? Die Kontroverse zwischen Paulus und der korinthischen Gemeinde um die Wahrung der Geschlechtsrollensymbolik." *ZNW* 90 (1999): 220–49.

Gill, David W. J. "The Importance of Roman Portraiture for Head-Coverings in 1 Corinthians 11:2–16." *TynBul* 41 (1990): 245–60.

Glick, G. Wayne. *The Reality of Christianity: A Study of Adolf von Harnack as Historian and Theologian.* Makers of Modern Theology. New York: Harper & Row, 1967.

Golden, James L., and Joseph L. Pilotta, eds. *Practical Reasoning in Human Affairs: Studies in Honor of Chaïm Perelman.* Synthese Library 183. Boston: Reidel, 1986.

Goldstein, Elyse. *ReVisions: Seeing Torah through a Feminist Lens.* Woodstock, Vt.: Jewish Lights, 1998.

Gorden, Pamela. "The Lover's Voice in *Heroides* 15: Or, Why Is Sappho a Man?" Pages 274–91 in *Roman Sexualities.* Edited by J. P. Hallett and M. B. Skinner. Princeton: Princeton University Press, 1997.

Gottwald, Norman K. *The Politics of Ancient Israel.* Library of Ancient Israel. Louisville: Westminster John Knox, 2001.

———. "Sociology of Ancient Israel." *ABD* 6:79–89.

———. *Studies in the Book of Lamentations.* SBT 14. London: SCM, 1954.

———. *The Tribes of Yahweh: A Sociology of Liberated Israel 1250–1050.* 2d ed. Sheffield: Sheffield Academic Press, 1999.

Gottwald, Norman K., and Antoinette Clark Wire, eds. *The Bible and Liberation: Political and Social Hermeneutics.* Berkeley: Community for Religious Research and Education, 1976.

Gottwald, Norman K., and Richard A. Horsley, eds. *The Bible and Liberation: Political and Social Hermeneutics.* Bible and Liberation Series. Maryknoll, N.Y.: Orbis, 1993.

Gracie, David McInnes. Introduction to *Militia Christi: The Christian Religion and the Military in the First Three Centuries,* by Adolf von Harnack. Translated by D. M. Gracie. Philadelphia: Fortress, 1981.

Grant, Robert M. *Paul in the Roman World: The Conflict at Corinth.* Louisville: Westminster John Knox, 2001.

Graverini, Luca. "Corinth, Rome, and Africa: A Cultural Background for the Tale of the Ass." Pages 58–77 in *Space in the Ancient Novel.* Edited by M. Paschalis and S. A. Frangoulidis. Ancient Narrative Supplementum 1. Groningen: Barkhuis, 2002.

Gray, John. *Straw Dogs: Thoughts on Humans and Other Animals.* London: Granta, 2002.

Greenblatt, Stephen. *Marvellous Possessions: The Wonder of the New World.* Oxford: Clarendon, 1991.

Greene, Ellen. *The Erotics of Domination: Male Desire and the Mistress in Latin Love Poetry.* Baltimore: Johns Hopkins University Press, 1998.

Grosz, Elizabeth. "Bodies-Cities." Pages 241–53 in *Sexuality and Space.* Edited by B. Colomina. Princeton Papers on Architecture. Princeton: Princeton Architectural Press, 1992.

———. *Space, Time and Perversion: The Politics of Bodies.* New York: Routledge, 1995.

Gundry-Volf, Judith M. "Gender and Creation in 1 Corinthians 11:2–16: A Study in Paul's Theological Method." Pages 151–71 in *Evangelium, Schriftauslegung, Kirche: Festschrift für Peter Stuhlmacher zum 65 Geburtstag.* Edited by J. Ådna et al. Göttingen: Vandenhoeck & Ruprecht, 1997.

Haines-Eitzen, Kim. *Guardians of Letters: Literacy, Power, and the Transmitters of Early Christian Literature.* New York: Oxford University Press, 2000.

Hall, Stuart. "The West and the Rest: Discourse and Power." Pages 275–322 in *Formations of Modernity.* Edited by S. Hall and B. Gieben. Cambridge: Polity, 1992.

Hallett, Judith P. "Female Homoeroticism and the Denial of Roman Reality in Latin Literature." Pages 255–73 in *Roman Sexualities*. Edited by J. P. Hallett and M. B. Skinner. Princeton: Princeton University Press, 1997.

Halperin, David M., John J. Winkler, and Froma I. Zeitlin, eds. *Before Sexuality: The Construction of Erotic Experience in the Ancient World*. Princeton: Princeton University Press, 1990.

Hamilton, Paul. *Historicism*. 2d ed. New York: Routledge, 2003.

Hamilton, Victor P. *The Book of Genesis: Chapters 18–50*. NICOT. Grand Rapids: Eerdmans, 1995.

Hammond, Dorothy, and Alta Jablow. *The Africa that Never Was: Four Centuries of British Writing about Africa*. New York: Twayne, 1970.

Handy, Robert T. "The Trials of Charles Briggs (1881–1893)." Pages 69–93 in *A History of Union Theological Seminary in New York*. New York: Columbia University Press, 1987.

Haraway, Donna. *Simians, Cyborgs, and Women: The Reinvention of Nature*. London: Free Association, 1991.

Harnack, Adolf von. *Adolf von Harnack: Liberal Theology at Its Height*. Edited by M. Rumscheidt. The Making of Modern Theology 6. London: Collins, 1988.

Harrill, J. Albert. "Invective against Paul (2 Cor 10:10), the Physiognomics of the Ancient Slave Body, and the Greco-Roman Rhetoric of Manhood." Pages 189–213 in *Antiquity and Humanity: Essays on Ancient Religion and Philosophy Presented to Hans Dieter Betz on His 70th Birthday*. Edited by A. Y. Collins and M. M. Mitchell. Tübingen: Mohr Siebeck, 2001.

Harvey, David. *The Condition of Postmodernity: An Enquiry into the Origins of Cultural Change*. Oxford: Blackwell, 1990.

Hawley, Richard. "The Dynamics of Beauty in Classical Greece." Pages 37–54 in *Changing Bodies, Changing Meanings: Studies on the Human Body in Antiquity*. Edited by D. Montserrat. New York: Routledge, 1998.

Hawthorne, Gerald F. *Philippians*. WBC 43. Waco, Tex.: Word, 1983.

Hawthorne, Sian. "Feminism: Feminism, Gender Studies and Religion." *Macmillan Encyclopedia of Religion*. 2d ed. New York: Macmillan, 2004.

———. "Gender and Religion: History of Study." *Macmillan Encyclopedia of Religion*. 2d ed. New York: Macmillan, 2004.

Heard, R. Christopher. *Dynamics of Diselection: Ambiguity in Genesis 12–36 and Ethnic Boundaries in Post-Exilic Judah*. SemeiaSt 39. Atlanta: Society of Biblical Literature, 2001.

Heine, Susanne. *Women and Early Christianity: Are the Feminist Scholars Right?* Translated by J. Bowden. London: SCM, 1987.

Hicks, D. Emily. *Border Writing: The Multidimensional Text*. Minneapolis: University of Minnesota Press, 1991.

Hillers, Delbert R. *Lamentations: A New Translation with Introduction and Commentary*. AB 7A. Garden City, N.Y.: Doubleday, 1992.

Hirdman, Yvonne. "Genussystemet—reflexioner kring kvinnors sociala underordning." *Kvinnovetenskapelig tidsskrift* 3 (1988): 49–63.

Hirschler, Horst. "Wir wollen kein Lehrverfahren: Der hannoversche Landesbischof zum Streit um den Göttinger Theologieprofessor Gerd Lüdemann."

Das Sonntagsblatt (23 February 1995). No pages. Cited 13 October 2004. Online: http://www.sonntagsblatt.de/1996/8/8–10.htm.

Hogland, Kenneth. *Achaemenid Imperial Administration in Syria-Palestine and the Missions of Ezra and Nehemiah.* SBLDS 125. Atlanta: Scholars Press, 1992.

Hohne, Karen, and Helen Wussow, eds. *A Dialogue of Voices: Feminist Literary Theory and Bakhtin.* Minneapolis: University of Minnesota Press, 1994.

Holloway, Paul A. *Consolation in Philippians: Philosophical Sources and Rhetorical Strategy.* SNTSMS 112. Cambridge: Cambridge University Press, 2001.

Holmes, Michael W. "Women and the 'Western' Text of Acts." Pages 183–203 in *The Book of Acts as Church History—Apostelgeschichte als Kirchengeschichte.* Edited by T. Nicklas and M. Tilly. BZNW 120. Berlin: de Gruyter, 2003.

Holter, Kurt. *Yahweh in Africa: Essays on Africa and the Old Testament.* Bible and Theology in Africa 1. New York: Lang, 2000.

hooks, bell. *Yearning: Race, Gender, and Cultural Politics.* Boston: South End, 1990.

Hopkins, Keith. *Conquerors and Slaves.* Sociological Studies in Roman History 1. Cambridge: Cambridge University Press, 1978.

Hopwood, Keith. "'All That May Become a Man': The Bandit in the Ancient Novel." Pages 195–204 in *When Men Were Men: Masculinity, Power, and Identity in Classical Antiquity.* Edited by L. Foxhall and J. Salmon. New York: Routledge, 1998.

Hornus, Jean-Michel. *It Is Not Lawful for Me to Fight.* Scottsdale, Pa.: Herald, 1980.

Horrell, David G. "The Development of Theological Ideology in Pauline Christianity." Pages 224–36 in *Modeling Early Christianity: Social-Scientific Studies of the New Testament in Its Context.* Edited by P. Esler. New York: Routledge, 1995.

Horsley, Richard A. *Jesus and the Spiral of Violence: Popular Jewish Resistance in Roman Palestine.* San Francisco: Harper & Row, 1987.

―――. "Subverting Disciplines: The Possibilities and Limitations of Postcolonial Theory for New Testament Study." Pages 90–105 in *Toward a New Heaven and a New Earth: Essays in Honor of Elisabeth Schüssler Fiorenza.* Edited by F. F. Segovia. Maryknoll, N.Y.: Orbis, 2003.

―――, ed. *Paul and Empire: Religion and Power in Roman Imperial Society.* Harrisburg, Pa.: Trinity Press International, 1997.

―――. ed. *Paul and Politics: Ekklesia, Israel, Imperium, Interpretation.* Harrisburg, Pa.: Trinity Press International, 2000.

Horsley, Richard A., and John S. Hanson. *Bandits, Prophets, and Messiahs: Popular Movements in the Time of Jesus.* Minneapolis: Fortress, 1985.

Horst, Pieter W. van der. *The Sentences of Pseudo-Phocylides with Introduction and Commentary.* SVTP 4. Leiden: Brill, 1978.

Hua, Bai, et al. *A Starless Night in June: An Anthology of Poems.* Hong Kong: Breakthrough, 1990.

Hunt, Mary E. "War: A Feminist Religious View." *JFSR* 18 (2002): 51–52.

Hurley, J. B. "Did Paul Require Veils or the Silence of Women? A Consideration of I Cor 11:2–16 and I Cor 14:33b–36." *WTJ* 35 (1973): 190–220.

Iggers, Georg G. *Historiography in the Twentieth Century: From Scientific Objectivity to the Postmodern Challenge.* Hanover, N.H.: University Press of New England, 1997.

———. *New Directions in European Historiography.* Rev. ed. Middleton, Conn.: Wesleyan University Press, 1984.

Iggers, Georg G., and James M. Powell, eds. *Leopold von Ranke and the Shaping of the Historical Discipline.* Syracuse, N.Y.: Syracuse University Press, 1990.

Ilan, Tal. *Integrating Women into Second Temple History.* TSAJ 76. Tübingen: Mohr Siebeck, 1999. Repr., Peabody, Mass.: Hendrickson, 2001.

———. *Jewish Women in Greco-Roman Palestine: An Inquiry into Image and Status.* TSAJ 44. Tübingen: Mohr Siebeck, 1995. Repr., Peabody, Mass.: Hendrickson, 1996.

Ingham, Patricia Clare, and Michelle R. Warren. *Postcolonial Moves: Medieval through Modern.* New York: Palgrave Macmillan, 2003.

Irigaray, Luce. *Ce Sexe qui n'en est pas un.* Paris: Minuit, 1977.

———. *Elemental Passions.* Translated by J. Collie and J. Still. London: Athlone, 1992.

———. *Speculum de l'autre femme.* Paris: Minuit, 1974.

———. *Speculum of the Other Woman.* Translated by G. C. Gill. Ithaca, N.Y.: Cornell University Press, 1985.

———. *This Sex Which Is Not One.* Translated by C. Porter and C. Burke. Ithaca, N.Y.: Cornell University Press, 1993.

Irvin, Dale. *Christian Histories, Christian Traditioning: Rendering Accounts.* Maryknoll, N.Y.: Orbis, 1998.

Isaksson, Abel. *Marriage and Ministry in the New Temple: A Study with Special Reference to Mt. 19.13–12 [sic] and 1 Cor 11.3–16.* ASNU 24. Lund: Gleerup, 1965.

Jack, Alison M. *Texts Reading Texts, Sacred and Secular: Two Postmodern Perspectives.* JSNTSup 179. Sheffield: Sheffield Academic Press, 1999.

Jameson, Fredric. "Postmodernism, or the Cultural Logic of Late Capitalism." *New Left Review* 146 (1984): 53–92.

———. "Postmodernism and Consumer Society." Pages 1–20 in *The Cultural Turn: Selected Writings on the Postmodern, 1983–1998.* London: Verso, 1998.

———. *The Political Unconscious: Narrative as a Socially Symbolic Act.* Ithaca: Cornell University Press, 1981.

Järlström, Margareta. "Förmoder: Emilia Fogelklou—teologen." *Kvinnovetenskaplig Tidskrift* 10 (1989): 80–83.

Jayawardena, Kumari. *Feminism and Nationalism in the Third World.* London: Zed and Kali for Women, 1986.

Jayawardena, Kumari, and Malathi de Alwis, eds. *Embodied Violence: Communalising Women's Sexuality in South Asia.* London: Zed and Kali for Women, 1998.

Jenkins, Keith, ed. *The Postmodern History Reader.* New York: Routledge, 1997.

Jobling, David. "The Salvation of Israel in 'The Book of the Divided Kingdoms,'or 'Was There Any Fall of the Northern Kingdom?'" Pages 50–61 in *Redirected Travel: Alternative Journeys and Places in Biblical Studies.* Edited by R. Boer and E. W. Conrad. JSOTSup 382. New York: T&T Clark International, 2003.

———. *1 Samuel.* Berit Olam. Collegeville, Minn.: Liturgical, 1998.

Jobling, David, Tina Pippin, and Ronald Schleifer, eds. *The Postmodern Bible Reader.* Oxford: Blackwell, 2001.

Johnselius Theodoru, Cecilia. "'Så ock på jorden': Emilia Fogelklous gudsrikestanke – en feministisk utopi." Idéhistoriska uppsatser 37. Stockholm: Stockholms universitet, Avdelningen för idéhistoria, 2000.

Jones, A. H. M. *The Later Roman Empire, 284–602: A Social Economic and Administrative Survey*. Oxford: Oxford University Press, 1964.

Jordheim, Helge. *Lesningens Vitenskap: Utkast til en ny filologi*. Oslo: Universitetsforlaget, 2001.

Joshel, Sandra R. "Female Desire and the Discourse of Empire: Tacitus's Messalina." Pages 221–54 in *Roman Sexualities*. Edited by J. P. Hallett and M. B. Skinner. Princeton: Princeton University Press, 1997.

Kadowaki, J. Kakichi. *Zen and the Bible*. Translated by J. Rieck. Maryknoll, N.Y.: Orbis, 2002.

Kahl, Brigitte. "No Longer Male: Masculinity Struggles Behind Galations 3:28." *JSNT* 79 (2000): 37–49.

Kähler, Martin. *The So-Called Historical Jesus and the Historic Biblical Christ*. Edited and Translated by C. E. Braaten. Fortress Texts in Modern Theology. Philadelphia: Fortress, 1964.

Kaiser, Barbara Bakke. "Poet as 'Female Impersonator': The Image of Daughter Zion as Speaker in Biblical Poems of Suffering." *JR* 67 (1987): 164–82.

Kant, Immanuel. "Idea for a Universal History with Cosmopolitan Intent." Pages 117–32 in *Basic Writings of Kant*. Edited by A. W. Wood. Translated by C. F. Friedrich. New York: Modern Library, 2001.

Kates, Judith A., and Gail Twersky Reimer. *Reading Ruth: Contemporary Women Reclaim a Sacred Story*. New York: Ballantine, 1994.

Kellenbach, Katharina von. *Anti-Judaism in Feminist Religious Writings*. AAR Cultural Criticism Series 1. Atlanta: Scholars Press, 1994.

Keller, Catherine. *Apocalypse Now and Then: A Feminist Guide to the End of the World*. Boston: Beacon, 1996.

Kelley, Shawn. *Racializing Jesus: Race, Ideology, and the Formation of Modern Biblical Scholarship*. Biblical Limits. New York: Routledge, 2002.

Kennedy, George A., trans. and ed. *Progymnasmata: Greek Texts of Prose Composition and Rhetoric*. SBLWGRW 10. Atlanta: Society of Biblical Literature, 2003.

Keppie, Lawrence. *Colonisation and Veteran Settlement in Italy: 47–14 B.C.* London: British School at Rome, 1983.

———. *The Making of the Roman Army: From Republic to Empire*. London: Batsford, 1984.

Kittredge, Cynthia Briggs. *Community and Authority: The Rhetoric of Obedience in the Pauline Tradition*. Harrisburg, Pa.: Trinity Press International, 1998.

———. "Corinthian Women Prophets and Paul's Argumentation in 1 Corinthians." Pages 103–9 in *Paul and Politics: Ekklesia, Israel, Imperium, Interpretation*. Edited by R. A. Horsley. Harrisburg, Pa.: Trinity Press International, 2000.

Knust, Jennifer Wright. "Paul and the Politics of Virtue and Vice." Pages 158–72 in *Paul and the Roman Imperial Order*. Edited by R. A. Horsley. Harrisburg, Pa: Trinity Press International, 2004.

Kolmodin, Adolf. *Bibliska Tids-och Stridsfrågor*. Stockholm: Evangeliska Fosterlandsstiftelsens förlag, 1906.

Kraemer, Ross Shepard. *Her Share of the Blessings: Women's Religions among Pagans, Jews, and Christians in the Greco-Roman World*. New York: Oxford University Press, 1992.

————. *When Aseneth Met Joseph: A Late Antique Tale of the Biblical Patriarch and His Egyptian Wife, Reconsidered.* New York: Oxford University Press, 1998.

Kraemer, Ross Shepard, and Mary Rose D'Angelo, eds. *Women and Christian Origins.* New York: Oxford University Press, 1999.

Krašovec, Jože. "The Source of Hope in the Book of Lamentations." Pages 679–88 in *Reward, Punishment, and Forgiveness: The Thinking and Beliefs of Ancient Israel in the Light of Greek and Modern Views.* Edited by J. Krašovec. VTSup 78. Leiden: Brill, 1999.

Kraus, Hans-Joachim. *Geschichte der historisch-kritischen Erforschung des Alten Testaments von der Reformation bis zur Gegenwart.* 3d ed. Neukirchen-Vlyun: Neukirchener Verlag, 1982.

Krentz, Edgar M. "De Caesare et Christo." *CurTM* 28 (2001): 341–45.

————. "Military Language and Metaphors in Philippians." Pages 105–9 in *Origins and Method: Towards a New Understanding of Judaism and Christianity. Essays in Honour of John C. Hurd.* Edited by B. H. McLean. JSNTSup 86. Sheffield: Sheffield Academic Press, 1993.

Kristeva, Julia. "Women's Time." Pages 31–55 in *Feminist Theory: A Critique of Ideology.* Edited by N. O. Keohane et al. Chicago: University of Chicago Press, 1982.

Kuchich, John, and Dianne F. Sadoff. *Victorian Afterlife: Postmodern Culture Rewrites the Nineteenth Century.* Minnesota: University of Minnesota Press, 2000.

Küchler, Max. *Schweigen, Schmuck und Schleier: Drei neutestamentliche Vorschriften zur Verdrängung der Frauen auf dem Hintergrund einer frauenfeindlichen Exegese des Alten Testaments im antiken Judentum.* NTOA 1. Göttingen: Vandenhoeck & Ruprecht, 1986.

Lacey, Marc. "African Anglican Leaders Outraged Over Gay Bishop in U.S." *New York Times.* (November 4, 2003): A21.

Landry, Donna, and Gerald M. MacLean, eds. *The Spivak Reader: Selected Works of Gayatri Chakravorty Spivak.* New York: Routledge, 1996.

Lang, Friedrich. *Die Briefe an die Korinther.* 16th ed. NTD 7. Göttingen: Vandenhoeck & Ruprecht, 1986.

Laqueur, Thomas. *Making Sex: Body and Gender from the Greeks to Freud.* Cambridge, Mass.: Harvard University Press, 1990.

Larson, Jennifer. "Paul's Masculinity." *JBL* 123 (2004): 85–97.

Lauretis, Teresa de. *Alice Doesn't: Feminism, Semiotics, Cinema.* Bloomington: Indiana University Press, 1984.

————. "The Violence of Rhetoric: Considerations on Representation and Gender." Pages 239–58 in *The Violence of Representation: Literature and the History of Violence.* Edited by N. Armstrong and L. Tennenhouse. London: Routledge, 1989.

Lee, Archie C. C. "Biblical Interpretation in Asian Perspective." *AJT* 7 (1993): 38–48.

————. "The Chinese Creation Myth of Nu Kua and the Biblical Narrative in Genesis 1–11." *BibInt* 2 (1994): 312–24.

Lee, Nancy C. *The Singers of Lamentations: Cities Under Siege, From Ur to Jerusalem to Sarajevo.* BibInt Series 60. Leiden: Brill, 2002.

Leeming, Joseph. *Yoga and the Bible.* Punjab, India: Radha Soami Satsang Beas, 1978.

Lefebvre, Henri. *The Critique of Everyday Life.* London: Verso, 1991.

Lentricchia, Frank. "Foucault's Legacy: A New Historicism?" Pages 231–42 in *The New Historicism.* Edited by H. A. Veeser. New York: Routledge, 1989.

Leonardo, Micaela di, ed. *Gender at the Crossroads of Knowledge: Feminist Anthropology in the Postmodern Era.* Berkeley and Los Angeles: University of California Press, 1991.

Levick, Barbara, ed. *The Government of the Roman Empire: A Sourcebook.* London: Croom Helm, 1988.

Levine, Amy-Jill. "The Disease of Postcolonial New Testament Studies and the Hermeneutics of Healing." *JFSR* 20 (2004): 91–99.

Levine, Amy-Jill, and Marianne Blickenstaff, eds. *A Feminist Companion to the New Testament and Early Christian Writings.* 13 vols. London: Continuum, 2001–.

Linafelt, Tod. "The Refusal of a Conclusion in the Book of Lamentations." *JBL* 120 (2001): 340–43.

———. *Surviving Lamentations: Catastrophe, Lament, and Protest in the Afterlife of a Biblical Book.* Chicago: University of Chicago Press, 2000.

Loader, James A. *Das Hohelied, Klagelieder, Das Buch Esther.* ATD. Gottingen: Vandenhoeck & Ruprecht, 1992.

Loomba, Ania. *Colonialism/Postcolonialism.* The New Critical Idiom. London: Routledge, 1998.

López, Alfred J. *Posts and Pasts: A Theory of Postcolonialism.* Explorations in Postcolonial Studies. Albany, N.Y.: State University of New York Press, 2001.

Loraux, Nicole. "Herakles: The Super Male and the Feminine." Pages 21–52 in *Before Sexuality: The Construction of Erotic Experience in the Ancient World.* Edited by D. M. Halperin, J. J. Winkler, and F. I. Zeitlin. Princeton: Princeton University Press, 1990.

Lorde, Audre. "The Master's Tools Will Never Dismantle the Master's House: Comments at 'The Personal and the Political' Panel (Second Sex Conference, October 29, 1979)." Pages 98–101 in *This Bridge Called My Back: Writings by Radical Women of Color.* Edited by C. Moraga and G. Anzaldúa. 2d ed. New York: Kitchen Table, 1983.

MacDonald, Margaret Y. *Early Christian Women and Pagan Opinion: The Power of the Hysterical Woman.* Cambridge: Cambridge University Press, 1996.

Mace, David R. *Hebrew Marriage: A Sociological Study.* London: Epworth, 1953.

Machado, Daisy. "The Writing of Religious History in the United States: A Critical Assessment." Pages 83–86 in *Hispanic Christianity within Mainline Protestant Traditions: A Bibliography.* Edited by P. Barton and D. Maldonado, Jr. Decatur, Ga.: Asociación para la Educación Teológica Hispana, 1998.

Mailloux, Steven. "Articulation and Understanding: The Pragmatic Intimacy between Rhetoric and Hermeneutics." Pages 378–94 in *Rhetoric and Hermeneutics in Our Time: A Reader.* Edited by W. Jost and M. J. Hyde. New Haven: Yale University Press, 1997.

Man, Paul de. "The Return to Philology." Pages 21–26 in *The Resistance to Theory.* Minneapolis: University of Minnesota Press, 1986.

Marcos, Subcomandante Insurgente. *Our Word Is Our Weapon: Selected Writings.* Edited by J. Ponce de León. New York: Seven Stories, 2000.

Martin, Dale B. *The Corinthian Body.* New Haven: Yale University Press, 1995.

———. "Heterosexism and the Interpretation of Romans 1:1–32." *BibInt* 3 (1995): 332–55.

Martin, Troy W. "Paul's Argument from Nature for the Veil in 1 Corinthians 11:13–15: A Testicle Instead of a Head Covering." *JBL* 123 (2004): 75–84.

Martínez-Vásquez, Hjamil A. "Postcolonial Criticism in Biblical Interpretation: A Response to Efrain Agosto." *Perspectivas: Occasional Papers* 6 (2002): 57–63.

Marx, Karl, and Friedrich Engels. *The German Ideology.* Moscow: Progress, 1976.

Masenya, Madipoane (ngwana' Mphahlele). "'. . . But You Shall Let Every Girl Live': Reading Exodus 1:2–2:10 the Bosadi (Womanhood) Way." *OTE* 15 (2002): 99–112.

———. *How Worthy Is the Woman of Worth? Rereading Proverbs 31:10–31 in African-South Africa.* New York: Lang, 2004.

———. "Is White South African Old Testament Scholarship African?" *BOTSA* 12 (2002): 3–8.

———. *Making the Context of African-South African Women a Hermeneutical Focus in Theological Education.* A National Initiative for the Contextualisation of Theological Education Publication 21. Johannesburg, South Africa: NICTE, 2000.

———. "Proverbs 31:10–31 in a South African Context: A Bosadi (Womanhood) Approach." Ph.D. diss. University of South Africa, 1996.

———. "Rereading the Bible the *Bosadi* (Womanhood) Way." *BCTSA* 4 (1997): 15–16.

———. "A Response to Himbaza and Holter." *BOTSA* 13 (2002): 9–12.

———. "A Small Herb Increases Itself (Impact) by a Strong Odor: Reimagining Vashti in an African-South African Context." *OTE* 16 (2003): 332–42.

Massa, Mark Stephen. *Charles Augustus Briggs and the Crisis of Historical Criticism.* Minneapolis: Fortress, 1990.

Maunier, René. *The Sociology of Colonies: An Introduction to the Study of Race Contact.* Translated by E. O. Lorimer. International Library of Sociology and Social Reconstruction. London: Routledge & Kegan Paul, 1949.

Mazlish, Bruce, and Ralph Buultjens. *Conceptualizing Global History.* Boulder, Colo.: Westview, 1993.

McEvenue, Sean E. "A Comparison of Narrative Styles in the Hagar Stories." *Semeia* 3 (1975): 64–80.

McKinnon, Catherine. "Feminism, Marxism, Method, and the State: An Agenda for Theory." Pages 1–30 in *Feminist Theory: A Critique of Ideology.* Edited by N. O. Keohane, M. Z. Rosaldo, and B. C. Gelphi. Chicago: University of Chicago Press, 1982.

Meeks, Wayne A. *The First Urban Christians: The Social World of the Apostle Paul.* New Haven: Yale University Press, 1983.

———. "The Image of the Androgyne: Some Uses of a Symbol in Earliest Christianity." *HR* 13 (1974): 165–208.

Meese, Elizabeth. *Crossing the Double-Cross: The Practice of Feminist Criticism.* Chapel Hill: University of North Carolina Press, 1986.

Meiling Bäckman, Ingrid. *Den resfärdiga. Studier i Emilia Fogelklous självbiografi.* Stockholm/Stehag: Brutus Östlings Bokförlag Symposion, 1997.

Menoud, Philippe H. "The Western Text and the Theology of Acts." *Bulletin of the Studiorum Novi Testamenti Societas* 2 (1951): 19–32.

Metzger, Bruce M. *The Text of the New Testament: Its Transmission, Corruption, and Restoration.* New York: Oxford University Press, 1968.

———. *Textual Commentary on the Greek New Testament.* London: United Bible Societies, 1971.

Meyer, Marvin. "Making Mary Male: The Categories 'Male' and 'Female' in the Gospel of Thomas." Pages 76–95 in *Secret Gospel: Essays on Thomas and the Secret Gospel of Mark.* New York: Continuum, 2003.

Meyers, Carol. *Discovering Eve: Ancient Israelite Women in Context.* New York: Oxford University Press, 1988.

———. "Returning Home: Ruth 1.8 and the Gendering of the Book of Ruth." Pages 85–115 in *A Feminist Companion to Ruth.* Edited by A. Brenner. FCB 3. Sheffield: Sheffield Academic Press, 1993.

———. "Tribes and Tribulations: Retheorizing Earliest 'Israel'." Pages 35–45 in *Tracking the Tribes of Yahweh: On the Trail of a Classic.* Edited by R. Boer. JSOTSup 351. London: Sheffield Academic Press, 2002.

———. "'Women of the Neighborhood' (Ruth 4.17): Informal Female Networks in Ancient Israel." Pages 110–27 in *Ruth and Esther: A Feminist Companion to the Bible.* Edited by A. Brenner. FCB 2.3. Sheffield: Sheffield Academic Press, 1999.

Meyers, William H. "The Hermeneutical Dilemma of the African American Biblical Student." Pages 40–56 in *Stony the Road We Trod.* Edited by C. H. Felder. Minneapolis: Fortress, 1991.

Michaelsen, Scott, and David E. Johnson, eds. *Border Theory: the Limits of Cultural Politics.* Minneapolis: University of Minnesota Press, 1997.

Miles, Margaret R. *Carnal Knowing: Female Nakedness and Religious Meaning in the Christian West.* Boston: Beacon, 1989.

Minh-ha, Trinh T. *Woman, Native, Other: Writing Postcoloniality and Feminism.* Bloomington: Indiana University Press, 1989.

Moallem, Minoo. "Transnationalism, Feminism, and Fundamentalism." Pages 119–45 in *Women, Gender, Religion: A Reader.* Edited by E. A. Castelli with R. C. Rodman. New York: Palgrave, 2001.

Moi, Toril. *Hva er en kvinne? Kjønn og kropp i feministisk teori.* Oslo: Gyldendal, 1998.

———. *'What is a Woman?' and Other Essays.* New York: Oxford University Press, 1999.

Moore, Carey A. *Esther: Introduction, Translation and Notes.* AB 7B. New York: Doubleday, 1971.

Moore, Stephen D. "Deconstructive Criticism: The Gospel of Mark." Pages 84–102 in *Mark and Method: New Approaches in Biblical Studies.* Edited by J. Capel Anderson and S. D. Moore. Minneapolis: Fortress, 1992.

———. *God's Beauty Parlor and Other Queer Spaces in and around the Bible.* Contraversions. Stanford: Stanford University Press, 2001.

———. *God's Gym: Divine Male Bodies of the Bible.* New York: Routledge, 1996.

————. "History after Theory? Biblical Studies and the New Historicism." *BibInt* 5 (1997): 324–63.

————. *Poststructuralism and the New Testament: Derrida and Foucault at the Foot of the Cross.* Minneapolis: Fortress, 1994.

————. "Revolting Revelations." Pages 183–200 in *The Personal Voice in Biblical Interpretation.* Edited by I. R. Kitzberger. London: Routledge, 1999.

Moore, Stephen D., and Janice Capel Anderson, eds. *New Testament Masculinities.* SemeiaSt 45. Atlanta: Society of Biblical Literature, 2003.

————. "Taking it Like a Man: Masculinity in 4 Maccabees." *JBL* 117 (1998): 249–73.

Mosala, Itumeleng. *Biblical Hermeneutics and Black Theology in South Africa.* Grand Rapids: Eerdmans, 1989.

Moy, Russel G. "Biculturalism, Race, and the Bible." *RelEd* 88 (1993): 415–34.

Moyise, Steve. "Does the Lion Lie Down with the Lamb?" Pages 181–94 in *Studies in the Book of Revelation.* Edited by S. Moyise. Edinburgh: T&T Clark, 2001.

————. *The Old Testament in the Book of Revelation.* JSNTSup 115. Sheffield: Sheffield Academic Press, 1995.

Munslow, Alan. *The Routledge Companion to Historical Studies.* London: Routledge, 2000.

Murphy-O'Connor, Jerome. "Sex and Logic in 1 Cor 11:2–16." *CBQ* 42 (1980): 482–500.

Myerowitz Levine, Molly. "The Gendered Grammar of Ancient Mediterranean Hair." Pages 76–130 in *Off with Her Head: The Denial of Women's Identity in Myth, Religion, and Culture.* Edited by W. Eilberg-Schwartz and W. Doniger. Berkeley and Los Angeles: University of California Press, 1995.

Nadar, Sarojini. "Power, Ideology and Interpretations: Womanist and Literary Perspectives on Esther as Resources for Gender-Social Transformation." Ph.D. diss. University of Natal, 2003.

Newsom, Carol A., and Sharon H. Ringe, eds. *The Women's Bible Commentary: Expanded Edition with Apocrypha.* London: SPCK; Louisville: Westminster John Knox, 1992.

Nicholson, Linda, ed. *Feminism/Postmodernism.* New York: Routledge, 1990.

————. "Interpreting Gender." Pages 39–67 in *Social Postmodernism: Beyond Identity Politics.* Edited by L. Nicholson and S. Seidman. Cambridge: Cambridge University Press, 1995.

Niditch, Susan. "Genesis." Pages 13–29 in *The Women's Bible Commentary.* Edited by C. A. Newsom and S. H. Ringe. 2d ed. Louisville: Westminster John Knox, 1998.

————. *War in the Hebrew Bible: A Study in the Ethics of Violence.* New York: Oxford University Press, 1993.

————. "War, Women, and Defilement in Numbers 31." *Semeia* 61 (1993): 39–49.

Nietzsche, Friedrich. *On the Advantage and Disadvantage of History for Life.* Translated by P. Preuss. Indianapolis: Hackett, 1980.

Niles, D. Preman. "Editorial." *Commission for Theological Concerns Bulletin* 5 (December 1984 – April 1985): 2–3.

Nissinen, Martti. *Homoeroticism in the Biblical World: A Historical Perspective.* Translated by K. Stjerna. Minneapolis: Fortress, 1998.

Nolan Fewell, Danna, and David M. Gunn. "Tipping the Balance: Sternberg's Reader and the Rape of Dinah." *JBL* 110 (1991): 193–211.

O'Connor, Kathleen M. "Lamentations." Pages 187–91 in *The Women's Bible Commentary: Expanded Edition with Apocrypha*. Edited by C. A. Newsom and S. H. Ringe. Louisville: Westminster John Knox, 1998.

O'Day, Gail R. "John." *NIB* 9:491–865.

Oakes, Peter. *Philippians: From People to Letter*. SNTSMS 110. Cambridge: Cambridge University Press, 2001.

Økland, Jorunn. "Feminist Reception of the New Testament: A Critical Reception." Pages 137–48 in *The New Testament as Reception*. Edited by M. Müller and H. Tronier. JSNTSup 230. CIS 11. Sheffield: Sheffield Academic Press, 2002.

———. "Men Are from Mars and Women Are from Venus: On the Relationship between Religion, Gender and Space." Pages 152–61 in *Gender, Religion, and Diversity: Cross-Cultural Approaches*. Edited by T. Beattie and U. King. London: Continuum, 2004.

———. "Sex, Gender and Ancient Greek: A Study in Theoretical Misfit." *ST* 57 (2003): 124–42.

———. "Women in Their Place: Paul and the Corinthian Discourse of Gender and Sanctuary Space. Ph.D. diss. University of Oslo, 2000.

———. *Women in Their Place: Paul and the Corinthian Discourse of Gender and Sanctuary Space*. JSNTSup 269. New York: Continuum, 2004.

Oldfather, William Abbott, trans. *Epictetus*. 2 vols. LCL. Cambridge, Mass.: Harvard University Press, 1926–1928.

Olsson, Birger. "Förändringar inom svensk bibelforskning under 1900–talet." Pages 68–135 in *Modern svensk teologi—strömningar och perspektivskiften under 1900-talet*. Edited by H. Eilert et al. Stockholm: Verbum, 1999.

Osiek, Carolyn. *Philippians, Philemon*. ANTC. Nashville: Abingdon, 2000.

Oster, Richard. "Use, Misuse and Neglect of Archeological Evidence in Some Modern Works on 1 Corinthians [1 Cor 7, 1–5; 8,10; 11,2–16; 12,14–26]." *ZNW* 83 (1992): 52–73.

Otzen, Benedikt. *Tobit and Judith*. Guides to Apocrypha and Pseudepigrapha. Sheffield: Sheffield Academic Press, 2002.

Parker, Holt N. "The Teratogenic Grid." Pages 47–65 in *Roman Sexualities*. Edited by J. P. Hallett and M. B. Skinner. Princeton: Princeton University Press, 1997.

Patte, Daniel, et al., eds. *Global Bible Commentary*. Nashville: Abingdon, 2004.

Penner, Todd. *In Praise of Christian Origins: Stephen and the Hellenists in Lukan Apologetic Historiography*. ESEC 10. New York: T&T Clark, 2004.

Penner, Todd and Caroline Vander Stichele. "Unveiling Paul: Gendering Ethos in 1 Corinthians 11:2–16." In *Rhetoric, Ethic, and Moral Persuasion in Biblical Discourse*. Edited by T. H. Olbricht and A. Eriksson. New York: T&T Clark International, 2005.

Perelman, Chaïm, and Lucie Olbrechts-Tyteca. *The New Rhetoric: A Treatise on Argumentation*. Translated by J. Wilkinson and P. Weaver. Notre Dame, Ind.: University of Notre Dame Press, 1969.

Pérez, Emma. *The Decolonial Imaginary: Writing Chicanas into History*. Bloomington: Indiana University Press, 1999.

Perez-Christiaens, Noëlle. *Le Christ et le Yoga*. Paris: Institut de yoga B.K.S. Iyengar, 1980.

Pervo, Richard. "Social and Religious Aspects of the 'Western' Text." Pages 229–41 in *The Living Text: Essays in Honor of Ernest W. Saunders*. Edited by D. E. Groh and R. Jewett. Lanham, Md.: University Press of America, 1984.

Peskowitz, Miriam. "Tropes of Travel." *Semeia* 75 (1996): 177–96.

———. "What's in a Name? Exploring the Dimensions of What 'Feminist Studies in Religion' Means." Pages 29–33 in *Women, Gender, Religion: A Reader*. Edited by E. A. Castelli with R. C. Rodman. New York: Palgrave, 2001.

Peterlin, Davorin. *Paul's Letter to the Philippians in the Light of Disunity in the Church*. NovTSup 79. Leiden: Brill, 1995.

Pilhofer, Peter. *Philippi I: Die erste christliche Gemeinde Europas*. WUNT 87. Tübingen: Mohr Siebeck, 1995.

Pippin, Tina. *Apocalyptic Bodies: The Biblical End of the World in Text and Image*. New York: Routledge, 1999.

———. *Death and Desire: The Rhetoric of Gender in the Apocalypse of John*. Louisville: Westminster John Knox, 1992.

———. "Peering into the Abyss: A Postmodern Reading of the Biblical Bottomless Pit." Pages 251–67 in *The New Literary Criticism and the New Testament*. Edited by E. S. Malbon and E. V. McKnight. JSNTSup 109. Sheffield: Sheffield Academic Press, 1994.

———. "Wisdom's Deviant Ways." Pages 143–53 in *On the Cutting Edge: The Study of Women in Biblical Worlds: Essays in Honor of Elisabeth Schüssler Fiorenza*. Edited by J. Schaberg, A. Bach, and E. Fuchs. New York: Continuum, 2003.

Pohlenz, Max. "Paulus und die Stoa." *ZNW* 42 (1949): 65–104.

Pollini, John. "Slave-Boys for Sexual and Religious Services: Images of Pleasure and Devotion." Pages 149-66 in *Flavian Rome: Culture, Image, Text*. Edited by A. J. Boyle and W. J. Dominik. Leiden: Brill, 2003.

Portefaix, Lilian. *Sisters Rejoice: Paul's Letter to the Philippians and Luke-Acts as Received by First Century Philippian Women*. ConBNT 20. Stockholm: Almqvist & Wiksell, 1988.

Porter, Frances, and Charlotte Macdonald, eds. *'My Hand Will Write What My Heart Dictates': The Unsettled Lives of Women in Nineteenth-Century New Zealand as Revealed to Sisters, Family and Friends*. Auckland, New Zealand: Auckland University Press, 1996.

Pressler, Carolyn. "Sexual Violence and Deuteronomic Law." Pages 102–12 in *A Feminist Companion to Exodus to Deuteronomy*. Edited by A. Brenner. FCB 6. Sheffield: Sheffield Academic Press, 1994.

———. *The View of Women Found in Deuteronomic Family Law*. BZAW 216. Berlin: de Gruyter, 1993.

Preston, Ronald, and Anthony T. Hanson. *The Revelation of Saint John the Divine*. London: SCM, 1949.

Price, David. *Love and Hate in Jamestown: John Smith, Pocahontas, and the Heart of a New Nation*. New York: Knopf, 2003.

Propp, Vladimir J. *Morphology of the Folktale*. 2d ed. Publications of the American Folklore Society. Biographical and Special Series 9. Translated by L. Scott. Austin: University of Texas Press, 1968.

Provan, Iain W. "Past Present and Future in Lamentations III 52–66: The Case for a Precative Perfect Re-examined." *VT* 41 (1991): 164–75.

Pui-lan, Kwok. *Discovering the Bible in the Non-Biblical World.* Bible and Liberation Series. Maryknoll, N.Y.: Orbis, 1995.

Rackham, Harris, trans. *Aristotle: Athenian Constitution. Eudemian Ethics. Virtues and Vices.* LCL. Cambridge, Mass.: Harvard University Press, 1935.

Räisänen, Heikki. "Biblical Critics in the Global Village." Pages 283–309 in *Challenges to Biblical Interpretation: Collected Essays 1991–2000.* BibInt Series 59. Leiden: Brill, 2001.

———. *Marcion, Muhammad and the Mahatma: Exegetical Perspectives on the Encounter of Cultures and Faiths.* London: SCM, 1997.

Ramsay, William Mitchell. *The Church in the Roman Empire before A.D. 170.* London: Putnam & Sons, 1893.

Ranke, Leopold von. *The Secret of World History: Selected Writings on the Art and Science of History.* Edited and Translated by R. Wines. New York: Fordham University Press, 1981.

———. *The Theory and the Practice of History.* Edited by G. G. Iggers and K. von Moltke. Translated by W. A. Iggers and K. von Moltke. Indianapolis: Bobbs-Merrill, 1973.

Reed, Betsy, ed. *Nothing Sacred: Women Respond to Religious Fundamentalism and Terror.* New York: Thunder's Mouth, 2002.

Reimer, Raymond Hubert. "'Our Citizenship Is in Heaven': Philippians 1:27–30 and 3:20–21 as Part of the Apostle Paul's Political Theology." Ph.D. diss. Princeton Theological Seminary, 1997.

Richardson, Peter, and David Granskow, eds. *Anti-Judaism in Early Christianity.* 2 vols. Waterloo, Ont.: Wilfred Laurier University Press, 1986.

Ricoeur, Paul. *Oneself as Another.* Chicago: University of Chicago Press, 1992.

———. *Time and Narrative.* 3 vols. Translated by K. McLaughlin and D. Pellauer. Chicago: University of Chicago Press, 1984–88.

Robbins, Vernon K. "Argumentative Textures in Socio-Rhetorical Interpretation." Pages 27–65 in *Rhetorical Argumentation in Biblical Texts: Essays from the Lund 2000 Conference.* Edited by A. Eriksson, T. H. Olbricht, and W. Überlacker. ESEC 8. Harrisburg, Pa.: Trinity Press International, 2002.

———. "The Dialectical Nature of Early Christian Discourse." *Scriptura* 59 (1996): 353–62.

———. *Exploring the Texture of Texts: A Guide to Socio-Rhetorical Interpretation.* Valley Forge, Pa.: Trinity Press International, 1996.

———. "The Reversed Contextualization of Psalm 22 in the Markan Crucifixion: A Socio-Rhetorical Analysis." Pages 1161–83 in *The Four Gospels 1992: Festschrift Frans Neirynck.* Edited by F. van Segbroeck et al. BETL 100. 3 vols. Leuven: Leuven University Press, 1992.

———. "The Rhetorical Full-Turn in Biblical Interpretation: Reconfiguring Rhetorical-Political Analysis." Pages 48–60 in *Rhetorical Criticism and the Bible: Essays from the 1998 Florence Conference.* Edited by S. E. Porter and D. L. Stamps. JSNTSup 195. Sheffield: Sheffield Academic Press, 2002.

———. *The Tapestry of Early Christian Discourse: Rhetoric, Society and Ideology.* New York: Routledge, 1996.

Robbins, Vernon K., and Gordon D. Newby. "A Prolegomenon to the Relation of the Qur'an and the Bible." Pages 23–42 in *Bible and Qur'an: Essays in Scriptural Intertextuality*. Edited by J. C. Reeves. SBLSymS 24. Atlanta: Society of Biblical Literature, 2003.

Rogerson, John W. *Old Testament Criticism in the Nineteenth Century: England and Germany*. Philadelphia: Fortress, 1985.

Rollmann, Hans. "From Baur to Wrede: The Quest for a Historical Method." *SR* 17 (1998): 443–54.

Ropes, James Hardy. *The Text of Acts*. Vol. 3 of *The Beginnings of Christianity*. Edited by E. J. Foakes Jackson and K. Lake. London: Macmillan, 1926.

Rosaldo, Renato. *Culture and Truth: The Remaking of Social Analysis*. Boston: Beacon, 1989.

Rosenthal Shumway, Suzanne. "The Chronotype of the Asylum: *Jane Eyre*, Feminism, and Bakhtinian Theory." Pages 152–70 in *A Dialogue of Voices: Feminist Literary Theory and Bakhtin*. Edited by K. Hohne and H. Wussow. Minneapolis: University of Minnesota Press, 1994.

Ross, Cathy. "More Than Wives? A Study of Four Church Missionary Society Wives in Nineteenth-Century New Zealand." Ph.D. diss. University of Auckland, 2004.

Russell, Letty, ed. *Feminist Interpretation of the Bible*. Philadelphia: Westminster, 1985.

Ryan, Thomas P. *Prayer of Heart and Body: Meditation and Yoga as Christian Spiritual Practice*. New York: Paulist, 1995.

Sábato, Ernesto. "Valores para la Paz." Paper presented at the Inter-American University of Puerto Rico. Puerto Rico, August 15, 2002. Translated by H. A. Martínez Vásquez.

Sæbo, Magne. "Who is 'The Man' in Lamentations 3? A Fresh Approach to the Interpretation of the Book of Lamentations." Pages 294–306 in *Understanding Poets and Prophets: Essays in Honour of George Wishart Anderson*. Edited by A. G. JSOTSup 152. Auld. Sheffield: Sheffield Academic Press, 1993.

Said, Edward W. *Culture and Imperialism*. New York: Knopf, 1993.

———. *Orientalism*. New York: Pantheon, 1978.

Ste. Croix, Geoffrey E. M. de. *The Class Struggle in the Ancient Greek World: From the Archaic Age to the Arab Conquests*. Ithaca: Cornell University Press, 1981.

Saldívar, José David. *Border Matters: Remapping American Cultural Studies*. Berkeley and Los Angeles: University of California Press, 1997.

Saldívar-Hull, Sonia. *Feminism on the Border: Chicana Gender Politics and Literature*. Berkeley and Los Angeles: University of California Press, 2000.

Sampley, J. Paul, ed. *Paul in the Greco-Roman World*. Harrisburg, Pa.: Trinity Press International, 2003.

Sánchez, Rosaura. "The History of Chicanas: A Proposal for a Materialist Perspective." Pages 1–22 in *Between Borders: Essays on Mexicana/Chicana History*. Edited by A. R. del Castillo. Encino, Calif.: Floricanto, 1990.

Sandmel, Samuel. *Anti-Semitism in the New Testament?* Philadelphia: Fortress, 1978.

Sandoval, Timothy J. and Carleen Mandolfo, eds. *Relating to the Text: Interdisciplinary and Form-Critical Insights on the Bible*. JSOTSup 384. Sheffield: Sheffield Academic Press, 2003.

Sandt, Huub van de. "1 Kor 11, 2–16 als rhetorische eenheid." *Bijdragen* 49 (1988): 410–25.

Sandys-Wunsch, John, and Laurence Eldredge. "J. P. Gabler and the Distinction between Biblical and Dogmatic Theology: Translation, Commentary, and Discussion of His Originality." *SJT* 33 (1980): 133–58.

Santosuosso, Antonio. *Storming the Heavens: Soldiers, Emperors, and Civilians in the Roman Empire.* Boulder, Colo.: Westview, 2001.

Sarna, Nahum M. *Genesis.* The JPS Torah Commentary. Philadelphia: Jewish Publication Society, 1989.

Sawyer, Deborah F. *God, Gender and the Bible.* Biblical Limits. New York: Routledge, 2002.

Schaberg, Jane. "Luke." Pages 275–92 in *The Women's Bible Commentary.* Edited by C. A. Newsom and S. H. Ringe. Louisville: Westminster John Knox, 1992.

Schäfer, Peter. *Judeophobia: Attitudes toward the Jews in the Ancient World.* Cambridge, Mass.: Harvard University Press, 1997.

Schenker, Adrian, ed. *The Earliest Text of the Hebrew Bible: The Relationship Between the Masoretic Text and the Hebrew Base of the Septuagint Reconsidered.* SBLSCS 52. Atlanta: Society of Biblical Literature, 2003.

Schlier, Heinrich. "κεφαλή." *TDNT* 3:673–81.

Scholder, Klaus. *The Birth of Modern Critical Theology: Origins and Problems of Biblical Criticism in the Seventeenth Century.* Translated by J. Bowden. London: SCM, 1990.

Scholtz, Gunter. "The Notion of Historicism and 19th Century Theology." Pages 149–167 in *Biblical Studies and the Shifting of Paradigms, 1850–1914.* Edited by H. G. Reventlow and W. Farmer. JSOTSup 192. Sheffield: Sheffield Academic Press, 1995.

Scholz, Susanne. "Gender, Class, and Androcentric Compliance in the Rapes of Enslaved Women in the Hebrew Bible." *lectio difficilior* 1 (2004). No pages. Cited 20 April 2004. Online: http://www.lectio.unibe.ch/04_1/Scholz.Enslaved.htm.

———. *Rape Plots: A Feminist Cultural Study of Genesis 34.* StBL 13. New York: Lang, 2000.

———. "Was It Really Rape in Genesis 34? Biblical Scholarship As a Reflection of Cultural Assumptions." Pages 182–98 in *Escaping Eden: New Feminist Perspectives on the Bible.* Edited by H. C. Washington, S. L. Graham, and P. L. Thimmes. Sheffield: Sheffield Academic Press, 1998.

Schottroff, Luise. *Lydia's Impatient Sisters: A Feminist Social History of Early Christianity.* Translated by B. Rumscheidt and M. Rumscheidt. Louisville: Westminster John Knox, 1995.

Schottroff, Luise, and Marie-Theres Wacker, eds. *Kompendium Feministische Bibelauslegung.* Gütersloh: Gütersloher Verlagshaus, 1998.

———, eds. *Von der Wurzel getragen: Christlich-feministische Exegese in Auseinandersetzung mit Antijudaismus.* BibInt Series 17. Leiden: Brill, 1996.

Schottroff, Luise, Silvia Schroer, and Marie-Theres Wacker. *Feminist Interpretation: The Bible in Women's Perspective.* Translated by M. Rumscheidt and B. Rumscheidt. Minneapolis: Fortress, 1998.

Schrage, Wolfgang. *Die Erste Brief an die Korinther.* EKKNT 7.2. Düsseldorf: Benziger. Neukirchen-Vluyn: Neukirchener Verlag, 1995.

Schroer, Silvia. "Bibelauslegung im europäischen Kontext." Pages 126–30 in *Hermeneutik sozialgeschichtlich: Kontextualität in den Bibelwissenschaften aus der Sicht (latein)amerikanischer und europäischer Exegetinnen und Exegeten.* Edited by E. S. Gerstenberger and U. Schönborn. EUZ 1. Münster: LIT, 1999.

Schroer, Silvia, and Sophia Bietenhard, eds. *Feminist Interpretation of the Bible and the Hermeneutics of Liberation.* JSOTSup 374. London: Sheffield Academic Press, 2003.

Schüssler Fiorenza, Elisabeth. "Biblical Interpretation and Critical Commitment." *ST* 43 (1989): 5–18.

———. *Bread Not Stone: The Challenge of Feminist Biblical Interpretation.* Boston: Beacon, 1984. Rev. ed. Boston: Beacon, 1995.

———. *But She Said: Feminist Practices of Biblical Interpretation.* Boston: Beacon, 1992.

———. "Challenging the Rhetorical Half-Turn: Feminist and Rhetorical Biblical Criticism." Pages 28–53 in *Rhetoric, Scripture & Theology: Essays from the 1994 Pretoria Conference.* Edited by S. E. Porter and T. H. Olbricht. JSNTSup 131. Sheffield: Sheffield Academic Press, 1996.

———. "The Ethics of Biblical Interpretation: Decentering Biblical Scholarship." *JBL* 107 (1988): 3–17. Repr. as pages 107–23 in *Reading the Bible in the Global Village: Helsinki.* Atlanta: Society of Biblical Literature, 2000.

———. *In Memory of Her: A Feminist Theological Reconstruction of Christian Origins.* New York: Crossroad, 1983. 2d ed. New York: Crossroad, 1994.

———. *Jesus and the Politics of Interpretation.* New York: Continuum, 2000.

———. "Paul and the Politics of Interpretation." Pages 40–57 in *Paul and Politics: Ekklesia, Israel, Imperium, Interpretation.* Edited by R. A. Horsley. Harrisburg, Pa.: Trinity Press International, 2000.

———. "Remembering the Past in Creating the Future: Historical-Critical Scholarship and Feminist Biblical Interpretation." Pages 44–55 in *Feminist Perspectives on Biblical Scholarship.* Edited by A. Y. Collins. SBLBSNA 10. Chico, Calif.: Scholars Press, 1985.

———. *Revelation: Vision of a Just World.* Proclamation Commentaries. Minneapolis: Fortress, 1991.

———. *Rhetoric and Ethic: The Politics of Biblical Studies.* Minneapolis: Fortress, 1999.

———. "Rhetorical Situation and Historical Reconstruction in 1 Corinthians." *NTS* 33 (1987): 386–403.

———. "Struggle is a Name For Hope: A Critical Feminist Interpretation for Liberation." *Pacifica* 10 (1997): 224–48.

———. "Text and Reality—Reality as Text: The Problem of a Feminist Historical and Social Reconstruction Based on Texts." *ST* 43 (1989): 19–34.

———. "Transforming the Legacy of The Woman's Bible." Pages 1–24 in *A Feminist Introduction.* Vol. 1 of *Searching the Scriptures.* Edited by E. Schüssler Fiorenza with S. Matthews and A. Brock. 2 vols. London: SCM, 1993.

———. "'What She Has Done Will Be Told....': Reflections on Writing Feminist History." Pages 3–18 in *Distant Voices Drawing Near: Essays in Honor of*

Antoinette Clark Wire. Edited by H. E. Hearon. Collegeville, Minn.: Liturgical, 2004.

———. *Wisdom Ways: Introducing Feminist Biblical Interpretation.* Maryknoll, N.Y.: Orbis, 2001.

Schüssler Fiorenza, Elisabeth, with Ann Brock and Shelly Matthews, eds. *A Feminist Commentary.* Vol. 2 of *Searching the Scriptures.* New York: Crossroad, 1994.

Schuster, John Paul. "Rhetorical Situation and Historical Reconstruction in Philippians." Ph.D. diss. The Southern Baptist Theological Seminary, 1997.

Schwarcz, Vera. "In the Shadows of the Red Sun: A New Generation of Chinese Writers." *Asian Review* 3 (1989): 4–16.

———. "Memory and Commemoration: The Chinese Search for a Livable Past." Pages 170–83 in *Popular Protest and Political Culture in Modern China.* 2d ed. Edited by J. N. Wasserstrom and E. J. Perry. Boulder, Colo.: Westview, 1994.

Schwartz, Regina. "Adultery in the House of David: the Meta-Narrative of Biblical Scholarship and the Narratives of the Bible." Pages 335–50 in *Women in the Hebrew Bible.* Edited by A. Bach. New York: Routledge, 1999.

Schwartz, Seth. *Imperialism and Jewish Society: 200 B.C.E. to 640 C.E.* Jews, Christians, and Muslims from the Ancient to the Modern World. Princeton: Princeton University Press, 2001.

Scott, Joan W. "Experience." Pages 22–40 in *Feminists Theorize the Political.* Edited by J. Butler and J. W. Scott. New York: Routledge, 1992.

———. *Gender and the Politics of History.* New York: Columbia University Press, 1988.

———. *Only Paradoxes to Offer: French Feminists and the Rights of Man.* Cambridge, Mass.: Harvard University Press, 1996.

Segovia, Fernando F. "'And They Began to Speak in Other Tongues': Competing Modes of Discourse in Contemporary Biblical Criticism." Pages 1–32 in *Social Location and Biblical Interpretation in the United States.* Vol. 1 of *Reading from This Place.* Edited by F. F. Segovia and M. A. Tolbert. Minneapolis: Fortress, 1995.

———. "Biblical Criticism and Postcolonial Studies: Toward a Postcolonial Optic." Pages 49–65 in *The Postcolonial Bible.* Edited by R. S. Sugirtharajah. Bible and Postcolonialism 1. Sheffield: Sheffield Academic Press, 1998.

———. "Cultural Studies and Contemporary Biblical Criticism: Ideological Criticism as Mode of Discourse." Pages 1–17 in *Social Location and Biblical Interpretation in Global Perspective.* Vol. 2 of *Reading from This Place.* Edited by F. F. Segovia and M. A. Tolbert. Minneapolis: Fortress, 1995.

———. *Decolonizing Biblical Studies: A View from the Margins.* Maryknoll, N.Y.: Orbis, 2000.

———. *Interpreting Beyond Borders.* Bible and Postcolonialism 3. Sheffield: Sheffield Academic Press, 2000.

———, ed. *What Is John? Readers and Readings of the Fourth Gospel.* 2 vols. SBLSymS 3. Atlanta: Scholars Press, 1996–1998.

Segovia, Fernando F., and Mary Ann Tolbert, eds. *Social Location and Biblical Interpretation in the United States.* Vol. 1 of *Reading from This Place.* Minneapolis: Fortress, 1995.

Setel, T. Dorah. "Feminist Insights and the Question of Method." Pages 35–42 in *Feminist Perspectives on Biblical Scholarship*. Edited by A. Y. Collins. SBLBSNA 10. Chico, Calif.: Scholars Press, 1985.

Shaw, Brent D. "The Passion of Perpetua." *Past and Present* 139 (1993): 3–45.

———. "War and Violence." Pages 130–69 in *Interpreting Late Antiquity: Essays on the Postclassical World*. Edited by G. W. Bowersock, P. R. L. Brown, and O. Grabar. Cambridge, Mass.: Harvard University Press, 2001.

Sherwin-White, A. N. *The Roman Citizenship*. 2d ed. Oxford: Clarendon, 1973.

Simkins, Ronald. "Patronage and the Political Economy of Ancient Israel." *Semeia* 87 (1999): 123–44.

Sissa, Guilia. "The Sexual Philosophies of Plato and Aristotle." Pages 46–81 in *A History of Women in the West: From Goddesses to Christian Saints*. Edited by P. S. Pantel. Translated by A. Goldhammer. Cambridge, Mass.: Harvard University Press, 1992.

Skogar, Björn. *Viva vox och den akademiska religionen. Ett bidrag till det tidiga 1900-talets teologihistoria*. Stehag/Stockholm: Symposion Graduale, 1993.

Smith, Craig S. "Where East Meets West Warily, She Makes Them Laugh." *New York Times*. (November 14, 2003): A4.

Smith, Jonathan Z. *Drudgery Divine: On the Comparisons of Early Christianities and the Religions of Late Antiquity*. Chicago Studies in the History of Judaism. Chicago: University of Chicago Press, 1990.

———. "Wisdom and Apocalyptic." Pages 67–87 in *Map is Not Territory: Studies in the History of Religions*. SJLA 23. Leiden: Brill, 1978. Repr., Chicago: University of Chicago Press, 1993.

Snyman, A. H. "Persuasion in Philippians 4:1–20." Pages 325–37 in *Rhetoric and the New Testament: Essays from the 1992 Heidelberg Conference*. Edited by S. E. Porter and T. H. Olbricht. JSNTSup 90. Sheffield: Sheffield Academic Press, 1993.

Snyman, Gerrie F. "From Text to Sermon: Reading and Creating Religious Texts." Pages 116–23 in *Congregational Ministry*. Pretoria: UNISA, 2003.

Soja, Edward W. "Thirdspace: Expanding the Scope of the Geographical Imagination." Pages 260–78 in *Human Geography Today*. Edited by D. Massey, J. A. Sarre, and P. Sarre. Cambridge: Polity, 1999.

Spivak, Gayatri Chakravorty. "Can the Subaltern Speak?" Pages 66–111 in *Colonial Discourse and Postcolonial Theory: A Reader*. Edited by P. Williams and L. Chrisman. New York: Harvester Wheatsheaf, 1993.

———. "The Politics of Interpretation." Pages 118–33 in *In Other Worlds: Essays in Cultural Politics*. London: Methuen, 1987.

———. *The Spivak Reader: Selected Works of Gayatri Chakravorty Spivak*. Edited by D. Landry and G. M. MacLean. New York: Routledge, 1996.

———. "Three Women's Texts and a Critique of Imperialism." *Critical Inquiry* 12 (1985): 243–61.

Stanton, Elizabeth Cady. *The Woman's Bible: A Classic Feminist Perspective*. Mineola, N. Y.: Dover, 2002.

Stearns, Peter N., Peter C. Seixas, and Samuel S. Wineburg, eds. *Knowing, Teaching, and Learning History: National and International Perspectives*. New York: New York University Press, 2000.

Steck, Odil Hannes. *Old Testament Exegesis: A Guide to the Methodology.* 2d ed. SBLRBS 39. Atlanta: Society of Biblical Literature, 1996.

Steinberg, Naomi A. *Kinship and Marriage in Genesis: A Household Economics Perspective.* Minneapolis: Fortress, 1993.

Stendahl, Krister. "Dethroning Biblical Imperialism in Theology." Pages 61–67 in *Reading the Bible in the Global Village: Helsinki.* Atlanta: Society of Biblical Literature, 2000.

Stenström, Hanna. "The Book of Revelation: A Vision of the Ultimate Liberation or the Ultimate Backlash? A Study in 20th Century Interpretations of Rev 14:1–5, with Special Emphasis on Feminist Exegesis." Ph.D. diss. Uppsala University, 1999.

———. "Is a Liberating Feminist Exegesis Possible Without Liberation Theology?" *Lectio Difficilior* 1 (2002). No pages. Cited 20 October 2004. Online: http://www.lectio.unibe.ch/02_1/stenstroem.htm.

Sternberg, Meir. "Biblical Poetics and Sexual Politics: From Reading to Counterreading." *JBL* 111 (1992): 463–88.

Strelan, Rick. *Strange Acts: Studies in the Cultural World of the Acts of the Apostles.* BZNW 126. Berlin: de Gruyter, 2004.

Sugirtharajah, Rasiah S. *Asian Biblical Hermeneutics and Postcolonialism: Contesting the Interpretations.* BS 64. Sheffield: Sheffield Academic Press, 1998.

———. *The Bible and the Third World: Precolonial, Colonial and Postcolonial Encounters.* Cambridge: Cambridge University Press, 2001.

———. "Biblical Studies after the Empire: From a Colonial to a Postcolonial Mode of Interpretation." Pages 12–22 in *The Postcolonial Bible.* Edited by R. S. Sugirtharajah. Bible and Postcolonialism 1. Sheffield: Sheffield Academic Press, 1998.

———. "The End of Biblical Studies?" Pages 133–40 in *Toward a New Heaven and a New Earth: Essays in Honor of Elisabeth Schüssler Fiorenza.* Edited by F. F. Segovia. Maryknoll, N.Y.: Orbis, 2003.

———. *Postcolonial Criticism and Biblical Interpretation.* Oxford: Oxford University Press, 2002.

———. "A Postcolonial Exploration of Collusion and Construction in Biblical Interpretation." Pages 91–116 in *The Postcolonial Bible.* Bible and Postcolonialism 1. Edited by R. S. Sugirtharajah. Sheffield: Sheffield Academic Press, 1998.

———. *Postcolonial Reconfigurations: An Alternative Way of Reading the Bible and Doing Theology.* London: SCM, 2003.

———. *Voices from the Margin: Interpreting the Bible in the Third World.* Maryknoll, N.Y.: Orbis, 1994.

———. ed. *The Postcolonial Bible.* Bible and Postcolonialism 1. Sheffield: Sheffield Academic Press, 1998.

Swancutt, Diana. "'The Disease of Effemination': The Charge of Effeminacy and the Verdict of God (Romans 1:18–2:16)." Pages 193–233 in *New Testament Masculinities.* Edited by S. D. Moore and J. Capel Anderson. SemeiaSt 45. Atlanta: Society of Biblical Literature, 2003.

———. "Sexy Stoics and the Rereading of Romans 1.18–2.16." Pages 42–73 in *A Feminist Companion to Paul.* Edited by A.-J. Levine with M. Blickenstaff. FCNTECW 6. New York: Continuum, 2004.

Swidler, Leonard. *Biblical Affirmations of Women*. Philadelphia: Westminster, 1979.

Tamarkin Reis, Pamela. "Hagar Requited." *JSOT* 87 (2000): 75–109.

Tanner, Kathryn. "Social Theory Concerning the 'New Social Movements' and the Practice of Feminist Theology." Pages 179–97 in *Horizons in Feminist Theology: Identity, Tradition and Norms*. Edited by R. S. Chopp and S. Greeve Davaney. Minneapolis: Fortress, 1997.

Thiel, John E. "The Universal in the Particular: Johann Sebastian Drey on the Hermeneutics of Tradition." Pages 56–74 in *The Legacy of the Tübingen School: The Relevance of Nineteenth-Century Theology for the Twenty-First Century*. Edited by D. J. Dietrich and M. J. Hines. New York: Crossroad Herder, 1997.

Thiele, Walter. "Eine Bemerkung zu Act 1.14." *ZNW* 53 (1962): 110–11.

Thiemann, Ronald. "Faith and the Public Intellectual." Pages 88–105 in *Walk in the Ways of Wisdom: Essays in Honor of Elisabeth Schüssler Fiorenza*. Edited by S. Matthews, C. Briggs Kittredge, and M. Johnson-Debaufre. New York: Continuum, 2003.

Thistlethwaite, Susan Brooks. "'You May Enjoy the Spoil of Your Enemies': Rape as a Biblical Metaphor for War." *Semeia* 61 (1993): 59–73.

Thompson, Cynthia L. "Hairstyles, Head-covering, and St. Paul: Portraits from Roman Corinth." *BA* 51 (1988): 99–115.

Thornham, Sue. *Feminist Theory and Cultural Studies: Stories of Unsettled Relations*. London: Arnold; New York: Oxford University Press, 2000.

Tolbert, Mary Ann. "Graduate Biblical Studies: Ethics and Discipline." No pages. Cited 20 October 2004. Online: http://www.sbl-site.org/Article.aspx?ArticleId=195.

———, ed. *The Bible and Feminist Hermeneutics*. *Semeia* 28. Chico, Calif.: Scholars Press, 1983.

Tompkins, Jane P., ed. *Reader-Response Criticism: From Formalism to Post-Structuralism*. Baltimore: Johns Hopkins University Press, 1980.

Torjesen, Karen Jo. *When Women Were Priests: Women's Leadership in the Early Church and the Scandal of Their Subordination in the Rise of Christianity*. San Francisco: HarperSanFrancisco, 1993.

Tov, Emanuel. "The Growth of the Book of Joshua in the Light of the Evidence of the LXX Translation." Pages 385–96 in *The Greek and the Hebrew Bible: Collected Essays*. VTSup 72. Leiden: Brill, 1999.

———. *The Text-Critical Use of the Septuagint in Biblical Research*. 2d ed. Jerusalem Biblical Studies 8. Jerusalem: Simor, 1997.

———. *Textual Criticism of the Hebrew Bible*. 2d ed. Minneapolis: Fortress; Assen: Van Gorcum, 2001.

Trible, Phyllis. *Texts of Terror: Literary-Feminist Readings of Biblical Narratives*. OBT 13. Philadelphia: Fortress, 1984.

Troeltsch, Ernst. *Religion in History*. Edited and translated by J. L. Adams and W. F. Bense. Fortress Texts in Modern Theology. Minneapolis: Fortress, 1991.

Trouillot, Michel-Rolph. *Silencing the Past: Power and the Production of History*. Boston: Beacon, 1995.

Turcan, Marie, ed. *Tertullian: De cultu feminarum / La toilette des femmes*. SC 173. Paris: Cerf, 1971.

Ulrich, Eugene. *The Dead Sea Scrolls and the Origins of the Bible.* Studies in the Dead Sea Scrolls and Related Literature. Grand Rapids: Eerdmans; Leiden: Brill, 1999.

Ulrich, Eugene, et al. *Qumran Cave 4—IX: Deuteronomy, Joshua, Judges, Kings.* DJD 14. Oxford: Clarendon, 1996.

Vander Stichele, Caroline. "Authenticiteit en integriteit van 1 Kor 11, 2–16. Een bijdrage tot de discussie omtrent Paulus' visie op de vrouw." Ph.D. diss. Katholieke Universiteit Leuven, 1992.

Vélez-Ibáñez, Carlos G. *Border Visions: Mexican Cultures of the Southwest United States.* Tucson: University of Arizona Press, 1996.

Venn, Couze. *Occidentalism: Modernity and Subjectivity.* Thousand Oaks, Calif.: SAGE, 2000.

Via, E. Jane. "Women in the Gospel of Luke." Pages 38–55 in *Women in the World's Religions: Past and Present.* Edited by U. King. New York: Paragon, 1987.

Walters, Jonathan. "Invading the Roman Body: Manliness and Impenetrability in Roman Thought." Pages 29–43 in *Roman Sexualities.* Edited by J. P. Hallett and M. B. Skinner. Princeton: Princeton University Press, 1997.

Wanamaker, Charles A. "A Rhetoric of Power: Ideology and 1 Corinthians 1–4." Pages 115–37 in *Paul and the Corinthians: Studies on a Community in Conflict. Essays in Honour of Margaret Thrall.* Edited by T. J. Burke and J. K. Elliott. NovTSup109. Leiden: Brill, 2003.

Ward, Roy Bowen. "Why Unnatural? The Tradition behind Romans 1:26–27." *HTR* 90 (1997): 263–84.

Warnick, Barbara. "Lucie Olbrechts-Tyteca's Contribution to *The New Rhetoric.*" Pages 69–85 in *Listening to Their Voices: The Rhetorical Activities of Historical Women.* Edited by M. Meijer Wertheimer. Columbia: University of South Carolina Press, 1997.

Washington, Harold C. "Violence and the Construction of Gender in the Hebrew Bible: A New Historicist Approach." *BibInt* 5 (1997): 324–63.

Watson, Duane F. "A Rhetorical Analysis of Philippians and Its Implications for the Unity Question." *NovT* 30 (1988): 57–88.

Watts, James W., ed. *Persia and Torah: The Theory of Imperial Authorization of the Pentateuch.* SBLSymS 17. Atlanta: Society of Biblical Literature, 2001.

Webster, Graham. *The Roman Imperial Army of the First and Second Centuries A. D.* London: Adam & Charles Black, 1969.

Weems, Renita J. "Do You See What I See? Diversity in Interpretation." *Church & Society* 82 (1991): 28–43.

Weidmann, Frederick W. "An (Un)Accomplished Model: Paul and the Rhetorical Strategy of Philippians 3:3–17." Pages 245–57 in *Putting Body and Soul Together: Essays in Honor of Robin Scroggs.* Edited by V. Wiles et al. Valley Forge, Pa.: Trinity Press International, 1997.

Weiss, Johannes. *Der erste Korintherbrief.* 9th ed. KEK 5. Göttingen: Vandenhoeck & Ruprecht, 1910.

Welch, Claude. *Protestant Thought in the Nineteenth Century: Volume 1, 1799–1870.* New Haven: Yale University Press, 1972.

West, Gerald O. *The Academy of the Poor: Towards a Dialogical Reading of the Bible.* Sheffield: Sheffield Academic Press, 1999.

West, Gerald O., and Musa W. Dube, eds. *The Bible in Africa: Transaction, Trajectories and Trends*. Leiden: Brill, 2001.

Westermann, Claus. *Genesis*. Translated by J. J. Scullion. 3 vols. CC. Minneapolis: Augsburg, 1984–1986.

———. *Handbook to the Old Testament*. London: SPCK, 1975.

White, Hayden. *The Content of the Form: Narrative Discourse and Historical Representation*. Baltimore: Johns Hopkins University Press, 1987.

———. *Metahistory: The Historical Imagination in Nineteenth-Century Europe*. Baltimore: Johns Hopkins University Press, 1973.

———. *Tropics of Discourse: Essays in Cultural Criticism*. Baltimore: Johns Hopkins University Press, 1978.

Williams, Craig A. *Roman Sexuality: Ideologies of Masculinity in Classical Antiquity*. New York: Oxford University Press, 1999.

Williams, Dolores. "The Color of Feminism: Or Speaking the Black Woman's Tongue." *JRT* (1986): 42–58.

Williams, Jay G. *Yeshua Buddha: An Interpretation of New Testament Theology as Meaningful Myth*. Wheaton, Ill.: Theosophical Publishing House, 1978.

Wimbush, Vincent L., ed. *African Americans and the Bible*. New York: Continuum, 2001.

———. "In Search of a Usable Past: Reorienting Biblical Studies." Pages 179–98 in *Toward a New Heaven and a New Earth: Essays in Honor of Elisabeth Schüssler Fiorenza*. Edited by F. F. Segovia. Maryknoll, N.Y.: Orbis, 2003.

Winkler, John J. *The Constraints of Desire: The Anthropology of Sex and Gender in Ancient Greece*. London: Routledge, 1999.

———. "Laying Down the Law: The Oversight of Men's Sexual Behavior in Classical Athens." Pages 171–209 in *Before Sexuality: The Construction of Erotic Experience in the Ancient World*. Edited by D. M. Halperin, J. J. Winkler, and F. I. Zeitlin. Princeton: Princeton University Press, 1990.

Winter, Bruce. W. "The Achaean Federal Imperial Cult II: The Corinthian Church." *TynBul* 46 (1995): 169–78.

———. *After Paul Left Corinth: The Influence of Secular Ethics and Social Change*. Grand Rapids: Eerdmans, 2001.

———. *Roman Wives, Roman Widows: The Appearance of New Women and the Pauline Communities*. Grand Rapids: Eerdmans, 2003.

Wire, Antoinette Clark. *The Corinthian Women Prophets: A Reconstruction through Paul's Rhetoric*. Minneapolis: Fortress, 1990.

———. "Response: The Politics of the Assembly in Corinth." Pages 124–29 in *Paul and Politics: Ekklesia, Israel, Imperium, Interpretation*. Edited by R. A. Horsley. Harrisburg, Pa.: Trinity Press International, 2000.

Witherington, Ben, III. "The Anti-Feminist Tendencies of the 'Western' Text in Acts." *JBL* 103 (1984): 82–84.

———. "On the Road with Mary Magdalene, Joanna, Susanna, and Other Disciples—Luke 8:1–3." *ZNW* 70 (1979): 243–48.

———. *Women in the Earliest Churches*. SNTSMS 59. Cambridge: Cambridge University Press, 1988.

Wittfogel, Karl. *Oriental Despotism*. New Haven: Yale University Press, 1963.

Wong, Angela Wai-Ching. *The Poor Woman: A Critical Analysis of Asian Theology and Contemporary Chinese Fiction by Women*. New York: Lang, 2002.

Wood, Mark D. "Religious Studies as Critical Organic Intellectual Practice." *JAAR* 69 (2001): 129–62.

Woolf, Virginia. *Three Guineas.* New York: Harcourt, Brace & World, 1966.

Wu, Xuanren, and Qing Yang, eds. *Lament Songs and Flaming Blood: Anthology of Original Poems from the Democracy Movement, 1989.* Hong Kong: Shi Fang and Zhongguo Deng Huo Xing Dong, 1999.

Wuellner, Wilhelm. "Putting Life Back into the Lazarus Story and Its Reading: The Narrative Rhetoric of John 11 as the Narration of Faith." *Semeia* 53 (1991): 113–32.

Yarbrough, O. Larry. "Paul, Marriage, and Divorce." Pages 404–28 in *Paul in the Greco-Roman World.* Edited by J. P. Sampley. Harrisburg, Pa.: Trinity Press International, 2003.

Yee, Gale. "Gender, Class and the Social Scientific Study of Genesis 2–3." *Semeia* 87 (1999): 177–92.

———. "Ideological Criticism: Judges 17–21 and the Dismembered Body." Pages 146–70 in *Judges and Method: New Approaches in Biblical Studies.* Edited by G. Yee. Minneapolis: Fortress, 1995.

———. *Poor Forgotten Sister of Eve.* Louisville: Westminster John Knox, 2003.

Yoo, Yani. "*Han*-Laden Women: Korean 'Comfort Women' and Women in Judges 19–21." *Semeia* 78 (1997): 37–46.

Young, Robert J. C. *Colonial Desire: Hybridity in Theory, Culture and Race.* New York: Routledge, 1995.

Yu, Guangzhong. *My Heart at Tiananmen: A Collection of Poems for the Memorial of June 4th.* Taipei: Zheng Zhong, 1989.

Ziervogel, Dirk, and Pothinus C. Mokgokong. *Comprehensive Northern Sotho Dictionary.* Pretoria: van Schaik, 1975.

Zilin, Ding. "Documenting Death: Reflections after Ten Years." No pages. Cited 20 October 2004. Online: http://iso.hrichina.org/public/contents/article?revision%5fid=2122&item%5fid=2121.

INDEX OF PRIMARY SOURCES

OLD TESTAMENT

NEW TESTAMENT

ANCIENT JEWISH/CHRISTIAN SOURCES

OTHER ANCIENT SOURCES

INDEX OF MODERN AUTHORS

CONTRIBUTORS

Roland Boer is Logan Research Fellow at the Centre for Studies in Religion and Theology at Monash University, Melbourne, Australia.

Athalya Brenner is Professor of Hebrew Bible/Old Testament at the University of Amsterdam, The Netherlands; and the Rosalyn and Manny Rosenthal Distinguished Professor-in-Residence of Jewish Studies/Hebrew Bible at Brite Divinity School, Fort Worth, Texas.

Ann Graham Brock is Adjunct Professor of New Testament and Early Christian Traditions at Iliff School of Theology, Denver, Colorado.

Kristin De Troyer is Professor of Hebrew Bible at Claremont School of Theology and Professor of Religion at Claremont Graduate University, Claremont, California.

Esther Fuchs is Professor of Near Eastern Studies/Judaic Studies at the University of Arizona in Tucson, Arizona.

Priscilla Geisterfer is a Ph.D. Candidate in Biblical Theology at Saint Paul University, Ottawa, Canada.

Archie Chi Chung Lee is Professor of Hebrew Bible and Asian Biblical Hermeneutics in the Department of Cultural and Religious Studies at The Chinese University of Hong Kong.

Joseph A. Marchal earned his Ph.D. at The Graduate Theological Union, Berkeley, California, has taught at Colby College and St. Mary's College of California, and is currently Lilly Visiting Assistant Professor in Religion at Austin College, Sherman, Texas.

John Marshall is Assistant Professor in the Department for the Study of Religion at the University of Toronto, Canada.

Madipoane Masenya (ngwana' Mphahlele) is Associate Professor of Old Testament in the Department of Old Testament and Ancient Near Eastern Studies at the University of South Africa, Pretoria, South Africa.

Judith E. McKinlay is formerly Senior Lecturer in Old Testament Studies in the Department of Theology and Religious Studies at Otago University, New Zealand.

Hjamil A. Martínez-Vázquez is Assistant Professor of Religion at Texas Christian University, Fort Worth, Texas.

Jorunn Økland is Lecturer in New Testament in the Department of Biblical Studies, University of Sheffield, England.

Todd Penner is Cloud Associate Professor in Religion at Austin College, Sherman, Texas.

Vernon K. Robbins is Winship Distinguished Research Professor of New Testament and Comparative Sacred Texts at Emory University, Atlanta, Georgia.

Susanne Scholz is Associate Professor of Religious Studies at Merrimack College, North Andover, Massachusetts.

Hanna Stenström is Lecturer in New Testament at the University of Uppsala and in Biblical Studies at the University of Linköping and Ersta Sköndal University College (Stockholm), Sweden.

Caroline Vander Stichele is Universitair Docent in Religious Studies at the University of Amsterdam, The Netherlands.